manager's

manual

ththth think thinkst fast thinking fast

PEARSON EDUCATION LIMITED

Head Office:
Edinburgh Gate
Harlow CM20 2JE
Tel: +44 (0)1279 623623
Fax: +44 (0)1279 431059

London Office:
128 Long Acre
London WC2E 9AN
Tel: +44 (0)20 7447 2000
Fax: +44 (0)20 7240 5771
Website: www.fast-thinking.com

First published in Great Britain in 2001

© Pearson Education Limited 2001

The right of Ros Jay to be identified as Editor
of this Work has been asserted by her in accordance
with the Copyright, Designs and Patents Act 1988.

ISBN 0 273 65298 2

British Library Cataloguing in Publication Data
A CIP catalogue record for this book can be obtained from the British Library.

10 9 8 7 6 5 4 3 2

Typeset by Pantek Arts Ltd, Maidstone, Kent.
Printed and bound in Great Britain by Rotolito Lombarda, Italy
Design by Kenny Grant

The Publishers' policy is to use paper manufactured from sustainable forests.

contents

introduction

When you work at the speed of life, you need to learn at the speed of life. You haven't got time to read a 400-page book on any subject, and why would you want to anyway? This manual is for people who can think smart and pick up the essentials of a subject at the speed the real world moves at. It is a collection of condensed guides to 15 of the most important management topics you need to know about. Everything you need is in here ... and nothing else. No wasted space.

When the panic's rising and you have only a day left before your big presentation, or only half a day to draw up a departmental budget, all you want is hard — and fast — facts. These *fast thinking* guides will cut through the thought jungle, switch off the panic, and give you simple, concrete things to say, do and remember so you'll have the shine that makes you look as though you've been polishing for weeks.

THE ANTIDOTE TO ELEVENTH HOUR PANIC

So what have you left to the last minute this time? Proposal? Appraisal? A major decision? Tackling that work overload? We all do it. However hard we try, there always seems to be something more urgent. And suddenly that vital meeting or interview is tomorrow morning, and you still haven't done a stroke of preparation.

Or maybe it's the first time you've had to do this. You haven't got time to wade through a weighty manual or attend a course. What you need is a smart and savvy guide to pulling it off as if you were a seasoned professional.

Or maybe you don't do it very often, and you need a refreshing refresher to bring you up to speed with minimal fuss.

Whichever is the case, you need a fast thinking lifesaver. A minimalist guide to everything you need to know about the subject. Short enough to read fast — you haven't got long — and full of cool ideas not only for getting through it, but for looking polished too. Tips for giving the impression you know more than you do, checklists to run through at the last minute, shortcuts for doing as little preparation as possible. And a clear, readable style so that you can understand it even through the fog of panic (which will subside once you read it).

ALL YOU REALLY NEED AND NOTHING ELSE

OK, some of us are just downright disorganized, but most of us just have too much life and too little time. Here's the good news, fast: knowledge is power. And the *fast thinking* guides give you the knowledge you need to face the job head on. Not only will they get you through it this time, but they will set you up for all the next times. Once you know what you're doing, you'll never worry about leaving it to the last minute again (but hey, why not keep the books on your shelf anyway).

You'll find that as you use the *fast thinking* guides, you'll start to become a natural fast thinker yourself. You'll pick up the *fast thinking* style of working with its smart approach:

- **Always start by setting an objective (it saves you masses of wasted time later).**
- **Do your preparation fast but thoroughly (using all the tips and shortcuts fast thinkers have up their sleeves).**
- **Choose the fastest route there is to get the job done (plenty of advice on that in here).**
- **Get it right first time (one of the smartest time-savers of all).**

It's a fast world with tight deadlines, and you squeezed in between. You simply need last-minute solutions to help you think at the speed of life. Each of these guides gives you only the most vital information to make the best of your last few hours before crunch time. You've come to the right place. You'll look good – they'll never know. It's a fast world with tight deadlines, and you squeezed in between. You simply need last-minute solutions to help you think at the speed of life.

introduction

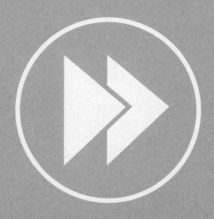

fast thinking manager

introduction

Handling people is one of the skills that marks out smart managers from weak ones. And it's one of the toughest skills to learn because it's so crucial. If you handle someone badly, you can damage their morale, even their career, and there'll be all sorts of negative knock-on effects for the people they work with too.

But don't worry, it's not going to happen. Not now. Here are the *fast thinking* guides to five key people skills that every manager needs to be able to call on. With the help of these guides, you can learn (or brush up on) how to tackle those thorny situations that other managers view with trepidation.

Feel nervous about interviewing people? We've all felt it sometime. And the key to escaping the nerves is confidence. The confidence that comes from knowing exactly what you're doing, and why you're doing it. The *fast thinking* guides to *selection interview*, *appraisal* and *discipline* will give you that confidence fast. This time tomorrow you'll wonder what you were ever worried about.

Inducting new beginners is another critical skill, and one that foolish managers fail to recognize the importance of. Did you know that most new beginners have decided within the first fortnight whether or not they'll stay in the job? So if you're smart, you'll act fast to make sure they want to stay after all the work you've put in. *new beginner* will show you how.

Even once you know how to deal with interviews and induction, there will still be other people problems to face. Some people are just plain difficult – perhaps only some of the time or maybe even all the time (in some cases I've known). What about difficult bosses? Or problems with rivalries in your team? *difficult people* will help you to deal quickly with difficult types, from overbearing bosses to whingeing team members.

This group of *fast thinking* guides will turn you from an ordinary manager into one of the few who are skilled and confident at dealing with people even at the toughest of times.

selection interview

SIFT CVS FAST

INTERVIEW WITH SKILL

HIRE THE RIGHT PERSON

fast thinking

ros jay

9

contents

introduction

Where did the time go? You advertised this post what seems like yesterday, but apparently it was a month ago. The interviews are supposed to be next week, and you haven't even started sifting through the applications yet, let alone compiling a list of likely applicants to interview. Or maybe you got that far, but the interviews are tomorrow and you can't even remember what the job description is.

You need a high-speed handbook to whisk you through the selection process at lightning speed, and still make sure that you end up selecting the right applicant. You wouldn't dream of picking a name out of a hat, but many managers might as well do, the way they go about selecting. No, you need to be fast but you also need to be smart. You've come to the right place.

Selection isn't just about chatting with a few applicants and then making a gut decision about who you want to appoint. It is a skilled process. You wouldn't buy a house without thinking hard about what you needed, what sort of potential the house should have, what features you would like but could manage without, and so on. A new employee may well, over time, cost the organisation as much as a new house, so the process warrants just as much thought and consideration.

That can seem like an impossible standard to meet when you're running out of time, but it can still be done. Maybe you've left the whole process to the last minute, or maybe it's just the interviews you're ill-prepared for. But even though the rest of your work is overtaking you, you can still make sure you select the best applicant. You just need:

 tips for getting on top of things fast

 shortcuts for avoiding any unnecessary work

 checklists to make sure you have the essentials covered

all put together clearly and simply. And short enough to read fast, of course.

And what if you really run out of time? If the interviews are tomorrow, you may just have to prepare for them this evening. But don't worry: it can be done. At the back of the book you'll find a brief guide to preparing for interviews in only a few hours. In fact, if you have as little as an hour, it can still be done – as the turbo-charged one-hour version right at the end will show you. Now that really *is* working at the speed of life.

So relax. Take a deep breath. You may have left things late, but there's still time if you think smart and act fast. Now you know it can be done in sixty minutes, it makes even a few hours look like luxury, doesn't it? If you have a whole day for this, it's practically time to start bragging about how organised you are (so long as you don't brag for too long). So take the phone off the hook, make a cup of coffee, and let's get started.

work at the speed of life

This book will take you through the seven key stages of selection interviewing:

1 Before you can do anything else, you need to identify your objective. What exactly do you aim to achieve at the end of this process?

2 There are two key documents you need before you can possibly decide who is right for the job: the job description and the employee specification. So the next chapter is all about what these documents look like and how you should use them.

3 If you haven't yet been through the applications, this is the next stage. Armed with your job description and employee specification, you need to slim down your pile of applications to a list of candidates worth interviewing.

4 Before the interview itself, you should prepare a set of questions to ask the candidates. So we'll look at the type of questions you need to ask.

5 You can't run selection interviews effectively in the wrong surroundings, or chaotic conditions. We'll look at the reasons why, and see how to set the scene for the interviews.

6 Now we come to the core of the process – the interviews themselves. We'll look at how to run the interview, how to glean the information you want from the interviewee, and how to tackle any thorny topics that may come up.

7 Finally, you have to make your decision. Which applicant will you give the job to? We'll look at how to choose the best candidate, how to check them out, and what to tell the rest of them.

We'll finish off with a quick look at other types of interviews, such as panel interviews and second interviews, since there are a few additional guidelines for these.

fast thinking gambles

So, is it a good idea to race through the selection process at the speed of a cheetah, or is there a price to pay? Well, if you're doing it smart as well as fast – following the guidelines in this book – you can't go far wrong. You'll pick a candidate who is well up to the job (assuming the quality of the applications was good), and you should be very satisfied with them. The nagging doubt, though, is whether there might have been an even better candidate whom you missed. That's the gamble you take.

Most of the time, a well (if speedily) thought through selection process will identify the best candidate. But sometimes you may miss a better but less obvious candidate. Or you may know that there are two applicants you are finding it hard to choose between: more time would have meant more opportunity to work out which was the more suitable.

- **The job description and the employee specification are your guidelines for picking the right candidate. They don't have to be long and wordy, but they do have to be accurate and informative. If you don't have time to prepare them effectively, you won't have a clear idea of what you are looking for. You may select a candidate who lacks a necessary skill, or who is unhappy when they find their job entails more time away from home than they realised.**

- **Sorting applications warrants a respectable time investment. Sure, you'll spot the blindingly good candidates pretty fast, along with the hopelessly unsuitable. But you may fail to identify the applicant who doesn't have all the qualifications you wanted, but who has flair that would more than make up for it.**

- **When you're under time pressure, you may miss details on the application form that would have been worth investigating. Perhaps there is a four-month gap in employment (you'll notice glaring gaps even at high speed), or a qualification in an unusual discipline, or a project they've been given that might indicate a particular talent, or a hobby that indicates a scientific bent. Following these leads could have revealed something very relevant – if only you'd had time to spot them.**

- **If your interviews give you the appearance of being unprepared, it will show you and your organisation in a poor light. So when both you and another company offer your best candidate a job, which one will they decide to take?**

- **When it is hard to choose between your top applicants, more time gives you more options – to follow up additional references, hold a second round of interviews, ask the candidates to take psychometric tests or whatever. When you're up against the clock, making the final decision can be tough.**

Fast thinking will get you through the selection process at speed, and you'll end up with a good candidate – often the best one. That's most of the battle won. But if you want to be certain of picking the very best candidate every time, you'll need to find a little more time so you can ease up on the gas.

1 your objective

Have we got time for this? The interviews are twelve hours away – maybe less – and you're supposed to worry about objectives? You're just trying to get the post filled, surely?

Not quite. It's more specific than that. You are aiming to appoint the applicant who is most suitable for the job. And no, that's not the same thing. There are subtle but crucial differences. Suppose you are interviewing for an assistant chef in the canteen. You have two applicants. One is eighteen, and has a basic City & Guilds catering qualification. The other is twenty-eight, has a degree in food biology, and has run their own restaurant for four years. Which one is more suitable?

Presumably – all else being equal – the eighteen-year-old. It's no doubt just the job they're after, and they will enjoy it and work well. The twenty-eight- year-old, on the other hand, is odds on to leave through sheer boredom within the first month. So the better candidate, in terms of qualifications and potential, is not the more suitable one.

In real life, of course, the distinction is rarely so obvious. But the point is the same: you want the most *suitable* candidate – not necessarily the best- qualified, or the one with most experience. So you need to be clearly focused on your objective.

It's rather like buying a house. The most expensive house is not necessarily the best one for you. You might well be happier in the one that has a shorter walk to the station in the mornings, or that has a double garage that would make just the workshop you want, rather than have the three of you rattling around in a ten-bedroomed mansion.

SERIOUS BUSINESS

When time is tight, it's very easy to be drawn into getting the process over with as quickly as possible, without recognising the importance of your decision. But it is worth reminding yourself quickly of how crucial it really is for everyone involved.

- ▶ *Your organisation:* **When you buy a house, you have to pay for stamp duty, removals, change-of-address cards, and all the rest of it. It's an expensive exercise, even before you launch into the cost of keeping and maintaining the building. When your organisation recruits a new employee, they have to pay for advertising the post, mailing application forms (and the time it takes), organising and running the interviews (your time now, in other words), induction, and the ongoing cost of the employee. If you employ the wrong person, that's a lot of money down the drain.**

- ▶ *Other team members:* **If you appoint the wrong person to this post, how are their team mates going to feel? They are likely to be demoralised – their productivity may drop – and if you have to let an unsuitable new employee go, it's even more damaging.**

thinking smart

SQUARE PEG ...

Have you ever worked with someone who was clearly in the wrong job? Remember what it was like – for you, for them, and for everyone else. Keep this in mind if you're tempted to rush through the process in a way that jeopardises your chances of appointing the most suitable candidate. We're going to do this fast, but we're not going to rush it.

▷ *The employee:* **Suppose you appoint someone who moves to the area to take the job. Or who gives up a job with good prospects for this post. Or who is close to retirement and unlikely to find another job if this one falls through. Quite apart from the short-term demoralisation and frustration, you may be doing someone long-term harm by offering them a job for which they aren't really suitable. If you could have identified this fact but didn't, you're carrying a big responsibility.**

So that's why we're going to do this selection stuff properly. We're going to take any shortcuts we can, but not if they increase the risk of appointing the wrong candidate.

for next time

We're going to do this properly, but it's going to mean some hard work. Another time, you'll be doing yourself a big favour if you block in sacrosanct time in your diary for this process. Not just for the interviews, but also for:

▷ preparing the job description and employee specification (see Chapter 2)
▷ going through the application forms to select candidates to interview (Chapter 3)
▷ preparing questions (Chapter 4).

We'll be looking at all these later on, but actually doing them is a lot less stressful if you've eased the time pressure by setting aside time when you first advertised the post.

2 the vital documents

Paperwork ... aargh! The clock's ticking away and you're supposed to be playing with bits of administrative paperwork? Yep, 'fraid so. But it doesn't have to take long. And you may be able to delegate parts of it (but not all of it – you need to be involved).

Let's be rational about this. You can't hope to appoint the most suitable person for the job if you don't know what the job is, can you? So you need a basic description of the job just to make it clear. And the candidates will need to see it too (in an ideal world you'd have sent it out with the application forms), so they can make certain that this is the job they want. So the job description is one of your two vital documents.

The other one is the employee specification. You must decide what sort of person you are looking for to fill this post. Do they need to be able to use certain types of software? Must they have an HGV licence? Should they be confident and friendly to deal with customers over the counter? This, together with the job description, gives you a full picture of the hypothetical person you are looking for. Then your job is simply to match the real candidate with this hypothetical one.

THE JOB DESCRIPTION

You must have seen plenty of job descriptions. They usually go on for two or three close-typed pages, detailing exactly what the employee has to do, from opening the morning post to the precise procedures for returning faulty items. Well, we don't want one of those. We haven't even got time to read it, let alone write it.

We only need the important bits – the bits that are relevant to choosing the right person to do the job. When you want to buy a house, you don't describe your ideal house to the estate agent down to the last detail. They don't need to know exactly what furniture you are planning to fit into it, or whether you prefer a high- or low-level cistern for the lavatory. They just want to know how many bedrooms, what sort of location, whether you want a garden and that sort of basic guidelines.

The same goes for the job description for this post you're advertising. It need only be an outline of the key facts about the job. It should give:

- **job title**
- **who they report to**
- **overall objective**
- **key responsibilities**
- **other information for the applicants.**

The easiest way to explain this fully is with an example. Let's suppose you're interviewing for a receptionist. The job description should look something like this:

JOB DESCRIPTION

Job title Receptionist

Reporting to Customer service manager

Overall objective To provide a telephone and face-to-face receptionist service for all callers and visitors to the building

Key responsibilities

1 Greet visitors in a friendly and helpful manner to give a good impression of the organisation, and notify staff promptly when visitors arrive

2 Answer the switchboard promptly in a friendly and helpful manner, and:

> Put calls through to the appropriate extension

> Take accurate messages and pass them on promptly

> Give information and help

3 Keep the reception area tidy

Further information

▶ Dynamic young company in central London office

▶ Training with a view to promotion within the company

▶ Childcare allowance available

Of course, some jobs have more key responsibilities than others, but you shouldn't need to list more than half a dozen or so at most, and three or four often cover everything.

It should be clear that you need to go through this thought-process yourself, as it will help you enormously when you come to review the applications and interview the candidates. But you can always get someone else to type it up into a standard format.

THE EMPLOYEE SPECIFICATION

You've established what the job is now, but you still need to decide what kind of person you are looking for to fill it. When you look for a house, you have a whole

thinking smart

NO RUBBER STAMP

If you are advertising an existing post, you presumably already have a job description for it. This may well provide a handy shortcut. But look through it and make sure it still describes the job as you want it to be. Perhaps this is a good opportunity to change some of the responsibilities that go with this job, or perhaps the previous incumbent never actually did half this stuff, and it shouldn't be down there at all. So never settle for simply digging out the old job description without reviewing it.

FROM THE HORSE'S MOUTH

If you're really pushed for time – or even if you're not – why not ask the person who is vacating the post to draft a list of key responsibilities that they feel describes the job they really do? Ask them to disregard what the old job description says (it may be very similar, or wildly different) and to come up with a short list. Then go through this yourself – properly – to check whether you want to change or add to it.

list of requirements that are not part of the description you give the estate agent. You told them what job the house needs to do – it needs to provide four bedrooms and a small garden not far from the shops and the station. But in fact, of all the houses in town that can do this job, only some will suit you.

You have your own list. For a start, it needs to have a bedroom that will take your huge old bed you inherited from your grandmother. It needs a big dining room or family kitchen because you often hold large dinner parties. And the garden has to face the right way to grow your prize sunflowers. Ideally, you'd like a range cooker, too, although you could always put one in yourself.

In other words, you have a list of requirements – some essential and some simply desirable – that any house will need to fulfil. And the same goes for the new employee you take on. They must have certain skills and attributes, and you need to identify these in advance. Otherwise you may not recognise them when you see them. And, just like your ideal house, some of these will be essentials while others will simply be preferences. For example, if you have a lot of foreign visitors, you might consider it essential for your receptionist to speak French, and desirable for them also to speak Spanish.

The best, and fastest, way to draw up an employee specification is to draw a matrix:

	Skills	Attributes
Essential		
Desirable		

Now you simply fill in each box with the relevant skills or attributes that your hypothetical ideal employee should have. Anyone you consider must meet every requirement in the top two boxes. You will want to find someone who also meets many of the requirements in the two bottom boxes.

Again, there's no need – and no time – to write an essay here. You are probably looking for around three or four skills and half a dozen attributes altogether. These might include:

- *Skills:* qualifications, foreign languages, understanding of particular software programs, problem-solving skills, supervisory skills, book keeping.

- *Attributes:* good teamworker, ability to work to deadlines, flexibility, ability to think analytically, good eye for detail, good at communicating, able to work under pressure.

So let's see what your employee specification for that receptionist's job might look like:

	Skills	Attributes
Essential	▶ Experience in switchboard operation ▶ Fluent in French ▶ Helpful telephone manner and clear speaking voice	▶ Able to communicate with people at all levels ▶ Able to work under pressure ▶ Friendly and helpful manner
Desirable	▶ Some clerical experience	▶ Flexibility about working hours ▶ General neatness and tidiness ▶ Good attention to detail

There, that shouldn't have taken too long. But it should have given you a much clearer idea of what precisely you're looking for. You now have the two vital documents you need to tell you what the job is, and what kind of person will be suitable for it.

thinking smart

DON'T GET PERSONAL

When it comes to personal attributes, make sure you remain objective. If a friendly and pleasant manner is necessary to the job – say, a receptionist – then include it in your employee specification. But don't put it in just because you think it would be nicer. It is unlikely to be a requirement for an in-house designer, for example.

for next time

The job description should really be prepared well in advance, so that you can send it out with the application forms to anyone who requests one. It's only fair that applicants should know what the job they are applying for is. Don't send out an old, out-of-date job description that you haven't quite got round to updating – it could be extremely misleading.

The employee specification, although it should be drawn up in advance, is for your own information, however, and not for sending out to applicants.

3 shifting the application

You may already have been through the application forms and shortlisted candidates for interview. In this case, you can skip on to the next chapter for now if you're pushed for time (but please come back and read this one next time you have a post to advertise). If you haven't yet been through this process, let's get cracking.

You have a pile of application forms in front of you, and you can't possibly interview all the applicants. You haven't got time to waste interviewing people who aren't suitable, and you don't want to waste their time either. So you need to sort these applications into two piles: those you want to interview and those you don't.

NARROWING THE FIELD

So just how are you going to narrow this pile down fast? It's simply a process of elimination. And how do you know what to eliminate? By using your job description and employee specification, that's how. See, they're coming in handy already.

Imagine that these applications are all the house details you've been sent by estate agents. They give you a photo of the front, a location, and measurements and details of each of the rooms, the garage, the garden and so on. If you're after a house, you can tell at a glance which are worth a visit and which aren't – you already know what requirements you gave the estate agents, and what else you need from any suitable house. If the information isn't comprehensive enough for you to be certain, you'll probably opt to take a look just in case. You're just doing the same thing now with job applications instead of house details.

So simply go through the applications and compare each one with your two vital documents. Weed out any applicants whose experience or attributes clearly don't fit these descriptions. Suppose your job description indicates that you need someone who must work closely as part of a team. An applicant who has always worked alone and shows no other team-working potential (such as listing formation parachuting under hobbies) is unlikely to be suitable.

Likewise, if your employee specification shows that you need someone with experience of operating a switchboard, applications from people without this experience are unlikely to be worth pursuing.

As well as comparing the applications with your job description and employee specification, you also need to look for any other obvious omissions or suspect areas in each application. Probably the most common of these are:

thinking smart

LOOK WITHIN

It makes sense to fill vacancies internally if you can, so always give consideration to internal applicants. Not only do they already know your organisation, but the very fact that you consider them shows all your staff that you are positive about finding them opportunities for promotion. So you are benefiting the morale and the commitment of your workforce by encouraging internal applicants.

thinking smart

BE FLEXIBLE

Although you need to measure each application against your two vital documents, it is worth bearing in mind that the best candidate doesn't always fulfil the criteria exactly. If a particular application really impresses you despite one or two reservations, there's no law that says you can't interview the candidate anyway. Some skills or attributes may be essential, but don't be too rigid over everything, or your best applicant may never make it as far as the interviews.

▸ **significant gaps between jobs with no obvious explanation**

▸ **an applicant who has taken drops in salary, perhaps when changing jobs, again without any clear reason.**

These factors prove nothing in themselves, but they are pointers to potential problems. Of course, employment gaps might be explained by illness, or taking breaks to have a family. A drop in salary might have been worth it for a more interesting job. On the other hand, the explanations might not be so innocent. In other words, if the application is otherwise impressive, you can still interview these applicants (and question them about these things, as we'll see later on).

But in general, gaps and salary drops add to the balance of points against, and may swing your judgement in favour of the 'no interview' pile. The important thing, of course, is to make sure that even though you're up against the clock, you still notice these kinds of omissions or areas of doubt.

SIZE ISN'T EVERYTHING

So how many applicants are you supposed to be narrowing this pile of forms down to? Well, it's hard to be precise, and you really shouldn't try. Remember, the object of the exercise is to appoint the most suitable candidate, not to get through the process fast (appealing though that might be). Clearly, if you've got a 'yes' pile with fifty applications in it, you're going to have to try harder to whittle them down.

But the real question is: how many promising applicants are there? If there are nine in your 'yes' pile, it's no good thinking that you'll have to get rid of one because there are only eight interview slots in the day. You might reject the one who would have been your best candidate. And anyway, you haven't got time to spend hours deliberating over which one should go. Just interview them all, and squeeze up the schedule or spend two long half-days interviewing instead.

Equally, if you have five applications that stand out, don't try to find three more just to fill up the day. You can't afford to waste that sort of time – and nor can they. So be as ruthless as you need to be to get the numbers down to a sensible level, and then interview everyone who meets these criteria.

THANKS BUT NO THANKS

What do you do about all those applicants you're not going to interview? No matter how busy you are, you must write to them as promptly as possible. Send

WHAT ARE YOU AFTER?

If suitability for this post rests chiefly on experience and skills, it will probably be easy to reduce the list for interview to only a few candidates. When personality is more important, for instance for a receptionist's job, you'll need to see more of the applicants in order to decide who is most suitable.

them a polite note of thanks for their interest, but let them know that you won't be inviting them for an interview. If you don't have time, delegate the job but sign the letters yourself. Remember that these people may not be suitable for this post, but they may be ideal for another job with your organisation in the future. So make sure you leave them with a good impression of your friendliness and efficiency.

SETTING UP THE INTERVIEWS

When you invite candidates to interview, try to be as flexible as you can about times. It may be hard for them to get time off, especially if you've left things a little late. So give them as much leeway as you can.

When it comes to allocating time for interviews, don't imagine you can interview each candidate successfully in fifteen minutes (much as you might like to be able to). As a rule of thumb, allow about three-quarters of an hour for interviews for a junior post (plus another ten to fifteen to make notes and then refresh your mind about the next candidate). If you're interviewing for a senior management position, you might well need to allow about half a day for each applicant.

PICK UP THE PHONE

Always get someone to phone candidates to arrange interview times, rather than writing. It makes it much quicker to agree a time, and it ensures that promising applicants know you're interested as soon as possible – before they accept another post elsewhere.

for next time

If you have received a large proportion of applications from people who are not suitable for the job, something has gone wrong. Most of these people would probably never have applied if they had realised they had no chance. You can save yourself and them a lot of time by making it clear in the original recruitment ad, and in the information you send out with the application form, exactly what your requirements are. So another time make sure you write informative job advertisements, and send out the job description along with the application form.

Another option when time is less pressing is to pay an agency to find you a shortlist of candidates. Ironically, although this will actually save you time, you need to get the ball rolling earlier than this. You'll still have to produce a job description and employee specification, show the agency around and brief them fully. But they will then take care of the advertising, sending out application forms and going through the replies, before giving you your interview list.

4 the questions

I know you haven't got time to waste preparing these interviews, but you're going to look a fool if you go in there and don't know what you want to ask. Equally, you'll look pretty stupid if it turns out when your new appointee arrives on their first day that they've never operated a switchboard, but you forgot to check that one out.

So planning your questions is a necessity, not a luxury. That said, you don't need a detailed list of fifty questions for each applicant. You need two sets of questions:

1 questions that you ask all the applicants

2 specific questions for each applicant.

If you design your questions well, you don't need that many of them. There's nothing wrong with letting the conversation flow, and asking questions that crop up as you go along as well as those on your prepared list.

GENERAL QUESTIONS

When you're looking for a house, you want to check certain things about all of them: have they got off-road parking for two cars? Do they have central heating? Are the fixtures and fittings included in the price?

The general questions, which you will want to ask all the applicants, are the key questions arising from the job description and the employee specification. You will want to find out how their experience relates to the job description, details of their qualifications, skills and work history, and their approach to customer care, corporate change, or integrated IT systems, or whatever is relevant to this particular job.

So assemble a list of broad questions to get them to discuss these things. For example:

▸ **'This job involves dealing with customers face-to-face and on the phone. What do you think are the most important aspects of good customer care?'**

▸ **'What experience do you have of handling customers?'**

▸ **'Tell me about your experience of working under pressure.'**

thinking smart

FEWER AND BETTER

The more open the questions you ask, the better. For one thing, you will need to prepare fewer questions, and for another you will get fuller answers. So instead of asking 'What switchboards have you operated?' try asking 'Tell me about the switchboards you've operated in the past.' Instead of their simply listing them, this encourages the interviewee to say which were easy or difficult, how much experience they have of each, and so on. With one question, you've found out plenty of detail.

PAST, PRESENT AND FUTURE

Aim to ask each candidate individual questions about their past experience, their present attitudes and circumstances, and their future ambitions. This will give you a broad picture of the applicant by the end of the interview.

You'll probably find that you need only devise half a dozen or so of these broad, open questions – which won't take you too long. And you can follow any interesting threads in the answer on an *ad hoc* basis. But it is important to ask everyone the same core questions so that you can assess each candidate on the same basis.

INDIVIDUAL QUESTIONS

You will also have individual questions for the applicants. Again, to follow the analogy of buying a house, these are like the questions you identified from the individual house details. For example: is the heating oil, gas or electric? Could the third bedroom be converted into another bathroom easily? Does the garage have a connecting door to the kitchen, or is the only access external?

You don't have to spend ages drawing up neat lists here – just annotate each application form or stick a post-it note on it (as long as it won't come adrift). You're simply drawing your attention to the points you want to raise. Yes, this means you're going to have to go through the application forms individually, but if you do this soon after the shortlisting process you'll probably remember most of the significant points from each application anyway (now there's one of the few real advantages of cutting the preparation fine).

You might make a note to ask about:

- a gap in employment
- a career change
- their reason for leaving previous jobs
- their style of working
- the fact that they appear overqualified for the post
- a useful-looking skill, such as fluency in a foreign language

CAREFUL WORDING

Generally, you don't need to design the individual questions exactly, but simply to note down the points to cover. However, if you want to raise a delicate topic that you think might be hard to bring up, it is wise to plan the precise wording of the question in advance to make it easy on yourself.

- a particular hobby that indicates a relevant attribute (such as determination, or a fondness for working alone).

These are only a few examples – there are many possibilities. The point is to make sure that you touch on any subject that you think is particularly relevant, whether positive or negative.

WHO'S ASKING THE QUESTIONS?

There's just one more thing. At the end of the interview, you should ask each candidate if they have any questions for you. When they do, it's going to look a whole lot better if you know the answers. So prepare yourself for this by anticipating any likely questions. For a start, you should arm yourself with a copy of your terms and conditions of employment. In addition, you should know the answers to questions about:

- **salary**
- **working hours**
- **holiday entitlement**
- **what training you will give the successful candidate**
- **career prospects**
- **how you will notify candidates**
- **whether you will hold second interviews.**

and any other topics you think are likely to be raised.

The process of planning the questions really doesn't have to be a long one at all. But it is an essential one if you want to be sure of appointing the right candidate.

for next time

It is well worth talking through your list of general questions with your boss or a colleague, to make sure you've covered the essentials. By the same token, it can help to ask someone else to look through the applications individually for you to identify any areas that are worth going into in more detail.

5 setting the scene

You're almost there. You've written your job description and employee specification, you've been through the applications, and you've prepared two lists of questions: one general list for everyone, and a brief list of questions or notes for each applicant individually. You're doing well, and it shouldn't have taken you too long to get here. This chapter is about the last few loose ends to tie up before the candidates arrive for their interviews.

The crucial thing to remember about selection is that it is a two-way process. I'm sure you remember what it's like looking for a job yourself. You are invited to several interviews and (you hope) offered more than one position. So you get to choose which organisation you would like to work for out of two or three, if you're lucky.

Your best candidate will have applied for other posts, and may well be someone else's best candidate too. So when they come to select which job they prefer to take, how will you ensure they accept your offer? This chapter is all about treating the candidates in a way that will make them feel that yours is the organisation – and you are the boss – they would most like to work for. Much of it is also plain courtesy, but it can make the difference between whether or not you get the candidate you want.

PREPARE THE ROOM

The traditional image of an interview has the candidate sitting across a desk from the interviewer. But in fact this is a very formal, intimidating set-up for an interview. It is far better to remove this psychological barrier, and seat both yourself and the interviewee (and anyone else present) in comfortable chairs. This will encourage the interviewee to relax and open up.

If your office can't accommodate this kind of relaxed seating, try to borrow another room that is more suitable. If you really can't even do this, at least move the chairs away from the desk.

MAKE THEM FEEL IMPORTANT

There are plenty of other small but important measures you can take to make each candidate feel that you value them. For a start, make sure that you are not the only one prepared for this interview: check that reception has a list of names and interview times, along with anyone who is showing them into the interview room.

> **Each candidate should be welcomed by someone – even if it's the receptionist – as soon as they arrive so that they know they are expected. The receptionist should treat them with the same importance as they would a member of the board or an important customer.**

 thinking smart

DON'T BE CLEVER

You've probably heard of all sorts of techniques to intimidate candidates, ruses for challenging them, and questions for baffling them. Once in a blue moon there might be a valid and justifiable reason for employing these techniques. But for the vast majority of posts it isn't a clever approach. It's far better to be pleasant and friendly, and to put the interviewee at their ease.

FIRST IMPRESSIONS

When the interviewee enters the room, you should stand up, smile, shake hands and address them by name. Tell them who you are, and invite them to sit down.

- **Forestall any interruptions. Divert calls and close the office door, with a notice on it if necessary to ensure that the interviewee has your full attention and knows it.**

- **Start the interview promptly. It is disrespectful to keep people waiting.**

- **Have the job description, employee specification and the candidate's application form to hand during the interview, to show you've done your homework and are treating this interview with the importance it deserves.**

HELP THEM RELAX

Here are a few more steps you can take to help interviewees to calm down if they are nervous, and to prepare themselves for the interview. Remember, this could be a deeply important time for them; they may really want this job.

- **Make sure someone offers to take their coat, and show them to the toilet if they want to visit it.**

- **Offer them a cup of coffee or tea, or a glass of water, either before or during the interview.**

- **Leave copies of the annual report or company newsletter in the waiting area for candidates to look at, and make sure the waiting area – whether it is reception or a corner of an office – is clean and comfortable.**

- **Make sure there is a mirror they can use somewhere in the waiting area.**

- **If you want to keep tabs on the time, don't unsettle the candidate by looking at your watch constantly. Make sure there's a clock you can look at easily.**

BREAKING THE ICE

If you sense that the candidate is nervous, try to put them at their ease for a minute or two before you start the interview proper. Find something to chat about informally on their application form. For example, 'I see you trained in Manchester. I used to work there. What did you think of the city?' Not only will it help them relax, it also proves you've read the application form.

for next time

Give yourself time to arrange a suitable room to hold the interviews in, and make sure every candidate has been given a time and date for the interview in writing, along with directions for getting to you, several days ahead of the interview.

If you sense that the candidate is nervous, try to put them at their ease for a minute or two before you start the interview proper

27

6 the interview

So here you are. All the preparation is done and you're ready to start the interviews themselves. You should have four pieces of paper with you for each interview:

- **the job description**
- **the employee specification**
- **the application form, with notes of questions arising from it**
- **your list of general questions that you are asking all the candidates.**

The room is set up comfortably and reception (and anyone else who needs to know) is expecting the candidates, so it's time to get cracking on the first interview.

This book is about how to think fast and get through the job as quickly as possible. However, you cannot rush an interview. What you can do, however, is to conduct it so effectively that you cover everything you need to, and ensure that your techniques will show up the best candidate first time. That way, you won't have to waste time on second interviews or, worse, appoint the wrong candidate.

When you're looking for your dream house, your best bet is to allow plenty of time to look at each house in detail. You wouldn't rush a viewing. Then the odds are you won't need another look to make up your mind – unless you need someone else to see the house too.

THE INTERVIEW STRUCTURE

Broadly speaking, you should always follow the same structure for an interview:

1 Welcome the candidate and put them at their ease.

2 Ask the questions from your general list, i.e. those arising from the job specification.

3 Ask the questions you identified from the application form, i.e. those that are specific to the candidate.

4 Invite the candidate to ask you any questions he or she has.

thinking smart

NO SECOND CHANCE
Except for the most high-powered posts, second interviews should only be necessary if you are shortlisting candidates for someone else (together with you or not) to interview later. A second interview is not just an opportunity for you to have another go at spotting the most suitable candidate. You don't have that sort of time to waste. So do the job properly first time, and you won't need a second attempt.

Depending on how much time you have, you can pace yourself according to this structure so that you don't get behind schedule. You need allow only a minute or two for the opening courtesies, and about five minutes for the candidate's questions (and for you to tell them what happens next and thank them for coming). Apart from that you can roughly halve the remaining time, using the first half to ask them your general questions, and the second half to ask individual questions.

THE TECHNIQUES

Interviewing is not as simple as just firing off a list of questions. There are techniques you need to use to draw out the candidate, and to get them to give you honest and illuminating answers. And the two key techniques – which go together – are listening and encouraging the candidate to talk.

Let's start with listening. It may sound like an obvious skill, but many managers fail to do it when interviewing (a lot of them fail to do it the rest of the time as well). However, if you don't listen well you will miss vital clues, as well as possibly unsettling your interviewee.

There's more to listening than you might think. Listening properly means taking it all in, not just hearing what the other person says. You know yourself that you can tell when someone is really listening to you and when they aren't; what you may not realise is *how* you can tell. It's something we sense unconsciously as a rule, but there are signs that show the other person you're listening. More importantly, the signs mean you *are* listening, so you won't miss a trick in the interview.

So what are these signs? Well, here are the key ones:

- ▶ **Make frequent eye contact with the interviewee.**

- ▶ **Look interested and show that your attention is on them – don't keep checking the time or getting absorbed in your papers.**

- ▶ **Make the occasional one- or two-word note if you wish, but don't spend the whole time writing while they are talking (don't worry: we'll sort out time for taking notes later).**

- ▶ **Make listening noises from time to time, such as 'uh-huh' and 'hmmm'.**

- ▶ **Don't interrupt them while they're speaking.**

- ▶ **Repeat key points back to them occasionally to show you were listening. For example, 'So you'd planned to go into engineering from the start? That's very dedicated.'**

It's easier than it sounds: these are both the symptoms and the causes of listening. Do them, and you'll find you're listening. Listen naturally, and you'll find you do all these things instinctively.

II thinking smart

BODY LANGUAGE

The way you sit helps to show you are listening – and the right posture will make it easier for you to listen. Sit in a relaxed position, but lean forward slightly to show you're being attentive. If you cross everything – arms and legs – you will appear defensive, which makes it harder for your interviewee to talk freely. So go for a reasonably open posture.

> ### PAST, PRESENT AND FUTURE
> You could break down the first main part of the interview – the general questions for everybody – into a series of questions that goes through each candidate's career from a suitable starting point (school for a candidate in their early twenties, but maybe early career for a fifty-year-old). Talk about their past, then their present job, attitudes, approaches to work and so on, and then their future ambitions.

The second key technique is encouraging the candidate to talk. With some, of course, this is no problem. In some cases, getting them to *stop* talking is more of a challenge (especially if they are nervous). But many people clam up in interviews, especially at the start. If you put them at their ease and listen well, they should open up quite quickly. However, there are plenty of ways of getting them talking almost from the start.

Start with the past

People find it much easier to talk about their past than about, say, their attitudes or their ambitions. It is safe ground, and they don't have to think too hard. So it's an easy place to begin. Ask them about their education or their early career, and watch them relax as they talk.

Let them do the talking

You want the interviewee to do about seventy-five to eighty per cent of the talking in the interview. If you tell them too much about the job, they'll adapt their answers to suit what they think you want. You want to hear about them, so ask the questions and then let them get on with it, while you simply steer them in the right direction. You'll do most of your talking in the opening welcome, and in the last few minutes when they get to ask you questions.

Ask open questions

A shy or nervous candidate may well restrict themselves to brief answers to your questions if they can. So make sure they can't. Don't ask them closed questions – ones to which they can answer 'yes', 'no', 'twelve' or 'green with red stripes'. Ask open questions, to which they have to give a full answer. Open questions tend to start with 'how', 'what' or 'why'. For example: 'How did you come to choose research as a career?' or 'What made you apply for this post?' Another useful phrase at interview is 'Tell me about … your interests at school / your ideas on how businesses can integrate more fully with the Internet / your long-term career objectives', and so on.

Empathise

The candidate may be doing most of the talking, but you're interjecting to ask them questions. You can help to encourage interviewees to talk by showing you're on their side, and want to hear more. So, as you go from one answer to the next question, be human and inject a little friendliness. For example, if you've just asked them what their least favourite subject at school was, you might say, 'I never got on too well with history either. Why do you think it was your least favourite?' You can throw in any comment that is honest and friendly, to make the encounter more

thinking smart

TAKING THE WHEEL

You're in charge of this interview. So it's up to you to keep garrulous candidates under control. You have to keep these interviews running on time. The best technique is this: take over the wheel; don't try to stand in front of the car. In other words, don't block them, just steer them on to the right subject. Find a link and use it. If they're talking at length about how good their university course was, you might say: 'That's what got you interested in a career in marketing, then? So how did you get your first job once you'd got your degree?'

natural, from 'That's an interesting answer' to 'I'm impressed. Nothing would induce *me* to jump out of an aeroplane at several thousand feet.'

DON'T HAVE OPINIONS

You know perfectly well that if you tell an estate agent that you're looking for a house with excellent views, they'll assure you the house they've just sent you details about has the kind of views you only dream of. Interviewees are much the same. If you tell them you think the latest legislation affecting your industry stinks, and then ask them what they think about it, what do you suppose their answer will be?

Yet many managers do precisely this. It may not be as obvious as this example, but they give away their attitudes before asking the interviewee for theirs. And of course any smart candidate will tell you what you want to hear. It can be hard to catch yourself leading the candidate to the answer you want to hear. You might, for example, say: 'I think the Internet is one of the most exciting developments of the last few years. Tell me what experience you've had with it, and how you feel about it.' Even this signposts the type of answer you want to hear.

This really can be tough, because it's the way we often talk to our colleagues and friends. But you're not having a cosy chat now, or even a business debate. You're interviewing, and that is something quite different.

DIGGING DEEPER

This all sounds very nice and friendly so far, and so it should. But things aren't always so easy. Sometimes there are delicate topics that you want to introduce – touchy areas, perhaps, where you're not sure how the interviewee will feel about the question. Perhaps you want to know why they changed career to what appears to be a less challenging and lower-powered job. Maybe you want to know why they haven't had a promotion in nine years with the same company.

thinking smart

STAY ON TOP

Just as some candidates clam up, others try to take control of the interview, and talk about what they want to say, not what you want to hear. Don't stand for it: it's your interview and you should be in control. A simple technique is to start asking a few closed questions. If open questions get people to open up, closed questions get them to close down. You can bring the interview back on to your territory by asking closed questions such as, 'How many years have you been in your present job?' or 'Do you have a driving licence?'

31

ELEMENTARY, MY DEAR WATSON

Try imagining yourself as one of your favourite detectives – Morse, Sherlock Holmes or Poirot – interviewing a witness to try to get at the truth (you'd be well advised to think of the candidate as a witness rather than a suspect). You're looking for clues, and giving away nothing in case it muddies the evidence. This approach may help you to keep your own views hidden during the interview.

We get very sensitive where other people are concerned – understandably. But think about your house-hunting for a moment. If the owners are showing you around a house and you notice a patch of discoloured wallpaper, do you maintain a polite silence? Of course you don't. You say, 'Is that a patch of damp there?' You're not going to risk spending all that money on a house that turns out to have a damp problem you hadn't budgeted for.

Well, you're about to spend as much money on a new employee, so you're going to have to adopt the same approach to any areas of concern: ask about them. And the technique is blindingly simple. You don't faff about, embroider the question or sound embarrassed. You simply ask.

- **What made you choose this career change?**
- **Have you applied for promotion while you've been with your present employer?**
- **What were you doing during the year between these two jobs?**
- **Why did you take a job that entailed a salary drop when you left Zedcon?**

Simple, huh?

The thing is, you *have* to ask these questions. Otherwise you can't find out whether the candidate is suitable for the job. They may look terrific on paper, but that one-year gap could be concealing a recent spell drying out from alcoholism – not ideal if the job involves entertaining a lot of corporate clients.

Equally, you may be tempted to reject them because of that suspicious-looking gap when a little questioning would establish that they were taking time out to look after a dying relative. So you must investigate these areas for both your sakes.

What is more, any candidates worth their salt will be expecting you to ask them this sort of question, so they are unlikely to be offended by it. So long as you're

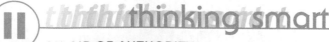
AN AIR OF AUTHORITY

It is much easier to keep the interview on course, and ask the questions you need to, if you have the air of being in charge. This doesn't mean dominating or bullying – far from it. It simply means coming across as confident and sure of yourself, and knowing what you're doing (this is one of the many reasons why the preparation was worth it). If you behave confidently from the outset – standing up, offering a hand to shake, and greeting the candidate with assurance – they will accept your authority without question.

thinking smart

CUTTING BOTH WAYS

Remember that selection is a two-way process. The candidate may have reservations about working for you which you want to set at rest. So probe and ask questions at the end of the interview to make sure they have no lingering doubts. If you suspect they do, put it to them straight: 'I wouldn't want you to leave with any unanswered questions. Please feel free to ask if anything is bothering you. I sense you may have misgivings about our training?'

not personal or rude in your questioning, but simply ask the question straight, they have no reason even to be surprised, let alone put out. Would you be?

Suppose, as sometimes happens, you get an answer to your tricky question that doesn't really satisfy you. What do you do then? The answer here is that you must keep asking the question: 'I'm still not clear why this job you took after Zedcon was worth a salary drop for you?'

And if this still doesn't get an answer that satisfies you (one way or the other), you can simply express your doubts squarely. Say what's bothering you. And, once again, tell it how it is. For example: 'Can I tell you what's worrying me? We're looking for someone with drive and ambition. The successful candidate is likely to find themselves well on their way up the career ladder here in a few years' time. You've been doing the same job at Zedcon for nine years now, and I have to ask myself whether you really have the ambition to take this job where we expect it to go.'

This gives the candidate an opportunity to put their case. Maybe the job at Zedcon has been expanding and growing, and, although the job title hasn't changed, the responsibilities and the expertise needed to do it have grown beyond measure in the last nine years. Then again, maybe this candidate just has no personal drive. Whichever is the case, you won't know unless you explain the problem.

THE LEGAL POSITION

There are laws governing what you can and can't ask candidates at interview. These can vary, but the object is to make sure that all job applicants are treated fairly and without discrimination. You will need to talk to your legal or HR department if you want detailed advice, but broadly speaking you cannot turn down an applicant for discriminatory reasons – and quite right too, of course.

If you reject a candidate who might be subject to unlawful discrimination, you must be able to demonstrate that you had some other, legitimate reason for turning them down. This means that it is very unwise to try to elicit any information you don't need, especially if it could be seen as discriminatory. For example, don't ask a woman if she is planning to start a family – an affirmative answer could be seen as a reason not to take her on, even if you in fact turn her down for some other reason altogether.

This whole legal area can seem like a minefield, but it doesn't need to be. As a basic guideline, if you have a sound business reason for asking a question, that's fine. If you don't, why are you wasting time asking it? If you want a checklist of topics to avoid unless you have a good reason to investigate them, here's a rough (but not exhaustive) guide:

Look after them all the way back to the front door

33

- colour, race, religion, nationality
- age (except to ask if they are over eighteen)
- sex
- disability, handicap, medical history
- marital status, maiden name, details of children, childcare arrangements, future plans for a family
- height and weight
- history of any compensation claims against a previous employer
- English-language skills
- details of arrests or spent convictions, or military service discharge
- credit rating or history of bankruptcy.

CLOSING THE INTERVIEW

Once you have asked everything you need to, and your time is almost up, ask the candidate if they have any questions for you. Give them time to answer this question, and tell them anything you think they might need to know that hasn't been mentioned yet – from the fact that you have a crèche to the training programme you're offering.

Finish the interview by signalling clearly that the end has come, and letting the interviewee know what will happen next: 'We'll be in touch at the beginning of next week.' Thank them for coming, explain any arrangements for claiming travel expenses, and tell them how to find their way out. Ideally you should post someone to show them out, find them their coat or whatever. Otherwise they may feel that now you've finished with them nobody's bothered any more. So look after them all the way back to the front door.

for next time

Make a note of the questions candidates ask you at interview, and make sure next time that you're ready with all the answers. Every time you conduct interviews you discover a little more about what the candidates want to know about your organisation. This means that you can be that little bit more prepared each time you run interviews than you were the last time.

7 decision time

Well, that's it. You've seen all the candidates and it's time to make a decision. What's more, you haven't got time to dither over it for hours or delay it for weeks. You've got to get on with it. But it has to be the right decision, too.

And it's never easy, of course. One of your interviewees may have come across as a confident and friendly personality for the receptionist job, but another was much more experienced in switchboard operating. And then there was the one who just seemed to have a natural rapport with people, but had never done any reception work at all. It is rarely obvious who the most suitable candidate is.

Your notes

But there is one thing that will help you make your decision. Your notes. You remember: the ones I told you not to take during the interview. Well, you can't take them during it, but you can make notes immediately afterwards, as soon as the candidate has left the room. And you must. It's amazing what you can forget after half a dozen or so interviewees have passed before your eyes.

These notes don't have to take long, but they are crucial. They will be your basis for the final decision on whom to appoint. So give them the attention they deserve. Allow yourself about ten minutes between interviews for making notes.

One of the most effective ways to take notes is to have a sheet of paper for each candidate, with headings on it such as 'experience', 'qualifications', 'attitude', 'technical knowledge', 'skills' and so on – whatever is relevant to this post. Then you can simply jot down key points under each heading.

You might also like to have a combined 'score sheet' for all the candidates. The candidates' names go down the side, and there are columns headed 'skills', 'experience', 'attitude' and so on. Give each candidate a score out of ten in each column. If some factors are more important than others, you can weight the scoring in their favour by marking these columns out of twenty. Fill in each candidate's row of marks as soon as their interview is over. At the end, you can see who has scored the most marks:

thinking smart

FINDING A BALANCE

Whatever your system, you'll want to see who has scored best or been given the best notes out of all the candidates. This is generally the most suitable candidate. However, it doesn't have to be, especially if two or more candidates are running neck and neck. The notes and scores count for a lot, but don't disregard your own gut feelings. Take them into account; it's possible they may swing the balance in the end.

	Skills /20	Qualifications /10	Experience /20	Technical knowledge /10	Attitude /10	Total /70
Candidate A	15	8	10	10	9	52
Candidate B	14	7	15	7	8	51
Candidate C	12	7	16	6	6	47
Candidate D	12	6	15	5	6	44

This is a useful approach, but you shouldn't rely on it totally. In the example above, you'll notice that candidate A has the highest score. However, look at the 'experience' column. This candidate is far less experienced than the others. You might decide that this is acceptable, in view of the outstanding performance otherwise. On the other hand you might decide that it still rules them out for the post, given that there is another promising candidate only one point behind on the scoresheet.

So those are your notes. There's no need for long essays; you just need to record enough information to help you make the right choice.

BACKING UP YOUR DECISION

You may be a naturally cautious decision-maker, in which case you will no doubt want to do whatever you can to be sure that your choice of candidate is right. So this section is really for the hasty decision-maker. If you are inclined to make snap decisions based on gut instinct, you won't like this bit. Especially if you're pushed for time too. But please hear me out.

The odds are that when you buy a flat or a house, however sure you are that it's right, you'll still get a survey and do a search on the property. For the money you'll be spending, you'd be daft not to. And you may be a fast thinker, but you're not stupid. When it comes to checking references and possibly even qualifications, these are simply the employment equivalents of doing a survey and a search. You're about to commit as much money as you would on a new house (the only difference being that it's not your own money – but that argument isn't going to impress your boss).

In the worst cases, the most successful bluffers are very often the most impressive candidates. After all, if you have no compunction about stretching the truth, you can make yourself sound pretty good, and such candidates tend to be brimming with confidence and self-assurance. More realistically, many candidates will not be hardened fraudsters, but they will obviously paint the best picture of themselves that they can. If they are naturally confident and personable, they will come across well even if their record isn't quite so ideal.

thinking smart

THE RIGHT CRITERIA

One of the key things to bear in mind when you are making your choice is that you must measure each candidate individually against the standards for the job. You are not measuring them against each other. A scoresheet, while not a final decider, can help you to look at the candidates in the light of the criteria you set at the start of the process (when you drew up the job description and the employee specification).

References

So when you think you know who you want to appoint, check their references first. It's always best to do this by phone, since people speak more freely than they write – they may not want a permanent record of their comments, for legal reasons apart from anything else.

Even on the phone, you're not likely to get any blatant negative comments from referees; they will probably be quite subtle in their hints. Apart from anything else, the law of slander applies to telephone references, and they will probably know this. So what they *don't* say may be as telling as what they do. You can, of course, ask specific questions, but there's no point trying to pressure a referee into answering a question they don't want to.

A referee's opinion is, of course, only one view, and as such it shouldn't influence you too heavily (unless they tell you something really terrible, such as that the candidate you're interviewing for the post of minibus driver was sacked for being drunk while driving a company vehicle; and how often is that likely to happen?). It is also possible that the referee wasn't a big fan of the candidate, so a single weak reference doesn't have to sway your view.

So what's the point of taking up references in that case? Well, what you're really looking for are any comments that reinforce your own reservations. If you suspect that this promising candidate may not work well under pressure, you should take note if a referee suggests this is the case (assuming it is important they should cope well). Obviously, if you talk to two or three referees and they all say the same thing, this too will start to give a more reliable picture.

Qualifications

Managers almost never check qualifications, and you may decide it isn't necessary. However, some people do claim qualifications they don't have in order to help clinch a job. And even if the qualification itself isn't that important to you, the fact that this person is prepared to lie about it might well sway your judgement of them. So check qualifications if you feel any kind of suspicion that they may not be genuine.

You should also check any qualification if it's essential, for example legal qualifications for a company lawyer. You should check them even if you feel no doubt that they are genuine. It's the only way to be cast-iron certain.

thinking smart

THE MISSING LINK

The most obvious references for anyone to give are their current employer and their previous one. But people don't tend to give references they don't think will speak well of them. Many people leave their current employer off their references because they don't want them to know they're looking for a new job. But if the previous employer is also missing, it should make you wonder why. The best bet is to ask the candidate straight during the interview: 'Can you tell me why your references don't include either your present employer or your last one?' There may be a good reason, of course, but you won't find out unless you ask.

thinking smart

ONE MAN'S MEAT...

The fact that a past employer has a negative comment about your candidate isn't necessarily a bad thing. It depends on your requirements for the job. Suppose two referees mention that your candidate isn't at their best under pressure. Does this actually matter to you? Some negative comments may even signal positive benefits to you. A comment such as 'He doesn't like having to stick to the rules' may be the sign you want if you're looking for someone who can employ initiative and work off their own back (so long as they're not going to lock all the fire doors, of course, or bring a loaded gun into the office).

thinking fast

PASS IT ON

Checking qualifications is simply a matter of phoning the college, university or training provider concerned and asking them to confirm the qualification for you. So if time is at a premium, get someone else to do this for you.

Tests

There are loads of psychometric, intelligence and aptitude tests around that some organisations like to use. Don't do them just for fun; use these tests only if you really feel they can shed valuable light on whom you should appoint. Bear in mind that all these tests have limitations and can fail to spot certain strong positive or negative qualities or abilities that fall outside their scope. So use them as an additional resource to feed into your decision, but don't rely heavily on them.

As a general guideline, run the tests on all the candidates before the interviews if you wish, but don't look at the results until after the interviews, and after you have written notes and filled in the scoresheet if you're using one. This means you will use the test results only as a back-up to check your own conclusions – a much more sensible approach.

OTHER CONSIDERATIONS

There are two other factors in particular that you may need to consider in making your decision. The first of these is the danger of making moral judgements about candidates. We're all guilty of making such judgements at times. Maybe we think people ought to show plenty of application and the ability to stick at things. Perhaps we think a strong imagination is better than a poor one. Maybe we feel it is better for people to have some drive and ambition, or that being very shy is a real handicap.

In fact, these are all judgements and many of them are ill-advised. It may be better for *you* to be a certain way, and you may prefer the company of people who are like this. But different jobs have different requirements. There is, for example, a popular belief that it's a good thing to be a team player. But if you want someone to work as a designer, spending all day alone in the graphics studio, a real team player is the last person you need. They would be frustrated and lonely, and would probably leave before long for a job in a more sociable environment. So avoid making subjective judgements of this kind.

thinkingsfast

CUT YOUR LOSSES

Almost without exception (the exception being aptitude tests related directly to the post), you might as well abandon doing any tests if time is short, whatever your usual company practice is. The value they contribute just doesn't justify the time and cost of running them.

Fitting into a team

The other factor to consider is the question of who your new employee will be working with. If you're selecting someone to work as part of a close-knit project team, you'll need to take into account how each promising interviewee would mesh with the rest of the team.

Clearly, personality is a factor in who will fit into an existing team. If the team works well at the moment, it shouldn't be hard to find someone who can slot in easily. If things are a little strained, perhaps you will want to look for a natural diplomat, or someone who isn't likely to try to take over. Maybe the team needs someone laid-back, could do with a bit of an injection of energy, or would benefit from someone with a good sense of humour.

But you also need to take into account the team's natural abilities. Some people are naturally good at coming up with ideas, or at problem-solving, getting on with the hard graft, or encouraging co-operation from outside the team. You need to take these factors into account and find someone who will expand the abilities of the team as a unit. For example, if all the team are great at generating ideas, but not so strong on carrying them through, it might not be wise to appoint yet another ideas person, even if they have all the right qualifications and experience.

LETTING EVERYONE KNOW

Make your decision as promptly as you can, for everyone's sake. Once you have all the information, from the application forms to your own interview notes and any references, there's nothing to be gained by prevaricating. Don't rush the decision, but don't put it off either. If you find decision-making difficult (and plenty of managers do), you can always read *fast thinking: Decision*, also in this series.

If you're pushed for time, offer the job to your preferred candidate by phone (although a letter is just as good when time allows). You'll need to follow up the call with a letter in due course. Don't reject the next two candidates until you have a definite acceptance from your first choice.

Write as promptly as possible to all the other candidates, thanking them for their time and wishing them success in finding a position. Remember that they may be – or may talk to – potential future employees or customers, so you want to leave them with a warm impression of your organisation.

WHAT IF YOU DRAW A BLANK?

Sometimes, there simply isn't a suitable applicant to give the job to. No one really satisfies you that they can do the job well. So what then? The answer, I'm afraid, is that you have to go through the whole process again (stop groaning). The thing is, if you give the job to someone unsuitable:

Find someone who will expand the abilities of the team

thinking smart

MEET AND GREET

You can always get the team – or key players in it – to meet each candidate informally. Get the team leader to greet each candidate at reception and look after them until the interview starts. Or call the candidates in fifteen minutes early so they can have a chat over coffee with the rest of the team. This is only an informal meeting, but it makes the team feel involved, and they can tell you if they found anyone particularly promising or if there was a candidate they really didn't warm to.

thinking smart

TEAM ROLES AT WORK

When you have a little time, it's worth studying Dr Meredith Belbin's work on team roles. Start by looking at his book *Management Teams: Why they succeed or fail*, published by Butterworth-Heinemann. This will tell you all about the key roles you need to fill to create an effective team.

- ▶ **They won't do the job as well as you'd like, and they'll probably leave before long – at which point you'll have to go through it all again anyway.**

- ▶ **It's not fair on them, since they won't be happy and they won't do as well as they could in a more suitable job. And that could hold back their career.**

Before you repeat the exercise exactly, however, it would be smart to ask yourself why it didn't work this time. If you simply do the same thing again, why should you be any more successful? It may be that your requirements are unrealistic. Perhaps you're looking for a very experienced receptionist with a lot of peripheral skills, at a salary that no experienced receptionist would accept. Maybe you should raise the salary – or lower your requirements. Or perhaps you're trying to find someone with a huge range of skills to do a very pressured job. It might be better to split it into two jobs, each calling for a somewhat narrower range of skills.

Most managers panic at the thought of not appointing someone, even if they're not ideal. After all, you've got to have a receptionist. It's no good putting up a sign for visitors saying, 'Sort yourselves out. We can't find a suitable receptionist. The coffee machine's over there.'

thinking smart

CHANGE YOUR ADVERTISING

Your inability to find someone suitable this time may not be down to the nature of the job you're offering. Maybe you just haven't caught the eye of the most likely applicants. Perhaps you should advertise elsewhere – nationally instead of locally, or in trade publications, or to graduates. Or maybe you should look harder for suitable internal applicants. Perhaps the right person is out there somewhere … but you haven't found each other yet.

But think smart. There's always a better way than appointing the wrong person. You could delay your present receptionist's promotion, or ask them to stay beyond their period of notice. You could hire someone on a short-term contract. You could get a temp in. You could get everyone in the sales office to cover for an hour a day. You could move someone over from another department for a few weeks. You could get your calls routed through an external switchboard service. You'll come up with something ...

for next time

When you have time, prepare well in advance for anything that will help you make your decision more easily. For example:

▶ If you want the team to meet the candidates informally, organise this ahead so the team can make sure they're around for the interviews.

▶ If tests are going to help you, prepare for these in advance.

▶ If you're trying to fill a technical post and you're not a technical expert yourself, you could arrange for a more technically-minded colleague to spend a few minutes interviewing each candidate after you.

8 other types of interview

We've covered the standard selection interview, which is most likely what you're conducting at the moment. But it's possible that you may be running a slightly different type of interview – or you may need to in the future – so it's worth running through the guidelines for a few key interview types.

SECOND INTERVIEWS

When a job is a key one, you may occasionally find that you really cannot choose between two candidates after the initial round of interviews. I said earlier that you should aim to do the job properly first time, and so you should for a receptionist, a PR assistant or a sales executive. But more high-powered jobs are different. Often, two applicants will bring very different skills and it is hard to be sure which is the better choice.

But there's no point just repeating the interview you have already done. When you find yourself in this position, you need to call the candidates back in order to investigate their secondary skills in more depth and to identify their differing strengths. So you'll need to work hard to prepare a list of questions that will reveal more than the first interview's questions.

The other typical reason for holding second interviews is that you have produced a second shortlist of candidates who you consider are potential appointees, and someone else also needs to interview them with you. In this case, you will need to repeat many of the original questions for the benefit of your colleague.

PANEL INTERVIEWS

These are far more intimidating for the poor interviewee, so you need to work extra hard to make sure you put them at their ease. Don't make them sit alone on one side of a desk or table with all of you lot facing them across it. Sit in easy chairs if you can, or at least all sit round a table together. And make sure you tell the interviewee who you all are and your positions in the organisation.

You need to be well prepared (second nature to you, I'm sure); otherwise you can give a poor impression by being unsure who is asking what questions in what order. Divvy up the questions in advance, and follow a logical thread.

INTERVIEWING INTERNAL APPLICANTS

The way you handle internal applicants at interview is important. It is essential that they feel they are being treated fairly, and on an equal footing with other applicants. If they don't get the job, they will have to carry on working in the organisation, probably alongside the successful candidate (most internal applicants apply for jobs in their own department, or one they work with closely).

PANEL SAFEGUARDS

Make notes individually at the end of each interview, and keep your own scoresheets, before you discuss the candidate with each other. Otherwise your views may be influenced by each other's, especially if someone has a particularly strong view about any of the candidates.

In order to treat internal applicants fairly:

- **Make their interview as formal as everyone else's, despite any temptation to be informal. If it doesn't feel like an interview to them, it won't feel right.**

- **Give them as much time as everyone else, and don't answer their questions for them, or say, 'Of course, I know you can handle this, so we don't need to go into it.'**

- **Ask them exactly the same general questions as everyone else. These form your basis for assessing everyone against the same yardstick, so make sure your internal applicant has an equal opportunity to measure up to it.**

- **Don't assume they know more than they do about the job. It's safest to tell them exactly what you have told all the other candidates – they won't mind if some of it isn't news to them.**

 thinking smart

LETTING THEM DOWN GENTLY

Be especially considerate if you have to reject an internal applicant, and make sure you don't damage their confidence. Be as positive as you can and – above all – make sure they hear it from you first.

interview in an evening

So the interviews are at nine o'clock tomorrow morning, and you haven't started on them yet? Whoops. Never mind: you can get yourself straight by morning, even if you have to spend most of this evening working. What you really need are a few tips for getting through this process as fast as possible.

- ▶ **Before you leave the office, collect the following documents:**
    - **– the application forms**
    - **– the job description**
    - **– the employee specification.**

    Skim through the last two of these and check they still apply to the post (they may have been drawn up ages ago). If they don't, rework them so that they are accurate.

- ▶ **If either the job description or the employee specification (or both) don't exist, you'll have to write one. This shouldn't take long; read Chapter 2.**

- ▶ **Also before you leave, make sure the receptionist and anyone else who needs to know is prepared for tomorrow's interviews. Promise them a list of candidates first thing in the morning, before the first one turns up (and make sure you remember to draw up the list). And check that your office, or whatever room you plan to use, will be available and set up for the morning.**

- ▶ **Write your list of general questions for all the applicants (see page 23) – you can do this before you go through the applications.**

- ▶ **Now go through the application forms, and make notes of the individual questions you want to ask each applicant (see page 24).**

- ▶ **Finally, read Chapter 6 on the interview itself before tomorrow morning.**

- ▶ **After the interviews are over, read Chapter 7 (on making the decision) before you finalise your choice.**

interview in an hour

Uh-oh. An hour to go, and you've only just cleared the rest of the work out of the way. Now you have sixty minutes to turn the pile of application forms in front of you into a well prepared interview plan. You need Rumpelstiltskin. Failing that, you need to move fast. Very fast.

1 Read Chapter 1 so that you know what objective you're trying to achieve. When you're in a rush, you need a clear head more than ever.

2 To begin with, you need a job description and employee specification. If you don't have these on file – maybe this is a new post you're creating – you'll have to write them now (see Chapter 2). If someone is currently doing the job in question, and the job description and employee specification are out of date or non-existent, show them Chapter 2 of this book and ask them to draft the documents for you in the next thirty minutes. Then you'll have to check them.

3 Now go through the applications. You shouldn't be doing this unless you already have the job description and employee specification in front of you, but this isn't the time to quibble. Use a highlighter pen to identify any specific areas that you want to question the candidate about – you don't have time to write out a list of questions.

4 Once you have a copy of the job description you can draw up a list of general questions to ask everyone (if you were lucky enough to have it from the start, it might be better to write these questions before you go through the applications). Take each of the key responsibilities on the job description and turn it into a question: 'One of the requirements of the job is [key responsibility]. What experience do you have in this area?'

5 Now do the same with the key attributes on the employee specification: 'This job calls for someone who can [key attribute]. Tell me what past experience you have of this.'

6 Finally, once you have your documents and your questions ready, arrange the room so that it is suitable for interviewing (see page 26).

Now take a deep breath, relax, and get ready to smile and greet the first candidate warmly. They're on their way down the corridor now.

appraisal

 **AVOID CONFRONTATION**

AGREE SMART OBJECTIVES

MOTIVATE YOUR STAFF

richard templar

contents

introduction

Goodness me, but doesn't time fly. It seems only yesterday that you sent out that appraisal notice. And now the appraisal is due – tomorrow – and you haven't even dug out their file or their appraisal form from last time, let alone sorted out a suitable room.

OK, so maybe you've done all that, but have you got a copy of their job description – yes, an updated one, of course? Have you worked out what you are going to say? Have you identified any training they may need? What about their performance as measured against standards? And surely you've got notes of any critical incidents that have occurred since the last review? No?

Well, in that case, what you need is an express guide to zip you through the appraisal system at breakneck speed and still make sure you end up conducting an appraisal that is useful both to you and the member of your team. You wouldn't dream of going into an appraisal interview with no notes, no job description, no employee personnel file, no nothing, would you? Well, you'd be surprised just how many managers do. But you're going to want to do it fast and smart, right? Then this is the very book for you.

Conducting an appraisal isn't about mulling over how they've been since their last interview or using it as an opportunity to slag them off about all the things they've done wrong. Neither is it an exercise in mutual appreciation. It's a skilled process and one that can do you both good. You wouldn't run your car throughout the year without some routine maintenance, would you? And neither would you let an employee just get on with their job without monitoring their performance – and once monitored they need to be told how they are doing and have a chance to explore that with you in some depth.

I know all this seems a lot to ask when time is so short but it can be done – and easily and efficiently at the same time. Doing something well doesn't necessarily mean doing it slowly – ask a champion racing car driver.

Maybe you've prepared absolutely nothing in which case we are going to have our work cut out – but we can still do it and have you looking pretty cool.

Or maybe you've prepared everything but haven't a clue what you're supposed to say or how to conduct the interview. We'll help you with that as well. You just need:

 tips and shortcuts for getting on top of this interview fast

 guidelines for running a successful appraisal

 speedy information about what to say and how to say it

 checklists to make sure you haven't forgotten anything

... and all presented clearly and logically. And short enough to take in quickly. You've come to the right place.

And what if you've really run out of time and the appraisal interview is scheduled for later this morning? In about one hour? Well, it can still be done – and still done well. At the back of this book, you'll find a brief guide to appraisal interviews in a real hurry. Now that really is thinking at the speed of life.

So chill for a moment and take a deep breath. You may have left everything to the last minute but help is at hand. You're going to have to think fast and think smart but you can do it. Now you know you could do it in 60 minutes if you were really up against the clock, having a whole day seems positively extravagant, doesn't it? OK, let's get started.

work at the speed of life

APPRAISALS AT THE SPEED OF LIFE

This book will guide you through the seven key stages of appraisal interviews:

1 Before you can proceed you need to identify your objective – what do you intend to achieve by holding this interview and what is the member of staff going to get out of it?

2 Telling the member of staff what is happening. You have to give them some time to prepare and let them know what is expected of them.

3 Get yourself ready. You need certain key documents and you need to have carried out certain key things beforehand – don't worry, we'll tell you what in a moment.

4 Hold the interview. There's a right place and a wrong place. We'll guide you through selecting just the right place and making it appropriate for the interview.

5 Structure the interview. We'll guide you through such things as setting an agenda – yep, you're going to need one. And setting a time limit, that sort of thing. Essential.

6 What are you going to say? And how are you going to say it? We'll guide you through asking the right questions, making the right noises and displaying the right attitude.

7 How to correct faults and improve performance – constructive criticism.

fast thinking gambles

So, we can get you through it quickly and smartly but there are risks. If you follow the guidelines in this book you shouldn't go far wrong; you'll conduct a good interview that is worthwhile for both of you, *and* for your organisation. But there is always a risk when you do things as fast as we are going to:

- You won't have had enough time to make sure their job description is really up to date – that it matches what they do now as opposed to what they were supposed to do when they first joined your company. These things do have a habit of getting out of sync.

- Their personnel file may not be up to date and you simply won't have time to run around collecting all the relevant information.

- You may not have time to find and prepare a suitable room and may have to make do with your own office with all the attendant interruptions and its inherent lack of neutrality.

- You can be so rushed you haven't had time to read their response to the employee preparation document.

- You can even be so rushed you are halfway through interviewing when you realise you have the wrong person entirely – not likely after you've read this book, but it does happen, although only to managers less smart than you.

- Your team member brings a whole lot of points to the interview and you haven't left yourself enough time to work through them.

Fast thinking will get you through the appraisal interview at speed and you'll end up doing a damn good job. And that's the point of the exercise. But for next time you really could do with leaving yourself a little more time. Not only can you do an even better job, but it'll ease the pressure on your heart a bit.

1 your objective

Have you got time for this? The appraisal interview is tomorrow – drawing nearer by the minute – and you're supposed to be worrying about objectives. You just need to talk to a member of your team about their progress, right?

No, not really. You have to do a bit more than just have a chat. You are trying to *appraise* a colleague and that means assessing their performance; evaluating their strengths and weaknesses; reviewing their implementation of company procedures; considering their future and possible training and development needs; valuing their commitment and input – and letting them explain what they need in the way of support, advice, guidance and motivational tools. Whew, bit more than just a chat.

Of course, you could just pull up a chair and have a bit of a chat or tell them off for what you consider they've done wrong, pat them on the back and send them on their way. How do you think they would feel?

You could hold this informal chat in the staff canteen with their colleagues listening in over tea and doughnuts. How do you think they would feel?

You could just summon them with no prior warning – the sort of 'be in my office in ten minutes' routine. Again, how do you think they would feel?

Yep, you could do any of these, but it wouldn't be an appraisal interview. I'm not sure what it would be except not the sort of thing we expect from a smart manager like you.

No, the correct procedure is to think it out beforehand – set an objective if you like. That way the staff will feel that you've taken the time, trouble and effort to really appraise them; that you regard it as important and considerate to give them a proper appointment in a suitably private place free from interruptions and noise; that you consider them worthy of getting your facts straight and that you have bothered to look at their personnel file and know who they are – and what they do.

An appraisal interview is an opportunity to review performance on both sides. They may have a lot to say about how they feel and you really have to set aside long enough for both of you to communicate effectively.

When you conduct proper, well-thought-out and stimulating appraisal interviews your staff feel cared about, motivated, encouraged and rewarded. We all like to know how we are doing, to have a set of guidelines against which we can measure our performance.

We like to be challenged to do better and to know when we've messed up. We like our performance to be assessed by people we respect and whose opinion we value. We are all motivated by a desire to please.

So, that's what we are going to do with every one of our appraisal interviews from now on. We are going to use them as an opportunity to:

- ▶ **assess**
- ▶ **consider**

thinking smart

▶ **evaluate**

▶ **review**

▶ **value.**

That way our team members are going to feel:

▶ **cared about**

▶ **encouraged**

▶ **motivated**

▶ **rewarded**

▶ **stimulated.**

And they will have a clear view of where they have been and where they are going. That's our objective: *to give our team members documented feedback so they know how they are performing and to let them have an opportunity to discuss how they see their progress and work.*

Now let's see how quickly we can achieve it and what good results it will produce.

for next time

If you haven't taken many appraisal interviews or find them exhausting, daunting, or just plain nerve wracking, make sure you ask for some guidance yourself at *your* next appraisal interview. And ask to go on a proper training course in personnel management.

An appraisal interview is an opportunity to review performance on both sides

53

2 preparing the team member

So the appraisal is tomorrow and your team member is all ready and expectant. They *are* ready, aren't they? You did notify them in advance what was happening and give them the opportunity to prepare themselves? You didn't? Then we have little time and a lot to do. Hang on to your hat – this is staff preparation at the speed of life.

THE OFFICIAL MEMORANDUM

OK, first things first. You have a note in your diary that tomorrow a member of staff is coming for their periodic assessment. Do they know this? Have you informed them? In an ideal world you would have told them at least ten days ago – and told them officially, in writing, in a memorandum. And the more senior they are the more you would have consulted them to make sure the time and day was mutually convenient. There is nothing worse than trying to give someone an appraisal when they are looking at their watch and fretting about an impending deadline of their own.

THE PRE-APPRAISAL INTERVIEW

For more junior members of staff for whom cover can be arranged easily you can be more managerial in your imposition of a time and day. But if the member of staff is very new you might like to have a pre-appraisal interview. This should only take about ten minutes but is invaluable for them. All you have to do is take them through the procedure and explain what is going to happen. Quick and productive – that's what we like.

The official notification for an assessment should be on official paper and logged and filed so there can be no dispute at a later date about who was supposed to be where. If you haven't already done this you had better do it now – and quickly. It should state:

- the team member's name
- their job title
- the purpose of the memo – their appraisal and the period it covers, i.e. six monthly, annual etc.
- the purpose of the appraisal – to provide feedback on their performance and to give them an opportunity to discuss their work performance and any future training or promotion needs
- when and where the appraisal is to take place
- roughly how long it will last – at least an hour

- who is issuing the memo – yes, I know it's you but give your full name and job title
- and finally sign it and keep a copy.

Do this now if you didn't at least ten days ago. And attach to it a copy of your organisation's *appraisal preparation document*. What? You haven't got one? Then you'd better draw one up quickly. After all, this appraisal is a two-way process. Not only do you get a chance to discuss your team member's performance but they also get a chance too, you know. And the appraisal preparation document also gives you a chance to see beforehand exactly how they regard their own performance. This could help you enormously if you think they are well below average and they think they are well above. You have a chance to clarify this before the appraisal gets off the ground on the wrong foot if you'll pardon the mixed metaphor.

THE APPRAISAL PREPARATION DOCUMENT

With such a document there used to be a trend to give the employee lots of boxes to tick but that was proved to be unproductive as they merely ticked boxes and you didn't get any feedback at all. Nowadays the current thinking is to give the employee lots of space to fill in their own comments – much better. The sort of thing you might like to provide could look like this.

Name

Job title

Date and time of appraisal

The purpose of this form is to give you an opportunity to prepare for your appraisal so that your assessment can be as productive as possible. Please fill in the spaces as fully as possible.

How do you consider you have carried out the main functions of your job?

Which tasks have you performed best, and why?

Are there any areas of your job which you feel to be unclear?

Do you feel the need for any extra training and, if so, what sort of training would be helpful?

What would be helpful to you in order for you to carry out your job more successfully?

Which aspects of your job interest you the most?

Which aspects interest you least?

Are there any functions of your job which you feel you have underachieved at, and why?

How do you see your future with the company?

If you haven't already issued one of these do it now and give them at least the rest of the day to complete it and get it back to you.

Keep a copy of this form in their file and have it with you at their appraisal of course. And make sure you have read it and fully understand where they are coming from before the assessment.

WHAT THEY CAN EXPECT

By sending out these two bits of paper you inform, reassure and include. Information is essential to any organisation's smooth running. Reassurance is imperative if the staff aren't to be intimidated by the appraisal system – and you certainly don't want that. And inclusion makes them feel as if they belong – which they do.

Their appraisal is important to them. It helps them know *where* they are going and *how* they are doing. Don't let them approach it with a feeling of fear or trepidation. Don't let them feel it means nothing to *you*. Let them know it is a two-way process and be ready to listen. Their appraisal is just that – an appraisal, with the emphasis perhaps on praise. It is not an interview. It is not a school report. It is not a court case. It is not an interrogation. It is an appraisal – an opportunity to *praise* and *raise* issues.

BE POSITIVE

Different organisations have different terminology for this periodic review. It might simply be called an appraisal. But then again it might be a staff development review; a performance review; a development needs assessment; a staff assessment; even a staff development and assessment appraisal. Whatever it is called try to make the staff feel it is friendly, productive and useful. Make sure that when you talk about it you use positive upbeat phrases and don't downgrade it by talking about 'those bloody appraisals I've got to do' – that sort of thing is bad for morale and makes the staff feel you're just going through the motions because you have to. If your heart's not in it, theirs won't be either.

NO SURPRISES

Reassure the team member in advance that there will be no surprises. You aren't suddenly going to launch an attack on them for a past misdemeanour or a lost order or late attendance. You will have dealt with all that at the time. Their appraisal is their opportunity to discuss jointly their performance on a grand scale, their future, their progress, their objectives and focus, their prospects and their approach to the job. It is not a nit-picking session, a telling off or a litany of complaints.

DOCUMENTATION

Make sure you keep copies of every document you send out and receive back, starting with these advance documents:

- ▶ **notification memo**
- ▶ **appraisal preparation document.**

This is protection for your staff as well as for you. If they later claim that you did not mention at their appraisal that you were dissatisfied with their performance but subsequently you have to let them go, how will you justify it if you haven't kept a copy of everything?

for next time

Make sure you get the forms sent out at least ten days in advance. Any new members of staff will need a pre-appraisal interview to let them know what to expect.

When you get their appraisal preparation document back take some time to read it and understand it. Check with colleagues who work closely with the team member if there is a big difference between how you perceive their performance and how they see it.

When you send out the memo informing the team member of the time and place make sure the tone is right – not so formal that it scares them and not so informal that they think they can take it or leave it.

3 preparing the team leader

Yep, that's you, that is – the team leader. OK, so you've got a date for tomorrow. A member of staff, one of your valued and trusted team people, is coming to see you for their periodic appraisal. You are ready, aren't you? You have gathered together all the relevant documents, haven't you? No? Well then, we'd better be quick. The clock is ticking and there are only so many hours in a day – this day, this one, the one before tomorrow when you have the appraisal to do. Quickly now. Let's run through a checklist of what you need – and why.

First, you need their appraisal preparation document back – and you need to read it. It's pointless them filling it in if you don't. Check it for any major differences. For instance, if you think that a particular aspect of their job is the most vital and interesting and they obviously think it the least important and most boring there is a fundamental assessment gap. You need to check with other supervisory staff to see if it is you or them that has hold of the wrong end of the stick.

THEIR JOB DESCRIPTION

Have you read their personnel file? No? Then go get it quickly and set aside at least half an hour to go through it and see what's there. And what most definitely should be there right at the front is their job description – and it should be up to date, of course. And of course it won't be, will it? It never is. And we don't really expect it to be so. Jobs aren't static and stagnant. They grow organically. The only time a job description is bang up to date is the very first day someone starts a new job. After that bits get added on and bits taken away. It happens all the time to all of us.

Trouble with an out-of-date job description is it is very hard to put it to someone that an aspect of their job isn't being carried out effectively if they can turn round and say, 'Well, it isn't part of my job officially anyway – so what's the beef?'

Go through their job description and make notes of any aspects that don't tally with what they actually do. You can then use these notes as part of the appraisal

thinking smart

PREPARATION IS IMPORTANT

We all like to look flash and think on our feet at times but an appraisal isn't one of those times. You want to be thoroughly prepared. After all a team member is an asset, a useful and productive contributor and an appreciated colleague – surely worth spending some time and effort on. Preparation makes them feel valued and that is important.

itself. You can check to see if they are happy with any duties that have been added on or unhappy with any that have gone.

The ideal job description

Their job description should be a clear definition of their overall work objectives broken down into key areas of activity. It shouldn't be too long – no more than one A4 sheet – neither should it be too detailed. It should list the key responsibilities, not individual items. It isn't a job breakdown sheet or a list of daily duties. It should be broad in its outlook and cover the focus and objectives of the job rather than the detail or the itemised specifics.

THEIR LAST APPRAISAL

Now you need a copy of their last appraisal. Obviously, if they have joined you since the last reviews you won't have one – but you will still have given them their pre-appraisal interview, won't you?

Hopefully, the last appraisal is completed satisfactorily and there was an action plan. Has it been carried out? If not, why not? If so, was it done effectively, did the team member benefit from it? Did they go on that training course they so desperately wanted? Did they get the extra set of safety guidelines for operating the new ZX4000 they requested? Have they been rewarded/thanked for taking on the responsibility for training the new apprentice? That sort of thing.

CRITICAL INCIDENT REPORTS

Does their personnel file have a critical incident report – the sort of thing that covers major breaches of security or discipline or performance? Their appraisal isn't the place to bring these things up – they should have been dealt with at the appropriate time. That's right, immediately the incident occurred. If they have had a critical incident or any disciplinary hearings then you should be fully aware of them. Have they had any written warnings? Or verbal warnings? (They should have been recorded in writing, yes, I know it's a funny old world.) What about compassionate leave? Any record of medical problems?

Make sure you know this team member as well as they know themselves.

APPRAISAL RECORDS

Naturally, you have a blank one of these, don't you? No? Heavens, we really do have our work cut out. OK, quickly now, we don't have much time. In an ideal world you

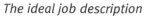

thinking fast

UPDATE JOB DESCRIPTIONS

Every couple of months set aside a little time and quickly check through all your staff members' job descriptions. If you monitor regularly, any changes are easy to spot and quickly put right. If you leave it too long it is a very time-consuming job indeed. A little and often is good maintenance and regular servicing. A long time between services is a breakdown on the motorway.

CHECKING WITH OTHERS

It never hurts to have a quick chat with other managers who come into contact with your team member just to make sure you haven't missed anything or been too hasty. They may know something you don't or have been aware of a drop in standards that you might have missed. They might also have praise for effort you might have overlooked or it might be outside your area of responsibility. Check also with the team member's immediate supervisor, of course, before their appraisal and make the supervisor feel included in the process.

would start an appraisal with a blank sheet of paper and fill it in according to how the appraisal goes. We don't, however, live in an ideal world and you need some sort of form to give you a structure and a checklist to make sure you've covered everything. If your organisation uses a ready prepared form hopefully it won't be just a case of ticking boxes or giving marks out of ten. You need to write something human and make real comments.

You could draw up something that looks like this.

Present duties

Approach to work

Motivation

Acceptance of responsibilities

Supervisory capacity

Technical knowledge

Planning, organising, co-ordinating abilities

Team qualities

Strengths

Weaknesses

Areas for improvement

Training/guidance/instruction required

Long-term goals

Employee's comments

Manager's comments

Obviously you may have to adjust this to suit your own working environment and organisation but it is a broad outline of the type of thing required. You will notice that there is no space for pay or conditions. These aren't discussed at an appraisal and should be avoided at all costs. Pay should be discussed at a pay review and conditions, benefits and bonuses should all be discussed at another meeting entirely.

That's the paperwork complete. You should have:

- **job description**
- **personnel file**
- **previous appraisal form**
- **employee's completed appraisal preparation document**
- **blank appraisal form**
- **any notes you have made.**

HOW ABOUT YOU?

Good, now how about you? Feeling confident? Nervous? What? It's vital that you approach an appraisal with the right attitude. You're not there to play God, be a judge or jury, be an interrogator or exercise any form of punishment or discipline. You are there to act as a conduit, a catalyst. The object of the game is to try to stay out of the way as much as possible and allow the *structure* of the appraisal to take over and run itself. If you are clever you will get the employee to point out their own defects and recommend their own correction or retraining. Lots more about this in Chapter 6 ('What to say and how to say it').

THE JOB, NOT THE PERSON

Now remember you are going to talk about the job – not the person. The job has to be done and this team member has the responsibility to do it. How well they do it is almost irrelevant. What you are interested in is whether the job is being done. Focus on the job and not the person and you will sail through this appraisal. This especially applies when you are gathering information – especially other people's opinions about the team member. You are interested in how the job is being done, not whether they wear an earring to work or slurp their tea or collect

thinking smart

AVOID GIVING POINTS

The smart manager knows that by giving points or marks out of ten they generate a feeling, in the team member, of being at school. Much better, and smarter, to make notes and comments in plain English that are easy to read and understand that relate to the job and whether or not it is being done well. Is a B+ better or worse than 6 out of 10? Smarter to say, 'You're doing this part of your job well but I feel it might be more efficient if you always filled in the NZ27 form in triplicate so we all had a copy. What do you think?

thinking smart

REPHRASE THE PHRASE

Never say, *'You are inefficient'*, it just causes alarm, hostility and anger. Try saying, *'The job isn't being done as efficiently as we might expect, what do you think?'* Much better, and no reason for the team member to feel threatened or antagonised.

furry gonks on their desk. All these things may make them a colourful person but it doesn't affect how the job is being done.

Concentrating on the job rather than the person makes it easy if you know the person quite well – they may even socialise with you after work – you aren't, in this sense, appraising them but the job instead and whether or not it is being done effectively and efficiently.

If you bear this in mind it makes it so easy to know what topics you can talk about. Lateness, for instance, may be thought of as a topic for an appraisal. Not so. Lateness is a disciplinary matter and should be dealt with at the time it occurs – or a little while after. Same with attitude, interpersonal staff relationships, dress sense or code, sickness, faults, mistakes or slipups.

This is an objective appraisal – not a subjective review. Note the distinction and stick to it. Discuss facts – not opinions, hearsay, rumours, feelings, personalities or prejudices.

Sticking to talking about the job makes it so much easier to correct any problems. You only need explain that certain aspects of the job aren't being fulfilled and the team member doesn't have to be personally criticised. Even the most difficult of employees responds to this approach. Obviously when you are giving praise or credit then you talk about the person rather than the job. It's fine to say, 'Despatch are complaining about late orders, how can we help remedy this? And thanks for helping out last Saturday when we had that rush print job on, well done.'

So, you see, there is no reason to be nervous, in fact your team member is much more likely to be nervous than you are and there's no need to play this any way other than helpfully and constructively.

for next time

Make sure you send out the memo at least ten days in advance, after you have discussed with the employee a mutually agreeable time and day. Send out the appraisal preparation document with it and make sure you specify a day by which it should be returned. Try to make this at least four or five days before the appraisal as this gives you lots of time to study it and make notes. It also gives the team member five or six days to complete it and get it back to you.

For any new staff who are coming up to their first appraisal make sure you have set aside a little time to guide them through the process at a pre-appraisal interview. This doesn't need to be anything more than an informal chat outlining what they are to expect.

4 the appraisal room

Good, we're cracking on at quite a pace now. You've prepared the team member and prepared yourself. All that's left is to decide *where* you are going to hold this appraisal. There are some places where you simply wouldn't ever conduct an appraisal under any circumstances and some situations which are also taboo:

- the work canteen
- in a corridor
- in an open-plan office
- in front of colleagues
- at home
- on the shop floor
- over the phone
- via email or fax.

So where are you going to hold it? In your own office? Well, you can but it is not ideal. There are various drawbacks with using your own office:

- It isn't neutral enough and the team member may feel intimidated – a bit like entering the lion's den.
- You may find it more difficult staving off interruptions.
- You, yourself, might be distracted and keep getting up to close the filing cabinet or quickly check a file that was in your pending tray and you suddenly think of a note to add – that sort of thing.
- The seating arrangements may not be suitable – we'll look at that in a moment.

GETTING TURFED OUT

So where? Well, most organisations keep an interview room for just such purposes. If you don't have one see if you can borrow a colleague's office for an hour or so – they could always use yours. A conference room or even the board room would be suitable at a pinch. You need somewhere quiet, away from interruptions, neutral and with the right sort of seating. You need to know you won't be turfed out unexpectedly or have people poking their heads round the door every five minutes to see who is using the room.

You need somewhere in which you can create a relaxed informal atmosphere so perhaps the board room isn't ideal. You may not be intimidated but your team member may well be.

LIGHTING

Now lighting. An easily overlooked aspect, but it is very important. Make sure you both have adequate light to see clearly and to be able to make notes. Check any spotlights and make sure they aren't behind you, shining in the team member's face. If they are, angle them away or your staff member will think they are helping the police with their inquiries.

NOISE AND INTERRUPTIONS

Choose a quiet meeting room well away from the hurly-burly of office life. If the builders are in next door don't try and shout above the noise – move rooms. Post a notice on the outside of the door requesting no interruptions and add a finish time on it. Switch off all mobile phones and make sure you're not interrupted by internal phones ringing for you.

Notify any secretarial staff that you are away from your office for (roughly) an hour and that you cannot be disturbed except in a dire emergency – and make sure they know you mean it, this is important. Your team member's appraisal should be very high up your priority list and being interrupted to sign something or to be asked where something is sends out the wrong message to your valued team member.

The key factors to take into consideration when selecting somewhere are:

- **confidentiality**
- **distractions**
- **furnishing and seating**
- **light**
- **peace and quiet.**

If you need to book a special interview room make sure you have done so. And make sure you have booked it for long enough – better to over-estimate than be turfed out before you've finished.

SEATING ARRANGEMENTS

It might be best if you went along now to the interview room and had a quick look to see how the seating arrangements can be adjusted to provide the most informal and comfortable atmosphere.

Traditionally, there are five seating arrangements for such an assessment:

You both sit in low chairs round a coffee table. This is certainly comfortable but impractical for making notes as you have to bend forwards or keep getting up to get files. The table itself may be too small.

You sit at opposite ends of a meeting table. This is good as you can both spread out papers in front of you but it is perhaps slightly too formal and perhaps slightly confrontational.

thinkingfast

WHO'S IN CHARGE OF BOOKINGS?

Find out who is in charge of booking meeting rooms and make sure you get on their right side. By winning them over well in advance you often get priority. If you then need a room at short notice they are much more likely to put themselves out to make sure you get one. Don't leave it to the last minute and then find they are on holiday or away from their desk for the morning.

WOOING A CLIENT

Try to create the same sort of atmosphere as you would use to woo a client. This isn't an interrogation or a disciplinary hearing. It is an informal business-style meeting between two colleagues, one of whom happens to be senior to the other.

You sit next to each other at a meeting table. Very good indeed. It is informal, friendly and practical. Ideally, one of you should sit at the short end and the other alongside at the other side. If you sit right next to each other it is harder to maintain eye contact (*very* important) and you have the feeling the other is looking over your shoulder all the time. If you sit opposite each other it is too formal and confrontational.

You sit behind a desk and the team member sits facing you on the other side. Very formal, very confrontational. Avoid it at all costs.

You both sit in office chairs on one side of the desk. Informal but not very comfortable. One of you gets to rest an elbow on the desk but the other has nowhere to spread papers.

So, you've chosen the meeting table and the 'next to each other but at right angles' approach. Good.

REFRESHMENTS

A cup of coffee or tea is always welcome and helps break the ice and settle your team member into the right sort of relaxed approach. Ask them at the start if they would like something and make sure you either have the facilities to make it or can send out for it. Don't offer if you can't provide it or if it is a lot of hassle. You don't need to take a break during the appraisals unless your team member requests it to use the lavatory.

You can impose the same sort of atmosphere as you would for any other business meeting – since this is what it is – such as jackets off or whatever. You don't need to be all formal and managerial. Relax and enjoy the process yourself – the other person is more likely to as well if you do.

for next time

Make sure you have booked the room well in advance. If you are doing a whole series of appraisals make a block booking to cover the lot. Make sure you have notified everyone who needs to know that you are away from your desk and are not to be disturbed. If you allow one petty interruption you open the flood gates. If this has been your style up to now, for next time, make sure you give this job the priority it deserves.

When you have a few minutes to spare, experiment with seating arrangements until you find the right one for you that is relaxed, informal, comfortable and practical.

5 structuring the appraisal and setting an agenda

You still have some time before tomorrow's deadline and you would be advised to spend a little of it thinking about the structure of the appraisal. Yep, you have to have a structure or you will flounder and lose your way. The structure doesn't have to be too detailed but it has to be there as a framework for building on. The same with an agenda – this can be loose and flexible but you do still need one.

Structure helps the team member have a sense of direction and also provides you with a means of controlling the discussion and making sure all relevant topics are awarded the appropriate time and importance. A structure keeps the thing moving along.

Like any good story an appraisal must have a beginning, a middle and an end.

THE BEGINNING

Take a few minutes to put your team member at ease. Offer them coffee or tea and show them where they can sit and put their papers. Spend a couple of minutes on very light chat just to lighten up the mood and relax you both. Nothing too controversial here. If you know them well you can ask about their children or how that new car they bought is going. Light stuff. Easy stuff. A few pleasantries.

Keep it light

You can keep it entirely to off-work subjects – 'So, how's that new Morgan you bought? Bet it goes like the wind?'

Or you can add in the odd work thing as long as it's light and praiseworthy – nothing heavy – 'So, Robin, I got a phone call about that print design you did and they were very pleased indeed, well done.'

Signal that the chat is over

After the chat create an opportunity to signal that the chat is over and it's time for the real business of the meeting to take place. You know the sort of thing – 'Now, let's

thinking smart

INSIDER INFO

If you know nothing personal about this employee then for heaven's sake find out something – they like football, they paint watercolours, they have six children, they used to be a lifeguard, they once won the lottery – from someone who works with them. Ask and find out – discreetly, of course. All you have to do is ask another manager or the team member's supervisor: 'What does Robin do outside work?' Then you've got your opening gambit for the appraisal. 'So I hear you once shared a dressing room with Eric Clapton? What was that like?'

get down to business', or 'Yes, I'd love to see the photographs of your hernia operation, but right now we've got an appraisal to do, okay?'

Explain why you're both here

Then explain why you are both here – 'As you know it's your yearly/six-monthly appraisal, Robin.' Then explain what is going to happen. 'The reason for this meeting is to look at how your job is going [not them, remember, *the job*] and to see if there is anything you need to help you do it better or improve what you do. We'll have a chat about training opportunities and some long-term plans.' Don't say, 'We'll look at your future' as it implies some doubt as to their security with the organisation.

Point out that you will be taking notes and they should feel free to do likewise. And that any action plans will be decided jointly – you won't impose anything from above.

CREATING AN AGENDA

This is a joint meeting. You may, in theory, be chairing it, but it is still a joint meeting and you have to create an agenda together or they simply won't feel included and involved. You can, of course, lead this creation. Start by saying, 'We need an agenda to decide what points we are going to cover. I thought we could start with a general review of how you see your job and then move on to any specifics you feel need covering. Then I'd like to have a bit of a chat about how the new machines are fitting in and any problems you've encountered. We also need to have a chat about the staffing levels and overtime rates as they've changed dramatically recently. Then we could look at any training you feel you need. And finally we'll talk about long-term plans. How does that sound to you?'

In most cases they'll be only to happy to go along with what you've put to them but they will feel included and involved. If they have items of their own then they can add them to the agenda just so long as they fit into the proper criteria of the appraisal.

Once you've worked out the agenda you can move on.

'Good, so we've got an agenda of sorts, a loose one, but one we can work with, right? Anything else you'd like to add in for discussion?' They may say they want the car parking arrangements added in – it's obviously important to them for some reason so agree and slot it in – it may not be part of their appraisal as such but still worrying them or needing some form of discussion. 'Right, the car parking

thinking smart

PUT YOURSELF IN THEIR SHOES

Before the actual appraisal take a moment or two to put yourself in their shoes. Imagine what their job entails – perhaps you once did it yourself back in the dim past – and what sort of issues are likely to come up. The issues that affect you are not the same ones that are affecting them and the way they do their job. You have to come down a notch or two and envisage what sort of problems they are likely to be encountering. Do this in advance. That way you'll be on their wavelength from the very first moment they enter the meeting room.

67

arrangements. Fine, how about we talk about that after overtime and before training, suit you?' They'll invariably agree.

Good, you're almost at the end of the beginning. All it takes now is an open question to get the ball rolling and the show on the road. 'So, how do you feel the last 12 months/six months have gone then?'

This is an open question – see next chapter for more information on this – but basically it cannot be answered with a simple yes or no and thus invites discussion.

You can of course follow the way the appraisal form is laid out and work through this as an agenda but it can feel a little stilted and formal.

Or you could use the job description as a basis for an agenda but again it might appear to be very formal.

THE BEGINNING OF THE MIDDLE

Ask them to assess their performance since their last review. Then give them your assessment of their performance since the last review. If there is a major difference you need to move straight onto the middle – see next chapter. If you are both in agreement move on to the next section.

THE MIDDLE

OK, you've opened the batting and got them talking. Now you can talk in some depth about training, the future, any problem areas that have cropped up – we'll look at that in the next chapter in some detail. Just make sure you stick to the point and don't let them wander about or off. Keep the discussion friendly at all times and remember that this is a joint meeting – let them have their say as well.

THE END GAME

Once you've covered all the ground you both want to it is time to wrap it up. There is no point going on any longer than is necessary. As before when you signalled the beginning of the discussion proper, now is the time to signal that it's time to finish.

So you could say, 'Well, that about does it for me, anything else you'd like to add?' Or 'Whew, we've worked through a lot today and I think we've just about covered everything we set out to. Pretty good going, what do you say, shall we call it a day?' Both of these signal that the end is drawing near. And that signalling is very important. It allows the team member to bring up anything else they may want to – and they should be allowed to, of course, just so long as it's relevant – and it brings you to the next phase of the appraisal neatly and effectively.

SUMMARISING

Once you've signalled the end you should summarise just so long as there are no further points to deal with. If there are, deal with them and then signal again. Then summarise. You don't have to summarise the whole appraisal – just the action points you have both decided on. You could say, 'So, that's about it. Anything else? No? OK, so you'll improve the credit control system as we discussed and I'll check out those cashier training courses you asked about. And we'll both check back in a week to report on progress.'

thinkingsmart

MAKE CONTACT

When they first come in make a point of shaking their hand and offering them a seat. Of course, you'd do this anyway but make the handshake very warm and friendly. If you don't know how your handshake feels – strong and reassuring or the wet fish one? – get a personal friend to shake hands with you and then ask them to be honest about how it feels. Nothing is more off-putting than the limp, clammy, barely grasped wet fish.

 thinkingfast

GET A SIGNATURE THEN AND THERE

Some managers like to have the whole appraisal form typed up and then sent to the employee for signature. Best to write clearly and get them to sign it at the end of the meeting. That way it is fresh in their mind and you save time.

Summarising like this is very good for two reasons. It makes sure you – or they – haven't forgotten anything. And it makes sure both of you fully understand what has been decided. They may turn round and say, 'What, I've got to upgrade the computer system? I thought we'd decided Harrison in R & D was going to do it.' Then you can clear up the misunderstanding and summarise again – and move on.

WATCH THEIR REACTION

Watch how the team member reacts when you summarise. If they are not happy about any action plan you've agreed on but aren't saying, they'll reveal their true feelings in the way they sit or fold their arms or sigh or just look blankly at you. (Lots more about body language in the next chapter.) If you pick up on such signals don't let it go unchallenged. Say, 'You don't seem entirely happy about having to go on a training course for print buying? What's the problem?' Or 'I thought we'd agreed you'd spend more time on production and less in dispatch and now you seem hesitant to include it in your action plan. Am I missing something?'

Once you've summarised you can move on to actually wrapping up the meeting. This should end on a light and friendly note even if you two might have gone a round or two during it. Remember:

- ▶ **signal the end**
- ▶ **summarise**
- ▶ **watch for reactions and amend action plan if necessary**
- ▶ **summarise again if required**
- ▶ **thank them for coming**
- ▶ **praise them for their contribution**
- ▶ **end on a pleasantry as you began.**

thinking smart

KEEP STAFF – SAVE MONEY

By giving your staff the opportunity to discuss how they feel, as well as providing them with lots of feedback about how well they are doing, you motivate them, make them feel cared about and include them in your team. They feel as if they belong and thus are much less likely to leave. Replacing staff is costly, time-consuming and unproductive. Appraisals help keep staff – and save money in the long run.

So you should say something like, 'Well, that was a good session. I enjoyed that and thank you for coming. Brilliant idea of yours to switch warehouse duties to Rotherham. I'll get onto that straight away. You're doing good work, you know, keep it up. Oh, and wish young Ben luck in his match. That kid's going to play for Chelsea one day, mark my words.'

There, all done – only another five team members to go.

for next time

Have a structure worked out in advance including the agenda, even though you let the team member think they are creating it with you. The structure you use can be varied according to the type of employee. For example, some older colleagues may prefer a more formal agenda such as working through their job description or using the appraisal form.

6 what to say and how to say it

Tomorrow is the big day and the clock is still ticking. Yep, tomorrow you have to carry out this appraisal. You have prepared the team member. You have prepared yourself and you have worked out a structure and pencilled in an agenda. That's about it, then? Sorry, but it isn't. What are you going to say? How are you going to say it? How are you going to get this person to really open up and discuss frankly and honestly their performance? What if they clam up and don't want to say anything? What if they turn the tables and begin to criticise you and your management style? What if they burst into tears? What if they are difficult? Or even aggressive?

Yep, you've still got quite a bit to do before you go into the meeting room if you are to handle this effectively and professionally.

You don't have time to learn interview techniques from scratch so what you need now are some practical guidelines to make this appraisal go with a zing. We are thinking – and learning – at the speed of life. Let's cut to the chase.

HOW TO ASK QUESTIONS

You'd have thought it was obvious, wouldn't you? You just ask. So let's try it:

> *'How's the job going?'*
> *'Fine.'*
> *'Any problems?'*
> *'Nope.'*
> *'Well, that's that then. Thank you for coming.'*

OPEN AND CLOSED QUESTIONS

See, it just doesn't work. You've asked *closed* questions – ones which allow the team member to give a one- or two-word answer. And this means they don't open up, don't discuss, don't enter into the spirit of the thing. And that usually means very short, ineffectual appraisals which benefit no one, least of all the team member. It is only fair to them for you to put a little bit more effort into it and ask

thinking smart

WE NOT I

You will find your team member much more responsive at their appraisal if you talk of 'we' rather than 'I'. 'We need to look at this problem area,' rather than 'I think there's a problem here.' That way they will feel much more involved, and that it is a discussion rather than a telling-off process.

open questions – ones which require more than a one- or two-word response. Let's try it again:

> *'So how do you feel the job's been going since the last appraisal?'*
> 'Oh, not too bad, but I have had problems with integrating the new software.'
> *'Why is that?'*
> 'Because the matrix doesn't mesh with the ZX4000 programs as we were promised. It makes us very slow completing our returns which means dispatch get held up. That causes all sorts of problems as Jackson simply hates delay and I've had to work a lot of overtime which has meant ...'

And so on. See the difference?

Quick recap:

- **Closed questions allow one- or two-word answers.**

- **Open questions require a fuller answer.**

Closed questions are this sort:

- **Have you met your targets?**

- **Are you happy with this part of your job?**

- **Are you concerned about the staff turnover in your department?**

- **How long did it take to get up and running again after the fire?**

Try these again as open questions and see if the response is different:

- **What do you think about the targets you were set for this year?**

- **Which parts of your job are you happiest with?**

- **Why are you losing so many staff?**

- **What was the biggest challenge in getting up and running again after the fire?**

OPENING UP A DISCUSSION

Open questions not only indicate that you are genuinely interested in the answers but they also offer an invitation to the team member to unburden themselves and open up.

thinkingfast

HAVING THE TABLES TURNED

It can happen at an appraisal – you get the tables turned on you and suddenly you are under attack for your managerial style or a complaint about the way you handle things. Be calm. Stay calm. Don't be defensive. Regard this as an opportunity to open up the discussion. Ask the team member for specific examples of what they are talking about. Listen to them and repeat back what they say. If they've brought it up it is because it means something. Look for a solution together.

Open questions open a discussion; closed questions close it down. For instance, closed:

'How's your new trainee getting on?'

'Fine.'

Open:

'How are you finding the new trainee?'

'Not bad, they seem very keen. I would like them to have a bit more practice on the rolling excavator machine but I simply can't spare them from the loading bay at the moment. I really could do with another pair of hands there if we want them to get some more experience. Do you think it would be worthwhile if we …?'

DISCUSSIONS AND FACTS

Obviously if you want to find out facts you need to ask closed questions. You don't ask open questions if you want figures, dates or percentages. But often asking a closed question first will demand an open question afterwards to get the discussion rolling:

'How many staff do you need then for the packing department?'

'Seven.'

'Why so many?'

'Because four of them are needed to actually do the packing but then we have to have someone to drive the lorry and at least two to shift the pallets from stores. Actually, I could really do with eight but I don't think the budget could stretch to that, could it?'

And as they've asked you a closed question you can safely answer *'no'*.

OTHER TYPES OF QUESTIONS

Open and closed questions aren't the only ones you can ask. Depending on what sort of response you want you have to vary the way you ask things. And there are certain types of questions you really don't want to use – ever.

Searching closed

This is where you need specific information to establish a definite point from which you can then lead the discussion.

'So how many copies can you collate now with the new machine?'

'Fifteen hundred an hour if only we could get it running properly.'

'And how is that affecting your delivery times for the Newman contact?'

thinking smart

BODY LANGUAGE

You don't need to watch individual gestures – arms folded, legs crossed, sullen face, head dropped, shoulders sagged – to know when you are not getting a positive response. Watch instead for clusters of gestures. Two or three or more indicate a resistant team member. Notice and ask why they are unhappy about what is being discussed. Don't leave it and hope they will perk up. Be aware that whatever their body language you will unconsciously 'mirror' it – copy it. You can't help this unless you consciously fight it and make sure you are open and upbeat in your own body language, otherwise you get a downward spiral.

Searching open

If you want specific information but also want the discussion to open up then you ask a searching open question:

'And then exactly what happened after you reversed over the MD's dog?'

Or:

'So you shut down the machine and cut the power, but what happened to the boy's arm?'

Empathetic questions

Use this sort of question when there is an emotional content to what the team member is saying. They offer a sympathetic compassionate approach which might be appropriate.

'And you are so upset about being transferred to the printing department that you are considering leaving?'

Or:

'So how did you feel when the client stormed out?'

Empathetic questions often include a measure of repeating back to the employee what they have just said to you – or at least repeating back the emotional content. Try not to put any interpretation on the emotional side such as:

'Don't you think being so upset about being transferred that you'd consider leaving is a bit silly?'

Or:

'Surely you realised it was your own fault the client stormed out?'

If an emotional issue like this is raised then there is a reason behind it – your team member genuinely feels something. Ask about feelings. You might think them silly – but think it only. Their feelings are real and to be taken seriously. You can't deny them the right to have the feelings and it is your job to allow them to express them.

'What if' questions

These take the form of asking the team member to imagine a scenario or put themselves into another's position or to get them to think about a new idea or situation. They can be very useful in getting a discussion going or getting the employee to consider their responsibilities in a new light.

They shouldn't ever be derogatory:

'What if we all behaved like that?'

thinking fast

TAKING NOTES

There is nothing more off-putting than someone taking down what you say verbatim. If you aren't filling in the appraisal form but just taking notes keep these to a minimum. Fast managers don't take notes but fill in the appraisal form as they go. If it ain't on the form you don't need it. Your notes are for you but this is a joint process. They may wonder what happens to the notes later or what you are writing. Be open and fill in the form as you go and get their assent on every category.

Or:

'What if we all wrote our own job descriptions – wouldn't get much done then, would we?'

Rather, try getting the team member to see things from someone else's point of view:

'What if you'd been in charge that day, what would you have done?'

Or:

'What do you suppose would have happened if that order had fallen through?'

You're not apportioning blame or telling them you think it is their fault that something bad happened, merely getting them to see the consequences of their actions or the repercussions throughout the organisation.

'What if' questions don't have to begin 'what if'. You can also ask:

- ▶ **What do you suppose ...?**

- ▶ **What would you do if ...?**

- ▶ **How would you have handled ...?**

'What if' questions ought to contain a word such as 'if', 'suppose' or 'imagine', however, to make sure the team member realises that it is a hypothetical question and not one which is likely to happen immediately. There's no point saying:

'What if you were in my shoes, what would you do with an employee like you?'

They simply don't have the experience to answer such a question and it only makes them feel and look small. So don't do it.

Leading questions

These can be useful if you want to set an agenda or formulate a structure that they feel part of but which you are actually not giving them too much choice in. The downside of them is that the team member may feel they are being led – they may agree but not *feel* in agreement. This can lead to resentment or regret later.

Leading questions may be useful for agendas but not for committed action plans. You can say:

'So we'll discuss the job description first and then specific problems if that's all right with you?'

But not:

'Bet you really regret doing that now, don't you?'

They may agree but not feel any regret at all and you have lost a valuable opportunity to find out how they really feel.

thinking smart

NO 'BUTS'

Never finish praising a member of staff at an appraisal – or any other time – with the word 'but'. Once they spot you do this it destroys any future praise as they know what's coming:

'That was a very good presentation, but ...'

'I liked the way you handled that client, but ...'

The same goes for 'however', 'although', 'nevertheless' and 'yet'. You will find that saying *'it might be worth bearing in mind'* is more helpful if you want to make a point and sharpen their performance.

II

> ### DON'T TALK DOWN TO THE TEAM MEMBER
>
> They may be a lot younger and less experienced than you but don't talk down to them. Avoid using jargon that they might not understand. Avoid foreign phrases – *'laissez-faire'*, *'Schadenfreude'*, *'sine qua non'* – that sort of thing. Don't use high-falutin' managerial speak. No acronyms that they may not be familiar with such as GIGO (garbage in, garbage out) or RDB (regional development board). If they don't know what you are talking about chances are they won't ask for fear of being seen as uneducated or stupid.

'Alternative close' questions

I'm sure you know this is a very useful sales technique but it also works if you are trying to get a team member to agree to an action plan. Basically, you give them a choice and they feel they have to go down one of the two routes you have put to them. Clever, eh? Not only that – it also gives them a feeling of control. It's *their* choice:

'So do you want to switch to print or design after Christmas?'

'Would you like to go on this training course now or leave it until next month?'

'Do you think you can patch things up with Sam or do you want me to have a word?'

The alternative close questions are good when you really do want them to take some action but feel that if you left it to them they might not do anything. It also works with children – *'Do you want to have one more swing then go home or a quick go on the roundabout before getting back into the car?'*

Rapid fire questions

Do not use this technique unless you are a police officer or a member of a foreign interrogation squad. Rapid fire questions are exactly that – fired so fast that the person simply doesn't have a chance to answer any of them. It confuses them and disorientates them. But there are some managers who do try to use this technique at appraisals so they can get the whole thing over with as quickly as possible. Pointless. You know the sort of thing I'm sure:

'So you think you're doing OK? But what about that incident in production last week? Bet you think I've forgotten those lost delivery notes? Well, I haven't and I still want an answer to this training issue – are you going or not? And I'd better have an answer to the staff recruitment problem as well – what are we going to do about it? And what's more important when are we going to do it? Come on now, cat got your tongue?'

Not useful and not to be used.

WORD THE QUESTIONS CAREFULLY

Good, so word your questions carefully. Take your time to think about *how* you are going to ask, as well as *what* you are going to ask. Any of the techniques just examined can be used in an inappropriate way as well as a beneficial one. For instance, you could use the 'alternative close' question to elicit a response that might be quite wrong and not what the team member wants to say at all:

'So do you feel you're doing OK or do you need a bit more training?'

What hope has the employee got? They have to answer that they're doing fine or submit to a training programme that they may not want or need. What if they *aren't* doing fine but don't feel the need for any training? Do they need some other support instead? What if they think they're doing fine and still feel they want some additional training?

Better to ask:

'Do you feel you are doing OK?' or *'How do you feel you are doing?'*

And wait for an answer before going on to suggest training or whatever – your response depends on their answer.

Make sure you give them space to answer, that you haven't filled in the blanks for them. Try not to phrase questions so that the answer is already implicit in the question such as:

'I suppose you reacted that way because you felt inexperienced, didn't you?'

This is a leading question gone wrong – leading them to a place they might not want to go. Better to ask:

'Why do you think you reacted that way?'

LISTENING

An important skill for any manager to learn. I'm sure you are very good at this or you wouldn't be the smart manager you are:

- ▶ **Good listening lets the team member take some time before they speak. You don't have to jump in and break the silence.**

- ▶ **Good listening allows each question to be answered fully without interrupting.**

- ▶ **Good listening means listening and not taking notes at the same time.**

- ▶ **Good listening means using appropriate phrases to encourage the employee to carry on such as 'go on', 'yes', 'I'm listening', 'take your time', tell it in your own words', 'there's no rush', 'good' and so on. Even just making the odd noise will encourage them to continue and prove you're not asleep.**

So, I guess we've pretty well exhausted questioning in a brief sort of way. This stuff can be studied for years and I guess all you need is this quickest of guidelines to get you through this appraisal tomorrow – or do you need some training?

 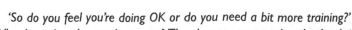 thinkingsfast

SUGGESTIONS NOT PROPOSALS

If you want their agreement quickly and without fuss try suggesting rather than proposing. A suggestion begins *'shall we …?'* A proposal begins with *'I think we should …'*

Suggestions are easy and quick to go along with. Proposals are sort of imposed and you may get resistance which slows the process down.

thinking smart

GOOD LISTENING SKILLS

If you want to show that you are listening and paying attention to what is being said try looking interested – lean your head slightly forward and to one side as if you were hearing intently.

▶ Ask questions to show you are listening.

▶ Repeat back what has just been said to you: *'So if I've got this right, you want to …'*

▶ Bring the discussion back on track – this really shows you're listening.

for next time

Make sure you have worked out which questions you need to ask – and the way you are going to ask them – in advance.

7 constructive criticism

We all need it but can we all take it and can we all dish it out? Many managers feel distinctly uncomfortable with appraisals because they don't like criticising their team members. However, failure to take the bull by the horns, so to speak, leads to a lot more problems than constructive criticism ever does.

DEVELOPING YOUR TEAM

A lot of managers fail to criticise staff properly whom they know to be 'difficult'. And, of course, if they know a team member is pretty easy going they may well criticise more than is necessary. The result is that the person who needs it the most gets it the least and the one who needs it least gets the most. Very unfair indeed. And all because the manager felt intimidated by or fearful of the process of proper constructive criticism.

And if you don't carry out a proper constructive critical stage in the development of your team then how can you expect them to improve? It is the manager's right to criticise. Without criticism poor performance will continue and any opportunities to improve will have been squandered. It's OK to criticise at an assessment – your team are expecting it.

WHEN TO CRITICISE

Criticism is best done at the time it is most needed – immediately. What we are concerned with here, of course, is criticism at an appraisal. But the rules of good constructive criticism apply in all circumstances anyway. If you are storing up criticism for the appraisal you are storing up trouble. A lot of managers do, but it is an unsavoury practice. Better to do it as soon as you spot something that needs correcting. Also criticism is often a bit of a shock to the employee. They didn't realise that what they were doing was wrong or not being done according to company procedures, or even just plain daft.

STOCKPILING CRITICISM

And remember what we said early on – no surprises at their appraisal. So you can't just suddenly turn round at the appraisal and produce a list of faults and begin criticising. It just won't do. You should have dealt with these things at the time – not stockpiled them like some picky squirrel. How would you feel if your boss did it to you?

STORING UP RESENTMENT

The other problem with storing criticism is you are also storing resentment. If the team member does something wrong and you fail to take corrective action immediately, chances are that by the time their appraisal rolls around they will have

thinking smart

CRITICISM SANDWICHES

A lot of managers use the criticism sandwich technique. It isn't a good one. This is where they sandwich the criticism between two bits of praise. They hope it will make the criticism a bit more palatable. It doesn't. It merely harms the praise. Better to be bold and upfront about it. Get the criticism over and done with and then have two praise puddings instead. Much tastier.

done it another 20 times. And what has that done to your temper? Chances are you will find out at the appraisal when all that resentment boils over and there is trouble with a capital ubble.

Criticism + storage = resentment
Resentment + appraisal = trouble

Criticising is correcting a fault. That's it. It isn't:

- nit-picking
- complaining
- deliberately finding fault
- being on their back
- looking for trouble
- moaning
- carping
- being finicky
- being hypercritical
- showing disapproval
- being fussy.

Criticism is correcting a fault. You do it pleasantly, politely, graciously, even. You spot a fault and you put it right. If the same fault is carried out often you need to look at retraining. If errors continue it might be a disciplinary matter and that's not criticising. Criticising is something done to correct a fault at the time. It's no good

thinking smart

YOU CAN'T EXPECT PERFECTION IMMEDIATELY

Or even eventually come to that. If a team member is going off track in a lot of areas you can't put them all right at the same time. Better to concentrate on one or two key areas first. Get them right and then tackle another couple of problems. None of us can take an infinite amount of criticism. Ration it a bit and take your time. You are building a productive team member here so don't expect miracles overnight. Invest in time and work it through in stages.

thinking smart

thhfihi thinking smart

THE WIN–WIN SITUATION

Don't let the team member go away after the appraisal thinking it was all one-sided. You need to concede ground, give a little, as well. If you want them to go on a training course and they seem reluctant you can always offer a trade: *'Look, you go on this course and I'll make sure Andy deals with your paperwork while you're away so you don't have too much to come back to.'* Or: *'You work the overtime we need and I'll make sure you get the extra days off you want next month.'* That sort of thing. This way you both come out feeling you have achieved a result.

having a team member coming into an appraisal and you launching into a list of things that need correcting if you've never said anything before. *No surprises.*

CRITICISM AND PRAISE

If criticism is correcting a fault, what is it when no faults need correcting? That's right, praise. And praise and criticism should go hand in hand. It is part of your job to notice when a task is being carried out well – and offer praise. But it is just as much part of your job to notice – and correct – any faults that are occurring. The smart manager doesn't just dish out praise but also gets the staff used to being criticised so they expect a degree of fairness. If they do something wrong they expect to be told and corrected. And obviously when they do something well they expect it to be noticed – and praised.

SO WHAT'S AN APPRAISAL FOR?

If you can't store up criticism for the appraisal you might wonder what it's for. Simple. It is to review progress. It isn't a correcting session where you go over old ground and try to put everything right. It is an opportunity to review why things go wrong in the first place. It is a chance for both of you to discuss what the team member needs in the way of support or training or encouragement or motivation to make sure faults don't occur in the future. It most certainly isn't a moaning session where you berate the member of staff for all their past errors.

CONSTRUCTIVE CRITICISM

If you do have to criticise a member of staff – at the time of the incident – then it should be constructive. This means you point out the fault – and then offer ways and means of doing it better, doing it properly and doing it again if necessary. Constructive criticism is just that – constructive. You are constructing a better way of doing it. Merely pointing out a fault is useless if you don't offer an alternative at the same time. The objective of criticism should always be to improve performance and create better working relationships. If your criticism doesn't work towards this goal then it isn't criticism but one of those listed earlier.

CRITICISM BASED ON FACT

All too often a manager will steam in and blow their top when something has gone wrong. This rather quaint and old-fashioned style of management is thankfully dying out. But there are still those among us who do it. All criticism should be based on fact. Find out:

- who did it
- why it was done
- what they thought they were doing
- what they thought they were supposed to be doing
- whose responsibility it was
- what can be done about it now
- what's to stop it happening again.

The same goes for appraisal. It's no good discussing something with a member of staff unless you are really sure of your facts:

'So, your job description says you are responsible for the production of the annual show brochures but we don't seem to have had any for the last year. What do you think is going wrong here?'

'Well, the annual show was cancelled last year so no brochures were needed.'

'Oh, was it?'

Don't you look foolish now?

Be sure of your facts – and have evidence

Always be sure of your facts for the appraisal – and any time you need to criticise a team member. You may be challenged so you'd better be sure of yourself. This means having the evidence. It doesn't mean snooping or playing detective. It doesn't mean collecting a police-type dossier on employees. It just means being accurate and having details of faults. You need to know when and how and where – that sort of thing. Otherwise:

'Ah Robin, I need to talk to you about all this lateness of yours. We need to do something about it, don't we?'

'What lateness?'

'Well, you have been late quite often recently.'

thinking smart

OFFERING AN ALTERNATIVE

Don't criticise if you can't think of a better way of doing things yourself. There isn't much point saying to a team member, *'Your presentation wasn't too effective because the overhead projector failed twice at crucial points'* when you both know the projector is defective and you have no plans for replacing it. You have to offer an alternative way of doing things – a better way – or you run the risk of the team member turning round and saying, *'Well, what should I do then?'* and then you'll be lost for words and have to mumble and slink away. Be prepared before you say anything.

'When have I been late? Name a single day when I've been late.'

'Um, well, er, I'm sure you have been.'

'Well, I haven't.'

'OK then, off you go.'

Much better to have the facts at your fingertips:

'Ah Robin, I see you were late on Monday and Tuesday of last week and again on Wednesday and Thursday of this week. What are we going to do about it?'

So have your facts to hand and the evidence collected. But before you talk to the team member you need to:

▶ **test the evidence**

▶ **substantiate the facts.**

Corroborate and discuss

Never criticise anything unless you have first checked with another member of staff that you've not been sold a dummy. It does happen and you need to both protect yourself from possible recriminations and the member of staff from false accusations. Never launch a critical attack. Always ask first:

'So, Sam, you've lost the Madison contract. Well, I'm not happy and we need to take some firm action to stop this sort of thing happening again.'

No, no, no. Try instead:

'So, Sam, what's happening with the Madison contract?'

'Ah, the Madison contract is being phased out, but a new one, and one much more in our favour is being drawn up now.'

'Good work, Sam'.

Of course, it might not have been *quite* so easy:

'So, Sam, what's happening with the Madison contract?'

'Ah, I think I've blown it.'

'Do you want to explain that?'

'Well, I thought I was pushing hard but it seems too hard. Madison didn't like being called a stingy badger and walked out. I'm sorry.'

'So let's look at where you think you've gone wrong and then we'll look at ways of making sure it shouldn't happen again. Suit you?'

'Thanks.'

A BLANK SHEET OF PAPER

Every appraisal should start with a mental blank sheet of paper. If you had to criticise staff during the period between appraisals then that is old stuff. It has been dealt with unless it's a recurring problem and then, as you know, it's retraining or disciplinary. Once you've criticised a team member and they have corrected the fault satisfactorily then move on and cover new ground. It doesn't even need mentioning at the appraisal if it has been successfully rectified. Nothing is worse for an employee than having all their misdemeanours dragged up at an appraisal. The body should have been buried, there is no need to pick over the bones. It is a spent conviction.

BRINGING UP PROBLEM AREAS AT AN APPRAISAL

Their appraisal is a chance to discuss how they have been doing their job. Not criticising doesn't mean you can't bring up problem areas – but they should be discussed. A discussion is quite different from criticising. You begin by asking them how they see things. Then perhaps point out that the organisation might need more or better and then formulate an action plan. At no point have you criticised the team member. You are reviewing the job, remember, and how effectively it is being done. Criticism is a personal thing. An appraisal is an objective review.

BE SPECIFIC

Bringing up problem areas at an appraisal is easy if you approach it correctly. It isn't criticism but a chance for the team member to focus on specific things that may need improving:

'So how are you finding the new ZX4000 machine?'
'Pretty good although it isn't as reliable as the old ZX3000.'
'Why is that, do you think?'
'Well, it has a tendency to recalibrate the steel rollers automatically when I've manually set them.'
'But doesn't it say in the manual that they have to be set automatically?'
'Does it?'
'I think you'll find it does. From my experience the ZX4000 is the bee's knees when it comes to reliability but you do need to follow the instructions pretty closely. It's much more complex than the old ZX3000 and you can't assume the operation is the same.'
'Oh, I thought it was identical.'
'Not at all. Do you think a quick refresher course might be useful?'
'Not 'arf. That would help a lot.'

Now you know they needed some retraining. You knew they weren't reading the manual properly. In fact, you knew their approach was lazy and lax. But did you need to say that? Did you attack them? Were you critical? Nope. But you've got the result you wanted, they feel good about themselves and they think you helpful and that your managerial style is rather friendly and effective. What's more, you've revealed your experience and they know they can't try to pull the wool over your eyes in the future. Good work.

JOINT ACTION PLANS

When you tackle problem areas at an appraisal always try to find a joint solution. Trying to impose a solution from on high is ineffective and rather pointless. The team member simply won't respond well if you try this approach. If you get their co-operation and involvement they are much more likely to stick to an action plan – after all, it's their baby too.

Why an action plan?

Even top people need plans to stretch them and improve their skills and give them more training. An action plan is always welcome as it gives you and the team

> ### BEING A CHOREOGRAPHER
>
> If you use all the techniques in this book to get the team member to open up and discuss things you may create an atmosphere that is both relaxed and informal. And sometimes it can get too relaxed, too informal. The discussion can turn into a general chat about goodness-knows-what. You have to see your role as a choreographer – directing the dance and keeping everyone in step, including yourself. Even managers can get distracted. You are there to participate but you are also the manager and have overall control. Any divergences have to be turned back quickly and politely: *'That's brilliant, Robin, I didn't know you knew so much about early nineteenth-century porcelain but we do need to get on and work our way through this agenda. Let's get back to the appraisal, shall we?'*

member a result. It gives them something to report back about to fellow team members and a sense of achieving something concrete. An action plan may be no more than a simple note of chasing up an order or telephoning a supplier and checking problems have cleared – for example, a review in four weeks to check there are no more problems with the ZX4000.

It might be a training course, a refresher course, a new responsibility, a transfer to a new department, increased duties, lessened duties, a new project, some hands-on experience of new technology. It might even be some guidance towards promotion.

It is only fair to give your team members all the help they need to carry out their role to the very best of their ability. After all you get lots of help. You've got this book.

WRAPPING IT UP

Make sure you summarise everything you've discussed and that you have both agreed the action plan. If you want them to sign their appraisal form get them to do it now. After that it's just a question of finishing on an upbeat note. Thank them for coming. Shake their hand and open the door for them. Again thank them and pass a pleasantry similar to the one you gave them when they arrived – *'And don't forget to wish Ben luck from me.'* Or: *'Let me know how the bungee jump goes.'* That sort of thing. Then they leave. You remove everything from the meeting room that you brought with you and go get yourself a well-deserved cup of coffee. Well done.

FOLLOWING UP

If you two have agreed an action plan then make sure you *both* follow it up. Don't just expect them to achieve results – you need to monitor them. You need to make sure that they know that you have their best interests at heart and are prepared to remember the action plan and work on it as much as they have to. You have to do what you have said you will do. So if you promised to look out those training manuals make sure you do. If you said you would check on a possible transfer to your Ipswich branch for them make sure you do.

Build in dates by which things have to be done or some form of monitoring results. That way you can make notes in your diary when you get back to the office and keep an eye on the situation.

DEALING WITH DIFFICULT PEOPLE

No matter how hard you try and how good you are at your job there will be times when you encounter difficult people at appraisals. These are the ones who seem intent on making your job as challenging as possible. Whatever you do you must not rise to the bait. Count to ten (under your breath, of course), practise a simple relaxation technique such as deep breathing, leave the room for a moment or two if it gets really heated. And if the worst comes to the worst you are quite within your rights to cancel the appraisal and reschedule it for another time. But do try to see these people as a challenge rather than as a difficulty – that way you'll think of ways and means of dealing effectively and productively with them rather than getting irritated.

for next time

Work out well in advance what you are going to say and how you are going to say it.

Make sure that any mistakes that are being committed have been criticised at the appropriate time and not saved up for the appraisal.

Practise asking open and closed questions and see the different responses you get.

Work out in advance solutions to any problem areas that you need to discuss – that way you won't be caught on the hop when they ask what they should do about it.

appraisal in an hour

If you really are up against it and only have an hour to prepare you have to think on your feet and act quickly – this is appraisal preparation at the speed of life. And it is preparation in an hour – not an appraisal in an hour, that takes as long as it takes:

- ▶ You probably haven't got time to check their job description (see pages 58–9) beyond making sure that they are still doing the job they are supposed to be and that they haven't been transferred to another department entirely or even promoted.

- ▶ If they've completed and returned their employee appraisal preparation form (see page 55) read it now, quickly. Use a highlighter to mark anything that you think you will need to discuss or focus on specifically.

- ▶ Make sure you've got their personnel file. You might not have time to read it in depth now but do open it at least and make sure you know who you are talking to.

- ▶ Grab a pad and the appraisal form that you're going to fill in as you go (see page 59). Work out a quick and rough agenda. You are lucky in the fact that working out the agenda is supposed to be a joint process anyway. All you are doing now is roughing some basic shape – the detail you two can thrash out at the appraisal.

- ▶ You don't have time to read the sections in this book on how to ask questions or give constructive criticism – you'll have to wing it this time but make sure you've read everything before the next appraisal.

- ▶ Hopefully the meeting room has been pre-booked and you won't have to use up any of your precious hour hunting down a room to use. You don't have time to read the section on arranging the meeting room so just make sure you greet them in a friendly way and offer them a seat. Try to sit at right angles to them rather than opposite them as that's a bit too formal.

- ▶ Do make sure you stick a notice on the door asking not to be interrupted. This time is important to the team member.

- ▶ If, during the appraisal, you are asked anything specific and you don't know the answer (because you are ill prepared or haven't done your homework) then admit it. Better to say, *'I don't know much about that training programme right now but give me a day and I'll have the details for you.'*

Time's up. Good luck.

difficult people

 AVOID CONFRONTATION

DEAL WITH THE PROBLEM

IMPROVE THE ATMOSPHERE

ros jay

contents

introduction

Life moves fast enough these days to keep you working at break-neck speed most of the time. What you can really do without is problem people who create unpleasantness and difficulties and just plain slow you down. Just because you didn't handle touchy Tessa just right, she's stalling on the paperwork you need. One wrong word to sulky Steven, and he won't give you the information to complete your report. And a simple misunderstanding with cranky Colin is causing ridiculous delays on the new contract.

In this age of fast working, difficult people cause delays and extra effort that you simply can't afford. Unfortunately, these people aren't suddenly going to change personality overnight. So you're going to have to do the work instead. And it's not so bad really. Once you know the techniques for handling these people, you'll find it comes naturally before long. Whether they are domineering, or they constantly pass the buck, whether they are sulkers or just plain whingy, there are techniques for getting the best from everyone and making your own job a damn sight easier.

This book is about difficult people wherever you encounter them at work, whether they are colleagues, bosses or your own team members. Most of the guidelines for handling them are much the same whatever their position – it's the person who is difficult, after all, not their role. But where there are different techniques, we'll highlight them.

Whoever is making your already hectic life more stressful, you simply want to know how to keep them out of your hair politely, so as not to cause any more hassle to yourself or anyone else. You just want:

 tips for dealing with any type of difficult personality

 shortcuts for getting what you want out of people fast

 checklists to make sure you haven't overlooked anything

… all put together clearly and simply. And short enough to read fast, of course.

So don't panic. Next time you see a colleague bearing down on you along the corridor red in the face with anger, or you catch two of your team members coming to blows, simply whip out this book and give yourself a crash course in handling the situation with diplomacy and assurance. And still getting the result you want, of course. This book will tell you everything you need to know about handling the tough cookies in the tin; you'll even find a lightning crash course for handling difficult people in five minutes at the back of the book, if you're seriously pushed for time.

This book will take you through the six key stages or groups of skills for dealing with difficult people, from bosses and colleagues to your own team members:

1 To begin with, you need to identify exactly what you're trying to achieve when you attempt to deal with difficult people – not quite as obvious as it might seem.

2 After this, we'll look at the underlying strategies for making all encounters with difficult people more pleasant and straightforward, including feedback techniques, and simply being more assertive without winding anyone up.

3 Next, we'll look at some of the basic types of behaviour that create difficult situations, such as anger, silent sulks and emotional blackmail.

4 Chapter 4 is all about handling difficult bosses – it can be a lot more nerve-wracking than dealing with other difficult people, but it's easy once you know how.

5 Sometimes the real problem is conflict between members of your team, rather than yourself and someone else. So here's the low-down on sorting out other people's squabbles and personality clashes.

6 Finally, Chapter 6 gives you a whistle-stop guide to handling over 20 of the most common difficult types, from prima donnas to rule-benders.

fast thinking gambles

This book is all about thinking on your feet: handling difficult people fast so you can concentrate your time on your core activities. But throughout the book, you'll find hints on how to handle difficult people next time – when you can allow yourself a little more time. So what's the point? Why not handle them as fast as possible every time?

Well, there's always an element of risk in doing anything at break-neck pace and giving yourself no leeway. Nineteen times out of 20 the guidelines and tips in this book will get you what you need out of people without wasting time. But just occasionally, a little more time will gain you a greater benefit. Let's look at a few examples:

- ▶ **Some of these techniques will give you just the solution you want. But some may give you only a short-term solution to a potentially permanent problem. If you want to find a lasting solution, it can take a little longer (as you'll find out later).**

- ▶ **People can't change their personalities, but they can change their behaviour – if they want to. The fastest way to deal with a difficult person may be a technique that removes the problem from your point of view. But persuading the person to change their behaviour (which may take longer) can ease the problem for your team members and colleagues too – enabling everyone to work more effectively.**

- ▶ **Just because you've overcome the problem thrown up by your difficult workmate doesn't mean to say that you necessarily feel good about it. You may be left with a feeling of irritation and frustration. Another solution – albeit a more time-consuming one – might have left you feeling happier.**

So when time is tight (and when isn't it?), you'll find this book full of great techniques as well as being a handy reference guide. But if ever the workload eases up for a few moments, find a chance to follow the advice on finding more lasting answers to some of the people problems that you encounter regularly. That way, you'll remove much of the need for quick-fix solutions.

1 your objective

This book promised you speed, and now we're messing about with fancy thing like objectives. It's a rip-off, that's what it is.

Actually, no. This isn't highfalutin' theory, it's real work. Setting your objective is as important to achieving success as getting out the road map before you embark on a long car journey to a new destination. In fact, it's very similar. Your objective *is* your destination, and without it you will be lost.

If you set off in your car and just follow your nose, the odds on ending up precisely where you want to are pretty slim. How can you possibly decide which route to take if you don't know where you're going? In the same way, when it comes to dealing with difficult people, if you don't know what you're trying to achieve, you can't have any idea how to go about it.

So, we begin by setting an objective. It won't take long – three or four minutes. About as long as it takes to read this chapter, in fact. Once it's done, you'll know where you're going with all the other techniques in this book.

And what is your objective? Well, here are some possible outcomes to handling difficult people:

- ▶ **You get them out of your hair but you don't get what you need from them work-wise.**

- ▶ **You get your immediate problem resolved, but you leave them feeling angry and resentful (uh-oh, sounds like trouble ...).**

- ▶ **You keep them happy, but it takes the whole afternoon just to get a simple piece of information out of them.**

- ▶ **You've broken up the row between your team members for the moment, but you know it's only a matter of time before they fall out again.**

In all of these cases, you have dealt with the difficult people, but none of them sounds like a perfect solution. Either it takes too long, or it's storing up trouble for later, or the people are fine but the work has suffered. So you need to set yourself a clear objective that resolves *all* these related problems, not just some of them.

 thinking smart

STOP, LOOK, LISTEN
The more rushed you are, the more worthwhile it is to take time out to set your objective. It doesn't take long, but it does ensure that you focus on the real issues. It's very easy when you're under time pressure to act rather than think, but this just leads to undirected – and therefore wasted – time and energy. So stop, set your objective, and then proceed.

When it comes to dealing with people problems, here's the sort of objective you need to aim for, at least if you're working at the speed of life: *To resolve the situation swiftly and permanently, in a way that meets work objectives and satisfies everyone involved.* That's more like it. Now you know where you're trying to get to, and you know you haven't succeeded until you have met the objective in full.

◀◀ for next time

If this is a relatively minor problem, and you need to resolve it fast, you can use the objective outlined here. But if you have a serious people problem, or one that could cause major disruption to work, it's worth taking the time to spell out your objective in a little more detail. In particular, you should specify:

▸ the key work objectives
▸ what it will take to satisfy everyone.

For example, your objective might be: *To resolve the situation swiftly and permanently in a way that doesn't delay the report, and that leaves Richard feeling he has been given responsibility without Pat feeling displaced.* A detailed objective such as this will help you to keep focused on the outcomes that are important without getting sidetracked.

2 the basic techniques

You'll be pleased to know that there are certain underlying techniques that, once learnt, you can apply to most difficult people. Yes, it does take a short time to learn them initially, but the investment is worth it. They will then help you resolve numerous problems with such ease that you will barely notice there was a problem – now that's fast thinking.

LEOPARDS DON'T CHANGE THEIR SPOTS

Before you can learn anything about handling difficult people, however, you have to understand one critical thing about them: you can't change them. That is to say, you can't change their intrinsic personality. And once you accept that, you find that your tolerance level shoots up. Someone who used to be difficult now appears simply to be different from you. But before you despair, there is something you can change. You can – with their cooperation – get them to change their behaviour.

Let's take an example from outside work. When you're at home, are you a tidy person or an untidy one? Most couples who live together differ in this to some extent, and it's a frequent cause of arguments. One thinks the other is trying to make them live in a pigsty, and the other thinks their partner is creating unnecessary stress, and if they'd just relax they'd see it wasn't that important. So the tidy one tries to turn their partner into a tidy person – which creates resentment. Meanwhile, the other tries to make their tidy partner into a more laid-back kind of person who isn't really bothered about whether the towels live on the towel rail or on the bathroom floor. The tidy partner is angry at this attempt to change them.

The fact is, we can't change. If we could, we would do it and save the arguments. But because we *think* we can change the other person, we're upset and annoyed when they don't change. Our expectations of creating the kind of person we want aren't being met.

How about a different approach? Suppose we accept that we can't change the other person, so we stop trying. However, we can encourage them to adapt their behaviour. So, if you're the tidy one, try saying: 'I know you're not a tidy person. Could you, sometimes, be a messy person who puts the towels back on the rail?' It helps to be specific about your requests, and to limit them to a maximum of two or three at a time. This has two effects:

thinking smart

ON TOLERANCE

I don't mean to sound preachy here, but it can help to think about ways in which you yourself might be classed as difficult – maybe at home, at work, or even by your mother. Are you neurotically tidy? Opinionated? Indecisive? Picky about food? Your difficult co-workers can no more change than you can, and probably no more see why they should than you do. Think on it.

חוזר 383490   Hazel

thinking smart

thhfihl

> **SHARING TASKS**
>
> Accepting that people won't change can lead to all sorts of other solutions – because you can now have a friendly discussion where you both accept the other one's standpoint. This often leads, for example, to divvying up tasks differently. When it comes to tidying the bathroom, for example, it's not that big a deal to hang up their towels for them on the odd occasions they forget – and in exchange, they can do a couple of the jobs you really hate, like cleaning the hair out of the basin U-bend when the plughole won't drain.

1 You have lowered your expectations, and no longer expect 100 per cent tidiness from them, so you'll be happier to settle for only 75 per cent.

2 They feel you're accepting them for what they are, so they have no need to feel angry or resentful.

This principle applies equally at work. If you try to change people, you create resentment and frustration on all sides when it doesn't work. But if you accept each other's intrinsic nature and work with it, everyone feels understood and respected – the first and biggest step to cooperation.

STOCKING UP ON SKILLS

So how can we build on this new, more tolerant approach to difficult people? What techniques will help persuade them to cooperate by changing their behaviour? Well, a lot of the work has to come from you. Presumably, the person concerned is happy to be difficult (that's if they even recognize that they are), or they would change their behaviour without being asked. Perhaps their behaviour suits them very well. If they are domineering, for example, and it seems to get them what they want, why should they change?

Even if they would prefer to be more popular, perhaps they feel unable to let go of their difficult traits. Maybe they don't feel comfortable behaving any other way – they are happier staying as they are.

Assertiveness

So you're going to have to make a fair bit of the running if things are going to change. And to do that, you need to arm yourself with the necessary skills. The first thing that many of us lack when it comes to difficult people is assertiveness. There are plenty of difficult types around, and some of them cannot be dealt with effectively unless you can be assertive with them. How about:

▶ **the team member who constantly criticizes you**

▶ **the team member who likes to get their own way by shouting and losing their temper**

▶ **the colleague who begs more favours than you have time for – and makes it extremely hard to say no**

▶ **the senior colleague who talks over your head, blinds you with jargon, or treats you with impatient irritation if you don't grasp their ideas instantly**

▶ **the boss who never asks for your opinion or takes your views into account, even on projects you're heavily involved in**

▶ **the boss who is always putting you down in front of other people**

... to name but a few. If you are troubled by these kinds of people, and find them difficult, you probably need to work at becoming more assertive. Some of them will no longer seem difficult if you do this, while others will still be difficult in principle, but far easier to handle in practice.

Being assertive is all about treating others as equals, and recognizing your own right to be treated as an equal by other people. They may be senior to you in the company hierarchy, but they should still recognize that we are all created equal as people. If they don't, your assertiveness will put them straight – or at least ensure that they behave accordingly whatever their private views.

Once you begin to behave more assertively, people will begin to show you more respect. You must have noticed how submissive people are often overlooked, even when their contribution is valuable. And dominant characters get listened to more, regardless of whether what they are saying is worth hearing or not. Assertive people fall between these two extremes: they neither dominate others nor allow themselves to be dominated.

So how do you do this assertiveness stuff? You're naturally slightly shy or underconfident, your mother brought you up to apologize even when it's the other person's fault, and now you want to change your behaviour. Well, there are three basic guidelines to being assertive:

▶ *Express your feelings.* **An assertive person must be able to say how they feel, good or bad. You don't want to upset people, but you have rights too. If someone else is upsetting you or making you angry, say so. Don't be unpleasant or inflammatory about it; simply say, for example, 'I feel angry when you don't allow me to express my view.' If you start by saying 'I feel ... when you ... ' you are far less likely to provoke conflict.**

▶ *Be honest.* **You are allowed to say what you think. From 'I disagree' to 'I have reservations about your idea; I think it needs reconsidering.' This means you can criticize people, but being honest means you must do it fairly. Don't just be rude. But if you are still learning to be truly assertive, you're not likely to take your comments too far.**

▶ *Stand your ground.* **Don't be intimidated into backing down. If you are put under pressure to change something you're not willing to, simply keep repeating yourself, politley but firmly. If, for example, a colleague tries to persuade you to support their**

❚❚ **NO, BUT ...**

When people ask favours that you simply don't have time for, say no with a very brief explanation: 'I'm sorry, I simply can't. I have to have this report finished by Thursday.' It's the guilt that often makes it hard for us to say no, so alleviate this by offering a suggestion or solution: 'Have you asked Meg? She's really good at that sort of thing.' At least you've shown your desire to help. (One thing: if you direct them towards someone else, pick on someone assertive enough to say no if they want to.)

idea (which you actually think is dreadful) at a forthcoming meeting, just say 'I'm sorry, I can't support it.' If they continue to insist, repeat 'I'm sorry, I'd like to be able to support it, but I can't.' Stand your ground and don't be bludgeoned.

Assertive behaviour will not instantly resolve every difficult encounter, but it will have two key effects:

- It will reduce the number of people problems you have at work.
- It will enable you to stand up for yourself when difficult people need dealing with.

As a matter of fact, you'll find that all the techniques in this book are assertive techniques for handling difficult people. They are neither aggressive nor submissive, but show equal respect to you and to the person you're dealing with.

Keeping calm

Another of the basic techniques you need in your repertoire for handling difficult people is the ability to keep calm even when you are irritated, angry or upset. Some people can generate a strong emotional reaction – which is often entirely justified – but showing your emotions is never going to resolve the problem quickly or effectively. It is far more likely to lead to conflict and a build-up of animosity.

That is not to say that you should never express your emotions. As we've seen, the assertive approach is to let the other person know how their behaviour makes you feel. But you should let them know with words, not with a flood of tears or a torrent of rage. That way, you can phrase it so that they don't become defensive but are more likely to cooperate.

Face it. If someone starts hurling abuse at you or bursting into tears in response to behaviour that you feel is entirely reasonable and justified on your part, you are more likely to become defensive and resentful, and therefore far less willing to resolve their problem. So stay calm. Some of us find this easier than others, but keep your mind focused on your objective, and recognize that this is the way to get what you want with the minimum of hassle and time.

Feedback

Feedback is a specific technique for addressing problems with other people in a nonconfrontational way. One of the big advantages of this is that it's a relatively easy way to approach someone, so you don't have to wait until you're at breaking point before you tackle them.

 thinking smart

PRACTICE MAKES PERFECT
It will take months of practice to feel truly assertive, but you'll get there. Start by being assertive with easier colleagues, or over minor points. Once you feel comfortable and confident, begin to assert yourself with more difficult types or in more emotionally charged situations.

thinking smart

COUNT TO TEN

If you are so riled that you cannot speak calmly and rationally to the other person, just extract yourself from the conversation altogether until you have calmed down. Say something along the lines of, 'I don't feel happy about this. I'll talk to you about it later,' and then leave. If you can't leave, just shut up (and count to ten under your breath). If you're too emotional to speak calmly, don't speak at all.

Feedback works especially well with persistent problems, which is what you tend to encounter with difficult people. Suppose you have someone on your team who is a persistent complainer. Talk to them in private, when neither of you is in a particular hurry. Here's how you can use the rules of feedback to resolve the problem:

1 Decide in advance the key points that you want to make, and prepare ways of saying them that do not include:

- **exaggeration, such as 'you're always complaining'**

- **judgements, such as 'you're hopeless at dealing with problems yourself'**

- **labels, such as 'you're a whinger.'**

2 When you speak to the person, focus on yourself and not them. Don't start sentences with 'You make me feel ... '; try saying, 'I feel ... when you ... .' For example, 'I feel helpless and frustrated when you complain about things that I feel are minor details.'

3 Explain why you feel this way: 'I can't deal with them myself because I have other claims on my time that take higher priority; but I feel helpless having to say no to you.'

4 Now let the other person have their say. Listen to them, and show you're listening.

5 Focus on how they *behave*, not what they (in your view) *are*.

7 Be prepared to quote actual instances wherever possible.

8 Suggest a solution and see how the other person feels. This is very important; as we saw in the introduction, you can't change people's personalities, only their behaviour. So you must have an alternative behaviour in your mind that you are asking them to adopt. If you can't think of any solutions, you'd be better off not tackling the matter in the first place. Remember, you're not asking them to stop being a complaining person – they can't do that – you're asking them (perhaps not in so many words) to be a complainer who doesn't complain about certain things or at certain times. For example: 'Could you suggest a solution when you explain the problem to me? Try to think of something that doesn't involve time

THE BIGGER PICTURE

If the person you are talking to is a member of your team, relate their behaviour to the task: point out how their behaviour is impairing the team's ability to get results.

thinking smart

GIVE THEM THE GOOD NEWS

When dealing with your own team, be positive as well. Tell them when they have done well by not complaining, or whatever the problem behaviour is. Show them they *can* behave cooperatively.

or resources that aren't available. Then, when you talk to me, I'll be better able to help and you'll find the complaint is more likely to be dealt with effectively.'

9 Listen to the other person's response and be prepared to compromise with them. (You may even learn something about how *you* appear to others, and be able to adapt your own behaviour and improve your performance.)

Many difficult people can be handled simply by using assertive behaviour, or by using the techniques we'll look at in Chapter 6 for individual types of difficult people. But when these approaches don't get the results you want, you can use feedback with any problem to meet your objective of resolving it swiftly and permanently, in a way that meets work objectives and satisfies everyone involved.

for next time

When you have more time to reflect on the people problems around you, there's one scary question you need to consider: could it possibly be – even just sometimes – that the problem is you? Some people seem to have more difficult people problems than others, and this can be a good indicator that at least part of the problem lies with that person themselves.

So here's a private little checklist for you to run through. You never have to tell anyone you even bothered to glance through it. But just for reassurance …

Which of the following lists of personality traits would you say most closely describes you? Be honest, now, or the exercise is pointless.

List A	List B
You are good at seeing things from the other point of view	You have a strong, commanding tone
You don't interrupt people	You interrogate people firmly
You express yourself assertively	You have a loud speaking voice
You have a sincere tone of voice	You sometimes threaten people
When you ask questions, you listen attentively to the answers	You raise problems even when you have no solutions to them
You enjoy change	You take things personally
	You judge other people
	You don't always plan ahead

There are no prizes for recognizing that problem people mostly possess character traits in list B. Mind you, we're all a mixture of both lists – the question is which list describes you most predominantly? If you recognize yourself frequently in List B, try to work on the behaviours it describes (without changing your personality, of course), and see if you can't tone it down. You don't want other people going out and buying this book to help them deal with you.

And by the way, if you identified with every point on List A and none on List B, you must be a saint. And they're the worst of all to work with.

3 tricky types of behaviour

OK, you've learnt the basic techniques for handling problem people. You're going to be assertive from now on, you're going to keep calm (or go away and come back calm), and you know how to use feedback if you need to.

Some difficult people have a particular recurring characteristic that drives you mad, and we'll be looking at those in Chapter 6. But there are certain types of tricky behaviour that almost anyone can exhibit. Some people exhibit them regularly, and some only occasionally. Whichever is the case, they can come at you out of the blue, so you need to be ready to deflect them instantly. That way, you can meet your objective of resolving the problem swiftly and permanently, in a way that meets work objectives and satisfies everyone involved.

So what are these behaviours? The key ones, which I'm sure you'll recognize, are:

- ▶ **anger**
- ▶ **silence**
- ▶ **emotional blackmail.**

ANGER

Some people are justified in getting angry – we all are from time to time. Others get angry frequently in order to bludgeon you into doing things their way. The way you handle these two types is very different, so we'll look at them separately.

Justified anger

I'm sure you never give anyone cause to get angry, but even so most of us have to deal with other people's anger occasionally. Maybe there's been a misunderstanding; maybe the system is unreasonable and you are its representative – who else are your team members going to take out their frustration on when the organization lets them down?

Anger is rarely the best way for anyone to get what they want; if they are dealing with someone reasonable, fair and sympathetic (like you), it is never the best way. But we're all human. The question is, how do you handle it and diffuse things as fast as possible?

▶ **People who get angry for a good reason do so because they feel they cannot get the response they want without getting angry. Usually they feel they are not being listened to. So the first thing to do is to listen to what they have to say. Hear them out, and they will begin to calm down.**

thinking smart

KEEP YOUR PROMISES
Whatever you agree, stick to it. If you don't, you'll be dealing with someone twice as angry next time. And quite right too.

- Show the person that you sympathize with their point of view. You may not be able to give them what they want, but you can still indicate that you appreciate their feelings. You can use phrases such as 'I can see that must be frustrating for you,' or 'No wonder you're feeling angry about it.'

- Don't wind them up by trying to justify your actions. It sounds as if you're making excuses, and are more interested in your side of the matter than theirs. Maybe they really need to know if their holiday dates have been approved before they can book their favourite hotel – which is about to become fully booked. And they've asked you twice already. The last thing they want to hear is a long explanation of how busy you've been and how difficult it is to schedule everyone's holidays.

- What angry people really want is a result. So the next step is to agree a resolution that they are happy with. Promise you'll do the dates by the end of the week; agree that if they miss their hotel thanks to you, you'll let them change their holiday time. Best of all, give them a choice – then they feel you've given them a measure of control: 'I'll do the dates by the end of the week but, if you prefer, I'll let you submit a different set of dates.'

Tactical anger

People who lose their temper in order to intimidate you into giving in to them are an entirely different matter. The worst thing you can do is to let them get away with it. If it works, they'll keep doing it to you, and everyone else.

The first thing you need to do is to brush up on your assertiveness skills. You'll need them. You mustn't allow yourself to be intimidated, and you're not paid to be shouted at by someone who has never grown up. You may also find that feedback (following the guidelines in Chapter 2) works with this person. But before you try that, here are a few tips:

- Don't allow yourself to be shouted or ranted at. Be assertive and say something along the lines of, 'I don't like being shouted at, and I shall leave if you don't calm down.'

- If they continue, do just that: leave. Say, 'I'll talk to you when you've calmed down,' or, if you find that hard to say, just say, 'Excuse me,' and walk out of the room.

- Continue this response at any subsequent encounters where they get angry, until they learn to talk to you rationally and reasonably.

SILENCE

People sulk because they want to let you know how upset they are. If they didn't sulk (they feel), you would think the matter wasn't important to them. Almost all of us are prone to sulk occasionally, but some people do it over such seemingly minor issues that it ends up happening frequently and creates an unpleasant and unhelpful

ththththinkingrtsmart

KEEP A LID ON IT

Never respond to anger with anger. It doesn't work, it inflames the situation, it makes a resolution to the problem far less likely, it stores up resentment and bad feeling, and it loses you the moral high ground. So bite your tongue before you're tempted to bite their head off.

attitude that can seriously sour the working relationship. Whether you are dealing with a regular sulker or an unexpected dose of the silent treatment, the guidelines for handling it are the same.

▸ **Silence is intended to make you feel guilty once you realize how upset the person is. Any approach to handling a sulker works only if you honestly have nothing to feel guilty about. So when you have the kind of discussion with this person that can lead to an unpleasant silence, make sure you genuinely listen to them with an open mind, explain the reasons behind your view of the matter, and act in a friendly and reasonable way. Once the discussion is over, if they choose to sulk you know that there is nothing else you could have done except give in for no good reason, simply to avoid it.**

▸ **The aim is that you will capitulate. Never, ever do so. If it works for them once, they will try it every time.**

▸ **Don't perpetuate the atmosphere by being short with them either. Behave as if everything were normal. If they give you the silent treatment, just say 'OK, we'll sort it out later.' If it really can't wait, force them to answer you. Ask them the question and then wait for their response. And wait ... and wait. Force them to break the silence by answering – it's their turn to speak after all. Once you've shown them that you can hold out longer than them, they won't try that technique again.**

EMOTIONAL BLACKMAIL

'I'm going to be in a real mess if you don't help me out with this.' 'Don't give me a hard time for being late, I find it so difficult to get up in the mornings.' 'Please don't be uncooperative.' Emotional blackmail is a popular weapon for getting people to do whatever the blackmailer wants. They are playing on your guilt, or your desire to be popular, in order to manipulate you into doing things their way.

But there's one thing you need to know about emotional blackmail: it doesn't work on assertive people. And the emotional blackmailers learn to recognize assertive people and they stop using this insidious technique on them. So apply a bit of assertiveness and become impervious to this kind of manipulation.

▸ **Recognize emotional blackmail for what it is. As soon as you start to feel guilty about saying no, or emotionally uncomfortable about your response to someone, ask yourself, 'Am I being emotionally blackmailed?' Once you're alerted to the possibility, you'll have no trouble recognizing when it's happening.**

- Tell yourself that emotional blackmail is not a fair, equal, adult behaviour, and that you owe nothing to those who use it. If they're prepared to use such an underhand approach with you, you are quite entitled to respond by not giving in to it.

- Now simply stand your ground, according to the assertiveness guidelines in the previous chapter. If they persist, adopt the stuck record technique. Don't allow them to make you feel bad – it is they who are behaving unreasonably, not you.

- Challenging people directly over this technique can cause unpleasantness, but with some people you may find that you can say – with a joke and a laugh – 'Careful! That's starting to sound like emotional blackmail ... ' It pulls them up short. If they think you're getting wise to them they'll back off.

for next time

Once you get used to using these techniques – and you may encounter these behaviours often enough to get plenty of practice – you'll find they get easier and easier to handle. The key is to recognize them early, and nip them in the bud:

- As soon as someone starts to sulk, simply leave them alone. Don't give them the satisfaction of knowing that you've even noticed.
- Recognize someone else's mounting anger before it goes too far, and stop yourself responding in kind.
- Learn to recognize emotional blackmail as soon as it rears its head, and don't allow yourself to be taken in and to start feeling guilty.

4 difficult bosses

In some ways, problem bosses are the most difficult of all to deal with. You inevitably worry because they have the power to influence your career, and whatever you do you don't want to upset them. This is a perfect example of where you really do need fast thinking to keep them sweet *and* get what you need from them too.

You'll find that many difficult bosses exhibit traits that you also find in colleagues and team members. If this is the case, you will probably find all the tips you need elsewhere in this book. But there are some difficult characteristics that are only – or chiefly – a problem when you find them in your boss. And that's what this chapter is about.

There are three main types of behaviour that fall into this category – see if you recognize any of these bosses:

- ▶ **the one who never backs you up**

- ▶ **the one who breathes down your neck**

- ▶ **the one who's always right**

THE BOSS WHO NEVER BACKS YOU UP

These people are often friendly, affable and easy to get along with. But when you need a decision made, or need someone to put your case to senior management – or even just need advice – they somehow wriggle, stall, or just plain disappear. They are the enemy of fast thinking.

Often, the problem is that they simply can't handle conflict. So, rather than tell you that your proposal isn't considered good enough to implement, they just avoid making a decision on it. Or worse, they send you off to do some extra research on it, or add another section, just to put off having to disappoint you.

And it's not only you they don't want to get into deep water with. They are nervous of arguing with their own bosses. So when you ask them to clear a budget increase for you, they somehow never sort it out. They take no for an answer without putting up any reasoned defence, and leave you in an impossible position.

Because they hate conflict, this boss is also very reluctant to give you constructive criticism or to put you straight if you go wrong. Consequently, you may well have little idea if your performance isn't up to scratch. This is demoralizing for you, and can be downright dangerous to your career if more senior managers can see the problem but your own boss hasn't enlightened you.

So what can you do to get these reluctant bosses to start doing their job properly? Here are a few techniques that will help:

- ▶ **If you ask them for a straight opinion on your performance, they won't be able to make any negative comments. It might upset you. They'll just insist there's nothing wrong. So if you sense there's a problem, try phrasing your question differently:**

thinking smart

RESIST TEMPTATION

The temptation with these bosses is often to go over their heads simply to get a decision or an answer. But doing this will rile them, and could well cause more problems than it solves. So avoid this if you possibly can.

'What do you think could improve my proposal to make it even better?' This allows them to feel they are being helpful rather than brutally honest, and they answer while still implying that the proposal was excellent.

▶ If your boss is stalling, there is some kind of conflict. Maybe they know that senior management don't want to see any budget increases this year. Or maybe they feel that their own boss doesn't support the project you want the additional funds for. So get them to tell you what the conflict is; then you know what you're dealing with. And they may find it easier to tackle the situation once it's out in the open. Try saying, 'I realize there's a conflict for you here. I'm pushing for a budget increase for this budget. So what's on the other side, holding you back?'

▶ If your boss is simply indecisive and puts off making decisions, try acting as an unofficial adviser, and see if you can't help them to find a firm solution. Or simply make the decision yourself. Talk to them about the problem, and then say 'That's really helpful. OK, I'll tell you what I'll do … ' Make this a statement rather than a question. This gives them the chance to disagree, but almost certainly they will leave you to get on with it, having effectively approved your decision.

▶ Don't pressure this kind of boss too hard. If the pressure feels worse to them than the risk of doing something, they will do anything just to get you off their back. And it probably won't be what you want them to do.

THE BOSS WHO BREATHES DOWN YOUR NECK

There are few things more frustrating at work than being denied the responsibility you know you can handle because your boss won't let go. Very possibly it's responsibility you actually hold on paper, but in reality you can't make a move without your boss's express approval.

These people may be control freaks, power hungry, perfectionists or just plain paranoid that you'll get more credit than them. Whatever their particular motivation, they need to be dealt with swiftly so you can get on with doing your job properly – by yourself.

▶ Check that you aren't doing something that gives your boss cause (however unjustified) to check up on you. If they don't seem willing to let you make decisions, or they seem to mistrust your expenses claims, ask them – without being defensive – what their reason is. For example, 'I realize you don't always trust my judgement. It would be helpful if you would tell me the reason.' Then sit back and wait for the response. You might not like it, but listen anyway.

▶ Once you've heard them out, acknowledge their worries even if they seem unfounded to you. Then you can reassure them that it won't happen again – with some concrete

107

> **GO NATIVE**
>
> Don't get defensive, especially if there seems to be a level of personal mistrust (such as a conviction that you're fiddling your time sheet). Perversely, what you should do is encourage your boss to check up on you (no that wasn't a misprint – I really did say 'encourage'). The point of this is that it will build your boss's trust in you, and although they may take the opportunity initially, they are more likely to loosen their hold once they see that you are trustworthy.

reason why it won't: 'I can understand why you've been concerned in the past. But I've devised a new monitoring system now ... '

- ▶ **Try to emulate your boss more.** I know that sounds like a recipe for madness, but the point is that if they think you work in the same way they do, they are more likely to trust you. So include the same level of detail in your reports that they do in theirs, and try to use the same approach as them to problem-solving or handling tricky situations.

THE BOSS WHO'S ALWAYS RIGHT

This boss won't listen to anyone else's point of view. Why should they? They already know the right answer. And once they've made up their minds about something (which doesn't generally take long) the subject is closed. Full stop.

Although this boss doesn't breathe down your neck, they have a similar constricting effect because they know exactly how to do your job, and they won't be happy if you don't do it the way they know is right. Here are the best ploys for dealing with the boss who's always right.

- ▶ **Never tell them they're wrong.** You've probably picked this one up already, but what do you do when they are wrong? The best way to get them to see it is by asking innocent questions: 'Can you explain how that will work in peak production periods?' 'I think I follow, but what happens after the initial promotion?' 'Could you just explain how that works with new staff?' Now sit back, and let your boss realize their error of judgement for themselves.

- ▶ **If you have trouble wresting responsibility away** from this expert who knows how to do the job so much better than you, be realistic. Find the area of the job they find least interesting or consider least important, and ask to be allowed to make decisions over that. For example, 'I know Scotland is our smallest territory, and none of our big customers are there. Could I look after those regional accounts, with authority to agree discounts? There won't be any really big figures involved anyway, and I've been watching the way you handle customer discounts in the south-east.' This way you can slowly build up a recognition in them that you know much of what they do, and must therefore be right quite often yourself.

- ▶ **Make sure you get things right as often as is humanly possible.** Do your homework thoroughly, so that your results always demonstrate that you, too, are invariably right. Well, almost ... you'll doubtless find that no one else is allowed to be quite perfect.

thinking smart

NEVER GLOAT

Bosses who are always right, and therefore never listen to anyone else, are actually wrong quite often (surprise, surprise). When this happens, resist the temptation to say 'I told you so,' and instead help your boss to save face: 'Of course, if it hadn't been a leap year, your projections for February would have been spot on.' There's a good reason for this. These people, once proved wrong, will always look for someone else to blame. (Obviously. It couldn't have been them, after all, because they're always right.) So align yourself with them fast, so the finger of blame points past you and elsewhere.

for next time

Learn to spot difficult bosses further up the organization, so that you can either avoid working directly under them (if possible) or at least lay the groundwork for being the kind of person whose work they respect. Get on the right side of them now, and when the time comes, the job of taming them will be a whole load easier.

Don't get defensive, especially if there seems to be a level of personal mistrust

5 conflict in the team

As a team leader, you'll know that even if you are an expert at handling difficult people, you can still have problems when they aren't experts at handling each other. Conflict within the team is your problem, even when you are not one of the protagonists. What's more, it is a problem that can disrupt everyone and waste the whole team's time. So you need to be able to sort out conflict promptly and effectively.

The first thing to recognize is that there is less conflict in well-run teams than in poorly run teams, so if you're doing your job properly things will be easier from the kick-off. The key guidelines for maintaining a happy team are:

- **Make sure everyone is doing a job that suits them and that they can enjoy.**

- **Make sure you are approachable and easy to talk to when your team members have problems.**

- **Ensure your team members are all well motivated (you'll find guidelines on motivation in *fast thinking: project*).**

- **Make sure everyone in the team understands the objectives of their jobs, and the team's overall objective. As with any individual project, so each person should also have their own objective (see *fast thinking: work overload*).**

- **Help ease the stress for any team members who have personal problems (you'll find a section on counselling interviews in *fast thinking: discipline*).**

I'm sure all of these are second nature to you; they are core skills that all good managers possess. However, even the best-run team suffers occasional conflict, so how can you nip it in the bud? The most common ongoing problem is a personality clash within the team. You have to address the two people involved by sitting down with them and talking through the problem. You have to get them together, otherwise they will each wonder what you said to the other, and they may even misrepresent you to each other. This could make the problem worse rather than better, and it could even turn into a three-way conflict that you have become entangled in.

- **Create a relaxed, informal setting to discuss the problem, at a time when no one is under time pressure.**

- **Make it clear from the start that your job is to focus on objectives and to ensure that the team works towards them as effectively as possible. Their conflict is inhibiting that process, and you want to resolve it for the sake of the team. Explain that you do not wish to allocate blame – you simply want to resolve the problem.**

- **Ask them to accept you as a mediator. Tell them that you believe that talking through the problem will resolve it, but get their agreement that if there are any points they cannot resolve they will accept your decision on them. These can always be reviewed later if the difficulties persist.**

Make absolutely sure that you give no indication whatever of any personal bias. If you think one of the team members is being more unreasonable or difficult than the other, don't let either of them see it. You are a referee only, so don't express an opinion.

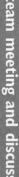

- Explain to them the techniques of feedback, which we looked at in Chapter 2. Tell them that you would like them to use the feedback format to discuss their conflict. Remind them that feedback rules state that they should each allow the other to finish what they are saying, focus on the problem and not each other's personality, and talk about their own feelings and reactions rather than focus on the other person's actions.

- Keep out of the discussion as much as possible, except to remind them of the rules if they start to stray from them.

- Don't allow them to finish the meeting without an agreement – a verbal contract – about their future behaviour. If one person is in any way coerced into this arrangement they are unlikely to follow it, so you need to make sure that it is a genuinely mutual agreement. Make sure that one of them isn't making all the concessions in order to keep things sweet, but that they are both taking steps to meet each other half way.

- Do anything you can to help in your capacity as team leader. For example, they may ask you to reallocate certain tasks, or reprioritize them, or to rearrange the office layout so the two work physically closer together or further apart. You brought these two people together to resolve their differences, so it's important that you are seen to cooperate when it comes to taking practical steps to achieve that resolution.

- At the end of the meeting, thank both of them for cooperating in trying to resolve the problem. Tell them you recognize that it isn't always easy, and that by managing to improve matters they have benefited the team as a whole.

Arrange a date to review things after a few days or weeks (whichever seems appropriate). This way, no one feels they have to commit themselves to an arrangement that they might not be happy with once they have tried it, and if it only partly solves the problem they have a chance later to discuss further action. At the review session, thank them for any success they have had in making their solution work.

FACTIONS WITHIN THE TEAM

There's one thing even worse than a personality clash between two members of the team, and that is when the entire team divides into factions. This is a major problem at the best of times, and when schedules are tight and deadlines are bearing down on you, it can become a waking nightmare.

If you have a well-managed team (and I'm sure you do), it's extremely unlikely your team will separate into factions. But it can occasionally happen to the best of us. In the unlikely event, you need to identify what kind of split it is. There are three factors that can cause a split in the team:

- **disagreement over policy issues**

- **a status battle between two senior team members**

- **rivalry between groups in the team.**

Each of these problems has a different choice of solutions, so we'll look them individually.

The policy issue split

There may be such strong disagreement in the team about the collective goal that it splits the group. For example, the team can't agree whether it should concentrate on the domestic or industrial market.

- **You need to identify the problem as early as you can (a standard fast thinking approach). In many cases, this is just a matter of not ignoring it in the hope it will go away. The sooner you take action, the better – and if you can pre-empt a split completely, that's even better. You can't act too soon.**

- **Call a team meeting and discuss the issues. The aim of the meeting is to reclarify the team's objectives. If you have built a strong team, its members will want to reach agreement and they will understand the importance of doing so. Your job is to make sure it happens.**

- **Once a decision has been made, you need to make it evident that it is final. There's no point in your team members continuing to discuss the merits and demerits of the various options because it's too late. So, whatever you do, don't let them think it's open for review later.**

- **It can help to follow up this session with an increased workload (within reason) or a major challenge to the team. You can often create this by bringing forward a project the team would normally have started work on in a few weeks' time. The object of the exercise is to unite the team in a common cause, and put them under just enough pressure that they don't have time to dwell on past decisions and emotions but focus on future plans instead.**

START A SMALL WAR

One of the best ways to unite the team is to focus them on threats, dangers, rivals or enemies outside the team. If you can make them feel that survival is at stake and the enemy is beating at the gates, internal disputes seem less important. It is on the same principle (if a little more dramatic) that dictators often start foreign wars to forestall revolution at home.

The status battle split

This can be a little tougher to deal with. What happens is that the factions form around two key players on the team who have different aims for the team, different styles of working, or different ambitions for themselves.

▶ **This situation can arise only if the two people involved are pulling in different directions. You need to refocus them on the team, its needs and its objectives.**

▶ **Call the two people together and mediate while they discuss their differences together, following the guidelines we have just covered.**

▶ **The greatest danger in this situation will come if you are weak in the way you handle it. You will need to be firm with these two people, and tell them that the split in the team would not be happening unless they were allowing it to. Point out that the team is suffering as a result of the split, and that if they are committed to the team they must smooth out their differences and work to reunite the team.**

▶ **The most important question to address with these people is, 'What is the best way for the team to accomplish the task?' Once you retreat to 'What is the best way to keep A happy, or stop B sulking?' you are on a very slippery slope. People will realise that success depends on the force of their personalities not the force of their arguments.**

TELL IT LIKE IT IS

If a status battle split has reached a critical point, or the people involved are not willing to cooperate, it may well be necessary to point out that if they do not have the necessary commitment to the team there is no place for them as a member of it.

GETTING TO KNOW YOU

Groups tend to have collective personalities. Other teams in the organization will be perceived as 'clever' or 'spoilt' or 'aggressive'. When two teams merge, each sees the members of the other team in this light. Encourage them to see each other as individuals and this feeling often dissipates. Try sitting members of each team at desks next to each other, organize team social events, hold regular team meetings and generally speed up the 'getting to know each other' stage. Hold contests at team social events in which the teams are mixed up, so that rivals become allies.

The group rivalry split

This happens most commonly when there are already two groups within the team – say, national sales and international sales – or when the team is made up of two smaller teams that have been merged. In this case, a natural rivalry springs up between the two teams just as, when I was at school, there was rivalry between the A stream and the B stream (despite the fact that we were streamed quite randomly, not according to ability).

- ▶ **Don't assume this is necessarily a bad thing. Sometimes it encourages healthy competition. If you have, for example, two regional sales forces competing, you need to make sure that the atmosphere remains friendly, that one team doesn't become demoralized by always being seen as the 'losers', and that the rewards are designed to motivate but are not valuable enough to create serious jealousies.**

- ▶ **Sometimes you can handle this a little differently and split the existing factions into smaller groups so that each competes with its previous 'allies' as well as with its previous 'opponents'.**

- ▶ **If the atmosphere has become tense and the rivalry is being taken too seriously, swap round some of the key people – have a reshuffle – so that they can't compete.**

Team conflict is a worrying thing, since it eats into everyone's time and productivity. But with some fast thinking and smart action, you'll find that you can keep any difficulties to a minimum and get on with the things that really matter.

Make it standard practice to train your team members (not forgetting any new members who join) in feedback skills. That way, they may well be able to resolve minor conflicts themselves. And when you *do* have to get involved, you can address the problem straight away without having to take time to teach them the techniques for resolving it first.

6 the fast guide to problem people

Right. You're under pressure, the workload is mounting, the deadlines are getting tighter. And just as you're trying to get to grips with it all, someone turns up and starts causing problems. Or maybe they've always been difficult but it seems more of a problem now that you've got no time to deal with it. What you need is a handy reference guide for dealing with the most common problem types. So here it is.

Simply run through the contents list at the front of the book, and find the one you need. Then look it up in this chapter for some much needed tips on how to get them off your back. Sorry, I mean how to resolve the situation swiftly and permanently, in a way that meets work objectives and satisfies everyone involved.

THE UNCOMMUNICATIVE PERSON

Some people are naturally slow to contribute to conversations and may genuinely not realize how unhelpful they are being. One of the problems associated with this behaviour is that these people often fail to commit themselves to anything because they tend to speak in 'Mmms' and 'Uh-huhs' rather than using phrases such as 'I'll have it ready by Tuesday morning.' Consequently, they often infuriate their fellow team members who feel they can't rely on them. Feedback is often very effective, but before you try it, here are a few tips that may ease the situation:

- ▸ **Ask these people a lot of questions to encourage them to talk, and make the questions as specific as you can. So don't ask, 'Can you get this report done next week?'; try 'This report needs to be about 5000 words, and I need it on Thursday week at the latest. Will you be able to do that?'**

- ▸ **Except when eliciting commitments from them, ask open questions (ones to which they cannot reply 'yes' or 'no'). This forces them to communicate more.**

- ▸ **Once you've asked a question, shut up and wait for them to answer. Don't feel uncomfortable – the onus is on them to speak first so tough it out.**

THE PERSON WHO NEVER LISTENS

Don't you just hate 'em? These people can be incredibly frustrating for everyone. Not only do you know damn well they're not really listening while you're speaking to them, but tasks frequently don't get done as a result. And when you tackle them, they claim you never told them about it in the first place. There is, however, a simple technique for dealing with this:

- ▸ **When you've finished speaking, say, 'I want to be certain I'm making this clear. Could you just repeat it back to me?'**

▶ **If you are worried they're repeating back to you parrot fashion and still won't remember, ask them questions – open ones, so they can't just say 'Mmm': 'What do you think about including case studies in the report, and how should we work them in if we use them?'**

▶ **These people will never remember what you did over the weekend – just concentrate on making sure they remember what they need to get the job done well.**

THE DAYDREAMER

The problem with daydreamers is that their productivity drops when they start to dream, and then they tend to make mistakes. As a result, they often let down their colleagues. The chief cause tends to be boredom, so the best treatment is to keep their attention going.

▶ **Give them tasks to share with someone else – the other person will keep them awake and on their toes.**

▶ **As far as possible, let them decide which tasks they want to do when.**

▶ **Set them productivity targets paired with accuracy targets, and with good incentives for meeting them.**

▶ **Accept that these people will never be suited to certain kinds of monotonous work and try to avoid giving it to them.**

THE LONER

Loners are happy that way. They like keeping their office door shut. The problem when they're on your team is that they aren't really team players. As a result, they can appear quite remote and often negative to the rest of the team, and can inhibit a free flow of ideas.

▶ **Loners tend to withdraw further if they are put under pressure to be social. As we've established already, you can't change them, so you might as well accommodate them. In fact, this will probably improve matters. Allow them their privacy and don't force them to attend large gatherings.**

▶ **Loners are often more comfortable talking to people on the phone than face-to-face. So call them on the internal phone sometimes instead of walking round to their office.**

THE SECRETIVE PERSON

Some people make a habit of keeping back information from the rest of the team, which makes it impossible for everyone to feel that they're pulling together. It helps

> ### IT'S NOT ALL BAD
> Recognize that loners have certain positive qualities: they tend to work well on their own, have a bent for detailed work, and can be very good at working on long-term projects. Exploit these talents, and make sure the rest of the team appreciates them as well – they may well be glad to pass these tasks on to someone who wants to do them.

to understand why people do this. There are two common reasons for it: one is that it gives them a feeling of power, and the the other is that they have a particularly strong need for recognition.

- ▶ **Make your requests for information very specific, and put them in writing if necessary.**

- ▶ **Alternatively, write down the information you already have and ask them to fill in the blanks for you; this should satisfy any need for power that they have. They'll get a feeling of satisfaction from being able to tell you what you didn't know.**

- ▶ **When they give you the information you wanted, be warm and generous with your thanks so they feel smart for having been able to supply it. Do this in front of other people when you can. This should satisfy their need to have their contribution acknowledged.**

- ▶ **You should be able to tell from their reaction to these approaches which of the two reasons for being secretive applies in their case. Once you've worked out which of the approaches suits them best, you can concentrate on that. In future, you should have no problems getting information out of them.**

THE OVERSENSITIVE PERSON
Every tiny criticism is taken as a personal slight with these people, making it almost impossible to discuss their work objectively. You'll always have to watch what you say, but there are ways to minimize the problem:

- ▶ **Never make any comment they could take offence at in front of other people; this will make them feel humiliated.**

- ▶ **Make sure that your criticisms are objective, specific and worded so as to be clearly critical of their work and not themselves. So don't say, 'I'm a bit worried about your performance lately'; say, 'I'm a bit worried that you've missed two deadlines in the last month.'**

- ▶ **Build their self-confidence. Always point out where they have done well when you discuss their weak points: 'Mind you, although you delivered the work a day late, it was a terrific report.' Comment on strengths of personality as well as work: 'You have a real knack for getting to the heart of an issue.'**

THE MARTYR
Martyrs are always taking on extra work and moaning about it. 'Still, someone's got to do it,' 'Go on, I'll add it to my in-tray,' 'Don't worry, I'll manage.' .... The problem with martyrs is that they often make other people feel guilty for not working as hard as

> **EASE UP**
>
> Remember that if people are very sensitive, a little criticism goes a long way. If you say, 'I'm a bit worried,' they'll feel they've turned in the worst month's work in history. If you say, 'I'm not satisfied with this report,' they'll be heading for the razor blades before you've finished the sentence. So go easy on them.

them, and their tension and negativity can spread through the team. They are also very prone to stress, which is disruptive for them and their colleagues.

You can't convert a martyr into a laid-back, relaxed person. But you can minimize the disruption they cause around them:

- **Don't allow them to take on extra work. Keep their workload to a reasonable level and politely decline any offers to help out with urgent or extra tasks. Encourage them to take full lunch breaks and to go home on time.**

- **If necessary, have a private talk to tell them you're concerned about the stress they put themselves under. Make it clear to them that you don't expect them to take on extra work, and you won't think them any less able if they keep their workload down.**

- **You could tactfully point out that their effect on the rest of the team is counterproductive. Bear in mind, however, that martyrs are often extremely sensitive, so be very diplomatic. You could imply, for example, that others are inclined to feel inferior because they don't have the martyr's stamina, and that this damages morale.**

- **Martyrs often feel inadequate themselves and are driven by a need to prove their ability and boost their self-confidence. So make sure you give them plenty of recognition for the work they do. Reduce this slightly when they overwork, and shift it to concern for their health and the team's morale. They are more likely to prefer the response they get when they work less hard.**

THE MOANER

There are two good points worth making about people who constantly complain (honest):

1. They will often be the ones who bring genuine problems to your attention — problems that you want to know about. Because of their natural tendency to

> **THE PRE-EMPTIVE STRIKE**
>
> Before they complain, ask them if they need any help. Occasionally, they may see this as an invitation to complain, but more often than not they will tell you things are fine (if they'd thought of a complaint they'd have voiced it already). Once they have committed themselves to the attitude that everything's OK, it makes it harder for them to start moaning later.

moan, the team will often unofficially appoint them as spokesperson for the group, and when they come to you they may be airing a commonly held complaint.

2 They are often very conscientious workers. If they weren't, they wouldn't care when things went wrong. It's because they care that they complain.

Bear these points in mind when they come to you with their latest complaint. But to minimize the minor whinges they come to you with:

▶ **Don't make decisions that affect them directly without consulting them first. If they feel involved in any changes or new procedures they will feel less inclined to moan.**

▶ **Try to avoid putting them under pressure – this almost always leads this kind of person to complain.**

▶ **When they complain, these people are prone to keep analyzing the reasons why the problem has arisen. Focus them on the solution instead: 'Well, it's happened now. What do you think is the best way to resolve it?' Just occasionally, it may be useful to know the background so you can prevent the problem recurring, but even so, suggest to them: 'Let's identify the reason for the situation later; for now, let's just worry about resolving it.'**

THE PESSIMIST

When someone says, 'It'll never work,' it's extremely frustrating as well as being unconstructive. On the other hand, the pessimists are often the ones who stop the group from making mistakes. But they need careful handling to exploit their ability to spot flaws, and stop them dragging the team down.

▶ **When they express a negative view, ask them to make it specific. Why won't it work? Are they guessing or are they basing their assessment on the facts? Is it just a hunch or do they have previous experience of this sort of thing? Be firm about getting them to be precise about which part of the project will create difficulties and why.**

▶ **Ask them how they think the problem can be resolved. Again, get them to be specific. Don't settle for 'I don't know – the whole thing looks like a waste of time to me.'**

▶ **Pessimists are often afraid of failure, and therefore avoid taking risks. They try to stop the whole team taking risks as well by adopting a negative viewpoint. Try asking them to tell you what they think the worst possible scenario could be as a result of following the course of action under discussion. This process often helps them to get their feelings in perspective.**

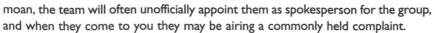

thinking smart

TURN THE TABLES

Don't get into arguments about whether women are as good as men, whether experience is everything, whether the immigration laws are too lenient, or whether all people educated at public school are snobs. Just remember, *you* have as much chance of convincing someone prejudiced of your point of view as *they* have of persuading you round to their way of thinking.

> Remove their fear of failure by relieving them of as much responsibility as possible. Then, even if the project does fail, it won't be *their* failure. Either tell them you will take responsibility for the decision, or make it clear that the team as a whole is responsible (which dilutes their personal ownership of the project). Often, with this burden lifted, pessimists can become helpful contributors – although they will never become optimists.

THE PREJUDICED PERSON

There are all sorts of prejudice you can encounter at work. The most commonly cited are sexism and racism, but some people dislike working for people younger than them, or sharing an office with someone from a different social background. You haven't a hope of persuading someone through reasoned argument to change this kind of attitude. Often the best way to resolve this kind of problem is the feedback approach outlined at the beginning of the chapter. But it is sometimes possible to change these sorts of behaviour without broaching the subject directly.

> Show them they're wrong. Let's take sexism as an example. If you have a sexist man on your team, make sure that the women on the team have the chance to demonstrate that their abilities aren't restricted by their sex. Give them traditionally male tasks to do. Once their sexist colleague sees they can do them perfectly well, their attitude may soften.

> Make sure you don't inadvertently reinforce their prejudice – you might want to talk about this to other team members who are affected. For instance, a woman who asks a sexist man to change the light bulb in her office is reinforcing his prejudice. It may be that she's only asking because she's not tall enough to reach it herself, but she still isn't doing her cause any good. Far better to stand on a chair and change the bulb herself, or at least wait until he's out of the office and then ask someone else.

THE JOBSWORTH TYPE

The jobsworth won't do anything that isn't down in black and white in their job description. These people can crush everyone else's collective motivation. Forget cooperation, forget mutual support – they're not interested. You need to find out why if you can. Often, jobsworths behave as they do because they feel unappreciated. If you thank them generously when they do you a favour they'll be more inclined to put themselves out for you next time. So how do you get them to do you the first favour?

> You need to appreciate, as they already do, that if it's not on their job description they don't have to do it. It's no good getting annoyed or frustrated. They're absolutely entitled to say no.

 thinking smart

LEARNING BY EXAMPLE

Encourage cooperation between all members of your team. The jobsworth may learn from the others' examples, and may sometimes be persuaded more easily by other members of the team than by you.

If you have a sexist man on your team, make sure that the women on the team have the chance to demonstrate that their abilities aren't restricted by their sex

- They know the rule book and their own job description like the back of their hand, so you'd better know it too. Then, at least you'll know whether you're asking them to do something they're paid to do, or whether you're asking them a favour.

- If you're asking them to do something outside their remit, let them know that you know you're asking a favour. Don't say, 'Please get today's orders over to despatch.' Say, 'I know you're busy but Kim's off sick today and today's orders need to go over to despatch. Would you mind taking them?'

- If they say no, accept it gracefully. If you say, 'That's fair enough, it's not your job,' you're showing them that you respect their rights. This approach might at least soften them up for next time.

- If you want them to do you a favour, make it a two-way deal and thank and reward them for it.

- Some jobsworths behave as they do because they suffer from a deep insecurity and fear of the repercussions that will result if they make a mistake. It is therefore important that you don't bawl them out if they do slip up.

THE CONTROL FREAK

These people are so nervous of being let down that they find it virtually impossible to delegate or share work. This both frustrates and excludes their colleagues. They are often perfectionists and they need recognition – that's why they find being let down so painful. Control freaks cannot change their innate fear of being let down, but they can learn – in the right circumstances – to change their behaviour and delegate more work to others.

- These people are happy if they know they can trust people to work to as high a standard as they do. So allow them to delegate or share work at a more gradual rate than most people, so they can learn one step at a time that the people around them can be trusted.

- While they are learning this, encourage people to keep them posted as to what is going on, and ask their advice where necessary. This way, they are continually aware that the task is being carried out satisfactorily.

- If anyone around them makes a mistake, let them see that it's an opportunity to learn and the mistake won't be repeated. Encourage people to admit their mistakes and actively demonstrate that they have learnt from them (this is a good general practice anyway): 'I arranged the meeting over a month ago and wrote it in the diary, but I never called back to confirm because the arrangement had been definite. I hadn't thought that the customer might change their schedule and forget to tell me. Still, after wasting an hour and a half travelling to see someone who wasn't there, that's one mistake I shan't make again. I'm going to confirm every appointment I ever make from now on.' This kind of self-assessment will give the control freak confidence that the lesson really has sunk in.

- As team leader, you can sit these people down and ask them what the worst possible scenario is if someone does mess up. Often it's not really that bad, and getting them to verbalize it helps them to see it in perspective.

121

- If you have people on the team who are prone to make the kind of mistakes the control freak hates, don't invite trouble by asking them to work closely together.

- Once a control freak has learnt to trust someone, you should find that they become excellent at delegating – at least to that person – and they'll be more open-minded about learning to trust someone else after a happy experience last time. So try to put them together with one of the most reliable team members while you're unofficially training them to trust their colleagues more.

THE KNOW-ALL

Know-alls are infuriating. You find yourself wanting them to be wrong even though the project and the team will suffer – and that's not healthy. But how do you stop them frustrating everyone?

- Know-alls are incapable of saying 'I was wrong.' Rather than pointing out their errors to them, ask them to explain their ideas or plans to you so that they can spot their own mistakes as they speak. If they don't identify them, ask them questions that focus on the area you feel needs closer examination.

- Don't try to humiliate them in front of other people, tempting though it may be – you will only antagonize them.

- Give them credit where it's due, but make them share it: 'That was a very good idea, Pat. Mind you, we'd never have got the results we did from it without Jason's inspired planning. And Jacky's presentation was first class.' Make sure the know-all recognizes everyone else's contributions as well as their own.

THE PRIMA DONNA

It's no coincidence that these people are prone to act like five-year-olds. This kind of behaviour is usually learned in early childhood; they discover that by creating a scene they can get what they want. In a work environment, however, you want people to focus on what is the best way to achieve the team's objectives, not on fulfilling their personal agenda.

- The prima donna has learnt that this kind of behaviour gets them what they want. All you have to do is to teach them that it doesn't – at least not here. It may take time after years of finding it successful, but if you're consistent they'll learn in the end.

- Don't respond to this kind of behaviour. Find an excuse to leave the room – make a phone call or grab a coffee – and come back when they've calmed down. Be responsive and willing to listen as soon as they're calm and rational, but opt out of the conversation whenever they become childish.

thinking smart

> **CONFIDENCE BOOST**
>
> Know-alls tend to knock people's confidence by crediting themselves with every good idea and every success. So keep everyone else's confidence boosted – particularly those who work closely with the know-all.

thinking smart

> ### IT'S AN ILL WIND
> You can't change these people's natural ebullience, and you really shouldn't try. There are times when it is exactly what the team needs. These are the people who keep everyone's spirits up in a crisis.

▷ **Don't meet their emotion with emotion of your own: meet it with cool, objective, factual statements and information-seeking questions.**

THE ROWDY PERSON
They sing to themselves while they're waiting for the phone to be answered, they burp loudly, they laugh uproariously at things they're reading to themselves – in short, they're cheerful, jolly and well meaning, and their colleagues are frustrated, irritable and underproductive.

▷ **It can help to have an informal word with these people. They generally have no idea that they are disrupting everyone; often they think they're being helpful in keeping everyone's spirits up. So be positive in your approach: 'It's great to have someone cheerful and optimistic around, especially when things start to get a bit pressured. The only trouble is … '**

▷ **If the problem doesn't diminish after this, the best solution can be to put physical distance between this person and the rest of the team. Put them in the corner of an open-plan office, or give them their own room if you have individual offices. It might be more tactful to give a different explanation for doing this. Instead of squashing their zest for life by saying 'No one wants to sit near you,' you could say, 'It makes sense for you to be nearer the fax machine' or 'you meet a lot of customers at the offices – you really need your own room.'**

THE OVERCOMPETITIVE PERSON
Colleagues competing with each other can work well if it's done on a friendly level, and especially if there's an element of luck involved – such as who happens to answer the phone to the customer placing the huge order. It can spur people on and help keep them motivated. But overcompetitiveness can be very destructive, as well as being demoralizing to anyone who can't keep up and so always loses.

▷ **Concentrate on focusing the team's performance on its customers (whether they are internal or external), not on each other. Explain to the team collectively (in a friendly, informal way) that you'd like them to channel their competitive drive outwards rather than inwards.**

▷ **If an overcompetitive person can't ease up, try to encourage them to compete against themselves and beat their own targets.**

▷ **Occasionally, someone takes competitiveness so seriously that they start to keep back information from other members of the team in order to give themselves a competitive**

Don't try to humiliate a know-all in front of other people, tempting though it maybe – you will only antagonize them

123

advantage over them. This does the team immeasurable damage and you will have to speak directly to the person about it explaining why it is bad for the team.

- A few people are born so competitively natured that they just can't help it. If nothing else works, your best option might be to allocate them tasks where they work independently and therefore have nothing to compete over.

THE BULLY

Bullying within the team destroys any chance of real team spirit, and it needs to be controlled. Of course, you can't eradicate it completely. That's all right, you just need to reduce it to a level where the rest of the team can handle it.

- Domineering people often pick on the weakest person around – often the youngest, least experienced member of the team. Stand up for this person until they learn to stand up for themselves. Don't be aggressive in their defence, or confrontational, but don't allow the domineering person to bully them. If they are trying to dragoon them into doing an urgent task that they don't have time for, come to their support and say, 'Actually, Peter has got his priorities right. The research he's doing for Jacky is very urgent and he can't do anything else until he's completed that.'

- Domineering people tend to try and shout other people down. Don't react. If everyone else stays calm, they will start to look rather silly losing their cool. They'll soon learn to stay in control rather than make a fool of themselves.

THE AGGRESSIVE TYPE

This type of person can upset other team members. Aggressive people tend to think and act fast, and they are often insecure and need recognition and personal power. These aspects of their make-up can guide you in dealing with them.

- Because they like to get on with things, it eases your relationship with them if you can move at their speed on projects you're working closely with them on.

- They need recognition and will sometimes put people down in order to make themselves appear superior. If you give them credit when they deserve it they won't need to do this.

THE MANIPULATOR

Good manipulators never leave any evidence; you can't actually *prove* that they've been manipulative. But you know it anyway. And so does everyone else. There's no point challenging them directly because they'll deny it. So make them feel that you want to help, not to point the finger.

- If they are manipulating a situation, they must have a reason. Think it through and work out what they are trying to achieve.

- Talk to them without accusing them of manipulation: 'I get the feeling that you'd like to run the ABC Ltd account. Is that right?'

- They will probably agree with you, but if they deny it give them reasons why you have this impression. 'I noticed at the meeting last Thursday that you highlighted one or

ASSERTIVENESS PAYS

Aggressive people don't necessarily want you to capitulate to them all the time – they often don't like people who are wet. They would much rather be able to respect you. So stand up to them assertively (but non-aggressively) when you need to.

two errors that Pat had made recently with the account. You don't normally focus on that kind of detail unless you have a particular interest in the subject – so I concluded that you were probably interested in the ABC account.'

▶ Once the manipulator feels they can talk confidentially and openly to you, without fear of accusations of manipulation, they will do so. After all, they are more likely to achieve their aim that way.

▶ If you can't give them what they want, explain the reasons to them. 'Pat is running the account well, albeit a little differently from the way you would do it. And the customers are happy and settled; I don't want them to have to get used to a new contact person here when it's not necessary.' But compromise with them if you can: 'If you feel you're ready to handle larger accounts, though, we can talk about finding a suitable large account for you to take responsibility for.'

THE RULE BENDER

Rule benders often get excellent results by playing the system or ignoring a few minor regulations – that's why they do it: because it works. These people are a problem for two reasons. One is that the team – or even the company – can be in trouble if their rule bending is uncovered; the other is that the rest of the team resent their getting away with it.

▶ Assuming this isn't the case, stand up to them for the sake of their colleagues. Resist their argument that their results improve when they bend the rules.

▶ If they agree to play by the book, give them at least as much recognition and reward for good results, even if the results aren't quite as good as they were when the rules were being bent. This should reduce their need to get results at all costs.

▶ Bring up the matter at team meetings. Don't accuse the rule bender personally; just raise the issue of rules in general, or the particular one in question. If they see that their colleagues are opposed to their behaviour, they may think twice.

▶ Obviously, if you cannot stop this person from twisting the rules you may have to warn them that you will report them next time, or take disciplinary action.

THE BUCK PASSER

These people are full of excuses for not having done things: 'Robin was away so I couldn't get at the research material,' 'The computer went down on Tuesday,' 'Pat needed me to produce a report really urgently at the end of last week.' You're just waiting for them to say, 'The dog ate my homework.' These excuses often implicate other team members, which can lead to conflict within the team.

DON'T MAKE ASSUMPTIONS

Before you tackle the rule bender, make sure they don't have a valid point. They may be breaking a rule of the team's own making that is better broken – so always make sure the best solution isn't to abolish the rule.

▸ Be very specific about the targets for tasks you give them to do. For example, 'I'd like this report to be fairly in-depth – say around 10,000 words – and I need it completed, printed and bound by 4.30 this Friday.' You may find that you need to put all instructions in writing for some buck passers.

▸ If they give you any excuses, just use the stuck record technique. If they tell you they couldn't get at the research material say: 'I can see that makes it harder. But I still need it on Friday.'

▸ Occasionally they may have a genuine problem in getting the work done, but don't help them unless it's really necessary, otherwise they'll never learn to sort out their own problems, and they'll always dump them on you. If they try to do this, stop them by responding to their excuse: 'I can see it's a problem for you not having access to the material you want; how are you going to solve it so you can still deliver on Friday?'

▸ If they try to blame someone else, don't get sidetracked. If they tell you Robin shouldn't have taken the key to the filing cabinet home, just say, 'That's a separate issue. At the moment we're talking about how you're going to deliver this report by Friday.'

▸ Make it clear that responsibility for something means being responsible no matter who actually does the work, and whether or not you're there at the time.

THE PUT-DOWN MERCHANT

These people like to belittle others by making snide remarks or ones that contain poorly concealed criticisms. They are full of remarks such as 'Late again, Kate? No surprises there,' or 'You actually managed to read it, did you? Mind you, I don't imagine you understood much of it.' If it's any consolation, other people aren't likely to take the implications seriously, since they will all be well aware of the type of person the comments are coming from. But how do you deal with it?

▸ The first thing is not to give them any ammunition. If you *are* always late, it's difficult to respond to the accusation, however unpleasantly they have chosen to put it. So make sure you give them no valid grounds for putting you down.

▸ If you rise to the bait, you will only create a row, which will get you nowhere. If you rile this person, they'll get worse and not better.

▸ If you respond submissively, on the other hand, you encourage them to carry on putting you and other people down. If you are happy to ignore the remarks with dignity, you can do so, but if you want them to stop, this isn't the way to go about it.

So you're left with the rational centre course – assertiveness. Reply with a polite question that challenges the put down. When they say, 'Late again?' you reply, 'Apart from last Wednesday, when there was a tube strike, I don't believe I've been late for several months. Which occasion are you referring to?' This will take the wind out of their sails and you'll find, if you employ this technique regularly, they'll soon learn that if they try to belittle you, it's them who will end up looking foolish.

Just remember that you can't change people's personalities. Once you accept that, you stop expecting miracles and you find you're satisfied with a reasonable improvement. Once you have the basic techniques under your belt, difficult people suddenly don't seem nearly so difficult after all.

for next time

As soon as you think you recognize one of these types in a colleague, a team member or a boss, look up the relevant section and learn how to deal with them from the off. You will always get results faster if you start out as you mean to continue, rather than changing your technique later on.

difficult people in five minutes

Y ou're off to a meeting, and you've just discovered that Valerie is going to be there. That's Valerie, the snide, sarcastic one. Or maybe you've got to discipline whinging Walter in five minutes. Or perhaps you've just been called into bully-boy Ben's office.

So what are you going to do? You've got five minutes to prepare yourself for an encounter with a prime example of a difficult person. Now just keep calm. Five minutes is plenty of time to get ready. Here's what you have to do:

- ▶ **Remind yourself that they are the difficult one, not you. What's more, everyone else knows that too.**

- ▶ **You need to stay calm when the time comes. If you are worried that you're going to lose your rag or burst into tears, try promising yourself a real treat on the condition you manage to keep your cool.**

- ▶ **See if the problem type is included in Chapter 6. If so, look up the technique for dealing with them.**

- ▶ **Remind yourself of the guidelines for assertive behaviour (page 97).**

- ▶ **If the problem is your boss, refresh your memory by looking through the relevant parts of Chapter 4.**

- ▶ **Whatever the difficult type, think about the reasons why they are difficult (you may find Chapter 6 enlightening on this point). Simply seeing the other person's point of view can make them far less frustrating, irritating or intimidating.**

- ▶ **If you're dealing with someone overbearing and you still feel nervous after all this, just try imagining them being given a rollicking by the MD (or if they are the MD, by a very important customer). It usually helps to put things in perspective.**

Whatever the difficult type, think about the reasons why they are difficult

discipline

- CHOOSE THE RIGHT PROCEDURE
- INTERVIEW WITH CONFIDENCE
- RESOLVE THE SITUATION

richard
templar

contents

introduction

So, things have got worse and you haven't taken action in time. Or maybe this matter's been dumped on your desk and you have to deal with it without knowing what it is all about. And now it's come to a discipline interview that has been pencilled in for tomorrow. The clock's ticking and you haven't really thought about what procedure you've got to adopt, what you are going to say, how you are going to handle this one if it gets difficult, what happens if you don't put in place some follow-up procedure to make sure it doesn't happen again – and you've got to do all this with diplomacy and restraint. And show the other members of your team that you are on top of your job, treat them all fairly and yet won't stand for any nonsense. Seems like a pretty tall order.

Here's the guide to help you through it with ease and expertise, and have you looking good at the end of it.

Now, we all know that time is our enemy – there simply isn't enough of it to go round – so what you have to do is cut out the irrelevant and work only with the necessary stuff. That's what this book will enable you to do. It will tell you how to handle a discipline interview clearly and precisely without any waffle or boring bits. It will show you what you have to do when the discipline interview is only a day away. And there is even a section for the discipline interview in an hour's time and one for taking disciplinary action in 15 minutes.

This book will also guide you through the process of handling ongoing discipline concerns, how to handle difficult people, how to be assertive yourself so you feel confident and comfortable administering discipline, and what to do in a real discipline crisis.

Sure, it's always better to have more time, but we live in the real world and we have to work with what we've got. There's no time to lose so what you want is:

 tips for looking as if you are handling this confidently when you know you're really quaking in your boots

 shortcuts to speed the process up

 checklists to run through so you make sure you've forgotten nothing

… and all put together clearly and simply. And short enough to read fast of course.

Let's assume you've got a day to prepare for this discipline interview. Ideally you would have had longer, but events have overtaken you and you've simply no room for manoeuvre or delay. You've got to prepare at the speed of life – so take the phone off the hook, make a quick coffee, and settle back to read fast.

 133

HANDLING DISCIPLINE AT THE SPEED OF LIFE

This book is going to get you through the five key stages of handling discipline:

1 The first thing to do is identify your objective so you know exactly what is required of you.

2 After this comes taking immediate action – what to do on a daily basis for dealing with minor problems of discipline.

3 The discipline interview itself – when all other forms of treatment have failed and you have to take serious steps – includes collecting the relevant information, handling the interview itself, and using your company's codes of practice and procedures. And, of course, we'll look at the most difficult of all discipline interviews – the termination of employment interview.

4 Handling difficult interviews: what to do and how to react when people respond in a less than helpful way, and how to remain calm and handle the situation effectively and diplomatically.

5 Lastly we'll look at what happens when it's not a discipline matter at all but really a counselling interview you may need to be holding – when you can't really take disciplinary action because the case is a much more sensitive issue.

fast thinking gambles

Of course we would all like more time but the fact remains – you've got to handle this discipline interview tomorrow. Ideally you would have had more time to prepare if only that had been possible. Fast thinking will stop you making horrendous mistakes and will achieve your objective comfortably. So what's the point of allowing more time if we can wing it effectively this time? Well, no matter how well you handle this, there are risks, and when your time is limited your options are also limited.

So what's the downside of preparing a discipline interview at the last minute rather than taking more time? Well ...

- ▶ **You may not have carried out sufficient research thus leaving yourself wide open to charges of unfairness or just plain being wrong – and you won't have time to make sure of all the facts.**

- ▶ **You may jump in at the deep end and react badly yourself if cornered by a difficult interviewee.**

- ▶ **You may not have carried out your company's discipline code of practice as well or as correctly as necessary – and that could lead to the dreaded tribunal.**

- ▶ **In your haste you might overlook some essential aspect of the matter that might indicate it is more of a counselling concern than a discipline interview – and hence risk upsetting people more than you need.**

- ▶ **You may be tempted to handle a termination of employment interview yourself without having time to seek the relevant legal advice – and again that leads to the dreaded tribunal.**

Fast thinking will enable you to handle this situation with care and tact as well as looking good and being seen to be fair – but for a truly magnificent display of team leadership qualities, do try and leave a bit more time next time. Of course, with any discipline matter you need to take decisive and effective action as quickly as possible to nip things in the bud but that should be done on a day-to-day basis as we will see shortly. A discipline interview, on the other hand, needs time to think about, prepare for and plan it. No good rushing these things even if you are at the cutting edge of management. We need to think fast but think effectively. Next time leave more time. But for this time we'll get you through it and have you come up smelling of roses and without leaving a trail of debris behind you.

1 your objective

One of the first things we usually do in a crisis is panic. We stop thinking about our long-term goals and how to manage effectively, and simply seek ways to get us through this quickly. Quick can sometimes be deadly, as well as slower than if we take a little time out to catch our breath and consider the best plan of action. Discipline interviews – and indeed any aspect of discipline – is fraught with danger. You are dealing with people here, and in their most vulnerable state – when they are on the defensive. It is a minefield of emotional pitfalls and potential outbursts. No one likes being disciplined – in fact no one likes doing the disciplining but it has to be done. And you owe it to your team to be as calm and effective as possible.

This means sitting down and thinking clearly about what you are doing. Yes, it means setting an objective. What are you trying to achieve? Easy to say 'Give old Bill a good roasting for being late so often,' but is that really what you want to achieve? What happens in the long term? You might well have expressed your anger at Bill, got something out of your system and ended up feeling better, but what about Bill? Have you encouraged him to turn up on time? Found out why he is late so often? Made it plain to the rest of your team that you care about them? Been seen to deal with discipline matters fairly and calmly? I think not.

Let's have a rethink about this. You need to work through the three key stages of discipline in order to set an objective:

1 Find out why – clarify the facts.
2 Take appropriate action – action that deals with the situation as and when it occurs without damaging morale amongst the other team members.
3 Make sure it isn't an ongoing problem – set up procedures to monitor it long term and to make sure it doesn't recur.

So, if old Bill is late on a regular basis you need to find out why – and why it hasn't been dealt with previously; decide on suitable action – this may not be a discipline interview matter at all but a quiet word on the side instead; then put in place systems to monitor it and correct it and prevent it occurring again as far as possible.

thinking smart

If you spend five minutes thinking about your objective you actually can create more time in the future. If you get it right now, you won't have to waste time attending a tribunal or dealing with potentially damaging litigation or simply rebuilding your team's morale. If you think five minutes is too much to spare, consider the implications of not thinking about your objective.

Thus your objective becomes a lot clearer: to establish the truth, to deal appropriately with it, and to make sure it doesn't happen again. That's better than just sounding off at Bill and getting his back up – as well as the rest of the team's backs.

Now you've identified your objective write it down. Spend five minutes thinking about it. This is your mission statement for dealing with all discipline matters in the future.

for next time

Set your objective earlier. That's it. And now you've done it this time you won't have to do it next time – it should always remain the same for all discipline matters.

2 taking immediate action

So, we've got to move on quickly now as the clock is still our worst enemy and we are thinking – and working – at the speed of life. Let's get cracking.

Administering discipline tends to take one of three approaches. There is the instant discipline, where you see someone doing something wrong and you correct it on the spot – the equivalent to a cuff round the ear.

There is the slightly more serious offence that requires pulling the person to one side and privately having a word – a sort of kick up the back side.

And then there is the more serious matter that requires a formal discipline interview (which we will look at in the next chapter) – the equivalent to six of the best.

Obviously the administering of any punishment never takes a physical form and these examples are just there to emphasize a point: please don't really hit your staff.

Each of these three requires a slightly different approach. Let's look at the first two. Both of these are for less serious infringements of company procedures, but they do need to be handled a little differently.

THE CUFF ROUND THE EAR

You have a team member that you catch coming in late – what are you going to do? Well, firstly think back to when you've come in late. How did you feel when you were ticked off? In fact, how did you feel being ticked off for any mistake that you made unintentionally and that you never really saw coming? Sure, it makes you feel resentful. The person telling you off obviously doesn't have a clue how you feel, whether or not you are genuinely sorry, what their treatment of you is doing, or indeed what effect it will have on your future performance or behaviour. This 'ticking off' might clear their congestion but it certainly doesn't do any good for morale, does it? And we saw earlier that maintaining morale was part of our objective. So what are you going to do knowing now that such a ticking off can be detrimental?

Well, the cuff round the ear might have worked way back when small boys went scrumping and got caught, but in this modern world of team leadership we cannot afford to rile people, put their backs up, or be caught on the hop. We have to handle

 thinking smart

KEEP RECORDS

Maintain some system of your own whereby you keep a record of your tolerance levels. If you accept that a team member can be late once a month without you saying anything then write that down on a card for your own private use. If you catch someone smoking in a no-smoking zone what action do you take? – write it down. Try to run through all breaches of discipline you've encountered in the last six months and make a note of what you did. This tolerance level record will serve you well as you can then treat the staff fairly and they will expect you to do so. And it's very quick just to pull out a card before you storm off and steam in and jump the gun; it gives you a slight breathing space and allows you to see what you did before when you weren't having such a bad day.

situations sensitively and diplomatically – and fairly of course. If Bill has been in late twice this week and you take action, be pretty sure that when Katie was late twice in the same week last month you followed exactly the same procedure. Don't haul Bill over the coals when you let Katie off. Likewise don't let Bill off if you gave Katie a hard time, she will remember her treatment and if you let Bill off she will be resentful.

So, be consistent at all times. Be fair and as just as you can. Now I know you might not like having to confront team members who are slipping, but confront them you must. Team leadership qualities involve being assertive and being prepared to be out there in the firing line to get the best from your team. If you let this go, it will get worse and the rest of the team will suffer. You have to nip things in the bud or they will bloom in an altogether unfortunate way. It is your job to maintain good order and discipline.

So what are you going to say?

Remember your objective – *find out the truth*. Don't tell Bill anything – ask him instead. Give Bill a chance to explain. He may have a good reason. He may have cleared his lateness with another manager or team leader who has inadvertently forgotten to tell you, or he may well be aware that he is late and he is now feeling pretty rotten about it. Charging in and telling him off also tells him you think little of him and that you don't care if he becomes demoralized. So always:

- ▶ **Find out the circumstances first.**
- ▶ **Give the team member a chance to explain.**
- ▶ **Accept their apology if it is offered in good grace.**
- ▶ **Respect their feelings about the matter and don't give them a hard time.**
- ▶ **Give them a chance to make amends.**

There, that didn't hurt too much, did it? And you didn't have to cuff anyone round the ear.

Point out to Bill he is late by all means but give him the chance to explain. Accept his apology and he might well say, 'sorry, the car broke down but I'll make sure it doesn't happen again. I'm getting a new battery tonight so this shouldn't be a problem again.'

End on a positive upbeat note. Pat Bill on the back and tell him it happens to us all from time to time. This is a first infringement so you don't want to make too big a thing of it. If Bill's car breaks down every Friday morning you will have to go to plan B – the kick up the backside, which we will look at in a moment.

 thinking smart

WE ARE ALL HUMAN

Don't expect too much of people and they will surprise you. If you allow them to be human they will occasionally foul up, let you down, run amok, slope off, be naughty, make mistakes, and generally behave as humans do. And you will be expecting it and not be surprised. What you might be surprised by is how infrequently they do so. If you expect them to be perfect you have only disappointment waiting for you – and you will be surprised how often you are disappointed.

GENUINE MISTAKES

The overwhelming majority of mistakes in any organization happen by accident. They are exactly that – accidents. Treat them as such. If the person making the mistake realizes what they have done and regrets it, your job is virtually done for you. There is then absolutely no point in giving them a hard time – they know what they have done and regret it. What more can you do to improve that situation? Make sure they understand how it happened and that they have learnt from it. Be magnanimous enough to thank them for owning up to their mistake – good one this as they'll be happy to tell you next time they foul up and not try to conceal anything.

But have we finished?

Not quite. There a few more rules to stick to:

- ▶ **Never criticize a team member in front of anyone else.**
- ▶ **Deal with things as and when they happen rather than letting them fester.**
- ▶ **Be very sure of your facts before diving in.**
- ▶ **Make sure the person understands the implications of their actions.**

Never criticize a team member in front of anyone else

This really is an unbreakable rule. You must be aware that bawling people out in front of their colleagues is unacceptable. It does nothing for their morale and certainly embarrasses the others. If you follow the rules of good discipline management outlined just now, you will realize that bawling anyone out is unproductive. All you have to do is pull them to one side – 'Bill, can I have a quick word?' – and you move to a corridor or out of earshot. Easy.

Deal with things as and when they happen

If you see someone coming in late, don't put it off until after your mid-morning coffee or later in the week. Talk to them there and then. Catch them before they've got their coat off, but do it nicely. Ask; remember, don't yell or tell. You can even be light-heartedly kind about it, 'So, Katie, get caught in the Tube strike? Well, you voted for him.' Don't be sarcastic or micky-taking, but you can be friendly. Obviously the friendliness evaporates if this is a habitual problem, but that is another matter. Nipping it in the bud should be your mission statement for dealing with infrequent minor lapses of discipline.

Be sure of the facts

But is Katie late? Are you sure? Has she pencilled in a dentist appointment since you last looked at the diary? Did she clear this with someone else? Has she been out on company business since arriving at work before you? Was she caught in idle chit-chat with the MD in the lift and couldn't get away? Was she out in another department organizing a whip round for your birthday present? (This actually happened to me many years ago when I was relatively inexperienced as a general manager of a large organization and, boy, did I feel dumb and embarrassed.) Do you have a good system of checking in so you can monitor lateness? Perhaps Katie is only taking advantage of sloppy time-keeping rituals that have gone on unnoticed for quite a while, until you noticed her this morning, that is. It happens sometimes that someone gets caught for an offence that everyone else is also committing but the team leader hasn't noticed. It is then very unfair to punish or blame anyone except yourself for poor systems. We'll look at implementing company codes of practice a little later. So make sure of your facts before taking action. And sometimes, the only way to make sure of your facts is to say something – ask if you're not sure. You can't be blamed for that just so long as you are asking and not accusing.

Make sure they understand the implications of their actions

If Bill is late, it means Harry can't finish the paper work, and Sue can't take the stock sheets over to Brenda, who then can't process them in time for the internal audit due this afternoon which means the rest of the team will be let down – that sort of thing. Emphasize the fact that you are a team and if one team member is not pulling their weight or taking their responsibilities seriously it undermines the whole shooting match. Don't make too big a thing of it for minor infractions, but it is worth pointing out how dependent on them you are – this makes them feel they are letting *you* down if they foul up rather than just themselves.

MAINTAINING DISCIPLINE

No one likes to be told off and no one likes to do the telling off. And if you maintain good discipline there is no need for either. Set standards yourself of course – don't be late or take home free pens if you don't expect the team to do so. But there will always be times when someone somewhere likes to take advantage. This then becomes the kick up the backside. Reserve it for persistent infringements. It is the informal discipline chat. It isn't a full-blown discipline interview which deals with major incidents, but rather a chance to try and put things right before they get really bad. The informal chat is for persistent infringements of minor company policy – habitual lateness rather than being drunk on duty, occasional sloppiness in work standards rather than serious misconduct, such as being caught having sex in the store room, persistent parking in the MD's parking space rather than writing off a company car showing off in the car park. That sort of thing.

The kick up the backside

One of the key rules for the informal chat is to catch it early. This isn't quite nipping it in the bud. You may have tried the ear cuffing technique and it failed. Now you have to move on to a more serious technique – the kick up the backside. Sometimes it is all someone needs to pull them back into line. Suppose Katie was late once and you had a quiet word. This had an effect at the time but now she is late almost every day. You can't let it go on. Once it has happened four or five times, you have to have the informal chat. If you let it go on for months, there is an implied agreement to her actions – she expects to come in late because you haven't said anything.

Tightening up their performance

At this stage you are still dealing with a fairly minor problem, so there is no need for any official action, such as written warnings. You don't have to get het up about it as you are dealing with it. All you are doing is tightening up the person's performance to get the very best from them. It isn't a major issue yet. If you announce it as a matter for a major disciplinary interview you've overreacted. Basically the informal chat takes place before you even need to issue a verbal warning – which you always do in writing of course to protect both yourself and the team member.

Rules

The rules for an informal chat are quite similar to those of the informal cuff round the ear:

- **Always go somewhere private – this is between you and the team member and there is no need for anyone else to know what is being said – or that you are even having this chat.**
- **Be pretty damned sure of the facts before calling someone in for an informal chat – you'll end up with egg on your face if you are wrong.**
- **Be consistent – you might think that you are being so, but make a record and check back that you always handle this particular problem in the same way.**
- **Give the person a chance to have their say – there may be more going on than you realize, or they may already feel pretty bad about the situation and don't need you sounding off to add to their troubles. Let them express their regret and offer solutions before you play the heavy-handed card.**
- **Focus on the problem not the person – it is their behaviour that is at fault, not them.**
- **Make it short and sweet – you are there to discuss this particular problem, not their entire career or anyone else's. Stick to the facts and don't go round the houses or get sidetracked by any other issues. Be assertive but fair, be succinct and brief.**
- **End on a positive note – no matter how you feel about the problem or the person, always end on an upbeat tone so they go away feeling good about themselves, you and the informal chat. Don't finish on a sour note whatever you do, as the ramifications can be long term and disastrous.**

Handling the informal chat

So, those are the rules but how do you handle the chat? Easy. Pop your head round the corner of the person's office or workplace and just say, 'Ah, Katie, can I have a quick word with you in my office in five minutes. Thanks.'

Then get them sitting down and remember, don't accuse, ask instead. 'Now, this lateness problem seems to be getting a bit out of hand so I thought you might like a chance to say how you feel we could resolve it. Got any ideas?'

Get them to do all the hard work

Katie is then not being bawled out or told off but given the chance to express herself, outline any problems connected with this matter, and have her say. You aren't being angry or irritated. You are a team leader trying to do what is right for the whole team. You can always point this out. You have a team member who isn't pulling in quite the right direction. That's all you want to accomplish. Get Katie to offer solutions. Get Katie to do all the hard work. That way she will feel part of the discipline process rather than like a small child being told off by her teacher at nursery school.

A lot of managers and team leaders do rather see their role as a parent or teacher when it plainly isn't. Your role is to motivate and encourage, lead and coordinate, inspire and direct. It isn't to tell anyone off or shout at anyone. You are a leader, a director, a guide; not a teacher, parent or police officer.

So, now you know what to say and how to say it all that remains is to call them in and get it over with. Take a deep breath and remember this is part of your job. I know you don't like it – no one does – but see it as an opportunity to rise to a challenge, a chance to improve your own experience and expertise, and a golden opportunity to do it better than all the times it was done badly to you in the past. The cycle of being told off then feeling resentful has to end somewhere. Make sure it is you that ends it – better management today by better methods and better people to inspire a better output. What could be better?

thinking smart

THE NAUGHTY CHILD

If you have a naughty child at home and constantly tell them that they are naughty, you are reinforcing the problem not solving it. If you tell them they are a good child who has done a naughty thing, then you are blaming their behaviour and not them. They are a good child who has done a naughty thing, not a naughty child. This works for team members as well. They are good team members who have done a naughty thing, not bad team members.

thinking smart

TAKING RESPONSIBILITY

For every breach of discipline by one of your team members, deduct five points from your own score. If they foul up, you can only blame yourself. Your job is to motivate and inspire them. If they wander off course, you must blame the guide not the porter. You are the guide. You must take responsibility. If they foul up, you must look at your own leadership qualities to see where you have gone wrong.

for next time

Keep records of what you did so you can maintain a consistent track record thus keeping the team members sweet and demonstrating your fairness.

Practise different ways of asking what the hell someone thinks they are doing coming in late or whatever without letting them know you are upset, riled or irritated. Make enquiries rather than demanding explanations. Ask open questions (ones that can't be answered with a simple yes or no – more about this later) so you elicit a response. Once you've got them talking, they will quite naturally and without prompting offer an apology and even suggestions as to how to stop it happening again.

Practise treating your team members like grown-ups and see if it doesn't generate a better response from them. Give them the space to be human.

3 the discipline interview

Quickly now, the clock is still ticking and you've got this discipline interview tomorrow – or in an hour if you're unlucky (see page 90) or even in 15 minutes if you've really drawn the short straw (see page 94). But not so quickly that you don't read this section carefully and take it all in. You are dealing here with a situation fraught with emotional fireworks and charged with sensitive dynamite. Tread softly for you tread on people's feelings, hurts, vulnerabilities and defensiveness. But you still have to enforce company procedure and policy and be an effective team leader. Maintaining good discipline is part of your job – this is what you signed up for.

Now before you go into this interview tomorrow there are five key areas you should have checked thoroughly so you aren't caught on the hop. Make sure that:

- ▶ **This really is a clear breach of company policy.**

- ▶ **The company policy is clearly understood by each and every member of your team and that they know they have broken the rules.**

- ▶ **This offence is a major one and warrants a discipline interview and not just a cuff round the ear or a kick up the backside – that this really is one for six of the best.**

- ▶ **This offence warrants a discipline interview and is not so serious that the only outcome could be a termination of employment.**

- ▶ **You've got the right person and that they did do it – whatever 'it' is. Make sure of your facts very, very carefully before going down this route.**

We'll quickly run through these so your checklist is in place and ticked off before tomorrow.

CLEAR BREACH OF POLICY

Is the offence a clear breach of company policy? There are two parts to any company policy – the written and the unwritten.

WRITTEN COMPANY POLICY

The written is what constitutes part of everyone's contract and usually states their working hours and duties, what the company expects from them, and what their job entails. Make sure this is all up to date. You can't bawl someone out for failing to carry out a task if that task isn't and never was part of their job description. They may have been expected to do it but if it ain't written down then they've got you and you have no defence. Make sure that the written part of company policy is kept up to date. Make sure it says what time they are expected to be at work – that sort of thing.

CHANGE THE LOCATION

You don't have to hold the interview in your office or a meeting room. Why not have it over lunch rather than just after lunch, or even in the team member's office. Changing the location to a somewhat unorthodox and unexpected one can change the attitude that such meetings can produce. You are there to be the good shepherd, not the parent, so you can be as inventive as you like, just so long as you get the job done with the minimum of resentment or tears.

Unwritten company policy

The unwritten part is the sort of normal behaviour you'd expect of anyone – not being drunk on duty, being civil, not taking part in any sexual harassment, being honest, being trustworthy – that sort of stuff. If you catch anyone breaking an unwritten part of company policy think very carefully before bawling them out as you may have found a legal loophole that they might exploit – but do it if you have to. Make sure a record of it is kept and make sure the powers that be are told in order to protect both you and the team member. It might also be worthwhile suggesting that it be included as part of the written company policy.

IS COMPANY POLICY UNDERSTOOD?

Make sure the company policy – written and unwritten – is clearly understood. When inducting a new member of staff (see *fast thinking: new beginner*) it is worth pointing out a subtle clause such as 'and of course we expect you to behave in a responsible and mature way when at work'. This covers you in the eventuality of them fouling up. They can't come back with 'but I never knew I wasn't supposed to be drunk on duty.'

Make sure they fully understand that they have broken the rules. There's not a lot of point in having a discipline interview – which is there, of course, to put things right, not to be a form of telling off sitting down – if they don't understand what they have done wrong or that it was wrong. They must be aware that their conduct was a serious breach of company policy.

IS THIS A MAJOR OFFENCE?

Some managers seem to think that having a discipline interview is a matter for routine and you should have one for any minor infringement of the rules. Others never have

thhfhk**thinking**smart

INVITE A FRIEND

Offer the person the opportunity to bring along a friend if they want. This could be a work colleague or their direct supervisor or a union representative. You have nothing to hide and it reassures them that you are not about to fire them or shout at them or bring up anything personal or anything they aren't prepared for.

Make sure the company policy – written and unwritten – is clearly understood

one if they can help it. Either extreme is just that – extreme. You hold a discipline interview as and when you need to: not for minor offences and not to be avoided at all costs. Every team leader will encounter behaviour that warrants a discipline interview – presumably you have recently, or you wouldn't be holding this interview tomorrow – and should be aware that they are not to be treated lightly, nor are they for minor violations of rules. Reserve the discipline interview for the big stuff.

Does the offence warrant termination of employment?

Some offences are so serious that the only outcome is termination of employment. These matters are certainly not for the discipline interview, although you may have to hold a form of one to:

- **establish the truth**

- **make the team member aware of the seriousness of their behaviour**

- **discuss possible options such as their resignation before you terminate anyway, or a transfer to your Outer Hebrides branch, or a written apology and repayment of all the money – that sort of thing.**

If the offence warrants a discipline interview, it has to be pretty serious anyway, but not so serious that you need to take advice or seek counsel from a higher authority.

Check you have the right person

It does happens that an offence occurs, you think you've got the person who did it, you hold the interview, only to find out it wasn't them. This leaves you feeling and looking pretty foolish. Make very sure of your facts before launching into this. Establish:

- **who did what**

- **when it was done**

- **how and why it was done – as far as possible**

- **who was responsible – this is different from who did it, they may have been acting under someone else's instructions about which you know nothing**

- **what has happened since it was done – they may have made efforts to make amends**

- **what the ramifications of what they did are – they may use the excuse or defence of 'Well, what does it matter anyway, nothing disastrous has happened'**

CHOOSE YOUR TIME CAREFULLY

You may not have realized that there are 'good' and 'bad' times to hold discipline interviews. The good time is just after lunch – we are all a bit more mellow when we've just been fed. The bad times are the high-stress times – between 9 and 11 in the morning and between 3 and 5 in the afternoon. In the morning, there is work to be done and an anxious need to be getting on with it. In the afternoon, there is a winding down and thoughts of going home. Best stick to just after lunch.

◉ **any previous convictions – you need to find out if this is habitual. Have they been transferred from another department because of this sort of behaviour? Is it likely to recur? Are they the only one doing it? Have any other team leaders had any experience of dealing with this issue?**

Whew. That's your checklist pretty well covered. That's what you need to do in advance. Seems a lot but it might take only a few minutes. If you are sure that you've got the right person, and that the offence has been committed, you're almost there. If you aren't sure at any step along the way then reschedule the interview. Don't go in half sure or even three-quarters sure. Be very, very sure, or postpone until you are.

ADVANCE NOTICE

OK, let's jump ahead to tomorrow. What preparations have you made? None? Well, you do need to make some. The team member needs to be told in advance that a discipline interview is scheduled – it's unfair to spring it on them at the last minute. You can't just march them to your office and begin a discipline interview without giving them the chance to marshal their forces and collect their breath as well. They may need to seek union advice, consult a friend, talk to anyone else involved, reschedule any important meetings of their own, or gather any relevant evidence they may have in their defence. I know this isn't a trial but they must be given a full opportunity to 'put their case' so to speak. So give them due warning. Make it a formal interview and set a time and a date well in advance. I presume you have done this for your discipline interview tomorrow? If not, do it now. Quickly, while there is still time. If you can't, then reschedule the interview.

WHERE TO HOLD THE INTERVIEW

Yes, you can hold it in your own office but there are risks involved. You are subject to endless interruptions. You gain an unfair edge by holding it on your territory – remember this isn't a trial or a battle of wits. You want this team member back on the case and anything you do to help this along will be recognized and respected.

thinking fast

THE PRAISE SANDWICH

We all hate discipline interviews from either side, and when we are the one holding the interview there is always a terrible need to start by giving praise to soften the blow of what is to come. This doesn't work. The person knows what is coming and can see through this technique. They also know you'll end on an upbeat note – some more praise. So the bad news gets sandwiched in between. Instead, begin by saying 'We'll discuss this problem area first then move on to a couple of points I'd like to make about your good progress in X.'

That way they know there is something good to come and you've removed the bread but left the filling – which is what they have come for. It also speeds up the entire process, which is good news for you.

Hold the interview, if you can, on neutral territory. Book a meeting room if your company has them. Borrow an office. Use a quiet room where you won't be disturbed. Make sure everyone knows you are out of contact for a specified time – usually half an hour should be sufficient at the most. No one wants these things to go on a second longer than necessary.

Seating

Traditionally, the boss sat behind the big desk and the employee stood in front of it and was duly rollicked for some misdemeanour. That practice has long since died out – and quite rightly so: it was unproductive, seriously undermined morale, and made the employee defensive and hostile. Nowadays we treat people with a lot more respect. Choose the sort of seating arrangement that reflects this. Sitting behind a desk sets up a whole string of assumptions, all of which you need to get rid of. You are not there to instil fear or to intimidate. You are there to nudge a fellow team member kindly back on track. This isn't a difficult process, but it is demanding. You have to tread warily. You are dealing with human beings with real feelings. Sit opposite them by all means, but get rid of the desk. Two chairs brought out to the same side of the desk works well. Sitting in low, comfortable armchairs doesn't seem to work well, as you both sink into an unwork-like relaxation. You need to be alert, professional and businesslike.

So, you've got the room and the seating right. You've got your checklist and obviously the employee's personnel file. You are ready to begin the real job of carrying out the discipline interview.

THE DISCIPLINE INTERVIEW

How are you going to begin? Let's try a few examples, which are all taken from real interviews:

'You're here because I'm bloody well fed up with your constant lateness.'

'You knew this was coming. You knew you were pushing your luck, didn't you?'

'This is a really serious matter and I don't know whether to bawl you out or fire you.'

'I knew when I took you on you'd let me down.'

'Let's cut the ****. You're useless at your job and if you don't pull your socks up, you're out.'

 thinking smart

WRITE IT DOWN

When we begin a discipline interview, there is often a tendency to have a somewhat confrontational eye-to-eye contact. You begin by outlining the problem verbally while the person stares at you. This isn't a good technique as it makes it uncomfortable for both of you. A better way is to hand them a piece of paper with a brief outline of why they are here. They are then obliged to read it – and thus break eye contact – and then you can ask them for their views. You have removed the initial confrontation, which makes life easier and the interview quicker and slicker. It also gives the person a chance to look away from you while receiving the bad news, giving them a greater feeling of control.

All real. All true. All unproductive and unhelpful. These openers do nothing to raise morale. They don't inspire or motivate. They immediately set the team member on the defensive and don't give them any room to explain themselves, make amends, seek new ways to improve, or even make them feel part of a team. They are old-fashioned and out-dated.

Let's see if we can't improve on these openers drawn from the age of the dinosaurs. Never begin with a statement such as:

'I expect you know what all this is about.'

'This is a discipline interview to discuss your behaviour last Wednesday at the conference.'

'You knew you were breaking company security procedures.'

Begin instead with a simple question. such as:

'Do you know what this is about?'

'So, what happened last Wednesday at the conference?'

'Are you aware that you have breached company security procedures?'

This sets the tone for the whole interview. It is going to be a full and frank discussion. It is not going to be a trial or an interrogation. You are there to set the person back on track. You are not there to administer punishment or haul them over the coals. You are not their parent. If you insist on being a relative, be an avuncular uncle or aunt – kindly and well meaning, friendly and forgiving. I know this might sound as if it goes against the grain of a discipline interview, but you really must ask yourself what you want out of this interview. Is it:

- ▶ **a confession?**
- ▶ **tears and guilty regrets?**
- ▶ **to find a suitable punishment?**
- ▶ **to make them feel really, really sorry?**
- ▶ **to extract a promise from them never to do it again?**
- ▶ **to make them realize that you are in charge and they must do as you say?**
- ▶ **to make them feel bad about themselves?**
- ▶ **to make them feel bad about the team?**
- ▶ **to make them want to leave?**

No, of course not. It is none of these. So what is it? It is to bring them back on track.

That's it. Nothing else. You don't have to make them feel anything – they'll feel it for themselves. You don't have to extract a confession. This is a simple matter of finding out what happened and why and to ensure they are clear about what they did and why it shouldn't have been done. There are no threats, no intimidations, no punishments.

See yourself as a shepherd. One of your flock has strayed and you bring them back into the field. You wouldn't beat a lamb so don't beat a team member. Reassure them, comfort them, explain kindly the error of their ways and bring them back on track.

GIVE THANKS

Make sure you make a point of thanking the team member for attending. You know they are obliged to – and so do they – but thank them anyway. This is polite and respectful and they will appreciate it. It also lightens the mood of what may be a difficult half an hour for both of you.

Have a quick tot up of how much it costs to recruit staff, train them and employ them and see if being a shepherd rather than a wrathful god of vengeance doesn't make more economic sense.

AFTER THE OPENER

Once you've outlined in the form of a question why the discipline interview is taking place you need to get the person to talk. You won't do this by asking closed questions (ones that require a one-word answer, such as yes or no). You need to ask open questions that require them to talk.

If you say, 'You know you've been late too often recently,' they can just say 'Yes'. End of discussion, and you've arrived nowhere.

Try instead, 'Why have you been late so often recently?' and you might find they open up and explain about their boyfriend borrowing the car to go rallying, which has left it unreliable, and it keeps breaking down, and they have to wait for the AA, who won't come because the car's been modified to unacceptably ferocious standards. You'll be surprised, perhaps, at what answers you do get. The straight, closed questions give you nothing to work with. Open questions give you something to bite on.

'So what happened at the conference?'

'Well, I helped Jimmy carry all the information packs in and hurt my back. I got some painkillers off the receptionist, and then I just had the one gin and tonic at lunchtime and before I knew it I was dancing naked on the table'.

'Ah, and what have you learnt from this?'

'Not to drink at lunchtime?'

'Well, yes, there is that but also not to take any medication from someone you don't know. And perhaps more importantly not to lift things that are too heavy for you. I'll have a word with Jimmy as he knows he's supposed to use that new forklift we bought specifically to stop anyone having to lift anything at conference.'

CONFIDENTIALITY

Make sure the person knows that nothing of what is said will go beyond the walls of the office unless they want it to. You won't gossip about them, but they can choose to tell anyone if they want to. None of us like being reprimanded, and if we think that everyone knows about it, it makes it worse. Obviously, if you have to place a note on their personnel file you will make it as objective as possible – outlining only the facts of the incident and what action was taken. Tell them this and make sure they know you keep your word.

thhfhltthinkingrtsmart

BOOKING THE INTERVIEW

You may well need to book the interview in writing. Drop the person a quick memo saying, 'There's something we need to discuss. I can make Tuesday at 2 o'clock, is that OK for you?' rather than 'I'm holding a discipline interview on Thursday at 10 – be there.' A little tact and diplomacy goes an awfully long way to improving working relations and making the team member feel like that – part of a team.

See, you learned a whole lot more than if you'd just said, 'This is a discipline interview because your behaviour was unacceptable last Wednesday. Can't have staff dancing naked on the tables, can we?' 'No'.

You've also found out that bad behaviour can be accidental and unintentional. Once you know this behaviour was not deliberate it can be forgiven much more easily – if you see that as your role. But your lost sheep can also be brought back into the fold much more easily because there is no anger or recrimination – they didn't let you down, they were merely the victim of circumstance.

But what if it had been different?

'So what happened at the conference?'

'Oh, I was so bored. I got a bit pickled in the bar at lunchtime – well, we all like a drink at conference – and then Jimmy dared me to dance on the tables and I just fancied stripping off. Not got a problem with nudity, have you?'

Now you're in the hotseat. You have an employee who has acted irresponsibly and on purpose. They have admitted their offence but seem quite unabashed by it. They have further compounded their problem by admitting to being drunk – to whatever degree – and they are now challenging you as well. What are you going to do now?

Let's lynch Jimmy

No, don't lynch poor Jimmy for suggesting the dare in the first place. And no, don't rise to the challenge. This interview is about the team member's behaviour, not your views on public nudity or anything else. We'll look in the next chapter at handling difficult interviews, but it is worth bearing in mind now that you must at all times keep the purpose of the interview uppermost in your mind and not be

thhfhltthinkingrtsmart

YOU DON'T KNOW HOW THEY FEEL

During the interview there may be a tendency to empathize: 'Look, I know how you feel.' Don't do this. You don't know how they feel. You may think you do, but you don't. At most, you can say, 'I realize you may be feeling pretty bad about this but we need to resolve this problem.' It is best to try and stay away from feelings altogether. You are there to bring a team member back on track. It is a business. You are there to discuss the facts – their actions – and implement ways of correcting their performance. It doesn't have to be an emotional experience at all.

distracted, nudged off course, irritated, made to feel rotten about having to conduct the interview in the first place, or deflected from your objective. Stay on course, stay calm and stay focused.

So, you've got the person talking and you've got them to admit their actions. Now you must get them to change course. Once they have accepted that their behaviour is unacceptable, you can move on. They may, of course, not see this, so you may have to point out to them how their behaviour affects the rest of the team and how it reflects badly on themselves.

The gap

You expect employees' behaviour to be of a certain standard. Their behaviour has fallen below this. There is a gap. You have to establish that you both acknowledge the same gap – that you are both singing from the same song sheet.

You must both agree what the expected standards of behaviour are. Unless you both agree you will leave the interview with a different set of standards and thus will never be able to reconcile your differences. Suppose you think occasional lateness is fine but frequent lateness is not. They may agree with you. Now define 'occasional' and 'frequent'. It's a bit like the Woody Allen film, where he says, 'We hardly ever have sex – only three or four times a week,' and Annie Hall says, 'We are always having sex – three or four times a week.' They see the gap differently.

For you 'occasional' and 'frequent' may mean once a month is OK but once a week isn't. Your team member may think once a week is fine but every other day isn't. The key rules for establishing the gap are:

- **outline the expected behaviour**
- **outline where they fall short**
- **define the terms used**
- **agree the gap.**

You must reach a common consensus of the terms used so you both know what the rules are – you must agree what 'occasional' and 'frequent' actually mean in real

thinking smart

*thhthithi*thinking*rthmant*

DON'T THREATEN THEM

You are allowed to outline the procedure for repeated offences of this nature: 'If this problem crops up again we shall have to try to resolve it in a different way,' rather than 'You step out of line again and I'm firing you!'

The problem has to be resolved. It has to be resolved in an appropriate way. You are not allowed to threaten the person with actions that are unreasonable or bear no relationship to the offence. You can't threaten to cancel their holidays or take away their company car (unless it is a motoring problem related to the car specifically). Nor can you give them a letter to take home to their parents. This isn't a school; it is a place of business and you are not there to punish them – merely to help them come back on track.

terms. Once you have done that, you can establish the gap. You may both have a dawning moment when you see the other's point of view: 'Oh, I see why you did this, you thought that dancing on the tables was fine and it was the stripping off that was unacceptable, whereas what I meant was no dancing of any sort.'

A quick example, and then we must really move on. Suppose the discipline interview is about someone taking decisions on matters way above their responsibilities. You establish that they ordered two million extra spare parts for the ZX140 when in fact they have no authority to order anything. They explain that in your absence, they ordered the spares because you said, 'While I'm away, deal with anything that crops up that isn't urgent.'

You didn't specifically tell them not to order anything and they were daft enough not to realize that they shouldn't. You have a gap. Now you've established it, define the terms and set an agenda for an action plan to make sure it doesn't happen again.

FORMALIZING AN ACTION PLAN

Once the employee has admitted that their behaviour is less that what you would have expected and they have appeared suitably contrite – and no, you don't want tears and sobbing, just an acknowledgement that they were wrong – you can move on to the next stage, which is to formalize an action plan.

This is actually a very simple exercise, but it goes a little beyond the 'I promise I won't do it again' sort of thing. You need to set a formal agenda for positive action. An extracted promise given in the heat of a discipline interview isn't worth the air it's sobbed into. You need a written agreement. But first you must establish the gap.

Setting an action plan

You have to define the terms of what the person should and shouldn't do. Only then can you monitor them to see if they have come up to your standards. It might be as simple as a quick chat in a month's time to make sure they haven't ordered anything in your absence or danced on any tables. Or it might be that they have to check in with you first thing every morning for a week to make sure you know they have arrived on time. Whatever action you jointly decide on – and it must be a joint decision or there is no point to this exercise – make sure you monitor it. If you forget about it, they will think you have no respect for them – they aren't worth the bother. But it also leaves you wide open next time it happens. You have no defence if you have failed to monitor them after a discipline interview.

⏸ **thinking smart**

NO EMOTIONAL BLACKMAIL

Don't be tempted to try emotional blackmail. You know the sort of thing – 'If you foul up you are not just letting yourself down but you are letting me down as well,' and 'I expected better things of you,' or 'Don't you feel ashamed of yourself?'

Stick to the facts and stay on course. Avoid any need to make the person feel more guilty than they already do. This speeds up the interview and stops it becoming difficult. A speedy interview is a good thing, just so long as you both stay calm and agree on all points.

DON'T TALK DOWN TO THEM

You may be senior to the person and more experienced and professional, but avoid talking down to them. Outline the problem. Suggest ways of correcting it and move right along. Don't reminisce, either, about how this happened to you when you were just starting out in their job or whatever. Stay focused on the reason you are both there and get the job done quickly and efficiently – and with the minimum of fuss. Talking down to them, or trying to make them feel small or bad, will only distract you both from the object of the exercise.

WRAPPING IT UP

The whole interview should never take more than half an hour. This isn't a long, drawn-out process. You don't need to get heated or angry. You are setting the person straight, not going back over their childhood to see where you went wrong as a parent.

1 Outline the problem – the person's behaviour, actions or performance.
2 Agree the gap between expected standard and actual standards.
3 Formulate an action plan.
4 Wrap it up.

Wrapping it up should take seconds. There is no further business. This isn't an appraisal. There are no other points to be raised. You can't keep the person here and prattle on about their long-term future or even ask them where they think they'll be in five years' time. It is a discipline interview. Even that sounds too harsh and old-fashioned. It is a formal meeting to discuss the person's shortfall in behaviour, actions or performance.

Anyway, whatever it is called, you've done it and now you both need to get out and have coffee. Once you have agreed an action plan, end on a positive note. Don't leave the meeting – or let them leave – on a note of gloom. Lift the air, have a laugh, find something positive to say about them so they feel good about the meeting.

Now go away and make a note to yourself to follow up on the action plan, have a coffee, and get on with the rest of your work. Well done. Good job.

VERBALIZE IN WRITING PLEASE

Obviously you may need to declare this offence as one which warrants a verbal warning. You may also have to log this in writing, but don't make it sound too serious or you risk intimidating the person. If it is a repeat offence, you may need to get a little more serious and declare it sufficiently irksome to warrant a written warning. You must know both your company's policy on these matters and current legislation – don't fall foul of either.

thinking smart

NO BRIBERY

Someone has fallen short of standards. You want them to make up the difference. They too must want to or the interview will lose its way. Don't be tempted to bribe them into good behaviour. No saying, 'Look, you pull your socks up and I'll see about that raise/promotion/new car/redecorated office/a longer lunch break.'

This technique may gain their quick agreement, but you are setting up a lot of long-term problems by doing it. They've effectively got you over a barrel and you will have lost their respect. They must want to come back on track for their own sake. You must be a sufficiently good leader to make them want to follow without having to bribe them.

for next time

Make sure you know and understand you own company's internal discipline procedures, and that you also know and understand any relevant current legislation.

Check out the next chapter about difficult interviews and how to handle them as you won't be able to stop and read it when you suddenly find yourself in the middle of one. Read as much as you can about how to handle difficult people (see *Fast Thinking: Difficult People*). Bear in mind that most discipline interviews need never happen in the first place if the team members are all on your side. This only comes about from good management practices – treat people with respect and they will reward you with improved effort and a desire to never let you down.

Treat people with respect and they will reward you with improved effort and a desire to never let you down

155

4 handling difficult interviews

Hopefully, if you have taken on board the techniques in the last chapter you won't need anything in this chapter. But life is never quite like that. Difficult interviews crop up from time to time – and you need to be prepared.

Read this chapter if there is the slightest possibility that tomorrow will contain anything unexpected. Yes, that's right, read it anyway as you never know when an interview is going to blow up in your face no matter how diplomatically you've handled it. You are dealing with a human being and they are tricky little beasts.

DIFFERENT TYPES OF DIFFICULT INTERVIEWS

There are various reasons why an interview can be regarded as difficult:

- ▶ **The team member gets emotional and expresses it as anger or tears.**
- ▶ **It is a follow-up interview to a matter that you thought had been dealt with.**
- ▶ **You've got your facts wrong and are caught on the hop (although if you have followed the advice given in early chapters this shouldn't happen).**
- ▶ **The team member goes all quiet on you and refuses to discuss their actions.**
- ▶ **The team member agrees with everything you say.**
- ▶ **It is a termination interview.**

We will look at each of these in turn – and ways to avoid them, of course – but quickly, as we are still thinking at the speed of life and you have a discipline interview tomorrow. I guess you need all the tips you can get if you are to deal successfully with a difficult interview. Let's hope you don't have to.

The emotional team member

Emotional outbursts of any sort are pursuing the same aim – to get you to change direction. If someone cries or shouts it is to get you to stop reprimanding them,

thinking smart

IT'S A DISCIPLINE INTERVIEW

The person is there to be reprimanded for a specific offence. They are not there to have their appraisal or a full review of their working life with your company. Stick to the one incident and that alone. This is faster and more efficient unless you want to be there for three hours going over old ground or discussing what happened two years ago at the Christmas party.

sacking them, telling them off, criticizing them – or whatever else you are doing that they don't like. To be blunt, it is a form of blackmail: 'See how you have upset me so much that I am now in tears/really angry?'

In a way, it is a bit like a small child throwing a tantrum. Now, I am not saying that they aren't genuinely upset and feeling emotional but this is a place of business and histrionics are out of place. Any grown-up, responsible person will accept being pulled back into line without crying or getting angry. And, like a small child throwing a tantrum, if you give into it they will do it again … and again … and again. Be firm (not harsh or cruel) and refuse to be swayed by tears or temper tantrums and they should get the message quickly – here is one damn good team leader who is not to be messed with.

If the person becomes emotional, be sympathetic but don't allow it to put you off or change your focus. Follow the five standard rules of discipline interviews:

1 Get the employee to talk.
2 Stick to the facts.
3 Focus on the problem, not the personality.
4 Remain calm yourself and uninvolved emotionally.
5 Be consistent.

Give them time to recover if they get upset but bring them back to the facts. If they become angry, ask them why discussing the facts should be a source of stress – and bring them back to the facts. If they shout at you, remain calm, but remember you do have the right to terminate the interview if you feel threatened. Obviously, you should immediately reschedule it for a later date (and with someone else in attendance) when the person has calmed down. You aren't backing down, merely giving yourself breathing space.

You will find that if you stick to the facts, don't issue ultimatums, and remain calm and businesslike, the chances of you having an emotionally difficult interview are remote indeed.

Follow-up interviews to a previous matter

Before you go in, ask yourself why you thought this matter had been dealt with. What more could you have done to prevent it occurring again? Is there some fundamental part of company policy that is flawed and encourages team members to stray off the track? Remember the analogy of the lost lamb? Well, they've got out of the field again. Did you repair the fences last time? Or leave a gap for them to squeeze through? You can't blame a sheep for getting out, it is part of their nature. But you do have to do something about the fences before they do it again.

thinking smart

TISSUE, PLEASE

Always have a discreet box of tissues handy just in case there is any chance of tears – or the person simply needs to blow their nose.

Then again, you may just have a troublesome sheep. If that's what you've got, you will have to be consider transferring them to another field or changing their responsibilities. Some team members simply don't fit in and will have to be relocated. Some are troublesome because it's in their nature. There is little you can do – you are not their father or counsellor, and you shouldn't take on board that responsibility. Remind them of whatever action plan you formulated last time and look at where it went wrong – together with the person of course. Formulate another action plan and institute more severe ways of monitoring it – yes, I know this means more work for you but it's what you get paid for. Remind them of where their duties lie and what happens if they fail to shape up – this isn't a threat but a timely reminder that ultimately you have to decide whether or not to keep them.

The follow-up interview can be a difficult one. You may need to issue a formal written warning to cover yourself in the eventuality that you decide to terminate their contract – after checking with your higher authorities of course.

You've got your facts wrong

If you are caught out like this – and it does happen, but hopefully not to you after you've read the earlier chapters – then you must terminate the interview immediately and apologize profusely. Don't try and bluff it. Don't try and make out it wasn't your fault. Admit your mistake and move along swiftly.

The team member refuses to discuss their actions

In this case, you should outline the facts and ask open questions to get them talking. If they refuse to do so, just ask an open question and then shut up. The onus is then on them to answer so they'll break before you do. No matter how uncomfortable you find this, remember: they are finding it even more so. Once you've got them talking, you can agree what action you require in the future – and action plans must always be agreed or they just don't work – and let them go. It will all have gone in. They may not be talking but by golly they are listening. You've done your job and stuck to the facts and formulated an action plan. If they aren't playing ball you may need to keep an eye on them for quite a while and find out what the real problem is.

The team member agrees with everything you say

Again, use the same procedure as above – stick to the facts but don't express any opinions – just ask for theirs. Then agree an action plan and move on. This team member thinks they will get away with murder if they just agree with you, so be consistent, treat it like any other discipline interview, and stay focused.

thinking smart

IN YOUR SHOES
Never begin a disciplinary interview with the phrase, 'And what would you do if you were in my shoes and this had happened?' It will only intimidate them. It is patronizing. They haven't been in your shoes. They don't know what it's like. They don't have your experience. And they may well not have your taste in crocodile lace-ups.

OTHER DIFFICULT INTERVIEWS
The other difficult interview types are:

- ▶ **The team member offers to resign – just say you aren't dealing with that issue at this time and stick to the facts.**

- ▶ **The team member denies stepping out of line – just make sure you have all the facts in front of you.**

- ▶ **The team member always has an excuse – and usually this means passing the buck. Again, stick to the facts and refuse to allow them to incriminate anyone else or blame anyone else. Don't get dragged into debates about details.**

You will meet a lot of others, from the barrack-room lawyer who always knows every point of law, to the 'but we're old mates' team member who doesn't believe you'll reprimand them if they remind you of how you once socialized together and have become blood relatives ever since. There's the out- and-out liar who will invent stories so fabulous you'll be tempted to believe them – don't. Then there's the gossip who, instead of accepting a reprimand, will try to fill you in on all the wrong things others have been doing – don't listen to such busybodying, stick to the facts of this discipline interview. And a hundred more. They're all delightful and should be seen as challenges. Their job is to get you to leave the holes in the fence unmended and for them to stray whenever they want. Your job, as humble shepherd, is to bring them back to the flock, mend the fences and keep an eye on them, naughty little lambs that they are.

THE TERMINATION INTERVIEW
This is the one we all hate. But it sometimes has to be done for the good of the team. Now it's your turn to do it and you feel trepidation and anxiety. Of course you do. You are about to make a decision that will deeply affect an individual's life, livelihood and long-term prospects.

The most important thing to remember when facing a termination interview (yep, a sacking) is that your team member has just ceased to be part of a team and now has nothing to lose. They can say what they want, do what they want, and tell you exactly what they think as well. Let's look at how these three things can be used constructively – or at least how you can defend yourself.

thinking smart

WHAT DO THEY TAKE WITH THEM?
The more senior the team member who has to have their contract terminated, the more likely they are to have sensitive information about the company. They will share this information if they leave feeling aggrieved or angry. Make sure they leave feeling you have done them a favour, as they will be much more likely to remain loyal and keep what they know to themselves. Also, if they leave feeling vindictive they can spread false rumours, leak information to the press, blacken your reputation as a team leader, play malicious practical jokes (it does happen), and generally make life difficult for you. The fast-thinking team leader doesn't allow this to happen – they make the leaving team member feel valued and respected even if they have been sacked.

thinking smart

LAST THING IN THE DAY

Don't give someone their cards and then expect them to return to their desk as if nothing had happened. If you give someone a week's notice, make it last thing on a Friday. They then have the weekend to compose themselves at least before having to face their workmates.

They can say what they want

OK, they can get angry but if you have followed all previous procedures exactly the person will know this is coming. Anger often comes as a reaction to a shock. If you've laid the groundwork well, there will be no shock – and thus no anger. Let them have their say if they need to, though. Your back is broad and you've heard a few choice expletives before so don't get all prissy and defensive. If they need to call you a few names, then so be it.

They can do what they want

Oh no they can't. They can't hit you or destroy the place. Make sure you have someone on standby whenever carrying out a termination interview just in case. If the person looks as if they might get violent, summon assistance immediately. Do not attempt to restrain someone you've just sacked – it ain't your job and you will only make a bad situation worse.

They can think what they want

… and tell you in no uncertain terms. Good. Let them. Ask them to do so. You will learn a lot about your company from them and about your management style. Let them sound off. Ask them to tell you exactly what they think of the team. You may hear grievances and disputes they've stored up but you may also hear one or two tiny gems that you'd never realized.

How to sack people

Hopefully you won't be doing this tomorrow – or in an hour or 15 minutes. But you may have to some day and you need to know the five basic key steps:

▶ **Present the termination in writing – this is both a legal requirement and also a useful technique. It avoids the eye-to-eye contact that is so intimidating, and gives the person something to look at while the bad news is digested. They will be grateful for the chance to look away.**

thinking smart

SWAP TEAM LEADERS

There is no reason why another team leader can't dismiss or discipline one of your team members instead of you – you may have to repay the favour. Sometimes it removes the heat of the situation if someone slightly more objective and neutral does the disciplining.

thinking smart

thhfhirsmart

TREAT THEM LIKE ROYALTY

Just because someone is having their employment terminated doesn't mean you have to treat them like a pariah. Instead, treat them like royalty. Don't sack them in a corridor or the tiniest cubicle you can find – use a decent office and even treat them to a lunch if they are potentially useful in providing information about where your system has gone wrong. Treat them like royalty, and they will respond accordingly. Treat them as if you don't care about them, and they will be much more difficult.

▶ **Stick to the facts – refuse to discuss anything except totally relevant bits such as termination pay, length of notice, references etc. The person will have known this was coming, so they may have prepared a list of reasons why they shouldn't get the sack, all of which are given to make you feel really bad about it.**

▶ **Use tact and creativity – don't be belligerent or aggressive, no matter how difficult you find this. Try to find ways to make it easier for both of you. The person may know it is coming and be glad to be gone, so it might not be as desperate as you think.**

▶ **Maintain confidentiality – if the person doesn't want anyone to know why or when they are going then respect their privacy.**

▶ **Maintain the morale of the team – let the team know after a termination has been successfully completed why it had to happen. In general terms, you don't have to discuss the specifics of the case and how it affects them. Chances are they will know as much as you do anyway, but they will appreciate being told the facts straight from the horse's mouth.**

So there you have it. That's the difficult interview sewn up. Well, it might be if life was as easy as that. But it ain't. People will always think of new ways to fool and fox you, and you will have to stay one jump ahead of the game. You will also have to stay one jump ahead of the legislation if you want to keep your own job. No one higher than you is going to be very tolerant if you discipline team members or even sack them without first following the specific guidelines laid down in both the company procedures and the law. Make sure you know them both well.

SELF-PROTECTION

Here are a few guidelines to enable you to carry out any disciplinary matter without ending up at a disciplinary interview yourself. I know we have little time but this lot is important, so take your time and digest them well.

It is a legal requirement for employers to provide written information to all employees about their disciplinary rules and procedures. This should form part of their contract of employment.

The law recognizes the importance of these rules and procedures when it comes to dismissals, and the way the dismissal has been handled will form part of any industrial tribunal's investigation. If the dismissal has been handled unfairly, the employer may well be ordered to reinstate the employee concerned and/or pay them compensation. It doesn't matter if the grounds for dismissal were fair. If the dismissal itself was unfair then you are liable.

Your job, as humble shepherd, is to bring them back to the flock, mend the fences and keep an eye on them

SQUARE PEGS

If you have done your job properly, people who end up being dismissed are invariably what you might term 'difficult'. The fact you have to terminate their employment therefore shouldn't reflect too badly on you, and you should bear in mind that they might well have been a square peg being forced into a round hole. Think of it as an opportunity to liberate them to find their perfect square hole somewhere else.

All procedures and disciplinary procedures have to be seen to be fair by both parties – the employee and the employer – or they won't stand up in an industrial tribunal. They must be reasonable and accepted by both sides.

Any disciplinary rules and procedures must relate to specific incidents and are not to be worded so vaguely as to be meaningless. An industrial tribunal realizes that you can't legislate for every eventuality, but the rules should cover basic safety and maintain satisfactory working relations with all staff.

Any disciplinary rules and procedures should be part of any new beginner's induction process (see *Fast Thinking: New Beginners*).

Team members should be made aware of what happens to them if they break the rules, and they should be made very aware of what would constitute grounds for a summary dismissal.

Any disciplinary procedures should always follow these guidelines:

- ▶ **They should be issued in writing – even if it is a verbal warning.**
- ▶ **They must specify to whom they appertain.**
- ▶ **They must indicate what disciplinary actions are being taken.**
- ▶ **They must be dealt with as quickly as is reasonably possible.**
- ▶ **They must specify which levels of management have what degrees of authority – basically who can sack you and who can't.**
- ▶ **No decisions are to be reached without the team member being informed of the complaints against them.**
- ▶ **Any team member to be disciplined must be given a chance to air their side of things.**
- ▶ **Team members who belong to a union must be given the opportunity to consult their union.**

BE AVAILABLE

A disciplinary interview can seem terribly intimidating to a team member, especially if they are fairly new. Conduct the interview, but always make sure they know you are available in a less formal setting to discuss any points that the interview may have raised. They may come and see you and have a chat, or they may choose not to, but they will feel reassured that you are available, human and caring. Score extra brownie points.

BRING ALONG A FRIEND

If you give your team member the right to bring along someone else to a disciplinary interview, then you must also have the same rights. If you think the interview is going to get emotional, bring along an assistant or someone from another department or even from personnel and say, 'Oh, this is Ann, she's just going to sit in on this, you don't mind do you?' Invariably they will agree and it diffuses the situation to have a third person there who seems impartial and merely observes, but in reality is there to safeguard your well-being. Obviously, don't bring along someone the person doesn't get on with or who was involved in any previous discipline matter.

- ▶ **No team member is to be dismissed for a first offence unless it is a gross violation of company procedures or rules.**

- ▶ **You must provide a right of appeal, and you must tell the team member what that appeal procedure is and how to follow it.**

- ▶ **You must keep records of any disciplinary procedure, even if it is only a verbal warning.**

- ▶ **There must be a reasonable time lapse on offences committed if satisfactory behaviour has been maintained – if a second offence occurs outside this time it is regarded as another first offence.**

- ▶ **It is up to every individual team leader, manager, supervisor, or whatever to keep abreast of current legislation. That means *you*.**

That should keep you out of court. Remember there is no legal duty to have a disciplinary procedure, but any industrial tribunal is going to look very unfavourably on you if you don't have a pretty good one.

COUNTING THE COST

If you have to give someone a week's or a month's notice, work out what that costs you financially. Now weigh it up against what it would cost you in lost orders, morale being dragged down, sabotage, poor work performance and the like. If the employee has the potential to damage you financially more by staying, then it sometimes works out cheaper to pay them a week's or a month's wages and let them go early.

◀◀ for next time

Make sure you know your company's dismissal procedure extremely well, and that you are up to date with current legislation. Keep records of any disciplinary procedure you have instigated, and make sure any discipline you dish out is backed up with a written record to the team member.

Follow up, follow up, follow up. The three key rules for maintaining good discipline. Be consistent with this, and make sure every team member knows you will be checking to see that if they were late, they are now on time, or whatever. Make notes in your diary to check regularly that minor infringements aren't creeping in and that the team understand's you are fair but firm.

It is up to every individual team leader, manager, supervisor, or whatever to keep abreast of current legislation. That means you

discipline v counselling

I know time is getting on, and you have a discipline interview tomorrow, and you think by now we've covered pretty well everything. But there is a special case to look at – the discipline interview that you suddenly realize should be a counselling interview.

We'll cover this as quickly as possible, but still do it efficiently – thinking at the speed of life. The discipline interview may turn into a counselling interview. If you suddenly decide you are holding the wrong sort of interview, stop what you are doing and rethink your strategy. Obviously you will need to discuss the problem, but you will need to ease off on the discipline and switch hats to a counselling one. Let me give you an example.

Sandra's work has always been good. She's on time and is a very conscientious team member. Of late, however, her work has been of a lower standard. She's misplaced files, burst into tears on more than one occasion, and blown up at quite trivial incidents. And now last Wednesday she stormed out of a meeting and missed another vital deadline. You've pulled her in for a discipline interview although you are sure there is much more to this than meets the eye. On the surface this is a discipline interview, and that is what Sandra is expecting, but you know that you will go easy and try to find out what is going on rather than reprimanding her and sending her on her way – which would undoubtedly exacerbate the situation. Several colleagues have tried asking her what is wrong, but have failed to elicit a response. Now it is down to you as her manager to find the truth.

You are not the counsellor

Now let's make one thing very clear – you are not in the business of counselling anyone. It is not your job and you are not trained for it. Even if you are a trained counsellor, it would be unprofessional to counsel someone for a personal problem – or even a work one – if they are directly under you or working as part of your team. What you are going to do is work counselling – finding a way to accommodate someone's personal problems within a working environment.

Back to Sandra. Now you've got her in, what are you going to do? How do you break the ice? Here are the key tips of getting someone to open up and confide in you at a counselling interview:

- ▶ **Outline the problem as you see it.**
- ▶ **Acknowledge that there might be an underlying problem that you can't see.**
- ▶ **Explain that you are here to help them find a work solution.**
- ▶ **Don't be frightened of silences – don't be tempted to fill them.**
- ▶ **Acknowledge the person's feelings once they do open up.**
- ▶ **Reassure them that their actions are quite normal and that you understand.**

- ► Don't tell them you know how they feel – you don't.

- ► Ask open questions that require more than a one-word answer.

- ► Focus your attention on the person and make eye contact.

- ► Sit in a relaxed posture and make encouraging listening noises – *aha, oh, ah, mmm*.

- ► After they answer each question, summarize to make sure you fully understand the situation – and that they know you understand.

- ► Don't offer any judgements or personal opinions – if their partner has left, don't say 'Well, you're better off single, I know I was when I got divorced.'

WHY HELP THEM SOLVE PROBLEMS?

Because if you don't:

- ► your team's productivity will drop

- ► their morale will fall

- ► mistakes will be made

- ► the situation will get worse rather than better.

You aren't being kind. You are looking after your team's best interests in the best way you know how. Remember that your team member's private life is none of your concern – unless it affects their work. Once it does, it becomes your business. You don't pry into the details, but you do need to take action. The counselling interview is not a 'soft' option, but the wise one.

OUTLINE THE PROBLEM

So Sandra comes in and you outline the problem – 'The problem seems to be that your work is going downhill and you are flying off the handle at the slightest thing. Now that's not like you, so can you tell me the reason?'

Now you will find out whether Sandra is just plain bored and looking for another job or, as you thought, has a real problem that is affecting her work.

If Sandra doesn't open up at once – and chances are she won't – you'll need to encourage her. Try saying something along the lines of 'I wonder if there's a problem I don't know about?' or 'If you can give me some idea as to what the problem might be, I might be able to offer some help.'

thinking smart

TENDING YOUR FLOCK

The smart manager watches for signs of any behaviour that is out of place, and corrects it before it has a chance to get worse by suggesting professional counselling and/or offering support. Much as a shepherd will constantly monitor the flock to look for signs of illness or underfeeding or lameness, so too must you tend your flock.

If you aren't frightened by the silences, sooner or later your team member will open up and start to speak. Perhaps she explains she is very worried about the health of one of her parents and is dreadfully afraid of losing them. Work seems trivial when such a situation occurs, and she gets angry because it all seems so meaningless when someone she loves dearly is in hospital and facing major surgery, for which there is only a slim chance of success.

HELP THEM FIND A SOLUTION

Now you can start to find a solution that will bring Sandra back on track, keep the rest of the team happy, and restore your faith in her work ability. But you do not offer solutions. Oh no. Part of the success of this interview must rest on Sandra suggesting solutions herself. She has to be part of this process to feel helped by it. It is important to get the team member to face up to owning their own problem. Unless they do, any offers of help will seem imposed on them and they might resent it later. They must come up with their own solutions – and you must agree with them, seeing as how you've given them the responsibility. In Sandra's case, it might be to take a couple of weeks off until the crisis has passed.

EXAMINE THE OPTIONS

You need to examine the options before arriving at a solution. Some options will already have been discounted, such as six months' paid leave, or flying Sandra's sick mother to South Africa to recover in the sun, before you arrive at solution time.

If you try to impose a solution from on high, it will backfire. 'Look, I'll give you a couple of weeks off and you can sort this out' will sound like 'I don't want you around while all this is going on.' If the person comes up with the idea of a couple of weeks off, it is their idea and they have owned their problem.

WHAT TO WATCH OUT FOR

The wise shepherd watches their flock and notices any changes. You too must watch your flock and look out for:

- **any falling off in productivity**
- **deadlines being missed**
- **bad temper or irritability**
- **shoddy work**
- **time wasting**
- **being quiet or distant**
- **poor communication**
- **negative attitude**
- **lack of enthusiasm**
- **absenteeism**

- ▶ **lateness**
- ▶ **any uncharacteristic behaviour.**

Any one of these on its own may not be important. And any one on its own may be quite normal. What you are looking out for are *changes*. If someone has always turned in good work and suddenly becomes shoddy and turns up late, then you need to look into it.

◀◀ for next time

Know and understand the real difference between a discipline matter and one that requires counselling. Don't be too ready to suggest professional counselling, though, as some team members may be insulted if they think you think they can't cope.

Know and understand your company's attitude to counselling. Know what systems they have in place and how to effect them. Know who to go to for advice about a counselling matter, and which door to knock on to get impartial advice if you are unsure.

discipline in an hour

Something has happened. Something bad. You've got to move fast. Discipline has to be enforced straight away.

Wrong. A few minutes must be taken first for consideration of all the facts. Do you know:

- who?
- what?
- where?
- when?
- how?
- and most importantly, why?

If you don't know the answer to any of these, then don't go off half cocked. Stop and take the time to find out. An employee's work record may depend on you investigating and finding out. If you fail to do so, you may fail them. You only have an hour, so you must get a move on. Get a sheet of paper and make as many notes as you can.

Get the team member's personnel file and see what their past discipline record has been.

You must know the facts. You must clarify the incident before you can take action. It is better to delay an interview than to go in unprepared. Bear in mind that any discipline interview may come back to haunt you one day at an industrial tribunal.

Remember you have an objective: to establish the truth, to deal appropriately with it, and to make sure it doesn't happen again.

Now you have to:

- **Find out the circumstances.**
- **Give the team member a chance to explain.**
- **Accept their apology if it is offered in good grace.**
- **Respect their feelings about the matter and don't give them a hard time.**
- **Give them a chance to make amends.**

That shouldn't take too long. A discipline interview is a serious matter and hopefully you can resolve most disciplinary matters without having to resort to one. If you've simply got to hold one in an hour, then you need to:

- **Outline the problem.**
- **Give the team member a chance to have their say.**
- **Focus on the incident that led to this interview, rather than be led astray by discussions, such as 'Well, everyone else thought it was a good idea if I abseiled down the building.'**
- **Accept an apology if it is offered.**
- **Formulate a plan to prevent it happening again, or set in place monitoring systems to make sure you are aware of future behaviour.**
- **End on a positive note and thank them for coming.**

There, that didn't hurt too much. Try to leave more time next time and prepare better. This may have been an easy one but you'd better read the chapter on difficult interviews before you get one.

discipline in 15 minutes

Don't. That's my advice. There is too much at stake to rush in and risk the repercussions of an industrial tribunal. If you have a discipline interview pencilled in your diary, and you've only just realized, the best you can do is reschedule. If you simply can't do that, at least make sure that:

- ▶ **You know what offence was committed.**
- ▶ **You've got the right person.**
- ▶ **You've got their personnel file in front of you.**
- ▶ **You stick to the facts – and you'd better know them or you'll have to reschedule.**
- ▶ **You give them a chance to explain.**
- ▶ **You jointly agree an action plan to prevent a recurrence.**
- ▶ **You end on a light upbeat positive note.**

That's about the best you can hope for. Next time, leave much more time. This is a serious matter and you need to give your very best to your team members, as you would expect them to give to you.

If it is a minor offence, such as being late, then an informal discipline chat (see page 142) might be sufficient, and this you can do in 15 minutes. Give yourself time to be calm and collect your wits. Remain calm and dish out discipline with all the care you can muster. You are the good shepherd and one of your flock has strayed. They don't need punishment, merely guiding back into the field, gently and kindly.

new beginner

- PLAN THEIR FIRST DAYS
- BRIEF THEM WELL
- INTEGRATE THEM SMOOTHLY

richard templar

contents

introduction

So, you've got a new beginner starting in your department tomorrow – a new team member. Brilliant. You sure could do with another pair of hands. But hang on a moment, isn't there something we're overlooking? Who is going to show this new team member their duties? Who is going to show them where the coffee machine is? Do we have any company systems to introduce this new person successfully to our working practices and conventions?

Yep, it's happened. You have less than 24 hours to learn, understand and put into place a full and complete induction programme. We're going to have to think at the speed of life. But don't panic. Help is at hand. *fast thinking: new beginner* is your bible, your guide to the wonderful world of induction – the new beginner's programme for starting a new job. This book is about thinking fast and smart. This book cuts out the waffle and tells you what you really need to know about how to introduce a new team member successfully and efficiently, and how to make them truly feel at home.

Sure – it's better to have more time, and this book will tell you what to do with it when you *do* have it. But for now, what you need is the fast thinker's version. You want:

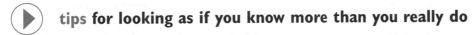 **tips for looking as if you know more than you really do**

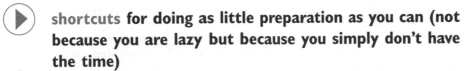 **shortcuts for doing as little preparation as you can (not because you are lazy but because you simply don't have the time)**

checklists to run through to make sure you've forgotten nothing

… and all presented clearly and simply. And short enough to read fast of course.

Ideally you would want longer and you would have started earlier – as far back as interview stage. But that's in an ideal world, and we're working in the real world where stuff hits fans at the last minute and there is never enough time to do things properly. All we can hope for is doing things well and looking good. You've only got a day and this is the time to wake up and smell the coffee – no time to drink it I'm afraid. If you're really up against the clock you may have only an hour to prepare, in which case there is a checklist at the back of the book to help you really get jet-propelled.

And if you've been given as little as 15 minutes (it does happen) there's a truly up-against-the-wall version to help you prepare faster than the speed of life.

So take the phone off the hook, take a deep breath and don't panic. It's all in here and this book will get you through the process of greeting and meeting, welcoming and installing a new beginner in your department in as little as 15 minutes if that's all you've got. Every minute you've got beyond that is a bonus. So stop thinking of your one whole day as too little and start thinking of it as a luxury. You've even got a little time to relax and have that coffee now.

work at the speed of life

NEW BEGINNER AT THE SPEED OF LIFE

This book is going to go through the five key stages of initiating a new beginner into a new job:

1. The first thing to do is identify your objective, so you know where you are going and the best way to get there.
2. Then we'll have a quick look at pre-employment preparation – what happens between interview and first day. Chances are, you won't have much time for any of this but at the very least it will be nice to know what should have happened so you can make sure it happens next time. You'll also need to know who is arriving, what job they are going to be doing, letting the rest of the team know, that sort of really basic stuff.
3. The next step is structuring a welcoming procedure so they feel right at home and you don't have to worry too much that they will get lost, bored or disenchanted with the job on their first day. And we'll have a quick look at training, including skills, knowledge and attitude, so your new beginner sees a long-term future ahead of them with you.
4. We will look at special need new beginners, such as women returning to work after having children, people with disabilities, ethnic minorities, older workers, part-timers, school leavers, graduates and executives.
5. And finally we'll look at follow-up procedures so you can keep an eye on your new beginner and not have them sink into the oblivion of the day-to-day running of your department.

fast thinking gambles

Of course we all know you should have had more time to prepare this induction process, if only it had been possible. But why? Fast thinking will have you coming up smelling of roses anyway. Why bother with more time? Well, no matter how well you are going to welcome this new beginner and help them find their feet, there are certain gambles in doing it in such a short time. Some things take longer than you think, and when your time is limited so are your options. So what are the downsides of preparing an induction programme for a new beginner at full throttle instead of at a steady pace?

- **In your rush to get the person in, and show them whe re everything is and who everyone is and what everything is, you neglect a vital part of their training programme – such as how to actually do the job they've come to do.**

- **You are so rushed into this process that you choose someone completely unsuitable to show them round and they both go off and get lost.**

- **You are so busy that you fail to welcome them successfully and they leave before they ever had a chance to learn the job properly.**

- **You may pitch your induction procedure completely at the wrong level – instead of a school leaver working their very first day ever and needing to be shown where the toilets are, you instead have a senior member of management who is experienced and would like to know if your computer system is compatible with the ZX4000 system they were using in their last job and whether it speaks Cobalt Blue with 3D cadmium background Doppler effect. Gulp.**

These are only a few of the risks and gambles – there are many more along the way – but you see why more time would have been helpful. But we can still do this and do it well if you follow this guide, which you've so cleverly bought and have open in front of you. This guide will turn a potentially fraught and embarrassing spectacle into a polished, efficient induction process that will leave your contemporaries gasping with admiration. But do try to leave more time, next time.

1 your objective

No matter how busy you are, no matter how short of time, there is always time to set an objective. Reason? Well, you wouldn't set off in your car with no destination in mind, would you? You wouldn't go and buy a train ticket to 'anywhere', would you? And you wouldn't ever embark on a business exercise without knowing:

- **what you want to achieve**
- **how to achieve your aim**
- **some form of monitoring system to check you have arrived at your goal.**

WHAT YOU WANT TO ACHIEVE

And what do you want to achieve? To get a new beginner settled in and off your hands as quickly and as painlessly as possible? No, not really. You want them to be welcomed, settle in, feel at home, understand their way around, know their duties, meet the other team members, have company procedures and policies explained to them – that sort of thing. So your aim might well be: *to induct the new beginner effectively and warmly.*

HOW TO ACHIEVE YOUR AIM

But how are we going to achieve that? I don't mean the detail but in general terms? Well, if money were no object we could give the new beginner a minder to follow them around for the first few weeks and explain everything. But in the real world – the one we live in – money *is* an object and we are limited in our resources. We have to induct the new beginner in a cost-effective way and still have them learn effectively and quickly. We can achieve this by inducting more than one new beginner at a time. And if we can't do this, we can have them follow a tailor-made package that will simplify things for them. We need to have induction systems in place *before* they arrive. So we can add to our objective by saying: *by following the guidelines already worked out.* (And don't worry if your company, for whatever reason, doesn't have an induction policy or guidelines for you to follow – we will look at setting that up a little later.)

A MONITORING SYSTEM

How will we know the new beginner has settled in well, is happy in their new employment and is working effectively and satisfactorily? We need some form of ongoing monitoring to make sure they don't get lost in the system. Our objective really should include something about this: *and to make sure their settling procedure is maintained satisfactorily.*

thinking smart

BUYING TIME

Allow yourself five minutes to think through your objective, and set a stop-watch. If you have only an hour before having to greet a new beginner then you may cut this down to three minutes. However, don't let it be any less than this. Tell yourself that, no matter how panicked you are, you will not use up less than your allocated five minutes. If you finish early, write it out again more neatly to pass the time. You will probably find five minutes is exactly the sort of time you do need though. Getting this bit right will save you plenty of time later on. This is the fundamental upon which everything else is built. Get it wrong or don't do it and you are building on shifting sands.

BAGGY TROUSERS

That's not too bad for a first go and it's only taken us a few minutes. I know the clock is ticking and you are anxious to be off, panicking like anyone else would in this situation. But there really is no need. Once you have an objective, you can work through it in logical and easy steps. Management can be by the seat of your pants or by calm and rational fast thinking. One will get you baggy trousers and the other will get you the job done quickly and efficiently. You choose. So let's have a look at this objective:

> To induct the new beginner effectively and warmly by following the guidelines already worked out and to make sure their settling procedure is maintained satisfactorily.

Not bad. Sounds a bit formal. Perhaps we could make it a little less so:

> To settle the new beginner in a warm and efficient way, using the standard company procedures, and to make sure they continue to feel motivated, enthusiastic and happy in their work.

Not bad at all. Now we have a destination, something to measure our success by. We can confidently go out to greet the new beginner tomorrow knowing that we have a goal in sight.

Now you have your objective, write it down. This is your touchstone for the rest of the preparation you need to do. If any aspect of the induction process doesn't further this objective, then don't waste your time on it.

2 before they start

So, tomorrow the new beginner turns up and what have they come to expect of you? Yep, they will by now have formed an opinion of you and your company by what has already happened to them. Their image of you will have started the very instant they first saw the job advertised.

Now you may have had no control over the job advertising, but you will have been part of the interview and candidate-selection process, and it might even have been your final judgement that swung it in their favour. But the way you notified them that they'd got the job, and what they were to do after that and before actually turning up on the first day, is all part of their induction process. Probably without realizing it you have set the ball rolling, and let's hope you have done so effectively, warmly and well – see your objective. In case you're in any doubt, we will go over this pre-employment induction process so if you have fouled up or not done it as well as it might have been you can make notes and tighten up for next time. If you've only just bought this book, then a lot of this chapter will tell you what you should have done – it might not be too late. You can put together a welcome pack with most of the information in it. Make sure the person's name is on the front and that it looks professional and well presented.

WHAT THE NEW BEGINNER IS THINKING

Before the new beginner actually turn up to begin their new job with you, they will be asking themselves a lot of questions:

- ▶ **Will I fit in?**

- ▶ **What sort of rules will apply to me?**

- ▶ **Can I cope with this new job?**

- ▶ **Will I be happy working here?**

- ▶ **How nerve-wracking is my first day going to be?**

thinking smart

DON'T ASSUME

Just because they came for the interview and were successful at it doesn't mean you can relax and let things go. You mustn't assume they will actually turn up for that important first day. Anything you do now between the interview and their starting date can influence their decision as to whether or not to join your organization. Send them a letter *offering* them the job. Don't assume they will accept it. They may have gone for several interviews and been successful at all of them. Their decision will now be based on how you appear to be as a likely employer. Be friendly and welcoming in everything you send out.

thinking smart

THE FIRST TWO WEEKS

Research has shown that people make their decision as to whether to stay or leave a company within the first two weeks of starting a new job – that's right, the *first two weeks*. And that's usually about the same length of time it takes for an induction process. It might just be that the two are linked. Get it right and they stay. Get it wrong and they leave. It really is as simple as that. And if you are going to spend the money in the first place training them, inducting them and employing them, then it makes economical and humanitarian sense to get it right. It costs you money to keep replacing staff and it simply isn't fair on them to induct them badly and make them suffer from poor management techniques. Not that that's you, as you are a fast and smart thinker – or you wouldn't be reading this.

▶ **What sort of company is this?**

▶ **What are my long-term plans?**

And a whole lot more. Think back to whenever you've started a new job. There is trepidation, excitement and intrigue. You want to know how working for this company is going to affect you, and how your new work colleagues will take to you. These fears are only natural, but they can cloud the enjoyment of the first day. Your job, as a fast thinking and effective team leader, is to dispel these doubts before the person ever sets foot in the building.

Answering the questions

So what are you going to do about all these questions? Well, hopefully you will answer a lot of them and set the person's mind at rest. To do this, you will need to write to them before their first day and send them basic literature about your team, their job, the company and the rules of behaviour expected of them.

COMPANY LITERATURE

The company literature you send out to your new beginner has a pretty major influence on the way they perceive your organization. When you are sending anything out to them, make sure it:

thinking smart

CONSISTENCY

You will have to make sure you are quite clear about what is *expected* of them as opposed to what is *accepted*. Make sure their first day is consistent with whatever literature you've sent out to them previously. There's not a lot of point in stressing that good timekeeping is a part of your requirements if they are immediately told by the rest of the team to ignore that as nothing happens if you're an hour late whenever you want to be. Make sure the rest of the team is in line before you introduce a new beginner.

Research has shown that people make their decision as to whether to stay or leave a company within the first two weeks of starting a new job

179

DEAR SIR OR MADAM

Make sure any letters are addressed to the new beginner personally and not to 'Dear Sir or Madam'. When you suggest that they write back, instead of formal phrases such as 'Please reply to Mr Owen', use 'Please reply to Bob Owen'. This way you will have already gained an advantage before they even begin their induction process.

- ▶ **isn't too formal**
- ▶ **isn't worded in a terribly old-fashioned way**
- ▶ **carries positive images**
- ▶ **doesn't imply any discrimination**
- ▶ **doesn't carry any false promises**
- ▶ **makes the new beginner feel part of a 'family' rather than merely a small cog in a vast machine.**

YOUR ATTITUDE

How you write to the new beginner is terribly important. They will get quite an insight into how you regard staff by the way you inform them that they have successfully got the job and what they have to do next. If your letters are pompous and full of unnecessarily formal phrases, they will see you as old-fashioned and out of touch. If your letters are short and brief to the point of rudeness, then that's how they will see you. Here are a couple of examples of what not to do:

Dear Miss Smith

It is with very great pleasure that I am happy to inform you that you have been selected as the successful candidate for the position of copywriter's assistant with MegaPlus and Company. We look forward to receiving you into our organization and would request that you commence your employment with us on Monday the 21st. If you would be so kind as to present yourself to the reception desk at 10 o'clock promptly, you will be instructed as to your duties and responsibilities.

We take this opportunity to enclose a formal contract, which you should sign and return to Mr Partridge in personnel by the 13th of this month.

We hope your employment with us will be mutually beneficial.

Your faithfully

Mr Owen, Senior Team Leader

Dear Miss Smith

You got the job. Be here on the 21st at 10 o'clock. Enclosed contract. Please sign and return to personnel by the 13th.

Good luck.

Mr Owen, Senior Team Leader

Both of these leave the new beginner feeling somewhat less impressed than they may have been. How about:

> Dear Barbara
>
> Congratulations. We are happy that you have been successfully chosen for the job as copywriter's assistant. Could you come in on the 21st around 9 o'clock? And please let reception know when you are here as I would like to welcome you in person.
>
> You will find enclosed a contract of employment. Please have a good read of it and if there is anything you don't understand feel free to give Tony Partridge in personnel a ring on extension 2341. He will be only too happy to explain anything you need him to. Once you are happy with the contract could you let us have it back – preferably by the 13th please.
>
> I look forward to seeing you on the 21st and also enclose a company information pack for you to have a look at. Any questions, give me a ring on extension 2345.
>
> Regards
>
> Bob Owen, Senior Team Leader

There, that should make them feel encouraged, wanted and respected.

- **You have addressed them by their first name, which always seems warmer and friendlier.**

- **You have *asked* them to come in on the 21st rather than telling them, but you have also repeated the date later so they know they don't really have a lot of choice. Even so, you have given them a get-out if they really can't make that day.**

- **You have signalled that 'Bob' and 'Tony' are OK names to use, rather than Mr this and Mrs that.**

- **You have been friendly and signalled warmth – the use of 'please' and 'happy'.**

- **You have given them vital information if they don't understand something – extension numbers and who to ring.**

- **You have indicated that you don't expect them to understand everything right from the word go and that you will be forgiving and understanding if they need to know anything.**

- **You have indicated that you genuinely look forward to meeting them and welcoming them into your company.**

THE OFFER LETTER

Good. Now what else? Quickly, as the clock is ticking and tomorrow is looming. Well, we need to have a quick look at what else you should have sent out prior to this new beginner joining you. Here's a checklist:

- **the starting salary/wages and any other financial packages on offer**

- **the job being filled, with a job title, objective and brief description of duties and responsibilities**

- **the starting date, where to report and at what time – include also where to park or nearest Tube station**

- how they are to be paid – monthly/weekly, by direct transfer/in cash, on a Thursday/last day of the month
- the grade of the job and what that means – such as Technician grade 4, salary band £x to £x
- where they are to work – they may have been interviewed at your Slough office but are actually working in the admin block at Maidenhead
- basic terms and conditions – sick pay, maternity leave, pension plans, holidays, hours of work, breaks, meals, accrued holiday pay entitlements, the probationary period
- any salary progressions
- any company discipline procedures (see *fast thinking: discipline*)
- details of any relocation packages on offer
- the name of their direct supervisor
- who to report to on their first day
- the size of the team they will be joining, and a rough guide to who they will be working with – 'There are 20 of us here in the finance office and the average age is 30, so you should feel at home'
- any special factors, such as dress standards, special clothing to be worn, e.g. hairnets, flat shoes, white overalls. Indicate where this special clothing can be obtained from, and who is paying.

You should also make sure that it is quite clear whether or not the job offer is subject to you obtaining satisfactory references and/or medical checks. If they do have to have a medical check, you will have to explain:

- where
- who is paying (the company of course)
- what the medical is for – for example colour blindness if you are employing a paint chart mixer.

NEGOTIATING AGREEMENTS

Obviously, a lot of the previously mentioned job offer details are not negotiable. But what if they are? Well, you should have cleared up a lot of things at interview stage. But make sure they know that if there is anything that they really are not happy about they can give you a ring, and that you are happy to discuss – and thus negotiate – anything with them.

THE CONTRACT

You don't legally have to offer an employee a written contract until they have been with you for 13 weeks. But the second they start, you have an unwritten one so you might as well go the whole hog and do the honourable thing and offer the contract before they begin the new job. We can't cover the scope of the legal

thinking smart

IT AIN'T OVER UNTIL ...

... they walk through the door on their first day – and even then it is still a trial period. For them of course. They have the right to walk out again. And before they do walk in, they have the right to not take you up on your wonderful job offer. They may change their mind, decide to tell you to stick it, be upset by something you send out, get a better offer, decide to throw it all in and go round the world. You simply don't know, so don't take chances. You obviously want them or you wouldn't have advertised the job, been through the selection process, held interviews, made a decision and offered them the job. Don't throw it all away at the last minute by sounding unfriendly or boring or old-fashioned.

niceties of the written employment contract in this book, but you should make sure that you have included:

- **the name of the employer**
- **the name of the employee**
- **the periods of notice on either side (you need to check the statutory minimum)**
- **the probationary period and how it can be extended (or not) if the work isn't quite up to standard**
- **hours of work**
- **salary**
- **starting date**
- **what the job entails**
- **how performance is judged.**

Remember that this is a legally binding document and must be prepared professionally.

WHAT THEY SHOULD BRING

Phew. Bet there is a lot more here than you realized. And we haven't finished yet. You should have told them what to bring with them tomorrow. Haven't? Might need to give them a ring now and tell them to bring:

- **P45 and National Insurance number**
- **bank account details, if that's how you pay their salary**
- **certificates of qualifications you might need to see**
- **any work permits required**
- **driving licence, if required**
- **birth certificate, if required**

But make sure they know that if there is anything that they really are not happy about they can give you a ring

183

- ▶ their sandwiches (no joke this – if you don't provide lunch or there isn't a canteen, make sure they know)

- ▶ any dates they can't work for some reason, such as a previously booked holiday

- ▶ any uniform or special clothing – you should have sorted this out already, but it helps to remind them

- ▶ special tools of the trade – again, they may well know this, but a reminder saves any embarrassment

- ▶ any forms that needed signing and returning, such as acceptance letter, contract, personnel record card

- ▶ any licence they may need to carry out their employment.

THE COMPANY INFORMATION PACK

Good. Now we're moving along. And what did you send out that wasn't part of their direct employment details? Why, the company information pack of course. You did, didn't you? Of course you did, but just to make sure yours was bang up to date and really useful, here is a quick checklist of what should have gone out. If you forget to send it, make sure you have one to hand the new beginner first thing tomorrow morning:

This is what the company information pack should contain in an ideal world:

- ▶ a letter from the company chairman or managing director welcoming them

- ▶ a chart explaining the hierarchy of the organization, showing job titles and names

- ▶ a welcome letter from any trade union or staff association they can join

- ▶ any literature on customer care

- ▶ any political, religious or philosophical ideology the company may have

- ▶ company history, size and subsidiaries

- ▶ the company mission statement

- ▶ any sales literature that is relevant

- ▶ financial reports and/or last annual report (probably included only for fairly senior staff)

- ▶ details of any social clubs or activities the new beginner can be part of.

thinking smart

NOT FIRST THING

If the rest of your team members normally start work at 9 o'clock, then don't schedule a new beginner to start at this time. They will get lost in the crowds and feel intimidated. Get them to start a little later – say 10 o'clock. This also gives you a chance to clear your desk of anything urgent, sort out any pressing problems, have a cup of coffee, make sure the team is in place and working effectively, and generally compose yourself.

thinking smart

THE TOUR

It is often considered a useful exercise to offer the new beginner a tour round the place of work before they start. About a week in advance is the right sort of time, as they then don't forget everything before starting. This tour gives them an idea of what they are to expect, and will also outline any future problems they may have before they crop up – 'Oh, I didn't realize you all sat on high stools like that at the work benches; I couldn't possibly sit up there as I'm frightened of heights,' or 'But you all smoke and I'm a non-smoker; what am I to do?'

Giving them a quick tour is a friendly thing to do, and it gives the rest of the team a chance to get to know them – even if only slightly – so that when they start they will know what to expect.

AND WHAT ELSE HAVE YOU GOT TO DO?

Bet you're wishing you'd never taken on this new beginner now. Don't despair. We're almost through the pre-employment stuff, and then we can get on to the really exciting briefing – the day itself. I know time is limited and there is so much to take in, but you are thinking fast, thinking smart and you can do it.

What is left to do? Well, here is a quick checklist. Oh no, not another one! Yep, but would you rather have to wade through pages of bumf to extract the key points yourself? I thought not. Here's the essence without the waffle:

▶ **Make sure you have provided adequate stationery and equipment for the new beginner.**

▶ **Make sure that they have been allocated a workspace/desk, and that it is suitably clean and fresh for their arrival.**

▶ **Make sure that they have any keys and security passes necessary.**

▶ **Door nameplates and business cards should have been ordered if they are needed (make sure you've used the name and personal title that *they* want, for example their preference for Ms Julia Newton rather than J. Newton).**

▶ **Other staff and colleagues should have been briefed about their arrival.**

▶ **Gate security and reception staff should have been notified of their arrival, along with their name, job title and where they should go.**

thinking smart

GO THAT LITTLE BIT FURTHER

You might like to provide some fresh flowers or a new potted plant if you really want to impress. Or how about a new coffee mug? Or a smart new blotter and telephone pad? A new set of pens/pencils? Anything that is relatively inexpensive could help them feel welcomed, and is a great personal touch without costing the earth. Be consistent, though – and provide an extra treat for all new beginners or none at all.

Have a cup of coffee, make sure the team is in place and working effectively, and generally compose yourself

185

- Make sure that you know exactly what you are going to do with this new beginner on their first day and during their first few weeks.

- Ensure you have scheduled time in to greet them and be part of the induction process.

- Any training that you think necessary should have been arranged, places on courses booked, and supervisory staff informed.

- The post room and switchboard should have been notified of the new beginner.

- The new beginner should have been allocated an extension number if necessary.

- Is there any information from the previous job holder that might prove useful you could supply?

- Have they been allocated a locker if required, and has it been cleaned out after the previous occupant?

- Do they need allocating a computer password? Has this been done?

- Are you ready? Do you need a refresher course on training new starters? (Of course not, you've got this book.) Do you know all the terms and conditions applicable to a new beginner, and are you totally familiar with company induction policy and practice?

- Have personnel been informed and do they have all the right information?

There, that will do for now. We have almost finished the pre-employment stages. The actual day – tomorrow – should seem like a doddle compared to all the stuff you have to do in advance.

THE LETTERS

We looked earlier at the letter you send out telling the new beginner that they have been successful in their interview and at this stage you are making them a formal job offer. That's the first letter.

They should reply, accepting – hopefully – your kind and generous offer.

Now you have to send out the welcoming letter. This should contain the joining instructions. In other words:

- details of what they need to bring with them

- where and when to start

- whom to report to

- details of the induction period with relevant training

- the welcome pack.

Good. That's the new beginner written to. Now you have to formally tell personnel. You will need to supply details, such as:

- **The person's name, address, National Insurance number and/or P45.**
- **Personal details, such as date of birth, sex, telephone number, nationality, and medical information.**
- **Details of the work itself, including references, proof of qualifications, pay-roll number, union number, bank account details, pension scheme details, previous occupation, holiday entitlement, details of the contract issued and signed, department, details of work permit, if required.**

And now you've finished. Well done. You now have a pretty comprehensive knowledge of what's required of you before the new beginner actually turns up tomorrow. Do go back over the checklists quickly and just make sure you haven't forgotten anything.

for next time

Check the lists regularly if you take on lots of new beginners or are unfamiliar with the protocol.

Keep records of everything you do so you have some form of history to refer back to.

Make sure that everyone on the team understands what is expected and required of them – they can make or break a new beginner's morale quicker than anything you can do to welcome them. If you feel it would help, train your team in how to help newcomers to settle in.

Don't use pre-prepared letters to offer a new beginner a job or to welcome them. Make each letter personal and friendly. There is nothing worse than feeling you, as a new beginner, are a tiny part of some vast, faceless organization before you've even started. Make your letters human.

There is nothing worse than feeling you, as a new beginner, are a tiny part of some vast, faceless organization before you've even started

3 on the day

So the big day has dawned and you are about to welcome the new beginner. You have done everything in your power already, by following all the checklists in the previous chapter, to make sure this is a successful and enjoyable day for them.

All you've got to do now is check that you know everything they will need to know about. Their first day is going to be pretty nerve-wracking, and anything you can do to reassure them and make them feel confident and happy will go a long way to making sure that they stay and that their induction process is effective.

FITTING IN

Some new beginners seem to fit in right away; they are confident and settle in easily. Others take longer and need more reassurance.

How the new beginner fits in with the rest of the team is very important. Obviously there will be a certain amount of caution on everyone's side as the old team make way for a new member. Judgements will be made if they are taking someone else's post, especially if the one who left was well liked and popular. Naturally, there will be a certain desire on the part of the old team to want the new beginner to shape up quickly and fit it.

Initiation rites and practical jokes

In some institutions there might well be practical jokes played on the new beginner or even more serious 'initiation rites' performed. If the job entails any danger where team members have to trust and rely on each other for their very lives – such as the fire brigade, the army or mountain rescue teams – these initiation rites can be extreme to say the least. How you view these pranks or rites is entirely up to you, but there does seem to be some evidence that a certain amount of 'bonding' may be necessary for the old team to accept the new team member. Bear in mind that when the new beginner is no longer seen as a threat they will have successfully passed their team's admittance programme – however unofficial this is. If the jokes continue too long, or are too harsh or personal, the new beginner will simply leave. You need to monitor the situation without being seen to interfere or discriminate.

THE BUDDY PHILOSOPHY

Many companies subscribe to the view that appointing each new beginner a 'buddy' will be beneficial. This system has been found to be extremely helpful to the new beginner and allows them to be inducted faster and more effectively. The buddy shows them the ropes and is on hand to answer any questions the new beginner will have – and there will be a lot of them. If you don't like the American term, you can call them a 'companion', a 'sponsor', a 'chum' or a 'starter's friend'. It's entirely up to you, but I shall continue to call them buddies.

The buddy performs many vital roles to enable the new beginner to settle in quickly. There are some ground rules, such as:

- The buddy should be a similar age to the new beginner.
- The buddy should be of a roughly equal status, and certainly never junior.
- They should have some things in common if possible, e.g. they both live in the same area of town, they both share martial arts as a hobby, they both drive 2CVs – that sort of thing.
- The buddy should also be relatively new to the company as well – but obviously not another new beginner – as they will still have a fresh memory of the rules and procedures.
- It should only be a temporary arrangement.
- The buddy should be a willing party to this and not press ganged into it.
- The buddy should be an accepted member of the team, not an outsider or an unpopular member of the team.
- The buddy should have a confident personality and be outgoing and friendly.

If you find someone who has all these qualities and requirements, let me know and I'll employ them as a buddy to my new beginners. Obviously this is a wish list – just make sure your buddy fulfils as many as possible.

What does a buddy do?

OK, we've established that choosing a buddy needs some thought, but what do you do with a buddy now you've got one?

Well, having a buddy is very useful to the new beginner, and to you as well. From the buddy, you can get useful information about how the new beginner is settling in, how they seem to fit in with the rest of the team, and any problems they may be having. All you have to do is trust the buddy to be your eyes and ears, and to report back to you at the end of the first day and the end of the first week.

The buddy should be responsible for:

- showing the new beginner where to hang their coat
- showing them where and when to go for lunch
- showing them where things are

 thinking smart

CLOSING-DOWN PROCEDURE

Make sure the new beginner knows what to do at the end of the day. This might be as mundane as making sure all the windows are shut, but it might also involve training in setting burglar alarms, signing out at reception, collecting a pager, taking work home, signing for a laptop, reporting to a supervisor or logging off a computer terminal. Whatever your closing-down procedure is, make sure the new beginner is well versed in it and doesn't feel confused at the end of the day.

INTRODUCE THE BUDDY BEFOREHAND

In an ideal world you would appoint the buddy long before the new beginner starts, and then get the buddy to make contact with them prior to their start day. This gives the new beginner a familiar face to help them feel at home on their first day. If you give new beginners a tour, then you could introduce the buddy at the same time. The buddy could even be the one to give the tour.

- ▶ **introducing them individually to the rest of the team**

- ▶ **letting the new beginner know about rules – both standard and unwritten ones**

- ▶ **demonstrating how to log on to computers, operate security systems, and operate equipment such as photocopiers, telephones, fax machines and shredders.**

- ▶ **explaining how the breaks work, what they do about the post, and basic on-the-job instruction**

The buddy basically takes the pressure off you. Make sure you tell the buddy what you expect of them and how they should report back to you. You need a sort of mini buddy induction training programme.

What a buddy doesn't do

The buddy shouldn't be the one to greet the new beginner. That's down to you. It is polite, courteous and friendly for the team leader to be the one to go to reception – or wherever the new beginner has to report to on their first day – and shake hands, welcome them warmly and escort them to their place of work. You can take them into your office to begin with and give them a chat about what you expect of them, but they probably just need to be handed over to their buddy to ease their shaking nerves.

The buddy shouldn't be responsible for collecting their personal details, their personnel records, their work permit or anything of that nature. Again, that's your job. You can take anything like that off them when you greet them at reception.

MANNING THE LUNCHTIME PHONES

A lot of offices insist that when everyone goes off to lunch someone remains behind to answer the phone. The new beginner should be immune from this chore for the first month. It is impolite not to make sure they get included in lunch and that way they also get to know the rest of the team better and socially. In any case, there is simply no point leaving them to staff the phones as they won't have a clue what they should be saying or doing, or who anyone is.

thinking smart

REQUISITIONING STORES

Make sure the new beginner knows how to get hold of the stuff they need to do their job properly. This might be paper, ink, toner cartridges, a laptop, pads, pens, staples, post-it notes, in-trays – whatever. There should be a system for requisitioning stores and they should stick to it – and so should the rest of the team.

The buddy doesn't introduce the new beginner to the whole team. You do that. Then you hand over to the buddy, and they do the rest of the introductions individually without you being there. If you are there, it will only serve to make it all terribly formal and stilted. You can say, 'Hi, team, this is Julia. She's starting with us today [as you told them all last week] as the new graphic designer. Andy is going to be her buddy for the next week or two. I'll let him show her where everything is, and then you can meet her and have a chat once she's hung up her coat and had a cup of coffee.' Then leave for a while. You can drop back a little later on to check her progress. After she has settled in a bit, the buddy can introduce her individually to the rest of the team, but maybe only the ones she needs to work with initially as too many new faces can be daunting – you never remember all the names and you forget which ones you need to know.

WHAT'S NEXT?

So the buddy has taken over a major part of your role, and you can now go back to the office, put your feet up and relax. Your job is done and the new beginner is settled in. In your dreams. There's still a lot for you to do. Time is marching on and we must work at the speed of life if we are to cover everything before tomorrow and the reality of your new beginner.

You need a plan of action – a sort of map of the new beginner's needs. We'll cover this as quickly as possible by using checklists without the waffle. You need to be aware that the new beginner needs to know:

The environment

- ▶ **surroundings**
- ▶ **the way round the building**
- ▶ **travel arrangements**
- ▶ **where and what the facilities are**
- ▶ **health and safety procedures**
- ▶ **fire drills**
- ▶ **security**
- ▶ **what they have to do about maintenance and repairs.**

191

The job

- what it entails
- what the job does not include
- what standards you expect
- what to do if things go wrong
- their limits of authority
- how their work standards will be measured
- what information they will need
- what equipment they have at their disposal
- the challenge of the job
- availability of information and feedback
- methods of communication
- any special jargon or language they need to know.

The company

- what it does
- its suppliers and customers
- its mission statement
- its subsidiaries
- its parent company
- the security it offers
- its history and future
- the facilities it offers its employees.

The team

- the hierarchy
- subordinates

 thinking smart

MAKE THEM FEEL SPECIAL

If your new beginner has to be given an in-tray, for example, make sure it is a new one and not one covered in the last employee's stickers, graffiti and used chewing gum. Make your new beginner feel special by making them feel as if they deserve the best. This is a quick and inexpensive way to get them feeling good about you and the company.

- peers
- supervisors
- other colleagues
- social contacts
- what is expected of them in terms of discriminatory policies
- group dynamics
- expectations of the team
- how the team meshes together
- who they have to work with.

Phew. That's a lot, and obviously you aren't going to give it all to them on their first day. You have to break it down into manageable chunks. And here, your buddy can become very useful. A lot of the above points can be introduced successfully over the first few weeks by the buddy. Your job is to make sure the buddy helps the new beginner learn the important things first, and that they are not overloading the new beginner with too much information. Your new beginner may well want to know all about the company, but their first concern undoubtedly will be with their actual job itself – what they have to do to earn their crust.

THE PRE-INDUCTION TRAINING WEEK

Some companies take the new beginner off for a week's training before their first day in the workplace. This can be successful as it teaches them what they are supposed to be doing, but a lot of new beginners find this very stressful as it invariably takes them away from home, often isolates them in a hotel overnight (or nights), and sometimes makes them feel that whatever they are being shown will be completely divorced from the reality of what actually goes on in the workplace.

On-the-job training may be more beneficial in the long run. But whatever you decide, make sure the tone of the first day – and weeks – is totally positive. Let them arrive later than the rest of the team and let them leave earlier. Praise them on settling in so well and so quickly. Try to remember your own first day and be aware that they have too much information to absorb, too many faces and names to remember, and too many new experiences to take it all in. They will be tired and unsettled. Let them go home without calling them in for a lengthy review.

thinking smart

AT THE END OF THE FIRST DAY

Make sure the new beginner reports to you at the end of the day for a final round-up of any problems – this should be a very quick chat as they will be anxious to get off home – and for you to monitor how they've done and how they feel about their first day. Make sure the buddy also reports back to you at the end of the first day and gives you a progress report.

Your new beginner may well want to know all about the company, but their first concern undoubtedly will be with their actual job itself

193

FURTHER READING

If you have any useful books on any aspect of their new job, it might be worthwhile lending them to the new beginner at the end of their first day. It will make them feel as if you care (of course you do, but you must also be seen to do so) and it gives them something to take home and read while they are relaxing in the bath after their first long, hard day – or short, easy one, depending on which school of induction you subscribe to.

Don't ask, 'So, what do you think of us after your first day?' This leaves them stumped for an answer – if they think little of you they can't really say it, and if they thought a lot they'll think they sound toadying if they say so.

Nor should you say things like, 'So, that was quite a quiet day – but you just wait until next week, that's when we get really busy!' You'll just discourage them and make them feel inadequate.

But we're jumping the gun here. They haven't even started and already we're sending them home after their first day. Still it pays to be prepared.

PLANNING THEIR DAY

For an inexperienced new beginner, you might be best leaving the day to shape itself. Let the buddy set the tone and pace. For more experienced staff, you need a timetable to keep them busy, get them involved and show them you trust their judgement and coping skills. You may need to discuss with them an agenda in case they just want to get on with it, meet the rest of the team first, have some training, have a tour of the building – whatever they feel they need to settle in quickly and effectively.

Encouragement

Make sure you encourage the new beginner during the day. Encourage them to ask questions by making sure they don't feel stupid or embarrassed. They will forget a lot and have to ask the same questions several times to become fully conversant with everything. Encourage them by letting them know that they are doing well and that no one expects too much of them on their first day. Encourage them to use their initiative and to set the pace themselves. Encourage them to get on with something useful if that's what they feel they need to do. If they don't do any actual

GOING WITH THE CROWD

If everyone disappears to the pub at lunchtime, make sure the new beginner doesn't feel they have to. They may not be able to afford it. They may not want a drink. They may need a bit of peace and quiet. They may feel intimidated by refusing, so make sure they have an easy get-out if they want and don't get press-ganged into going.

If they do go, monitor their alcohol consumption and make sure they don't drink too much to cover up any nerves they may have.

work, they may go home feeling like a spare part. Obviously you have to set realistic goals for them to achieve, but you can get them helping other team members, which encourages social contact. Encourage them to feel free to wander about a bit so they can get their bearings rather than sitting at their desk or workplace all day long. Finally, encourage them to come to you with any problems to do with work or settling in.

Their arrival

There really is only one person who should greet the new beginner at reception – and that's you, as we've already seen. But the receptionist should certainly make them feel welcome. You will have informed reception that they are arriving – at what time, their name and department, and all that – so all reception staff have to do is invite them to wait and inform you.

A priority engagement

As you have put this in your diary, consider it an important priority engagement. There simply is no reason to be delayed or late unless the office is on fire. If it was a client booked in, you'd make pretty damn sure you were on time, so do the same for your new beginner. It sets the tone for politeness and respect that should hopefully last their entire working life with you.

If, for reasons of layout, you can't get to reception to greet them, it is permissible to have someone show them to where you are. But they must never be told where to go and set off alone. That is simply unforgivable and potentially frightening for them if they get lost.

Make sure you remember who they are and why they are there. Once you've greeted them warmly, you might like to hand them over to personnel if that is appropriate. Personnel can then take over the completion of their initial documentation. The sort of things they will need to know are:

- ▶ **national Insurance number, P45 details and bank/ building society numbers**
- ▶ **proof of qualifications, driving licence and birth certificate**

thinking smart

DON'T SPOIL THEIR FIRST DAY

Don't allow the person's first day to be spoilt by unintentionally making a gaffe such as parking in the MD's car parking space, hanging their coat on someone else's peg, sitting in the wrong chair at the wrong desk, using someone else's favourite coffee mug, not bringing their lunch when they should have, getting lost, getting told off for using the wrong entrance, inadvertently addressing someone by the wrong name or title and being made to feel small for doing so, having to ask to use the lavatory, having to ask the same questions over and over again and being made to feel stupid for doing so, forgetting something vital such as their P45, or just being late. Be kind and fairly forgiving on their first day. It will pay in the long run if their initial impression is one of tolerance and consideration.

> **FALSE EXPECTATIONS**
>
> No one can start a new job and do well immediately without supervision, training, encouragement and support. Fail to give any of these and they will flounder. Give them all and they will reward you with a job well done. Their productivity goes up in direct relation to the amount of help they get. Leave them alone to make a mess of things and your investment will not pay off. Your job does not stop when they start – it begins. Don't expect them to do well immediately. They won't. They are only human.

- details of next of kin, and name and address of doctor
- full name and address
- pension details.

We have already covered all of these, with the exception of next of kin details, but these are only for use in an emergency and hopefully won't be needed.

The first chat

Before you move the person along to meet their buddy, you need to have a little chat with them. You can do this in a very informal way over a cup of coffee. The important thing is to make them feel welcome, relaxed and 'at home'. Put them at their ease and explain that you want to have a chat to make sure they:

- understand the job that they have been employed to do
- are fully aware of what their contract means
- know how and when they will be paid – and how much of course
- understand why certain policies are in force
- know the hierarchy (not in too much detail at this stage)
- have, and will read, their copy of the employee handbook
- have been given instructions on using their company car (if applicable)
- understand rules about dress codes, conduct, house styles, discipline procedures and equal opportunities
- understand any company instructions about dealing with the public, press or any complaint procedures.

You must avoid the 'here's a load of bumf' technique, in which you hand them armfuls of papers and pat them on the head before sending them on their very confused way. Take your time and go through things with them. You don't have to go through everything in a lot of detail, just enough so that they know what it is you are giving them – or telling them – and so that they will be able to find any document again and know what it refers to and why.

INVESTING TIME

I know time is valuable but so too is your new beginner. The more time you invest in them, the better they will settle in. There is no short cut to spending time with them. It pays dividends later.

GETTING TO KNOW THEM BETTER

This shouldn't take too long at all – probably about 15 minutes. You can even get personnel to deal with a lot of this if you prefer. Once all the documentation is out of the way you can get to know the new beginner better. Give them an idea of what they can expect today and for the next week or two. Explain about the buddy system and how it works. Find out how they got there this morning and what the journey was like. Ask about their personal preferences for music, food or whatever to establish some rapport and bonding.

Things to avoid

- **intimidating them**
- **overloading them with information**
- **patronizing them**
- **hurrying them**
- **making them feel you are really too busy to deal with them**
- **forgetting their name or what they are there for**
- **dismissing them too quickly and handing them over to someone else to get rid of them**
- **being irritated at having to repeat yourself because they didn't understand you the first time**
- **telling them how much money you've invested in them**
- **telling them how good their predecessor was**
- **failing to reassure them or make them feel welcomed.**

CHOOSING THE BUDDY

Make sure you choose a buddy who toes the party line. If you all take 15 minutes for a tea break mid-morning, then make sure this information is conveyed correctly by the buddy, not, 'Oh, and we are supposed to take 15 minutes but we all stretch that out to half an hour.'

Obviously the buddy will convey any unwritten rules so you might need to tighten the team up a bit if they have got lax before the new beginner latches on to bad habits.

Walk around your work area and notice anything that may need pointing out to a new beginner unfamiliar with your working practices

197

EMERGENCIES AND SAFETY

Have you briefed the new beginner in all relevant emergency and safety procedures? These include bomb scares, fire drill, being trapped in the lift, building evacuation, first aid (including first-aid points and first-aiders), sickness at work (including company doctor if you have one), accidents, health and safety risks (dangerous substances, food contamination, no-smoking zones, keeping passageways clear, keeping fire exits clear), protective clothing (if relevant), electrocution, carcinogenic substances (photocopier toner, paints, acetates, inks), radiation hazards, and repetitive strain injury (RSI). There may be others not listed here but relevant to your business. Walk around your work area and notice anything that may need pointing out to a new beginner unfamiliar with your working practices.

I'm sure you won't do any of these but it is always best to know which ones you are likely to do – and thus be on the lookout for them. We are human after all, and prone to being too busy or too stressed to do things properly. Obviously not you, as you have taken the time and trouble to get it right by buying this book. Score extra brownie points for diligence and smart thinking. Well done.

IT'S A TWO-WAY PROCESS

So, you are on your best behaviour and doing it all right. But what about them? Are they reading this? Probably not. Which means they won't be following an up-to-date business programme written specifically to put them at their ease. Instead they are going to be pretty nervous and likely to make appalling gaffes. They are quite likely to turn up at the wrong time, in the wrong place, and on the wrong day. And this isn't just school leavers. Executives, graduates and senior managers have been known to go to pieces on the first day in a new job and get it all wrong. It isn't just nerves about meeting new people. They're likely to be worrying about whether or not they can do the job, especially if this is a promotion. Different people worry about different things. The younger they are the more they tend to worry about fitting in, making friends and being accepted, whereas older people tend to worry about the responsibilities of the job.

THE OFFICE GRAPEVINE

Like it or not, there is one. There always is. And it can be quite an influence on how the new beginner views your organization. If the office grapevine is abuzz with rumours of take-overs, redundancies, sackings and relocations, they'll feel unsettled and nervous. It's your job as team leader to know what the latest gossip is – and it's also your job to make sure it stops. Gossip is the result of poorly communicated information and, as a smart thinker, you regularly hold team briefings to stop this sort of nonsense. You can warn the new beginner if rumours are flying around and tell them that if they don't hear it from you they can ignore it. You are the official line. Brief your team that they too should give the official line to new beginners.

GETTING LOST AND GETTING TIRED

So your job is to reassure all these different people with their different worries that they are all unfounded and that everything is going to be fine for them. They will all worry about getting lost, being taken seriously, being liked, getting enough information to do the job and not being left floundering, satisfying superiors sufficiently to stay in the job and finish the trial period and avoiding mistakes. They are on their toes and highly nervous, which makes it more likely that they will make mistakes. They will also get tired. Tiredness is a natural way for the body to handle stress such as a first day. Give them lots of breaks and a chance to sit down as frequently as possible.

Reassurance

You will also need to reassure them about all the other worries. Show them charts of the company structure and point out exactly where they fit in. If you are their immediate supervisor or manager or team leader, you will need to go through with them their exact duties and what is expected of them. If you are at one remove from them, you can hand this over to their immediate supervisor.

GETTING THEM STARTED

A lot of what we have talked about up to now has been the admin and reassurance part of the package. But there is another side to all this. They are here to do a job of work. This is their first day. The best thing you could do for them is to get them to do some meaningful work.

Doing something useful

New beginners need to do something useful on their first day if they are to feel worthwhile and that they have achieved something. Giving them something real to do will make them feel a part of the team much quicker than if you leave them to read through company literature.

Your aim should be to stop them getting bored, and finding real work for them will achieve this. It also shows you trust them and are prepared to throw them in at the deep end.

thinking smart

THE OFFICE AFFAIR

It happens from time to time. And what do you say to the new beginner? If you say nothing, they risk putting their foot in it. If you say anything, you risk breaking confidences, alienating staff, spreading rumours that may not be as true as you think – and generally putting yourself in the firing line. The smart thing to do is to pitch your presentation in the middle by saying something like, 'Oh, and you may hear some rumours about Alice in your department and Charlie in production. I've no idea whether they're true or not but I thought you should know.' This way you've left yourself in the clear if it's not true – although you know full well it is – and you've given them some warning so they don't say anything negative about Charlie without realizing. Obviously this applies only to people they are working with directly. It is also worth pointing out who is married to whom as a similar precaution.

thinking smart

WHAT IF SOMETHING GOES WRONG?

Does your new beginner know what to do if equipment fails? Is there a proscribed way of getting repairs done, calling an engineer, or notifying maintenance? There should be, and everyone should tackle the problem in the same way. Repairs should be left to qualified professionals, not handled by team members. Even if Billy from despatch knows exactly where to hit the photocopier to get it to work, it shouldn't be encouraged. Get it fixed properly by the proper person and make sure the new beginner knows the procedure.

thinking smart

HANDLING A POTENTIALLY DIFFICULT SITUATION

What if the job they've successfully applied for and got was also applied for by someone they have to work with closely? What are you going to do about this potentially difficult situation? Do you tell the new beginner? Evidence suggests that telling them is the smart thing to do. If the team member who applied for the job was considered too junior or not right for the promotion, then your new beginner won't have too much of a problem once they convince the team member of their suitability. If the team member is of equal status, then the new beginner will have to find ways to work with them without upsetting them – no boasting, bragging, or rubbing salt into wounds. It has to be handled diplomatically, which is why the new beginner always needs to know.

The jobs you give them on their first day need to help them feel important. Therefore there are certain rules that apply:

- ▶ **Don't give them mundane jobs.**

- ▶ **Don't give them the worst jobs to do, such as filing or making tea.**

- ▶ **Give them something to do that is directly relevant to why they have been employed.**

- ▶ **Don't dump too heavy a workload on them on their first day.**

- ▶ **Give them things to do where they feel challenged but not snowed under.**

- ▶ **Make sure they are supervised.**

That should about do them for a first day. They will be exhausted but reassured, stretched but not overwhelmed. They will have met some of the people they will be working with and bonded with their buddy. They will have had a tour of the building and found out where all the really useful amenities are, such as the lavatories, canteen and coffee-making facilities. They will go home feeling satisfied and confident that they made the right choice.

And you can also go home knowing you've done a great job and that you too made the right choice.

Day two

You've successfully done day one. So what do you have to do on day two? Well, you don't have to take any forms or information off them. And you get them to turn up at the same time as everyone else, and work a full day. No letting them go home early today. Apart from that, pretty much the same as yesterday. If everything was in place for day one, then day two should be a doddle for everyone concerned.

- ▶ **They report to you.**
- ▶ **You hand them over to their buddy.**
- ▶ **They do some meaningful and useful work connected with their real job.**
- ▶ **You leave your door open all day for any questions that might arise.**
- ▶ **You monitor them at regular intervals to make sure they are doing fine.**
- ▶ **You get them to report to you at going home time.**
- ▶ **You get the buddy to report to you at going home time.**

thinking smart

NO COLLECTIONS

Make it a rule that a new beginner is immune from all office collections for the first month. Chances are they won't know the person for whom you are having a whip-round and couldn't care less if Betty is getting married, or Trevor is leaving to work his way round Australia. They also shouldn't have to sign get-well cards, chip in for birthday presents, or fork out for retirement presents. They do, however, have to contribute to any funds, such as a coffee fund or tea box.

for next time

Make sure all your checklists are ticked off this time so that you haven't forgotten anything. If anything crops up that we haven't covered, add it to your checklist. Monitor how this new beginner slots in and you'll get a good understanding for next time of what works and what doesn't. Watch out for any mistakes they make, and take action to stop them happening again. This might include getting lost, going to the wrong entrance, or failing to find reception.

Monitor how well your team takes to a new beginner and make a note of anything that needs improving on next time. Take notes of how well the buddy system works and how your choice of buddy turns out. This is also a good chance to monitor the buddy, especially if they are in line for increased responsibility or promotion. Think ahead to how your new beginner can be someone else's buddy next time. You can tell them this so they know the score and already feel trusted and ready to take on a task in the future.

4 different needs

People come in all shapes and sizes, with different levels of aptitude, experience, needs and abilities. Throughout this book we have assumed that your new beginner fits into some framework of your past experience. But there are occasions when we have to induct a new beginner who, for whatever reason, needs different priorities or alternative working procedures, or even different access to the building. The variety of different needs that people have is pretty big, more so than you might think at first. We are all aware of the needs of people with disabilities and those from ethnic minorities, but what about school leavers? Or ex-offenders? Women returning to full-time employment after having children? Expatriates? They all need to be thought about when it comes to induction programmes.

These are some of the people you might be expected to consider and plan for:

- **people with disabilities**
- **people with ethnic differences**
- **part-timers**
- **shift workers**
- **long-distance workers**
- **professionals**
- **women returners**
- **older workers**
- **school leavers**
- **graduates**

- **managers**
- **expatriates**
- **transferees**
- **promotees**
- **people returning to work after long unemployment**
- **ex-offenders**
- **temps**
- **job sharers**
- **home workers.**

We'll look at each of these individually, but quickly as I'm aware that precious seconds are slipping away.

PEOPLE WITH DISABILITIES

Nowadays these people are usually referred to as 'people with different abilities'. They are not disabled but *differently* abled. As long as you think like this you should be able to plan an induction programme to suit their particular needs. If you think of them as disabled, they may seem helpless. If you think of them as differently abled, they seem capable, but in a different sort of way to you.

Don't make the mistake of assuming that 'disabled' means a wheelchair. It doesn't necessarily. Not all differently abled people are the same. They are as varied as any other group of workers. Epilepsy, cerebral palsy, partial sightedness, partial hearing and diabetes all fall into the category of differently abled.

You will need to be aware of any special emergency or first-aid treatment the person may need, for example in the case of epilepsy or insulin shock from diabetes. You must also be aware of access problems and what account has to be made of the person's differing abilities in the event of fire or evacuation of the building.

The best thing is to talk to the person concerned before taking any action. You will probably have found out a lot at interview stage.

According to research, people with different abilities often more than make up for any interference with their working practices by keeping better time, taking less time off for illness and sickness, and being more productive. Just concentrate on what they *can* do rather than what they *can't*.

PEOPLE WITH ETHNIC DIFFERENCES

Your job as team leader is to make sure that no new beginner is subjected to any racial harassment. But this should also include cultural, language, background, social and religious differences. People with ethnic differences need to be accepted into your team easily and effectively. This may mean briefing your team in advance. Differences may include special times of day for prayer, special diets, or written instructions in a different language. All of these things may have to be done to facilitate a smooth and easy introduction into the team.

PART-TIMERS

Everything you do for full-time workers you should also do for part-time workers. They are no different – they just work fewer hours for you. Any induction should take place during their normal working hours – just as it would for a full-time worker – and not in their own time. They may need more thorough training or training more often, as the gaps between sessions may be longer and thus they may retain less information. As a consequence, you may have to extend their probationary period to take this into account.

SHIFT WORKERS

The same goes for shift workers: training should take place in their normal working hours, and they are entitled to a full and complete induction programme.

LONG-DISTANCE WORKERS

These workers have little contact with the office and can be hard to include in an induction programme. But include them you must. You have to engender a feeling of belonging to the company, even if they work at considerable distance from it, such as oil-rig workers, sales representatives and travelling maintenance staff. They may need special induction training in reclaiming their expenses, reporting into the office, reporting in sick, queries and questions, acting on their own initiative, or making decisions. They may also need pairing up with a professional buddy for a while to make sure they are being trained fully in company procedures.

thinking smart

SEEKING PROFESSIONAL ADVICE

If you need any further information, contact your local Job Centre and ask to talk to the Disablement Resettlement Officer. The Royal Association for Disabilities and Rehabilitation (020 7637 5400) can also give very useful advice.

ETHNIC DIFFERENCES

If in doubt, contact the Race Relations Employment Advisory Service at your local Job Centre. Seek advice from someone else in the company who knows and understands the differences.

PROFESSIONALS

The biggest problem you're likely to come up against with inducting a professional is exactly that – they are professionals. They are already trained with a relevant qualification. They may be someone such as the company doctor. You know they can cure the sick – or at least alleviate the symptoms – so why on earth do you need to induct them? But they too need to know their way round, who to report to, how to get paid, what to do if things go wrong, the fire drills and emergency procedures, and where the canteen and the lavatories are. They too are human, and need to be reassured to feel that they are part of a team and are fitting in.

WOMEN RETURNERS

Ever tried bringing up children and running a home? Try it for a while and you'll find it needs a lot of skills and talents, such as budgeting, discipline, motivation, consistency, planning, decision making, supervisory skills, team building, inducting new beginners, maintenance and repair skills, diplomacy, negotiating skills and many, many more. Your biggest challenge with women returners is to imbue them with confidence. They have the skills but they need to realize they are valued and valid in the workplace. Once you are over the confidence hurdle, you can induct them as any other group of workers.

OLDER WORKERS

They may have become set in their ways. They may have seen it all. They may well have been 'doing this when you were still having your bottom wiped, kiddo.' But they do come with a wealth of experience that shouldn't be ignored or overlooked. Inducting an older worker may require a little more tact – giving them a buddy of a similar age rather than a young upstart will help – but you do inherit an awful lot if you do it right. They fear failure and rejection just like the rest of us, so work hard at reassuring them and don't patronize them or treat them as if they are old timers.

SCHOOL LEAVERS

People fresh from school have many obstacles to overcome including:

- **being trained on outdated equipment**
- **having no work experience**

PHONE WORKERS

These can be regarded as long-distance workers, and the same provisions should be made to make sure they feel they belong and that they have any special procedures under their belt.

- having a poor attention span due to never having had a lesson that lasted longer than an hour
- having poor self-motivation skills
- having little experience of working alongside equals of vastly differing ages
- working on their own
- being unused to work discipline
- having no experience of working conditions and rules
- having no experience of equipment
- being nervous and unconfident
- having no experience of safety and health regulations
- having little decision-making experience.

But they do bring with them enthusiasm, an ability to learn fast, keenness to try new challenges, youth, energy, vitality, life and no bad habits (except maybe chewing gum, being late and dressing in a weird and strange fashion). Get them young and you have fresh clay to mould. You will have to spoon-feed them information to begin with and mollycoddle them a bit. But they want to learn and haven't yet got out of the habit of it. They may well have had a part-time job or a newspaper round or a summer job, so they might not be quite as bad as you expect. They may have done a little work experience and understand what is required of them. You will need to be patient and considerate.

GRADUATES

Like the school leavers, graduates may have had no work experience; if they have only recently been to university or college, they may have very little in the way of work discipline. They have the potential to take badly to time keeping, attending meetings and being there every day. They may also have specialized in a very narrow discipline, which means they may find it hard to branch out or to take risks. They may think that what they have been doing will automatically lead to immediate responsibility and real work and find the reality very different and quite hard to take. They may also have no practical skills.

But they do have knowledge, enthusiasm, youth, a remarkable ability to learn, and great reasoning powers. Be considerate with them and give them as much responsibility as they can manage and you can trust them with. The faster you bring them on, the better they will respond.

MANAGERS

They may well be experienced in the job but they will still need inducting into your company's procedures and disciplines. They usually don't want inducting – and the rule is the higher the post the less they want it – but they do need to know basic information as we have outlined before. You might not need to give them a buddy – in fact they may be insulted by such an idea – but get them alongside another manager of equal status to show them the ropes. They may need to know more about the company's politics than about how to use the photocopier, but they still need initial help and advice. They also need to get on with real work as quickly as possible if they are to feel happy.

A KINDRED BUDDY

If your new beginner is a recent school leaver, give them a buddy who didn't leave school too long ago themselves. This way you establish an instant rapport. The new beginner will look up to the buddy, and the buddy has someone for whom they feel responsible, which makes them feel grown up themselves.

EXPATRIATES

Expatriates need time to adjust if this is their first employment since returning to the 'old country'. Customs and work practices will be different and people will treat them differently. They need sympathetic induction.

TRANSFEREES

This group of people is usually easier to induct because they already have a knowledge of company procedures. But this can cause problems if there are discrepancies: the 'But we never did it like that in Durham' mentality can prevail. Transferees still need guidance on their new job, even if it is the same job as they were doing previously. They still need to learn new faces and names, know the layout of the building, and understand your routines and procedures. Transferees are often ignored on the basis that they should already know everything. They don't of course, and they need their own induction process just like any other group of workers.

PROMOTEES

The same goes for promotees as transferees – they often get overlooked, forgotten or ignored. You still need to train them in their new job. Failure to do so can be disastrous, as it gives them the right to take you to an industrial tribunal if you dismiss them for failing to reach the proper standards for the job.

Promoting within a company is financially sound, as you save on advertising and interview costs, but it does have drawbacks as sometimes the team member doesn't get treated with the respect their new job warrants. Your induction process will take care of this, just so long as you are aware of it.

BRIEFING YOUR TEAM

Your team needs to be briefed in the sort of differences likely to be encountered when taking on an expatriate as a new beginner, such as how to treat different groups of workers, how to address superiors and juniors, how to cooperate in a multicultural workplace, travel, language and currency. Returning home after a long period living abroad can be a bit of a shock. The expat has an expectation of what they will find on their return and is often sadly disillusioned. They will need help to overcome this, and help with modern equipment, which may well be vastly different to what they have been using.

PEOPLE RETURNING TO WORK AFTER LONG UNEMPLOYMENT

These workers need the same degree of induction process as any other group, but they may well need extra care in bolstering their confidence and guidance with modern working practices and procedures.

EX-OFFENDERS

You will have known at interview stage what their offence was. Once employed – and you have already made that decision – their future with the company should be based entirely on their current performance. They are being employed to do a job and the only thing relevant to how well they do that job is their current performance. Nothing else. You mustn't inform the team or make a fuss – they have a right to have their background kept confidential unless they themselves wish it to be disclosed. Treat them as a returning worker who hasn't worked for a while, in the same way as someone who has been unemployed, but also be aware that they may well have acquired new skills or training in prison. Don't treat them like school leavers.

TEMPS

They too need to know the layout of the building, your procedures, and how to relate to other people within the organization, and should be trained in the job they are there for. Temps are often very good at adapting and fit in quickly – it's in the nature of their vocation. Nevertheless, they should be shown what to do and where everything is. If they fail to meet your standards, it almost certainly isn't their fault and it's no good just sending them back and asking for another temp.

JOB SHARERS

Don't give each job sharer half of an induction process. Give both equal treatment and a complete training programme. You need to qualify with them what happens if one of them is on holiday or leaves. You need to know exactly how the job is split and what that entails. And you need to know exactly who is responsible for which aspects of the job. Inducting job sharers is not without its challenges, but as long as each is treated as an individual and given full training you shouldn't encounter too many problems.

HOME WORKERS

People working from home for a company still need to know the procedures and company policies. They still need inducting. If they have reason to visit the offices then they will need to know their way around. They may suffer from being isolated and not feeling part of a team. Regular checks are essential to make sure they are

thinking smart

HOME WORKERS NEED TO SOCIALIZE TOO

Home workers should be invited to department lunches, drinks after work, staff parties and all that sort of thing. They too need to socialize with other team members and it makes them feel as if they belong and that you care.

following the company guidelines for work. You can stay in touch with them via e-mail and telephone. They may need extra training in modern technology; they will be relying on it heavily and won't have the same back-up and support that an in-house employee would have.

for next time

Be aware at interview stage which category of worker your intended candidate will fit into, and be prepared to adjust your induction programme accordingly. Obviously this won't influence your decision as you will want to employ the best person for the job anyway.

If you are in any doubt about how various groups should be inducted, such as disabled workers, ex-offenders or long-term unemployed people, then contact your local Job Centre for further advice.

Find out what your company policy is regarding such things as disabled access, job sharing, flexitime, temps, teleworkers and others working from home. This way you can tailor your induction package in advance and have a set of guidelines already laid down before the interview stage. To be prepared is smart thinking.

5 follow-up procedures

So, you've successfully got through the first day – or couple of days. Now what are you going to do with them? Your new beginner is settling in, making friends, and learning their new job. Seems like you can relax. No way. This is when you really need to be on your toes to stop apathy setting in and the new beginner getting overlooked in the hurly burly of everyday office life.

Your new beginner is a valuable resource that you have invested in heavily. To get a decent return on your investment you have to follow a four-point plan:

- ▶ **You have to be *committed* to their development.**
- ▶ **You have to *plan* their future.**
- ▶ **You have to put your plan into *action*.**
- ▶ **You have to *judge* how effective your plan is.**

You might like to remember this as the *committed plan of action is judged*.

Let's have a quick look at how this plan operates.

COMMITMENT

Unless you see team members as instantly replaceable, you have to be committed to them both as people and as a resource. They are a valuable tool in your job. Without them you can achieve very little. It makes sense to want them to be stretched, challenged, motivated, stimulated, encouraged and praised. You have to want the best for them as workers and as people. You have to take a genuine interest in them. You have to care.

As a team leader it is often easier to see team members as units of work rather than people with all that entails, such as having problems, making mistakes, getting it wrong, being unhelpful at times, feeling depressed, being late, having off days, shirking responsibility and generally behaving in an all-too- human way. But the more committed to them you are, both as a team and individually, the easier it is in fact to be realistic and accept them with all their faults. You set your expectations at a realistic level and work with what you've got. Slotting a new beginner into such a philosophy is easy because you don't expect them to be perfect. But if you are committed, you expect them to do their best and, with your help, to rise to the challenge, enjoy their work and want to improve and get on. Your commitment to them is to treat them well and be the best team leader they've ever had.

PLAN

Every new beginner, no matter how humble their first job, has the potential to reach the top; to take your job one day, and eventually go higher than that. Every new beginner is an embryonic company chairman or managing director. Their time with you is part of their first step along that route. Some will fall by the wayside but all of them must be given the opportunity to reach as high as they want. This is where your plan comes in. You must have a plan. Not just for the first day or the first week, but for the next year and beyond that. You must start this plan before they start their first day. You have to map out their future – with their cooperation of course. If they start as a clerk, you must be looking ahead to the time when they will be a senior accountant. If they start by making the tea, you must see them as a potential finance director.

Obviously you want them to do a specific job. That is what they were employed for. You need to:

- **train them in the job**
- **encourage them to look ahead to their next position**
- **start their training for that position while still doing their original job.**

This way you have an ongoing training programme. As soon as they get promoted, you start them off on their next step, the next position.

ACTION

Every day at work should be a training day. That's a simple rule. Every day there should be some challenges towards the next step in the new beginner's career. When you train them in their job, you will be explaining to them why that job is so important – how the cogs mesh together to make the bigger picture. You explain their vital role so they feel very much a part of the team. And you begin to explore how they can contribute more by knowing the next step.

This training has to be realistic and ongoing. You must work out your plan and stick to it. There will be times when training is the last thing you want to do but as team leader it really is important to bring new beginners on. Just doing the job should never be good enough. They must be encouraged to take on more responsibility, increase their workload, try new duties, and expand their horizons. Having a team is a bit like having children. You wouldn't expect children to remain static. They don't. They grow and learn, change and adapt. Team members are your children and as their work parent you have to bring them up by training them.

JUDGING

No training is effective unless you monitor and assess it. You have to have an ongoing evaluation programme where you regularly assess the performance of each and every individual in your team (see *fast thinking: appraisal*). You must also have a process to judge how effective your induction programme is, and a feedback programme to let the new beginner know how well they are doing.

In any of these four key stages, you must use your discretion as to how to implement them; all staff are different and all teams operate differently. You have to look at your needs and adjust your training accordingly. But every day is a training day. Now you can confidently go out and greet your new beginner.

for next time

Make sure you understand and implement the four-point plan – *the committed plan of action is judged*. Work out how each and every one of your new beginners can progress. Try to see where they will be in one, five and ten years' time. Make sure each new beginner is given:

- ▶ support
- ▶ encouragement
- ▶ guidance
- ▶ feedback.

Make sure the goals you set them are:

- ▶ fair
- ▶ specific
- ▶ measurable
- ▶ attainable
- ▶ realistic.

new beginner in an hour

If you really have left it this late there is only so much you can do. The first thing is to set an objective (see Chapter 1) and make sure you stick to it: to *induct the new beginner effectively and warmly*. Make sure reception know:

- **who is turning up**
- **what they are to do with them**
- **who is to be informed when they arrive.**

Make sure you go and greet the new beginner personally and that you know their name, which department they are working in, what their job is and who their direct supervisor is. If you haven't chosen a buddy for them, do so now (see page 188). Select someone of a similar age and with similar interests, and quickly go and ask them if they would very kindly agree to do you this favour at such short notice.

Run through the checklist on page 183 of what they should have brought with them, such as their P45, National Insurance details and bank account details.

Introduce them to the rest of the team – but especially those they will be working closely with. Introduce them to their buddy. Have a cup of coffee and promise never to leave it this late again.

new beginner in 15 minutes

Under normal circumstances, if you'd really left it this late, I'd advise you to reschedule. But this time you can't. Even as you read this your new beginner is driving in through the main gates. You have only 15 minutes before they present themselves at reception.

Grab a notebook and write down their name, the department they will be working in, and what job they are going to be doing.

Make a quick decision as to who is going to be their buddy, (see page 180) choosing someone of roughly their own age. Ask the buddy nicely if they would be prepared to take this on at such short notice.

You just have enough time now to make it to reception and greet your new beginner. If they are late don't, for heaven's sake, give them a hard time. You've cut it pretty fine yourself.

guide to praising

ros jay

fast thinking manager's guide to praising

Smart managers use carrots rather than sticks wherever possible. Your team will be far better motivated by knowing you'll praise them when they do well, rather than fearing the backlash if they fail. Praising is one of the most important parts of a manager's job. But it's not as simple as saying 'Well done' every once in a while. It's a real skill, and one you can master quickly and use effectively.

There are seven key guidelines to using praise to its maximum effect:

1. *Make it specific.* Let the person know you are being sincere and genuinely appreciate their work by saying exactly what you're praising them for. Don't just say 'Well done for yesterday' – which could be a pat phrase that rings hollow; instead, say, 'Well done for yesterday; that was one of the most succinct presentations I've heard, and it was delivered very professionally.'

2. *Discuss it.* Show your interest is genuine by talking about people's successes. People love to talk about themselves, especially in such a good light. Say, for example, 'I knew you were nervous because you told me so, but I'd never have guessed it.' Or ask them questions: 'How did you come up with that brilliant analogy about the octopus?'

3. *Never put a sting in the tail.* You undermine the praise completely – in fact you score a negative point – if you include a criticism alongside the praise. So don't say, 'I think we should sort you out some training in how to use visual aids before your next presentation.'

4. *Make a record of the praise.* A lot of praise can be given verbally and informally. But if someone has done particularly well, put it down on their personnel record, and let them know you have.

5. *Publicize it.* For significant achievements, give public praise. Write to senior managers about how well your team member has done, put it in the staff newsletter, or – if the success doesn't quite warrant this – announce it at a meeting in front of the person's colleagues or superiors.

6. *Pass it on.* If someone praises one of your team members make sure you let them know about it: 'The PR director was telling me how impressed he was with the way you handled some of our key customers on the exhibition stand.'

7. *Be on the lookout.* Don't hang around waiting for obvious successes and achievements on the part of your team to hit you in the face. Look for opportunities to praise them. Remember, every piece of praise is a piece of motivation.

Praising, if you follow these guidelines, is one of the fastest and best ways to motivate your team and get them to give you one hundred and ten per cent. Now that's fast *and* smart.

introduction

fast thinking leader

Your team look to you to guide them when they hit trouble. They need you to be a strong leader on whom they can depend. It's easy to cope when things are going well, but it's the conflicts and crises that sort the strong leaders from the average managers.

How are you going to handle that tough meeting tomorrow, when you'll be pulled both ways? You've got to be fair, but you've got to make sure the outcome is right too. Do the job well *and* keep everyone happy. You need *team meeting* to lead the way. Follow the guidelines, and then it will be your turn to become the leader.

Meetings are tough enough, but what about coping in a real crisis? What if the computer system goes down or the building catches fire? You can't prepare, surely, if you don't know it's going to happen. Oh yes you can. *crisis* is a crash course in handling those unexpected emergencies when leadership qualities are vital – including preparing for them.

Projects may not be quite the emergency that a life-or-death crisis is, but isn't it amazing how late you can find you've left them? From organizing a product launch to getting the customer newsletter out, we realize all too often with horror that there are only 48 hours to the deadline and we haven't even started yet. Well, don't panic. You'll find everything you need to know to guide you through the last-minute planning to the heart of the action in *project*.

The final guide in this group is *decision*. You know you sometimes put them off. Maybe you frequently put them off. Who doesn't? The smart manager, that's who. We put off decisions because we're not sure how to make them (at least, not the right ones). Once you've read this guide, however, you'll know exactly how to make decisions in future and there'll be no need to put them off again. Your team can confidently look to you for direction.

It doesn't matter how well you manage your team in terms of organization and people handling. You also have to be a leader who also they feel they can follow in order for the team to gel and reach its full potential. So get wise – read the guides.

team meeting

KEEP YOUR FOCUS

MOTIVATE YOUR TEAM

ACHIEVE YOUR GOALS

ros jay

contents

introduction

So which team meeting is it this time? Project team? Inter-departmental meeting? Team briefing? Whatever it is you need time to prepare for it effectively – but what time? You meant to start planning for it days ago, but somehow the work caught up with you (doesn't it always?) – probably even overtook you – and you're down to your last few minutes. The meeting is in an hour and you haven't started thinking about it yet. Until now.

What you need is a brief guide (definitely brief) to planning and running effective team meetings on the hoof. Well, you got it. This book contains everything you need to know to plan and prepare for your meetings. And once you get to the meeting, you can't afford to waste time. You need to run meetings that occupy the minimum time so you can get on with your life. And of course they need to be truly productive: it's hard enough scheduling the time in the first place, without wasting it when you get there.

This book is about preparing and running team meetings. You could argue that any meeting by its nature is a team meeting. It is attended by several people who, for the purposes of the meeting, are working together as a group. But the phrase 'team meeting' implies that the members of the group also work together outside the meeting, as a department or a project team, or at least in the same organisation. This is the assumption you will find in this book. (Mind you, almost exactly the same rules apply to chairing any other meeting.)

Most team meetings, though not all, are regular. However, this doesn't mean to say that the preparation you did for the last meeting will do for this one. The advance work needs doing afresh each time. And you may well feel that your regular meetings are always hampered by being underprepared, running too long or being unproductive. You want to do something about it, but you don't have time to go on seminars or read long books on management practice. You simply want:

 tips for looking as if you know more than you do

 shortcuts for doing as little preparation as possible

 checklists to run through at the last minute

… all put together clearly and simply. And short enough to read fast, of course.

Let's suppose your meeting is tomorrow. In your dream world you would have finished preparing your meeting by now. The agenda, in all its detail, would have been circulated ten days ago, and you'd have blocked out in your diary a relaxing couple of hours this afternoon to go through all the background papers thoroughly. Before the meeting tomorrow you've allowed 15 minutes to get into the right frame of mind and think through the key results you expect from this meeting.

Wake up! This is the real world, and you'll be lucky if you make it to the meeting on time, and luckier still if you get 30 seconds before it to remember where you are. That's why this book will take you through the whole process fast, with a section at the end for preparing the meeting in ten minutes if you're working at the speed of life.

So take a deep breath, and relax. It's all in here, and by the time you've worked through this book your meeting will be planned and prepared, and you'll be ready to get through it with lightning efficiency and maximum productiveness. What's more, you'll also find all the information you need to do the job when the heat is off (just in case that ever happens).

work at the speed of life

This book will take you through the five key steps of preparing and running a team meeting:

1 Begin by setting the objective for the meeting so that you can be faster and smarter in your planning and execution.
2 The next stage is to prepare the agenda – more than simply scrawling a list of items for discussion, a well-prepared agenda will make the meeting far quicker and more productive.
3 Now you need to involve the other people by circulating the relevant paperwork.
4 After this comes the task of chairing the meeting itself; we'll begin by looking at the practical skills you need so your meetings can be halved in time and doubled in effectiveness.
5 People skills are equally important when it comes to getting the most out of your meetings, so we'll look at these too.

Finally, we'll look at the particular guidelines for specific types of team meetings:

- ▶ regular departmental meetings
- ▶ inter-departmental meetings
- ▶ project meetings
- ▶ team briefing sessions.

fast thinking gambles

The accepted thinking is that you should leave longer to prepare for team meetings (although the accepted thinking doesn't seem to have thought about how you're supposed to find the time). The idea is that you can't plan and run meetings effectively under time pressure. But is this really true?

So long as you are acting smart as well as fast, there's no reason why you shouldn't run team meetings that are better than those most of your colleagues run, even when you're spending only half the time on them. But there are disadvantages to meetings at breakneck speed. Here are some of the key ones:

▶ **If the agenda is not prepared well in advance, it won't be circulated well in advance. This means that the other participants may not have time to prepare fully (you're not the only one with more work than time, you know). Missing information and ill-prepared arguments do nothing for the productiveness of meetings.**

▶ **If you are pushed for time, you may well not get around to reading all the background papers before the meeting (surely not?). Appearing ill-informed about the content of your own meeting does nothing for your credibility, quite apart from diminishing the effectiveness of the meeting.**

▶ **Problems and conflicts can arise at meetings, which are easier to handle if you have allowed time to think about them in advance and prepare for them.**

Fast thinking will ensure that your team meetings are professional, speedy and effective. But you'll always have a better chance of getting the most out of the time you spend in meetings if you start preparing well in advance. So always aim to give yourself a good run up to a meeting. Failing that, trust to fast thinking.

1 your objective

An objective? For a meeting? And we've just established that time is short. We haven't got time to mess about with objectives, surely? Well yes, we have got time and I'm afraid it's got to be done. But before you slam the book shut in annoyance and write it off as another waste of money, just let me explain.

Objective setting can help make your meetings faster. You see, once you know what your objective is, you can see which of your agenda items meet it and which don't. And often, you can scrub the ones that don't. There, that's starting to sound more like fun. In fact, sometimes you can scrub whole meetings if they don't help to further your objective. Yep, just like that. Cancelled. Go away everyone, we're not having a weekly meeting this week. Find something else to do instead.

I hope that makes objective setting seem more worthwhile. Of course, much of the point is to make sure that the meeting achieves what it sets out to (by defining just what it *does* set out to do). But it is also important in this fast-moving age to avoid wasting time on anything else. So you need to start the process with a clear objective.

Almost without exception, the objective of the meeting as a whole will be the objective of the team, for example:

- **to ensure that this project is successfully completed on time and on budget**
- **to build company profits and customer satisfaction**
- **to keep the running costs of the organisation down and productivity up**
- **to ensure that this department meets its targets.**

That is why you are holding the meeting, and you need to keep sight of your objective. It should take only a couple of minutes to phrase it; when you have done so, write it down. One of the first things we tend to do when we are in a hurry is stop thinking. But a few moments' thought now will save you plenty of time later. What's more, if this is a regular meeting, you won't have to go through this every time. The objective of the monthly team meeting will always be the same; you will simply need to remind yourself of it each month.

 thinking smart

TIME OUT
Make yourself stop everything until you have identified your objective. Time yourself for three minutes and don't allow yourself to do anything else in this time. That way, you can't be tempted to skip this bit just because you're up against the clock.

Once you have a clear objective you can view each suggested agenda item in the light of it – as we'll see later. If the item does not help the meeting to achieve its objective, it may well not belong there at all. Of course it may still need attention, but perhaps in informal discussion, exchange of e-mails or memos or at a separate meeting.

WHY ARE YOU HOLDING THIS MEETING?

Most regular meetings are held for the same reason: because it's the weekly/fortnightly/monthly meeting so we hold it every week/fortnight/month. But do you really need to? If holding the meeting doesn't further the team's objective in any way, why hold it? The first question you should ask when you plan a meeting is: 'Do we really need this meeting at all?' If the answer is no, cancel the meeting. It's your meeting, after all – you can do what you like. You haven't got the time to hold meetings that you don't need:

- ▶ **Perhaps you usually need the weekly meeting, but you could skip it this week.**

- ▶ **Maybe you could switch your fortnightly meetings to monthly meetings, or the weekly meeting to a fortnightly one.**

THE SOCIAL SIDE

Although cancelling unnecessary meetings is often the best course, it is worth being aware that team meetings do have an important social function. Sometimes it is worth holding a meeting more frequently than you might, or face-to-face rather than on the phone, in order to reap the social benefits:

- ▶ **It establishes and reinforces the identity of the team.**

- ▶ **It reinforces each person's role in the team, from their place in the hierarchy to the value of their contribution (including reinforcing your position as leader of the team).**

- ▶ **It establishes collective commitment and responsibility – decisions arrived at democratically are more likely to be supported by everyone, even those who didn't vote for them.**

So don't hold a meeting just for the social side – a team drink down the pub after work might do the job just as well – but do bear it in mind as a point in favour of holding a meeting rather than cancelling it.

thinkingfast

PICK UP THE PHONE

Could you replace your meeting with a conference call? These tend to be much quicker. Regular meetings can sometimes alternate a face-to-face meeting with a phone meeting to save time.

PREPARING MEETINGS AT SHORT NOTICE

Let's be frank. You cannot run a truly polished and professional meeting at an hour's notice. This is because you should have circulated the agenda at least a week ago. You can certainly do the preparation in an hour and often far less, but not now. Last week.

The agenda needs to be circulated to give everyone time to read any background papers, and collect any information they want to present to the meeting, or find the figures to back up their view on an important agenda item. It also gives people time to get back to you if they feel strongly that another item should be included or an existing one should be deferred until the following meeting.

Without this opportunity, you may well find that time is wasted at the meeting because people haven't mugged up on the background to an item, or vital information is missing without which you can't take the decision you wanted to. Or people try to argue about what should or shouldn't be on the agenda.

So what can you do about it now? Well, you have three options:

1 My best advice is: postpone this meeting if you possibly can, even for just three or four days. You may even be able to cancel it altogether if it is a regular meeting with no urgent items to discuss. Use the time you have set aside now to prepare and circulate the agenda, and hold the meeting once everyone has had time to read and act on it.

2 Failing this, hold a brief meeting to cover only those agenda items that simply cannot wait. Defer anything else until the next meeting.

3 If you must hold the meeting, you must. But promise yourself you'll start planning earlier next time (and a promise is a promise … isn't it?)

for next time

Remember, you don't need any more time to prepare well for a meeting. You need the same time, only sooner. So before the next meeting:

- Ask for any background papers you need for circulation in reasonable time for people to submit them (often you will ask for them at the previous meeting).
- Prepare the agenda a week to ten days ahead of the meeting (or three days for a regular weekly meeting). Block this time in your diary well in advance. In fact, for regular meetings, you could go through your diary now and mark in the time for the rest of the year.
- Circulate the agenda, with all the necessary background papers, in plenty of time — remember, most of your colleagues have more work than time, too.

2 the agenda

Most people write pretty pathetic agendas, if the truth be told. They are little more than a list of items to discuss. I suppose that's better than nothing, but really it is only an aide-mémoire to make sure you miss nothing out.

The genuine article, however, will make your meeting faster, more productive and clearer for everyone. It will avoid confusion and time-wasting, and ensure that each item achieves a concrete end result. You'll be able to zap through your meetings, scattering results, decisions and action points all around you as you go.

To indicate the value of a proper agenda, it might help to remind you what can happen with one of those list things that so often passes for an agenda. How often do any of the following happen in meetings?

- **You spend 20 minutes debating which of two proposals to accept: the pricey or the cheaper option. The cost of those 20 minutes – in terms of the value of your time and everyone else's – far exceeds the cost saving you are debating.**

- **You spend half an hour discussing an agenda item but reach no conclusion, and have to discuss it all over again another time.**

- **You discuss next year's targets for 15 minutes, and then spend three quarters of an hour haggling over the new car park allocation of reserved spaces.**

- **Someone turns up without the necessary information to feed into the meeting because they misunderstood the agenda item. For example, when it said 'NEC exhibition' they assumed it meant the scheduling was being discussed, so they didn't bring the quotes and draft designs for the stand.**

- **You come away from the meeting still unable to get on with certain tasks because the meeting never made the decision you were hoping for.**

Well the good news is, such time-wasting and inefficiency is now a thing of the past, at least in your meetings. A clear, well-planned agenda means your team meetings will be swift, time will be allocated effectively and items will have a purpose – no more vague discussion that leads nowhere. So how is it done?

The agenda items

The first step is to establish which topics should be on the agenda. You'll have a mental list, no doubt, and perhaps requests from other people. The other key source of agenda items is the minutes from the last meeting (assuming this is not a one-off meeting). This may well stipulate certain action points to be completed in time to feed into this meeting.

Once you have your list of items, the most common problem at this stage is finding that your list is too long. A regular team meeting shouldn't really run much longer than an hour – people have neither the time nor the concentration to do it justice.

MEETING YOUR OBJECTIVE

Check all the agenda items against your objective to make sure they belong in the meeting. Eliminate any that don't belong there – perhaps they should be discussed or agreed outside meeting time by a smaller group of people or maybe one person alone can take charge of them rather than waste the meeting's time.

A project team or inter-departmental meeting might need longer, but shouldn't go beyond two hours, as a rule of thumb. You're trying to keep this meeting short and your list of items is fighting you all the way. So if you need to slim down the agenda, here are a few tips:

 If this agenda is looking longer than usual, hold over any non-urgent items to the next meeting (of course, this doesn't work if your agenda is bound to be this long next time, too).

- **See if any items can be covered by a sub-group. Either they can have decision-making authority, if necessary, or they can feed into the main meeting without the whole debate having to be repeated.**

- **It can be easier to schedule, and more productive in the long run, to hold more than one meeting. Not everyone will have to attend both if you plan them sensibly, which will also help speed them up (small meetings are always quicker than large ones).**

- **Some agenda items are generally for information only. We'll look at these in more detail later, but often they don't need to take up meeting time at all – they can simply be circulated as a document and the item can be cut from the agenda.**

ORDERING THE AGENDA

The next stage is to put the agenda items into a logical order. This doesn't just mean the most important item goes first: your meetings aren't going to overrun so everything will get discussed for the appropriate amount of time. Here are several useful tips for ordering the agenda as effectively as possible:

NO OTHER BUSINESS

One of the best ways to save time at meetings is to ban 'any other business' from the agenda – it is an invitation to people to dream up things to discuss for the sake of it. It is also sometimes used by schemers as a ruse to spring items on the rest of the meeting for Machiavellian purposes, knowing that no one else has prepared for them. Occasionally you can allow a request to add a last-minute item when there is good reason, but don't invite it.

- Really urgent items should be near the top of the agenda. Your meetings may run on time, but there's always the chance the building will catch fire or some other unforeseen happening will halt the meeting.

- Sometimes one item will depend on the outcome of another, and this will affect the order. For example, there's no point discussing the schedule for the NEC exhibition until you've established whether you are definitely going to attend it.

- It makes sense to group related items together so that people don't have to make too many huge mental leaps during the meeting.

Those are the logistical considerations, but there are also psychological factors that affect the ordering of the agenda:

- People tend to be more wide awake and creative at the start of a meeting, so any items that will need bright ideas and inventive thinking are best off near the top of the agenda.

- An attention lag sets in after about 15 or 20 minutes, so that's a good place for any hot topic that people are capable of getting animated about, even at this stage.

- Some items will unify the group, while others will divide it. Be aware of this when you draw up your agenda. You may want to start by unifying the group before you introduce the more controversial topics, or you might prefer to do things the other way around. But be aware of which you are doing, because it makes a difference to the mood of the whole meeting.

ADDING THE DETAIL

What you have now isn't yet an agenda; it's still just a list of topics to discuss. Now you need to turn it into an agenda. And you do that by fleshing out the detail. An agenda needs clarity more than it needs brevity. It doesn't matter if your agenda runs to two or even three pages, so long as it helps everyone to understand what the meeting is about.

That's not to say you should write an essay under each topic. In any case you haven't got time for that. But you should make it clear what aspect of the topic is in the spotlight, otherwise people won't be able to prepare effectively for the meeting. So instead of putting simply: 'New brochure'; it is far more helpful to put: 'To discuss the format of the brochure in the light of the budget and costings' – and then attach the costings, of course. Otherwise most people won't know whether you're discussing the format, the design, the content or the schedule.

thinking smart

UNITED WE STAND

Whatever order you choose for the items that bring the team together or divide it, you should always end with an item on which everyone is united – preferably against a common cause. This might be anything from another department to new legislation; the point is that it will strengthen team spirit as everyone leaves the meeting.

thinkingfast

SPEEDING BULLET

If there are several points to discuss under one item, one of the fastest and clearest ways to indicate this on the agenda is to use bullet points.

So if you state your subject clearly, your agenda item might read:

To discuss the new sales brochure in the light of the budget and costings:

- **format**
- **design**
- **content**
- **schedule.**

Now we're getting somewhere. Everyone can tell exactly what they are supposed to be discussing, and can prepare ideas or read background material accordingly. But there's more. We may all know what we're talking about, but where is the discussion leading?

Meetings aren't about open-ended discussions just for the fun of it. Who's got time for that? Certainly not you. They have to go somewhere, have a point, achieve something. But what? There are only three reasons why you should include an item on your agenda:

1 for information
2 for action
3 for decision.

Let's take a quick look at each of the three, and you should see how everything can fall into one of these categories.

INFORMATION

There is no point wasting everybody's time passing on information that can be circulated easily on paper. The only reason to bring up an information item at a meeting is if it needs to be passed on in person. This might be because:

- **It needs clarifying or explaining, and people might need to ask questions for this purpose.**
- **It should come from a particular person.**
- **It has deep significance for the members of the meeting.**

Progress reports on projects often need to be passed on at a meeting so that people can ask for clarification.

232

ACTION

These items are usually preceded by at least some discussion. At the end of this, an action point determines what will happen next. There are all sorts of options, which might include:

- agreeing to find specific data to feed into the next meeting

- setting up another meeting or committee to deal with the matter in more depth and to report back

- taking specific action: anything from commissioning a designer, to cutting the confirmation time for online orders to ten minutes, to redesigning the delivery packaging so it's easier to open – you know the sort of thing that gets actioned in meetings.

DECISION

This covers the matters that the meeting as a whole needs to decide. In a sense, many action points are delegated decision points – we all agree the policy, but someone else can take the decisions without wasting the meeting's time. But decision points are too important to delegate. They often start with a policy, but the meeting has to decide: 'How shall we implement this?' Often, you need to get the meeting to agree a decision for the psychological purpose of making everyone feel they have a stake in the decision.

So you will certainly need to discuss some items, but the discussion should leave you further on than you began. It is not just a vague conversation that leads nowhere. At the end of it you should make a decision or agree an action point to take the matter further.

You may know where each item is leading, but it's no good keeping it to yourself. State it on the agenda so everyone knows. You will find that this can lead to a slightly longer agenda: good. All the more information so everyone can prepare for the meeting thoroughly.

So your 'new brochure' agenda item will now look more like this:

1 **To discuss the new sales brochure in the light of the budget and costings:**

For decision:

- format – number of pages/size/colours etc

For action:

- design – agree brief and invite designers to tender

- content – agree pitch (paper attached) and agree to brief writer

- schedule – discuss outline so schedule can be prepared.

You may be wondering how you are supposed to find time to draw up this agenda. Well, don't worry, it really doesn't take long. You already have all the information, you're simply writing it all down. And, once you've done it, you've got your own notes, and the thought process functions as a valuable preparation. Writing a good agenda is all the preparation you need.

TAKE NOTE

You know what meetings you have coming up. So why not keep a sheet for making notes on each? As anything crops up, or thoughts occur to you, jot them down. Think about the odd agenda point while you're waiting for someone to answer the phone, or for your modem to connect. By the time you come to write the agenda, you should have most of the key items already jotted down along with the details you need to itemize on the agenda.

ALLOCATING TIME

You're almost there. But there is just one more ingredient you need to add to create a thoroughly indispensable agenda. You need to allocate timings to each item. I know almost nobody else does it, but two wrongs don't make a right. If you can't waste time, you need to know how much time you aren't going to waste.

Suppose you have eight agenda items and you don't want this meeting to run over an hour (you haven't the time and there's no need for it), how are you going to make sure the first item doesn't take too long and squeeze others out? By working out how much time you can spare for each item, that's how.

It's no good simply dividing the hour into eight equal sections, obviously. It takes far longer to consider the proposal to integrate the sales and marketing functions than it does to agree the date of the next meeting. So allocate time on the basis of how long it:

a needs

b deserves.

Some relatively minor items genuinely take a few minutes to get through and, conversely, some important items don't actually need very long. But judge your timings on experience and common sense and make sure they add up to the total time you want to spend at this meeting.

PRUNING RAMBLERS

If you have someone at your meeting who is likely to ramble on about a particular pet topic, ask them in advance how long you should allow for it on the agenda, and steer them towards agreeing a sensible time. It makes it much easier to rein them in when it comes to it. You can even start by saying: 'Right, item 3. Robin and I both reckon we can cover this comfortably in ten minutes, don't we Robin?'

Then write down your timings next to the agenda item, so everyone else can mentally prepare themselves for a meaty debate or a quick flit through the basics of the topic. The simplest way to do this is to write a start time next to each agenda item – it's also a quick way to check you're on course as the meeting progresses. So your finished agenda item now looks something like this:

1 To discuss the new sales brochure in the light of the budget and costings: 10.35am

For decision:

▶ **format – number of pages/size/colours etc**

For action:

▶ **design – agree brief and invite designers to tender**

▶ **content – agree pitch (paper attached) and agree to brief writer**

▶ **schedule – discuss outline so schedule can be prepared.**

And that's it. The art of writing a really effective, productive agenda. And the smart way to make sure everyone arrives at the meeting prepared for each item and knowing what to expect. So when it comes to running the meeting, you'll find that half the battle is won already.

for next time

This is already the smartest way to write an agenda, and it's pretty fast too. But if you have the luxury of more time, it can be worth talking to one or two key people who will be at the meeting, if only to get them on your side.

There are always items that particular people feel they 'own'. They are in charge of the project in question or they are the acknowledged authority on the computer or on direct mail. Asking for their input when you prepare the agenda can be helpful in making it realistic, and it also makes the other person feel involved.

3 involving other people

To be honest, it's a bit late for this chapter if you have to go into the meeting in half an hour. But if you managed to take the advice in Chapter 1 to defer the meeting, you'll find the contents of this chapter valuable for saving time when you do finally hold the meeting.

Once you have prepared the agenda, you need to inform the other people who will attend the meeting. So the first thing to do is decide who will be there. Small meetings are always quicker, and often more productive, than large ones. This means that you want to include as few people as possible in this meeting. As a general guide:

- **The ideal number for a meeting is between four and seven.**
- **Up to ten people is manageable.**
- **Do whatever it takes to avoid meetings with over a dozen people – you'll be there all day.**

Now that's all very well, but it's not that easy dropping people from meetings. We all complain about meetings, but we hate being left out. People may feel they aren't thought important enough to be there or they may simply want the opportunity to put their case. Well, there are ways round these difficulties. The important thing is to keep in mind that you simply have to keep the numbers down because you haven't time for a big, unwieldy meeting. So here are a few ideas:

- **Look through the agenda and see if some people can be scheduled to leave half way through the meeting or arrive in time for item 4 (another benefit of putting timings on the agenda). You don't want a constant traffic of people arriving and leaving, but the agenda will often split into two or even three sections very simply, and not everyone will need to be there for everything.**
- **An alternative to this is to hold two separate smaller meetings to cope with large numbers, just as we saw earlier for coping with an overlong agenda.**
- **Ask a small group to meet in advance and discuss certain items, and then ask just one representative from that meeting to attend yours and feed in any comments or proposals.**

Having said all that, remember that there are times when the team needs to come together as a group in order to reinforce their identity as a team. Team briefings (which we'll look at in more detail later) can be larger, along with other meetings, where most items are for information rather than discussion leading to action or decision.

PROVIDING BACK-UP

You've decided who you will include in this meeting, but before you circulate the agenda to them you need to add any supporting paperwork to it. Assuming you're normal, you probably find your stomach sinking at the thought of background papers. All those wodges of documents you know you won't have time to read.

thinking smart

TOO IMPORTANT FOR A MEETING

If people are likely to have their noses put out of joint by being excluded, call them in advance. Say: 'You're far too busy to come to this meeting; if I can pick your brains now for any comments or ideas we don't need to waste your time by dragging you along when you have more pressing things to do.'

If this has always been your private view of background papers, congratulations. Your instincts are right. Huge piles of documents with an agenda precariously balanced on top are, frankly, a stupid idea. Do you read them all from cover to cover? Of course you don't. And nor does anyone else.

Mind you, background papers circulated in advance do have some value, so we wouldn't want to abandon them completely:

- ▶ **It's better than everyone reading the papers in the meeting. You must have played that game – you all sit round in silence reading ... and then waiting for the slowest person to catch up.**

- ▶ **It means people can think about the topic ahead of the meeting and come armed with useful comments or ideas.**

- ▶ **If anyone wants to add any data to what is already there, they have time to find the information before the meeting.**

So if we don't want lots of paperwork, and we don't want no papers at all, the middle way should be clear. Short papers. Ask people to provide *brief* background papers, giving them as much advance notice as possible.

Once you have decided who to include in the meeting, and you have collected the necessary (short) background papers, you can circulate them with the agenda. And that's your preparation done.

thinking fast

DEALING WITH DOCUMENTS

If ever you do find yourself without time to go through documents you should have read, you can still give the impression you've done your homework. Stick a few Post-it notes in the pages and make random underlinings and question marks in red ink in the margins.

thinking smart

TECHNICAL PROBLEMS

A few papers, such as financial or statistical documents, can be better presented at the meeting rather than in advance. They may need explanation or people might want to ask questions to clarify their meaning.

for next time

Make it a rule for your meetings that all background papers should be as brief as possible. If they run to any significant length, they should have a one-page summary attached. (Since this is all anyone is going to read, the rest of the paper might just as well be dropped.)

Sometimes you need to circulate a longer report or document; again, you should attach a brief summary if it is not already included. This should save a huge amount of time for you and everybody else, both before and during the meeting.

4 chairing the meeting

Let's get the worrying bit over with first. As a manager, you are judged on your results. Results only happen after action and decisions – which are the product of effective meetings. In other words, the effectiveness of your meetings will determine your results, and therefore your reputation.

There's no getting away from the fact that the success or failure of a meeting is down to the skills of whoever chairs it. However, this has a plus side: when the meeting is successful, everyone knows it is thanks to you (not that they will actually *say* thank you, mind). If your meetings achieve results, and achieve them fast, your reputation will be formidable.

Your preparation has already set you well down the path to a successful meeting. You already have:

- ▶ **a clear objective**

- ▶ **a detailed and useful agenda, stating what result to expect from each item and how long it will take**

- ▶ **only those people you really need, all well prepared with brief background papers where necessary.**

Now you want to get through the meeting as fast as you can without cutting corners or leaving out anything important.

STRUCTURE

The first thing to address is the way in which you tackle each agenda item. It's no good arriving at an item randomly from any direction, leaving some people wondering where it is coming from or where it is leading. You need to approach each item logically so that everyone in the meeting is clear about it. Some people may be deeply involved, while others haven't been concerned with the matter until now or know nothing of it at all.

So each item should be introduced. You can ask the person most responsible for it to do this or you can give an introduction yourself. Either way, the introduction should briefly cover:

1 why the item is on the agenda
2 a brief background to it up until this point
3 what needs to be established, proposed or decided at this meeting
4 the key arguments put forward so far on both sides of the issue
5 the possible courses of action this meeting could take.

The introduction should rarely take more than a minute or two and you should explain this to other members of the meeting – and demonstrate it by example. For instance, suppose the agenda item is the new sales brochure. You might introduce it by saying:

DOING THE INTRODUCTIONS

If someone else is responsible for a particular item, generally you would ask them to introduce it. However, if they are incapable of being brief you can always introduce it yourself – just find a way of doing it without putting their nose out of joint. It can also be wise for you to do the introduction for a controversial item, where neutrality is important. Otherwise, whichever side of the argument is represented in the introduction might appear to have your blessing.

> *We need a new sales brochure before the product launch in September, and we need to decide how best to spend what resources we have on it.*
>
> *The old brochure is out of date, and we get complaints that it isn't comprehensive enough. So we need to decide broadly how we can get the most out of the available budget.*
>
> *There is an argument that we should produce a lengthy and comprehensive brochure, even though this will mean a fairly simple and economical design. On the other hand, we could keep the main brochure short but glossy, and then back it up with a black and white catalogue listing of the more detailed product range.*
>
> *So we need to decide whether we have one smart but simple brochure, or two brochures – one glossy and one fairly cheap black and white.*
>
> *We also need to press on with the design and content, and outline a schedule so we can keep on top of the project.*

No doubt you can see that this brief introduction will occupy little time, but could save a great deal in the way of questions, confusion about the nature of the discussion and so on.

Once the introductions are over, there is a four-stage structure that will take you through the rest of the item without wasting time:

1 Examine the evidence.
2 Discuss the implications.
3 Arrive at a conclusion.
4 Form a decision.

Examine the evidence. You need to go through all the relevant details that back up the arguments now. Anything substantial should have been circulated earlier so you don't have to waste time reading it all at the meeting. But you need to produce figures, costings, sample brochure styles, research results and so on – all the information necessary to carry the discussion forward.

Discuss the implications. This is the real debate. All the evidence has been put before the meeting, so now is the time to invite views and arguments and discuss what it means.

Arrive at a conclusion. Once everything that needs to be said has been, people are inclined to start repeating themselves if you let them. Once you sense that everything useful has been said, steer the team towards forming a consensus about what the best course of action is.

thfhk**thinking smart**

WRITE IT UP

It can help to write up key questions on a flip chart or whiteboard – such as *What do these facts mean for us?* – in order to keep people on track.

Form a decision. Now summarize the conclusion and record it, along with any action points arising from it (we'll look at keeping minutes later in this chapter).

When it comes to your role in the chair, it's your job to make sure that the team follows this route through each agenda item. Keep reminding them what stage the meeting is at, whenever they start to stray. For example: 'Hang on, we haven't heard all the arguments yet so we can't start drawing conclusions' or 'We don't need to discuss the facts – we all know what they are. We need to move on and discuss their implications.'

You need to be firmly in control. Once you allow any kind of unhelpful behaviour – from intimidating to time-wasting – you invite everyone else to do it too. So don't permit the group to stray from the central purpose of the meeting. But don't wield an iron fist – unless it wears a velvet glove. In other words, be firm but don't intimidate people.

You may need to intervene occasionally to make sure that quieter members of the team get their chance to speak, or to invite a contribution from someone whose opinion you think would be valuable. Or you might want to summarize part way through a complex discussion if you sense confusion in the group.

You don't want to waste time here, but if you have a sensible agenda and you stay in control, you should be able to keep the meeting running on time without any sense of rush or people being bulldozed into making decisions before they feel ready.

KEEPING TO TIME ...

... which brings us to another key part of your job. You don't want to bulldoze people, but you certainly don't want to waste their time either. You need to crack on with your meeting and create an atmosphere of urgency without rushing.

The first step towards this is to make sure your meetings start on time. Don't you hate hanging around for ten minutes at the start of every meeting while people turn up? The solution is simple: just start your meeting on time (of course, you have to set the example). If anyone isn't there, they will miss out on the chance to contribute. And don't go back over the first part of the meeting when they finally turn up: they'll find

thfhthfhk**thinking fast**

RABBIT, RABBIT, RABBIT

One of the toughest challenges when you want to keep things brief is handling someone who is naturally garrulous. The thing to remember if you want to stop the flow is: take the wheel; don't try to stand in front of the car. Pick up on a remark and use it to move the discussion on. For example: 'That's a very good point, Jim, and worth thinking about. What do you reckon, Brenda? Have we got enough staff to cover a three-day exhibition?'

241

thinking smart

LATE ARRIVALS

Record on the minutes of each meeting anyone who arrived late or left early. Ostensibly, you are recording who was present for any decision or discussion. But in fact it will help to shame people into turning up on time.

out what happened when they read the minutes. It won't take long before everyone learns to turn up to your meetings promptly.

Another popular form of time-wasting is for people to give long briefings or try to circulate papers at meetings, simply because they didn't get their act together to circulate the information with the agenda. Don't stand for it. Unless they have a very good reason, such as an item that had to be added late, make them wait until the next meeting to have their topic discussed. That'll learn 'em.

As far as the general course of the meeting is concerned, you can encourage people to keep to time by various means:

- **Get them to stick to the point. If you never allow digressions and amusing but barely relevant anecdotes, people will stop trying to insert them into your meetings. Be consistent and it will get easier all the time. By the way, that's not to say you shouldn't allow humour, which can be invaluable at meetings; just don't allow it to ramble off the point.**

- **Remind them of the time: 'We've only got ten minutes for this item, so we need to move towards a conclusion'.**

- **If your own contributions are concise and relevant, people will follow your lead (not every time, but broadly speaking).**

- **Adopt a dynamic, urgent tone of voice to show that you want to crack on.**

- **Hurry people along with your body language: lean forward, make eye contact with the speaker, raise your eyebrows, and nod quickly to indicate when a point has been made.**

You can also make sure that each agenda item reaches the intended conclusion or, if it can't do so for any reason, abandon it swiftly and get on with the rest of the meeting. The kind of indicators that an item should be abandoned include:

- **You don't have all the facts you need to reach a conclusion.**

- **You need input from people who aren't here.**

thinking fast

TURNING THE TABLES ON TIME-WASTERS

If you know your meeting is likely to be plagued by timewasters, schedule it for an hour before lunch, or at 4.30 pm. Few people are eager to procrastinate if it's going to cut into their personal time.

242

thinking fast

WRITING BY COMMITTEE

A common time-wasting factor in meetings is discussions of papers that degenerate into a general redrafting of the paper by committee. If you spot this happening, get everyone to agree what the problems with the paper are and then delegate someone to do a fresh draft later and circulate it.

▸ **Everyone needs more time to think and to discuss the subject with other colleagues.**

▸ **Things are changing in a way that may negate any decision you make now.**

▸ **You don't have time to do the subject justice at this meeting.**

▸ **It is clear that this matter can be settled more quickly and more effectively outside the meeting.**

In any of these cases, you should close the item and move on, but make sure that the necessary action is taken to keep the matter moving – agree what facts will be circulated before the next meeting, set up another meeting or whatever.

MINUTES

Your whole meeting will be a waste of time if everyone leaves at the end of it and nothing happens. Perhaps they all thought someone else was going to take action. Maybe they didn't realize that a final decision had been reached. It is essential that there is no room for doubt about what happened at the meeting and what is going to happen next. That's what minutes are all about.

Whoever actually writes down the minutes, *you* are responsible for them. They don't have to be lengthy, but they must be clear. They should include:

▸ **the time, date and place of the meeting, and who chaired it**

▸ **the names of those who were present and apologies for absence – and names and times for those who arrived late or left early**

▸ **each agenda item discussed. For each item the minutes should state key arguments, decisions or action points, and the name of the person responsible for carrying out the action points**

▸ **the time the meeting ended**

▸ **the date, time and place of the next meeting.**

thinking smart

BEYOND REASONABLE DOUBT

If there is any room for doubt or argument, you can read out the minutes as you write them at the end of an agenda item and check everyone is in agreement.

thinking fast

SETTING A DATE

It is generally much quicker to get your diaries out at the end of a meeting and set the next date (assuming it isn't a regular meeting), rather than spend ages back and forth on the phone fixing it up later.

for next time

Running meetings faster and more productively doesn't take any longer than running them unproductively – in fact, of course, it's quicker. So you can get it right this time as well as next time.

But there are ground rules that you can follow for all the next times to make sure that it gets easier and easier to hold fast, effective meetings. Once your team gets to know your style, they will adapt to it naturally. And the more consistent it is, the sooner and the better they will get to know it. So to keep your meetings swift be consistent about:

- ▶ starting every meeting on time, whether or not everyone has arrived
- ▶ keeping the introductions to agenda items as brief as you can
- ▶ discouraging digression
- ▶ insisting that papers are circulated in advance (unless they accompany a late agenda item)
- ▶ keeping your own contributions brief and to the point.

5 handling people

We've already covered everything you need to know about running meetings … so long as everyone who attends your meetings is permanently affable, amenable, confident and co-operative. However, if you never have to handle any conflict, aggression or domineering behaviour in any of your meetings, I can only assume you work for a Trappist order.

If you are living in the real world with the rest of us, you are going to need to know how to handle people if you want to keep your meetings fast and effective. Some meetings will go smoothly, but others will test your skills to the limit. If you can't stay well in control the meeting will degenerate, take far longer than it needs to, and achieve less. Worse still, it may leave behind resentment and ill feeling in the team. So people skills are vital to chairing meetings productively.

SERVANT NOT MASTER

You may be the most senior person at the meeting, but your function while you are chairing it is to be the servant of the team. It is not your job to pull rank, impose decisions, give opinions or wield power. If you do this, you will have a seriously detrimental effect on the meeting:

- ▷ **You will intimidate less confident people, who may be put off making comments or proposing ideas that could have been useful.**

- ▷ **People will not offer opinions if they think they will be shouted down or made to feel foolish.**

- ▷ **The team members will not feel a shared responsibility for decisions that they feel were imposed on them.**

You are there to make sure the meeting achieves its aims. You should:

- ▷ **Maintain the focus of the group.**
- ▷ **Explain and clarify where necessary.**
- ▷ **Keep the discussion moving towards a resolution in the shortest reasonable time.**
- ▷ **Remain neutral.**

Whoa there! Remain *neutral?* You're the boss and you're supposed to let decisions go through without even expressing an opinion? That can't be right, surely.

But it *is* right, and it's very important. Think about it for a moment. Your interests are the interests of the group and it is essential, for a free flow of ideas and opinions, that you are seen to be on everybody's side. That way, you can be seen to be fair and the task of keeping discipline becomes much easier. You are the servant of the group – you simply want the meeting to reach the best decision.

245

MAKING YOUR CASE

If there is a danger that your views might not be expressed as well as you would like, or that certain arguments might be omitted, have a private word with a like-minded colleague before the meeting. Make sure they will express the points you want made, and furnish them with any useful arguments they might need.

What's more, if you give an opinion – especially early on – it can deter junior members from expressing a contradictory view for fear of arguing with the boss. Not only should they feel able to say how they feel, there is also a good chance that they have an important point to make that is worth hearing.

And what about your opinion? Well, someone else is almost bound to share it and they will express it for you without the meeting having to know how you feel. Then, assuming the debate hasn't changed your view, you can sum up in favour of the colleague who expresses your opinion.

THE GROUND RULES

One of the advantages of team meetings is that everyone knows everyone else, and the meetings are probably regular and certainly fairly frequent. So if you can set up a clear meeting style from the start, people will learn to stick to it without being told. Of course, this isn't much use for today's meeting, or tomorrow's, but you can start laying down the ground rules now. In a short time you should start to see the results in easier, pleasanter and quicker meetings.

You need to spell out the ground rules so that everyone is clear about them. Disagreements are fine – indeed they are often necessary to find the best course of action – but they should never become personal or unpleasant. To make sure your meetings follow this principle, you need to foster a sense of respect for the meeting and everyone in it. So set out four 'rules' for everyone in the team to follow:

1   Always ask for clarification if anything is unclear.
2   Conversely, always be willing to give explanations or answer questions for other members of the meeting.
3   Everyone can help to encourage quieter members of the team to have their say and keep the more dominant members in check.
4   Team members should listen to each other and treat every idea with respect even if they disagree with it.

HANDLING AGGRESSION

Disagreements can be a healthy way to force new ideas out and often lead to even better solutions. Trouble is, people can become emotionally involved and rational disagreement quickly changes to aggressive argument. Sometimes people become very attached to their own ideas and don't want to see them rejected or they feel they are being personally criticized. Sometimes a certain decision will cause extra work or problems for them so they argue heatedly against it.

From your point of view this is unproductive and a waste of precious time. And you want to keep relations in your team on good terms both in and out of meetings. So you need to find ways to make sure that strong feelings are kept in harness and that the meeting doesn't become unpleasant.

Ideally, you should be able to spot trouble brewing and stop it before it starts. It is much easier to keep the peace than to regain it once it has been lost. So as soon as the mood starts to heat up, take action. Respond to the first personal snipe you hear with: 'Let's not get personal. We're not discussing what went wrong last time. We need to decide what lead times we need on this contract.'

There is a four-stage process for bringing overheated discussions back off the boil and keeping the meeting moving forward in the process:

1 Let people let off steam.

2 Be neutral.

3 Involve the rest of the group.

4 Keep to the facts.

The sooner you bring these techniques into play when you see trouble brewing, the less heated things will get.

Let people let off steam

The first principle is that once strong feelings are aroused, it is counterproductive to attempt to repress them. You know yourself that if you are angry and someone tells you to calm down, it just makes you want to clout them. And the thing that irritates most of all is feeling that no one is listening.

So as soon as you sense heated emotions, ask the person concerned to express them. This opportunity to let off steam will help them feel that the group is at least listening to them, and will enable them to calm down by themselves. Ask what's wrong and insist that the rest of the team listens without interrupting for a few moments, until the person has got their feelings out in the open.

Of course, you don't want a fight to develop. If you feel this is a danger, come down firmly on any remarks that are getting personal, and don't allow this sort of bickering or arguing to start. You can intervene and let each person have their say in turn, but get them to speak through you rather than directly to each other until tempers begin to cool.

thinking smart

GET THE FEELING

It isn't only aggression that you need to be on the lookout for. If someone is sulking or withdrawing you need to recognize this, and handle it in the same way. Use the word 'feel' rather than 'think', to encourage them to express their feelings. So you might say: 'I sense you're not feeling happy about this. What's the trouble?'

YOU'VE GOT TO LAUGH

Humour is one of the best tools for restoring calm and good relations, and the opportunity to laugh can act as a safety valve for everyone, not only those who are at the centre of the argument. Just make sure the laugh is not at the expense of anyone at the meeting.

Once people have had their say and got their aggression out of their system, they tend to calm down by themselves. When angry they will often be pigheaded, but once they are calmer it is easier to get them to listen to rational argument and to express their own point of view more reasonably.

Be neutral

We've already looked at the need to be neutral yourself, and this is never more important than when feelings are running high. It is essential that you are seen to be on no one's side but the group's as a whole. Your focus is on resolving the debate amicably and sensibly, and without wasting time on it. So whatever you do:

- **Avoid getting drawn into the argument.**
- **Don't start allocating blame.**
- **Don't criticize anyone for having strong feelings – they are entitled to them so long as they express them without getting personal.**
- **Don't lose your cool, or you will also lose credibility and respect.**

There are times when someone's behaviour at a meeting really is out of line, of course. No matter what the provocation, it isn't on to threaten violence or to be deeply personal. But if one of your team deserves to be pulled up for this kind of behaviour, do it later and in private. Giving them a dressing down in front of the meeting will only increase their anger, as well as being thoroughly unprofessional.

Involve the rest of the group

When two angry people lock horns, they often lose sight of what is going on around them. One of the best techniques for diluting their emotions is simply to bring other people in to the debate. Of course, if you ask other people just to stick in their twopenny worth you are simply encouraging the argument to expand and dragging in the rest of the team.

The trick is to change the subject subtly. Keep to the same topic, but ask someone else for a new angle on it. Look for something that will move the discussion on (you're still working to the deadline of whatever finish time you specified, don't forget). You want to add new facts, bring in a new perspective or shed light on the cause of the problem.

Suppose the argument is about whether the new brochures should be delayed to incorporate the new autumn product range or whether they should be ready in time for the May mailshot. You could bring in someone else by saying, for example:

- Ellen, you've been involved in this for four or five years now. What has happened in the past?

- Tom, would it be possible to get the brochure out by May?

- Hilary, how about giving the new products their own supplementary brochure? That's what you used to do at your last company isn't it?

The aim here is not to shut out the warring parties, but simply to calm them down. Even angry people can have a valid point to make, and they may well be right. So don't exclude their point of view; just give them some time to relax and calm down while others are speaking.

Keep to the facts

This technique is another useful way to keep tempers from flaring. If people express their opinions, they are bound to take sides in some way, whether they want to or not. So avoid opinions and stick to facts. They are much harder to argue with. Ask questions such as: 'What have we done about this in the past?' or 'How much more would two brochures cost?' If anyone tries to respond with an opinion, simply say 'Let's stick to facts for the moment …' and then repeat the question.

CONTROL THE DOMINANT TENDENCY

One of the other key people problems you may encounter at your meetings is the dominant people who are inclined to squash the weaker members of the team. This isn't necessarily an aggressive urge at all. It's just that some people are naturally confident and garrulous while others aren't. And some of the more confident people aren't necessarily considering the opinions of those who aren't prepared to butt in. You, on the other hand, *should* be considering them. But what is the best way to handle them?

You need a two-pronged approach. First, you need to keep the bigger personalities in check. And second, you must encourage the quieter ones to speak out. It's not too difficult: the important thing is to notice when it needs doing. If you spot anyone trying to speak you can say: 'Hold on a minute, Ellen. Hilary, did you want to say something?' Let the dominant members of the group have their say, but then create a space for the others to comment too. (Don't try to force an input from people who have nothing to say, however, or you will simply intimidate them.) The one thing to look out for here is that you shouldn't take sides, as we know – and that includes not seeming to side with the weaker members of the meeting.

If you need to use more forceful methods, here are some tips:

- Go round the meeting occasionally and ask each person in turn to say what they think. People generally co-operate with this slightly more formal process and keep quiet while others speak.

- If some people are intimidated because they are juniors and don't like to disagree with the more senior members of the team, ask them to give their opinion first, before you ask the more senior people.

GET IT IN WRITING

If your team includes people who tend to dominate by repeating their ideas endlessly, record all ideas on a flip chart or a board. Once it's on display they will be reassured that they don't need to repeat it again. And you can save time and get on with the meeting.

> **Have a rule that no one can either interrupt or disagree unless they first summarize what the previous speaker has said. This ensures everyone listens properly, preserves clarity, and it slows the faster ones down.**

BE POSITIVE

One of the biggest dangers in running meetings is that you will get through the whole agenda in the allocated time, with all the decisions and action points you needed, but ... they are not the best decisions and action points.

When time is tight, it is especially crucial that you reach the *best* decisions. You can't afford to be unproductive, and you have to live with these decisions. You don't have time in your life to go back over the meeting in six months' time looking for a better way or clearing up the mess created by a wrong decision.

There are three key rules for making sure your meetings arrive at the best decisions:

1 Set the right tone.
2 Don't settle for the first solution.
3 Be creative.

Set the right tone

You've been at enough meetings to recognize this one. How often do meetings become focused on the negative points, the problems, the difficulties? Is there even a decent solution at all? People are happy to pick holes in each other's ideas, without putting forward any viable alternatives of their own.

Staying positive is largely down to the mood you create in the meeting. Make it clear that there is always a good solution, and it can be found if everyone looks for it. Encourage new ideas – even if they don't seem particularly promising – and keep the enthusiasm going with positive remarks: 'We can certainly build on that,' 'Good thinking' or 'I'm sure we can find a way round this.'

You will also need to keep negativity to a minimum. Some people are naturally cautious and that's fine – in fact, without them the rest of us would get into a lot of

THE POWER OF POSITIVE THINKING

If the team seems negative about the existence of a good solution, remind them of what Henry Ford said on the subject: 'Whether you believe you can or whether you believe you can't: you're absolutely right.'

trouble. But don't allow hole picking for the sake of it. Negative remarks should have a relevant and useful point.

Once an idea has been rejected, don't allow further debate on it. There isn't time and it will damage the mood of the meeting. So don't allow comments such as: 'I'll tell you another reason why it wouldn't work …'

Don't settle for the first solution

There's a Woody Allen film in which someone says: 'I know the answer!' and relates it. Allen replies: 'That's not *the* answer; it's *an* answer. And it's the wrong answer.' Just because a solution fits, it doesn't make it the only one or even the best one. But often a meeting will reach one possible solution and then stop looking.

For example, in the case of those brochures, you might decide that you should have a single brochure for now and add a second brochure for the new products in the autumn. But if you continued to look for better ideas, you might have found one. How about a short run of brochures for now and extra pages stapled into the centre for the next print run?

That's all very nice in theory, but how can you tell when you've got to the end of the possible solutions? After all, you haven't got time to keep the discussion going indefinitely on the off chance there's a better solution somewhere if you can only hit on it.

The answer is that you can rarely know for certain, but you can know that you've given it your best shot. A positive atmosphere is a good start, but there are other techniques too:

- ▶ **Encourage ideas from everyone; don't let one person shout down the others.**

- ▶ **Record all ideas and suggestions on a flip chart or a board. This encourages positive thinking – you can all see where you're getting to. People want to see their ideas written up, and they can use other suggestions as a springboard for their own ideas.**

- ▶ **Go round the group every so often, asking for positive ideas and suggestions.**

The core principle behind all these techniques is the same: the more solutions you can come up with, the less chance you have of omitting the best one.

Be creative

Clearly, if you want people to come up with useful ideas and suggestions, you are asking them to be creative. Contrary to popular belief, we are all capable of being creative, but most of us need encouragement to do it. That's *your* job.

thinkingfast

SEE IF YOU CAN DO ANY BETTER

If you are cursed with a negative bunch of people on your team, you could institute a rule that no one is allowed to say no to an idea unless they have a better alternative to offer. If this is too constricting, just bring the rule into play when you sense that the meeting is being dragged down.

The way to generate good ideas is to create lots of ideas. The most famously creative people in history, from Archimedes to Einstein, didn't have a much higher hit rate of good ideas than the rest of us. They were simply prolific. If every tenth idea is a good one, and every fiftieth idea is a great one, a meeting that generates a hundred ideas has a better chance than one that generates only five ideas. It really is that simple. So to encourage a hundred ideas instead of five:

- **Allow all suggestions, however unpromising – they may be the jumping-off point for a great idea.**

- **Record all ideas on a flip chart so others can build on them.**

- **Don't allow anyone's ideas to be criticised or put down – it will discourage people from volunteering any more suggestions.**

- **Encourage people to be wacky, bizarre and adventurous in their ideas.**

- **Accord each idea the same value.**

- **As always, you should remain neutral and not be seen to favour any ideas over any others.**

Once the ideas seem to have dried up, you can pick out the most promising by finding the ones with the most positive points in their favour – no need to get picky and negative about any ideas that are rejected. Look at all the most positive ideas before making a final selection.

REACHING CONSENSUS

When it comes to taking decisions at a team meeting, you are generally looking for a consensus – at least for any decision of importance. You want everyone in the team to buy into this decision and share responsibility for seeing it through, so everyone has to agree to it. In other words, you need to reach a consensus.

There is a popular misconception that a consensus decision is one that everyone has voted for unanimously. If this were true, it is hard to see how most decisions could get made at all. However, insisting on a consensus decision avoids going with a majority decision in which the minority is strongly in disagreement. If you did this, you would have a small faction within the team that did not feel committed to the decision.

No, what you need is a consensus – a decision that, while not necessarily everyone's first choice, is nevertheless acceptable to the whole team. A decision everyone can live with, even if it's not what they really wanted. If you explain the value of a consensus to your team – that no one has to abide by a decision they fundamentally disagree with – you'll be surprised to find that they will manage to arrive at one.

The techniques in this chapter are as easy to implement when you're under time pressure as when you aren't. In fact, under pressure is when you need them most. But some of them take a little more practice than others.

Handling difficult people at meetings is an invaluable skill. Start by learning how to handle the difficult types you already have on your team. If you know all your meetings are attended by a prima donna, a whinger or a cynical sniper, begin by learning what you can do to curtail these people's more negative characteristics. You might want to read one of the companion volumes to this one: *fast thinking: difficult people*.

Another area where you can develop your skills to make your meetings more productive without being any longer is creative thinking. If you can teach your team to be creative in meetings, you'll find there's a knock-on effect and they will become more creative outside meetings too. Before you know it, you could have an explosion of ideas and brainwaves around your department.

There are numerous creative techniques you can usefully employ at meetings, from brainstorming (as we saw earlier) to Edward de Bono's six thinking hats. They make meetings both fun and hugely productive, and could earn you quite a reputation if you use them regularly. Buy a book on business creativity and start feeding some new techniques into your meetings – now there's an idea.

The way to generate good ideas is to create lots of ideas

6 the type of meeting

All the guidelines we've looked at so far are generic ones for running team meetings. But certain types of team meetings have specific guidelines attached. Running a team briefing session, for example, is not exactly the same as running a project meeting. So this chapter provides a rundown of what you need to know for the most common types of team meeting, for example:

- **regular departmental meetings**
- **inter-departmental meetings**
- **project meetings**
- **team briefing sessions.**

If you're rushed, just read the one that applies to you now. You can still come back later and read the rest of them.

REGULAR DEPARTMENTAL MEETINGS

The key thing about regular departmental meetings (you know, the Monday morning one or whatever it is in your case) is that it is the only time the department really exists except on paper. The rest of the time people are working in ones, twos and threes. This is their chance to come together as a team and reinforce their group identity. So this is your chance to cultivate real team spirit. This means you want the meetings to be as upbeat and unifying as you can manage.

The biggest threat to this is the status battle. When the whole team is together, many people see it as a golden opportunity to assert their position in the hierarchy. This can lead to point-scoring and even battles for supremacy over certain issues. What you want to do, however, is to ensure that while ideas can clash, people don't.

Your neutrality, of course, is all important. But neutrality doesn't have to be silent – it can show favour so long as it is equal. When people are battling for status and position in the hierarchy, it is your approval they seek. So make them all feel they're doing OK. Cool down arguments before they get out of hand with interventions such as: 'You've got a good point there, Charlie, but Ellen is quite right that delivery times should be a higher priority.'

Why are we here?

A common danger at departmental meetings is that they become repetitive, drawing on old agendas for a list of this week's or this month's items. It is easy to forget the real function of the department – which goes back to your original objective. So make a point of livening up the meeting, and reinforcing the real focus of the team, by adding 'why are we here?' items (unless the agenda is really packed this week).

Look at the big issues. Why are delivery times so slow? Why are we losing a lot of new customers? Don't get bogged down in overtime staffing issues and machine repair

KEEP IT SHORT

One of the chief mistakes people make when they chair departmental meetings is to put too many items on the agenda. Specifically, they tend to include items that only concern one or two people there. Since you can't afford to waste time in meetings, make sure these items are addressed outside the meeting. Informal chats or smaller meetings, with or without you, can take care of a lot of items and free up everyone's time.

updates. You may get some invaluable ideas, people will feel involved in the stuff that really counts, and they will be reminded why they are there.

INTER-DEPARTMENTAL MEETINGS

The biggest problem you tend to face at inter-departmental meetings is turf wars. Each department head fighting their own corner. Department heads, what's more, tend to be pretty confident types, and you can end up with a roomful of them slugging it out. But more often, there are two key combatants – at least at any given time. Marketing is always sniping at distribution perhaps, or accounts and personnel are frozen into a permanent cold war.

You can't expect to bring universal peace and the end of all conflict – nor should you. The problem arises from people's genuine loyalty to their own team. So what can you do to keep the meeting productive and reasonably good-natured? Well, here are a few tips:

- **If you know there will be conflict, call the two parties privately in advance. Say to one: 'This is a sensible plan, but it's going to give marketing some problems. Can you think about ways to ease things for them?' When you call the marketing manager you might say: 'This is a problem for you, I can see. But it will be a huge improvement for distribution. I'd like you to consider whether there isn't a compromise that would suit you both.'**

- **If two members of the inter-departmental team really are at loggerheads, ask them to get together and come back to the next meeting with a joint recommendation (that should make them think twice next time they want a barney at one of your meetings).**

- **Use any opportunity to unite the team by talking about threats from outside – competitors, worrying new legislation, recession, the strength of the pound or some other collective worry. Schedule these kinds of items to follow divisive issues so you can reunite the group.**

WATCH THE COSTS

Meetings are expensive, but few people realize how expensive. It is easy to calculate the cost of a regular team meeting such as this, and it's highly illuminating. Once you have done the sums, you can apply them every time. Calculate the cost of each person's time – you know their salaries – and then add the lost income they could have been earning if they hadn't been in the meeting: missed sales, uncompleted units in production or whatever. Your meeting could easily be costing hundreds of pounds, perhaps even thousands, an hour.

Ideas should clash, but not people

CONGRATULATIONS!

There are all sorts of undercurrents at meetings, of course, and especially inter-departmental ones. Everyone will be vying for your approbation, so use meetings to congratulate people publicly on their contributions. 'Pete, that idea of yours about improving call-out times has already cut call-out complaints by 45 per cent. Well done.' You don't have to congratulate each person the same number of times, but make sure you are fair about what earns praise and about who gets it.

PROJECT MEETINGS

Project meetings are, by their nature, very focused. There may be many different aspects of the project to discuss, but they are still limited to the range of the project itself. You need to keep the enthusiasm for the project high and keep everyone working to deadlines, so the mood of the meeting should be positive and upbeat with a sense of urgency about it (good news if you want to spend as little time as possible in meetings).

Project meetings require discipline, both about the meeting and the project itself:

- ▶ **Discipline about the meeting is essential. Project meetings are all about checking budgets, schedules, quality and problems. And about ironing out snags. So don't let the meeting wander off the point. Keep it very focused, and focused on the future. This isn't the place to hold post-mortems into why we are behind schedule; just concentrate on how to get back on course. The past is important only in as much as it sheds light on the future. If understanding why the schedule slipped helps prevent it recurring, fine. But don't start making recriminations and allocating blame.**

- ▶ **Discipline about the project means that once it is under way, you should stick with your plan. It can be very tempting to change things because someone has a great idea about doing things differently. But this is how projects go off course and get behind schedule. Unless there is a really exceptional reason to change, don't.**

TEAM BRIEFING SESSIONS

One of the most successful approaches to communication within organizations is team briefing, a system pioneered by The Industrial Society. If you don't already hold team briefings, it is a good idea to introduce them (just as soon as you have the time). They are unlike other team meetings because all the items are for information only, not for decision. So the best news of all is that you don't have to get your act together to circulate an agenda in advance.

BLURRING THE LINES

Try handing over chairing your project meetings – or parts of them – to different members of the team. The nature of project teams is such that everyone needs to work for the team as a whole, rather than focus on working just for their immediate boss. Hierarchies can get in the way of this. A junior member of the department may be in charge of part of the project in which they have authority over more senior members. So it can help to blur the traditional lines of command.

The overall approach ideally involves the whole company, led from the top down, in which all team leaders are briefed and, in turn, brief their own teams. If your team is part of a larger organization that doesn't operate team briefing, you would do well to recommend it. In the meantime you can still operate a reduced system with your own team, even without the support of top management.

The principles behind team briefing are:

- **People cannot co-operate fully unless they know what's going on.**
- **The best way to bond a group of people into a team is to talk to them as a team, about team concerns.**
- **The fact that you are the one doing the briefing strengthens your position and demonstrates in an effective but non-confrontational way that you are in charge.**

In order for team briefing to work effectively, The Industrial Society has identified five rules to which you must adhere. The briefing sessions need to be:

1 face-to-face
2 in small teams of between 4 and 15 people
3 run by the team leader
4 regular (preferably monthly or thereabouts)
5 relevant to the team.

Monitoring

If your team is part of a larger briefing system, or if there are teams within your team that have their own briefings, there is a sixth rule: briefings should be monitored. This means that if you brief several senior members of your team who go on to brief their own teams, you need to:

- **Check any information they are adding to your brief, that is 'local' to their own team.**
- **Sit in on their briefing sessions from time to time (but as an observer *only*).**
- **Make occasional random checks with members of their team to see how effective their briefing has been.**

These precautions should ensure that the system remains effective and that no misunderstandings or Chinese whispers work their way into the system.

The briefing

Team briefing sessions should last for about half an hour. The Industrial Society recommends that you have four categories of information on which you brief your team – the four 'P's:

1 **Progress.** Give the team performance results. Did they meet last month's targets? How do they compare with other teams in the organization or with competitors? What new orders have there been? Any special successes or failures? Has the competition brought out any new products?
2 **Policy.** This section covers any changes in systems, new deadlines, holiday arrangements, new legislation affecting the team, training courses, pensions and so on.
3 **People.** New team members, members leaving (including why and where they're going), new MD or senior management, changes in other departments that the team

deals with, promotions (including why), overtime, relocation, absenteeism, exhibition stand staffing and so on.

4 **Points for action.** Practical information such as new security measures that must be taken, suggestion schemes, maintenance priorities, correcting rumours, housekeeping details and the like.

A brief is just that – a brief; it's not a discussion. You have set (though not circulated) your agenda in advance and you should work through it:

- **Encourage questions, but not debate. If people want fuller information, explanations or reasons you should try to help, but don't get into arguments. If you feel an argument brewing, explain that this is not the time for it but you are happy for team members to raise the issue another time.**

- **Encourage comments and suggestions and note them down, but don't discuss them now. You can arrange an individual or team session for that later, if necessary.**

- **If anyone asks you something you don't know, find it out for them in the next day or two.**

- **Check that team members have understood anything complicated by asking questions to make sure it's clear to them.**

- **Summarise the key points at the end of the briefing.**

- **Find something positive to finish with so that people leave on an upbeat.**

- **Don't run over time – 30 minutes should be ample.**

- **Give the date of the next briefing so that everyone can mark it in their diary and make sure they are available.**

- **If anyone is absent from the briefing session, brief them yourself when they return.**

Like all team meetings, team briefing not only deals with the items on the agenda, it also cements the group and reinforces your position at the head of it.

thinkingsfast

ONGOING FILE
Rather than sit down before the briefing session and agonize over what you might have left off your agenda, it makes sense to have a file where you continually put notes or papers for the next team briefing. When you come to prepare, you should find everything in there – a much quicker way to prepare and you make sure your agenda is comprehensive.

fornext time

Think about the type of team meeting you're holding, and what particular type of handling it calls for. Take into account the personalities at the meeting, and spend a little time thinking about likely conflicts and the best ways to handle them. Once you can run fast and productive team meetings, your reputation will rocket and – best of all – your diary may even begin to have empty spaces in it (only joking).

team meeting in ten minutes

Whoops! Ten minutes to zero hour and you still haven't started planning your meeting. Your best bet is to phone round and put it off for an hour – or better still cancel it. But that isn't always possible. In that case, you'd better stick to the essentials. That's all you have time for.

Since you're reading this book, you clearly want the odd tip. So here goes:

- ▸ **Read the first bit of Chapter 1 so you know how to set an objective. I know you think it's a waste of time but you haven't got time to argue, so just do it.**

- ▸ **On your word processor, put down a list of items you think should be on the agenda.**

- ▸ **Check this list against your objective. If any item doesn't help further your objective, it doesn't belong on the agenda. Get rid of it.**

- ▸ **Now delete anything that can wait until your next meeting or be handled outside the meeting – by you or by anybody else (but make a note somewhere so it doesn't get forgotten permanently).**

- ▸ **Now you should have the shortest possible agenda. It doesn't matter how short it is – when was the last time you heard anyone complain that a meeting hadn't gone on long enough?**

- ▸ **Now knock the list into some kind of order. Urgent items first. Items that require the team to be awake and creative near the top of the agenda. Keep items in logical groups. And don't try to discuss anything that depends on the outcome of an item you haven't got to yet.**

- ▸ **Now read the bit of Chapter 2 about adding detail to the agenda. Use any remaining time to do this. Include the particular aspects of each item you want to cover and also state whether this agenda item is for information, action or decision.**

- ▸ **Print off a copy of this agenda for everyone at the meeting. It may be rushed and not circulated in advance, but it'll still knock spots off most agendas.**

crisis

DELIVER BAD NEWS

MANAGE TOUGH SITUATIONS

LIMIT THE DAMAGE

ros jay

contents

introduction

Don't panic! There you were, carrying on as normal when out of the blue … disaster. Computer crash? Half the department off sick and it's the day of the big launch? Food poisoning in the canteen? Redundancies? Customer collapsed in reception? There are so many possible crises that it's amazing really that they don't happen more often. But thank goodness they don't.

And were you ready for this one? No, of course you weren't. It wouldn't be a crisis if you were prepared, would it? It would be routine, and you wouldn't have needed this book. As it is, you just want to get it over with as quickly as possible and get back to normal. Well, you've come to the right place. This book will get you through any crisis fast, because once you've learnt the basic rules for crisis handling, you can apply them to every disaster.

That's lucky because, when a crisis hits, your top priority is not generally to send out to the bookshop. So the bulk of this book will help you with those crises that, like it or not, take a little longer to resolve. For example:

- ▶ **the after-effects of natural disasters – fire, flood and storm**
- ▶ **redundancies**
- ▶ **sackings (the crisis being their impact on the remaining team members)**
- ▶ **computer or switchboard crashes**
- ▶ **chronic staff shortages**
- ▶ **product recalls**
- ▶ **strikes and other industrial action**
- ▶ **pollution (when it's your fault)**
- ▶ **morale crises (such as the team's failure to win a crucial contract)**

… and all the other crises, which you can't think of now, but that will certainly happen to someone sooner or later, and it could be you.

This book will also help you prepare for future crises of the more immediate kind – the ones where you don't have time to read a book first:

- ▶ **fire**
- ▶ **serious injury**
- ▶ **sudden illness**
- ▶ **missing vital equipment on the morning of the launch or exhibition**
- ▶ **bomb scare.**

If you use this book as a preparation, you'll find that when disaster strikes you're far better equipped to cope. And the sections at the back on crisis handling in an hour and crisis handling in ten minutes flat will get you through even the most urgent crisis at the speed of life.

Of course, the aim is not simply to come out the other side alive. You may have thought that would do, and indeed it will do far better than *not* coming out alive. But we can do better than that. With cool, well-thought-out crisis handling (no, that's not a contradiction in terms), you can come through disaster looking even better than you did before you started. Don't believe me? Read on …

Whether you have a day to prepare or only a few minutes, you are going to have to think fast. Not only fast, but smart too if you're going to hit the ground running. You want:

 tips for looking as if you know more than you do

 shortcuts for doing as little preparation as possible

 checklists to run through at the last minute

… all put together clearly and simply. And short enough to read fast, of course.

So whatever the crisis, don't panic. I know that's like saying that if you scratch a mosquito bite it'll only itch more. Easily said, but not so easy to do. But really, you've nothing to panic about, because everything you need is in this book. And nothing else. You have here a fast but comprehensive guide to becoming an expert crisis handler within the next hour.

 ## work at the speed of life

This book will take you through the key stages of crisis handling:

1 You'll have to begin by defining your problem (not as obvious as it might seem) and setting priorities accordingly.

2 The next step, for all but the most immediate life and death crises, is to hold an emergency planning session. You might do this on your own but you are far more likely to involve others too.

3 After this, it's time to crack on with the disaster recovery operation. You can't do it all yourself so you need to allocate tasks and, crucially, you have to allocate the right tasks to the right people.

4 Throughout the operation, it is essential to adopt the right attitude towards everyone involved. People skills are key to creating a success out of a crisis. So we'll look at the guidelines for keeping everyone positive and motivated.

5 Some crises have a PR dimension, as news of them spills over into the outside world. The press will want to know all about the toxic waste you've been leaking into the local river system or the redundancies you're making. Getting the press on your side is an important part of your role as crisis leader.

6 And finally … when all the tasks have been completed and life is back to normal, you need to acknowledge that the crisis happened and tie up any loose ends.

fast thinking gambles

When a crisis hits, you've no choice but to scramble your resources and handle it as best you can. With the help of this book, you'll come through it with the least possible fuss and the greatest possible credit. But you are still, inevitably, merely turning off the fan and scraping off the walls whatever it was that hit it.

How much better to turn off the fan before impact. When you think on your feet, you can never come up with as many options as when you think with your feet up. So in the long term, it's wise to put your feet up and think through how you will handle future crises. Make a crisis plan. You'll find out how to do this as you go through the book but, in case you need any convincing, here are a few reasons why it's better not to leave everything until you hit red alert:

- ▶ **Many crises can be planned for, and it saves you a huge hassle in the event if you already have a back-up system in place.**

- ▶ **Whatever the crisis, you can work out a set of priorities that you simply and speedily apply in every case – for example, what are the most essential items in the building to rescue in any kind of physical catastrophe, from storm damage to bomb scare?**

- ▶ **Even when you couldn't have predicted the disaster, you can still shortcut the recovery process if you have planned which personnel you will allocate to which type of task (maybe Jake is great with people or Phil is your best problem-solver).**

- ▶ **Planning may not give you every answer, but it can highlight problems that you might otherwise miss in the heat of the moment. For example, if your plan draws attention to the fact that your most essential electronic machinery is in the basement, you're less likely to forget, as the burst pipe drenches you on the second floor, that your priority is to get downstairs fast and protect the hi-tech equipment in the bowels of the building.**

Fast thinking will pull you through any crisis with panache, but if you want to lead your team through it rather than be pulled through, you need to back up your fast thinking with forward planning. That way, you'll be so cool in a crisis you'll make 007 look like an amateur.

1 define your problem

So you've got a problem? That's putting it mildly. You've got a crisis. A major-panic-stations-drop-everything-oh-God-what-are-we-going-to-do disaster. And the first thing you're going to do is stop and think.

If you have someone collapsed on the floor in front of you, unable to breathe, you should act immediately. For any other kind of crisis – however disastrous – you should take at least a few moments to think before you do anything else. This has two particular purposes:

- ▶ **It means that when you take action it is far more likely to be the right action, rather than simply action for the sake of it.**

- ▶ **It helps you to stay calm. Instead of rushing headlong into panic, a moment of reflection will stabilize your emotions.**

So what are you supposed to do in these few seconds or minutes of reflection? Just stare at the walls trying to conceal your mounting panic? No, there is a more useful train of thought than that. You need to define the problem. It may take seconds or it may take minutes (if you have them). But it must be done.

You might think that when a major water pipe bursts, when the computer crashes or the truck delivering everything for the exhibition breaks down a hundred miles back along the motorway, it would be blatantly obvious what the problem is – the building is filling up with water, we have no computer or there's no exhibition stand.

However, these are not the *real* problems. They are the problems too many people focus on exclusively in a crisis, but they are actually disasters only because of their knock-on effects. Let's take the computer crash as an example. This is a crisis because it means:

- ▶ **you can't take orders**

- ▶ **you can't fulfil orders**

- ▶ **you can't issue invoices**

- ▶ **you can't generate a despatch list**

thinking smart

PLAYING BOWLS

Taking a few moments to think when a crisis hits keeps everyone else calm too. They will be so impressed by your cool approach – like Sir Francis Drake playing bowls as the Spanish Armada approached – that they will be filled with confidence in you and your ability to handle the situation.

… and so on. These are your real problems. If your computer crashed but you had a simple mechanism for duplicating all the computer's functions in some other way, it wouldn't be a crisis, would it? It would be just a glitch.

So your priority when the computer crashes is not to get it fixed, but to get the orders out on time. Obviously getting the computer fixed is a great way of achieving this, but it is only a means to an end, it is not the end in itself. Your top priority should be to find a temporary way of getting orders despatched, and worry about fixing the computer later.

If you don't take time to identify your real problem, you are likely to put all your energies into fixing the computer instead of getting the orders sent out. That's why you need to spend a few minutes identifying the real problem first so you can invest your resources wisely in resolving it. Here are some more examples:

- **When the building floods, the real problem is that valuable equipment or stock is being damaged and that work is being disrupted.**

- **When the exhibition stand doesn't turn up, the problem is that you can't sell your organisation and its products or services so effectively to the visitors.**

- **When you have a chronic staff shortage, the problem is that your team can't perform certain specific basic functions or can't perform them as effectively as it should.**

PRIORITIZE

So that's your first step: define your real problem so you can focus your resources on it. The next step follows on naturally: set your priorities. As you can see from the previous examples, a single crisis can generate a raft of problems. A burst water tank in the roof causing a flood might generate several problems:

- **valuable equipment is being damaged**

- **expensive stock is being ruined**

- **work is being disrupted.**

One of the defining laws of crises is that there are never enough resources to go around. So where are you going to concentrate your efforts? Saving your equipment? Rescuing your stock? Keeping work flowing – and if so which work most needs to carry on regardless? You must decide which of your problems is the most pressing, so you can put your scant resources to the best use.

thinking smart

URGENCY OVER IMPORTANCE

Keep in mind that the most pressing tasks in a crisis don't have to be the most important ones – they are the most urgent ones. For example, if your computer is likely to be back in action within a day or two, processing orders might be able to wait quite easily and catch up later (so long as you can take the orders manually). On the other hand being unable to generate pay cheques until two days late could have far greater repercussions.

LONG STOP

The planning process may lead to setting up a permanent fallback position. You can install automatic back-up computer or website systems in case of failure. You could build up a list of emergency staff to call on when you have a staff shortage. Or you might consider it worth having a spare exhibition stand and displays.

And that's the point of defining and prioritizing your problem. Instead of fixing your crashed computer in half a day and losing half a day's work, how much better to spend a whole day sorting it out but to achieve it without losing any work at all.

for next time

FOR NEXT TIME

You're never going to have a lot of spare time when a crisis hits – not this time, next time or the time after. So you need to find time *before* there's a crisis. This logic is not as flawed as it seems, for one simple reason: few crises are as unpredictable as we make out.

All right, there are some crises for which we simply can't prepare. I know someone who was trapped in a lift for two hours with about a dozen other people. Among these were a small child, who was sick after the first few minutes, and a woman who was phobic about vomit. Obviously you can't be expected to plan for this sort of emergency. I also know of a business where a horse was found inexplicably wandering in a third-floor corridor. And one where an irate customer decided to embarrass the staff by stripping stark naked in the middle of a busy shop.

But you can plan for a lot of other emergencies. Hold a session with your team to plan out your priorities in any likely crisis. In each case define the problem and identify your priorities. When the crisis occurs, you'll have your answers ready. OK, not every crisis will happen, but sooner or later at least one of the ones you've prepared for is likely to – and you'll be ready for it. We already prepare ourselves for what we will do in the event of fire: here are some ideas of what else to plan for:

- ▶ Computer crash – if your business relies on a computer, sooner or later it will let you down, you know it will.
- ▶ Physical damage to the buildings – this is relatively common too. It might be a major storm, a burst water pipe, or a fire in a neighbouring building which doesn't require immediate evacuation, but could eventually spread.
- ▶ Bomb threat – some organisations, such as public transport companies, utilities, theatres, galleries and cinemas, are particularly vulnerable to this. If you are a likely target you should be prepared.
- ▶ Dangerous chemicals – if you keep these on site, you should plan what happens if there is a spillage, a fire or if you pollute the local watercourse.
- ▶ If you keep valuable materials or equipment in a vulnerable place – a basement with a risk of flood or a building that is exposed in the event of extreme weather conditions – think through what you need to focus on in an emergency.
- ▶ If you use dangerous equipment on site that could cause serious injury, be prepared.

- If you manufacture potentially dangerous machinery or equipment, be prepared for product recalls.
- If you're planning an exhibition stand and there's any potential for a major catastrophe, such as the stand supplier letting you down or a vehicle breaking down with disastrous consequences, be ready for it.
- If you have a busy period for staffing coming up, such as a special event or a peak ordering time, plan what you will do if a severe flu bug strikes and 50 per cent of your staff are off sick.
- If you run a website that is important or even central to your business, don't be caught on the hop when it crashes or your server goes down.

Many organisations also have their own specific potential disasters, which you need to identify. In each case define your problem and set your priorities in advance, when you can think clearly, so you save yourself time when it really happens.

The process of thinking through these potential emergencies will show up all sorts of things you can do now to minimise the damage when calamity knocks at your door.

2 emergency planning

Now you know exactly what problem it is you're tackling, and what your priorities are. But you still have to decide *how* to deal with the problem. Again, if you have a serious accident on your hands, call an ambulance before you do anything else. But for most crises, however urgent, you will need to hold an emergency meeting. Even a serious accident calls for an emergency meeting if it is an ongoing crisis (for example, if people are still trapped). Just hold the meeting *after* you've called the emergency services.

Hang on. A meeting? Are you kidding? One of those interminable things we managers spend all our time in, where people talk for hours and nothing gets done? Surely meetings are a waste of time even when you *have* time to waste. Isn't it the very last thing you need in a crisis?

Well, that sort of meeting would be, yes. But that's not the sort of meeting you're going to hold. You're going to hold a quick – if necessary, very quick – meeting that is directed entirely towards generating fast action. No, that's not a contradiction in terms; this sort of meeting is perfectly possible.

ASSEMBLE YOUR TEAM

When you find yourself in the midst of a crisis, you have to scramble everyone who is available until the crisis is resolved. But although the entire organization might be involved in some way, they cannot all be part of the crisis team. Trying to recover from a disaster whilst co-ordinating a team of five hundred is a cumbersome and slow process. And you ain't got that kind of time. So you need a select crisis team around you who can, if necessary, mobilize other forces when they need to.

Generally, your crisis team will consist of your immediate team. Or, if you manage several teams, it might be the team most immediately involved in the problem. Whoever your team is, you want about half a dozen people at the centre of this recovery operation. So call them all together for an emergency meeting.

SUMMARIZE THE SITUATION

It might seem redundant to summarize what is happening but, in fact, it's easy to assume everyone knows the score when they don't. Even if they realise the computer has crashed or half their colleagues haven't turned up for work, they still need to hear it from you. And they need you to tell them the implications. They may have forgotten that today is supposed to be the day for the pay cheque run, for example.

Only by stating clearly the problem and its implications can you be absolutely certain that everyone is as clear as you about why this is a crisis. And when you're co-ordinating a crisis operation, it is even more essential than ever that everyone is working to exactly the same set of information, rules and priorities. Even a slight wrong move now could turn a crisis into a disaster.

thinking smart

SHOW THEM THEY'RE IMPORTANT

In an ideal world, you'd have about four or five people around you. But you may not be inhabiting an ideal world – if it were an ideal world it wouldn't have a crisis in it, after all. If your immediate team has, say, seven or eight people in it, you may have to involve them all. If you leave out a couple of people they will feel deeply unwanted, and it is generally better to involve them to keep them motivated and feeling valuable.

This is especially true of those crises where staff morale is involved. Suppose you are about to make several staff redundant, or perhaps your bosses are. You'll need to get together with colleagues for a crisis meeting (with a little less urgency than if the building were on fire, but no less importance). If you aren't all giving exactly the same version of events to your teams, rumour and gossip will quickly spread and you'll have a nightmare to deal with. So it is always worth summarizing the situation.

This summary may take only a few seconds: 'OK guys. The computer's down and we don't know yet how long it will take to fix or how much data we've lost, if any. So we can't process orders or issue invoices, and we've no idea what orders we're supposed to be despatching today.'

DEFINE THE PROBLEM AND SET PRIORITIES

You have probably been through this process already, as we saw in the last chapter. If so, tell your team exactly what the real problem is, and the priorities as you see them. But check to see if anyone else has identified any further problems or priorities that you hadn't got covered. Maybe you've been dealing with a couple of major complaints this morning and now can't access the customer data to resolve them – that could be a priority you'd overlooked.

BRAINSTORM YOUR OPTIONS

Get everyone to come up with all the ideas they can for coping with the problem (the *real* problem, that is). If you have identified several problems, spend as long as you've got – even if it's only a minute or two – on each of the priorities in turn (starting of course with the top one).

thinking fast

AN AIR OF AUTHORITY

You'll have to adopt a brisk, confident tone for this meeting, but not a domineering one. You have two considerations to balance: on the one hand, you want to transmit an air of urgency (without panic), so people don't think they can spend hours debating the finer points of the problem. This is a meeting on the hoof, not a sit-down discussion. On the other hand, you don't want to squash valuable contributions before they are even uttered by implying there's no time for anyone but you to speak.

For most crises, however urgent, you will need to hold an emergency meeting

Maybe you could take orders manually over the phone. Or explain the problem to customers and arrange to call back when the computer is fixed, and take the order then. You could still take urgent orders manually. Or you could invite phone customers to fax an order through.

When it comes to despatching today's deliveries, maybe you could identify them by going through the paper copies of the invoices sent when the order was made. Perhaps you have a lot of regular customers and can call them up, explain the problem and ask if they have a delivery due in the next few days. Or perhaps your best option is to give up trying to meet deliveries, wait for customers to call in a couple of days to ask where the delivery is, and then courier the packages to them.

The brainstorm session needn't take long, but may bring to light all sorts of ingenious ways round the problem, or at least ways round part of it.

DON'T TAKE UNNECESSARY DECISIONS

You haven't got time to waste, so don't do anything that doesn't *have* to be done. This includes not wasting time taking decisions you don't need to. So don't say: 'We'll just take customers' phone numbers for now, and see if we can get the computer back by lunchtime. If we can't, we'll start taking orders manually this afternoon.'

Why decide now what to do this afternoon? By lunchtime you might have established that the computer will be fixed by half past two. Or you might already have arranged two hundred call-backs to take orders. Or only four. You don't know until lunchtime what you will do then if the computer isn't fixed, so don't worry about it now. For the moment, simply decide to take phone numbers and to review things at lunchtime.

ALLOCATE TASKS

By now, your meeting should have been going on for no more than ten minutes. If you're really pushed, it may have taken as little as two minutes to get to here. Now it's time to start sorting out the crisis on the ground, so you need to allocate tasks to each of your team. You may allocate tasks directly, or you may allocate responsibility for tasks that the team members can delegate – or both, of course. The next chapter is all about allocating tasks as effectively as possible, so we won't waste time on it here.

thinking fast

NO 'WHAT IFS'

As a rule of thumb, never take a decision that is dependent on information you don't have. No 'what if' decisions. The only proviso here is that you shouldn't take a decision now that will back you into a corner if certain events ensue. So don't agree to promise customers you'll call them back tomorrow if it's possible you still won't be able to take their orders then.

CHECK EVERYONE UNDERSTANDS

The impulse now is to tell everyone to get cracking. But there's one last thing before you close the meeting. Make sure everyone is entirely clear about the problem, the decisions you've just taken, and their own tasks. If you don't, catastrophe may follow as people misdirect their energies, waste precious minutes on the wrong activities, or duplicate each other. In the worst instances, they may even make things worse.

Suppose you ask your team to evacuate everyone from the building into the car park because someone's phoned to say there's a bomb in the cafeteria. In the rush, one of your team evacuates all the customers into the staff car park – which is next to the cafeteria – instead of into the public car park. They heard the words 'cafeteria' and 'car park' and, in their panic, put two and two together to make three and a half.

So it's vital to recap and check people understand clearly, especially if they may be panicking and therefore not thinking as rationally and clearly as usual. Showing people that there is always time to check that everyone understands helps to calm them down, and reassures them that it's OK to ask if they are in doubt.

for next time

Print out an emergency meeting aide-mémoire and keep it to hand for the next time you have to hold a crisis meeting. It should read:

- Summarize the situation and its implications.
- Define the problem.
- Set priorities.
- Brainstorm the options.
- Make any necessary decisions – and no others.
- Allocate tasks.
- Check everyone understands.

Hold a crisis planning meeting every year with your team to talk through what you should do in each of the crises you have already decided to plan for (the ones we identified at the end of the last chapter). In effect, hold the crisis meeting for each of these potential emergencies. This will save you loads of time when they happen, as well as pointing up any yawning flaws in your system. 'You mean if the computer crashed we'd have no way of knowing which orders to send out? We should do something about that before it happens.'

You need to repeat this exercise every year or everyone will forget there even *was* a plan by the time the next major crisis hits. And if they do remember, they'll find that the key contact person left the organisation two years ago or the plans for evacuating the building involve mustering everyone in the car park that disappeared last year when you built on the new engineering workshop (which doesn't feature in the evacuation plans either). So update your crisis plans annually.

3 allocating tasks

Coping with a crisis is all about action. As we've seen, the more thinking time you can muster the more streamlined and effective your actions will be. But most of the exercise is likely to consist of doing rather than talking. Even with a morale crisis you have to decide on a plan of action, which is likely to involve calling people together for briefings or establishing new ways of working. In a short-term emergency you'll be doing anything from mopping out the basement to cobbling together an exhibition stand from empty cereal packets and sticky-back plastic.

So if it's action you need, you'd better make sure it is the right action, and carried out by the right people. Your emergency crisis meeting should have identified the key tasks by defining the problem and setting priorities. You know that you need to evacuate the top floor, persuade the directors to staff the sales office because no one else is available, move all your sensitive equipment away from the danger area or get a replacement demo model sent over from Hull.

For speed, you will also have to allocate groups of tasks to responsible people who can cope with them. For example, you might allocate to one or two people the job of clearing out the basement or getting the pay cheques produced manually. These jobs will incorporate several tasks, which you haven't time either to identify or to allocate individually, so they need to be taken on by people who can use their initiative in identifying the individual tasks themselves and getting them done.

DON'T GET BOGGED DOWN

Someone needs to keep an eye on the overall picture and co-ordinate the whole crisis operation. And that someone is you. You need to be available so that:

▶ **You know what is going on.**

▶ **People can come to you with fresh problems (just what you need) or ideas (that's more like it).**

▶ **You have time and a clear head to keep on top of the operation, make decisions and call any review meetings you consider necessary.**

thinking smart

HANDING OVER THE REINS
Sometimes you're not the best person to be in charge of the crisis operation. I know you're the boss, but maybe your marketing manager is better equipped to handle the situation. Or your shop manager, or your computer expert. So delegate: your most important job is to decide who to put in charge. Then get out of the way. Don't abdicate responsibility; be around if they need you. But let *them* make the decisions.

DON'T TREAD ON TOES

If you're doing something manual, which you can abandon when you need to, you'll presumably be working on a task allocated to someone else. Maybe you've put Liz in charge of moving all the equipment and you're shifting all the archive disks. In this situation, remember who is in charge. Liz. Don't try to take over – otherwise when you're called away Liz will be left at a distinct disadvantage, not to mention being mightily hacked off with you just when you need her support and enthusiasm. You're just an extra pair of hands for Liz. You're only the manager in charge when something outside the equipment rescue operation crops up.

This means that you should do your best to avoid taking on any other important tasks yourself. If fixing the lorry is the only thing that will save the situation and you're the only trained mechanic available, I guess you'll have to do it. But otherwise, stay free of any tasks that require concentration.

This doesn't mean you have to do nothing at all. Your most sensible course is to be an available pair of hands for a task that doesn't have to occupy your brain and that you can stop at a moment's notice if something that needs your attention crops up. So help out with mopping the floor, moving equipment, digging out paperwork – something menial. Your staff will love you for it, too.

WHO GETS WHICH TASK?

So to whom are you going to give each task, or group of tasks? Well, I obviously can't answer that precisely because I don't know what your crisis is or who you've got there to choose from. But there are certain types of people and there are certain types of task. And you should aim to pair the right person with the right task.

So here's an outline of eight key types of people you do (or don't) want around you in a crisis, and which type of task to give them. Identify as many of them as you can within your team.

1   **The 'yes' person.** It's worth having someone who takes directions well next to you in emergencies. If you say: 'Call an ambulance' or 'Move those things onto the top shelves first', they do it. Some people will respond with: 'don't you think a doctor would do?' or 'Why don't we move these ones before those ones?'

    There are times when people can help by coming up with better ideas than your own, but in an emergency the speed of the decision is often more important than its precise nature. If you think on your feet pretty well it's going to be a fine line between which decision is best, and action is better than debate. A reliable yes person at your side will not only get on with carrying out your instructions, but in doing so they will set a good example to the rest of the team.

2   **The cool-headed person.** This is the person to put right in the thick of things. They may be good at thinking on their feet, or they may not. It doesn't matter. You can tell them what to do if they're not a great decision maker, you just need them to do the nerve-wracking jobs. They are probably your first aider. If not (you may be lucky enough to have more than one cool-headed person on your

team) they can assist the first aider, or be the one to check there are no customers left in the building when you evacuate.

3 **The decision maker.** Often in an emergency there are two places where things are happening; the fire is on the first floor and the people evacuating the building are being checked and counted in the car park. Or someone has to go and stop the flooding while someone else starts to limit the damage. You can't be in two places at once so you need someone to go and be you somewhere else.

4 **The panicker.** This is someone to get out of the way as fast as possible. Problem is, you can't tell them that. So find a plausible job that needs doing urgently and that gets them out of the way: 'Pat, Robin's not going to be able to fix this leak without some tools. Can you go and see what you can find?'

5 **The gregarious one.** Some crises can be solved only by asking for outside help. Someone needs to call the stores and plead for spare hands to help move the equipment away from the flooding, and beg an emergency plumber to come round within half an hour – failing that they need to see if anyone in any other part of the organization happens to have plumbing experience. Some people are particularly good at this – they know who to call and they don't mind asking favours.

6 **The genius for detail.** If someone *knows* that their job is to stand next to you and tell you what you've forgotten to do, they're much more likely to think of things you've missed. For this role you need someone who is going to limit themselves to important things, but it's invaluable having a team member who occasionally reminds you that if there's a power failure, that means the electronic gates in the car park won't open for the fire engine, or points out 45 minutes into stemming the flood that it might be wise to cancel this afternoon's appointment with your top client *before* they leave their office to come and see you.

7 **The problem solver.** How are you going to get that machine clear of the flood when it's too big to go through the door and up the stairs? Leave it with the problem solver – and an assistant if you can spare one – while you get on with sorting everything else out. This kind of problem can take up too much of your time in an emergency, so give it to someone else.

8 **The sympathizer.** It's often vitally important to have someone to calm people down – to reassure customers who are being evacuated because of fire or to hold someone's hand while they're waiting for the ambulance. This is not a job to give to whoever hasn't got anything else to do. It's a skilled role and some people are far better cut out for it than others. It may even be something that your panicker is good at once their initial shock has worn off.

thinking smart

DECIDING ON A DECISION MAKER

Your decision maker should not only be adept at thinking on their feet, they should also carry authority in the team. This could be because they are older or more senior but it doesn't have to be – they may simply be someone the team has a natural respect for. That way there are no arguments when you say: 'Would you three please go and help Robin evacuate the second floor.'

thinking smart

LET EVERYONE HELP

Some crises are over in an instant and take only one or two clear-headed people to deal with them. But some last longer – perhaps you need to ask for volunteers to stay late or work over the weekend cleaning up your flooded basement and rescuing your sensitive electronic equipment. In these cases it's important to involve everyone, or the ones you leave out will feel they're not wanted. So find ways to make everyone feel they helped save the day.

BUILD A STRONG TEAM

When it comes to dealing with the crisis there are no hard and fast rules because it depends so much on what exactly the emergency is. But things will go far more smoothly if you follow these guidelines for which roles to allocate to which team members. In general, a strong team that is used to working together will always cope better in a crisis – even a totally unrehearsed and unanticipated one – than a weak or disparate team or group.

This is because each member understands their own role and function and their relationships with each other, so they can short-cut past many of the communication barriers that confuse or slow down other groups of people. For example, a good team will instinctively turn to the most appropriate person to take control, regardless of seniority, where a disparate group will often fail to 'appoint' a suitable leader.

thinking smart

DON'T PUSH IT

You can't force people into something like being a first aider; they need to be enthusiastic about it. So if someone prefers not to do it, move on to the next person on your list and ask them.

Plan in advance the best people to fill each type of role in an emergency. When you hold your annual crisis planning meeting (which I mentioned at the end of the last chapter), this is a useful exercise to go through with your team. If everyone has agreed who the 'decision maker' is, for example, they will feel involved and loyal when this person's skills are put into play in a crisis.

It should go without saying that not all the roles we have covered in this chapter should be discussed openly among the team. Identify your 'panicker' in advance, but keep it to yourself. The key roles to agree with your team are:

- ▶ cool-headed person
- ▶ decision maker
- ▶ gregarious person
- ▶ problem solver
- ▶ sympathizer.

When it comes to it, the more aware people are of their primary role (everyone's secondary role is to do anything else that's needed) the more smoothly they will work together, the more valuable they'll feel and the more effectively they'll solve the problem.

There is another vital step you can take to prepare in advance for a crisis: make sure your own team has at least one qualified first aider. Don't simply ask for volunteers, though. Draw up a list of people in the team who are usually on the premises, and then cross off the names of all those you suspect would be likely to go to pieces in an emergency. You now have a viable list of potential first aiders. Decide who would be the best in a crisis and ask them if they would be happy to train.

If groups within the team are often elsewhere – for example they attend a lot of trade shows with heavy display stands to set up – you may decide that one of them should also take first aid training. After the course, it can be very helpful to ask the new first aider to talk to the team about the main things they got out of the course.

Take their training seriously. I can tell you from personal experience that if your organisation sends you on a one-day first aid course and never mentions the fact again, five years on, if faced with someone who has stopped breathing or is bleeding profusely, you haven't got a clue what you're supposed to do. First aid training has to be topped up regularly.

4 setting the right tone

You would have thought that having to cope with the crisis and sort out the practical problems surrounding it would be enough for you. But oh no. You don't get off that easily. Managing a crisis is one of those situations that makes you feel that either there isn't a god or, failing that, we're saddled with a god who has a wicked sense of humour.

You see, the way you handle this crisis not only affects the outcome of the crisis itself, it will also have a huge impact on the morale of your team and on your position within it. Whether you lead a team of five or five hundred, these few hours will set a pattern that will be very hard to change in a hurry. Handled badly, this crisis will lose you respect, loyalty and the morale of your team. But handled well (which is how you're going to do it), it will boost your team's enthusiasm, reinforce its identity and confirm you at the head of it.

So this chapter is all about the psychology, if you like, of handling a crisis. How to get your team behind you and keep it there all the way. This is especially important in the face of crises that damage the team's morale, such as sackings, a death in the team, collective failure and so on. So the second part of this chapter focuses on these kinds of emergency situations.

THE BLITZ MENTALITY

A crisis generates heightened emotions, from excitement to fear. And you know yourself that you are far more sensitive when you are in an emotional state. So your behaviour now will make a strong impression on everyone. The right approach will pull the team together and make it stronger for the future as well as for now.

A blitz mentality often develops in which the group has no choice but to pull together, and its identity is positively reinforced. Often, people's positions in the team are strengthened as their colleagues discover talents in them they never knew existed. Someone senses a new admiration as everyone discovers that they speak fluent Polish, that they can memorize half a dozen phone numbers on the spot or that when the keys to the company car go missing in an emergency, they know how to hotwire the ignition.

But the wrong attitude can create strong resentments, splits in the team and a blow to morale. And the key to the whole thing lies not in what action you take, but in how

thinking smart

NOT A LOT OF PEOPLE KNOW THAT

A crisis is a great opportunity to bring out hidden talents in your team. The traditional team roles largely break down under pressure and become much more flexible. So if someone volunteers for a job you wouldn't normally have associated them with, try to give them a chance. It could work wonders for their morale.

you communicate. So you need to follow the seven key rules of communicating with your team in a crisis, to make sure you keep everyone pulling together.

THE SEVEN RULES OF CRISIS COMMUNICATION

So here they are: the seven core principles for making sure the team you're leading through the crisis comes out stronger at the end of it.

1 **Keep everyone informed.** Make sure you pass on any relevant information to your team throughout the crisis. Don't wait until your next crisis meeting tomorrow morning to tell them something they need to know now. Ignorance and misinformation lead to mistakes during a crisis.

   For example, if you know that the roof of the engineering block is unstable due to last night's major storm, don't rely on everyone following your general instruction not to go in there. Tell them it's unstable. Otherwise someone might decide to use their initiative and go in to check the electrics are turned off or to rescue expensive equipment or vital data files.

2 **Assemble the team together to give important information or instructions.** We all know how to play Chinese whispers, passing a message along the line until it becomes distorted beyond recognition, but this isn't the time for it. The only way to be certain that everyone has the same information, and is working to the same set of instructions, is to collect them all in one place and talk to them all at once. Do this even if the switchboard is down and this means that the one incoming line you've rigged up can't be answered for five minutes while you brief the team. In the long run, you will save time, as well as further problems.

3 **Encourage your team members to ask questions.** I know you want to get the briefings over with as fast as you can and then get back to work. But if people aren't allowed to ask questions – at the briefing or one-to-one – they may get their facts confused, fail to understand the priorities, or misinterpret your instructions. Don't forget, some of your team may be panicking, and that does nothing to aid clear thinking. If you don't allow them to ask questions, time consuming though it may seem, you are asking them to tackle the crisis armed with incorrect information, false priorities and faulty instructions. Is that really wise?

4 **Involve people in key decisions.** This is the ideal approach, because if people are involved they feel committed to the decision and responsible for making it work. Obviously, you cannot, in the thick of things, start organizing questionnaires and focus-group meetings to discuss the best solutions to your crisis. But make sure you go as far as you can to involve people.

 thinkingfast

WORKING BRIEFING
If you really can't afford to stop work for a second, you can talk to people while they work – but *only* if the work is so mindless they can listen easily while they're doing it: get them all moving piles of books or bailing out with buckets while you talk to them.

> **GENTLE TONES**
>
> When you talk to your team, try to be aware of your tone of voice. You may be out of breath, worried or up against the clock, but it is your job to stop your team from panicking. So don't let them hear anything in your voice that might alarm them. Let them see that *you're* not panicking, so why should they?

If you are responsible for tens or hundreds of people, you generally can't involve them all. But usually you can involve your immediate crisis team in most decisions. 'Who thinks we should call an ambulance, then?' may not be a wise decision to try to share, but you can ask for input on whether you should put your energies into replacing the exhibition stand or whether to forget the stand and worry about replacing the display materials instead.

When you have more time – in those equally critical but slower moving crises – you can certainly involve people in decisions. For example, if a member of your department has died, you can consult their colleagues about who should attend the funeral.

5 **Be available.** If the crisis you're dealing with is in any way upsetting or emotionally charged – anything from a damaged building to asking people to work unscheduled overtime – your staff may need to talk to you. They may be worried, frustrated, upset, even angry. If they feel they can't approach you because you're too busy for them, they will be alienated and demoralized. So make time for them to get their feelings off their chests, or to ask your advice, or just to have a whinge: they need you.

6 **Show your staff that you're on their side.** Make sure everyone who works for you knows that their welfare is a top priority. Let them see that you are working to rescue their property, to get a decision on overtime out of top management or to get their project deadline extended. If they can see that you're working for them, they'll be keen to work for you in return.

7 **Never lose your sense of humour.** Laughter is the best way in the world to reduce stress. If you join in or even initiate the humour, the rest of the team will see you as being even more cool and in control. And it takes the pressure off them because it indicates that you're not about to bawl them out for the slightest mistake.

Unless this is a life or death crisis, it's worth keeping in the forefront of your mind that in the long term, the team is more important than the crisis. Yes of course you need to get the website up and running again or the building restored to normal or the exhibition stand erected. But by next week or next month, the crisis will be all but forgotten. The team, however, will still have to work together. So generating a positive and enthusiastic atmosphere, which binds everyone together, is critical to the future of the team.

281

UNDER THE MICROSCOPE

If you're smart, you'll have noticed that the key rules of communicating under pressure are key rules for communicating all the rest of the time as well. They just matter more in a crisis because everything is magnified – emotions, results (good or bad) and everyone's level of attention. This is why good managers are generally good in a crisis too: they may not necessarily be the world's most cool-headed people, but they instinctively foster a positive attitude in those around them.

A CRISIS IN THE CAMP

This is especially true when the crisis is one that affects the team as a unit. Many of the crises that fall into this category are ones that last for days or even weeks, rather than hours. But they are still serious crises and are worth discussing on their own here because their impact on the long-term welfare of the team can be huge. The kind of crises I'm talking about are, for example:

- ▶ redundancies;

- ▶ major overstretching of the team – excessive demand for overtime, for example;

- ▶ major change – from a corporate merger or restructure to an office move or relocation;

- ▶ bad news – the team can't have the resources it wants to complete a project successfully or the department's request for more office space has been turned down;

- ▶ team failure – to win a contract or meet a vital project deadline, or maybe the team's negligence has caused a serious accident;

- ▶ theft in the department;

- ▶ death or serious illness in the team;

- ▶ disruptive office affairs (which can reach crisis point);

- ▶ sacking a member of the team.

All of these have long-term repercussions even if the initial crisis is relatively short-lived. So you need to make sure that you deal with them in a way that strengthens the team or department, rather than undermines it. The seven rules of crisis communication, which we've already looked at, are critical here, but there are other guidelines you'll need to bear in mind too, depending on the kind of problem. So let's look at each type of crisis in turn.

Redundancies

You presumably can't prevent the redundancies, so the way to keep this crisis to a minimum is to handle it sensitively and to recognize that even those people who are not made redundant feel threatened – next time it could be them.

- Keep everyone fully informed from the earliest stage possible. Don't wait until you have more information. People always get wind of trouble and their imaginations will blow it up into something bigger than it really is, so you're not protecting them by keeping quiet.

- Don't just tell them the basics – tell them whatever they want to know. How many redundancies? What departments? What are the criteria for deciding who should go?

- Don't, however, give them guesses. If you haven't got the information, you can try to find out, but don't speculate. They'll take it as gospel, having nothing else to go on.

- Once the redundancies have happened, assemble the rest of your team. Reassure them that you are now a smarter, tighter outfit than before. And give them any genuine reassurances you can that they are not about to go the same way.

Overstretching the team

Your team or department may be overstretched because of unreasonable demands from senior management or because of long-term absence by someone in the team – because of illness, for a sabbatical or on maternity leave, for example.

- Be available. Yes, this is always important but especially so here. It's not just that people are working harder, they are often doing jobs they are unfamiliar with or at speeds they are unused to. So they may well need more understanding, may need to ask a lot of questions or want help with prioritizing.

- Be prepared to lower your standards. Again, if people are trying to do more work in the same length of time, something may well have to give. Accept that not everything can always reach the same standard it does when the team is relatively relaxed.

- Share the extra workload. If someone is away, say on maternity leave, and you are sharing their tasks between the rest of the team, take some of them on yourself. Or you could free someone else up to do extra by relieving them of one of their regular tasks – though not their favourite one or one that means a lot to them for status reasons or whatever. To be safe, ask them: 'I could probably take over some of your work for a while so you're free to look after Angela's customers as well as your own. Is there anything you'd like to pass on to me?'

- Do something about the workload where possible – and be seen to be trying to reduce it. Sometimes the pressure lasts for a predetermined length of time. But sometimes it can go on indefinitely. Eventually your words of sympathy and understanding will begin to sound hollow and the team will start to feel that, as long as you keep telling them they're wonderful, you think that excuses you from ever having to do anything about the problem.

thinking smart

STATE OF EMERGENCY

When your team is working under any kind of long-term stress, recognition is vital. Acknowledge that they are under pressure and give them plenty of thanks and rewards.

Managing change

This could be caused by mergers and takeovers, restructuring, new legislation that affects the team's working practices, relocation and so on.

- ▶ **To start with, warn the team of impending changes as far in advance as possible, and fill them in on all the details you can.**

- ▶ **Involve them in any decisions you can by holding team meetings and inviting comments, questions and suggestions.**

- ▶ **Encourage people to express any negative feelings and listen sympathetically – they may resist change because it threatens their security, because they know they are slow learners or because they think it will make their role less important or their job less stimulating. Ask them to be very specific about their objections.**

- ▶ **Deal with each objection individually. Naturally there will be some genuine disadvantages resulting from the changes; admit to these but explain how they are more than offset by the benefits.**

- ▶ **When the changes are made, make regular checks with the resistors to see how they are adapting. Keep doing this until they tell you they are settled.**

It's worth examining the office move briefly, because it's something that most team leaders find incredibly frustrating. An effective group of people will handle the practical side of the move with little difficulty; the disruptive nature of the process is caused by status issues rather than operational ones. These can reach crisis dimensions, causing splits and ructions within your department, if you don't handle them sensitively.

- ▶ **Some desks or offices are considered more 'important' than others. But the argument never admits this – it's always conducted in operational terms: 'I need to be near the car park to carry in boxes of samples' or 'How can I conduct selection interviews in an open-plan office?'**

- ▶ **It's rarely any use bringing the status subtext out into the open; people always deny it. But if you are aware of it you can often adjust some other status factor upwards: the person's name on the door, their own business card, a change of job title from 'operator' to 'executive' or something else that will placate them.**

- ▶ **Take into account that status doesn't float in mid-air: it is relative to the people around. So it may be that the only reason John isn't happy with the office you allocated him is because he doesn't think it's as good as the one you allocated Pat,**

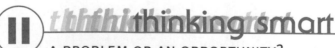

A PROBLEM OR AN OPPORTUNITY?

Some people love change and revel in the challenge of it. You have to make sure that these team members don't either belittle or leave behind the people who are more resistant to change and who regard it as a crisis to be endured rather than a challenge to be surmounted.

and he sees his role as being just as important as Pat's. In this case, you can use the same approach, but if you also give Pat business cards or a new job title you won't have achieved anything. Try to give these kinds of rivals completely different status symbols so it becomes hard for them to compare themselves with the other person. Which is better, a plusher office or a better sounding job title? Hard to say really – and hopefully John and Pat will find it pretty hard to say too.

Bad news

- You won't be moving to the smart new offices after all – your team is one of those staying in the grotty old building.

- You've been through the budget and there's just no way you can find the money to take on a temp for three months to help get a key project finished on time; the rest of the department is going to have to carry all the extra workload itself.

- The board has just announced that it is planning redundancies, which will probably affect your team.

Some types of bad news affect everyone and it's not a pleasant task having to break it to them. Their morale is likely to be seriously damaged and it can take a while to rebuild it. So you need to be as positive as possible when you tell them the bad news – within reason: unbounded cheerfulness and optimism would be out of place.

- Tell them the reasons why the decision has been made. If you didn't make it yourself, find out the reasons from whoever did.

- Let them know that you are sorry they missed out, and that you feel they deserved to move into better offices or to have extra help on the project. However, the wider picture didn't allow this to happen.

- Sometimes compensation is an option. For example, if they can't move offices perhaps you can arrange to refurbish the present ones. Or if you can't afford a temp for three months perhaps you *can* afford to contract out at least some of the work.

Failure

Sometimes bad news isn't simply a matter of bad luck. Perhaps the team has lost a contract they've been working to win for months, for the simple reason that their pitch wasn't as good as their competitors'. Or your team's negligence caused four deaths when a car crashed through a safety barrier that should have stopped it – your

❚❚ ~~thhfihk~~thinking~~rrsm~~ smart

THE VALUE OF DISTRACTION

Following bad news, try to give your department another challenge to put their energies into, preferably something you are pretty confident will work out well. For example, if your team has a real talent for organizing and giving presentations, try to arrange a key presentation sooner rather than later after bad news, to help distract them.

team built the crash barrier and never noticed the fault. All the points above apply, along with a few more techniques.

- Don't try to cover up failure; admit it. 'We failed.' Make it clear that *you* are not displeased with *them* – after all, you're one of them. Let them see that you recognize that as team leader you carry the greatest responsibility.

- Your job, in relation to your own superiors, is to take the blame yourself but to give credit to your team and its members (as the old army maxim says: there are no bad soldiers, only bad officers). Your team members need to know that you are in it with them, and that you aren't putting the blame on them when you talk to people outside the team.

- Hold a session to analyze the mistakes or weaknesses. Point out to them that if you can learn from your mistakes you should be better than anyone next time – you'll be the last people to make that mistake again. But it's crucial to identify and accept your failings.

- Once the team has done this, remind them that nothing is all bad. There must have been some things that you did well and you need to know what they were so you don't reject them along with the mistakes. This gives you a strong positive note on which to end the crisis meeting.

- Once a day or so has gone by, start to joke about it. You might as well – you've got nothing to lose. It keeps the atmosphere light and shows your team that it may not be good to fail, but it's not the end of the world. It will ease the pressure on everyone. There are a couple of points to bear in mind:

  - be wary of joking about a failure that has led to serious illness, injury or death;

  - don't direct jokes against any member of the team (except yourself, if you wish);

  - don't make jokes that reinforce the team's sense of inadequacy. Every joke has a butt, so try to focus your joke on things like the competitor that won the contract, the specification for it, any minor mistake that was caused by the whole team and not just one member, minor details that were out of the team's control – anything else but the team and its members.

Theft

Theft is a matter for the police; it's not your job to find the culprit, although clearly it *is* your job to do anything you can to help the police find them. The potential crisis in the team arises when there is a suspicion that it is an inside job – one of your team may be the thief.

- You must carry on as normal. Pass on to the police – in confidence – any information you feel may be useful, and leave it at that. Keep your eyes open, but don't go rummaging in people's desks when they're not there or manically checking up on their petty cash records. They'll realize instantly what you're doing.

- If your team members think for a moment that you don't trust them, it will do virtually irreparable damage to your relationship with them. Then, when the culprit is caught, all the innocent members of your team (which may well be every one of them) will have to work with you knowing that you considered them all capable of theft from their own employer. If you only suspect one or two of them, who turn out not to be guilty, your relationship with them will be even worse.

- Set your team an example. Until proven otherwise, your attitude must be: 'None of my team would do this. We'll be vigilant, but since none of us is guilty we shan't allow it to get in the way of our work.'

Death or serious illness in the team

This is about the most shocking thing that can happen in a team, and one that needs to be handled very delicately. Your team members will be at their most sensitive and will judge you harshly for any insensitivity you show. Having said that, don't be too nervous – they will see that you're stunned too and they will forgive you any mistakes made through being shell-shocked or inexperienced in dealing with this.

- When you hear the news of death, accident or diagnosis of serious illness, call the whole team together and tell them all at once.

- Be prepared for some colleagues to be extremely upset; if you have a company counsellor or doctor, arrange to have them on hand. If the news is unexpected and shocking, give the person's close colleagues the rest of the day off – maybe longer. Never mind what happens about today's important meeting or presentation: if the team think you put work before people they will lose respect and loyalty towards you in a big way. And the strength of the team is more important than whatever is in the diary for today. Just about anybody will understand your cancelling an event or appointment, or shutting up shop for the day, because of serious accident or death.

- If the person has died, give their fellow team members time off to go to the funeral, and go to it yourself. Make sure the organization sends flowers, quite apart from anything that members of the team may do jointly or separately.

- Give the team plenty of time – maybe several weeks – to get back to normal (depending on the nature of the tragedy). Let them feel they can talk about it – don't allow it to become a taboo subject.

- If you make any mistakes, say so: 'I'm sorry I didn't give you all the day off on Friday. With hindsight I can see that we were all much more shaken than I realized at the time.'

- If one of your team members is diagnosed seriously ill, but is still working, let them decide how to play it. They may want to keep it quiet or they may wish to tell people themselves, singly or as a team. Or they may want you to tell the team.

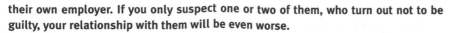

thinking smart

BE GENEROUS
If you're not sure what concessions to make to the rest of the team, or what action to take towards the injured person or the family of an employee who has died, always err on the side of generosity. Whether you're considering how much time off, how big a wreath to send or whether to send gifts, no one's going to complain about a generous decision, but they won't like feeling that they work for a skinflint.

287

Affairs

One of your team is having a fling with one of the directors of the company. Two married team members are having an affair. What do you do about it?

- The good news is that 95 per cent of the time you do absolutely nothing. It's not a crisis at all. In fact, it's none of your business.

- It only becomes a crisis if it seriously interferes with the department and its work. Maybe there's a suspicion that one of the team is being given special treatment because they are involved with someone higher up the organization. Perhaps they are even viewed as a management 'spy'. Worse still, if one or both of the people involved is married, someone in the department may have spilt the beans to one of the partners. That can really cause team relations to hit crisis point.

  You'll have to take the person – or people – on one side and let them know that you're not happy about the effect this is having. If two team members are involved talk to them separately, not together, since each one is independently contributing to the problem. They might also feel inhibited and unable to talk freely in front of each other.

- Behave as though the affairs weren't happening, in terms of how you treat the people concerned. If the rest of the team think that one of their colleagues suddenly has more clout with you just because they have a special relationship with a member of senior management, you will lose the loyalty of the rest of your team. Let everyone see that it makes no difference and there shouldn't be a problem.

- The other occasional, and certainly uncomfortable, situation you may encounter is when two of your team have a relationship with each other and then split up acrimoniously. Worse still, the rest of the team may even take sides. Again, talk to the two people separately and let them know that they are damaging the team and they must resolve things, at least while they are at work. Tell them you hold them at least partly responsible if their colleagues take sides.

  Then speak to the other members of the team one at a time, briefly. Tell them: 'It's none of our business what is going on privately between Robin and Kim, but I am making it clear to everyone on the team, including them, that it mustn't get in the way of work. If you have an opinion on the subject, I'd like you to forget about it during working hours. I understand that this may not always seem easy, but it's important for the good of the team.'

 thinking smart

KEEP MUM

Whatever happens, don't give members of your department any confidential information about their ex-colleague's misbehaviour. Quite apart from any legal implications, they will assume that if they ever leave the department you'll feel free to give away their confidences too.

Sacking a team member

▶ **In the unlikely event that you have to dismiss a member of staff, talk collectively to the rest of the department after the person has left. Tell them that you regret that it had to happen and there was nothing personal in your decision. Explain that you dismissed the person because their presence in the department was preventing the team from achieving its full potential – their colleagues were probably well aware of this and will understand. If it's appropriate, point out that the person was not a failure in themselves, they were merely unsuitable for the team.**

▶ **Let them know that you are confident that you were acting in the best interests of the department as a whole and you are sure that now they will be even more successful. You feel that all the remaining members are valuable to the team and each has an important contribution to make.**

It's not always pleasant or easy to deal with these difficult situations, but remember that it's often just as bad for the rest of the team – and sometimes even worse for them. So always treat them with respect, even when you're under immense pressure, acknowledge their difficulties and give them credit afterwards for handling the situation so well. When things ease off and you have the chance to breathe again, you will find that if you've handled the problem effectively your team will be even closer and stronger than it was before.

for next time

FOR NEXT TIME
Learn the seven key skills of crisis communication and practise them in your everyday approach to work. That way, when the next crisis strikes, you'll find it far easier to keep your team right behind you.

5 handling the press

Everyone loves a drama – except perhaps the people caught up in it. Inevitably, then, many crises will attract the attention of the press. They gather like hyenas around the kill, each hungry to get first bite at the story. And not only do you have to deal with the crisis itself, you also have to cope with the press, ready at any moment to turn on you if you make a wrong move.

The press can be either a blessing or a curse in a crisis, and the balance can lie in how you handle them. Of course, sometimes the press are on your side from the start. If your buildings have been damaged by severe weather or a lorry has careered off the road straight through your shop window, you have the sympathy of the media from the outset.

But the press always want someone to blame, and all too often they will pick on you. If you're making redundancies, if you've polluted the river that runs past the factory, if an accident has been caused by faulty equipment – they'll be sniffing round for evidence to pin the blame on you.

GETTING IT RIGHT

So what can you do? The good news is that there is a wealth of advice, derived from the experience of thousands of organizations over many years. There *are* ways to handle the press (and other media), which will at least minimize the damage and at best turn their attitude around to one of support for your case. So here are the key rules for handling the press in a crisis.

Keep in touch

Tell the press what's going on right from the start. Keep them sweet by holding press conferences; don't wait to be asked. Get outside the front gates and tell them what is happening. The more information you give them, the less they will need to dig the dirt to get a decent story. Don't wait until you've resolved the crisis – keep them posted from the moment they turn up asking questions.

Be honest

Remember Richard Nixon? If you get caught lying, you're done for. It's *never* worth the risk.

thinking smart

REMEMBER YOUR OWN

It's no good keeping the press informed if you don't also keep your own people posted. Otherwise disgruntled staff, who are being kept in the dark, may well decide to pass on to the press their own outdated or misunderstood version of the facts.

thhthithinkingtsmart

UP FRONT

Many years ago, the BBC accidentally double-booked two key political figures to give one of the prestigious Reith lectures. One had to be cancelled, of course, and the press were full of how and why he had been snubbed. The Director General of the BBC adopted a simple, but ingenious, approach when questioned by the press. He just said: 'It was a cock-up, OK?' He was open, honest and wrong-footed the press completely. We all have cock-ups from time to time and the press understand that as well as anyone.

Keep it simple

There are three rules to remember to keep things simple. (I know there should only really be one. Sorry.) First: the press don't know your organization or your industry as well as you do and they want to print a clear, simple story for their readers. So don't confuse them with unnecessary details, jargon or background information they don't want. Just keep your message uncluttered. If they ask for more, give it to them if you can. But don't volunteer it.

The second rule of keeping your story simple is to make sure you have only one spokesperson if you possibly can. Otherwise there is a danger that they may contradict each other. One single point of communication means one single, consistent voice.

And the third rule is: never speculate. This simply adds to the confusion. Speculation may be reported as fact – it often is. So if you're asked to guess at the cause of the chemical leak, how many redundancies there are likely to be or when the building will be operational again, politely decline to comment. Or just say, 'I don't know.'

So these are the three rules of keeping it simple:

1 Don't give more information than you need to.
2 Have a single, consistent message delivered by a single spokesperson.
3 Never speculate.

Get your priorities right

You will horrify readers, listeners or viewers if you start to talk about the financial cost of this disaster when people have been killed or injured. Likewise, they aren't concerned about your faulty equipment when you've just killed all the wildlife for a ten-mile stretch of the river. So talk about the crisis in the light of the public's priorities. These are:

1 people
2 environment
3 property
4 financial implications.

Be aware how things look to other people

Be aware of what the public perception of your crisis handling will be. It's not enough to be right – you have to be *seen* to be right. Suppose a press story breaks

291

NEVER 'NO COMMENT'

What do you think when you hear an interviewee say 'no comment', or when a report says that 'the company declined to comment'? You think they're guilty, don't you? You reckon they've got something to hide. That's what everyone thinks. And it's what they'll think about you, if you say 'no comment'. So don't. If there's nothing you can tell them, it's better to say: 'I'm afraid I don't have any more information at the moment.'

reporting that many supermarket eggs are infected with salmonella and there is a slight risk of serious illness. You are an egg producer. If you react by insisting that there is no danger at all, people will just think: 'They would say that, wouldn't they?'

There may indeed be no danger – or there may be. It doesn't matter. What matters is that people will *think* you are trying to cover up the facts for your own ends; that you're prepared to lie to people about their health rather than lose profits.

So consider how your version of events, which people will consider potentially very biased, will look. Better to say that you are very concerned about the health scare over eggs. You have no evidence that there is any risk at all, but you're taking action to find out the facts as fast as possible. Support any research – maybe donate funds to it – and invite inspectors to check out your operation. Say you would welcome official guidelines on how your organization can remove any risk and generally be seen to be taking the action the public wants, not just paying lip service to it.

Be positive

If you seem worried or downbeat in interviews, people will assume you're in trouble. If you come across as angry they will take a dislike to you. People will read a great deal into your attitude, so make sure it is always friendly and positive, especially when you're talking to the broadcast media. If people have suffered, it doesn't do to look too cheerful about it, of course. But you can still be open and courteous. Make sure you show sympathy for any victims of the disaster, whether or not you accept responsibility.

Be friendly

The press are only doing their job. If you want them on your side, you need to accept this and not hold grudges against them. Let them use the phone and the cafeteria (if it can cope), and give them a warm room if the weather's atrocious outside and you can spare one.

Always treat the press politely and with respect, whether or not they show you the same courtesy. Be as helpful as you can in giving them press packs, background information or whatever else they ask for.

thinking smart

GAGGING ORDER

There are some people you just know are going to put their foot right in it. Maybe they have a grudge against the organization, maybe they love gossip or maybe they just don't know when to shut up. In a crisis – or preferably before it – identify these people and keep them away from the press. Do whatever you have to. Send them on an impromptu business trip to Sydney or Rio de Janeiro if you must, but don't let them speak to the media.

Get your friends on your side

If the press are against you, recruit people outside the company who will speak on your behalf. Satisfied customers, trade association contacts, suppliers, ex-employees … anyone to whom the press will be interested to talk and on whom you can rely to back you up. They will assure the press that your safety standards are exemplary, that you're a great company to work for, that you are known for your reliability or whatever it is you need said. Outsiders always have more credibility than insiders.

Go the extra mile

If you've made a mistake, or are believed to have made a mistake, do everything you can to put it right. Even if people blame you for the crisis itself, don't give anyone an excuse to complain about your response to it. Do even more than you have to. Give people extra time off, replace their damaged property without quibble, even upgrade it, pay to clean up the river *and* fund a new wildlife reserve along its banks. Show that you're sorry you messed up, but you genuinely want to make everything better.

Remember, you don't have to deal with very many crises (thank heaven), but the press deal with them for a living. They are bound to be smarter than you at it, so don't try to fool them – they'll make *you* look the fool. Just play it straight, honest and open.

 thinking fast

NEVER A BAD WORD

You may remember a few years ago a cross-channel ferry ran aground on a sandbank. Due to the vagaries of the tide it was a day or so before they could float it off again. Meantime everyone was stuck on board. But the ferry company and the crew leapt into action as soon as the disaster struck. They kept everyone informed, refunded the cost of the tickets, gave away all the free food and drink they could and generally bent over backwards to make up for the discomfort and inconvenience.

When the ferry finally docked, the press were waiting to interview the passengers as they disembarked. But much to their disappointment (I should imagine), they couldn't find a single passenger who had a bad word to say about the ferry operator. They all insisted, 'It was just bad luck, and they looked after us beautifully.'

Just make sure that everyone understands that the key thing is to treat the press warmly – however hard

Either you or your organization – or both – should be prepared for dealing with the press. You may not know what kind of crisis will strike, but you know sod's law states that it's only a matter of time before something hits the fan.

The more high-profile your organization, and the greater the potential for disaster, the further you should go to prepare for it. But however small the risk of a PR disaster, you can still take some steps to prepare. The process is a valuable exercise in itself, focusing your mind on possible dangers and on how you might handle them.

Here are the key steps well-prepared companies or departments take to limit the damage in the event of a crisis:

▶ You will need a spokesperson to talk to the press, so decide ahead of time who it will be. Maybe you'll have more than one person standing by, according to the nature of the disaster. Train this person (or people) in how to deal with the media.

▶ We've already looked at preparing a list of 'likely' crises. Once you know what these are, you can also write the press releases in advance. Just fill in the gaps when the time comes, so you won't have to cope with writing a press release from scratch as the flood waters are rising.

▶ You can also prepare any other letters that the press might want to see, such as product recall letters to customers and so on.

▶ Prepare emergency press packs with details of your safety record, your evacuation procedures and so on. Make sure these are checked, and updated if necessary, every year.

▶ Think about how you would manage a horde of media people invading your premises. Where would you set up a press room? Could the cafeteria cope?

You can take all these steps fairly quickly and they will be invaluable when you need them. Go through the planning process with your team and it will help them to be prepared in an emergency, too. Just make sure everyone understands that the key thing is to treat the press warmly – however hard – and try to win them over to your side.

6 handling the aftermath

It's all over. The pollution wasn't nearly as bad as everyone first thought, the flood waters have receded, the website's back online, the redundancies are completed or the exhibition went amazingly well and your makeshift stand was a hit with your sympathetic customers.

So that's it. Or is it? Well, not quite. Before you settle back to work as if nothing had happened, there are still some loose ends to tie up. When the crisis is over, it's time to consider the people involved in it.

You're not the only one who has spent the last hour, week or day in a state of crisis. All around you, your colleagues, and maybe members of the public too, have been suffering as a result of the emergency you've just come through. Or perhaps they've been rallying to your side and helping you to get through the crisis quicker and more smoothly. Either way, you need to acknowledge them.

SYMPATHY MESSAGES

If people have suffered, they will be hurt if they feel you've forgotten them as soon as the crisis has passed. So make a gesture of sympathy now and it will count for a lot. Maybe it's a case of sending a card or a note, or perhaps a bouquet or a bottle of wine. It depends on the circumstances – err on the side of generosity. If someone has to spend six months in bed following an accident on your premises (even if you weren't to blame), a get well soon card might seem a little lame. Perhaps financial help might be better or a new, large-screen television to keep them entertained while they're laid up.

If customers have been put out by delayed deliveries or unrepaired faults, again you should get in touch. Offer them a discount on their next order, send them a bottle of champagne or invite them to your next shindig, at the same time as sending them a note thanking them for their understanding. They'll probably end up more loyal than before.

thinking smart

GET PERSONAL
If you have business customers, do something for the customer personally rather than for their employer. A discount does them no good at all – it's not *their* money you're saving. Send them a personal gift instead.

thinking smart

DON'T LET GO OF THE REINS

Don't be tempted to slacken off too much, soften the rules or change the system (except to prevent a recurrence of the crisis). People need the consistency of a structure and a system they recognize to give them confidence and security at a difficult time.

SAYING THANK YOU

The people who helped you get through the crisis want and deserve your appreciation. It's probably the only reason they worked their socks off in the first place. So don't be coy about it. Tell them how wonderful they are. And to show you're not just being glib, tell them exactly how they were so wonderful: 'I don't know how you kept all those customers calm' or 'Where did you learn so much about electrics? We'd have been lost without that.'

Don't just tell your team how great they were. Tell everyone else too. Send a special report praising them to the board of directors, write an article for the corporate newsletter, put them forward for a corporate award.

And give them a thank you present. If they worked together to get the computer back up, take them all out for a slap-up meal. If they saved half a dozen lives, buy them a car. Match the reward to the action. But make sure you reward them.

POST-CRISIS RECOVERY

If your switchboard crashes and takes the best part of the day to fix, you can assume that life will be back to normal by the following day, barring any backlog of calls that still needs clearing. But some crises take time to recover from and you need to be ready for this.

Not surprisingly, the hardest disasters to get over are those that leave people injured or dead and the ones that involve deep human emotions such as loss, failure, guilt and the like. You cannot expect your team to get over the failure of a major project or the responsibility of having caused major pollution in only a day or two.

So what should you do? Give up? Of course not. Pretend the crisis never happened? No, it would demoralize the team still further if you appeared to deny their feelings. Here are a few guidelines, then, to get you through the recovery period:

▶ **Once the immediate crisis is over, call everyone together and explain that you recognize that things are tough at the moment, but it's time to get back to work as usual. Be sympathetic but upbeat. Tell them that the team is strong enough to come through this.**

▶ **Be understanding and sympathetic towards your team and let them feel they can talk to you. Don't give the impression that the subject is closed. The crisis may be over, but their concerns are an ongoing issue.**

▶ **Be prepared to lower your standards a little. If it takes a while for your staff to recover their previous level of efficiency, don't be too tough. Just make sure the trend is upwards.**

So there you have it: crisis handling. With the help of this book you should sail through this crisis and every other one, closely followed by a strong, effective and loyal team. And when it's all over, I hope your boss buys you a bottle of wine, at the very least.

◀◀ for next time

There's one last thing you need to do. Sit down with your team, once the dust has settled, and analyse what went wrong and how you handled it. You're not trying to allocate blame and the mood of the meeting should be upbeat and positive, without fear of recriminations, otherwise you'll have wasted all the good feeling you generated when you thanked everyone.

But you do need to establish two things:

▶ Can we reduce the risk of this crisis – or a similar one – happening again?
▶ Another time, could we handle it any better?

If you don't learn the lessons of this crisis – about what you are good at, as well as where your weak spots are – you won't find the next crisis any easier to handle. So reap the benefits of hindsight and use them to prepare the ground for the next crop of emergencies.

crisis in an hour

Don't panic. This is luxury. A whole hour to prepare for a crisis? It can happen. Many crises take a while to get off the ground: suppose you've just had half your department call in sick on the day of your big product launch. You've probably got an hour or so before your customers and the press turn up in which to avert the catastrophe. Or maybe your boss has just called to tell you that there's going to be an announcement at lunchtime about the restructuring – and your department's in for a big shake-up.

So what do you do when you have a brief warning of an imminent crisis? You might have forty minutes, or you might have two hours. Either way, how can you best use the time to turn the crisis into no more than a bit of a drama?

1 You'll need to begin by defining exactly what the problem is, as we saw in Chapter 1. For example, it's not that you are short-staffed, it is that you can't give as impressive and slick a launch presentation as you wanted, you can't show each visitor to their seats personally, you can't provide refreshments during the mid-morning break.

2 Call together your immediate team – assuming the crisis isn't confidential at this stage. Hold an emergency crisis meeting (see pages 270–3). If you aren't able to talk to your team at this stage (or if they're *all* off sick) you'll have to work through this process on your own.

3 Begin by identifying the top priorities – is a slick presentation more important than the refreshments, for example?

4 Now brainstorm ideas for resolving the problem. Suppose someone nips out now and buys cold drinks and juices for everyone – then no one would need to make teas and coffees mid-morning. You could just set out an unstaffed refreshment table. As for the presentation – think through which sections or visuals might need to be cut if there's no one to operate the equipment. Or is there time to train someone else up quickly?

5 Delegate everything you possibly can, following the guidelines on allocating tasks (see pages 274–7). You need to be free to co-ordinate and deal with any other problems that come to light over the next hour, so don't get bogged down in jobs you don't have to.

6 Make sure you are somewhere everyone can find you fast if they need to. Don't disappear.

7 Remember the seven rules of crisis communication (see pages 280–2) and follow them to the letter, and you should come through this as smoothly as anyone could.

crisis in ten minutes

You are moments away from disaster. In ten minutes the flood waters will be lapping round your ankles, half your shop-floor workers will walk out or five hundred guests will turn up to a dinner that won't be cooked because power to the kitchens has just failed.

Terrific. It's not as if you didn't have enough to do already … and now this. You'll definitely hand in your notice next week. But you'll still have to deal with this first. So what can you do? You've got ten minutes, and you can't afford to waste even one of them. So here's the form:

1 Take a long, slow, deep breath. Literally. Calm the initial rush of adrenalin before you start to act. Five seconds of inaction will set you up to stay cool and set a calm example to everyone else.

2 Identify the real problem underlying the crisis (*see* pages 266–7).

3 Remember the key priorities for dealing with any crisis: people first, then the environment (if that's an issue here), then property, then money. So the first thing to ask yourself is whether there are any people at risk. If so, forget everything else while you deal with that and get them to safety.

4 Once there is no risk to people, identify your priorities. If there is more than one problem, decide which you will address most urgently.

5 Think. Alone or with your team, think through your options. There is an overpowering urge in an emergency to do something, no matter what. But it *does* matter what. It is a tough, but necessary, part of crisis management to quell this urge and take a few moments to think calmly.

6 Take firm control and delegate as many tasks as possible – keeping yourself free to handle the next developments. Make it clear by your manner and tone that you are in charge. You welcome constructive, relevant suggestions but there is no time for argument or dithering.

7 Always keep the crisis in perspective. Keep your sense of humour and imagine yourself regaling your friends and colleagues with the drama. Taking this kind of approach helps you to stay calm and act logically. This may all seem like a nightmare now, but unless people are badly hurt, it's going to be a great story to dine out on when it's all over. Good luck!

project

- **IDENTIFY THE LEADER**
- **CREATE A MASTERPLAN**
- **DELIVER ON THE DAY**

ros jay

contents

introduction

You've got 24 hours to go, and a list of jobs as long as your arm. Well, you would have, anyway, if you had time to write out the list. Why is it that so many projects seem to come on top of the rest of the work, rather than in place of it? If you have a press launch or an office party to organize, a corporate newsletter to get out or an exhibition appearance to arrange, your boss never removes any of your routine work to make way for it: 'Here, give me the minutes of Monday's meeting. I'll action your points for you while you get on and sort out the open day.' Huh … in your dreams.

That's why small but vital projects so often get pushed to the back of the queue. Obviously if your entire career involves project managing the design and build of out-of-town shopping centres, for example, you at least have time scheduled to get the job done. But no one has time set aside for organizing a one-off conference or getting a demonstration model up and working – it just has to fit around everything else.

There is good news, however, the basic guidelines for managing a project are consistent whatever the project, and whatever its size. And they're all in this book. Yes, in here you'll find everything you need to get your project completed on time, even if you're not starting it until the eleventh hour (or even later).

And we can do better than that. After all, you don't simply want to get the thing finished, do you? You want to look good, too. You want the conference to go with a bang, the newsletter to wow everyone, the research findings to impress the board or the press launch to lead to major national coverage. Everyone will be saying how incredible you are to pull so much together in so little time.

It can really happen. It just takes fast thinking and smart working. You need:

 tips for finding out what you need to know

 shortcuts for doing as little preparation as possible

 checklists to run through at the last minute

… all put together clearly and simply. And short enough to read fast, of course.

If your project is a last-minute one, you may be starting from scratch. If it's been planned for ages and involves other people, you have presumably already invited guests, arranged speakers, booked stand space, printed brochures or whatever is needed – and it's the final stages that have become a bit too tight for comfort.

But whichever is the case, don't panic. You may not have long, but it's long enough. This book will show you how to plan, carry out and complete your project in only a day or two. In fact, if you're cutting things fine, there's a half-day version at the end of the book, and you'll even find a 'project in an hour' section if you're truly working at the speed of life.

This book will go through the key stages of planning and carrying out a project at the last minute:

1 The first thing you need to do with any project is identify your objective. It's the only way you can be sure of staying on course. And the less time you have to spare, the more important this is.

2 Your next task is to identify the project owner – the person who is your boss on this project (not necessarily your immediate manager). Once you know who this is, talk to him/her about your budget in terms of money, people and other resources.

3 Now you have to create a masterplan – even if you only have time to scribble it on the back of an envelope.

4 That's enough thinking and planning; it's time to get on with the doing. This stage is all about working through your masterplan.

5 You've got no chance of getting this project finished, least of all successfully, unless you can get the people around you on your side. So there's a chapter at this point all about getting the best out of everyone.

6 It's the big day – the party, the launch, the exhibition, the delivery of the finished report, the conference or whatever it is you've been building up to. So you need guidelines on how not to fall at the final hurdle. Here are plenty of checklists and tips for putting on a polished performance despite your total lack of sleep.

Some projects start in a flurry of activity ahead of time – planning, making bookings, ordering stuff from the printers, sending out invitations – and then lie dormant until the last minute. In recognition of this type of project, at the end of the book you'll also find a guide to this initial planning process. Just because the final culmination of the project may be months away, this doesn't mean that you've got loads of time to plan it now. Often the reverse is true, and these early stages get left far too late (obviously not by you – I'm just talking about other people here). So the final section is a fast thinker's guide to advance planning.

fast thinking gambles

So if it's that easy to carry out a project at the last minute, why bother to get started earlier when time allows? Well, the thing is you certainly can get the job done fast, but it has a distinct skin-of-your-teeth feel to it (to you, even if no one else notices). This is because there are a lot of things you can't do, or can't do so well, when you run your projects right up to the deadline. Here are a few examples, just to convince you (if you need it) not to cut things so fine if you can help it:

- **When time is limited, options are limited. Maybe the menu options for the buffet are narrower, perhaps there's only one electrician who can get to you by tomorrow morning (and not necessarily the best or the cheapest), perhaps you haven't time to find the paint colour you really wanted for the exhibition stand and you'll have to make do with what's in the stores. The more time you have, the more choices you have.**

- **It's as much as you can do to get the project completed or ready on time, and you may not have time to prepare any back-up if things go wrong. The MC for your charity auction may be terrific and reliable too, but what if he's taken ill at the last minute? You won't have had time to prepare and rehearse a standby.**

- **The more time you have to plan, the more likely you are to spot any potential pitfalls. If you're doing everything in a rush, you're more likely to overlook the fact that the display stand you're building down in the basement won't ever leave the premises in its present form because it doesn't fit through the doors. And any printed materials aren't likely to be so thoroughly proofread.**

- **There are always tasks in any project that you need to ask (or wheedle, beg or bribe other people to do). The less time you give them, the less likely they are to say yes.**

- **Projects always cost more if you leave them until the last minute. There's overtime, express delivery costs, emergency call-out fees, and simply lack of time to shop around.**

There. That doesn't cover every possible reason to get started in good time, but hopefully it's enough to put you off leaving things so late another time. You may have been overloaded with work, but deep down you knew all along you should have got cracking on this sooner (I know because we all do it). Sure, fast thinking will get you out of a hole and no one else will know the difference. But *you'll* know it could have been even better if only you hadn't left it so late. So next time, do yourself a favour – start sooner and save yourself a lot of those sleepless nights.

1 your objective

If you can feel the panic rising with the realization of just how little time there is left and how much there is to do, you might think that sitting around setting objectives is a bit of a waste of time. That's an understandable first reaction. But in fact setting a clear objective now will streamline the work that needs doing. Instead of rushing about like a headless chicken, you'll be able to get the essential work done without wasting time on details you simply don't have time for.

So taking a few moments out to think through your objective will set you up famously for the impending day or two of frantic activity. What's more, it will help you to calm down and take a deep breath before you begin. So make yourself a cup of coffee, sit down, and get your objective clear before you do anything else.

You might be forgiven for thinking that your objective is simply to get the project done. In a sense this is true. But it is such a broad objective that it isn't really very helpful, and an objective should be immensely helpful – that's why it's worth finding time to get it straight. So to make it really useful, let's narrow it down a bit.

Suppose you work for a charity and you're holding a charity auction tomorrow night – that's your project. Your initial objective – to organize the charity auction – doesn't give you a lot of clues as to how to go about it. Try thinking a little deeper: what are you doing it for? Presumably to raise money. And presumably you have a minimum figure in mind that you aim to raise. So this should be part of your objective: *to organize the charity auction to raise at least £6000.*

That's more like it. Now, is there anything else? We're not considering minor aims such as not muddling up the lot numbers – we're looking at overall objectives you aim to have achieved at the end of the project. Well, there is another important one. You want the guests to have a good time – not just out of generosity but because you want them to come to your next fundraising event. So how about this for an objective: *to organize the charity auction to raise at least £6000, and to give the guests a memorable and enjoyable evening.*

And what's so useful about this objective now you've identified it? I'll explain. Given enough time and resources, there might be thousands of tasks you'd like to get done for this project. However, under the circumstances you may not have time for half of them (and that could be a generous estimate). So which tasks should you do and which should you manage without?

thinking smart

TIE YOURSELF DOWN

Allocate yourself five minutes to set your objective. The rule is that you're not allowed to do anything else until your time is up. So now you might as well set the objective. This approach should prevent you rushing what is an important process, as well as giving you breathing space before you get cracking on everything else.

thinking smart

thhfhthtthinkingrtsmart

THIRD TIME LUCKY

It often takes three stages to set a clear objective. First, identify your broad objective (for example to organize the auction), then give the key reason for it (to raise £6000), and finally incorporate any other essential reason (give the guests a good time).

Sometimes the third stage may not be another key reason but a matter of making your single key reason more specific. For example, you might identify your broad objective (to mount an exhibition display), give the reason for it (to attract visitors), and then make this reason more specific (who are potential customers).

Whichever way you reach your final objective, try to go through three stages to get there in order to ensure it is specific enough to be useful.

The answer is that you do the tasks that further your objective and don't do those that don't. Suppose one of the most expensive items being offered to you to auction has to be picked up from somewhere 20 minutes' drive away. Is it worth collecting it, or should you abandon it? Well, since it will contribute in a big way to your objective of raising £6000, you'd better go and fetch it. If it's going to raise enough money, it's worth paying for a taxi to collect it if you don't have the time to go.

Now suppose one of the loos at the venue has packed up. It could take ages on the phone to organize a plumber at short notice. Is it worth it? Not if there's another toilet your guests can use – it doesn't further your objective in any way to have this particular one working. So just stick up a sign that says 'Sorry, out of order' and get on with the real work.

You see? A good, clear objective is a touchstone against which to measure any task to give you a quick check on how important it is. Without an objective, it's all too easy to get bogged down with unnecessary activities you just don't have time for. This is your defence against such accidental time wasting.

for next time

fffnextrttime

Next time, of course, you'll have allowed yourself more than enough time to organize your project (won't you?). But you'll still find that a clear objective, set right from the start, means you can focus on the essential tasks and streamline your workload. Set your objective before you do anything else, and you'll find it helps right from the earliest stages of planning.

Make yourself a cup of coffee, sit down, and get your objective clear before you do anything else

2 who owns the project

You may be carrying out this project, but that doesn't mean you necessarily own it (in fact you almost certainly don't). So your next task is to identify the project owner and get them on your side. So who owns the thing? In other words, who is taking ultimate responsibility for it? Who is championing it? Who is providing the money?

If the demonstration model isn't ready and working in time for the big presentation, who is going to get it in the neck (other than you, of course)? If no one turns up to the press launch, who will have to explain things to top management? You may be doing all the hard work, but presumably someone else has initiated the project, or asked you to take it on, or assumed responsibility for it. And that's the project owner.

The project owner is often your immediate boss. But you can't assume that it is. If you're working on an interdepartmental project, for example, the project owner may be one of the other departmental managers, or perhaps a more senior manager or director. Maybe this open day you're organizing is really the marketing director's baby, although you've been drafted in from PR to organize it.

Whichever is the case, you've got to identify the project owner because you need information that only they can give you. So decide who they are, and then arrange to see them as soon as possible. If you can't speak to them face to face, get hold of them on the phone for a short (but crucial) session. But read this chapter first so you can prepare for the meeting.

GET THEM ON YOUR SIDE

You need the project owner to be on your side. Their role is to provide the resources you need to do the job, and to support and back you up. The odds are that they are already enthusiastic about this project, but if not, you will have to enthuse them yourself. It doesn't matter whether they want this thing to succeed because they believe in it or because their head will roll if it doesn't – it only matters to you that they want it to go well. So they'll have to support you if they want to ensure it does. The chances are that they will support you fully. If they don't, you're in deep trouble and you need to go back to whoever has dumped this project on you and ask for a different project owner.

So your first task is to check they are positive about the project and – if they're less than enthusiastic – persuade them that it's worth having the project succeed. There. Now you're both working together towards the same objective.

 thinking smart

THE COMPANY PROJECT

Some projects, such as open days or corporate events, may be projects you are carrying out for the company as a whole rather than one or two departments. In this case, the project owner is effectively the MD. However, the MD may be far too busy to deal with you directly, so you'll have to report to someone else. Identify the most senior manager you can deal with who has a vested interest in the project and wants to see it succeed.

thinking fast

THE BIG PICTURE

The project owner doesn't need to know about the details of the project, and hopefully doesn't want to. Their job is to keep an eye on the big picture. So don't give them a chance to waste time talking over details with you – the details are your job. Don't even mention them in the first place. Keep quiet about the problem with the caterers, or the fact that three of the contributors to the newsletter still haven't delivered their articles.

CHECK THE OBJECTIVE

Speaking of objectives, that's the next thing to deal with. You've already set your objective for this project; now run it past the project owner to check they agree with it. If they have a different objective in mind, now is the time to find out about it. Suppose they think the key purpose in exhibiting is not to attract new customers but to reinforce relationships with existing ones. Much better to find out now than after the event.

It's tempting to rush off now and crack on with the job. But wait. There's a couple more things to clarify with the project owner first. After all, they are central to the project, so you want to get everything you can out of them while you're here. It's quicker than referring back to them frequently as you go along.

The most important aims of the project are set out in the objective. But check whether your project owner has any other key requirements. Maybe they feel strongly that the newsletter should include a tribute to a long-serving member of staff who's retired, or that the exhibition stand should be much less cluttered than last year, or that a strip-o-gram should be organized for the MD at the office party.

Again, now is the time to find out about these kind of requirements. You don't want to wait until afterwards to learn that you didn't do what they wanted. But finding out what they feel strongly about requires a delicate touch. You have to ask them, sure, but ideally you hope they won't have any specific stipulations. After all, they only add to your workload.

So ask them briefly if they feel strongly about any aspects of the project, but don't press them to come up with anything. If you encourage them, no doubt they'll think of dozens of important conditions and requirements. So don't encourage them. In fact, keep it to a minimum and then leave the room fast. As long as you've asked, they have no comeback if they're not happy afterwards. If they complain that they wanted a hot dog stall in the car park for the open day, you can point out (diplomatically) that you gave them the chance to say so and they never mentioned it.

thinking smart

INSURANCE POLICY

There's another reason for checking the objective with the project owner: once they've agreed it, they really can't argue later. If they're not one hundred per cent happy with the way the project goes, you can demonstrate that you still met the objective that *they* agreed. That'll put any gripes they may have in perspective.

GETTING FULL VALUE

Resources such as money are not the only things your project owner will provide for you. They should also be able to get hold of key people for you, solicit the support of other departments, get you introductions to senior people or outsiders, and a host of other things that they are better placed to arrange than you are.

THE BUDGET

There's one last topic to cover before you leave your project owner to put their feet up with a cup of coffee, while you race off to carry out your Herculean task in an improbably short time. Budget. This is the person who is in a position to give you everything you need to get this project completed on time. In theory, all you have to do is persuade them to give you the money to buy in everything possible, a team of a dozen people to help, and access to all the equipment and resources in the organization, and you'd be laughing (I mean with relief rather than hysteria).

OK, that may be a little optimistic. But now you've got them on your side, make the most of it. They want this project to work as much as you do, so give them a chance to contribute. Tell them what you need.

MONEY

To begin with, get a budget allowance out of them. You should have some idea how much money you're going to need, whether it's petty cash or authorization to spend thousands. You may need very little for assembling a major report or getting the corporate newsletter typeset and finally off to the printers. On the other hand, if your project is some kind of event, you may need a lot. And money for taxis, buying in or hiring equipment, paying contractors and so on is also going to be a big help. Not to mention a contingency allowance for those unforeseen but inevitable hitches that only money can sort out fast.

Let's be realistic. Your project owner is going to need to see some figures. Do you really need £1000? Wouldn't £750 cover it? You'll have to show them what you need, and add a percentage for contingency expenses. This is clearly not the time for writing a lengthy budget proposal (although if you do have any time in hand – or for next time – *fast thinking: budget* will be a big help).

But for now, make do with the back of an envelope or the equivalent. The project owner doesn't want to see you wasting precious time any more than you

EMERGENCY FUNDING

Add a contingency of about 15 per cent to your total budget. This is generally pretty realistic, and still gives you some scope to be negotiated down if your project owner really can't stretch to the full amount. But remind them that there won't be time to keep authorizing additional expenses if you run out, so you need to be sure you have a realistic budget. Otherwise when your top customer gets so drunk you have to book a taxi to get them home, you won't be able to pay for it.

Let's be realistic. Your project owner is going to need to see some figures

> **WHISTLE-STOP AGENDA**
>
> Here's a quick recap of your agenda for your meeting with the project owner:
>
> 1 Get them on your side.
> 2 Double-check the objective.
> 3 Any more key requirements?
> 4 Budget: money, staff, other resources.

do, so forget about presentation. Just get the figures straight. Work out your key expenses and calculate how much they will amount to as accurately as you can. Aim to spend no more that 10–15 minutes on this process.

Now you should be able to get the green light to spend any money you need to to get this project completed successfully. What else do you need?

OTHER RESOURCES

Money isn't all you need from the project owner. For a start, you need people if you can possibly get them. Whether you need 10 people for two days, or just an extra pair of hands for the last hour or two, someone is going to have to authorize it for you. You may already have some staff at your disposal, or you may not. But if you need any more – or need specialists from other departments – it's your project owner's job to get them for you. Sometimes the readiest source of extra help is from contractors and freelances outside the organization. So again, work out what you really need. Be realistic; don't undermine your credibility by asking for luxury staffing levels. Be ready to justify your requests.

And then there's equipment and other resources. Do you need a company vehicle to go and pick up the leaflets for the exhibition stand? Do you need authorization to clear 10 car park spaces so the catering van can unload? Will you need exclusive use of the binding machine all afternoon? Do you want to take all the chairs from all the meeting rooms after four o'clock? The project owner is the one who can wave a magic wand and get you whatever you need. Well, it might take a bit more than that, but that's their problem.

So that's your meeting with the project owner. You start by clarifying that you both have the same aims in mind, and then you get them to earn your loyalty and dedicated enthusiasm for the project by providing you with the wherewithal to do it properly.

for next time

> Next time you run a project like this, get the project owner on board as early as possible. Make time to prepare your budget more carefully (there's always a risk at the last minute like this that you'll miss some vital and expensive item in the rush). And also think through what people you'll need when, and any other resources you're going to want.
>
> If you do all this a couple of weeks ahead of time it will be easier to arrange for extra people and allocate other resources. And if you still find you've left the bulk of the work to the last minute again (as if!), at least this will be one job already out of the way.

3 your masterpiece

It's still not time to start doing any of your long mental list of tasks yet. But trust me. We're going for the 'more haste, less speed' approach here. It will honestly be quicker and more effective in the long run.

The only exception at this point is if there are just one or two key tasks that really, really can't wait. Perhaps the caterers told you they couldn't cater for more than 60 unless you gave them final numbers before 9.30 this morning. If it's now 9.28 and you're expecting 75 people, you'd better call the caterers before you do anything else.

But don't get sidetracked into doing everything that seems urgent before you create your masterplan, or you'll never do any planning at all – at this point in the proceedings, what *isn't* urgent? And the plan will speed things up once it's done, because you'll be able to focus on the important tasks and streamline the entire workload to make it quicker and more effective. Can't say fairer than that.

The key to the masterplan is to recognize that you must have everything down in writing. If it isn't written down, it won't get done. You may forget it, and no one else will ever find out about it if it's not down in black and white. Once it's written down, it's safe – it can't get lost (at least, not so long as you look after the piece of paper properly). You can stop holding that long list of jobs in your head. And you have something to work through until it's all done.

BUILDING THE FRAMEWORK

The way to sketch out your masterplan is simple – you just build it up in layers. Begin by writing a list of headings across the top of your page (or envelope). These are the main categories of tasks you have to deal with, and between them they should encompass everything you have to do, which may mean including a 'miscellaneous' heading to cover one-off tasks. Depending on the type of project, your headings will be this sort of thing:

- ▶ caterers
- ▶ transport
- ▶ printing
- ▶ visitors
- ▶ press information
- ▶ venue

- ▶ speakers
- ▶ equipment
- ▶ final checks
- ▶ items for auction
- ▶ miscellaneous

… and so on. Groups of tasks, in other words.

> ### ADD-ONS
> If you think of more headings after you've reached the edge of the page, don't start again. Just tape a fresh sheet to the first one so you double the width of the page.

ADDING THE DETAIL

Once you have all your headings written down (you can always add more later if you find you've missed anything out), the next stage is to list all the individual tasks beneath each heading, from booking a taxi, to collecting the key speaker from the station, to photocopying handouts.

Again, the essential thing here is to write everything down, no matter how small. If it needs doing, it needs to be written down – right down to double-checking there's enough loo paper in the toilets. Don't get hung up on which heading to put things under, by the way. Most tasks are obvious, but where there's a choice it probably doesn't matter much – it certainly isn't worth wasting time over. Take the job of booking the taxi to collect your key speaker, for example. You can put that under either 'transport' or 'speakers' (if you have both headings), whichever you fancy.

The only important thing to consider, in terms of what you write where, is the order in which you need to do things. Aim to write down anything that needs doing urgently at the top of the list it comes under. And write down anything that has to be done before something else ahead of the something else. So if you can't book the taxi until *after* you've phoned the speaker to find out what time they'll arrive at the station, write it down below the task of phoning the speaker. This means you can adopt the simple route of working down through the lists in order, without finding you've snookered yourself at any point.

After this, and assuming you have help on this project, it's time to start writing down who will carry out which tasks.

TRIMMING THE PLAN

There is always the possibility that once you've written everything down, it may look like more work than you (and anyone else who might be helping) can get done in the time you have left. What then?

Well, this is where your objective comes in handy. You're obviously going to have to be prepared to abandon certain things. Maybe the tables will have to be

> ### JUST GET IT DOWN ON PAPER
> If you were a professional project manager, working months ahead, you would put together a complex and detailed plan that would be mapped out carefully using a sophisticated computer program. However, under the circumstances, feel free to use a pencil and the back of an envelope.

laid more simply, or perhaps the newsletter will have to go out without that article that's going to take ages to research. If any task looks like a candidate for abandonment, simply check to see whether it furthers your objective. If not, put it on a separate list of tasks you can forget about unless you find yourself with time to spare at the end (don't laugh, it happens). But don't try to do without any tasks that are central to your objective.

You haven't got time to waste going through this process, of course, so the trick is to select a few time-consuming tasks to skip, rather than spending ages trimming off items that take less time to do than it takes you to cross them off the list in the first place.

If the work has expanded to exceed the time available, you'll find that a bit of confident and well-judged pruning at this stage will make what's left of the project run far more smoothly and successfully.

ANNOTATING THE PLAN

You may well find it helpful to make marks and highlights on your plan to make it easier to see how it all fits together. You want to avoid ending up with an intricate mosaic of pattern on the page, which is too complicated to follow. On the other hand, certain annotations will probably help you a good deal. Use whatever you think will work for you, but here are a few ideas:

 Mark urgent tasks that need to be done first. **I know we just agreed everything was urgent, but give yourself a time allocation according to how long you have, and mark everything that must be done within that time. If you have two days for this project, mark as urgent any task that must be done by lunchtime today, for example. If you've got to be finished by tonight, mark tasks that have to be completed in the next two hours. If you're writing your list by hand, you might like to write these ugent tasks in**

KEEP IT POSTED

One of the best ways to cope with a plan that has a lot of call for arrows on it is to write each task on a post-it note. You can then move these around to make sure they are in the right order, and only use arrows to link tasks that occupy different columns.

red ink as you draw up the plan. Or you could use a highlighter pen to indicate them. They should, broadly speaking, be at the top of each of your lists.

▶ *Use arrows to show that one task leads to another.* Where one task has to wait until another is completed, you can use an arrow to indicate this. Many arrows will lead down from one item to the next in the same list, but sometimes they will cross from one column to the next. For example, you may not be able to set the reception table (under 'venue') until after you've completed everything in the 'press information' column, since the press packs have to go on the table. So an arrow could lead from the bottom of 'press information' to the 'set table' task under 'venue'. This will prevent you trekking over to the venue to check the equipment and lay out tables and chairs, only to realize that you have to return later just to add the press packs.

Don't draw arrows for the sake of it, or your plan will soon resemble one of those children's puzzles where you have to help teddy find the right path out of the maze. As a general guide, don't start by thinking 'Where should I put an arrow?' Much better to put them only where they spring to mind as you're writing the list or once you start working through it.

▶ *Put guide timings next to tasks.* This is especially useful if you're planning to delegate, but it can be helpful for you too. It's easy to get bogged down in a task that simply doesn't warrant the time it's taking. It can't be worth devoting half an hour of your valuable time to folding each table napkin to look like a rosebud, pretty though it may be. If you spot any tasks that are likely to eat up more time than they warrant, allocate a sensible time at this stage – in the cold light of day – and you're more likely to stick to it when you actually come to do the thing.

▶ *Tick off the tasks you have done as you work through them.* This always feels good, and it prevents any duplication of tasks – especially important if more than one person is carrying out the masterplan.

THE PSYCHOLOGICAL ANGLE

Whether or not you are a natural list-maker, you'll find you get a huge psychological boost from getting everything down on paper. It clears your mind hugely, because once a thing is written down, you no longer have to remember it. The project will instantly look and feel more manageable.

You may well have other annotations you want to use, and we'll look at one or two more options in the next chapter. The important thing is not to let it get too complicated, otherwise it will cease to mean anything to anybody.

Broadly speaking, it shouldn't take more than half an hour to fling together an accurate masterplan for a project that is going to take about two days. Once you have written your masterplan, added the detail and made any annotations you want to, you're ready to get on with actually doing the work.

thinking smart

DON'T LET GO

Once you've created your masterplan, on the back of an envelope or a print-out from your word processor, carry it around with you all the time. Take it home with you overnight and sleep with it by the bed (that's assuming you have time for sleep). That way, if anything occurs to you, you can add it at once. If you need to check anything, it's right there. If you panic you haven't done something, you can look and see if it's ticked off. So long as you and the masterplan are inseparable, you're fully in control.

for next time

When you have more time to prepare for a project, you have more time to start drawing up your plan, too. Get it started as soon as the project is launched, even if it lies dormant for a few periods in the middle. Add everything to it as it arises. When you've held the design planning meeting for your exhibition stand, add all the design-related tasks.

Where time is at less of a premium, you can also involve other people in the planning stages that feed into the masterplan. In particular, you should consult with:

- ▶ whoever originated the idea for the project
- ▶ the project owner (if this is someone different)
- ▶ your internal customers
- ▶ your suppliers (caterers, electricians, designers, computer services companies and so on)
- ▶ your own team (in other words, anyone working directly on the project with you).

Aim to talk to all these people at the same time if you possibly can; not only does it save time but a meeting always catalyses the participants and you get a better meeting that way.

All of these people will be able to tell you what needs doing and when, and what else needs to be in place first. When you have enough time to consult fully, you'll find that it makes the project planning process much easier and more reliable.

4 getting the job done

Right, enough of all the planning and paperwork. You should be only about an hour into the day, and it's time to get cracking on the meat of the project — working through the tasks. And now you have a clear objective and a masterplan, it should all be a doddle (albeit a very fast one).

Essentially what you have to do is simply work through your list of tasks, starting with the most urgent, until they are all done. But some ways of doing this are more effective than others, so let's look at the top techniques for getting the job done fast and well.

CLEAR YOUR DESK

No, you don't have to sort out that enormous pile of filing left over from last year before you start on this project. But if this project hadn't happened along just now, I don't suppose you'd have been twiddling your thumbs for the next day or two, would you? If you don't get all your usual, routine tasks out of the way, you'll never get this project completed on time. You probably haven't booked yourself into any meetings or appointments for the next day or two (I do hope you haven't), but if you don't tell everyone who you generally deal with that you're out of commission for the duration, you'll be pestered by interruptions you could well do without.

So start by sending a blanket e-mail to all your regular contacts, in or out of the company (including your family and friends who like to ring you at work), politely explaining that you'd be delighted if you didn't hear a peep out of them until this is all over.

GROUPING TASKS

I know we've already put the tasks into logical groups under headings, and often it makes sense to work through one whole category of tasks at a time, or at least a good few under the same heading at once. It's also a useful way to design your masterplan because it means you can see at a glance where you are in each area of the project.

But when it comes to carrying out the tasks, there's another form of grouping that often makes sense: grouping by activity. The more streamlined your activities, the less time you waste moving from one to another. So spend half an hour in your office making all your phone calls, for example, then spend 20 minutes at the word processor typing up everything from guest lists to press releases, before you go over to the venue and knock off a dozen or so tasks over there.

 thinking smart

GET OUT
Even better than clearing your desk is evacuating it. Find yourself a 'project desk' as far away as possible where you can concentrate on the project and other distractions will leave you alone.

317

EFFICIENCY OR EMERGENCY?

If you're going to group a lot of your tasks by function, you'll have to balance this against getting the urgent tasks done at once. Should you make all the phone calls first, or just the urgent ones? The answer is that it is better to group them all together if you can still get through all your urgent tasks in time, but if it means that some tasks won't be done on time, you'll have to sacrifice this efficiency to break off and complete other urgent tasks before it's too late.

Your masterplan means you can move from category to category without losing your thread. You can visit the venue and do all the tasks that need doing there at once, whether they come under 'final checks', 'catering' or 'technical equipment'. You can have a single session on the phone, getting all your phone calls out of the way at the same time, whether they were listed under 'printers', 'press packs' or 'items for auction'. This is far more streamlined and efficient, and will save you heaps of time.

DOING TASKS IN ORDER

Clearly there's another balancing act going on here. Try to keep tasks in groups of related activities, but also work through certain tasks in order. Suppose you need to e-mail the printer to find out what format they want the material supplied in, then you have to check with your designer on the phone if they can do this, and then you have to get back to the printer by e-mail. Obviously you can't do all your e-mails at once. So keep an eye on any tasks that are dependent on others, and make sure you get the primary tasks done in good time.

DELEGATING

Almost certainly, if you have a sizeable project to organize, you'll have somebody to delegate to. You may have one part-time junior, or you may have a dozen skilled people from various departments or from outside. Whoever you can call on to help you get through this workload, you need to know how to delegate effectively and fast. So here are the key steps to delegating successfully:

1 *Review the task and set the objective.* Here we go, setting objectives again. Have you noticed how setting the objective is the first step in almost all management skills? That's because if you don't know where you're going, your chances of

CATCH 'EM OUT

Sometimes you need to phone someone who you know is likely to trap you on the phone. If you are one of those many people who is underassertive about extricating yourself, either e-mail them or call when you think they'll be out and leave a voicemail message instead.

thinking fast

> ### WHEN YOU'RE PUSHED FOR TIME, GO FOR EXPERIENCE
>
> If you're in a hurry, it's a good idea to delegate to someone who will already know how to do the task with relatively little support from you. You *can* train someone up – and indeed when you can afford the time it's an important part of delegation – but now is not the time for it.

arriving there are seriously hampered. An objective is a destination: once you know it you can plan your route, estimate the time you will take, identify whether any alternatives or shortcuts will be helpful or not, and know when you have reached the end of the journey.

So start by identifying the task and setting an objective for it. Bundle together groups of tasks with the same objective. So if you need some research done for your last two or three newsletter articles, get one person to do it all. The objective is to find the information that will make the articles interesting and useful.

2 *Decide who to delegate it to.* Like beggars, people in a hurry can't always be choosers. At the same time, there's no point giving someone a task that simply doesn't suit them and wastes their talents. If you want someone to do your research, find someone who is quite methodical, and good with people if they need to coax information about competitors out of suppliers, or to persuade someone busy to spend time tracking down data. Don't delegate the tasks to a brash ideas person who is great at getting things started but then wants to move straight on to the next task without seeing the thing through. (And when you've decided who to delegate the task to, write their name next to the task on the masterplan.)

3 *Set parameters.* You're setting an objective for the person you delegate this task to. They need to know what they are supposed to achieve and why. But they will need more than just this. They will want to know how long they've got (even if it's only five minutes), what authority they have (to ask for input from other people, for example) and so on. So you need to provide:

- ▶ **objective**
- ▶ **deadline**
- ▶ **quality standards**
- ▶ **budget**
- ▶ **limits of authority**
- ▶ **details of any resources available.**

You are not, however, telling them how to do the job. You are telling them everything they need to give you the results you want – including when you want them, at what cost and so on. But how they get there is up to them. To return to the analogy of the objective as a destination, they are free to plan their own

IN IT TOGETHER

When you're delegating to younger or junior people, always say 'we' rather than 'you', especially if something has gone wrong and they come to you looking sheepish or worried. By including yourself in 'What shall we do about this?' you up their morale.

route so long as they arrive on time, having consumed an acceptable amount of fuel and not crashed the car. By all means ask them to outline their route to you, but don't make them change it to suit you. If you can see a problem they haven't anticipated, point it out and let *them* find the solution.

Apart from being a standard rule of delegation because it helps to develop the other person's skills, this also has benefits for you when you're pressed for time. The more specific you are about how they should do the job, the more they will feel they have to keep referring back to you every time some little thing goes wrong: 'I can't get hold of Mike on the phone until after 3 o'clock. What do you want me to do?'

What you really want them to do is to get out of your hair. You've enough to do getting your own tasks done. So do yourself a favour and give them as much free rein as you can. If they have clear parameters (which take only a few moments to set out for them) they will feel confident enough to use their initiative about how they get the task done. Then they will only refer back to you with problems you'd rather hear about (well, you'd rather they didn't exist, but if they do you want to know).

4 *Check they understand.* Encourage them to talk to you about the task, so you can make sure they understand exactly what is required and why. You can suggest ideas, so long as you are not railroading them into adopting your approach.

5 *Give them back-up.* Help all you can. Clear the way with another department head for them to get support from their team (or get your project owner to do it); tell them where to find information that you know about and they don't; and give them copies of any useful documents, such as the diagrams for the demonstration model, or the schedule for the big day.

DOUBLING UP

You can always delegate a task to more than one person. This is a good way to get the venue prepared, or phone round all the suppliers to check they're on time and know when and where to deliver or supply whatever you need. Generally the best approach is to appoint a task leader, and brief everyone at the same time so they all know what's needed.

thththt # thinking smart

KEEPING TABS

Just because you're up against the clock, it doesn't mean you can't monitor progress. After all, you still need to be sure that the task gets done properly. If you've delegated an urgent task to be done by the end of the day, you can still call or pop your head round the door half way·through the afternoon to check that it's going OK.

Those are the basic principles of delegation as far as last-minute projects are concerned. You need to find the time to brief people properly – which usually only means a couple of minutes – or you'll end up spending twice as long going round after them clearing up.

It's always worth remembering that if a delegated task goes horribly wrong, it's almost certainly your fault – at least mostly your fault. It happens because the task has been delegated to someone unsuitable, or because the poor sod wasn't briefed properly. It's your responsibility to get the task done, so if you do it through someone else invest a little time in delegating properly, and you'll save yourself plenty of time in the long run.

for next time

If you get started ahead of time, you'll find the tasks that would have been on your urgent list by now have already been done, giving you far more time to concentrate on the real last-minute tasks that couldn't be done sooner. With plenty of advance planning, there'll always be the odd urgent tasks, but far fewer.

Identify tasks for delegating as soon as possible. This gives the maximum time to get ahead of yourself, and for the person to whom you delegate the work to get it done. You can even (in an ideal world) build in time to check it and, if it's really necessary, add to or tweak it.

5 getting people on your side

You've got a lot to do in very little time. You probably can't get it all done unless you have help – even if you might just make it, help would be more than welcome. It will buy you time to give more attention to the most important areas, or simply to cope with unforeseen emergencies. After all, your job is to manage the project, not necessarily to do it.

You may have some help already. Perhaps you have your own team of people to help you; perhaps other staff have been allocated to you; maybe you've bought in outside help. Then again, you might be relying on your powers of persuasion to talk people into giving you their time even when they're not obliged to.

Whether your help is coming from people who've been told to help you or from people who are doing you favours, you still need to motivate them to do their best to make the project successful. It's down to you to make sure that they say yes to helping out, and that they really put everything they've got into it. So this chapter is all about the techniques you can use to make sure you get all the support you need from other people. The people you need most are always, by definition, people who are already on overload.

MOTIVATION

The key to the whole thing is motivation. If other people want to help and want to make the project work, you're laughing. The question is, how can you motivate them? The first thing you need to appreciate is that in other people's eyes, working for you and working for the project amount to much the same thing: you are the project. However much they care about the success of the project, they must also want to do the best they can for you in order to feel fully motivated.

Your team might want the office party to go with a swing, but if you demoralize or upset them they won't do their best. Even if they work hard, they'll work hard at the bits they're interested in, which may not be what you want them to work at. They'll all be happy to blow up balloons, but no one will want to count out 300 napkins and arrange them in alternating colours to suit your colour scheme.

Clearly this is even more important if the project *doesn't* motivate the people working with you. Perhaps it doesn't matter in the least to your colleague in

thinking smart

CLEARING TIME
Part of what demotivates people is being asked or expected to do work they just haven't got time for. The stress of fitting everything into the day makes them resentful. So always give people as much notice as you can, even if you can't tell them exactly what you'll need until nearer the time. That way, at least they can free up the time for you.

another department whether you get this newsletter to the printer on time. Maybe your receptionist is dead against the idea of an open day. But you've still got to persuade them that they want to put a real effort into it. They'll only be doing it for you. If they don't care about you either, you're sunk.

WHAT'S IN IT FOR THEM?

People are motivated by the prospect of reward. And different rewards suit different people. So the question you need to ask yourself of each helper individually is 'What's in it for them?' The answer won't be the same for each person.

There's a limit to what you can offer them, too. You're presumably not in a position to offer a company car or an extra two weeks' annual holiday, or even a salary rise. But that's OK. You're not asking them to sacrifice their marriage or risk serious personal injury. You're only asking them for a few hours of their time, so the reward can be more modest.

There are two types of reward you can give people. There are the rewards you can flag up in advance ('If you help out this evening I'll give you the afternoon off on Friday'), and there are rewards that you don't necessarily promise in advance but which experience should soon teach people that they'll get from you (such as writing an official note to their department head about how tremendously helpful they were).

So what you need now are ideas for the kind of rewards you can give to people who help you complete your project. People should still be rewarded whether they are doing you a favour or whether they haven't been given a choice about helping you. Here are some of the typical motivating factors you can use to encourage people to put real effort into this thing:

- ▶ *Money.* **Here's one of the most obvious motivators. You may not be able to use it but you often can, especially if you're using your own team members to help. If you expect them to work extra hours, it's quite reasonable to let them know that this will be reflected in their Christmas bonus, or taken into account at their next salary review.**

- ▶ *Status.* **Some people don't care two hoots about this, but others get a big kick out of it. For people who want status, give them the job of looking after the speakers – especially if they're famous ones – or interviewing the CEO for the newsletter. Or tell them that since the valuable demonstration model has to be loaded into their car, you've cleared it for them to park in the MD's parking space since it's nearest the entrance. Or put them in charge of a particular task with their own team of helpers.**

- ▶ *Recognition.* **This is different from appreciation (which we'll come to in a moment) because it involves broadcasting their achievements to other people. Whether or not you tell them you'll do this, you can recognize people's efforts with an article or thankyou in the company newsletter, or by writing to their head of department, or even the MD, to say how pleased you were with their help.**

thinking smart

TIME TEACHES

Every time you run a project, you should be generous in your appreciation in ways that mean something to the person concerned. They will soon learn to trust that you will reward them even if you don't spell out the reward in advance.

▶ *Responsibility.* Some people are itching to prove – to themselves or to you – that they can handle responsibility. So put them in charge of finding, organizing and distributing all the items for auction, or give them responsibility for the layout and presentation of the major report you're trying to get finished. These people may well get a big kick out of being given a team of assistants to help them.

▶ *Job satisfaction.* For many people, knowing they have done the job well is a big part of their reward, even before you've noticed it and thanked them. Give these people a complete job to look after, from start to finish, which they can take pride in. It might be organizing the car parking, decorating the venue for the party, or putting together all your disparate notes into a smart and informative press pack.

▶ *Challenge.* This is often related to job satisfaction, but it involves stretching people – giving them something to do that is difficult, or which they've never done before. Ask these people to get the demonstration model working, or to handle all the contact with outside suppliers.

▶ *Appreciation.* Just about everyone will want to know that you appreciate the fact that they are working extra hours for you, or that they have had to delay their other work to fit this in. So notice good work and thank people for it. Not just at the end of the project, but throughout it. As you rush past the recently laid out buffet table, it doesn't hurt to say 'That looks nice.' When someone hands you a neatly typed contents page and summary for the report, you can say 'Thanks – that was quick!' Always be ready to show appreciation; it's what makes people feel it was worth putting in the effort for you.

Clearly you can combine two or more of these motivating factors for most people. In any case, you should always show appreciation. That may be plenty for someone who's given you five minutes of their time, but for people who are putting in a few hours or even a couple of days, give them a little more to go on.

Before you allocate tasks to your team members and volunteers, think about which tasks will motivate each person. It may be that no one is going to find the job of sweeping the floor of the venue very inspiring, but someone will do a good job of it for enough reward – and thanks from you may be sufficient.

CREATING AN ATMOSPHERE

Everybody works better when they're enjoying themselves. So make this fun. Your aim should be that anyone who isn't involved in this crazy, rushed project will feel they've missed out. So put on your best sense of humour, and create a party atmosphere if you can – or failing that a blitz mentality – in order to create a sense of team spirit and shared objectives. Send out for cream cakes for everyone, have a competition to see who can set out their row of chairs fastest (without sacrificing neatness), or offer a bottle of wine to the first person who completes their newsletter article.

 thinking smart

SPECIFIC THANKS

A quick thanks in passing is fine, but when someone completes a task, give them more detailed thanks to show you're sincere and genuinely appreciative. So always aim to comment on a particular aspect of the task that they've done well: 'That was fast!' or 'I like the way you've allowed plenty of space in the layout so it looks really readable,' or 'That's a good idea, I'd never have thought of setting the chairs out that way round but it works much better like that.'

DON'T DO TOO MUCH

If you are lucky enough to have several people to help you, don't even attempt to get any of the tasks done yourself. You won't be able to, and you'll end up achieving less rather than more. With several assistants, your job is solely to coordinate everyone else, check completed tasks, brief on fresh tasks and distribute thanks and praise. That's more important than anything else. You can combine it with a mundane task that you don't mind being called away from frequently – such as setting out the glasses, plates and cutlery, but don't try to do anything demanding.

If there are any boring tasks going, put people in pairs or threes to do them. Give three people three tasks to do together instead of dishing out one job each. They'll have more fun that way. Putting people together to do groups of jobs is how Volvo build cars.

This is easiest to do when everyone is working in the same geographical area, but even with, say, newsletter contributors sending in material from different offices you can still generate enthusiasm with humorous but genuine e-mail updates to everyone. Yes, it takes a few moments, but if it speeds everyone else up it's worth it.

YOUR OWN ATTITUDE

It's vital that you should be popular – even under stress. These people are working hard to keep you happy. So make sure they want you to be happy. If they make mistakes, be generous. Otherwise they'll do it on purpose next time. Don't be too bossy, and always ask people to do tasks rather than telling them (even if they are obliged to do what you tell them).

And however stressed and frustrated you get, don't take it out on your workers. They're doing their best, and if you add to their stress their work will deteriorate. If necessary, hide in a cupboard and scream or punch the walls until you feel better. A general air of being fun and friendly but in a hurry should deter people from wasting your time.

STRIKING THE RIGHT TONE

If you're trying to persuade people to do something for nothing (or to do a lot for not very much), you may need to put some effort into how you ask. Some people will naturally be very cooperative, but others may resist helping and you need to think through how you're going to ask them for help or favours in advance. Whether it's a supplier, a colleague, your boss or the head of another department, the key is to decide what you're going to say before you speak to them.

MUCK IN

You will make yourself far more popular if you muck in and do the boring or unpleasant jobs along with everyone else. If they see you cleaning or pinning up notices, they can hardly complain if you ask them to do something equally mundane. And your popularity rating will shoot up. The key to good management is popularity.

325

It's no good pretending to be someone you're not – it will simply sound false – but most of us have a range of personas we can draw on. You might feel quite comfortable saying, 'Listen, mate, any chance of a favour?' to one person, and 'Sorry to bother you, but I wonder if you could possibly help me out?' to the next. So think about the best words to use to suit the person you're dealing with. This applies to the actual favour, too. Should you give them the background first, or just come straight out with it? Should you try to make it sound like less work than you suspect it really will be, or should you tell it like it is?

And it's not only the words – it's the tone, too. Some people respond well to cajoling, others just get wound up by it. Some people don't want to be told they owe you a favour, even if they do – it feels like emotional blackmail – while others are happy to have it pointed out. This isn't as complicated as it sounds – the point is that many people just don't think these things through in advance, but you'll have more success if you do.

Make sure your body language isn't overbearing or aggressive, either. Don't hold constant eye contact, lean too close to the person, or use any dominant gestures such as finger-wagging or thumping the table. All these types of body language give the impression you're trying to intimidate the other person into saying yes. It will work with submissive people (although they will do the work reluctantly rather than enthusiastically), but it will have the opposite effect with stronger personalities.

If this all sounds horribly complicated to remember, it really isn't. Don't worry. If you're not feeling intimidating or aggressive, you won't appear as if you are. So convince yourself you're asking for a favour that the other person has every right to refuse, and you should find that the tone and the body language take care of themselves.

thinking smart

FAIR'S FAIR

You're asking people for favours here; that means they're entitled to say no. And for all you know, they may have good reason to. You don't want to say yes to every favour *you're* asked, after all. So be gracious when you're refused. Don't sulk, or you can bet that the person concerned will never want to say yes to you in future. If you're magnanimous, on the other hand ('Fair enough – I can see you're really busy'), they are much more likely to feel guilty and say yes next time.

for next time

Make life easier for yourself if you possibly can. If you give people plenty of warning, they are far more likely to be able to schedule in the time to help you. If you leave things to the last minute, you make it harder for them to help you.

Even if their work does pile up at the last moment, if they promised you help three weeks ago it's difficult for them to wriggle out of it now. If you don't ask until now, however, they're bound to say no. So the moral is: the further in advance you ask for help, the more likely you are to get it. What you don't want to hear is 'You should have told me.'

6 the big day

It's finally here: D-day. You may virtually have started here, of course, or you may have taken a day or two to reach this point. Either way, it's the moment of reckoning. The research report has to be printed out (ready or not), the auction guests start arriving in an hour, the exhibition opens this morning, the newsletter is off to the printer any moment, the conference begins this evening, the party kicks off in half an hour.

The key thing when it comes to organizing your time for today is to arrange to have nothing to do. If the project is a specific event, make sure you have cleared all your tasks by at least an hour before it begins. Your schedule should now be blank. What you have left is just contingency time. And believe me, you ain't going to be twiddling your thumbs. Even in the smoothest, most clockwork projects, you don't end up thumb-twiddling.

Your task now is to stand back and watch, but be ready to intervene anywhere if anything begins to go wrong, and to prevent any dramas turning into crises. You are a coordinator and nothing else, and you need something to coordinate.

YOUR TEAM

For anything but the smallest of projects, you need a team of people to coordinate. If staffing resources were really low, these people may not have been working on the project up until now. But clearly if you're organizing a press launch the PR and marketing departments will be well represented, if you're holding a presentation someone will have to welcome the guests while someone else is running the technical side, and so on. These people may even be senior to you off the project; it doesn't matter. If they want things to run smoothly, they are going to have to liaise with you.

What you need is to allocate one person to be in charge of each key function – your task chiefs: one to oversee the erection of the exhibition stand, one to make sure all the deliveries arrive on time, one to deal with visitors or guests, one to look after the technical equipment and run final checks, and so on. Your job is to check with each of them at intervals that everything is still on target, and to wait for something to go wrong.

Each key person must stay at their post, so if problems arise and they don't have a minion to send out for gaffer tape or fresh orange juice or two AAA batteries

thinkingfast

CONSTANT CONTACT

For an event of any size and coordination, equip yourself and any other key personnel with mobile phones. That way, if anything goes wrong, you will be the first to know and you can pass on revised instructions accordingly as quickly as possible.

or whatever it is they need, they can contact you. You too must stay at your post, but your job is somehow to get hold of fresh orange juice at six in the morning in Shepton Mallet, or whatever the demand is.

WEAVING THE THING TOGETHER

The biggest and most dangerous problems you are likely to encounter involve hiccups in the scheduling that have knock-on effects. Here are just a few examples of the kind of things that can happen at the last minute:

- **The truck delivering the TV equipment is blocking the main entrance and the food van can't get access to the kitchen.**

- **The portaloos have arrived but the crane isn't here to position them and the crane company have no record of the order.**

- **The brochures have been delivered but they can't be unpacked because the carpenter hasn't installed the shelving yet – he's been called away to fix the presenters' table, which is in imminent danger of collapse.**

These are the problems you are waiting to resolve. That's what you're there for on D-day. You have someone in charge of the TV equipment for the press launch, and someone else sorting out the catering. But only you have the responsibility and the knowledge to coordinate the two. If the catering van doesn't get through soon, the person controlling the preparation of the venue is going to be on to you about their inability to set out the buffet table.

So the vital thing is to catch these problems early and resolve them before they snowball. If everyone understands that you are the liaison point, they must recognize too that you need to be told about every hitch because only you will know what implications it might have for other aspects of the project.

CHECKLISTS

OK, you need lists and schedules to get you through this smoothly, and I can't write them for you. But since you're short of time, I'll give you some pointers to the more general check points.

To begin with, if you are running any kind of event – exhibition, conference, open day, press launch, charity auction – you will need a stage-management-style emergency kit to cover any standard tasks, hitches or hiccups, from sticking up notices to nailing down loose floorboards. So here's a checklist of items for your emergency kit:

thinking smart

ALWAYS CARRY A SPARE

If it is absolutely essential for certain things to work, organize standbys – you don't have time to send out for a plumber or a spare video camera. You can arrange anything from back-up PowerPoint equipment, to standby carpenters or electricians, to a spare vehicle (insured as necessary) for emergency fetching and carrying. If it's important enough, it's worth paying for back-up.

- a range of basic tools, such as hammer and nails, adjustable spanner, Stanley knife, screwdrivers (flathead and crosshead)

- gaffer tape (for taping down trailing leads that could be tripped over)

- string

- fishing line (for tying things invisibly, such as wobbly demonstration models on the presenters' platform)

- tape measure

- scissors

- Blu-tack

- masking tape (to label objects)

- hairspray (stops shiny objects flaring under the lights on a lit stage)

If you have guest speakers, presenters, an MC or the like, include anything they might suddenly want, such as spare pens, highlighter pen, safety pins, basic sewing kit and so on.

That's your emergency kit taken care of; now what about the other areas you need to consider? You'll need to draw up sets of checklists of tasks in each area, from catering to technical support. Your masterplan is the blueprint for this. Give a copy of each list to the person in charge of that area on the day so they can make sure everything gets done.

I don't know what your precise project is, obviously, but here's a list to kick you off with the kind of things you need to remember to sort out – or arrange to have sorted out. They won't all apply to every project, but they give you an idea:

- technical equipment: PowerPoint, PA system, microphones, video, TV, telephones, electricity supply

- space: auditorium, private rooms – to accommodate speakers, or items for auction, or for your team to assemble the press packs at the last minute

- furniture: tables, chairs, lectern, tables for food, flipchart

- toilets: including directions to them

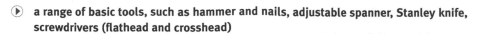 thinking smart

THE GOOD BOOK

You will need to give people copies of checklists that apply to them, but you yourself should have a master file of all checklists and any other paperwork, such as order confirmation notes from suppliers, copies of your invitations to check what arrival time you advertised and so on, copies of any handouts or brochures – anything that could conceivably be needed.

Keep these in a ring-binder file, properly hole punched, so they cannot fall out. This is your bible and you should keep it with you at all times. *Do not lose it.* But – just in case – label it very clearly on the front cover so if it ever did go astray it would be easy to find.

- guests: name badges, handouts/packs, notepads, parking, coats
- catering: meals, tea, coffee
- office services: phones, e-mail facilities, photocopying, fax, paper supplies
- carpentry and electrics: shelving, lighting, display frames
- rubbish: bins, clean up afterwards.

That should give you a starting point for planning your checklists and making sure everything gets done. Of course some projects will have special checklists too, like items for auction (including where they are kept, how they will be distributed and so on), or decorations (for the office party), or typesetting/proofreading checks (for a key report or a newsletter).

And here's an unexpected twist. Now that we've got to the end it's time to tell you that when you create the masterplan, you effectively do it by starting at the end and working backwards. If you get the D-day checklists right, everything that precedes them will fall effortlessly into place. The bulk of the masterplan consists of enabling the checklists; doing what is necessary to make them happen.

REHEARSAL

It is impossible to exaggerate the importance of rehearsing everything you can for an event. Obviously your conference speakers or your presenters will want to rehearse what they're going to say, but the technical equipment should also be rehearsed. And you need to check that people can find their way on and off stage down the steps in the glare of a spotlight, or that the demonstration model still works as well after its arrival at the venue as it did when it left the production depot.

Make sure it really is possible for the strip-o-gram to fit behind the top table to get round to the MD's seat (you may need to use a stand-in to test this – costume optional). And how many visitors can you realistically fit on your exhibition stand if you put the display shelving down the middle like that?

Test and rehearse, test and rehearse. Schedule in time for it, and don't let it get squeezed out. Rehearsal is not a luxury, it's a necessity.

for next time

Clearly, the earlier you start your planning the less sleep you will need to lose to get ready for the big day. So, start preparing your checklists well in advance, and add to them whenever anything else occurs to you. In this way, they will be largely written by the time you get there.

Allow plenty of time to brief your key people so that they know what they are doing, and what sort of hitches they need to let you know about as soon as they can. If you can arrange a spare person as your own gopher for the event itself, so much the better.

Always schedule in rehearsal time for anyone who will need it, technical or otherwise. Never assume that anything will work out fine without testing or rehearsing it: play it safe. It's just so embarrassing when you discover in front of an audience of 500 that Lot 22 won't make it on to the stage without bringing the curtains down on top of the auctioneer.

project in half a day

Whoops! Cutting things a bit fine, aren't we? Still, I assume it's a relatively small project or you wouldn't have left things this late. And you're doing better than the poor devil who's reading the next section (project in an hour).

So if you only have an afternoon or an evening to get your project organized, what do you need to focus on? Well, begin by reading this book; it'll take you an hour at the most, and it will give you an overview of what you need to do. Apart from that, here are a few more guidelines:

- ▶ **Set your objective first – this is not a task that you can afford to skip (however much it might look like it on the surface).**

- ▶ **Keep your meeting with your project owner down to five minutes if you can. You haven't got time to spend any money, so you're only dealing with petty cash anyway as far as the budget is concerned. But you may well want to get them to arrange for some extra pairs of hands for you.**

- ▶ **After this, begin by talking to anyone you need to get on board in order to give them maximum notice that you need their help. If you can't get hold of your first choice, you'll have to find substitutes. Don't hang on for ever waiting for someone to get back from lunch and call you back. If their lunch goes on until four, it could be too late by then – or they might say no anyway. So cut your losses and call someone else now.**

- ▶ **Now draw up your masterplan. This is essential and you cannot hope to get this project completed successfully without it.**

- ▶ **Now just work through your tasks, but keep a firm handle on the time and don't let anything eat up more time than it can justify.**

project in an hour

Blimey! You like to live dangerously, don't you? Still, for a project that is modest in scope (but which may still be hugely important) I guess it's possible. Well, don't let's hang about; here's the score:

1 You don't have to read this whole book right now, but you're going to have to read Chapter 1. You have to set your objective before you do anything else. It will keep you streamlined and efficient – which is going to be essential for the next 60 minutes.

2 Forget Chapter 2 – too late to worry about all that now.

3 If you need help getting this project completed – and I have a hunch you may find it helps – go and ask for it now. But however much of a rush you're in, don't forget to ask nicely, and don't pressure people too hard who want to say no. You'll only blot your copybook for next time.

4 Chapter 3, is vital. It's all about the fastest way to work out exactly what you need to do.

5 I'll précis Chapter 4 for you: just get on and do the work. (Before your next project, when you find time to read Chapter 4, you'll find it puts it more helpfully than that and is well worth reading. But save it for later this time.)

That should just about get you there for now – and no one will know you haven't been planning it for days. But next time, do yourself a favour and find the extra time, however busy you are. If nothing else, at least you'll have time to enjoy it.

the fast thinker's guide to advance planning

Some projects have to be planned well ahead of time. You have to book the exhibition space or the venue, organize the invitations, order new brochures from the printer and so on. Very often, the whole project then goes into hibernation – apart from processing returned invitations and taking deliveries from the printer – until the final mad rush at the last minute (which is what the rest of this book has been about).

But just because the final culmination of all your work won't come round for a few weeks or months, that doesn't mean you have plenty of time on your hands for this initial planning process. You have other projects and pressures to cope with right now, and finding time to plan a project that won't happen until next month or next year isn't something you can spare a lot of time for.

So here is the fast thinking approach to getting this early planning out of the way as quickly as you can so that you can get back to the rest of your mounting pile of work, and at the same time make the project – when it finally does come round – as easy for yourself as possible. Sounds tempting? Then read on.

GETTING STARTED

You'll need to start by finding out as much as you can about the project. To do this, you should find out (if you don't already know) exactly who the idea came from. Then collar this person and sit down with them for a discussion about it. They will have proposed it, whether formally or informally, so now you want to know exactly what is in that proposal.

The sort of questions you want to find the answers to include:

- (▶) **What departments are involved in this project? And which particular people?**
- (▶) **What other suppliers, partners or other outsiders are concerned?**
- (▶) **What is the objective?**
- (▶) **What is the budget (and where's it coming from)?**
- (▶) **What specific plans have been proposed – in other words has a venue been set? A date? Names of key speakers ... and so on.**

Whoever thought up this project in the first place will be able to pass on to you all the ideas and decisions that have so far been formed.

Once you've had this conversation, you now need to identify the project owner (who will not necessarily be the same person) and follow the guidelines in Chapter 2. Find out exactly what resources are at your disposal, and get the project owner firmly on your side.

DECISION MAKING

This is the stage at which most of the major decisions are going to have to be made. Will you launch a full-colour newsletter or go for two colours only? What size space will you book at the exhibition? When should you hold the open day? Which keynote speaker will you build your conference around?

You need to get these decisions out of the way because plenty of other decisions will hang on them. A full-colour newsletter will eat up a big chunk of the budget, which means you won't be able to pay contributors for articles. The size of the exhibition space will determine the size of the stand and its design … and so on. If you make the wrong decisions now, you could find yourself in big trouble later (I don't mean to panic you, but let's be realistic).

There are five essential stages to making the right decision, and you need to go through them all:

1 Set your objective.
2 Collect the facts.
3 Consult.
4 Consider the options.
5 Make the decision.

Let's take the size of your exhibition space as an example. To begin with, what is your objective? Precisely what do you intend to achieve through this decision? We've already looked at setting objectives earlier in the book, so we won't go through the process again. Let's say your objective is to decide what size space to book to attract the optimum number of visitors at an acceptable cost.

That will do fine. Now, the next stage is to collect the facts. To begin with, you'll need to know what the various sizes available are, and what the cost would be for each.

thinking smart

INFORMATION OVERLOAD

Having too much information is one of the curses of modern business. We all have piles of papers, articles, reports, books and magazines on our desk, and endless people telling us we should subscribe to this or that journal as well. But console yourself with this thought: no one else is reading all their stuff, either; they're just not admitting to it. One of today's key management skills is being able to dump loads of bumf in the bin with a clear conscience. So learn to speed read, and to select the few things you do need to read, and offload the rest. You'll go far.

Then you'll want to get the best estimate you can of how many visitors you'll get. So look back at company records of past appearances, find relevant trade press articles, talk to the exhibition organizers, calculate the average value per visitor, and so on.

Before you go on to analyze your options, you need to consult people. For one thing, they may have valuable ideas to offer, and for another you need them to feel involved and included. That way, they are much more likely to be behind you and the project than if they feel left out of it. So talk to anyone else in the company who regularly plans exhibitions appearances – perhaps for another section of the organization – and to anyone in marketing or sales (or any other department) who has experience of staffing the stands.

Now it's time to clarify exactly what sensible options you have. You may well be able to rule out the largest sizes because the cost is simply prohibitive. The smallest sizes may also be bad for the company's image, or may simply not attract the visitors. Look at what's left, and list the options.

If an obvious option doesn't stand out, think through the pros and cons, work out the best and worst possible scenarios, and eliminate any option that isn't the best one until you arrive at a decision.

If you need more help making crucial decisions, you should find *fast thinking: decision* very helpful.

thinking smart

WITHOUT PREJUDICE

When you're considering options, you may have to be strict with yourself about ignoring any personal prejudice. You might prefer a particular decision because that option was your idea. Or you might dislike certain options because you or your department will not do so well out of them. For example, if you're considering what exhibition venue to choose, you might be tempted to go for one that is easy for you to travel to. But force yourself to disregard such personal bias, and weigh up your options objectively.

PRACTICE MAKES PERFECT

Once you've loaded your project software, and spent a few hours learning its principles, one of the best ways to get yourself fully conversant with it is to use it to help somebody else run a project – perhaps a smaller project in your own department.

DRAWING UP THE PLAN

The final stage of the advance planning – before you put your plans largely to sleep for a few weeks – is to draw up the masterplan. You can do this according to the guidelines in Chapter 3, using index cards or paper lists. But since you have a little more time at this stage, it's well worth investing in a PC project-planning system (assuming you don't already have one) and the time to learn it. These systems are now very easy to use, as well as being fun.

Once your plan is completed (for the time being), you have one final task: go through your diary and mark in any tasks that need to be done between now and the final few days of preparation so they can't get forgotten. And contact anyone else who needs to carry out any tasks and make sure they also mark their diaries accordingly. Contact them in writing – memo or e-mail – so there can be no room for confusion or crossed lines.

Remember to mark in your diary any dates when you expect other people to get back to you or to complete tasks, so you can check that everything is on schedule. For example, a date to make sure you have received confirmation of your stand booking, or the date the designer is supposed to get back to you with the first draft design for the stand.

Although you should now be able to all but forget about your project for a while, be prepared to add tasks to your masterplan as they arise (or occur to you) at any time.

thhfhh thinking smart

THE KEY CRITERIA

You might not have any kind of preset conditions for making the right decision. You might have to find a solution that involves using two-colour printing only, or that won't interfere with peak production times. But there are four key criteria to consider when setting your objective for any decision, and it is useful to run through them all mentally each time, to see which apply in this case:

- ▶ cost
- ▶ time
- ▶ quality
- ▶ people – many decisions can cause upset, rifts and loss of motivation, so you may well have to decide on a course of action that won't upset a particular supplier, or that means the MD won't get wind of the plans for the party in advance.

for next time

As you work through your plan over the weeks ahead, make a note on your plan of how long each task or group of tasks takes you to complete. Next time it will be far easier for you to schedule your time. The best initial plan for a new project is the final version of the last time the same project was carried out.

decision

 GATHER THE FACTS

WEIGH UP THE OPTIONS

MAKE THE RIGHT CHOICE

ros jay

contents

introduction

It's decision time. You've been putting it off through pressure of work, or simply because you've no idea what decision to make. But now it's crunch time. It has reached the point where not making a decision is worse than having to make it. People are yelling, problems are mounting, the pressure is piling up ... and all because everything is waiting on your decision. But what should it be?

You're worried you'll make the wrong decision. You're worried you won't be able to make a decision at all. You're worried the yelling will get even louder. Well, you can stop worrying now. This book will guide you quickly and cleanly through the process, and before you know it the decision will be clear. Obvious, even. And once you've learnt the system this time, decisions will never seem so scary again.

As a manager, you may not have to make that many big decisions. But their importance is out of all proportion to the time they occupy: it is one of the most important parts of your job. The kind of decisions managers have to make can cover a massive range of possibilities. Here are just a few of them to give you a flavour of the kind of decision this book is about:

- ▶ **which candidate to appoint following last week's selection interviews**
- ▶ **what to do about the bottleneck in the production line**
- ▶ **which supplier to sign with for the next year**
- ▶ **whether to give a big customer the extremely big discount they're demanding**
- ▶ **whether to put the entire marketing budget into one huge campaign next year, or whether to spend it on several smaller campaigns**
- ▶ **which product name to go with for the new range**
- ▶ **whether to stop providing company cars for employees who don't travel as part of the job.**

They may not be earth-shattering decisions on a global scale, but they're a good deal more important than what time to take your coffee break. And, invariably, they affect other people. That's why they've all started yelling. They have decisions to make – whether large or small – which are hanging on your decision. And all that pressure just seems to make the whole thing worse.

Don't worry. This time tomorrow, they'll all have the decision they need (even if it isn't the one they want). In an ideal world you'd have given yourself longer to make this decision, but this isn't an ideal world. Anyway, now you know, you'll leave longer next time (won't you?). This book will fill you in on how to invest the extra time in future. Meantime, you want to get this decision made – and you need to be sure it's the right one. So you need:

tips for pulling together the information you need fast

 shortcuts for avoiding any unnecessary work

 checklists to make sure you have all the essentials covered

… all put together clearly and simply. And short enough to read fast, of course.

And what if you've cut it even finer than I was allowing for? What if the decision has to be made by this afternoon? Well, don't panic. Anything's possible. At the back of the book you'll find a brief guide to making a decision in an evening. In fact, even if you've squeezed the decision into the final hour before the deadline, you can still manage it. The one-hour version at the end shows you how to pull out all the stops and work at the speed of life.

So relax. Take a deep breath, and go and get yourself a cup of coffee before you start. You're not just going to make the decision here, you're going to make the very best possible decision. After all, the wrong decision can be worse than no decision at all. So we're not only going to act fast, we're going to think smart too.

▶ work at the speed of life

This book will take you swiftly and simply through the seven key steps of decision making:

1 The very first stage is to identify your objective. It may sound obvious, but it can go dramatically wrong if you don't think before you start, and be sure you're making the right decision.

2 Next, you need to decide to take the decision. I know it sounds pathetically obvious, but actually managers often go wrong by taking a decision that they should have passed on to someone else, or that should have been deferred.

3 Once you're clear about exactly what you're aiming to achieve, it's time to assemble all the facts you need. Without them, you cannot be sure of making the best decision.

4 I've already mentioned that your decision is bound to affect other people. This is why you must consult. It can take days or even weeks, but we're going to do it in a matter of hours, because that's all we've got.

5 You can't possibly decide what action to take until you know what the options are. So this next stage is all about identifying your options.

6 Here it comes: decision time. But once you've been through the earlier stages, you'll find it's nothing like as daunting as it looked from a distance. And we'll be looking at all sorts of tips and tools for helping you reach the right decision.

7 Once you've made the decision, it's no good keeping it to yourself. You have to communicate it to all those yelling people. And since it's your decision, you have to look after it and make sure it's followed through.

fast thinking gambles

This sounds easy. Shall we make all our decisions in 24 hours from now on? What's the point in spending any longer on them if we don't have to? Well, it can be done in 24 hours, but it really isn't the best way. Just because you're getting away with it this time, doesn't mean your luck can hold out for ever. There are reasons why you really need to leave longer for this kind of important decision if you possibly can.

- ▶ **The most obvious gamble you take is that you may not come up with the best decision. If you follow the guidelines in this book you'll certainly avoid making bad decisions, but that isn't the same thing as making the best possible decision.**

- ▶ **One of the vital, and sometimes the most time-consuming, stages of the process is collecting all the facts. Sometimes certain key facts simply can't be found this fast. It might take a few days – perhaps the only person with the vital information is on holiday, or maybe you have to run tests to find out what outcome certain actions would have.**

- ▶ **You need to consult other people for the vast majority of decisions. This can take a while to organise, particularly if you want to talk to a group of employees or colleagues.**

- ▶ **Consultation has a psychological angle too: people like to feel involved. If they feel they are being consulted at the last minute, without time to prepare their response fully, they will be resentful whatever decision you finally arrive at. For controversial decisions this can be catastrophic.**

Fast thinking will ensure that you reach a decision – and a good one at that – in minimal time. Right now, I imagine that's the most important thing. But if you want to make the best decision every time, and keep everyone else happy into the bargain, you'll need to leave yourself a little more time in future.

There are reasons why you really need to leave longer for this kind of important decision if you possibly can

343

1 identify your objective

The most vital part of the whole process is the bit that comes right at the beginning. If you're even slightly adrift at the start, you could be way off course by the end of the thing – the decision itself. So setting your objective is not a waste of precious time (I'm sure that never crossed your mind); it's your means of navigating your way through the decision. Set your course correctly from the outset, and the whole journey will run more smoothly, and you'll arrive at the right destination.

And you do all this by identifying your objective. Suppose the problem that you are trying to resolve is that there is a bottleneck in the production department. It's creating frustrations and slowing down production to a point where you can't fulfil orders on time. You have to decide what to do about it. But you'll run into difficulties early on if your objective is simply: *To decide how to clear the bottleneck in production.*

The problem is that this just isn't specific enough. It sets no boundaries or conditions. It doesn't state whether there is a cost limitation, or how soon optimum production levels should be re-established. This is going to make it pretty difficult to make the right decision. You might come up with the perfect decision – except that it costs too much to implement, or takes too long. So make your objective more specific: *To decide how to clear the bottleneck in production without exceeding the annual budget, and so that normal production levels are reached within two weeks.*

If you think about it, this makes it far easier to take the decision. Too much choice always makes it tough, but once you narrow it down it's far more likely that the best option will jump out at you.

thinking smart

thinking smart

THE KEY CRITERIA
You might have any kind of preset conditions for making the right decision. You might have to find a solution that involves using two-colour printing only, or that won't interfere with coffee break times. But there are four key criteria to consider when setting your objective for any decision, and it is useful to run through them all mentally each time, to see which apply:
- ▶ cost
- ▶ time
- ▶ quality
- ▶ people – many decisions can cause upset, rifts and loss of motivation. So you may well have to decide on a course of action that won't upset a particular supplier, or that means the MD won't get wind of the problem.

for next time

Before you reach this stage – the point where you have to get on and take the decision – you should already be aware of the criteria you have to meet. You presumably have a file on this matter, so jot down any key criteria while you're building up the file in advance of making the decision. Make sure they really are essential preconditions, and not just desirable results.

For example, it may be essential that you clear the bottleneck in production within two weeks of your decision on how to do it. On the other hand, it may be that you'd really *like* to clear it within two weeks, but you could just about fulfil your orders if it wasn't cleared for another four weeks.

So make sure that the criteria you set down in your objective really are essential. By the time you come to set your objective, you should already know what all of them are.

The most vital part of the whole process is the bit that comes right at the beginning

2 decide to take the decision

For crying out loud! First of all we're supposed to be in a tearing hurry, and now we're expected to waste time messing about with word games. 'Decide to take the decision' – what's that supposed to mean?

Well, if you'll be patient, I'll explain. You may be in a hurry, but you could be about to waste yourself a lot of time. You wouldn't be the first person to do it. The fact is that a lot of people agonise for ages over a decision they shouldn't be taking at all. Only they haven't noticed they shouldn't be taking it.

So now you've identified exactly what your decision is – what objective it must achieve – you're in a position to double check that you really need to take it at all, before you go any further. This is actually a decision in itself, of course.

Why on earth (you may be wondering) would you decide not to take the decision? We're only here now because this decision has absolutely got to be taken, and you can't put it off any longer.

Not necessarily. There are several reasons why you might decide against going ahead. Here are the most obvious ones to consider:

- ▶ **It may become apparent that this is really a decision for someone else entirely. Clearing the production bottleneck might be a job for the production director, and not for you as production manager at all.**

- ▶ **Perhaps the decision is yours, but only partly. Maybe you are authorised to decide what happens to the production line, but it's up to personnel to decide how much overtime can be worked. So a joint decision will be needed to integrate these two factors.**

- ▶ **Sometimes you can resolve the issue by tackling a different or bigger problem, and thereby avoid a decision on this one altogether. Perhaps there's a proposal on the**

thinking fast

ONE-WAY TICKET TO NOWHERE

Sometimes it becomes clear at this point that the decision is impossible under the criteria you're working to. Perhaps there is no option that will enable you to clear the production bottleneck without exceeding your budget by at least 50 per cent, and one of your criteria is that you should do it within your existing budget. You won't have all the facts yet (we're doing that bit later), but you may well have enough to see that the decision isn't feasible as it stands.

In this case you should stop now. Save yourself several hours' fruitless activity. Go to your boss, or whoever has set you this impossible task, and get the criteria changed before you go any further. Otherwise you are heading straight down a decision-making dead end.

table to outsource production. If this goes ahead, you won't want to have wasted resources on clearing a bottleneck that was expensive to sort out. Maybe you're better off making a decision on a stop-gap solution, rather than on a permanent one.

- ▶ This decision may depend on another one that hasn't yet been made. Maybe the root of the problem is with your suppliers, who can't deliver key components ready assembled. If they did, the bottleneck would resolve itself. So in fact, you can't make a decision until you've sorted out the issue of your supplier. If the bottleneck doesn't disappear, *then* you can decide what to do about it.

- ▶ Maybe you should be taking the decision, but not now. Perhaps this is the busiest time of year in production and, slow as it is, the present devil you know is better than the horrendous disruption you could cause by changing the system. Better to wait, perhaps, until a quiet time of year before you get this one sorted out.

It should be clear by now that it is deeply unwise to take it for granted that you should be making this decision, or making it now. Always ask yourself whether or not to take the decision. And the answer will be a decision in itself. So once you've been through this process, you've already got one decision tucked under your belt. That should make you feel a bit better about the whole process.

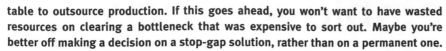 for next time

You should be on the lookout for this kind of thing as soon as you plan to make a decision. If it is better not to take it, the sooner you know, the sooner you can prepare someone else to take it, or find a short-term alternative, or get on with the other decision on which this one is dependent.

And, of course, as soon as you offload or defer a decision, you cut down your own workload in the process. And I strongly suspect that's always welcome.

3 assemble the facts

$a = 2$
$b = 3$
What is $a + b$?

That was pretty simple wasn't it? (At least, it was if you reached the answer 5. If not, you're in trouble.)

Let's try another one:

$a = 2$
$b = 3$
What is $a + c$?

Aha! Not so easy this time. In fact, downright impossible. And why? Because you simply don't have the information you need to decide on the correct answer. All you can do is make a random guess and hope it's the right one.

It's obvious when you're doing algebra, but when it comes to making decisions, far too many managers fail to spot the obvious. They try to take decisions when they simply don't have all the information they need to find the correct solution. But just as with algebra, if you don't have all the facts, you can't expect to get the answer right.

That's why the next stage in the process is collecting together all the information you need. No matter how urgently you need to make this decision, you cannot do it without the necessary facts, or you risk making the wrong decision.

WHAT FACTS?

Collecting the facts is often the sticking point for decision makers, for one of two reasons:

- ▶ **You have far too much information, and you don't know where to start sifting it all (or you simply can't face it).**

- ▶ **You haven't got the information you need, and you can't get your head round the process of collecting it – you haven't the time, or you don't know where to go for it.**

You may well recognise one – or even both – of these. They usually explain why the decision has been put off until the last minute. So our job now is to assemble all the facts

 thinking smart

INFORMATION OVERLOAD

Having too much information is one of the curses of modern business. We all have piles of papers, articles, reports, books and magazines on our desk, and endless people telling us we should subscribe to this or that journal as well. But console yourself with this thought: no one else is reading all their stuff, either; they're just not admitting to it. One of today's key management skills is being able to dump loads of bumf in the bin with a clear conscience. So learn to speed read, and to select the few things you do need to read, and offload the rest. You'll go far.

you need without tripping ourselves up on either of these stumbling blocks. And the way we go about it is the same, whether you have too much or too little information.

The tendency is to start with the information you've got. And that's what can make the process so difficult. You need to approach the whole question of facts from the opposite angle: what information do you need?

Take a sheet of paper and divide it into two columns. Head the first column 'must know' and the second column 'prefer to know', like this:

Must know	Prefer to know

Now forget the information you actually have available, and just think about what information you need. Suppose you're trying to decide which of three suppliers of key components you're going to sign a contract with for the next 12 months. There are certain things you absolutely have to know, such as:

- ▶ their prices
- ▶ their reliability
- ▶ the quality of their components
- ▶ their billing system

… and so on.

Then there are other factors, which aren't so essential, but which may influence your decision, especially if it's fairly borderline. These could include:

- ▶ how flexible they are
- ▶ which of your competitors they supply
- ▶ how high their customer service standards are.

Your list will start to shape up something like this:

Must know	Prefer to know
Price	Flexibility
Reliability	Which competitors they supply
Quality of components	Customer service
Billing system	standards

thinking smart

BALANCING ACT

The facts that go on your 'prefer to know' list should be weighed up carefully. We know they should not be essentials, but neither should they simply be whims. For example, you might be interested to know whether you personally like the person you'd be dealing with regularly at each supplier company, but is it actually going to influence your decision in any way? Hopefully not. So don't put it down on either list.

MAKING SPACE

Leave enough space on your list to fill in the answers – or a précis of each – once you have them. This will give you a really useful single-sheet summary of key facts later on, when you come to weigh up the decision. You can staple longer documents or summary sheets from reports to the back of it, so you have all your key information in one sheaf of papers.

So now, before you've even started looking at a single report, price list, catalogue or record, you have narrowed right down to the minimum the field of information you need to bother with. If you don't need to know it, it never has to pass before your eyes at all. When you're working against the clock, this will save you a lot of time. And, as you can see, it's also a much smarter way of working.

FINDING YOUR FACTS

So now you know what information you need, it's time to go fetch. Of course, you're limited by your time constraints, so you won't be able to do any lengthy research. There isn't time to get hold of samples of each supplier's components and test them exhaustively. Maybe you've already done this, or maybe you don't need to. But you'll be able to get most of what you need by talking to people, digging out papers from files (or from the pile on your desk), e-mailing and using the Internet. (If you need to dig out a lot of information, it's worth reading one of the other books in this series, *fast thinking: finding facts*.)

Look at each piece of information you need to find, and think about where the best place to get it is. By best, I mean the most reliable source but also the fastest where there is a choice. In the case of the example here, I should imagine you could get most of it from the suppliers over the phone. But of course it's not always that easy.

Here's a checklist (though not an exhaustive one) of places to consider for getting the information you want:

- ▶ **talking to people – suppliers, customers, experts, colleagues**
- ▶ **books**
- ▶ **competitors' annual reports**
- ▶ **minutes of past meetings**
- ▶ **internal management reports and monthly figures**
- ▶ **other internal reports and survey results**
- ▶ **magazine and newspaper articles**

FACE THE FACT

If you are missing an essential piece of information that will take longer to find than you have, go back and have another look at Chapter 2. You should have decided not to take this decision now, as without essential information you cannot take the right decision (except with pot luck on your side). If you *can* manage without it, it shouldn't be in your 'must know' column, but your 'prefer to know' column.

(▷) **publicly available information and statistics – from trade associations, market research reports, government departments, and so on.**

You should be able to access most of these within a day, using the phone, e-mail, the Internet and your feet (at least within the building).

So the process is simple. Here's a recap:

1 List the facts you need in order to take the decision, categorising them as 'must know' or 'prefer to know'.

2 Work through your list, deciding on the best (fast) source for each piece of information.

3 Go and find each fact.

Clearly there's no point in separating your facts into two lists if you're going to treat them both the same, so you're not. The second list is not compulsory. However, in an ideal world, you should aim to collect about 80 per cent of these facts. Actually, that's not really true: in an ideal world you should collect 100 per cent of them. But in the real world, when the pressure's on, aim for about 80 per cent. If there are some you feel would be more useful than others, you will presumably give them priority.

Having said all that, if the facts on the lists are allocated to the correct columns, it should be possible to make the right decision without any of the facts on the 'prefer to know' list. However, they will make it much easier for you to decide when the time comes. And they will, collectively, account for a significant percentage of the weight of argument, even though individually each one is not essential.

FACT-FINDING PITFALLS

Some facts are easy to find, and reliable once you have them. The example of which supplier to choose might fall into this category. If you're selecting the right candidate for a job, you should have all the information you need already, once you've completed the interviews (*see fast thinking: selection interview*). But some decisions are complicated or technical (or both). For example, you might be trying to decide into which of several possible campaigns to put a large chunk of your marketing budget.

The process for assembling the facts you need is exactly the same, but there are certain pitfalls into which the unwary decision maker may fall. So here's a quick guide to alert you to the most dangerous heffalump traps in the information jungle.

Trusting statistics

Some statistical information may not be as reliable as you need it to be. For example, while you will no doubt trust figures from the Institute of Direct Marketing on the relative value of different types of campaign (advertising, direct mail or whatever), data assembled by, say, a big publishing company might be biased in favour of press advertising. A trained historian's standard question is 'Why did this document come into being?'

You will have to use your own judgement to decide which data to rely on – and go for the most reliable sources in the first place if you can. You will also have to make up your own mind how much it matters. If you think a certain figure may be slightly biased but you only need a ballpark estimate, perhaps you will decide to use the figures anyway. The important thing is to recognise when the data you're using is not wholly reliable.

351

TIMING OUT

Obviously, you have to have all the information on your 'must know' list. That's the point of it. But the best approach to the 'prefer to know' list is to collect all the information you can quickly, but forget anything you can't find fast. One way to do this is to set yourself a time limit. If you haven't got hold of each fact on this list within a certain time, give up (unless you can see you really are almost there). The time limit is up to you, and depends on how much of a rush you're in. But try five or ten minutes as a starting point. This may mean you can abandon some facts before you even start, because you just know you won't get hold of them that fast.

Making assumptions

It's frighteningly easy to do this without even knowing it. Many managers fall into the trap of thinking they know more than they do. It's easy to see it with the more overconfident, arrogant type, but even charming, humble people like us do it sometimes. The problem is, we have a fair amount of experience of our subject, so we assume our 'knowledge' is reliable. For example, as a marketing person, it's easy to think 'direct mail is better targeted than advertising, so it's got to be a more cost-effective option.'

You may be right but, then again, you may not. So do the research and verify your assumptions, otherwise you could go very wrong. If you collect (or assume) misinformation, you're almost bound to make a wrong decision. Lord Kelvin, an eminent scientist who was president of the Royal Society at the end of the nineteenth century, has gone down in history for saying 'Heavier-than-air flying machines are impossible.' Presumably he was making inaccurate assumptions to arrive at this conclusion.

Treating estimates as facts

It's often necessary to make your own calculations of the probability of a certain outcome, in order to feed this information into your decision-making process. You might want to calculate, for example, the income from a direct mail campaign. You're going to have to estimate certain figures to work on, such as the likely response rate, the size of the mailing and so on. You'll have checked your estimates, of course, and you'll judge the best figures to use. But it's very easy to start taking these figures as gospel.

Suppose you've assumed a 7 per cent response to your mailing. You know how many customers you're going to mail, and you know your average order value. Anyway, you can do several calculations for different sizes of mailings. And for different order values. The danger is that you will forget that your response rate of 7 per cent is only a best guess. If you treat it as a fact rather than an estimate, you may rely too heavily on your calculations. So remember that the response rate might turn out to be 8 per cent, or only 5 per cent.

Looking for information that doesn't exist

Believe it or not, even in this electronic age, there are some pieces of information that have never been recorded. Or if they have, you ain't never gonna find them. You

thinking smart

WORD OF WARNING

Research indicates that our minds are unconsciously biased towards whatever estimate we settle on, even though we know it is only an estimate. So if you decide to estimate a response rate of 7 per cent to your mailshot you are likely to find, if you have the sense to remember that it's only an estimate, that you calculate for anywhere between 5 and 9 per cent. Very wise. But the true figure might actually have been 2 per cent, or 14 per cent. Your initial estimate anchors you to it, and can close your mind to wider options. So look out.

can waste hours or even days looking for stuff that isn't there. Some managers even put off decisions to the point of causing major disruption, because they are holding out for information that doesn't exist. And sometimes, it is even information on your 'must know' list that you can't track down.

The sooner you can recognise that the information simply isn't going to materialise, the sooner you can find an alternative and get on and make your decision. Think about those heavier-than-air flying machines again. The early inventors could feed in all the scientific data available, but I can tell you what would be top of my 'must know' list: is this thing going to fly or not? And there is no way that information is available until *after* you've made the decision on whether or not to jump from the top of the tallest building with the thing strapped to your back.

So face it. If the information isn't there, stop looking. Collect all the information you can to make a best possible estimate, and settle for that.

At the end of this stage, you should have collected all the facts you need to make the decision. And I hope you'll be feeling a whole lot happier. But although you may have all the hard facts, there's still one more ingredient you need: other people's input. That's what the next chapter is all about.

for next time

Some facts take longer to collect than others, so give yourself plenty of time for the information that it will take a while to pull together. Maybe you need to get it from other people who are hard to pin down, or maybe you need to run tests or trials and feed the results in to your decision.

The more time you allow, the easier it is to delegate fact-finding, too. It's pretty difficult to free up someone to dig out data for you at a moment's notice, but tell them you don't need it for a fortnight and suddenly they are much more cooperative.

4 consult

Winston Churchill would never have taken a key decision without consulting his Cabinet and his military advisers. Julius Caesar listened to advice (although famously he didn't take it from the soothsayer). Napoleon consulted his generals. But some managers think they can make key decisions all by themselves.

Well you can't. You almost always need to consult other people before you make any important decision, and especially one that will affect them. You need to do this for two reasons:

1 *To collect their input and opinions*. There's every chance that someone else will know something you don't, or will have thought of an option that you hadn't. Or perhaps you need to know that if you make a particular decision the whole of accounts is going to be up in arms, or production will slow down by 5 per cent.

2 *To make them feel included and involved*. If people who are affected by your decision feel that they haven't had an opportunity to put their case, they are likely to be resentful of any decision that doesn't exactly suit them. Lack of consultation can lead to general demotivation and frustration and, of course, people will be far less committed to a decision they feel they had no part in.

WHO TO CONSULT?

So who are you going to talk to about this decision? Well, obviously the people who you think are most likely to have something useful to say about it. This might mean colleagues, outside experts, your own team, your senior managers, your customers or your suppliers. Phoning an IT expert is a form of consultation, just as much as calling a team meeting to discuss the issue.

Think about who might have information you don't know about, or don't know you need. For example, maybe your predecessor as marketing manager might be happy to talk to you about previous campaigns and what did and didn't work – whether they are still in the organisation or not. But you are not simply fact-finding here – the information is doubtless on record anyway. You are looking for interpretations of those facts from your predecessor: why did this campaign work and that one fail?

HOW TO CONSULT

If your decision is relatively uncontroversial, consulting is easier. When you speak to senior colleagues or outsiders, a phone call will often do the trick. But if anyone is likely

thinking smart

GET THE BOSS ON BOARD
Whether or not your boss has to approve your decision, it is always better to involve them in the process. Not only are they likely to have a useful input, but they are much more likely to back your decision if they feel they contributed towards it.

QUALITY NOT QUANTITY

The more people you consult, the longer it will take. So when time is as precious as it is now, think carefully about whose input you most need. Look for a spread of expertise between your advisers, rather than talking to several people who are likely to cover much the same ground.

GO TO THE TOP

However pushed for time you are, don't exclude anyone who is likely to be upset by a controversial decision. However, you don't have to consult every last person. If another department is going to be affected by your decision, consult the department head. It is their responsibility to collect input from their team, if they want to, and pass it on to you.

to be upset by the outcome of your decision, or if they will be deeply affected by it, always consult them formally. This means three things:

1　Agree a time and place to discuss the issue face-to-face.

2　Give them as much warning as you can.

3　Talk to them alone.

Right now, the time and place may be your office in half an hour. But the more time people have to prepare, the more satisfied they will feel that they've had a chance to put their case to you properly. An element of formality reassures them that you are taking their views seriously. If you simply stop someone in the corridor and say: 'By the way, which floor do you reckon your department should get when we move to the new offices?' they may not even realise they've been consulted.

LISTENING IS NOT THE SAME AS FOLLOWING

Just because you listen to someone's advice, it doesn't mean to say you have to take it. This is your decision, it's not being taken by vote. There's no point asking anyone for a view if you're not going to take account of it, but neither should you follow it for the sake of it. After all, you are the one in possession of all the necessary facts, and you know what the other people you've consulted have said, too.

However, make a note of what the people you've consulted have said; you'll be needing it later (as you'll see when you get to Chapter 7). You will also want to feed

PHONE VERSUS E-MAIL

You can ask people's advice or opinions by e-mail – and if you're in a hurry it may be the only way. Speaking face to face or by phone is better if you can manage it – it gives you a chance to question and listen to nuances of tone. On the other hand, you can blanket e-mail a lot of people quickly if you want a quick 'yes/no' or 'pick option A or B' type response from a lot of people. So pick the best medium for the job.

You almost always need to consult other people before you make any important decision

LESS IS MORE

The more opinions you ask, the more likely they are to conflict with each other. So don't let it get to the point where you simply become confused (as if you had the time to talk to that many people, anyway). You avoided information overload successfully when you assembled your facts; stick to the same approach here.

these views into your final decision making, by which time you may have forgotten who said what, or even what it was they said. It may make a big difference to know from whom a certain opinion came, or exactly what the opinion was. What's more, they may have forgotten what they said, and your notes will serve to remind you both if they deny they said it. So jot it down, and keep it with your sheet of ready facts.

for next time

If you allow more time for consultation, it opens up new possibilities. You might get in a firm of consultants to advise you on the departmental reorganisation before you make the final decision. If you're really pushed for time, phoning someone in the USA or Australia might be out simply because you haven't got time to get hold of them. A little more time could have been a big help.

More time is also a huge advantage for a controversial decision. If you consult people this afternoon and then announce your decision tomorrow morning, they are likely to feel you had already made up your mind and the consultation was only a token one. And there's the danger that they will feel they haven't had the opportunity to prepare. So consult well in advance, especially where the decision is likely to provoke an emotional response.

5 identify the options

Many people reach this stage and then make their decision intuitively. Once they have all the information and input, they simply decide. This is certainly fast, but we set out to reach the *right* decision, if you remember, not just a fast one. So we're going to do this properly.

Having said that, an intuitive decision is fine at this point for small decisions, such as where to hold next week's appraisal interviews or how to organise your filing cabinet (the earlier stages won't have taken long, either). You haven't got time to go through a methodical decision-making process 20 times a day. But I don't imagine you bought this book to help you with that sort of decision.

If your decision is important enough to be reading this book, it's important enough to get right. And research has shown time and again that a methodical approach gives you a better chance of making the right decision than intuition does – although it often seems otherwise because we tend to be happy to live with wrong decisions taken on gut feeling.

You've done all the preparation, and you can now begin to make your decision. And the very first thing you have to do is to identify your options. These are what you'll be deciding between, so you'd better know what they are.

Some options will be obvious, of course. You knew all along that one of the options for cutting down on company cars was to provide them only for employees who travel as part of their job. And another option was to leave things as they are. But a classic error many decision makers commit is to limit their options. Too often, they give themselves an either/or choice. So the first thing to do is to come up with more options.

In the case of the company cars, there could be other routes you might take; maybe someone else has suggested another option to you during your consultation period. For example, how about:

- ▶ **letting anyone who already has a company car keep it, but not allowing anyone else to have one (unless they need it to work)**
- ▶ **giving employees a travel allowance instead of a car**
- ▶ **giving company cars only to people who have been with the organisation for more than five years.**

All of these ideas cut down the total expenditure on company cars, and you now have five options instead of two. That has to equip you better for making the best decision.

thinking smart

THE FORGOTTEN OPTION
Remember that doing nothing is often one of your options.

thinking smart

GIVE ME MORE

Alfred Sloan, the former president of General Motors (and universally acknowledged as one of the greatest businessmen of all time), had a habit of adjourning meetings in which he was presented with an either/or choice. He would insist that his executives went away until they could come up with more options.

thinking smart

THE VALUE OF INTUITION

If you are one of those people who has a strong sense of intuition, and confidence in your own gut feelings, you certainly shouldn't disregard these. However, don't rely on them to the exclusion of all else. If the decision matters, it's worth putting all your resources into getting it right, not leaving it to intuition alone.

KEEP IT FEASIBLE

You want to give yourself as many options as you can, within reason. That is to say that 500 options is more than you can deal with (especially in the time you've got left), but half a dozen – at this stage – is certainly better than only two.

However, there's no point generating just any options, however unrealistic. You need to come up with feasible options. Setting your objective right at the beginning will help with this – you're looking for options that fit the objective, including any constraints such as cost or time. But some options that fit the objective clearly aren't feasible. For example, there's not a lot of point suggesting that employees share company cars one to every six employees, so each one has the car for a month and then passes it on.

GENERATING OPTIONS

So how exactly are you supposed to come up with all these options? You have very little time to play with here, and suddenly you're supposed to generate ideas at the drop of a hat. That's right. Your thinking hat. It's time to put it on and come up with some creative ideas.

If there was only one, blindingly obvious option open to you, you'd have made the decision weeks ago, wouldn't you? You're in this position because the best course of action isn't clear to you. Perhaps none of the options seems very appealing. In these situations a highly creative, unexpected solution can often turn out to be the best. But you have to think of it first.

If you think you're not creative, you may feel yourself starting to panic at this point. You're not really an ideas person. Only hours to go and you've got to come up with new, fresh and creative solutions. You can't do it, can you?

thinking fast

DON'T GET BOGGED DOWN

You don't have to conduct a detailed feasibility study on every option at this stage – we'll do that later if it needs doing at all. Just think briefly through each option to make sure that it isn't obviously unfeasible.

thinking smart

As you think about the problem allow your mind to wander towards sleep. Very often, your unconscious mind will show you the solution to your problem

> **BELIEVE IT**
>
> One of the keys to arriving at creative answers is the belief that there is a solution. The psychological effect of doubting that the answer exists is strong enough to prevent you finding it. Henry Ford said: 'Whether you believe you can, or whether you believe you can't, you're absolutely right.' So be confident: the answer is out there and you're going to find it.

Of course you can. We're all capable of being highly creative, if we know how to be. Creativity is a skill you can learn. Sure, some people find it comes more naturally than others do, but we can all learn it – and fast (which may be more to the point right now). All you need is a few creative techniques for generating ideas quickly.

Problem reversal

This is a quick and easy creativity technique. All you have to do is to phrase your problem – 'we're spending too much on company cars' – and then reverse it. So you get 'we're not spending enough on company cars'. Now try to think of solutions to this reversed problem. How about these:

- ▶ **We should buy bigger and better cars for everyone.**
- ▶ **We should give company cars to everyone, right down to the part-time cafeteria trainee.**
- ▶ **We should give some employees two cars.**

You might be wondering where this has got you. Well, it's opened up new channels of thinking, that's what. You can now look at these apparently barmy ideas and use them to generate new and feasible ideas to the real problem:

- ▶ **The idea of bigger and better cars might give you the idea of grading the type of cars you give people. Long service enables you to progress from a much cheaper car than the present standard to a much better one. If you grade the progress correctly the overall bill will be cheaper, but the cars are still there, and so is the motivation to stay with the company.**
- ▶ **Company cars for absolutely everyone could lead you to think of other forms of transport. Perhaps you could give junior people bicycles (depending on your location). Or you could have a collective form of transport. If you're five miles, from the nearest station, you could run a company shuttle bus to and from it each morning and evening.**
- ▶ **Two cars per employee sounds daft, but what about two employees per car? What about allocating cars to certain people on the condition that they use it to give other employees who live nearby a free lift to and from work?**

You see, this is a quick and simple technique for coming up with some original options. Everyone is different – you would probably have come up with different solutions from the same problem reversal. That's fine. So long as you generate original and realistic ideas, you have a better chance of making the right decision.

Random stimulation

Like most creativity techniques, this one's fun too. And fast. The idea is really to knock your mind sideways into a different way of thinking – so you come up with different ideas from last time.

QUANTITY EQUALS QUALITY

One of the best things about creativity is that whoever you are – Einstein or just an ordinary mortal like the rest of us – the number of good ideas you have will be a fairly consistent proportion of the total. Einstein had more good ideas than most of us, but then he had more bad ideas too. The point was that he just had lots of them. So the route to having good ideas is simply to generate plenty. If one idea in ten is good, you're better off having 200 ideas than just 20.

Start by selecting a word at random. Try opening a dictionary with your eyes shut, pointing at a word, and then opening your eyes. This is the word you have to work with. If you haven't got a dictionary to hand, pick the name of the first object you see, or take a random word from another book. Suppose you pick the word 'sugar'. Now think about sugar for a while:

- ▶ **It's sweet.**
- ▶ **It comes from a plant.**
- ▶ **It comes in lumps or grains.**
- ▶ **You can eat it.**
- ▶ **There are lots of varieties.**
- ▶ **It makes you fat.**

It's up to you what attributes of sugar you come up with. You don't have to be comprehensive. After thinking about it for a while, go back to your company car problem and think about the two things in tandem – sugar and company cars. See how thinking about sugar can help to stimulate ideas:

- ▶ **Lots of varieties might lead you to a much wider range of company vehicles, planned to reduce the overall bill. Perhaps you could offer everyone a bicycle, certain people a travel allowance, further up the scale people could qualify for a small second-hand car, and on up to a Rolls for the MD.**
- ▶ **Eating sugar might take your mind on to corporate entertaining, and expense accounts. Perhaps you could offset company cars against the expense account – the more expensive the car, the lower the expenses allowance.**
- ▶ **Sugar makes you fat, and so does driving – compared with walking, jogging or cycling. Perhaps you could get rid of the company cars as part of a corporate fitness campaign. Spend some of the savings on putting in a really good gym in the basement, and offer a free bicycle to anyone who wants it. That way, you may be taking away with one hand, but you're giving with the other.**

Sensory images

One more for now, and then it's time to get on with making your decision. All you do here is think about your five senses in relation to the problem, and see if any of them helps to generate an idea. What does the idea of 'sound' in relation to company cars make you think of, for example? It can help to sit back, close your eyes and relax for this technique (if you can). Here are a couple of ideas:

- sound. If you take away people's company cars, give them a really good sound system to put into the car they have to buy for themselves as a compensation.

- smell. This might make you think of the smell of leather seats. How about another form of compensation? Why not upgrade the offices of employees who lose their company cars: large-screen monitors, swivel leather armchair, that sort of thing?

Hypnogogic imagery

This technique works well for many people, but you have to be tired enough to go to sleep (you don't actually have to have a nap – I doubt you have time). Or you may be able to wait until bedtime to do it.

Hypnogogic images are those dream images you see as you are starting to drift into sleep, but before you completely lose consciousness. The idea is to close your eyes, relax and clear your mind of any other thoughts. Then focus on the decision you have to make, and on the question you want answered: how can I reduce spending on company cars?

As you think about the problem, allow your mind to wander towards sleep and to generate its own images. Just before you fall asleep, rouse yourself and record the images before you forget them. Very often, your unconscious mind will show you the solution to your problem.

You can vary this technique – if time allows – by actually falling asleep and recording your dreams when you awake. This method is commonly known as 'sleeping on it', and it really can work. One of the best examples is the guy who invented the sewing machine (a chap called Elias Howe). He was having problems with the design of the needle, which he couldn't get to work. One night, he dreamt he was attacked by a band of savages carrying spears. The spears all had holes in the tips. Howe realised when he woke that this was the answer to his problem; the hole should go in the tip of the needle, not in the other end as it does on an ordinary needle.

Drawing techniques

The creative function is located in the right side of the brain, along with visual perception, while verbal skills are handled in the left brain. So if you use visual rather than verbal techniques, they can connect with your creative powers more readily since they are closer together. This is why many people find that doodling and drawing are more creative than verbal techniques.

One of the simplest methods is simply to draw the challenge as you see it. To decide how to handle the company cars problem, maybe you draw cars all over the page, or someone tearing up banknotes, or irate staff waiting on station platforms. You might doodle bicycles everywhere, or lots of people balancing on one car. Everyone's drawings and doodles will be different, but as you focus on the problem and draw whatever comes into your head, you often find you've stimulated an idea that gives you a new option.

 thinking smart

STAY COOL

Although these techniques are effective whatever your mood, you will find that the more you can relax the better you free up your unconscious mind to generate creative ideas for you. I know this isn't a great moment to say this with a crucial decision impending but ... try to relax.

Doodles are more abstract than drawings, and some people find this freeform approach more stimulating. The idea is to concentrate on the decision you need to make and simply doodle at random. When you've filled the page, look at what you've drawn and somewhere in it you should see something which gives you a new perspective on the decision in front of you.

Some people like to experiment by creating different doodles. You can do this by, for example:

▶ **Using coloured pens, paints or even finger painting – whatever you fancy**

▶ **Doodling with your eyes closed**

▶ **Using the other hand from usual to draw with**

RING THE CHANGES

Well, you should have more options on the table now than you had a few minutes ago. I'm not suggesting you use all these techniques – at least, not right now. Use whichever appeals to you. And then use a different one next time. If you always use the same technique your mind will get stuck in a rut, and the creativity level will start to drop off. So vary your methods. There are plenty more you can learn about if you want to – buy a book on the subject.

By now you should have a list of at least four or five perfectly valid options to decide between. So now you have all your ingredients ready, let's get cooking.

◀◀ for next time

Given a little more time, one of the very best ways to produce a list of options is to call together a group of colleagues for half an hour – perhaps your own team – and brainstorm a list. Between about half a dozen and a dozen people is the optimum number. We've all heard of brainstorming, and we know the gist. Everyone comes up with as many ideas as possible and you write them down on a board or flip chart.

But to get the best out of brainstorming, you need to follow the rules. If you didn't realise there were rules, you're not alone. But they are designed to maximise the number of ideas the session generates. There are just four of them:

1 No one is allowed to judge or criticise any idea. This is the most important rule of all. If people start to criticise, it inhibits others from making suggestions for fear of ridicule. And since the wackiest ideas can often be the best, it will probably cost you some of your most promising ideas.

2 All ideas are welcome, no matter how off the wall. The strangest ideas are the ones that open up everyone's creativity. Even if they aren't feasible in themselves, they often lead to really useful, feasible ideas.

3 The more ideas the better. Quantity generates quality.

4 No idea is sacred – aim to combine ideas, refine them or build on ideas already put forward, as well as generating new ones.

It's your job, as group leader, to make sure all these rules are adhered to. So next time you're in this position, give yourself time to call a brainstorming session. You should find it fun, exhilarating and highly productive.

6 decision time

You're on the home straight now. You've collected all the facts you need, and you've generated a list of options. Now you simply have to decide which is the best one. Sometimes, by the time you get to this stage, the right decision will have become clear. But even when it hasn't, the odds are that you can see it comes down to one of only two or three options, and you can discard the rest.

The best approach to reaching the right decision is to adopt a process of elimination. Suppose you started with six or seven options. Once you've done all your preparation – assembling facts and consulting other people – it should be easy to narrow this down to a list of three or maybe four. Then you simply go through them all – using the techniques in this chapter – and keep knocking out options as you establish that they are less good than any of the others. It won't be long before you're down to just one option – or perhaps two (we'll look at what to do when you have two equal options later on).

EVALUATING THE OPTIONS

You need to look at each option in turn in order to establish its merits. You'll want to use the notes you assembled with all the facts – or a précis of each – on a single sheet, with fuller details attached. And you should keep your objective written down in front of you all the time as a reminder of what your winning option must measure up to.

The most important thing you need to establish is the level of risk and reward involved in each option. Consider this for each option – we'll see how in a moment. Beyond that – if that alone doesn't make your decision clear – there are various methods you can choose from to help you make your mind up. But we'll start with the risk/reward evaluation.

This is the most important evaluation for every viable option. You cannot decide which is the best course of action until you know what might result from it. So you need to examine the potential negative results *and* the potential positive ones. The simplest way to do this is to envisage the worst possible and best possible scenarios.

For each option, write down the worst thing that could possibly happen as a result: production would grind to a halt, you'd lose a major contract, the wrong person in the job would be less effective and leave sooner, you'd have wasted half your budget, the building would collapse.

thinking smart

WITHOUT PREJUDICE
When you're considering options, you may have to be strict with yourself about ignoring any personal prejudice. You might prefer a particular decision because that option was your idea. Or you might dislike certain options because you or your department will not do so well out of them. For example, if you're considering what to do about company cars, you might be tempted to go for an option that allows *you* to keep your company car. But force yourself to disregard such personal bias, and weigh up your options objectively.

363

Next to this, write down the best possible scenario: productivity would double, your best customer would become more committed to you, the right person in the job would revolutionise its effectiveness, you'd have doubled the income generated by your department, morale and productivity would rocket as a result of brighter, bigger, more sociable offices.

There are two more points to make about the risk/reward evaluation before you can draw any conclusions from it:

▶ **The risk and the reward are balanced at either end of a see-saw.**

▶ **The likelihood of these scenarios taking place is also a factor.**

Let's look at each of these in turn.

The see-saw

You are not simply considering the scenarios here in isolation – you have to look at how they balance each other. A very high risk might be worthwhile if the other end of the see-saw gives a very high reward. If the worst possible scenario involves a risk of imprisonment for several of your senior directors, you can rule out that option (I'm afraid) regardless of the potential rewards.

In fact, a very high potential risk often rules an option out, but it shouldn't always. Many of the most successful decisions ever made have involved an element of high risk – this is often the pay-off for a high reward.

Likelihood

You obviously need to take into account the likelihood of the worst and best possible scenarios actually happening. If the worst possible scenario is pretty bad, but the odds on it happening are minimal, it might well still be a viable option. You'll be balancing it against the potential reward, too, and if this is both high and likely, the option still looks promising. Set against a lower reward, which is also fairly unlikely, the option seems less appealing.

You might like to estimate the likelihood of each scenario and pencil it in on your notes. Bear in mind that it's only a very rough guide, but give it marks out of ten, or a percentage, if this helps you to weigh the balance. And remember that the two added together don't have to come to 100 per cent. The actual outcome might be somewhere in between these two. It may well be that you estimate the worst possible outcome as a 10 per cent likelihood, and the best as around 20 per cent. In other words, the most likely outcome is neither of these.

So you can see that the balance of risk and reward, and their relative likelihoods, have to be factored in before you can evaluate the option properly. At the end of your risk/reward evaluation, you can eliminate some of your options:

- **where the potential risk is high but the reward is low**
- **where the potential risk is insupportable, such as a risk of personal injury or, worse, to other people**
- **where the likelihood of the worst possible scenario is significantly greater than the likelihood of the best possible outcome.**

OTHER TYPES OF EVALUATION

You may well find at the end of the risk/reward evaluation that your course is clear. At the very least, you should have narrowed down your options. After all, as soon as you can see that an option isn't the best, just strike it off the list. You don't have to prove it's unworkable or would be catastrophic. But you want a list that contains only those options that you still think might turn out to be the best. By now, there should be only two or perhaps three possibilities left.

So how are you going to eliminate all but one of these? Different methods of evaluating work well for different people, so choose one that you feel comfortable with. Some of us like to rely heavily on intuition (although you're trying to resist that for the moment), some like to weigh everything precisely, some worry deeply about the risks, while others are inclined to overconfidence when we fix our sights on the potential rewards.

You want to get on with this decision now because time's running out, so we're not going to bother with long, complex methods of assessment that involve drawing graphs and matrices filled with figures, or flow charts that occupy most of one wall. The approaches here are simple and straightforward, and will work for all but the most complex technical or financial decisions.

Write down notes as you work through whichever method (or methods) you choose on your 'master sheet' on which you've already noted your risk/reward evaluation for each option.

Thinking through the consequences

The risk/reward evaluation looked only at the opposite ends of the scale of possible outcomes. As such, it makes an excellent instant eliminator round. However, it's now time to look at the consequences in more detail – not only the best and worst but those in between as well.

365

> ## DON'T WASTE TIME
>
> You probably don't need to be told this when time is precious, but you need to match the time you put into this process to both the importance and the complexity of the decision. If the decision is not of huge importance, don't waste two days evaluating it when an hour or two would get you to much the same answer. Equally, a simple decision (in other words, non-technical and without complex ramifications) simply doesn't justify several hours of your time after you've identified the options.
>
> A complex and important decision, on the other hand, can demand hours or even days of evaluation – but if you've left it this late I don't imagine that's what you're dealing with right now (I certainly hope not). So assess how much time the decision needs and warrants before you bury yourself in lengthy evaluations.

The risk/reward evaluation looked at the *possible* results of your decision. This approach, however, not only takes a less extreme approach but it also looks at the *known* results rather than the possibles. All you need to do is to note down everything that you know will result if you choose each given option.

Note down the consequences in two columns: positive and negative. And think through all the areas where there will be consequences. For example, there may be consequences for:

- ▶ **the organisation**
- ▶ **the department**
- ▶ **you**
- ▶ **the budget**
- ▶ **production schedules**

… and so on. And don't forget to include the emotional consequences. If you know that despatch will be very upset by a particular decision, put this down on your list.

So when you've finished working through the option of giving your top customer an unprecedentedly big discount, your list might look like this:

Positive	**Negative**
It will increase the customer's loyalty	It will cut margins
	It will set a precedent with this customer
It will guarantee bulk sales	
It will improve the stage payment arrangements	
Production will be easier to schedule	

Remember, you're writing down what you know, not what you think *might happen*. Concentrate on the direct and certain consequences of your decision. So, for example, you haven't included the point that it will set a precedent with other customers if they get wind of it, because you don't *know* that they will.

You will find that going through this thought process is as valuable as having the result of it on paper in front of you. And with any luck, by the end of it, you'll have knocked another option or two on the head.

DON'T HOLD BACK
Almost every decision involves an element of uncertainty. If you wait until you can guarantee the outcome, you'll never make the decision – which may be as damaging as the outcome you fear that is holding you back. So get as close to certainty as you reasonably can (even if it's not as close as you'd like), and then just go for it.

List the pros and cons

This technique is similar to the last, but not the same. You're listing arguments in favour and against, rather than listing consequences. However, the consequences obviously feed the arguments.

You will end up with a more comprehensive list this way. But balance that against the fact that it will contain fewer certainties and more predictions. Let's try the same option again: to give your major customer the big discount they're demanding.

Pro	Con
The customer's layout should increase	It will cut margins
The bulk sales will be guaranteed	It will set a precedent with this customer
The stage payments will be better than otherwise	It may set a precedent with other customer sif they find out about it
Production will be easier to schedule	Our suppliers will give us good bulk discounts to offset the cost of our discount, but they may not maintain them
They are likely to increase their order in future if the price to them has reduced	If we hit serious production or delivery problems, our margins could be cut severely, or even wiped out

As you can see, you now have far more positive and negative points than you had with the previous 'consequences' technique. On the other hand, those were certain, and many of these are only guesses. You may prefer one or other of these techniques, or you might like to try both – assuming you have time. Once you've tried them both, you'll generally find in future that you only need to use one, and you can choose whichever seems most appropriate. Just make sure you always apply the same technique to all the options. Don't use 'consequences' for option A and 'pros and cons' for option B.

Can I sleep at night?

This technique really is called Can I Sleep At Night (CISAN for short). What you do is ask yourself, for each option: 'What will I most regret if I take this option?' And then: 'What will I most regret if I don't take it?' (The idea is to ask if you'd be able to sleep at night if you did or didn't choose each option.)

Suppose you're trying to decide which of your top two candidates for the post of PR assistant you will appoint. For candidate A, ask yourself these two questions:

▶ ***What will I most regret if I appoint this candidate?*** **You might answer that you'll regret committing yourself to putting in a lot of time to training up someone with huge potential but minimal experience.**

What will I most regret if I don't appoint this candidate? Perhaps you'll regret not appointing someone who has a natural confidence and rapport with people – an important quality in a PR person.

Now repeat the questions for candidate B. This approach often throws up a new angle on the decision that you hadn't previously considered. Not only that but, as you'll have realised, it's a really quick technique.

Involve others

You should be getting pretty close by now to seeing which option is the best one to take. However, if you're still troubled by the choice, there's no rule that says you can't ask advice. You consulted with other people to draw up your list of options – so now do it again if it helps.

You should find – especially given the time constraint at the moment – that you only need to talk to one or possibly two people. Or you might call in a small group of two or three immediate team colleagues for a quick meeting. Either way, simply pick up the phone and ask if you can have a few minutes of their time (over the phone or face to face). Then simply outline the options and ask them if they can see whether one is better than the other, and why.

Discuss it with them if it helps, but if they have no clear view there's not a lot of point wasting everyone's time going round in circles. You can do that much more quickly by yourself. So don't go for a long meeting – just ten or fifteen minutes at most to see if they can raise any important points you'd overlooked.

MAKING YOUR CHOICE

You've done everything you can to arrive at the best decision (and in a short time), and the chances are that you can now see which way to go. If at this stage you still really can't choose between the last two options, just toss a coin. No, seriously. If it's that close a call, it doesn't matter which you decide on. Never forget the importance of making the decision as a factor in itself. Putting it off may be worse than any of the other options.

There's another thing that can occasionally happen at this point: you don't like any of the options. None of them seems very promising, so what do you do? In this case, you will have to settle for the 'least worst' option. Not much fun, but there it is. A decision has to be made, and the best decision – even if uninspiring – is still the best.

thinking smart

NEGATIVES ARE EASIER TO PROVE
When you're examining whether a course of action will or won't work, remember that it is always easier to prove a negative than a positive. In other words, you may well be able to prove an option is not going to succeed, but you are far less likely to find conclusive proof that it will. So be prepared to settle for the fact that absence of negative proof may be as good as it gets.

thinking smart

SLEEP ON IT

The old trick of sleeping on a decision really does work. It gives your unconscious mind the opportunity to rearrange all the pieces into a pattern that makes sense. You may wake up with a blinding realisation of which choice to go for. Even if you don't, the picture may be much clearer by morning. So if you can leave the decision until tomorrow morning, do.

Bear in mind, however, that the least worst option might be to do nothing at all, and simply leave things as they are. However, making a firm decision that this is what you will do is still far better than leaving things alone simply because you haven't made the decision yet. This way everyone knows where they stand, and can get on with making decisions that were waiting on yours. So you still need to commit to a firm decision to do nothing.

By now you know which option you want to take, and there's just one more thing you have to do: commit to it totally. The time for dithering is over, and you must now throw your weight 100 per cent behind your decision. Yes, even if you only arrived at it by tossing a coin, or if it's a least worst option that you didn't want to have to choose. If you – its originator – aren't behind it, you can be sure as hell no one else will be.

So be totally committed yourself, and you can then transmit that commitment to everyone else when you communicate the decision to them, which is the next and final stage.

for next time

If your decision is complicated, or has many ramifications, you will need to leave yourself longer to reach it. You may even think through the consequences and then want to make secondary decisions along the 'what if ...' route to check that it is still feasible. For example, you might decide that option A for clearing your production bottleneck looks best, but there's a danger the machine you'd have to install might become obsolete within a couple of years. So what if you need spares for it after that?

At this stage – given enough time – you can decide what you will do if this happens. You shouldn't waste a lot of time on 'what if' decisions – they may never happen – but you may need to get far enough to establish that you will be able to find a workable solution if you need to.

Even with less complex decisions, it's always worth at least allowing yourself enough time to sleep on a decision, or to mull it over if you need to. Time away from the decision after you've evaluated the option can be a huge help. When you come back to it, everything slots into place. So schedule in a day or two's gap between evaluating the options and making the final decision.

7 communicate your decision

You've made your decision, and you can breathe a sigh of relief. Well done! But the job's not over yet. You've still got to tell everyone else. And not only tell them, but get their support too. So you need to find the right way to tell them, and then you have to sell them the decision and convince them it really is the best one, even if they aren't happy with some of its effects.

Needless to say, if people were consulted in the first place, they will be far more likely to go along with your decision now even if it isn't the one they want. They will feel they had their say, and that you took their views into account.

You will realise, when you read this chapter, that you will have to spend a few minutes preparing what you're going to say to everyone before you walk into the briefing session.

WHO TO TELL

Many managers make a big mistake at this stage: they don't tell enough people about their decision. If you want people on your side, the very first thing to do is show them they are important enough to hear the decision from you personally. If you let them hear it from someone else, it signals that you didn't consider them important. And that's not a good start if you want their commitment.

So tell everybody, whether they are senior or junior to you, who is going to be affected by this decision. Tell everyone that you consulted. And if you're in any doubt at all about whether you need to tell certain people, err on the side of caution and tell them anyway.

HOW TO TELL THEM

Ever heard of the grapevine? Of course you have. And the best way to feed the grapevine is to talk to people individually or in small groups. Then they have plenty opportunities to say: 'Well, I heard …', and 'Ooh, no, that's not what I was told …', and 'Apparently, according to Pat …' and so on. Everyone will have a different version of the decision, rumours will fly, and the grapevine will be at its most fruitful.

Or you could do it properly. Get everyone together and brief them collectively. That means that everyone hears the same version of events, at the same time, from the same person. It gives the poor grapevine precious little chance to flourish. (And it's far quicker than telling people individually – you only have to go through it all once.)

WHAT TO TELL THEM

So you've decided who to tell, and you've collected them all together. Now what are you going to say to them? Well, obviously you're going to tell them what you've

FLATTERY WILL GET YOU FAR

Since telling everyone at once involves a meeting of some sort, there is a sense of formality that flatters the people you are briefing. They are worth calling a proper meeting for – you obviously felt it was important that they should know, and should have a chance to ask for clarification if they need it.

decided. But there's more to it than that. You can't just call everyone together and say: 'Right, all of you, I've decided that you've all got to wear uniforms from now on. Off you go now, and pick up your new outfits from the box by the door on your way out.'

You need to communicate all the information that people will want to know about this decision:

- ▶ **what the decision is**
- ▶ **who it will affect**
- ▶ **when it will happen**
- ▶ **what changes to expect**
- ▶ **how and by whom the decision will be implemented**
- ▶ **why you have arrived at this decision.**

That's all pretty straightforward, apart from the last bit: explain why you've chosen this option. If you've gone for the option everyone wanted, you may not have much trouble with this. But suppose you *are* making everyone wear uniforms? Or banning all overtime? Or moving accounts into an even grottier office than the one they're in now?

You've got to sell this decision to everyone. Show them why it's the right one. Persuade them that, in your position, they would have reached the same conclusion. To do this you need to:

- ▶ **Outline the key arguments in favour of the decision.**
- ▶ **Present the decision in a way that emphasises any benefits to them ('We'll provide the uniforms, so you no longer have to buy yourselves clothes to wear to work ...').**
- ▶ **Explain the key reasons why this option didn't come up to scratch if everyone favoured another option you rejected. Most people will submit to rational argument, however reluctantly.**

thththth thinking smart

QUESTIONS NOT CHALLENGES

You need to give people an opportunity to question you for clarification and understanding, but make sure you don't get into a slanging match, or let people think they can persuade you to change your mind. So allow reasonable questions, but make it clear that this is not the forum for arguing the toss. If you allow people to challenge your decision you will undermine your own authority, and give the impression that there's a chance they might overturn the decision. In fact the decision is made, it is the best decision, and you are committed to it. Make this clear for everyone's sake.

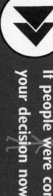

If people were consulted in the first place, they will be far more likely to go along with your decision now

371

Show you took their views into account. Remember you took notes when you consulted? Well, now's the time to use them: 'Most of you in accounts told me that improved storage was your top priority, and you have that in the sub-basement.' 'Sarah pointed out to me that your clothes often get marked and damaged by the machines. You won't have to worry about that any longer.' (But don't make it sound as if it's all Sarah's fault they have to wear uniforms from now on.)

You have to become a salesperson for the duration of the briefing session, and be prepared to sell the decision to your colleagues and staff just as you would sell your products or services to a customer.

CONFIRM IT IN WRITING

Finally, once you have finished the session, reiterate the main points in a written memo. Not only does this add weight and finality to your decision, but it also ensures that everyone continues to have the same version of events. The grapevine withers and dies in the face of written communications. They leave no room for doubt or speculation.

In your memo, restate the points listed above reminding people what the decision is, how, when and by whom it will be implemented, and what to expect as a result of it. After going through this communication process, you should find that you have the support and the commitment – or at least the consent – of everyone you need, and hopefully their enthusiasm as well.

for next time

On this occasion, you have been so pushed for time that you have no option but to pass on your decision as soon as you've made it. In future, however, when you'll have more time (of course you will), it can be wise to wait a day or two before imparting your decision. The reason for this is that it helps you get it straight in your own mind, and allows time for any deep-seated, barely conscious niggles to come to the fore. If there is a nagging doubt in the back of your mind, you need to address it – perhaps even change your mind if you realise you'd missed something vital.

Nineteen times out of twenty, you won't even consider changing your mind. But a break between deciding and communicating the decision still doesn't hurt. It gives you a couple of days to feel really committed to it.

If you do give yourself the luxury of a break before you impart your decision, however, for goodness sake keep it to yourself. Otherwise the rumour-mongers will have time to start up, if anyone gets wind of what you're about to announce. And even if you put everyone straight within a day or so, they will still feel put out that they weren't the first to hear.

Decision making is always easier without the clock ticking, even if you're not going to waste time over it. The best approach is to do it fast (but not too fast), do it smart, and do it without pressure. That way you'll be effective, confident, and you'll join the ranks of the great decision makers.

decision in an evening

So, you've got to make an overnight decision. You've got this evening (or perhaps you have a morning or an afternoon) and then the decision has to be made. People are waiting for you. There's a temptation to panic, and to come out with any decision just to meet the deadline. But deep down you know that if it's the wrong one, it'll be worse in the long run than no decision at all. But you simply don't know which option to choose.

Don't panic. By the end of the evening you'll have a decision, you'll be confident it's the right one, and you'll be ready to defend it if you need to. Just follow the guidelines in this book, and speed it all up a bit:

- **Set your objective properly at the start. It won't take a moment, and it will ensure that you stay on track. This isn't the place to cut corners.**

- **Make sure you have to take this decision at all. Are you sure it isn't someone else's decision really? Or that it isn't dependent on another decision? If you don't need to take it now, you could have this evening off – so don't launch into the process until you're sure you have to.**

- **Give yourself a strict time limit for assembling the facts – about an hour and a half. Decide which are the 'must know' facts (see page 348), and just stick to these.**

- **Ignore all the bumf on the subject in your file (you've got a file on this, I trust?), unless it happens to be on your 'must know' list. If it's not, it's simply a distraction.**

- **Make any phone calls to collect information first, before you look elsewhere for it; it can be hard to get hold of people at short notice and you don't want to miss them.**

- **if you're collecting facts on the phone from someone you also need to consult, do this at the same time. Don't call them back again in an hour.**

- **You'll have to do your consulting over the phone (unless you're in the office and the person you want to speak to is right next door). Keep your consultations short, but ask people what their preferred course would be and why. At least they'll feel they've been included in the decision.**

- **Write down your options, and if you feel you may be missing something, try one of the creative thinking techniques on pages 358 to 362 to help generate more. They don't take long, and if the right decision isn't down on your list somewhere, you'll have no chance of choosing it.**

- **The right decision may be jumping out of the list at you. But if it isn't, do a risk/reward evaluation for each option (see pages 363 to 364). Eliminate as many options as possible this way.**

- **If you're still uncertain, slim down your options using the 'Can I sleep at night?' process (page 367) – it's the quickest.**

- **You should be there now – the decision should be clear. If it's so close you really can't decide, and you're running out of time, just toss a coin. Go on. But whatever side it comes down on, commit yourself to that decision.**

decision in an hour

Wow! You like to live dangerously. I can only assume, if you've cut the decision this fine, that you've done most of your homework already. If this is a really important decision and you haven't even started assembling the facts, you're in big trouble. Bigger, in fact, than deferring the decision. So the logical thing to do is to delay the decision, no matter what hits the fan. It's still got to be better than making the wrong decision.

But let's suppose that you have assembled your facts. Maybe they've been sitting on your desk for weeks but you've been putting off the decision because the facts don't seem to be helping. In that case, we've still got time to tango.

1 Set your objective (page 344). Yep, sounds a waste of time, I know. But it's quicker than arguing, so just do it.

2 I imagine you've consulted already. I hope you've consulted. If not, pick the three or four key people who will be affected – or whose departments will be affected – by your decision, and speak to them. Ask them what they would like to happen and why. Keep the conversations brief – but make it very clear you're listening and you're really keen to know what they think. Feed this information into the decision.

3 Write down your options. Decide whether you reckon you've covered everything or if there may be another option you've missed.

4 If you need more options, use the problem reversal technique (page 359) – it's quick and highly productive.

5 Now it's down to a process of elimination. Any option that clearly isn't the best can go – even if it's not bad. As soon as you can see any other option is better, the less good option gets struck off. So get rid of any options you can.

6 Now do a risk/reward evaluation on the remaining options (see pages 363 to 364).

7 Time's running out, so knock any other options on the head that you feel you can.

8 If you have time, do the 'Can I sleep at night?' techinque (page 367) on the remaining options.

9 Now decide. If it's completely impossible to choose between what's left, just toss a coin. Any option that's still left has got to be a reasonable decision at least. And taking the decision is probably more important than which of these you actually plump for.

Well done! You've reached the end of the beginning: the decision. Now all you have to do is communicate it and implement it. But if you've decided wisely, it should all be plain sailing from here.

guide to constructive criticism

fast thinking

ros jay

guide to constructive criticism

When someone on your team does something wrong, it's your job to tell them so and put them straight. But handle it badly and you shatter their confidence and morale. No one enjoys having to criticize people (apart from the odd sadist among us), but if you handle it well it can be a positive experience for both of you. So here's the fast guide to using criticism as a positive tool.

1 *Do it fast, to their face, and in private.* If someone does something they shouldn't, you have to tackle it at the first opportunity – don't leave it for days, or even (a cardinal sin some managers commit) until their next appraisal. Address them face-to-face out of consideration and so you can discuss it properly. And make sure no one else can hear the conversation. Humiliating your team in public isn't helpful.

2 *Agree what happened.* You might think that your team member forgot to fill out the delivery forms for the next day before they went home. But before you take them to task about it, make sure they agree. Perhaps they legitimately handed the job on to someone else because they were called away. So make sure you are both agreed on the facts.

3 *Ask the reason, then listen to the reply.* You're agreed that they forgot to fill in the forms, but why? Maybe they'd just had a phone call to tell them their mother had been rushed to hospital. On the other hand, maybe they were busy chatting to their mates. It makes a difference as to how you handle it. So get them to tell you how the mistake happened.

4 *Criticize the action, not the person.* Don't make them feel small by saying, 'You're such a chatterbox, that's your problem.' If you label people, you reinforce the behaviour. Focus on the action: 'The problem with chatting while you work is that it can throw your concentration.'

5 *Put the mistake in the wider context.* Maybe your team member doesn't fully appreciate the ramifications of their mistake. So explain why it matters: 'If the forms aren't filled in, the delivery drivers can't start on time in the morning. That means they run late all day, the customers are unhappy, and the delivery drivers can't go home on time.'

6 *Agree a solution.* The mistake has happened now, and you can't go back. So the important thing is to make sure it doesn't happen again. You need to find a solution you're both happy with and, if possible, get your team member to suggest it themselves. That way they'll be committed to it. Maybe they could fill in the forms in a separate office in future, where there are no distractions.

7 *End on a positive note.* You don't want your team member to leave feeling upset or with their confidence dented. That's not going to help their performance. So always finish with a compliment, related either to the issue or on some other topic: 'We rely on you for those forms because you have such a high standard of accuracy,' or 'By the way, thanks for the report you gave me on Tuesday. I'm half way through it and it makes fascinating reading. You've done your research really thoroughly.'

If the criticism is constructive and non-personal, and leads to a better performance in future, it's in everyone's best interests. That's why smart managers never shy away from criticizing but meet it head on.

introduction

fast thinking doer

Many of the management and leadership skills mentioned earlier are about getting the best out of other people. But what about yourself? There are tasks you can't delegate – at least not always – and that you have to be able to master alone. Not only are they essential to your success as a manager, but you also need to set the lead so that the rest of your team can use you as a role model when they come to learn the skills themselves.

Finding Facts is one such skill. We frequently need to dig out reliable information to back up proposals or presentations, or to help inform our decisions. Often, there isn't time to delegate the job to someone else. You need to know what you're looking for, where to find the information and – increasingly – how to get what you want from the Internet *fast*. This guide will show you how.

The mere thought of drawing up a budget is enough to make the stomach sink. But like so many things, despair is caused by ignorance or underconfidence. Once you know exactly how to do it – and *Budget* will tell you – you'll view the prospect with equanimity, and carry it off with style.

Presentations and proposals are two sides of the same coin. One is written and the other spoken, but both aim to persuade someone else – your bosses or your customers – round to your way of thinking. The trouble with both of them is that they call on skills you haven't had to use for anything else: writing, public speaking, visual presentation. Where are you supposed to learn those sorts of things from? From *Fast Thinking Presentation* and *Proposal*, that's where.

Management techniques – from interviewing to handling a crisis with cool confidence – are an essential part of your job. But you also need hard skills to show that you're a rounded manager who can deal with anything from a budget to a presentation with equal panache.

finding facts

- SUPPORT YOUR CASE
- FIND SMART QUOTES
- EXPLOIT THE INTERNET

richard templar

contents

introduction

So, you've managed somehow to find a few scant hours to write your proposal or report, or prepare your presentation and now you realise that you're going to have to spend half of it frantically searching for data to back up your arguments. How on earth are you going to find so many facts in so little time? You don't even have time to get up from your desk and walk to the filing cabinet, let alone get down to the library or the nearest decent newsagent. And the Internet ... well, once you log on your computer just mutates into a machine that eats time.

Maybe you're lucky and you need just one key fact with which to stun the opposition at a vital meeting. Then again, maybe the meeting is only ten minutes away. Not so lucky, then. Or perhaps your boss wants the information for a presentation this afternoon and has just thrown a list of data at you and told you to come up with the answers by lunchtime.

Whatever the reason, you need facts and you need them fast. Well, help is at hand. This book is about getting hold of vital, relevant information quickly and accurately. In fact, without even having to leave the building. No more spending hours on the Net cruising when you should be surfing. It will all be explained clearly and simply.

This book is about finding facts fast. It does exactly what it says on the cover. It will give you:

 Tips for getting away with only the data you really need

 Shortcuts for locating data as fast as possible, and

 Checklists for making sure you have every option covered.

... all put together clearly and simply. And short enough to read fast, of course.

This book will assume that you have a day or two at most to get your facts, but you'll find a section at the back which deals with the tighter deadline of a couple of hours. And there's even a getting-the-facts-instantly section too.

So take a deep breath, and roll up those sleeves. We've got some work to do and there's no time for sleeping. We are thinking at the speed of life.

work at the speed of life

This book will take you through the key stages of finding facts fast:

1 Set your objective before you do anything else. It keeps you focused and prevents you getting side-tracked down blind alleys.

2 Next, you need to know exactly what information you're searching for, so we'll look at the questions you need to ask yourself before you begin.

3 Where are you going to go for these facts? You're pushed for time, but there's still likely to be a choice of sources. You need to make the right choice first time – you can't afford to go the long way round when there's a shorter route to the same data.

4 If you're serious about finding data, you need to know how to use the Internet. It's quick, easy, cheap, and available 24 hours a day (good news if you're still up working at three in the morning). It is also, however, a minefield: unreliable in parts and extremely large. You could get lost if you didn't have this *Fast Thinking* guide at your elbow as an excellent route map and encouraging companion.

5 The final stage is verifying your facts. OK, so you've collected your information, but how reliable is it? And how much junk can the Internet throw up? (Answer: More than you think.) You need to verify your facts and make sure their accuracy is unquestionable.

You'll also find a couple of useful chapters to read when you have time:

▶ 'fast but not now': a guide to the best software and hardware for finding facts now, from fast modems to mirror sites. Update your system ready for next time, and you'll be able to lay your hands on all that cyber-data even faster.

▶ 'smart but not fast': a guide to other valuable sources of information which you don't have time for today, but which could save you time in the future if you have a longer lead time to get them rolling.

fast thinking gambles

Of course you need more time to get these facts. Of course, in an ideal world, you wouldn't have a million and one other things to do at the same time. But hey, wake up and smell the coffee. It ain't an ideal world. No good blubbing; let's get on with it. This book will give you all the help you need given the tight deadline, but it's always some kind of gamble:

▶ **You won't have time to verify all the facts as accurately as you might like to. We'll give you the key pointers to identifying reliable sources – and unreliable ones, of course – but this means taking some facts on trust.**

▶ **You may not have time to collect all the facts you need. Perhaps you'd like to round up 20 facts to support your case, but you may have to be content with only half a dozen key facts – just enough to get you out of trouble this time.**

▶ **Some information simply isn't available in the time you have. Maybe you don't have time to trek off to the library, or the one person who knows the answer is out of the office until next week.**

▶ **Maybe the information is out there, but at a price. And you haven't time to get clearance for exceeding the budget.**

All that said, you can certainly keep yourself out of trouble with this book at your side. But for added reassurance next time, and to get hold of the best data around, clear yourself more time if it's humanly possible.

1 your objective

know you're on the verge of panic, but just stop and think for a moment. It will save you a huge amount of time in the long run, I promise. You need to think about what it is you're really trying to achieve.

The facts you want to find are simply a means to an end, not an end in themselves. What are you going to do with the information once you've found it? You're going to use it, that's what. So your starting point is to identify what you want the facts *for* – without this you can't hope to identify which facts you need.

The odds are that you need this information for one of three purposes:

1 to back up your arguments and persuade people to accept your proposal, your presentation or your standpoint at an imminent meeting

2 to include in a report you've been asked to write in order to add credibility to it

3 to enable you to make a decision.

By far the most frequent of these is the first one. If you're this pressed for time, and it's this important, the odds are you're trying to produce facts which will support your case and persuade a customer, colleague or boss to adopt your proposal. What's more, if you're putting together a proposal or presentation, you may have to find a lot of facts – and in a hurry, too.

So you should begin by identifying the objective of the overall proposal you are making (whether you're writing it, presenting it or putting it across at a meeting). This will help you focus on what the facts you are looking for will need to achieve. And it will help you save time, as you'll see.

SETTING YOUR OVERALL OBJECTIVE

This thought process should take you only a few moments, but will help hugely in setting a clear objective. Suppose you are proposing to your board that staffing levels in your department be increased. A statement of your aim might be simply: *to persuade the board to increase staffing levels in the department.* But the more detail you add, the more helpful your objective will be.

It's just like planning a journey: you need to decide not only where you are going, but also how you are going to get there. In other words, what are the main requirements of your journey? Speed? Plenty of interesting stop-offs on the way? Low fuel consumption? A convenient place to stop for lunch? Flesh out the objective a little more. Here's a fresh version: *to persuade the board that increased staffing levels in the department would be more productive.*

Now we're getting somewhere. But we need to be still more specific. What does 'more productive' mean? More cost-effective? Or will it generate more income? Or speed up the system? What benefit are you trying to sell to your board: what turns them on? Cutting costs? Increasing output? Improving customer service? Operating a faster system?

thinking smart

THIRD TIME LUCKY

It often takes three stages to set a clear objective. Identify the broad objective first, then state a broad reason why your reader or listener should accept it, and finally make the reason more specific. For example:

1 persuade the board to up staffing levels
2 to make the department more productive
3 in terms of customer service and income/cost balance.

OK, let's try again: *to persuade the board that increased staffing levels in the department would improve customer service and generate more income than it would cost.* That's more like it. You've thought about who the proposal is for and what they want to hear, and you've given yourself an objective that tells you where you're going and the key elements to focus on en route.

So that's your one-sentence objective. It should have taken you only a few moments to write, but you're going to be referring to it frequently over the next few hours.

USING YOUR OBJECTIVE

This objective helps you to focus on the facts you most need: the ones which further your overall objective. Suppose you have dozens of points you'd like to support with facts, but not enough time to dig them all out. Which do you spend time on? In the case of our last example, the ones which demonstrate that additional staffing will:

▶ **improve customer service**

▶ **generate more income than it will cost.**

So don't get bogged down in dragging out data on past staffing levels, or facts which show that increased staffing will speed up admin procedures. If time is short, concentrate on the data which support your overall objective. If you have the luxury of time left over (when did that last happen?) *then* you can dig out additional information.

AN OBJECTIVE FOR EACH FACT

Don't panic: setting an objective for each fact isn't going to take hours. It's just a matter of how you approach it. Suppose you want your board of directors to accept

thinking fast

CLOCKING OFF

If you have time to find more than the absolutely essential facts – congratulations. But your objective is still valuable. It is very easy (especially if you use the Internet) to get hung up on trying to find one particular but highly elusive piece of information. This can waste hours. You could set yourself a time limit, determined by how much time you have. If data do not directly support the overall objective, you'll give up if you haven't located the information within, say, ten minutes.

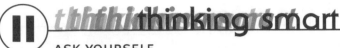
ASK YOURSELF

If you have any difficulty working out what your mini-objective is, simply ask yourself a question: 'What am I trying to prove?'

your proposal to introduce a new production system incorporating the recently developed jertain-based process. You need to back up your claim that jertains are much more cost-efficient to run than the old-style wockets. And you're lucky here – you remember reading a report in one of the trade publications about this not long ago. So all you have to do is dig out the article and you've got what you need.

Two hours later, you still can't track down the article you want. It would help if you could remember which publication it was in, but you can't.

You've fallen into a classic trap here: you've got hung up on the *fact*, instead of focusing on the *objective*. The fact, remember, is only a means to an end. And the end purpose was to demonstrate that jertains are more cost-efficient than wockets. But if you keep your eye on the objective, you'll realise that there is more than one way of proving this point.

You could, for example, contact both manufacturers and ask them each to fax or e-mail you the relevant, verified data. Then you can make the comparison yourself. Or you could search the Net for any relevant reports on the subject.

There is usually more than one way to make your point, and you need to focus on what you're trying to achieve in order to pick the fastest approach that will do the trick. And you do that by setting a mini-objective for each fact, such as: *to demonstrate that jertains are more cost-efficient than wockets.*

Armed with your overall objective, and mini-objectives for each point you want to back up with facts, you can approach your fact finding in a far more focused way, and you have a framework to stop yourself wasting time on unnecessary detail.

for next time

If you are writing a proposal or report, preparing a presentation, or making a key decision, you should already have set the objective for this. (You might like to read the relevant books in this series: *Fast Thinking: Proposal*, *Fast Thinking: Presentation* and *Fast Thinking: Decision*.) This gives you your overall objective for finding facts.

Armed with this, you can make yourself a quick list of all the points you would like to support with hard data and put them in priority order, according to how closely they fit the overall objective. Draw a line below the facts which directly further the overall objective: anything above this line is essential information. Anything below it is desirable but not essential. Then simply work through the list, until you run out of time. You can still set yourself a time limit for each fact, as we saw earlier, and also for each mini-objective.

2 getting your facts straight

OK, so you've set your objective and you are now ready to get out there and find what you want. But hold on. Do you know where to go? And what you are looking for? Take a little time – and I know you don't have much to spare but this is important – to think clearly about what it is you are researching.

ASKING QUESTIONS

If you know *exactly* what it is you are looking for – fine. But if not then ask a few questions first. When you need to know something ask yourself exactly what it is you are researching. Better to spend five minutes thinking at the beginning than wasting two days later on. If this research is for your own proposal or report then just sit down and ask yourself these few key questions before rushing out there:

- ▶ **What sort of fact is it?**
- ▶ **Who is it for?**
- ▶ **What will it cost?**
- ▶ **How much data can I handle?**

We will quickly nip through these questions so you have some guidelines before rushing off and wasting time.

What sort of fact is it?

Facts can be broadly divided up into three categories:

- ▶ *Hard facts.* **These are things such as historical facts – things that have happened and are well documented.**
- ▶ *Data.* **This is really a sub-set of hard facts but it is the sort of numerical information you might need, such as statistics, financial information, numerical data, scientific information, that sort of thing.**
- ▶ *Views and opinions.* **Perhaps not technically facts but relevant nevertheless. For instance you might need, to know that 78 per cent of people consider facts to be essential to good research – that's their opinion anyway but it is a fact: that's what they think.**

Who is it for?

Important one this, as it isn't the *user* of the fact that is important but the end customer, so to speak. You may be the user – the researcher – and you may think the fact is for you. But it isn't. It is for whoever the report or proposal or presentation you are including it in is for – they are the customer. You have to bear them in mind. It is imperative that you know who your customer is and which way to go.

Sometimes you *may* be the end customer. Perhaps you have to make an important decision and you need the relevant facts to make that decision. In which case you will have to be both judge and jury, so to speak. You will have to tailor your search to your own specific needs.

THINK LATERALLY

Don't get bogged down in always using the same avenue of research. The smart manager will chop and change as the circumstances change. You might usually go to the Internet for information, but this time there might be quicker, slicker sources. Take a moment to consider if you aren't using one source from habit rather than expediency.

SHOTGUNS AND PISTOLS

The smart manager will know that one clear, well-presented fact that is well documented and verified might swing the balance in their favour considerably more than a whole range of facts badly researched and lacking in authority. Having said that, the shotgun approach *may* be more effective: smart managers choose their weapon carefully!

What will it cost?

The Internet, on the whole, is a free source of facts, but they may not be either verifiable or accurate. Some site owners – especially the more reliable ones – may well have to be reimbursed for their trouble.

Some organisations charge for information: trade bodies, magazines and newspapers for archived articles.

How much data can I handle?

How much data can you handle physically? For instance, you may need to read and understand a 50-page document on the Internet just to find out one tiny piece of data. And on screen at that. Are you up to it? Can you read fast and accurately? Can your computer handle such vast amounts of information? Have you got time to read it all? We will look at ways of speeding all this up later but bear in mind when we first set off to hunt down our fact that we must be ready for information overload – and have contingency plans to deal with it.

GET A CLEAR BRIEFING

If someone else has asked you to research these facts, you will need to know how many, how big, how detailed. For instance, you might be asked for the number of washing machines sold in Germany in 1998. Fine and off you go. But before you waste time ask your boss a few other questions, such as:

PHONE A FRIEND

One well-placed phone call to someone in the know can save you an awful lot of time and effort. Before you log on take the time to think about who might have this information. Asking a friend takes but a second but might save you a lot of time in the long run. If they don't know the answer, they may know someone who does.

thinkingfast

WHO'S BEEN HERE BEFORE?

The smart-thinking manager will look at who might have had or needed this information before. Why waste time and effort researching facts when someone might have done all the donkey work for you? Take a moment or two to think about possible fact users that have gone before you. This might be previous company reports, sales statistics, financial documents, even books written on the subject.

thinking smart

CHECK YOUR FACTS

Before adding a fact to any document always ask yourself: 'If asked to justify or verify this fact, can I?' If you can't then don't put it in. Don't try to wing it: you'll get caught out, if not this time then next time for sure. Always have the back-up information to hand so you don't have to memorise vast chunks of data but can quote your sources at the flip of a page.

- ▶ **New or second-hand or both?**
- ▶ **Just German machines or all makes?**
- ▶ **Imports or only home sales?**
- ▶ **Retail or wholesale?**
- ▶ **Include exports?**
- ▶ **Domestic or industrial?**
- ▶ **Home sales or trade sales or both?**

Each one of these questions can refine your search and if you hadn't asked you may well be off on the wrong trail altogether. Once you have asked you might be told that the only information required is for domestic sales through retail outlets for home use of new German machines – there, that simplified things, didn't it?

Now let's get on with finding facts for real.

for next time

When you are planning your next report or presentation or proposal, check what facts you are going to need to support your case or argument. And check what facts you need well in advance of needing them. This will give you much more time to collect them and also allow time for emergencies. It's simply no good to wait to the last minute to log onto the Internet for a few quick relevant facts only to find your server is down or your computer is crashing or your phone line is out of action. The smart manager plans in advance and leaves nothing to the last minute if they can help it.

As soon as you know there is a report or presentation to do, start collecting facts: cut out articles from newspapers that may be relevant. These things take only a second but can prove very valuable at the last minute. If you don't need them then you haven't lost much at all.

We must be ready for information overload – and have contingency plans to deal with it

3 your options

OK, so time is getting on and we haven't even switched on the computer yet. We looked briefly in the last chapter at the sort of information you might be likely to need. Next, where can you get it from? Look at your requirements and decide what sort of facts you need. This makes it easier to determine your source.

Where can I find it?

For most people the top of the list will be the Internet but it really depends on the type of facts you are looking for. The Internet is a vast virtual library of information that is unbelievably diverse, covering any and every topic imaginable. But it also has its drawbacks:

- **It can eat up time you just don't have.**
- **Some of the information is quite deliberately biased or incorrect.**
- **It is too big to use for research unless you really know what you are doing (which you will do by the time you've finished reading this book).**
- **It provides distractions and dead ends that will entangle and ensnare you.**

Probably the best source of information is the Internet, but before you log on don't discount other sources such as:

- **accountants' reports, audited accounts and financial reports, stock market reports, treasury statements**
- **biographers and historians**
- **company library and company reports, internal records, minutes of meetings**
- **a friend, colleague or expert**
- **financial journals, digests, magazines, manuals, newspaper archives, pamphlets, periodicals, scientific periodicals, magazines**
- **publishers**
- **reference and university libraries (they may be online)**
- **competitor information**
- **resource directories**
- **trade associations and professional bodies**

You probably don't have time to leave the building, but you may be surprised at what you can find out with a quick phone call, fax or e-mail to any of these sources.

For instance, you might need to know who supplies your competitor with the three-inch widgets that they fit in their giggle pins for their revolving jertains. You could spend ages on the Internet cruising and surfing and getting side-tracked. A quick trip to your sales office, however, might give you a copy of your competitor's latest leaflet proclaiming in large bold type **'and with the new unbeatable three-inch widget from Pearson Industrial!'** See, I told you this stuff was easy.

thinking smart

BEING A DETECTIVE

Smart managers regard themselves more like a detective than a researcher – they look for clues as to where they might find the information, they follow up leads, they root around, they follow hunches and their nose, they ferret out information others might miss, they aren't afraid to phone up an expert or a friend, they have an uncanny sense of where information might lurk. They take research to a new and interesting dimension.

thinking smart

USE THE EXPERTS

Whatever fact you need to know, there will be someone who regards this fact highly. For you it is just ammunition for a report or proposal but for some anorak somewhere it is their life and blood. Find them and ask what you need to know. They will be flattered to be asked and invariably will part with the information free of charge. These people don't know things because it is their business but because they study them out of interest.

Or you might need the investment value of Georgian silver over the last 200 years. And whereas you could eventually find this on the Internet after a great deal of searching, a quick phone call to an antique dealer specialising in Georgian silver may well turn up trumps. It's the sort of information they may well have merely by chance – because they are interested in all aspects of their business.

If you need to research public opinion – or anyone's opinions come to that – then check the sources just given. For instance, to back up your argument you might like to show, from market research surveys, that 88 per cent of people, when asked for a preference, declared that they thought having a jertain in the home was a good idea and they would definitely buy one if the price was right. Simply brilliant if you are trying to persuade your board to branch out into the home jertain market.

If you are researching opinions then don't forget: politics, advice, counselling, warnings, government positions, conventions, guidelines, management topics and regulations. For instance, you might want to know if it is feasible, or even considered ethical, to keep jertains in the domestic environment without a licence. This is still a fact – not data, not a hard fact, but a view, a position, an opinion, a guideline.

So where do we get this stuff from? Well, for public opinion obviously market research, although this is limited when you're up against the clock (when time is less tight, see 'smart but not fast', page 420). Then there are loads of government offices simply dying to give out juicy titbits of information to those who ask.

THE OUTERNET

You could always subscribe to an Internet information database if this would throw up the results you wanted. Basically, these are online research agencies with computerised facilities. They are known as pure knowledge databases or knowledge indexes and are part of the Outernet – outside the Internet for fee- paying customers. You have to pay

thhfihhi thhthi

> **E-MAIL ROUND ROBIN**
> You can always send a round robin e-mail to a number of colleagues or friends or experts asking their advice as to where to go for certain information. They may well already have it or could certainly point you in the right direction.

for them but they are reliable and trustworthy sources. You can usually subscribe directly online using a valid credit card and have instant access.

You get what you pay for

Unlike the Internet where it is all free and thus anyone can post anything they want including illegal, misleading, faked, hoaxed and silly information – and they do, believe me – the Outernet is based pretty much on a 'you get what you pay for' sort of basis. These databases are selling data so they are updated very frequently – after all, their reputation depends on their data being accurate. They would go out of business fast if they weren't reliable.

A lot of these are American and they work by charging you a yearly subscription (around £50 per annum) and then you pay a per hour fee while you are online. This can range from as low as £10 per hour to as high as £200. Some also charge you if you print out any information – usually around 50p a page. The biggest of these is to be found at http://www.dialog.com/. This isn't a recommen-dation – merely a fact.

Different data

Beware the fact that most of them are American and the information can sometimes be misleading or very different from ours owing to the different way we handle data and figures; for instance, we are only just beginning to use 'billion' in the same way. Until recently our billion was one million million, whereas the American billion is only one thousand million – could throw your data out by a long way, stuff like that!

for next time

Make yourself acquainted with online newspapers, journals and other publications. Surf when you have a little time to spare – not now. Try:

http://www.publist.com/ This website covers over 150,000 magazines, journals and newsletters, with many links to publishers. It also has pre-launch listings.

http://www.mediafinder.com/ This one covers over 100,000 publications and includes mailing list vendors. It has a user database research section with free search by keyword or category.

http://ajr.newslink.org/ This has coverage of over 3,000 US and 2,000 foreign newspapers and links to campus newspapers.

4 sourcing your facts

Now we know what we need to find out. It's time to switch on, log on and get started. We simply don't have the time to learn about the history of the Internet or how it came to be. All we need to know, and quickly, is that it is a useful tool for us to use for research – and how we can use that tool effectively and fast. Above all fast. We may need to learn some new terms and commands but they will be simple and clearly explained. What we are looking for here is the essence of speed, not a retraining programme in the art of the Internet. We are thinking at the speed of life and need only the barest essentials along our journey.

Until a few years ago researching on the Internet was a bit hit-and-miss. Today it is vast and comprehensive – too vast, some might say. But if you know how to refine your search, you can find what you want. Quickly now: the seconds are ticking away and we have a lot to learn if you are to find these facts to make your presentation or report the best there is and capable of doing exactly what you want – backing up your argument and proving your case.

Let's quickly run through finding facts on the Internet and see if we can track down what you are looking for.

HOTLINKS

If you find a web page you think is relevant, you will also find hotlinks. These jump you to the next site of interest but you can find yourself wandering off course and getting lost. You could follow hotlinks for hours without turning up anything of any use. What you want is a website that lists all the sites relevant to your search. These are known as jumpstations and are put together by:

- ▶ **businesses**
- ▶ **interested people**
- ▶ **universities**
- ▶ **trade associations**
- ▶ **libraries.**

Add these to your bookmarks if they seem useful. To open any web pages simply left-click on them and you will be taken there. Left-click on your 'back' button to return to the jumpstation. You'll usually find jumpstations listed at the top of search engine pages.

SEARCH ENGINES

Search engines do exactly that – they search for you. They have databases of keywords used on website pages and they will quickly trawl through them to locate any that match your search. You simply type in a word and the search engine will find any sites that use that word. They work by searching out words on the opening page of a website. They often only check the first paragraph or two, so if your keyword doesn't appear until later on you won't be given that page to check. The software that does the checking is known as a spider and spiders check the metatag of a website, which is a series of HTML lines – the title, the address (its URL – uniform resource locator), the description and, most important, the keywords. They also check that the keywords listed for the site agree with what's on the opening page.

The downside of this is that search engines are almost impossible to keep up to date and if you use a common word you will be inundated with sites. Try typing in a simple word like 'facts' at Yahoo! and you will be given some 2,680 sites to look at.

"Quotation marks"

To speed up your search – and speed is of the essence here – add words to your search. The more words you add, the greater the chances your search engine will find what you are looking for. But if you use more than one word as a keyword search, remember that you should put those words into double quotation marks "like this" or the search engine will try to search out each word individually.

For instance if you type in *German washing machine manufacturers,* the search engine will find you all sites using the word German, as well as all sites using the word washing, plus sites using the word machine and finally add in all sites including the word manufacturers. It's been done for you:

German washing machine manufacturers – 4,259,712 sites

"German washing machine manufacturers" – 22 sites

Not putting your keywords into quotation marks also throws up some interesting additions. For instance, you don't just get all sites using the word washing in the last example: you also get all the sites using washing in any other context, such as *Washington* – both the place and the president.

Most search engines are free as they collect their revenue from advertising. Some are larger than others – they use more keywords – and some are faster. Remember that no one search engine is ever capable of searching more than around 15 per cent of the Internet. This is why you always need to use more than one. We will look at faster ways of refining your search under Boolean searching on page 43 – go there now if you need to know really urgently.

Search engines worth using (and bear in mind that there are around 350 of them currently) include:

- **AltaVista**
- **Lycos**
- **Yahoo!**
- **Direct hit**
- **HotBot**
- **Northern Light**
- **Snap!**
- **Deja**
- **Google**
- **GoTo.**
- **Excite**

To get to them just type in their name plus .com. For instance, to get to AltaVista type in AltaVista.com and you'll be taken there. Don't worry about the exact name as these search engines seem to have all possibilities covered. For instance, you could type:

- **altavista.com**
- **Alta-Vista.com**
- **AltaVista.com**
- **alta-vista.com**
- **Alta Vista.com**

… and you'll still be taken there. You can even miss out the .com and you'll get taken there. And don't worry too much even about the spelling – altavist will get you there, as will altivista.

Once at a search engine type in "search engines" to be given more.

METASEARCHES

A metasearch engine is one which searches the search engines. They look through the databases of several search engines at once and report back to you with a list of the results. If you haven't found what you are looking for or need a lot of information then trying a metasearch may pay off, especially if you are looking for a lot of obscure information. The downside of metasearches is that they can be overwhelming – they open up each new search in a new window and do tend to bombard you with information. Good to use when you are really proficient. Also most metasearch engines aren't too happy with the maths or Boolean commands – see later. But you could try:

- **All4one**
- **Searcha-z**
- **Savvy Search**
- **Cyward**
- **Web-search**
- **Matchsite.**
- **Suite101**

ACRONYMS
If what you are looking for is often known by its acronym then use the Boolean command OR to widen your search. If you need information on NATO then type in both the acronym and the full name: *NATO OR North Atlantic Treaty Organization.*

MULTI-SEARCH ENGINES
Basically the same as metasearch engines, except they don't try to combine all the results. Instead they open each result in a new window for you. They still send your search item to a number of search engines but each is displayed individually. This can be confusing or time-saving, depending on how many results you get. Multi-search engines are very good at presenting you with new search engines that you might not have tried before. Try:

- ▶ **Searchspaniel.com**
- ▶ **Theinfo.com**

SEARCH ENGINES WITH DIRECTORIES
By narrowing down your search you can get a better response. Most search engines will allow you to confine your search, if you want to, to certain key areas or categories of interest, such as:

- ▶ **health**
- ▶ **entertainment**
- ▶ **business**
- ▶ **companies**
- ▶ **travel**
- ▶ **sport**
- ▶ **money**
- ▶ **news**
- ▶ **jobs**
- ▶ **people finder**
- ▶ **real estate.**

It makes sense to use one of these directories if you want to exclude data from other areas that may not be relevant. For instance, if you want to research jertains you might like to know which companies import them but you might not want to know anything about their history, development or capabilities. Limiting your search to companies only would throw up relevant data but exclude all the stuff

HYPERLINKED SEARCH ENGINES
Most search engines list other search engines at the bottom of their opening page. If you type in a keyword and fail to get a decent response, simply click on the hyperlinked search engines listed to be taken there; they will begin your search again without your having to retype your keyword/s.

CAPITALS

If what you are looking for is a proper noun then make sure you put it into capitals. If you are looking for Apple computers instead of the apples you eat, make sure you put the capital in for the Apple or you'll be inundated with fruit.

you don't want. Most of the search engines allow you to refine your search in this way but you could do worse than try:

- ▶ **Magellan**
- ▶ **Yahoo!**
- ▶ **Excite**
- ▶ **Webcrawler**
- ▶ **Lycos.**

Again no specific endorsement, merely an observation.

WEB RINGS

Once you start surfing you might notice, usually at the bottom of a page, what is known as a web ring. This is a series of very similar sites which have got together to link to each other. One site might not have quite what you are looking for but another, on the same subject, may have exactly what you want. They can be a little time-consuming to follow but are often worth a search if you are looking for detail on a particular subject. For instance, perhaps you need to know a detail about the latest development of fuel-injection systems for jertains. You log on to the official jertain site at jertain.com but that only tells you that a new development has been made. You notice a web ring and click on it. It shows you five other jertain sites including jertaindevelopment.com. Off you go and there is the detail you wanted. You might never have thought to try jertaindevelopment.com but the web ring has taken you there.

ARCHIVES (GOPHERS)

When the Web first started, many universities and library facilities put a lot of text-based information on to it so other similar organisations could browse them. These text-based archives are still out there and can be accessed by anyone. Sometimes a particular bit of information you seek will be lying dormant just waiting for you to reactivate it. Such archives are very similar to encyclopaedia entries – just much more comprehensive and detailed. Use them if you want more information on a particular subject than a reference book or a CD of an encyclopaedia would give you. They are often updated as well, so they will give you up-to-the-minute political stuff as well, as current events.

These sites are known as gopher archives and you might like to search them out at:

- ▶ **Archie**
- ▶ **Veronica**
- ▶ **Galaxy**
- ▶ **Jughead.**

They may be useful, especially if what you want is typical archive material. Gopher archives are not technically part of the Web and if you type a gopher address into your web browser you need to use gopher:// rather than http://. They are best for academic research and anything to do with government offices.

NEWSGROUPS

If you haven't found what you want by now (and you probably will have), then you'll have to widen your search. Out there, in or on the Web (whichever you prefer) there are millions of people. Some of these have similar interests and like to communicate with each other. They do this through newsgroups. Newsgroups deal with very specific topics and exchange views and information freely and successfully. By subscribing to a newsgroup (joining it) you have access to whatever that newsgroup discusses.

You can post a message asking for particular information and receive replies by e-mail. This can be very useful sometimes, as you can gain access to someone who is heavily into a particular subject and as such may even be an expert. You may be inundated with e-mails or, as is more likely, receive only a few which answer your queries.

Vigilant and InReference both allow for keyword searches with the results being sent to you via e-mail. This saves a lot of time having to read every article about items. Both allow filtering so you can specify exactly what you want.

VALIDATING THE INFORMATION

Through newsgroups you can access the latest developments in some pretty fundamental research. You can also be led astray or receive misleading information. With a newsgroup there is no way, except through a sort of sixth sense, in which you can determine the validity of any information you are getting. And a sixth sense might not cut much ice with your readers or audience. Newsgroups, however, can often put you on the right trail of vital information that *can* be validated.

Most servers (this is the medium through which you access the Internet yourself; they serve you and you are their client) will have a list of newsgroups; you could try searching the search engines, or Deja News is a specific newsgroup search engine.

There are over 24,000 newsgroups currently. That's over 24,000 different subject areas – good for research. Always visit a newsgroup's FAQ – frequently asked questions – page first to see if the sort of thing you are looking for is being talked about within the newsgroup, as some have misleading titles and you might have accidentally stumbled into the wrong place.

REFINING YOUR SEARCH

Search engines work by looking for keywords in the title (usually) page of a website. They work by searching through words. Logically then, if you give them more words to search they are more likely to come up trumps for you. We looked earlier at the example of German washing machine manufacturers and how to put this search into quotation marks; well, there are a lot of other ways of refining your search. The two principal methods are known as maths and Boolean. Maths works

thinkingfast

THE + SYMBOL

Use the + symbol when you want to narrow your search down: it is useful when you're being overwhelmed with information. You can refine your search to anything you want. For instance, if you want to search out a Bogart movie such as *Casablanca*, type in *Bogart + Casablanca* and you'll omit any pages which might give you his other films, as well as omitting any pages which give you biographies, fan clubs or well-known quotations, sites selling photos and posters, and even sites selling the T-shirt.

by inserting symbols such as + or − into your request. Boolean works by inserting the words AND, NOT, NEAR and OR.

MATHS SEARCHES

The more specific your search, the more likely you are to come up with good, useful material – and quicker, which is what we are really interested in. By adding in a maths symbol you refine your search in great detail. Perhaps you want to know all about car manufacturers. Typing in *cars* would give you a lot of pages including ones on racing cars, kit cars, repairing cars, spraying cars and driving cars. Typing in *manufacturers* would give you a lot as well – and include a lot of manufacturers of other things such as washing machines. But both would contain irrelevant information which you would waste time sifting through.

Typing in "*car manufacturers*" would throw up only pages which use that exact phrase. By typing in *car +manufacturers* you would get only pages which used both words – not necessarily next to each other but on the same page. The more + symbols you put in, the narrower your search becomes. For instance, *car +manufacturers +Europe* would exclude all manufacturers from other places as well as manufacturers of washing machines or anything else.

You should use the − (minus) symbol when you want to *exclude* specific information. For instance, you might like to know about European car manufacturers but not Volkswagen or BMW as you already have enough information on them. So you would type in *car +manufacturers +Europe −Volkswagen −BMW*. That should omit anything to do with Volkswagen or BMW.

Boolean searches

Boolean searches are used by many professional researchers, although they are, as often as not, being replaced by maths searches these days. They are still extremely useful and can speed up your search considerably. Boolean searches work by allowing

thinkingsmart

CLOSE UP THE GAPS

Make sure that when you are typing in maths commands (+, −) you place these symbols next to the word which refines your search and don't leave a space. It should be *Shakespeare +Othello*, not *Shakespeare + Othello*.

KNOWING THE DIFFERENCE

The plus and minus symbols narrow your search down to pages which contain the information you want but not necessarily in any set order. Quotation marks narrow your search down to a specific phrase as it appears on a web page.

WATCH YOUR LANGUAGE!

If your word search includes any of the four words used in Boolean searching then make sure you place them in quotation marks or you will confuse your search engine. For instance, you might be looking for references to the book *Sons and Lovers*. If you type this in, you will get pages on sons and pages on lovers but you might not get any pages listing the book you want. Instead type in "Sons and Lovers" and you will get your result.

you to substitute one word for another without having to search twice. For instance, you might like to know about hair colouring. You can type in *blonde OR* blond and get pages listing either or both.

Most major search engines allow the use of OR (except Google because it does it automatically).

If you want to tie in two words, you use AND. For instance, if you want to find sites that cover both Tony Blair and Gordon Brown, type in *Blair AND Brown*.

Most if not all major search engines allow the use of AND, and in those that don't you can substitute + instead and it will do the same job.

Likewise Boolean searches allow you to omit certain sites. In the example about British politicians you might like to have sites for Tony Blair only and ignore any mentioning both. Type in *Blair NOT Brown*.

All major search engines support the NOT command except Google and Look Smart but they will allow the − symbol instead.

SAVING NANOSECONDS

If you really want to save time then learn the commands that replace Boolean:

AND	&
OR	|
NEAR	~
NOT	!

There, that should save you a nanosecond or two but it might be necessary if you really are in a tearing hurry.

thinkingfast

LEAVE A SPACE FOR MR BOOLES

Make sure that when you are typing in Boolean commands you leave a space between the words. Thus it should be *car NOT Ford*, rather than *carNOTFord*.

thinkingsmart

UPPER-CASE BOOLEAN

Some search engines require you to type in Boolean commands in upper case. Others are less specific. If you always type them in upper case, you will not fail. If you type them in lower case, you may have difficulty with some search engines such as Excite.

If you want to find pages which have two words close to each other then you use the NEAR command. For instance, *car NEAR manufacturers* will refine your search considerably. Most major search engines have their own convention as to what NEAR means. In AltaVista it means within 10 words, in WebCrawler within two words and in Lycos within 25 words. The way to improve this is to type in your own convention, such as *car NEAR/15 manufacturers*. That will give you your two words within 15 words of each other.

NESTING

These commands can be used with each other. This is called nesting. Nesting allows you to search within very specific parameters. For instance, you might like to find out more about *investments AND (Georgian silver OR glass)*.

Or you might need information on pets but you have enough information on dogs and tarantulas – so you would type in *pets AND (NOT dogs OR tarantulas)*.

Or you might need to limit your search to specific items with a subject. Let's say you needed to know about carburettors and specifically Zenith and Webber but you weren't too bothered about the rest. Then type in *carburettors AND (Zenith OR Webber)*.

Boolean, by the way, is named after Mr Booles who invented it.

Some search engines require you to use their advanced search facilities. You will see this as a box to click on within their home page.

thinkingfast

POOR SPELLING

If you are not sure how to spell a word but you think you know the beginning then type in what you know and add the $ symbol. For instance you might need to research Boolean commands but have forgotten how to spell Boolean. You know it begins with *bool*, so type that in and add the $ symbol: *bool$*. Your search engine will fill in the blank for you. This may not work with all search engines but it certainly does with Lycos. Don't try this with common words or you'll get a whole lot of pages thrown at you.

thinking fast

TURN OFF FRAMES

If a website gives you the option of turning off frames then do so. Frames take longer to load and serve no useful purpose if you are looking for text-based documents only. Frames are the windows that surround extra documents that you may see on the screen and can be scrolled up or down without affecting the main document.

WILDCARDS

You can search for variations or plurals of words using what are known as wildcards. A wildcard symbol is usually * or sometimes *.* and these symbols, especially the first, are used by all major search engines. Wildcards work by replacing the ending of words or pluralising them. For instance:

- ▶ **Type in *danc* and the search will throw up dances, dancing, dancer.**
- ▶ **Type in *theat* and the search will expand to theatre and theater (UK and US spelling variations).**
- ▶ **Type in *exhaust* and you'll get exhausted, exhaustion, exhausting.**

With some search engines you don't have to do this as they support what is known as stemming; they already give you all the variations you're likely to want. You may have to turn stemming off by using maths or Boolean (we've already covered that!) in order to reduce the number of results to a manageable level.

for next time

Bear in mind that some newsgroups don't take too kindly to being used for your own research in this way. If you need to access a newsgroup for research another time, it is best to give yourself time to lurk there for a while until you have acquainted yourself with their conventions and also checked out their FAQ pages – just in case what you want to know has already been answered.

Newsgroups are not there to provide you with answers and might react badly to you if you barge in and demand information. Best to tread lightly and seem genuinely interested, or you might be 'flamed' – sent rude messages by lots and lots of people. And don't 'spam' newsgroups – send lots of newsgroups the same message. They will spot this at once and flame you for your cheek.

Subscribe to any of the online research magazines such as the *CyberSkeptics Guide*, which you can find at: http://www.bibliodata.com/skeptic/ and this will keep you up to date on all avenues of Internet research.

5 verifying facts

OK, you've now collected as many facts as you need to add to your report or proposal or presentation. But just hold on a moment. Just because you got them off the Internet doesn't mean they are accurate, genuine, reliable or up to date. And just because you read something in a newspaper or journal doesn't make it true or trustworthy. At some point someone somewhere is going to ask you to justify these facts – and won't you look daft if you are proved to be wrong?

Best to check quickly that what you are putting in is accurate. You may think you've not got time for this but you will look foolish if someone asks you to verify any data you've presented and you can't or quote sources that can't be checked.

There are four key factors to checking that what you are getting via the Internet is good and useful:

- ▶ **Accuracy**
- ▶ **Authenticity**
- ▶ **Ageing**
- ▶ **Accessibility**

ACCURACY

There are no checks on the Internet. No one supervises the information being posted. No one looks after accuracy in any way, shape or form. There, now you know. There is simply no way, to verify that what you are getting is accurate. There is no editorial control as there would be if you were writing a medical textbook or a law journal. However, discrepancies can creep into both of those.

An example of how lax the Internet is is that of copyright law. There is a lot of information posted on the Internet about such a complex subject. To which country does it refer? Is it the same for all countries? (No, of course not.) Is it accurate? (No, it isn't.) It has been estimated that some 90 per cent of copyright law on the Internet has been found to be incorrect. Don't try it out in a court of law.

But don't panic. There are ways you can verify data quickly and effectively:

- ▶ **Collect facts from several different sources if you have time. Compare them. Are they telling you the same thing? If they are then chances are they may well be accurate.**
- ▶ **Do a quick telephone check with a known expert in the field. If they say it is so, then it probably is so. You may not get them to provide you with all the data in the first place but they may be happy to verify what you've got.**
- ▶ **Check the site you are getting the information from – see later in this chapter.**

AUTHENTICITY

Technically, the Internet is subject to international law regarding misrepresentation, libel and codes of advertising. However, getting anyone into court is another matter indeed. Sites may look good and appear to be quite genuine but may not be all they seem. For

thinking smart

CHECKING THE DOMAIN OWNERSHIP

Every domain name – the web address or URL – has to be 'owned', registered to someone somewhere. If you go to a domain register site such as DomainRegister.com, you can carry out a simple search of who the website you are using is registered to. This may throw up some interesting stuff you wouldn't have thought of. All you have to do is type in the URL and the register site will tell you the 'real' owner unless they have covered their tracks pretty carefully.

example there are a lot of drug companies running 'anonymous' health sites which appear to give independent and unbiased advice or the results of clinical trials which you would think to be authentic. But are they? Checking the domain name (such as sugarisreallygoodforyou.com) doesn't tell you anything.

So what do you do?

▶ **Check that any facts collected come from reliable sources and verify them with reference books (if you've got time), experts and your own common sense. Check with other sources and look for the origin of the web page (see 'What's in a name?' later in this chapter).**

▶ **Check with electronic versions of newspapers and journals – these will have been through some editorial process before they appear online.**

Ageing

Websites have no start date on them so you have no way of knowing how old they are or whether the information has been updated recently or has sat there twiddling its thumbs for the past three years. Some websites change almost every day and you'll never keep track of the information. What you obtain may be almost out of date before you've even entered it into your report. Obviously for some data, such as who ran the first four-minute mile, this won't be true – but what about stock market prices? Or how about population figures, which change by the minute. You may not need to verify data like these at all, which is lucky for you – saved yourself some more time.

What do you do about this?

▶ **Often on a website there may be a message saying 'last updated 23/9/00' or 'updated every Wednesday'. Check that that has been done – or if it hasn't been updated for a long time you might be best abandoning this site at once unless it contains the sort of data which do not need updating. If there's no message referring to its last update, the chances are it hasn't been done in a while.**

Accessibility

How accessible are the facts to anyone else who may want to verify them? You should quote your sources but go beyond this and make it easy for anyone else to access them also. Tell your audience or readers where the information is, give them

thinking smart

thhfhhh

USE YOUR BROWSER

On your browser you will find – along the top – a drop-down menu marked **edit**. Drop this down and you will find a box marked **find in page** [find (on this page) in Internet Explorer]. Click on this and a small browser will open up into which you type your key word/s, and this will seek out, in the web page, what it is you want to find. This speeds up your search considerably and can be used for as many web pages as you've got open without your having to retype your keywords each time.

the website address and the page number if relevant. Help them find their way around the site if you have to. Also bear in mind that websites close down, become inoperative at times and change their address from time to time. Print out your data as well, along with any help you can give for someone else to find their way there.

And how about you? You may find the site you want, and you may know the information lurks there, but it is simply buried in so much data that you can't find it. What can you do about this?

- **Learn to speed-read (see the next chapter) so you can quickly scroll down the page looking for useful information without having to read every word.**

FILTERED DIRECTORIES

Search engines are run by computers, which means the spiders they use aren't intelligent. They are told to look for keywords and they come back with them. That's all they do. There is no attempt to judge the information for reliability or authenticity. Directories, however, are chosen by human beings and are 'filtered' for out-of-date information, irrelevant sites, wrongly selected sites and sites which are to a greater degree what you are looking for. These filtered directories also give ratings to the sites as to how much pertinent information they contain. If they say a site is 100 per cent then there's lots of information on your keyword search. If they reduce this to 25 per cent, you know there's probably not a lot of point even looking at that site as the level of information that is pertinent has dropped off. For filtered directories try:

- **Magellan**
- **Excite**
- **Clearinghouse**
- **About**
- **Britannica.**

IDENTIFIED SITES

Look for sites which you know you can trust more than others. Any sites posted by professional institutes are likely to be much more reliable than commercial ones. Same goes for government sites and universities. Trade bodies are usually reliable, as are electronic versions of well known publications, newspapers and journals.

Don't be taken in by the domain name alone. Many domain names which sound impressive are used by commercial sites to fool you into thinking they are much more prestigious than they really are.

INSPECT THE WEBSITE

Before trusting a website take a good, long, hard look at it. Ask these questions:

- **Is it updated regularly?**
- **Is it run in a professional manner?**
- **Is it well written and logical?**
- **Is it well organised?**
- **Is it clear and well presented?**
- **Does any information it has cite sources and references?**
- **Is there a clear indication of who owns the site?**
- **Is there a contact address or e-mail address?**
- **Are there any links to other similar sites?**

If the answer to any or all of these is no, then move on to other sites which can answer yes to most, if not all, of them.

WHO PAID FOR THE SITE?

Websites cost money to put up and run. Someone somewhere is paying for it. Ask yourself why. Ask yourself if there is some catch. Are they trying to sell you something? If the site relies on advertising, they may be getting their running costs from that. If there is no advertising then someone is paying for it themselves and you have to ask why. You have to look for the hidden agenda.

Any website should fulfil certain fundamental criteria if it is to be of any use to you:

- **The site's purpose should be clear and that purpose should be reflected in its content.**
- **Sites should contain data, not the opinions or views of the person managing the page – the web master.**
- **The advertising on the site shouldn't overshadow the content of the site.**
- **The information should be easy to access.**
- **It should be easy to move around the site.**
- **The site should load (appear on your screen in its entirety) in a reasonable amount of time.**
- **The information should be updated where appropriate and a last-update date be given.**
- **The website should be accessible at all times and not subject to constant shutdown for redesign (you want your audience or readers to access it if necessary to confirm your data) – stability of the site is important.**

thinking fast

SAVE AND PRINT

If you don't have time to read an entire document carefully then simply save it for reading later or print it out for later. This frees you to continue searching. Also, reading from the printed page is a lot quicker than trying to read vast documents on screen.

thinking smart

LOOK FOR THE TILDE

If a web address contains the tilde symbol (~), it means that the name following the symbol is a personal name. These are personal web pages stored on a commercial server and, as such, are probably best avoided because they tend to contain one person's opinion.

WHAT'S IN A NAME?

Quite a lot, actually. Once you've found your website you need to know how reliable the information is, and this means checking the top-level domain name. This is the bit that comes after the domain name. Let's look at Jertain.com. Jertain is the domain name and .com tells you it is run by a commercial company – this is its top-level domain name. There are five main top-level domain names (apart from .co, which is the same really as .com):

- ▶ **.edu for educational sites such as universities**
- ▶ **.gov for government sites**
- ▶ **.org for non-profit-making sites**
- ▶ **.com for commercial sites (and .co.uk or .co.au etc., depending on what country it is)**
- ▶ **.net for technology-related commercial sites.**

There are other top-level domain names being currently suggested but as yet they haven't been introduced.

QUOTING YOUR SOURCES

It makes sense if you are including data in a report or proposal or in a handout at a presentation to quote your sources. This leaves the reader or audience free to check them if they want to themselves. Remember, though, that you are trying to prove a point, make a case, swing an argument – not necessarily to justify or verify a fact. The fact is there to back up your argument, not as a standalone.

If the Institute of Marketing says that a recent survey indicated that seven out of ten people preferred to shop online then that should be good enough for your audience or readers. You can quote this source with some confidence and don't have to worry too much about 'proving' it. You can quote the data, quote the source and allow anyone to check it themselves if they want to.

If a personal web page says that seven out of ten people prefer to shop online then be much more wary about either quoting it as a 'fact' or using it as a source. After all, if you write in your presentation that Joe Bloggs says seven out of ten people prefer to shop online, what do you expect your audience to think?

By now you should have not only found the facts you wanted but probably been inundated with them. Too many facts can be as daunting as too few. In the next chapter we will look at ways of speeding up the process – finding ways to prune all those data and updating your hardware to make it quicker and slicker to collect and process facts. And after that we'll look at ways of getting you up and out of the office to extend your search out into the real world.

⏪ for next time

Make sure you are using reputable websites which you have had the time to check for authenticity and reliability. When you can, take some time to check them for other related links, as you'll find that sites which are linked are more reputable than ones which aren't. Check back with sites from time to time, especially if they are useful for research purposes, to make sure they are updated regularly.

Try to stay abreast of Internet development. Such things as top-level domain names change from time to time and the smart manager knows about these changes before they take place and can take advantage of them.

Keep track of where you are getting information from by bookmarking (favourite in Internet Explorer) the sites. This makes it a lot easier to go back to them when you need them. Edit your bookmarks from time to time to keep them fresh and up to date.

If you do lose a site and didn't bookmark it then go to the top of your browser to **tools** and drop down the menu marked **Communicator**. Within this you will find another menu marked **tools**. Click on this. In here you will find a menu marked **history**. In Internet Explorer, click on the history button on the toolbar. This will give you a list of every web page you've visited for the last few weeks. Simply click on the web page you thought you'd lost to be miraculously transported there.

You can reset this history page to keep information for as long or as short a time as you want.

finding facts in an evening

If you have relatively few facts to pull together for your proposal, report or presentation, having a whole evening might look like a breeze. But suppose you need to find lots of data. Or maybe they are just very hard to track down. How do you handle finding facts when the time pressure is really building up?

Clearly you simply can't do as much in half a day as you can in a whole day or more. So the key question is: which bits do you leave out? Here are a few tips for digging up data at the double:

- ▶ **Remember your objective (Chapter 1). Only search for information you *really* need.**

- ▶ **Restrict yourself to looking for data from the fastest sources you can. You simply can't afford to waste time scouring the building for the one remaining copy of a five-year-old report that you're not even certain will contain what you want. Broadly speaking, stick to the phone (including your modem).**

- ▶ **Don't even start on facts you aren't confident you can verify. The second you can see that a website, for example, may contain doubtful information, abandon it. Find the information elsewhere.**

- ▶ **If you're working into the evening, be sure you make all possible phone calls first, before everyone goes home.**

- ▶ **The Internet gets very busy in the evenings and at weekends. If you can't use it first thing, you may be better off using it really late. If you're at panic levels watching data download at the rate of a snail with a hangover, just go to bed early, get a few hours' kip, and go back online at four or five in the morning. It'll be much quieter.**

- ▶ **If you've got any friends with faster equipment than yours for accessing the Net, don't be shy. Call round with a generous bottle or two of really good wine and ask them if you can borrow it for the evening. (The wine's for them.)**

finding facts in an hour

Blimey! This is cutting it fine, isn't it? But sometimes there's no choice. Work is piling up around you, or maybe you didn't know you'd need the data until now. Perhaps the meeting you want it for to put your case at has just been pulled forward to this morning. Whatever the reason, don't panic. If you're smart, you can do it. Here's the lowdown:

1 However short of time you are, establish your objective (see pages 388–9). No, I'm not kidding. I know the clock's ticking but this is the only way to do the job effectively and fast, instead of just fast but wrong. There's no point having your proposal or presentation ready on time but so ill-prepared it doesn't convince anyone. You need to identify your objective because you're going to have to slim down the number of facts you're looking for and this is your magic tool for doing just that.

2 Focus on this objective to decide which points or arguments absolutely have to be included in your meeting, proposal, presentation or whatever it is, and must have factual data to support them.

3 Now go fetch. If you can, delegate the job of finding some (or even all) of this information. But make sure the person you delegate this to understands the argument you are using these data to support.

4 When you're this pushed for time, you have to stay on your toes. You may have to be very inventive about what data you pursue and where from. Who can you call or e-mail who might know? Could you find a different piece of information to make the same point?

5 Don't, whatever you do, succumb to the temptation of using data you can't verify. Just avoid from the start any sources which aren't going to be quick to verify or corroborate once you have the information.

The key thing to remember is that it is more persuasive to present a case hinged on three or four core arguments, well supported with verifiable facts, than one based on a dozen or more flimsy, irrelevant or dubious arguments. In other words, when time is tight, focus on quality not quantity of arguments and supporting facts. That should speed things up nicely – *and* make your case far more convincing into the bargain.

fast but not now

If you intend to do a lot of serious research – especially on the Internet – then you do need to make sure that the tools you are using are up to date, fast and efficient. There is nothing worse than being in a hurry and having to wait for web pages to download or trying to peer at pages of data on a tiny 14" screen.

UPDATING THE HARDWARE

We all get used to using whatever computer happens to sit on our desk. It may be more than a year old, in which case it simply isn't the most efficient tool on the market. The old adage that computers double in capability and halve in price roughly every year happens to be true. The second you walk out of the showroom with your brand- new RX2000 tucked happily under your arm it's already out of date, as the sales staff had the RX 3000 tucked away waiting until they'd shifted surplus stock of the old 2000 models. Of course they weren't going to tell you. They are there to make a living, same as all of us.

Your computer is a tool, nothing more, nothing less. You deserve to have the best, the latest, the fastest if you need that tool to do your job quickly, efficiently and skilfully. No one would expect a surgeon to operate with blunt scalpels or rusty needles. Yet we are often given old and slow equipment and, therefore, are expected to operate with out-of-date stuff that should have been recycled long ago. Modern computers cost a fraction of what they once did and you can now buy a slick, efficient machine very cheaply indeed.

MODEMS

If you need to talk to your office manager about upgrading, make sure you have the latest specifications with you – and the justification. If you do Internet research then you need a fast machine capable of handling and processing data in big bites. This means a fast modem – the bit that links your computer with the World Wide Web. Modems were considered fast at 28 kbps (bits per second) a few years ago but now 56 is considered slow and ISDN lines are available. This is a special line that enables very fast connections and fast download times for data. You don't need to know how the technology works. The faster the baud rate (the bps), the better you can get on with your job.

thinking smart

DON'T SPEAK THE LINGO?

You may well come across sites which are in a foreign language – and they are the very ones you know contain the data you so desperately need. It happens. Don't rush off and learn a new language just so you can read them. Instead try Babelfish. This is a site which will translate for you. It isn't perfect but it will translate whole chunks of text from one language to another. Babelfish is run by AltaVista and will currently handle German, Spanish, Italian, French, English and Portuguese.

415

BOOKMARKS

For really speedy research – particularly if you specialise in one or two key areas – you can't beat a decent set of bookmarks. These can be found on your browser. Adding a bookmark is a simple click. Make sure you back up your bookmarks so in the event of a technology malfunction (I hate the word 'crash': it sounds so melodramatic) you can still access them. Update them regularly and delete any you haven't used in a while.

Next you need a machine capable of handling that fast baud rate. And that means junking your old 286 and investing in a proper modern computer that is run by a fast processor – the bit that processes the information. Now, at no point along this journey to improved efficiency and faster work rate do you need to put on an anorak – you simply don't need to become a geek or a nerd.

JUST BUY IT

You don't need to know how anything works – just that it does, and quickly. Go to the showroom and buy the latest, the best and biggest you can. Make sure it is loaded with the latest software and take it back to the office and get on with it. I know what I said earlier about sales staff but there's no way round it. As soon as you walk out with it I can guarantee you someone will come out with a bigger or faster one at half the price. But don't let this stop you. Buy it and work with what you've got. Update it approximately every 12 months. If you work for yourself, it is tax-deductible and you owe it to yourself to work with the best.

HARD DISK

To process data quickly you need a large storage area – gigabytes of it. No one would expect a filing cabinet the size of a matchbox, so buy as many megabytes as you can. A few years ago 10 or 20 megabytes was considered extreme, but nowadays software takes up megabytes of disk space in a vast and inexplicable way. You need the most you can get. Believe me, size does matter – at least when it comes to computer storage.

A WORKING TOOL

Your computer is your working tool. It is there to help you in your search for perfect research to put into the perfect report or proposal. It is not there to entertain you. Delete any games you may have acquired – games are time-consumers. If you need a break or to relax, go for a walk around the office.

Surf the web for research purposes only and save the other stuff for when you get home. Same with e-mails. Tell friends to stop e-mailing you the latest Clinton/Lewinsky jokes. You'll be surprised how quickly you can empty your mailbox when you know it is only work-related items that you're likely to find there.

thinking smart

THE SLEEPING GIANT

Ever noticed that websites take longer to load in the afternoon than in the morning? That's because in the afternoon the sleeping giant awakes – America. Once America wakes up and goes online it clogs up the entire system. You can avoid this by going online when the sleeping giant is still asleep – in the early morning. Yep, you gotta get in the office early.

CHECK OUT YOUR BANDWIDTH

You access the Internet via a service (or access) provider. This is a company which gives you your route into the World Wide Web. Some charge for this service and others don't – making their money from advertising. These providers need computers themselves, and the faster, bigger and better they are, the faster and better you can access the Web yourself. You aren't tied to any one provider or limited to only one at any time. Compare their performance by asking about their bandwidth – the rate at which they exchange information with the Web and you – and then choose the best. Ask about modem/user ratios. Once you have seen a few you'll know which is faster and better. The bandwidth is usually measured in bits per second. An A4 page of text is about 15,000 bits, whereas an on-screen video would take about ten million bps to run. You need a server with a minimum of 100 megabytes per second to run such a video and that is about the minimum you'd want anyway. Free providers operate at around 90, which is considerably slower – this matters when you are in a hurry and need information fast.

SCREEN SIZE

In the old days when computers were clockwork we all sat in front of a 14" screen and thought we were the bee's knees. Today 14" looks positively antique. By upgrading your screen to at least 17" you do two things – first, you give yourself much more room to work in. A big screen can show almost a whole page of A4 without the type being so small you can't read it. Secondly, you can move text around easily – and that text stays fully viewable. It makes sense to go even bigger. A 22" screen will make your working life tolerable in a way you wouldn't believe. Screens aren't expensive – and again are tax-deductible, if you are self-employed.

thinking fast

MIRROR SITES

A lot of popular sites now carry mirror sites. You'll know which ones these are as they will ask you where you want to go to. The American ones always ask 'West Coast or East Coast?' Others will suggest the nearest site to you and others, often the ones where you can download software, will give a list of suggested sites. These are identical but located in different parts of the world. If you are accessing a site which carries a mirror site, look for one which is in a time zone that is least likely to be used. This is usually between 11pm and 7am local time.

NETWORKED SYSTEMS

If you work from a networked system then upgrading what's on your desk may simply not be an option open to you. You may be best getting a decent PC or laptop at home and doing your research in the evenings – or, better still, get up early and go online first thing before everyone else does. It's the smart manager who catches the facts.

So you've updated your modem, screen and hard drive. What about software? Usually this is supplied already installed when you buy a machine, but it too does need updating from time to time. I know we all think software manufacturers only bring out new updates to make us spend money but the updates do improve your working life. If you're still using Word 1 on a 286 with a 14" screen and 64K of memory, don't expect to get any real work done today.

APPLE MAC OR PC?

As for the debate about whether you should go Apple Mac or PC, simply ask yourself what you need your computer for. If you run lots of graphics-based software (pictures) then go for an Apple, but if your data are text-based then a PC is fine. And obviously you need to know who you send files to and receive files from. If your clients or colleagues all use Apples then you might well be advised to go that way. But if everyone around you is using a PC then opt for that.

SPEED-READING

Once you've got all your hardware and software set up there is one aspect of your tool usage that also needs updating – you. There's not much point in having the latest technology importing data fast and efficiently if you can't handle it fast and efficiently yourself. Time for a personal makeover.

Slow readers vs fast readers

We simply don't have the time or space to train you completely in speed-reading. For that you need to invest in a good book on it and a little training yourself. The important thing to remember is that quick readers and slow readers move their eyes differently. Slow readers follow each line from left to right. When they reach the end of a line they go right back to the beginning of the left-hand margin and start again. Fast readers tend to read, or rather glance, down the page keeping

 thinking smart

> **WINDWEAVER**
>
> Smart managers spend a little time learning as much about the Internet as possible and it makes sense for you to do some homework. A book, even one as slick and as fast as a *Fast Thinking* guide, can only teach you so much. Log on to Windweaver Web Resources for an up-to-the-minute Internet guide which will outline all the search engines with their strengths and weaknesses. This site will also guide you through links and resources. And if you want to go into more academic detail about research, try the Information Research FAQ, which publishes articles relating to a wide range of Internet research.

thinking fast

SAVE AND PRINT

When you are reading web pages you can save them and print them out later, which makes them a lot easier to read. Save them as a 'text only' file rather than as an HTML file and you'll be able to open them in a word-processing software package and read them as a plain document – or print them – without all those annoying colours or moving graphics.

their eyes roughly focused on the middle of the page. Fast readers scan, looking for phrases and bits of information that seem pertinent. They miss out all the common words such as 'and', 'the', 'that' and suchlike.

Don't read and drive

A useful analogy is the way police drivers are trained. They don't focus directly on the road ahead but tend to stay slightly unfocused and can thus widen their field of vision. They get to see what is happening at the edges just as much as what is happening in the middle. With a little practice you too can do this – not when you are driving though! Scan the page with slightly unfocused eyes and key phrases and words will seemingly jump out at you.

Waffle and diarrhoea

Some writers, especially if they are using a word- processor rather than a pen or old-fashioned typewriter, have a tendency towards textual diarrhoea. They allow themselves to run on too long and to waffle. Not something, you will have noticed, that happens in a *Fast Thinking* guide. By not reading the waffle and only going for the real bits of information you can speed up the process considerably. If they start to wax lyrical, move your eyes down the page to where they get back to the real meat.

PERSONAL SERVICE

Don't expect to do good research if you come back to the office after a large liquid lunch. And similarly if you are tired, stressed or confused, you won't be at your best. First thing in the morning is good for logging on, as you should feel brighter and more enthusiastic. Make sure you are ready to concentrate and are feeling fresh and awake. Take a break every 20 minutes or so just to rest your eyes. Get up and walk around the office. Make sure you sit comfortably and aren't straining your back. Be relaxed and keep your feet firmly on the floor. Research has shown that by keeping your feet flat on the floor you do tend to stay much more alert and upright.

for next time

Make sure you stay ahead of the game by keeping abreast of the latest Internet search engines and facilities. You should keep your equipment updated and serviced.

Make sure you do regular back-ups and maintain your bookmarks. Back up your URLs (web addresses) so you know where you got the facts from. If you need them again in a hurry you have easy access to them and, more importantly, your audience can also access them.

By not reading the waffle and only going for the real bits of information you can speed up the process considerably

smart but not fast

Although the Internet may be the fastest and best means of accessing information in this day and age, there are still valuable sources waiting for you outside the office if you have the time to get up and get out there.

TYPES OF INFORMATION SUPPLIER

These can be broadly divided up into two categories – those you have to pay and those you don't. Obviously if you have the time and budget you can simply hand over your fact-finding mission to a researcher and let them get on with it. Perhaps you'd better make a note of this for next time. However, employing a researcher yourself does have drawbacks:

- ▶ **You might not get the information you actually wanted.**
- ▶ **They may waste valuable time and money without any results at all.**
- ▶ **You might get the information you wanted but it might not be in the format you wanted or is perhaps out of date and you'd have to start all over again.**

By the same token, employing a researcher does free you up to get on with life and work, and they should be professional at their job, which could pay dividends. You pays your money and you takes your choice. You could always try an Internet research agency to do your stuff for you. These usually charge a quarterly fee, and the more you pay, the better service you are going to get. Try MindSource, which you will have to access via memo.net.

But if you haven't the time or budget then you're going to have to do it yourself. And this means knowing exactly where to go, how much you want to pay and exactly what you want.

MARKET RESEARCH

If you need to use market research then you need to know there are various options open to you:

- ▶ **in-depth interviews with consumers**
- ▶ **group discussions among consumers**
- ▶ **at-home product testing**
- ▶ **business-to-business telephone surveys**
- ▶ **brief face-to-face interviews with consumers**

A THOROUGH BRIEFING
The key when asking someone else to do research for you is in giving them a thorough briefing on exactly what it is you want – and why, of course.

The key when asking someone else to do research for you is in giving them a thorough briefing on exactly what it is you want – and why, of course

thinking smart

THINKING AHEAD

The smart manager thinks ahead and collects newspaper cuttings (or already subscribes to a newspaper-cutting website), magazine articles, videos and relevant television programmes, and listens to the business programmes on the radio. In general they stay one jump ahead by thinking ahead – you never know when some fact you've collected along the way is going to come in useful.

- ▶ **questionnaires**
- ▶ **telephone tracking and attitude interviews.**

They're all different, throw up different views and opinions, and all cost different amounts. Sometimes, someone else may have done the sort of research you need and thus won't have to be commissioned to do fresh research but can simply sell you their previous results.

OMNIBUS RESEARCH

You could always combine your research with others. Suppose you needed public opinion about a couple of things. Commissioning your own survey of a couple of hundred thousand people would be frightfully expensive. But if a research company is already going out there asking questions, it is a lot cheaper to add your couple to theirs. This is called omnibus research. Most market research agencies will have details.

LIBRARIES

These are usually free but you may have to pay for photocopying, and also watch out for the old copyright trouble. I was once refused permission by a librarian to photocopy a page from a book I had written myself! And don't just think in terms of public libraries – there are also university libraries and company libraries.

thinking smart

E-MAIL RESEARCH

It doesn't take a moment to e-mail a group of clients, customers, friends or experts to ask quick questions that may throw light on where you should go for information. Your e-mail recipient may already have it. If you don't ask, you won't know. Always ask politely and appreciate that other people may be as busy and as rushed as you are. But surprisingly few people seem to mind being asked and will often spare the time to answer by e-mail, whereas a letter or telephone call may be ignored or the reply delayed.

thinking fast

TAKE A MOMENT

The smart manager always takes a moment to consider the type of facts they are researching before rushing off to their usual source. A quick trip to a library may save you a lot of wasted time surfing the Internet for information that hasn't yet been posted or might never be posted.

421

budget

GATHER GOOD INFORMATION

FORECAST EFFECTIVELY

DELIVER YOUR NUMBERS

richard templar

contents

introduction

So, you found yourself having to do the departmental budget and you haven't got a clue where to start – and the clock is ticking. OK, let's be charitable and assume you're doing this budget because either you are newly promoted and this is the first time you've had the responsibility or your departmental manager is off sick with Wimbledon flu and you're stepping into the breach.

Whatever the background, you've put it off owing to pressure of work (see *fast thinking: work overload*) and the days have flown past and now the budget has to be done and on someone's desk first thing Monday morning. This only leaves you a couple of days.

So what are you going to do? Panic, of course. No, you're not. You are going to work through the stages easily and quickly following the guidelines in this book so the budget will be done – and done well – and duly on the right desk at the right time and in the right way.

Panic doesn't get the job done. Only by thinking at the speed of life can you accomplish all you need to. Trust me, you *can* do the impossible.

We all have too much to do, and let's face it budgets don't sound much fun, but with the help of this book you will come through not only on time and with your budget, but also with flying colours and looking cool. Here's how. This book will explain what is required of you: what a budget is and how it is put together; how to get the information you require; what you're supposed to do with the thing once you've done it; how to check it against reality; how to put it right if it all falls apart; and how to make sure you prepare better in the future (this means leaving more time). So let's get on with it.

It may well be better to leave more time in the future but all you are interested in is right now, right? You want the fast thinking version of budgets, which is:

 tips for putting together a budget that looks as if you know what you're doing

 shortcuts for producing the maximum while doing the minimum

 checklists to glance through to make sure you've got it all down on paper.

… and all put together simply and clearly. And short enough to read, learn and inwardly digest, of course.

This book is going to take you through the key stages of preparing, delivering and maintaining a budget – your budget, the one you've got to do *now*.

1. The very first thing you've got to do is establish the objective so you can understand how to prepare a budget – without a destination, the map is useless – your budget is the map, your objective is the destination.

2. Next, we have to know what sort of budget we are preparing – and there are all sorts from cash flow forecasts to profit and loss to distribution. And even the departmental budget varies enormously from company to company, and even from department to department.

3. After this comes the basic preparation – collecting the information, finding out how it was done last year, establishing what figures go where and why, adding on and subtracting to allow for growth and slump.

4. The next step is filling in the actual budget – entering figures into boxes and balancing it all out.

5. Then you'll need to know how to present it and to whom and how to justify it. And you'll need to know how to maintain it and keep up with the variances – those bits which differ from what you said they would be – so you get a lot of good use out of it.

6. Last of all, it's looking at what to do next time – when you've got more time – and all the speedy tips and hints you might like to file away ready for next year's budget – and the year after and so on. And we'll do the really fast budget: the budget in an evening and the budget in an hour.

fast thinking gambles

So, don't panic. It's all in this book, everything you need to know – and no more. You don't need a long, rambling history of 20th-century economics or a lot of statistically pompous information about standards and variances. What you need is here, the minimalist guide to budgets for those of us who haven't got time to catch a breath let alone read waffle. You're thinking at the speed of life so you just want to get on with it.

Well, patience. First, you must be advised of some of the pitfalls before you can rush ahead. Let's face it, you've left this to the last minute either by choice or foolishness or accident and in an ideal world you would have a lot more time. But you haven't so you have to work with what you've got. The downside is that:

- ▶ **The people whose help you need to prepare this budget may be reluctant to provide vital data at such short notice or may find it physically impossible.**

- ▶ **You may not be able to get hold of a copy of a previous budget this quickly, and without knowing what the 'house style' is you can waste a lot of time and effort.**

- ▶ **You don't have the time to check all your figures as accurately as you might have wanted to – this can lead to mistakes creeping in unnoticed.**

- ▶ **You may be tempted to take shortcuts and put in more assumptions than would otherwise be advisable – data are facts, assumptions are exactly that.**

- ▶ **You may be tempted to lump together a lot of items in the hope that no one will ask you to justify a final figure. Forget it. If you are shaky on some aspect then that's the area you will be asked about – it's an irony of life and there is no escape.**

- ▶ **You might be tempted by the urgency of this project to take other people's data at face value – don't. They may have their own mission, one of throwing you off course for their own ends. You need time to be vigilant, and check everything.**

This fast thinking guide will get you out of trouble this time and have you coming up smelling of roses – but for next time allow longer, prepare better and enjoy the journey more. Now let's do it.

1 your objective

Faced with panic we all want to do something, anything. Well, you can't. Just do nothing for a moment or two. No panic. No activity at all. Except close your eyes for a moment and think about your objective. There, that's easy isn't it? Yep. Your objective is to get this darned thing filled in, on the boss's desk first thing Monday morning and save your job, bacon and reputation. Fine. There, that *was* easy. Trouble is that isn't your objective at all. First, you have to take a brief look at what a budget does.

DRAWING THE MAP

Apart from being a part of your job, what is a budget? It's a map. A map of the future. It might well be a treasure map of the future if used well. It tells you what is going to happen to your department over the next 12 months within the confines, obviously, of the fact that you cannot see into the future. But you can make reasonable guesstimates.

You can make assumptions based on sound managerial experience. You can use past form to produce a theory of what is going to happen. Then you can be on top of any events because you have predicted them:

- **No more panicking because staff are off on holidays and you have no cover – you will have budgeted for that.**
- **No more frenzied terror when summer sales slump because you produce umbrellas and there is no demand in August for them – you will have budgeted for that and be expecting it.**
- **No more waking up at night in a sweat because there's no money left in your budget and you still have to pay for the Christmas party – you will have budgeted for that.**

YOUR OBJECTIVE

So a budget is a map of the future – accurately and well defined and beautifully put together. It sings with perfection and you have orchestrated it with all the dedication and skill of a composer *par excellence*. But what is your objective? First you have to identify the objective and be very specific. It's no good saying: 'My budget is a plan of what is going to happen in my department over the next 12 months.'

That covers pretty well everything but what about the sales conference? Is that in there? Good, it should be. And the cost of paper clips? A new photocopier? Extra staff for the Christmas rush? Good. So you can refine your objective some more: 'My budget is a realistic plan of the next 12 months expressed in quantitative terms of what is going to happen to the finances of my department.'

That's better. It is a plan. Write it down.

thinking smart

GOOD MAP READING

Set a destination you know you can get to but still have to strive for. Commit yourself to your budget and make sure you achieve it.

REALISING YOUR BUDGET

When you compile a budget it has to be realistic or there is simply no point doing it. Your budget has to be attainable and realistic, and you have to be committed to it. If you set a target of selling 1,000 widgets a month then you have to move heaven and earth to achieve that goal. If you know in your heart of hearts you can only shift 600 then there is no point planning to sell more. If you also know that with a bit more effort and motivation you are going to move nearer 1,400 then say so in your budget. Use your budget as a tool for, not a hindrance to, good management.

INSPIRATION AND MOTIVATION

Under-budgeting is as bad as over-budgeting. It's your plan and it has to both inspire you and motivate you – and all your staff, of course, with whose help you will compile this budget. Without them you can do nothing (see Chapter 3 but not at the moment as you are busy finding out about what a budget is).

Under- or over-budgeting is a bit like setting out to arrive in Birmingham and settling for Stoke – near enough you think, and quite similar. It's like crossing out Birmingham on your map and writing in Stoke. You ain't fooling anyone. The perfect budget is one which is realistic and achieved.

A FEW RULES

OK, so you've got an objective. You also need to be realistic and aim for the truth. Technically, there is nothing difficult about preparing a budget. There are a few rules and as long as you stick to them you can be successful. If, however, you go that little bit further you can produce not only an effective budget but also a really useful tool that will make you look good, be sharper and stay on top of your job better. Interested? Here's how.

Making it manageable

Budgets can cover any period. Let's say yours is for the next financial year. Break that down into manageable chunks. It's pretty useless to have a budget which just gives a year's expenditure and a year's income. If you have a bad month (or a good one) there is no way of knowing. Thus you cannot make any adjustments to staffing levels or production or take any action based on the new information.

CHECKING THE DETAIL

Don't accept that a bottom line figure agreeing with what is budgeted is enough – you might be under in one area and over in another and these two are cancelling each other out. Someone, somewhere will spot this and you will be caught out.

Break your budget down into the smallest time periods which actually mean something to you. It will probably be months but may even be weeks. A daily target is probably unrealistic. So let's assume you will break your budget down into 12 months. That makes it easy to handle, easy to see what's happening and easy to take evasive action should you need to.

Noticing where the money goes

So you've looked at the objective and you've decided on what sort of budget is required – this may well be dictated to you by a regional director or a senior manager and you have no choice in it – and next you will see how you can gather all the information needed. Relax. You are already a long way towards reaching your goal. Now, take a quick mental walk through your department and see it with a financial eye. Try to notice:

- ▶ **what costs money**
- ▶ **where money is spent**
- ▶ **what staff you have and need**
- ▶ **what furniture and equipment you have and need.**

This shouldn't take long – now you can have a break.

Always allow yourself peace and quiet to think seriously about your objective. Be aware that your budget is one of your most effective management tools and try to put aside lots of time to work on it. No more leaving it to the last minute and having to panic. Be determined to be realistic and truthful in your budget and be committed to coming in exactly on budget – over and under are as bad as each other. Next time you will have this budget to follow on from so your job should be a whole lot easier.

2 types of budget

Y ou still have a lot of work to do and the clock is ticking those precious seconds away.

TYPES OF BUDGET

Now what sort of budget are you going to prepare? You might think there's only the one but there are several sorts of budget:

- sales
- production
- stocks
- capital expenditure
- cash flow
- profit and loss (including balance sheet)
- purchasing
- credit control.

Of course, all of these can be incorporated in one form or another into what is called a 'control budget' – a sort of master budget that covers everything. You have to determine which aspects of your department fit into your budget. Obviously if you are in the service industry you may not have sales as such or production. You don't make or sell anything. But you still need staffing costs, cash flow, credit control and capital expenditure. Or perhaps you only make and sell things, in which case a sales and production budget combined with profit and loss is your baby.

A *WHAT* BUDGET?

Let's briefly run through these different types of budget so we all know what we are talking about.

Sales

Simple really. A sales budget is exactly that – how much or how many are you going to sell? This may be broken down into distinct types of sales:

- credit sales
- cash sales
- sold items – i.e. $1\frac{1}{4}$" widgets, $2\frac{3}{4}$" widgets etc.
- delivered items/collected items
- trade sales/public sales.

Obviously if you are involved with sales you will know what sort of sales you make and thus what sort of costs you will have to budget for, such as:

- ▸ **sales staff**
- ▸ **delivery staff**
- ▸ **buying in stock**
- ▸ **overheads**
- ▸ **general running costs.**

Production

Again, simple when you think about it. Production is exactly that. Perhaps you are the manager of a production department, in which case your budget is all about how many of things you make. Your budget will stipulate how many each month set off against what it is going to cost you to make them.

Stocks

A stock control budget is one which deals with how much of anything you are keeping on the premises. Perhaps your business is very affected by seasonal changes. In this case a stock budget is essential. It's no good having money tied up in stocks of umbrellas over the summer months when trade is slack if that money would be better off invested in the high-interest account.

Capital expenditure

You need to budget for buying big things that your business needs. Perhaps that old photocopier in your department is going to need replacing sometime in the next 12 months – when are you going to buy it? Where is the money coming from? These things have to be budgeted for or events will have a nasty habit of sneaking up on you unannounced.

Cash flow

Perhaps your department needs more money at certain times of year than others – your cash flow budget will determine these slack times or over-rich times and allow you to make decisions and plan effectively.

Profit and loss (including balance sheet)

Suppose you buy in a second-hand car at £500 and spend £50 getting it through an MOT and another £25 on a new set of seat covers. And then you sell it for £600. You have made a profit of some £25. Brilliant. Now take out the cost of your time and the tank of petrol you put in and you will see what you actually made. Oh, so you cost yourself at £100 a day and the petrol was a fiver. Made a profit or loss?

But suppose your department plans to buy ten cars a month and sell them; then you need a profit and loss budget to make sure that you aren't unexpectedly making a loss without realising it – or planning it. The balance sheet is a statement of where the business is at any one time – a sort of Polaroid snapshot.

Purchasing

If you are the manager of the purchasing department then you need a purchasing budget. This is concerned with buying stuff in and allocating which months you need more or less in – simple.

thinking smart

DIFFERENT BUDGET TYPES

All budgets are different. The format varies a lot. Don't get into thinking budgets must always look the same – they don't. They vary from organisation to organisation. Smart managers know how to be flexible and think on their feet.

Credit control

If you are the manager of the credit department then you need a credit control budget which will tell you when you need more money or less, how to dish it out or call it in, and what to do with it once you've got it.

Sorry about the brevity of these budget explanations, but we really haven't the time to go into them in great detail. This isn't a textbook of budgets but a fast thinking guide to helping you with your budget – today.

YOUR BUDGET

In your budget some or all of these examples may appear – but equally they may not. In an ideal world you will only be concerned with a simple budget which deals with what you spend, your staffing costs and your overheads. This may be set against some form of income or you may well be allocated an expenditure for the year.

Negotiating your budget

What happens is you tell the manager above you what you need in terms of finances for the year and they give you this amount or less. If you are good with your budget and prove a couple of things, you'll be a smart cookie and they will trust you and give you what you say you need. If you are sloppy and prove yourself unable to manage or are deliberately over-estimating some costs so you have a little slack to play with then they will pare you down accordingly. So:

- ▶ **If you need six staff members, say so and budget for six – don't say seven and hope to have some money left in your budget to play with.**
- ▶ **Check your budget every month (or more frequently if necessary) so variances can be dealt with quickly and decisively – a variance is a difference between what you said would happen and what has actually happened.**
- ▶ **Be realistic when you budget and be truthful.**

thinking smart

DIFFERENT BUDGET TYPES

All budgets are different. The format varies a lot. Don't get into thinking budgets must always look the same – they don't. They vary from organisation to organisation. Smart managers know how to be flexible and think on their feet.

Things have to be budgeted for or events will have a nasty habit of sneaking up on you unannounced

433

- Don't make too many assumptions – data are facts, assumptions are guesses (OK, they may well be based on experience but they are still guesses); an assumption built on another assumption will always go wrong.
- Update your budget and stay on top of it – information is only valuable if you use it.

A QUICK EXAMPLE

If this is the first departmental budget you've ever had to prepare, you may feel daunted by what it actually is supposed to look like. So, let's look at an example.

A simplified version

This is obviously a very simplified version. The column for this year would be broken down into 12 – one for every month – and some of the costs might well be broken down again, such as staffing costs, which may be broken down into full- and part-time or service staff and sales staff. Only you know what is required in your department.

Fleshing it out

OK, a quick rundown of each area in your budget. Your departmental budget may look nothing like this example – so learn to think laterally and put whatever you need into the boxes to compile your budget.

Staff costs

These are what they say – how many people you have and what it costs to employ them including:

	Last year	This year	Variance +/–
Staff costs			
Travel			
Stationery			
Capital expenditure			
Furniture and equipment			
Heat/light			
Overheads			
Maintenance/repairs			
Petty cash			
Telephone costs			
Refreshments			
Totals			

thinkingfast

UNDERSTANDING A BUDGET

Look at the bottom line. The expression means exactly what is required of you. Don't get bogged down in detail – look at the very last line, the 'totals' line, and that will give you a pretty good overview of a budget.

- ▶ **wages**
- ▶ **cars**
- ▶ **national Insurance**
- ▶ **private medical insurance**
- ▶ **pension contributions**
- ▶ **perks**
- ▶ **expense accounts**
- ▶ **clothing.**

Ask yourself: am I going to need more or fewer staff this year? Will I be recruiting or downsizing? Is there anyone to be made redundant? Do I need extra cover at any particular time of year?

Travel

These costs may include any of the following:

- ▶ **train tickets**
- ▶ **petrol**
- ▶ **first-class plane tickets**
- ▶ **bus fares.**

Ask yourself: do my staff move around at all and if so what does it cost me and is it a seasonal or varying cost that changes depending on the time of year?

Stationery

Obvious really. What paper do you use and how much? Postage stamps? Put them in as well and:

- ▶ **envelopes**
- ▶ **computer consumables (they may go here or in another section)**
- ▶ **pads**
- ▶ **invoices**
- ▶ **pens**
- ▶ **paper clips**
- ▶ **sticky tape**
- ▶ **post-it notes.**

A variance is a difference between what you said would happen and what has actually happened

435

Ask yourself: are my paper needs going to change through the year? Are there brochures to be printed? Do I have mail shots to be done? Can I economise anywhere here?

Capital expenditure

This may make accountants do a double take. It doesn't really go here according to them but we are talking budgets in general and learning not to get hung up on where things go – merely that they have to be budgeted for. Your own house style of budgets will tell you exactly where it all goes. You will have to work with your own house style even if you dislike it or it looks as if it was designed by monkeys. So, capital expenditure – big stuff, machinery, plant, not stuff consumed but stuff becoming part of the business.

Ask yourself: what big things am I going to need to buy this year? What needs replacing? Has everything been realistically valued?

Furniture and equipment

This might be chairs, or it could be computers. Again, it depends on your house style and what the finance department stipulates should go in here. (We'll talk about how you talk to them in the next chapter.)

Ask yourself: what furniture will need upgrading this year? What equipment is going to need replacing?

Heat and light

You've got to be able to see at work and be warm. It all costs money. Where's it coming from? Out of your budget, of course. Perhaps you may not even have to think about these as they may be taken care of as part of a control budget fixed by head office. But it doesn't hurt to know what they cost and how much you consume of them.

Ask yourself: what are my heat and light running costs? What do we spend the money on? Can we economise in any area here?

Overheads

These are sometimes known as fixed costs. They include the rent on the building or mortgages, leases on machinery, ground rents, that sort of thing. You may well have no control over them. They may not even be included in your budget or they may be allocated to your budget as a fixed percentage of their overall cost. Head office may dictate to you that you have to include such and such a figure for overheads without your even knowing how they arrived at the figure. It all varies.

Ask yourself: even if I have no control over them, do I know what everything costs? Do I have a full breakdown of the figures from the finance department?

Maintenance and repairs

Things go wrong. Things have to be fixed. Someone, somewhere has to pay for it and you have to budget for it. You may well wonder how on earth you are expected to know what is going to break and how much it is going to cost to fix it. You aren't; you budget a certain amount as a sort of reserve. At the end of the year you will know how close you were and what to include in next year's budget.

Ask yourself: have I anticipated everything and anything that could get broken, fall apart, cease working, become out of date?

Petty cash

Some departments don't have this any more. Some do. It's a small amount of money kept for buying things such as the odd bottle of milk when you run out. Whose job was it to budget for the milk? Who got it wrong? But you may have to budget a bit for very small emergencies.

Telephone costs

Calls and phones all have to be paid for. If you need an extra line put in, it has to come out of your budget. Catch the staff phoning their relatives in Australia during the lunch break? Well, it's coming out of your budget. And, no, you can't budget for your own private calls. Email calls may well go in here as well so don't overlook them.

Ask yourself: have I explored every aspect of telephone costs? Do I get charged a percentage for general switchboard finances?

Refreshments

Could be anything from the office coffee (which in some departments would come out of petty cash) to entertaining clients. Mind you, entertaining clients may come out of your travel budget if you go out to eat. You see what I mean about not getting bogged down about where it all goes until you actually come to fill it in? By then you should know, as you will have a copy of last year's. And you'll be armed with a lot of information about all this stuff – next chapter, wait for it.

Ask yourself: are there any categories of spending not covered in these examples? Have I missed anything?

◀◀ for next time

Make sure you have fully and completely explored every avenue and aspect of your departmental finances. Make sure you know where money is spent and what everything costs.

Make sure you understand the house style – and if it sucks try to get it changed to a better style or a more usable one.

Ask yourself: even if I have no control over them, do I know what everything costs?

3 gathering information

Let's just take a moment to recap before plunging ahead:

- ▶ **Your budget is a financial statement of what you expect to happen within your department over the next 12 months.**
- ▶ **It is no better to be below budget than it is to be above it.**
- ▶ **Budgets vary from organisation to organisation and it is better to know about budgets in general than to become bogged down with how your lot do it – you need to learn to be flexible in your thinking.**
- ▶ **Don't make too many assumptions when you come to fill in the detail of your budget.**
- ▶ **Be realistic and truthful.**
- ▶ **Any budget you do, you are going to have to justify and live with.**
- ▶ **A budget is very simple – you get a sum of money either allocated to you or from sales and you have to run your department financially by spending that money to ensure an efficient and successful office.**

LAST YEAR'S BUDGET

So let's see what we have left to do. First thing first: last year's budget. Unless you really are taking over a very new department there will be an old budget from last year. A good manager will have had this on their desk all year to check it against *variances* – a difference between what was expected to happen and what really happened financially – and to provide valuable financial information about the successful running of their department. So perhaps you are just taking over, filling a breach, stepping into someone else's shoes for a while or newly promoted. I'm sure you can be forgiven for not having last year's budget already to hand.

OK, so priority now must be given to getting hold of a copy. Whose shoes have you stepped into? Are they around to ask? Is their office still intact and their desk worth raiding? Does the finance department have a copy? Does your boss have a copy? It doesn't hurt to ask these people. It doesn't hurt to admit you haven't got a copy. It doesn't hurt to be seen to be efficient and doing your job properly. No one can really compile a budget (unless it really is a brand new department) without knowing what has gone on before. So get it now before you do anything else. Off you go.

 thinking smart

A VALUABLE TOOL

A good manager never lets the current budget out of their sight for a moment. It is the most valuable tool in departmental managing. Without the budget you are lost at sea with no charts and thus no way of getting to where you are supposed to be.

Got it? Good. Now you can begin to take it apart.

Ask yourself the following questions as you examine last year's budget very carefully:

- **Who compiled this budget?**
- **How accurate was it?**
- **Can I do better?**
- **Where are the biggest variances?**
- **What can I do about adjusting them?**

Now go through it again and check that:

- **there is nothing there that is now obsolete or irrelevant**
- **there is nothing there that is missing from this year's figures.**

Follow-ons and zeros

There are two ways of doing a budget – following on from last year's or starting afresh. Following on is known as a *follow-on* budget – see, this stuff is simple – and a new budget not based on last year's figures is known as a *nil* or *zero* budget. And obviously there are two reasons for this:

- **a follow-on budget where you use the same categories and merely update the figures makes your job a lot easier, but**
- **it may contain data that are now irrelevant or misleading, subject to the changes your department has gone through in the last 12 months. And a brand new budget may be much more accurate – and thus make you look better as a manager.**

So, what have we got – last year's budget? Does it have figures from the previous year all neatly totalled up so you can see a sort of running history? Or does it look as if it was prepared only last year? Whichever one it is, you have to decide what sort you are going to do this time. If you are really pushed for time then a follow-on budget is quicker. You merely have to update the figures but be careful that you don't miss a new expenditure or include one that is now irrelevant.

But what if I haven't got last year's budget?

Then you'll need last year's accounts – which you should have anyway to compare to the budget. If you've got the accounts, you can use them in the same way you would the budget. And if you haven't got the budget or last year's accounts, you'll have to wing it. Go round the department and find out what money is spent on. But no one in their right mind would ask you to compile a budget with nothing to go on – it is unrealistic, unfair and just plain stupid.

Asking the right people

Now you need to ask some important questions of your last year's budget assuming you've got it:

- **How much money was your department given – what did it earn – last year?**
- **How many staff did you have and how many do you now need?**

ADDING ON 15%

If you want to see what this year's budget *might* look like – not what it *will* look like or what it *should* look like – merely add 15% on to last year's figures. This won't give you an accurate budget or even one that is workable – but it will give you a budget and if you are really pushed for time, at least you will have a piece of paper with some figures on it. Then when you've got a bit more time you can redo it properly.

▸ **What is the cost of those staff?**

▸ **What, apart from staff, is the single biggest expenditure you need to make over the coming year?**

Some of these answers you may well get from the budget itself or from your knowledge of the department. Some you may need to get from another source – the finance department (that's right, you got it in one). Now how are you going to approach them? You could just pick up the phone and demand the information – but that would be a mistake. Get up from your desk armed with the questions you want answered and make the journey in person. Face to face is so much harder to turn down.

So, off to the finance department and politely enquire if it would be possible for them to give you the information you need. Words such as *favour* and *grateful* should tumble forth from your lips with such an enquiry, as should such phrases as *I know you're frightfully busy* and *I'm sorry to disturb you*.

Also be aware that other departments are compiling their budgets as well as you. They, too, may have recently asked for such information and the poor finance department might be overloaded with requests. Make sure yours stands out by being the politest or the most unusual – perhaps you could include a free round of drinks in the bar at lunchtime or a gift of some sort.

Have a ring round

And now that you are aware that other departments are compiling their budgets at the same time as you are it doesn't hurt to ring round the other managers and have a chat to see what problems they are experiencing or what information they may have access to that is unknown to you. Perhaps a new directive from head office limiting the amount of overtime worked has escaped your attention and you might be reminded of it. Or the fact that the new photocopier you wanted has just doubled in price and you didn't know – it pays to talk.

ASK POLITELY

If you want information from someone to help you complete your budget then go in person and ask humbly, ask nicely, say please and thank you and make it clear that you are asking a favour rather than demanding.

Now go back to your list of expenditure. Look at what costs you the most. This can be done, hopefully, while the finance department is on your case and is sorting out your staffing costs. What costs you the most? Is it computer consumables? Stationery? Telephone calls? Whatever it is there is bound to be a person in your office in charge of it or monitoring it in some way. Make your way to their desk and get them to tell you all about it. Talk to your staff. The successful departmental budget is based on agreement and co-operation – not hierarchical dictate. Spend the next 20 minutes or so busily looking round at what costs you money – and talking to those who spend it for you. Ask for their advice, their views, their opinions. You don't have to include whatever they say but they may give you useful hints and tips that you might otherwise have overlooked.

Now you can have a break. You've sent out your runners to get information. You've talked to other departmental managers. You've talked to your staff. You've earned a break. But while you're having it you might need to know a few bits of useful information about collecting data for budgets.

Bear in mind that not everyone is as nice, as friendly or as co-operative as you are. They may have their own reasons for putting you on the wrong track. Always accept all information arriving in as useful but check its accuracy. Some people might not like to give you the information as quickly as you want purely because they want to see you fail or not be as successful as you'd like to be. Always try to ask for information face to face as it's so much harder to be stabbed in the back when you are looking at the person. Always be polite and humble.

When you talk to your own staff bear in mind they may well have their own agenda and be asking for more than they actually need. This might be to make their job easier or to come in under budget (which they may think is a good thing, but which you now know is a bad thing).

Bear in mind that some staff will always ask for the impossible and others for the absurd. Nod and smile as if you are taking it all in and then go away and do your own thing.

How well do you know your boss?

OK, so you have marshalled your information. You've gathered some useful data and now you need to think about how you are going to present it and to whom. Remember it's not what you know but whom you know. How well do you know your boss?

Here are some questions to help you along the way:

▶ **Is your boss a stickler for detail?**
▶ **Do they see broad strokes rather than fine detail?**

ASK THE RIGHT PEOPLE
Try asking various people to gather information on expenditure for you. Whoever it is that monitors items of expenditure such as stationery should have a good idea of what it all costs and recent price changes.

KNOW YOUR OPPONENT

Your boss's job is to keep down expenditure. Your job is to run your department smoothly. These two may not be compatible. You need to know how to get your boss round to your way of thinking. You both need to be in a win-win situation. You can only do this by knowing your opponent, seeing them as a colleague and talking to them as a friend.

▶ **Are they creative or accountancy-trained?**

▶ **How much leeway have you got for negotiation?**

▶ **Are they helpful or hindering?**

▶ **Are they part of the problem or part of the solution?**

Once you've got them pretty well tagged you can begin compiling the budget. You need to know how much detail to put in or collectively group. For instance, they may want details of every computer consumable listed separately under paper, laser cartridges, floppy disks and so on or they may only want a rounded figure for the whole lot. The first departmental budget I ever did was brilliant (at least I thought so) and the only question I got asked was, 'Where's the figure for light bulbs?' Yep, that sort of senior manager. If you know what your boss expects, you can save yourself either a lot of extra work for nothing or a lot of embarrassment and explaining later.

I think we're about ready to start fleshing the whole thing out now so get a calculator and be ready to go.

thinking fast

HAVE IT ALL TO HAND

Before you go into a budget meeting – and you will be called to one to explain all this – have all the information you need to hand and keep it all in neat, easy-to-read notes. This way when you are asked questions you don't need to shuffle through papers to see if you have the information – you will know you have it. And you won't be made to look a prat by having to say you'll look it up later.

thinking fast

Make sure you've asked the right people for the right information long in advance of when you need it to give them plenty of time to be as helpful and co-operative as you'd like them to be.

Make sure you've got a copy of last year's budget and check that it has been updated for any variances.

Make sure you know exactly what is expected of you and how much detail you are going to be asked to provide.

4 filling it in

So, thus far we have worked out our objective, looked at the types of budget there are and gathered all the information we need, and now we are ready to fill it all in. Jacket off, sleeves rolled up and let's get on with it. But hang on, there are a few rules you should understand first:

- ▶ **Don't use a budget as a weapon. It is a tool.**
- ▶ **Don't use it as an excuse to take on extra staff so you can cruise.**
- ▶ **Don't budget for resources you know you'll never need.**
- ▶ **Don't update last year's budget by simply adding on a set percentage to every figure unless you really are pushed for time – there may be a lot of changes to circumstances and this plan will come adrift very quickly.**
- ▶ **Don't set an 'easy' budget on the grounds you can say later that you've come in under budget.**
- ▶ **Don't pad a budget on the grounds that you think there may be cutbacks in subsequent years.**
- ▶ **Don't indulge in wishful thinking – be realistic at all times.**

FIRST DRAFT

Get a piece of plain paper. You're going to do some work. Write down everything that you can think of that costs your department money. Look at last year's budget. What did you spend money on? What has changed since then? Do you spend more or less on each thing?

Write down these 'things' as a list and put a plus or minus by each of them if you think they have changed their priority. For instance, you may have had six staff last year and you know full well you are up to eight already this year. Then put a plus by staff costs – they've gone up. But what about transport? Maybe last year you all travelled a lot to meetings but this year you do most meetings by conference call. Put a minus sign by transport if you think it's come down. But remember you may need a plus by telephone costs to cover the increased usage by all those conference calls.

Now you're getting somewhere. You should, by this time, have your staffing costs back from finance so you can begin to flesh this out. Once you've got your list of things that cost you money you can divide it up into things you have control

thinking smart

NOT JUST MONEY
The smart manager doesn't just budget for money but also for time and resources. A little time well spent with staff can have enormous benefits and should be budgeted for.

DON'T ASSUME

Don't assume last year's budget was correct. Keep thinking of what may have been missed off or included when it shouldn't have been. This is your chance to shine by pointing it out and putting it right.

USING THE SPREADSHEET

Remember your computer has a calculating function on spreadsheets – and use it. You can type a budget and use the calculating function to add up and insert figures into your document. If you are really good with spreadsheets, it can also keep running totals – thus if you alter one figure, it will automatically adjust all the other figures for you. This will save you time.

over and things you don't. These are known as fixed and variable costs. Fixed costs are usually set by head office or your boss. Variable costs are the real ones you can budget for as they are the ones you have some control over.

FIXED AND VARIABLE COSTS

Divide your expenditure into fixed and variable costs. The fixed costs are usually divvied up into 12 equal instalments so you can spread them over the 12-month period. The variable costs may not be. You have to look at all of them and decide if any or all of them are seasonal or subject to change for various reasons that would indicate you need to budget them differently during different times of the year. For instance, you might need more staff just before Christmas to cope with the rush. Or you need to budget for the extra brochures you always send out in the early spring. Or you know you'll get an increase in costs in the autumn to cover the annual sales conference.

By now you should have a pretty good list of things both fixed and variable and with a note of any hidden costs as well as a plus or minus next to them to indicate their changes from last year. You can now fill in a year budget in rough. Draw out 12 columns (one for each month) and jot down in pencil what you think these costs will be in each area. You already know what sort of detail is required so you can lump things together if you can get away with it just so long as you can justify them if asked to do so.

There are a few other things to take into consideration as well.

HIDDEN COSTS

Whatever the item ask yourself what its concealed or secret cost is. The cost to you is not necessarily the cost that is visible. You may know that you pay a member of staff x amount as basic salary. But what about National Insurance (NI)? Sick pay? Holidays? Pensions? That's why it's so important to get on the right side of the finance department. You need them or you'll go badly awry.

STANDARDS OF PRECISION

Don't forget: 'We've all got to sing from the same hymn sheet.' The standards of precision are how much you are allowed to round figures up or down. For instance you might earn £56,000 a year (it's possible!) and with NI and pensions and car that might come out at £85,396.15. Is that the figure you are going to put into your budget? I hope not. It is too unwieldy. You need to round it up or down depending on the standards of precision allowed within your organisation. Staying up late calculating everything to the nearest penny is unproductive and not cost-effective. Let's say we round your salary up to £85,400. That's neater, simpler and understandable. Usual standards include:

▶ **Rounding pounds to the nearest hundreds – above 50 is 100; below 50 down to the lower hundred. For instance £57.95 would be £100, and so would £112.56.**

▶ **Rounding hundreds to the nearest thousand in a similar manner: £879.15 would become £1,000 and £2,391.22 would be £2,000.**

Find out what your industry standards are and use them.

RESOURCES AND USING THEM

Remember when you are compiling a budget that it is a social document as much as a financial one. It requires the help and co-operation of a large number of people to get it accurate and keep it sweet.

Here are the main resources and what you should use them for. Let's start with those nearest home:

People who work in your department

These are the people working directly under you and reporting to you. Use them for their experience and for bouncing ideas off. They may come up with things you'd never have thought of. They are also your colleagues and, as such, must be included in goal setting and agreeing their role in supporting you in fulfilling the departmental budget.

The boss

This is the one to go to for your goals and targets. They need to be sounded out for anything they're not saying as much as for what they are – what's their hidden agenda? And they will have one, believe me. You need to liaise with them, to support them and be part of the agreement process for your budget.

Your peers

Check these buddies out for how they are doing with *their* budgets – they may have information you don't – as well as offering support and encouragement (you're supposed to be a team, remember?) and getting them to buy their own copy of this book rather than borrowing yours. They may also have ideas and experience worth listening to.

The finance department

Tricky little devils these – and yes, I used to run a finance department so I know what it's like from the inside and what our (entirely justifiable) reputation is – so approach with caution and politeness. Once in get them to part with:

- payroll information
- accounts
- spreadsheet templates
- profit and loss information
- asset register (a list of everything the company or organisation owns with its value)
- accounting policies on key areas such as accruals and depreciation
- financial background to the organisation.

The personnel department

Usually slightly more approachable but still tricky. Be polite and charming and get them to part with:

- salary structures including pay grades and ranges
- details of bonus schemes
- details of pension contributions
- company policy on promotions and cost of living increases
- policy on employment levels.

Others

You would well be advised to check out the marketing department for sales reports and market trends as well as projections, and any sales promotions that are being planned. And don't forget colleagues working for other organisations – they might identify information which you don't have that it might be useful to know in advance, such as changing industry standards. Keep abreast of your industry standards by reading the newspapers.

SETTING GOALS

Right back at the very beginning of this process we looked at setting an objective. You had to set one for your budget. How about getting your staff involved as well? You don't have to call it an objective – merely a goal. Set a goal for each person to do with collecting information or monitoring costs for this budget. That way you have lots of helpers all rooting for you and your budget. Get them involved and they will take care of your budget for you – then it's their baby too. Leave them in the dark – so-called mushroom management – and they will rip your budget to shreds just for the sheer fun of it. Get them to set goals for the people working under them – and so on. Then you have a sort of pyramid, an ant colony all working away keeping your budget in good shape.

PLANNING THE FINANCIAL CALENDAR

A year might be 12 months but those months are different lengths. February is a devil as it is so short whereas August is longer. You have to take these things into account. You also have to take into account bank holidays, Christmas, Easter, summer holidays and so on. You need a financial calendar which will show you when staff have to cover and be paid, but might actually be earning overtime or being paid at a higher rate such as double time or time and a half.

thinking smart

ASKING IN ADVANCE

The smart manager doesn't wait to be asked to do a budget – they're already in there months in advance asking. Make sure you put your boss on the spot and ask for a budget package which should include last year's budget, a set of guidelines, a specific goal/objective of what is expected of you, a financial calendar, a description of the department along with an historical perspective, any expansion plans and a breakdown of staffing levels required. If you don't ask you won't get.

You need to be aware that each organisation has a different accounting period – the financial calendar. You might have a budget that covers 12 months or is divided up into four – one for each quarter. Or you might even have to operate one on a 52-week basis. Some seasonal businesses operate on two six-month periods. There is no right or wrong in any of this – they merely take into account differing needs. You need to know which your organisation uses – and use it yourself.

SECOND DRAFT

There. Now you can sit back and bask in the glow of a finished draft budget. Good. Now total it all up and be horrified at how much it is going to cost you to run your department. How does it compare with last year? A whole lot more? How are you going to justify it? How are you going to ask for so much? Well, you're not. This is your draft budget and as such will need to be slimmed down.

Shaping it up

First, you need to look at what areas you can trim money off. These will be the less prioritised areas that can be shaved without loss of efficiency or productivity. Take this first draft budget to the most senior person in your department whom you can trust and work well with. Show it to them. Ask them if they can see areas that can be slimmed down. After all, they are going to have to work with this as much as you are so their input is valuable. Ask them if they can see anything you might have missed. Even ten minutes doing this can prove useful as often someone else will spot things you have overlooked.

Now back to your desk. By now you should have a pretty good idea of what you are doing and where you are going with it. Trim and trim and trim until you have shaved off every excess pound and every surplus ounce. The ideal budget is the one that is realistic and gets passed at the first budget meeting. There's not a lot of point putting in all this hard work only for it to be sent back again with the sort of 'good effort, now try again' note we all hate.

Having trimmed, total up the whole thing again. This time you should have a much more realistic figure to work with. Check the individual months' totals to make sure it all balances.

Now you have draft two it is time to really check the detail – and remember that too much detail will render your budget meaningless.

SEEING THE WHOLE PICTURE

The smart manager realises that their budget is only a tiny part of the whole picture. It is only a part of an overall budget strategy which is being built up department by department to cover the whole organisation. Once you see that your part is essential but only a part and not the entirety you accept changes to your budget more easily.

- ▶ **Look for costs which are non-essential. Maybe they are there from last year and are no longer really necessary.**
- ▶ **Have you identified all the hidden costs?**
- ▶ **Have you checked other people's figures for accuracy?**
- ▶ **Will this budget motivate your staff?**
- ▶ **Does this budget fulfil your objective?**
- ▶ **Have you been realistic and honest in all areas?**

Once you've answered these questions it's time for another quick cuppa and then on to preparing the third draft – the final budget.

Your budget should look something like the example shown if you've got it right. Let's suppose you are the departmental manager of the local fire department. You don't have any sales as such – merely call-outs – but you have staff, overheads and general running costs.

This is, of course, a very simplified version and yours may be much more complex but this will give you the general idea. You will notice some asterisks dotted throughout the budget. These will take the form of notes to make sure anyone else looking at your budget such as your senior fire chief will understand and know what you are talking

	Jan	Feb	Mar	Apr	May	Jun	Jul	Aug	Sep	Oct	Nov	Dec	**Totals**
Fixed costs													
Site rental	1000	1000	1000	1000	1000	1000	1000	1000	1000	1000	1000	1000	12000
Insurance	150	150	150	150	150	150	150	150	150	150	150	150	1800
Council tax	200	200	200	200	200	200	200	200	200	200	200	200	2400
Variable costs													
Staff	27000	27000	27000	27000	27000	27000	27000	27000	27000	27000	35000*	27000	332000
Heat/light**	4000	4000	3000	3000	2500	2500	2500	2500	3000	3000	3500	4000	37500
Staff meals	10000	10000	10000	10000	10000	10000	10000	10000	10000	10000	12500***	10000	122500
Maintenance	550	550	550	550	550	550	550	550	550	550	550	550	6600
Office admin	450	450	450	450	450	450	450	450	450	450	450	450	5400
Capital expend-iture****	25000	25000	25000	25000	25000	25000	25000	25000	25000	25000	25000	25000	300000
Totals	68350	68350	67350	67350	66850	66850	66850	66850	67350	67350	78350	68350	820200 820200

about – we will look at presenting your budget in the next chapter but for the moment you could add notes such as:

*   Increased staff costs in November to cover Bonfire Night

**   Heat and light costs adjusted throughout the year for seasonal variations – less heat and light in summer months

***   Higher staff meal costs in November to cover increase in staff

**** Capital expenditure budget for new fire appliance

Obviously, some or all of these will apply to you in some form or another. For instance, the capital expenditure may well not go in your departmental budget as it may be allocated elsewhere by head office or a senior manager, but this is the sort of thing you'd be expected to negotiate.

You will also notice the very bottom right-hand box. It has two totals which are – and must always be – identical. These are your monthly totals and your overall expenditure totals. They must always agree because if they don't you have got your sums wrong somewhere.

Now you know what you are spending every month and what on. What could be simpler? Or easier? Or faster? But time is passing and you still have to know what to do with this budget in the way of presentation and updating it regularly. If you haven't got time to read the next chapter in its entirety just read the bit about presentation – variances can wait until you come to do them, but I would recommend a quick glance just in case you get asked questions when you present your budget.

for next time

Be prepared for budget reviews. Yep, you gotta have 'em. Every now and again you will have to update your budget based on accurate accounting information flowing into your department. You have to keep on top of your budget and review it. You need to ask yourself if it still holds water or if it has all gone to pot. Ideally, you will do this over a cup of coffee with your boss in an atmosphere of calmness and mutual respect. I have, however, known no coffee, no respect and lots of shouting. If you are already prepared perhaps the shouting isn't necessary. Ask these questions of your budget before you are called in, to account for it.

▶ Is it consistent throughout?
▶ Is it accurate?
▶ Has it been trimmed to the bone?
▶ Does it have any data which you haven't checked?
▶ Are there assumptions based on assumptions?
▶ Can you talk through your budget without hesitation, repetition or deviation?

You are expected to answer: yes, yes, yes, no, no, yes.

5 updating the budget

The final finished professional budget

Nearly there. Your budget just needs a few additions now to become a full and final budget. You need to add a couple of columns. After the final totals column on the right add another column and jot in it last year's figures. If you want to be really flash add two columns – one for the budgeted figure and one for the actual figure.

Now add another column alongside this and use a plus or minus symbol along with the percentage increase/decrease this year. So the whole thing should look a bit like the example (you may need to print it landscape to get it to fit on an A4 sheet).

There, now that's a professional budget. It includes figures for this year broken down into the 12 months and grouped according to whether they are fixed or variable. It includes figures for last year. It has its percentage increases or decreases. It is all totalled and it balances. Put it on one side for the moment and let's have a look at how to present it.

Budget makeover

So, where are we going with this budget? We've set our objective, talked to our staff, gathered information, compiled and trimmed the thing – and now? Now we are going to turn it into the most professional-looking budget you've ever clapped eyes on. Yep, we're going to do a budget makeover that will make it so impressive you'll have it approved straight away and you'll look seriously cool.

	Jan	Feb	Mar	Apr	May	Jun	Jul	Aug	Sep	Oct	Nov	Dec	Totals	Last year (actual)	Increase/ decrease
Fixed costs															
Site rental	1000	1000	1000	1000	1000	1000	1000	1000	1000	1000	1000	1000	12000	9000	+33.3%
Insurance	150	150	150	150	150	150	150	150	150	150	150	150	1800	1500	+20%
Council tax	200	200	200	200	200	200	200	200	200	200	200	200	2400	2200	+9.1%
Variable costs															
Staff	27000	27000	27000	27000	27000	27000	27000	27000	27000	27000	35000*	27000	332000	285000	+16.5%
Heat/light**	4000	4000	3000	3000	2500	2500	2500	2500	3000	3000	3500	4000	37500	36000	+4.16%
Staff meals	10000	10000	10000	10000	10000	10000	10000	10000	10000	10000	12500***	10000	122500	135000[1]	−9.25%
Maintenance	550	550	550	550	550	550	550	550	550	550	550	550	6600	6000	+10%
Office admin	450	450	450	450	450	450	450	450	450	450	450	450	5400	6700[2]	−19.40%
Capital expend-iture****	25000	25000	25000	25000	25000	25000	25000	25000	25000	25000	25000	25000	300000	270000[3]	+11.11%
													820200	751400	+9.16%
Totals	68350	68350	67350	67350	66850	66850	66850	66850	67350	67350	78350	68350	820200		

[1] Reduced food costs due to improved catering contract
[2] Reduced admin due to improved telephone contract
[3] Increase due to inflation / supplier's figures

CALCULATORS AND PERCENTAGES

There's a very simple way to work out your percentage increases or decreases over last year's budget. The simple way to do it is – take this year's figure. Take away from it last year's figure. Divide by last year's figure and hit the % button. There, that was easy. Let's work a quick example. Last year we budgeted for £1,200 for uniforms. This year's figure is £1,500. Thus 1,500 − 1,200 = 300 Divide by 1,200 and hit the % button = 25%.

You can also do this by taking this year's figure minus last year's figure, dividing by this year's figure and multiplying by 100 – same result.

Carry a calculator and be prepared to work out any percentage increase and look flash while doing it. Very good.

When chancellors of the exchequer present a budget to the house they don't just hold up a sheet of paper with some impressive-looking figures on it. Oh, no, they talk it through by way of a speech. Relax, you don't have to make a speech. But what you do have to do is talk your budget through on paper.

Let's run through the exact stages:

- ▶ **Use A4 paper.**
- ▶ **First page should be a title page giving the name of your department, the year the budget covers and the word 'budget' (and your name, of course).**
- ▶ **Second page should be a contents page which is a clear listing of what the reader should expect to find in the following pages.**
- ▶ **Third page should be the actual budget – and no budget needs to stretch beyond one sheet of A4 paper, although you may need to print it landscape to get it all to fit – all neatly typed and looking very professional by now. Any notes will appear on the next page and you can link them with an asterisk or a footnote number [1].**
- ▶ **Fourth page should be your notes expanding on anything that might need explaining but try to keep these notes to a minimum and never more than one page.**
- ▶ **Fifth page is reserved for any subsequent information that needs clarity. In the budget example in the previous chapter we had a monthly figure for office admin. Let's suppose your boss wants to know exactly how that figure is arrived at. You could take the annual figure of £5,400 and break it down:**

A SLOPPY PRESENTATION CUTS NO ICE

A well-presented budget looks professional and looks as if you know what you are doing. If people are filled with confidence by your presentation they will transfer that confidence to your figures, your calculations and most importantly to your budgeted requests. A smart budget presentation gets more money for your department.

---

[1] They look like this.

		5400	
Office admin		5400	
Stationery	2200		
Computer consumables	1200		
Telephone	2000		
Total	5400		

Thus page 5 is a sort of mini-budget that can run to several pages. You might need to do a mini- budget for staff costs, a breakdown of staff meals, a breakdown of heat and light costs (remember the light bulbs) or a mini-budget for maintenance. Label each page 5a, 5b, 5c and so on. Any explanatory notes for any page 5s can go at the bottom as footnotes rather than on a separate sheet.

Now present the whole thing in a nice plastic folder with a clear cover and you have a good-looking document which will get the job done.

Now you are nearly ready for that deadline tomorrow morning. You've done your budget and presented it professionally. Well done. If you've still got a bit of time in hand, read the next bit about variances and what to do about them.

Maintenance	Budgeted figure	Actual figure	% variation	Notes
January	200	197	1.5%	Normal month
February	200	210	(4.7%)	Had to repair coffee machine
March	200	145	37.93%	Nothing broke down so saved money
April	200	1000	80%	Lift broken down – engineer called out 3 times
Sub-total	800	1552	48.45%	Service contract being looked into
May	200			
June	200			
July	200			
August	200			
September	200			
October	200			
November	200			
December	200			

VARIANCES AND WHAT TO DO ABOUT THEM

We all get them. They are nothing to be ashamed of. They can be treated. Variances are the differences between what you said would happen and what has actually happened. Suppose you budgeted £200 a month for maintenance and suddenly, in April, you have to spend nearly £1,000 getting a lift engineer in to sort out a particularly trying problem. Your budget may look like the following.

April's budget may be some 80 per cent over but your sub-total shows you are only 48 per cent above budget overall. So you've got the rest of the year to pull back and you are on top of the variance:

- ▶ **You know what happened.**
- ▶ **You know why it occurred.**
- ▶ **You are taking steps to make sure it doesn't happen again.**
- ▶ **Already you are negotiating with the lift company for a service contract.**

When questioned by your boss you can show you are on top of your job, you are efficient and you are ahead of the game. Well done. You are also noting down when you are under budget – which we know is just as bad – and you are demonstrating that you are aware of what is going on in your department.

Good. That's about it for today. Go home and enjoy a well-earned rest. You can be relaxed and even look forward to the morning knowing you have done a good job and pretty well tied up all the loose ends. There are a few more things you really should know before having to sit in a budget meeting but not for now. If you have time this evening, read the next chapter.

thinking smart

STAYING ON TOP OF VARIANCES

The smart manager gets the staff to report any expenditure that is above or below the normal. That way there are no surprises at the end of the year – you already know or can anticipate when your budget is wandering off course.

for next time

Make sure last year's budget has been updated for variances and all the columns are complete and balanced.

Make sure you understand percentages and what they can tell you about your department's finances.

Leave enough time to produce a really professional- looking budget neatly presented in its own folder with a clear plastic cover and no coffee stains. Get somebody to do it for you if you are pushed for time or if you are hopeless at this kind of thing.

Update your variances as you go through the year – it is all too easy to forget about them but a smart manager concentrates on them and stays ahead of the pack.

Take appropriate action to deal with any major variances before they get worse.

6 for next time

So you've got through the budget and produced a professional working document that you can be happy with – and so can your boss. Now you need to turn into a budget expert. You're going to have to present your budget tomorrow morning, and you will doubtless have to attend some sort of meeting where you will be questioned about your figures.

You don't have to do anything except read this chapter – make notes if you want to – but sit back and pay attention. Read slowly and carefully and if you don't understand anything read it again slowly until you do. There is nothing difficult here or complicated or even daunting. It is all easy stuff that may simply be new to you or unfamiliar territory.

WHY BUDGETS GO WRONG

It doesn't matter how hard you try or how on top of your job you are, bad things happen to us all. Just when you thought you were coming out spot on budget something terrible happens or a memo arrives from head office that throws your budget completely off track. This happens to us all and can't be helped. We have to live with it and get on with the job.

There are a few things we can do, however, to minimise the occurrence of bad things. Look again at your budget – mentally, you don't have to go and get it: what is your biggest cost? Bet it is staffing. It always is. People cost money – lots of it. And staff costs change. Staff costs change a lot and invariably these changes are outside your control. They can change for a variety of reasons:

- Someone gets an increase in salary because they are promoted.
- There is an across-the-board increase to cover a cost of living rise.
- Someone gets an increase because the time they have served warrants a step up to the next salary level.
- Someone gets a bonus for good performance.

Now you can see at a glance that some of these – if you are really on top of your job – could have been foreseen and budgeted for. Promotion, long service increases and bonuses are all expected. An across-the-board rise to cover inflation may not have been foreseen but you should have allowed for it as it probably happens nearly every year.

Being on top of your salary costs is the best thing you can concentrate on. Here are a few tips:

- Very few organisations – or even departments – are up to their full quota of staff at any one time. Use the slack to counteract any rises in salaries you hadn't allowed for.
- Working out a *total* cost for an employee including all the hidden costs, such as National Insurance, takes a lot of time. How much better if you know the basic salary and then can add on a *payroll overhead percentage*. Easy to do if you know how. Here's how. Take the total cost of your payroll and take away the cost of basic salaries and overtime. Divide this figure by the cost of salaries and hit the % button. This gives

thth*th*th*th*thinkingsfast

KNOW YOUR PAYROLL OVERHEAD PERCENTAGE

You really should always know what percentage of your total expenditure your staff costs are. They contribute the biggest chunk of money and are worth staying on top of. This is where the bulk of your expenditure will be and you should know it off by heart.

you the payroll overhead percentage. Now you don't need to trouble the finance department too much as you are using the same calculation they will be.

▶ Don't let staffing levels creep up unnoticed – it's easy to do so. Whoever, within your department, is responsible for taking on new staff has to be made to justify each new employee individually. Make them answerable to you in blood if necessary but monitor your staff levels like a hawk. Staffing is the biggest single area where your budget will fall apart if you don't watch it.

▶ Watch out for temporary staff and emergency cover. These two areas can again turn your budget into so much wastepaper if you don't monitor them. Same goes for consultants. If they are called in, they have to be paid for – and it all comes out of your budget.

STAFF BUDGET

Yep, you need one. Even if your boss doesn't want one as a breakdown of staff costs in your main budget you certainly need one – and you need to refer to it a lot. No manager can keep track of their finances without knowing their exact staffing requirements and the overall payroll costing.

Shown opposite is a simple example so you know what we are talking about.

There, that wasn't too difficult, was it? That's a payroll budget. You could break it down into months if you wanted or quarters or even six-monthly periods. Use whatever you need to be the smartest manager around.

BUDGETS FOR OTHER EXPENSES

Let's look at a few hints and tips to turn you from an ordinary manager into a really smart cookie – a supermanager of budgets.

▶ Remember not every month is the same length – we will look at how you calculate a calendar budget in a little bit.

▶ Irregular expenses. Some things you pay for only once a year – perhaps a business licence – and you need to know in which month it is to be paid, so you can budget for it, and how much it will be. Or you could allocate $\frac{1}{12}$ per month.

▶ Watch the seasonal expenses. These could be gas or oil for heating. And watch for seasonal variations in price – oil is cheaper in the summer.

thth*th*th*th*thinking*smart*

DONKEY WORK

Get your staff to do the donkey work for you – collecting information, checking key areas of the budget for variances and watching out for changes. Try offering an incentive bonus for various areas of the budget – 'Look, if we stay within budget for staff travel I'll take you all out for a slap-up meal at the end of the year' – that sort of thing.

455

Name	Position	Gross	NI	Pension	Benefits	Payroll cost	Notes
F Burrows	Department manager	60000	4638	9000	10000/car	83638	
T Bear	Assistant manager	40000	4380	6000	8000/car	58380	
W G Keldfelt	Section leader	30000	3120	4500	4000/car	41620	Due to retire in June/July
C Milton	Assistant sec leader	24000	2496	Nil	Nil	26496	Promotion July?
J Willis	Admin clerk	20000	2080	Nil	Nil	22080	Due pay rise in November for long service
R Jay	Apprentice	14000	924	Nil	Nil	14924	Qualifies Feb – pay rise to cover – need new apprentice
Totals		**188000**	17638	19500	22000	**247138**	**Payroll % 31.45**

thinkingfast

USE WHAT YOU KNOW

We all think size matters. But does it? You may be persuaded to upgrade your computer programs constantly, including spreadsheets. The trouble with this is it all takes time to learn – and the bigger and newer you go the more glitches, gremlins and gobbledegook you are going to encounter. Stick with whatever package works best for you. Sometimes even ignoring the computer and working out your basic budget with a pen and paper can be quicker, simpler and easier to play around with.

▶ **Make sure you have a clearly defined policy for such things as travel expenses. This way your staff will know what they can spend in advance. For instance outlaw first-class travel or specify a price band for hotels – and don't let them get away with anything the first time or your budget will go haywire by the end of the year.**

▶ **A lot of expenses can be directly related to the number of staff. As staff levels rise so do your telephone costs, office supplies and travel. Set limits if it helps you keep costs down.**

▶ **Analyse your department's history so you know when money is being spent, why it is being spent and how it is being spent.**

thinkingsmart

KNOWING YOUR PERCENTAGES

The smart manager knows what each category in the budget costs as a percentage. Thus you might say, 'Oh, staff costs are 57% of my budget, heat and light 14%, maintenance 2.7% and admin costs 23%.' If you keep tabs on these percentages you will know what is going up or down, what is happening and why. You will look seriously flash and all you need is a calculator and a simple equation (total budget minus the individual cost, divided by the total budget, hit the % button and minus 100). Need an example? Of course you do.

Total budget is 820,200 less the staff costs of 332,000 = 488,200 divided by the total of 820,200. Hit the % button = 59.52 less 100 = 40.47%. Easy.

Another one? Total budget of 820,200 less staff meals of 122,500 = 697,700 divided by the total of 820,200. Hit the % button = 85.06 less 100 = 14.93%.

> **SETTING REALISTIC TARGETS**
>
> If your staff exceed your budget you need to know – and take action. But at what level do you step in and get heavy? You need to set a realistic level under which you are not bothered. For instance, if your stationery budget is £240 for the month and your senior admin person spends £245, does it warrant your being involved? The time taken to inform you and for you to choose either to take action or ignore it may cost you more than the amount by which the budget has been exceeded. Set a target of say 5% or 10% above or below and stick to that. Only if spending creeps beyond that do you need to be involved.

There. That will do for now. We need to look at some of the technical terms you might come up against during budget meetings. After all it doesn't help to feel you've been made to look small just because someone uses a technical expression that you don't understand.

BUDGET TERMINOLOGY MADE CLEAR

Every organisation uses different terminology, often to mean exactly the same thing. If you are new to the company it can be a bit daunting to have to ask what they mean. Here are a few terms to help you along:

- ▸ *Variable budget*. **This is one of two things. First, it might well be where the budget figures are all expressed in percentages rather than pounds. Or it can be used to denote a budget that uses variances to provide running totals throughout the year – you use less so less gets transferred into next month's budget. Always ask 'Which sort of variable budget are you referring to?' This throws the onus back on to the enquirer and makes it look like you really know your budget stuff.**
- ▸ *Historical trend budget*. **Simple. This is a budget that uses last year's figures and merely updates them by a fixed percentage. It's quick but not very accurate.**
- ▸ *Line itemised budget*. **This is very similar to the examples we have used in this book: a simple budget that is basically a list of expenditure.**
- ▸ *Fund budget*. **This is a budget that allocates a large sum of money (a fund) to a department and then allows the department to spend it and allocate it later.**

◀◀ for next time

> Make sure you've got a budget package long before you need to sit down and do your budget. If your boss isn't too keen on giving you a package, ask why not and be assertive. You cannot be expected to do your job properly without the necessary tools. Keep your budget updated for variances and that way you won't be taken by surprise at the end of the year.
>
> *Monitor and monitor and monitor*. Check every detail so you stay on top of it. Your budget is one of the most important tools you can have as a manager. If it is used properly, efficiently and well it turns you from an OK ordinary manager into a kick-boxing Ninja manager who inspires awe and admiration. All you need is a decent calculator and the knowledge given you in this book. Practise the simple equations until you know them off by heart and can work out your payroll percentage or what percentage a particular expense is within the total of your budget at the drop of a hat.
>
> I know you can do it.

457

7 special budgets

So we have looked in some detail at your yearly departmental budget – and you've successfully completed it, handed it in, been praised for all your hard work and excellent presentation. So what's left? Well, there are times when you need a one-off budget – a special budget which might form a sub-part of your yearly budget or not. Suppose the MD calls you up and asks you to do a special three day exhibition to launch the new MX21. By now you know what your first question should be, don't you? That's right: 'what's my budget?'

Suppose the MD says you can spend ten grand – and not a single penny more – well, now you know what you've got to work with.

It might, of course, not be an exhibition. It might be:

- A conference
- A Royal visit
- A sales promotion
- A new product launch
- A PR event
- A trade show
- A commemorative lunch
- A retirement party
- An award ceremony
- A Christmas party
- A works outing

But back to the chase. It's no use just going to the trade exhibition and hoping that the ten grand will see you through. What if you run out of money after only one day? What you gonna do then? Pack up and go home, and tell the MD that you decided to prune the three days into one? I don't think so. Stuff would hit fans.

THE SPECIAL BUDGET
So what are you going to do? The special budget of course. And the first thing you need to do is plan the exhibition. Now that is outside the remit of this book (see *fast thinking: project*) so come back when you've done that.

Back already? Good. Now you know how many staff you'll need, what the stand is going to cost you, whether or not you need to put staff up in hotels, travel arrangements, sales material, refreshments, that sort of thing.

THE INTERESTING BITS
Now the interesting thing about a special budget is that there is always an overlap between it and your normal departmental budget, for instance staff costs. The staff you take with you – and yourself of course – are already budgeted for moneywise

> **PRINTED BUDGETS**
>
> When you start to work out your trial budgets, map out a table on your word processor and print out several copies. This saves time when you are filling them in, in rough. As you do each one and it is superseded by another you can throw the initial one away but you still have lots of blank tables printed to keep you going. Saves time and effort and makes your trial budgets a lot easier to work with.

out of your regular departmental budget for salaries. But what if they work overtime? Is that to be taken out of your special budget or out of your departmental budget? Only you can decide but normally they would receive their normal salary from departmental budget and the overtime payment from the special budget. But, and this is where things get complex and you have to think at the speed of life if you're not to come a cropper, the job they normally do back in the office ain't gonna get done while they're strutting their stuff on the exhibition stand.

So not only do you have to budget money, you also have to juggle people (no, don't even think about that). Who is going to replace them – and you – while this exhibition goes on? Do you need to get in replacement staff? Temps? Can you get existing staff to cover? Pull in someone from another department? Let it all go hang until you get back? You have to make that decision – and quickly if you're to get on with this budget (see *fast thinking: decision*). Once you know how you are allocating your staff you can move on to the really interesting stuff such as paying for the stand, getting in exhibitor organisers, hotels, travel, and refreshments of course.

You should now be ready to start a trial special budget which is basically a list of expenditure. You add it up, and hopefully you haven't forgotten anything, and it comes in at less than the £10,000 you were given to play with. It might look something like this:

Ah, we have a problem. You only have ten thousand pounds and already you've allocated over sixteen. This is why a special budget is so important. If you hadn't done this exercise, you would have overspent. That means you would have had to make up the shortfall out of your departmental budget which would have thrown that off track. OK, let's regroup and rethink. What can we cut down on?

Staff costs for overtime	£3000
Exhibition stand rental for three days	£600
Sales material and printed matter	£500
Hotel accommodation	£4500
Staff meals/refreshments	£800
Travel	£240
Exhibition organiser	£6500
Total	£16140

SECOND DRAFT

Firstly look at your biggest expenditure – staff overtime, hotels and exhibition organisers. Which of these can you pare down?

Staff costs and hotels go hand in hand so let's look at these two first. You need to pay the staff overtime, of course, as they will be working longer hours and away from home. But what if you sent them home at the end of the day instead of putting them up in expensive hotels where they will only run up colossal bar bills and probably get themselves into trouble? You need to find out if it is practical to send them home at the end of each day. How far away is the exhibition? Are there frequent trains? Can they drive there and back in reasonable time?

Are there cheaper hotels? What about a B&B? Do you need to pay them overtime or could you give them time off in lieu? If you don't know the answer to this one, go and ask them – hypothetically, at this stage. What if you paid them an exhibition allowance and let them spend it in anyway they chose, then they could drive home if they wanted to or stay in whatever accommodation they preferred. They might even have friends in the area and stay somewhere for free – no, you can't ask for the allowance back if they do this. Let's suppose you choose to pay them an allowance and you set it at £400 per person per day. And you need three staff with you – forget about yourself for the moment – that would cost you £3600. Damn. Too much. Cut it down and pay them £200 per person per day – that's only £1800 – saving £1200 – good. This also cuts down on your overtime bill as you officially dispense with the staff once the exhibition closes at the end of the day rather than paying them for all the time they are away from home. Most exhibitions start earlier and go on later than normal office hours, but you are paying them this very generous exhibition allowance so you might get away with not paying them any overtime at all – if you are clever and present it to them in such a good light

thinking smart

BROADEN YOUR HORIZONS

If you like organising then this job is for you – the special budget. It makes life easier and faster if you know how to budget well and keep control of expenditure. You'll be more than likely to be offered the plum jobs organising special projects – this gets you out of the office and allows you the chance to shine and look good.

thinking fast

NEGOTIATING UPWARDS

Just as you can haggle with suppliers and the like, so you can negotiate with your boss. If they say they want you to organise a conference and your budget is five thousand and you know this to be a bit on the light side – then say so. And make sure you have enough evidence to back up your claim. Keep records of all special budgets you do so you can justify an increase. Quickly whip out your proof and you take the wind out of their sails and pull the rug from under their feet – so to speak. If you catch them on the hop, they'll be much more likely to grant an increase than if they have time to think about it.

that they think you're doing them a favour. Let's suppose you sell it to them well and they accept. You've slashed your overtime to nothing and reduced the hotel bill to a mere allowance of £1800 – simply brilliant.

NEGOTIATING COSTS

Now what about these exhibition organisers. Seems to me they are taking you for a ride. Go back and negotiate them down. I know that sounds easier said than done, but we are all in the market place and no one objects to a little haggling. Phone them up and question their quotation. Believe me most will drop their price a little if you query it, or suggest a slight amendment. Suppose you say that the quote seemed a bit steep and you'd like it for less as your budget doesn't allow for such a high price – good one that, always blame the budget and not yourself for querying a quote – for you next tactic, suggest that you and your team will be responsible for clearing up afterwards instead of them and that you will provide staff to put out all the promotion material instead of them – obviously they have to be allowed to do their very professional job of putting the stand up, providing an impressive display, putting in the lighting and electrics and all that. Now they might well come back and agree a discount. Say they suggest £5700. You say 'make it five and a half and you've got a deal', chances are they will agree. You've now cut your exhibition organiser's budget by £1000 – again, brilliant. Let's have a quick look at a revised trial special budget:

OK, now we're getting somewhere. You've got a budget that falls below the ten grand you have to play with. Excellent. But you have forgotten one thing – yourself. What are you going to pay yourself for this exhibition? Strikes me you should pay yourself the same as your staff – the £200 per day – total of £600, I think. That takes you up above your target by £40 and you have no contingency to play with. A contingency is an emergency amount for emergencies – simple, huh?

Staff costs for overtime	Nil
Exhibition stand rental for three days	£600
Sales material and printed matter	£500
Hotel accommodation	Nil
Staff exhibition allowance	£1800
Staff meals/refreshments	£800
Travel	£240
Exhibition organiser	£5500
Total	£9440

ANTICIPATING THE SPECIAL BUDGET

Smart managers think on their feet. So if you hear that there is going to be a royal visit in six months time, then you know it's sod's law that you'll be given the job of organising the painting of the lavatories – or whatever is required. Stay one step ahead of the game and already have quotes, brochures, information to hand so you can give a rough idea of expenditure seemingly off the top of your head. Looks good and keeps you one step ahead of the rest.

LOOKING AT THE DETAIL

OK, let's now look at the lesser expenditure. You probably won't be able to negotiate the rental on the stand down so forget that. The cost of the sales promotional material is also pretty fixed. That leaves travel and staff meals/refreshments. No, you can't haggle with the rail companies or Shell Oil over the cost of petrol. That leaves the cost of feeding your team. £800 for three days – seems a bit on the generous side – that's £200 each (including yourself) for three days. What are you going to be eating, caviar? And drinking champagne? I think not: you're there to work. You could cut this down to a total of £400 and not starve anyone. Good, you've saved a bit so let's do a final budget – the one your MD will probably want to see before you go.

Exhibition rental	£600
Sales material	£500
Staff exhibition allowance (including you)	£2400
Staff meals/refreshments	£400
Travel	£240
Exhibition organiser	£5500
Total	£9640

Good, you're in under budget and have a little to play with. Pat yourself on the back and get on with organising that exhibition.

The rules for a special budget almost always follow the same lines and now you should have no difficulty doing one – and doing it quickly, professionally and smart.

for next time

Always be ready for the special budget – they crop up quite often – and always ask what your budget is before agreeing to organise a project. Keep a good record of any expenditure over and beyond your normal departmental budget so you have something to refer back to – this is especially important when it comes to staff costs which can be complex to work out anew each time.

Be ready to delegate the task of organising a special event but retain control of the budget at all times. The budget is your most important tool and you should stay well in charge of it.

budget in an evening

Throughout this book we have assumed that you are under pressure – the pressure to produce a budget in a couple of days at most. But what if you really are under pressure? The pressure to produce a budget now, today – and you only have an evening to prepare? Well, it can be done. First, you'll need to have a copy of last year's budget. Go through it and check it against the actual figures for what really happened last year.

Now sit down and work out exactly what staff you have and what staff you need. Use the equation on page 454 to calculate your payroll percentage. Add this on to your basic payroll budget. You should know what you are paying your staff as a basic salary. From last year's figures you can see the actual amount. Calculate the total you will need to find to pay the staff everything including NI, pensions, cars and bonuses. This is the biggest single expenditure and the one that probably accounts for around 50 per cent of your budgeted total. Get this one right and you are more than half way.

Don't worry at this stage about a monthly breakdown. Work only with total figures for the year. Look at the actual figures for last year. What was your next biggest expenditure? Is this going to be around the same or more this year? Why? Check the next two biggest expenditures and by now you should be around 80 per cent of your budgeted total. The rest should now slot in, leaving you room to manoeuvre.

Now you can divide everything by 12 to give you a monthly figure. It won't be very accurate but at least you have some sort of figure to enter. You won't have any seasonal differences but that can wait until you've more time.

That's about it. There's little more you can do now. Buy more time by getting into your boss's office early and start firing questions. The more questions you ask, the fewer there will be for you to answer. Fight fire with fire. They've put you on the spot by asking for a budget in an evening. Now make them pay by putting them on the spot and demanding all the information you obviously haven't been given.

Someone, somewhere isn't doing their job properly. Make sure it isn't you.

budget in an hour

OK, so a budget in an evening isn't enough of a challenge for you. How about a budget in an hour? It has happened. What do you do if it happens to you? Well, apart from burning your budget and claiming it was an act of God …

You have an hour. Quickly now:

1 Get last year's budget.

2 Do a quick check to make sure there is nothing there that shouldn't now be. Make sure there is nothing missing that you've now got to account for.

3 Do a quick check that your staffing levels are about similar.

4 Run through the figures and add 15 per cent on to all of them.

5 Fill in as much as you can.

6 Take one or two items and make a note about them – any note, it doesn't matter. You now have a budget which looks about right.

That's all you can hope for in an hour.
This temporary budget should buy you enough time to do a real one. Let's hope so.

presentation

- MAKE YOUR CASE
- GET IT ACROSS
- WIN PEOPLE OVER

ros jay

contents

introduction

You've got an important presentation to give in a couple of days – maybe even a couple of hours. The clock's ticking, and you haven't even started yet. But it had better be good, because this one matters. You have to sell your big idea, win a major order from a key customer, or maybe persuade your board of directors to invest big-time in a fully integrated website. Or perhaps you have to sell management's case for restructuring to a sceptical staff.

Whatever the objective, you know you should be giving a lot more time than this to preparing the presentation. But life's too fast in the modern business world, and you just don't have that time. So what's the solution? Fast thinking, that's what. And whether the time pressure is high or merely moderate, you need to think smart.

This book is about thinking fast and smart to prepare a presentation in a day or two. You can't possibly do justice to an all-day presentation to 300 people in this time, so that's not what we're about.

This section is about preparing a presentation of between a few minutes and, say, an hour, probably on your own or with just one or two colleagues, to a small audience. This is the most common type of presentation, and it can easily be done in a short time. But if you're working on a bigger presentation and want some last-minute ideas for pepping it up, *Fast Thinking* can help you add gloss.

Sure, it's better to have more time, and this book will tell you what to do with it when you *do* have it. But for now, what you need is the fast thinker's version. You want

 tips for looking as if you know more than you do

 shortcuts for doing as little preparation as possible, and

▶ **checklists to run through at the last minute.**

all put together clearly and simply. And short enough to read fast, of course.

Let's assume you have a couple of days to prepare your presentation. Ideally you would have longer, and you would have started early in case some research material took a while to get hold of, or visuals took some time to prepare. But that's fantasy land. You're here, now, with only a day or two left. If you're really up against the clock, you may have only an evening to prepare for a presentation tomorrow morning. If that's the case, you'll find a checklist at the back of the book to help you really step on the gas (see page 500). And for the truly up-against-it, the one-hour version (page 507) will show you how to prepare faster than the speed of life.

So take the phone off the hook, take a deep breath, and don't panic. It's all in here, and this book will get you through the process of preparing for your presentation in as little as an hour, if that's all you've got. Every hour you have beyond that is a bonus – a luxury if you like – so if you have a whole evening to prepare, you've got time to relax … and even make yourself a coffee before you start.

This book is going to go through the seven key stages of preparing and delivering a presentation.

1 The first thing to do is to identify your objective, so that you can prepare the presentation faster and smarter.

2 After this comes the basic preparation, collecting together all the information you can in the time you have.

3 The next step is structuring the presentation to give it the kind of clarity which makes it look really slick and which drives its message home.

4 After this, we'll look at how you can get everything you want to say into usable note form.

5 Next you need to think about the kind of language you use to be clear in your arguments and to make your audience feel they can relate to you.

6 Visual aids are a valuable part of most presentations, but if they aren't right they can damage rather than improve it. So the next stage is to design your visuals to be really effective.

7 And finally, you arrive at the finished presentation. The last lap involves rehearsal, delivery, handling questions and coping with nerves.

fast thinking gambles

Of course we all know you should have left longer for this presentation, if only it had been possible. But why? Fast thinking will stop you looking like a fool, and will achieve your objective comfortably. So what's the point of making more time? Well, however good you are at fast thinking, some things take more time than you've got. Basically, when your time is limited, your options are limited.

So what is the downside of preparing for a presentation at full throttle instead of at a steady pace?

- **Research is an important stage of preparing for a presentation. Some research takes time, and therefore can't be done at all when you're up against it. For example, you might want to get hold of a copy of your customer's annual report before you present to them, or talk to various suppliers to get a clear estimate of the cost of a proposal you're presenting to the board.**

- **Your audience is likely to ask you questions at some point. The better prepared you are, the more likely you are to be able to answer them effectively. The corollary is that the less preparation you've done, the greater the chance that they will identify a gap in your knowledge.**

- **Visual aids are a traditional ingredient of presentations. While they are often overused (the good news), there are nevertheless times when they lend considerable weight to your argument. Some potentially valuable aids take more time to prepare than you have, and you are therefore missing out on a useful source of persuasive material.**

- **Things can go wrong, technically, during presentations. Your notes fall to the floor, shuffling themselves in the process. The slides get out of order. The power supply to your computer fails. Your audience asks you to cover the topics in a different order because one of their number has to leave early. All these calamities are reduced or removed by preparation and practice, and the time to arrange fallback positions to cover likely emergencies.**

- **Your own delivery is the key to the effectiveness of your presentation. Unless you are a real natural, you will need time to learn how to deliver your presentation well.**

- **For the nervous, the real solution is rehearsal. The better you know what you're doing, the more confident you will feel (stands to reason). So cutting down the rehearsal time will leave you more susceptible to stage fright.**

Fast thinking will turn a potentially embarrasing spectacle into a polished, professional and persuasive presentation. But for a truly top-notch, first-class, five-star performance every time in the future, your best chance is to start a good couple of weeks ahead … next time.

1 your objective

One of the first things we tend to do when we're short of time is to stop thinking. We want to get on and *do* something. So we frantically collect up paperwork, start scrawling notes, dig out handout material and trawl through documents looking for something we can turn into a visual aid. It feels more productive – but it isn't. A little calm, clear thinking at the beginning of the whole process will save you a great deal of time later.

And the single most important thing you can think about is your objective. What is the idea you're trying to sell? What is this presentation for? We're not talking general stuff here, such as 'to win an order'. We need to be specific. How about 'to persuade the customer that our website design service is better than the competition'? That's getting better, but it could still be more specific – better in what way? What are this customer's key concerns – cost, effectiveness, technical superiority?

Here's a clear, concise objective, then:

> *To persuade the customer that our website design service will attract more visitors and repeat visitors to their website than the competition, and will be easily upgraded as new technology becomes available.*

Now we've set out clearly what precisely it is that we want to achieve as a result of the presentation.

Once you've identified your objective, write it down. This is your touchstone for the rest of the preparation you will do. If any research, information, visual aid or whatever doesn't further this objective, don't waste your time on it.

 thinking smart

BUYING TIME

Allocate yourself five minutes to think through your objective, and time yourself. If you only have an hour, you could cut this down to three minutes. However, don't allow yourself to take any less time. Tell yourself that, however panicky you are, if you finish early you'll just have to twiddle your thumbs until your five minutes is up. This should help you to give the exercise the time it deserves. Getting this bit right will save you plenty of time later.

2 preparation

Preparation is a large part of what makes a presentation work. The point of a presentation is to bring the audience round to your point of view, and well-researched and prepared arguments, with data to support them, are a key part of this. So don't be tempted to feel that you are wasting time you can't spare here. You can usefully occupy at least half your available time with preparation, excluding the time you spend physically preparing visuals and writing out notes.

Again, much of this is thinking time, and a cool, unflustered approach is what fast thinking is all about. Just because you aren't doing anything beyond jotting down notes, it doesn't mean you're wasting your time; quite the reverse.

RESEARCH

Aargh! This sounds like something that takes ages. Well, yes, it can do. But on this occasion you haven't got ages, so obviously it isn't going to take long today. But research is important. This is because if you don't do any research, you can make a real prat of yourself. Let me give you a few salutary examples.

- ▶ **You don't learn the names of the customers you are presenting to, and your boss walks in unexpectedly and asks you to introduce everyone.**
- ▶ **You spend several minutes explaining why it's worth investing in a website only to discover that they already have one – they just want a better one.**
- ▶ **You are asked the cost of a maintenance contract after the installation is completed, and you have no idea.**

Right. So you clearly need to do *some* research. But how little can you get away with? Or, better still, how much can you do in a limited time? Let's begin by identifying the areas you need to research:

1 your audience
2 your product or service
3 shared history
4 facts to support your case.

As you think through each area, jot down any salient points on a sheet of paper.

Your audience

This might seem obvious, but there's plenty that can get missed out if you're not thorough. Here are the basics to cover:

- ▶ **their names and job titles**
- ▶ **their likely attitude to your presentation – are they keen or reluctant to be persuaded?**
- ▶ **their level of knowledge – don't throw technical jargon at them if they know little about the subject, or talk down to them if they are experts.**

ON-THE-SPOT RESEARCH

If you're good enough at thinking on your feet, you can save a large chunk of the research until you begin the presentation. Start by asking the audience questions, and build their answers into your presentation as you go along. You can't ask things you blatantly should know already ('Sorry, what's the name of this company again?') but a useful tip is to stick to questions about their thoughts, feelings and opinions. Ask them open questions about what they consider the single most important feature of a telecommunications system, or what they most dislike about organisational change.

Luckily, you can answer most of these questions by thinking, or referring to the memo inviting you to give the presentation. You can often make a quick phone call too – an enthusiastic buyer or a boss who has asked you to give the presentation to convince their colleagues will happily fill you in on the background of the other audience members.

If the presentation is to a customer, the more you can learn about their organisation the better. Sales leaflets, background on their current supplier, press articles and so on are all useful here.

Your product or service

By this I mean whatever it is you are trying to sell. You might be trying to sell enthusiasm to your staff to get behind a project, or you might want to sell top management the idea of employing three extra staff. But whatever it is, you need to know your stuff. Don't get caught out with simple questions like 'How does it work?' or 'How many people do you already employ in that department?' Customers will expect you to know the basic facts about a product or service you're trying to sell them, such as:

- **size**
- **price**
- **colourway**
- **add-ons/accessories**
- **performance data**
- **competition**
- **delivery methods and times.**

and so on.

CALL IN THE EXPERTS

A brief, perhaps grovelling, phone call to an expert – inside or outside the company – can save you hours of research at libraries, in books and on the Internet. You could call an in-house technical whizz, a supplier, or perhaps a journalist who specialises in your industry.

The good news here is that you should know most of this already. But think it through again. Have new models been added lately? Has the price changed? Or the price of add-ons? If you're selling a project or an impending change to your staff, how long will it take? What exactly will it entail? What will the benefits be?

Shared history

Has your audience had any previous experience of the thing you want to sell them? Have they rejected it in the past? Have they used it before? Did they ask you to give this presentation or did you offer it? Have they ever seen the product? Has this customer had generic problems with you, such as late deliveries or product failures, which may influence their attitude?

You may well be able to access this kind of information quickly by viewing computer records, or perhaps in the same phone call where you were asking about the audience background. Or you may have notes from meetings, or copies of other people's reports.

Facts to support your case

A presentation is all about persuading the audience round to your way of thinking. And your best ammunition for this is hard facts. So you need performance data, costings, timescales, technical information, and so on.

The more facts you have at your fingertips, the harder it is for your audience to disagree with you. And apart from basic product knowledge you don't have to learn the facts by heart. Jot them down neatly on a piece of paper or a notecard, and have them to hand during the presentation.

DECIDING WHAT TO SAY

Don't begin to think about what order you're going to say things in – structure comes later. But this is the time to make a note of all the things you most want to say: the key arguments you'd kick yourself for if you left them out. Suppose your research has identified that your management board has a history of frowning on employing extra staff who don't directly generate more in income than they cost the organisation. In this case you want to be sure to include all your data to back up your assertion that they will each generate double their own salary within the first year.

 thinkingfast

CONDUCT A MINI-SURVEY

Sometimes you need to present evidence showing how people feel or think about something – survey information. For example, nine out of ten shop floor employees would work flexitime if they had the option. If you're pushed for time, you can still conduct mini-surveys of colleagues, friends, customers or suppliers. The best way to do this is by e-mail. Just ask one or two simple, quick questions with a cut-off time for replying.

If your audience is very cost-conscious, you want to focus on the figures. If they are nervous of new technology, you want to include a bit about how easy it is to use, or how the really terrifying thing would be falling behind their competitors technologically. And so on. Jot down all the key points so they are safely on paper instead of floating around tenuously in your head.

⏪ for next time

Ideally, it helps to write each separate point you want to make on a fresh slip of paper. This takes longer of course (which is why I don't recommend you do it when you're up against the clock), but it does make it easier to keep moving them around when you come to structure the presentation until you're happy with the order.

If you had more time, you would have access to other sources of research information which you haven't got time for now. Here are some ideas for good sources of data when time allows:

- ▶ annual reports
- ▶ press archives
- ▶ management reports and figures
- ▶ trade associations and regulatory bodies
- ▶ government departments, such as the Central Statistical Office
- ▶ surveys – conduct your own or study existing ones
- ▶ interviews.

If you're short of a lot of important data for an imminent presentation, get yourself a copy of one of the companion volumes to this one: *fast thinking: finding facts*.

3 structure

One of the most convincing ways of appearing practised and professional is to use a clear structure for your presentation. There's nothing worse than a presenter who jumps from point to point, backwards and forwards, interspersing their talk with remarks like 'Oh, yes, I forgot to mention…' and 'Actually, I should have said…', and so on.

When you're pushed for time, a good structure will help you to prepare your presentation more easily and to keep a clear head while you do it. And it will convince your audience that you have really put time into working up this presentation. You obviously take them seriously to have put in so much effort.

There's a simple structure you can use for all presentations, whatever the subject and whoever you are addressing. It divides into four main sections, sandwiched between two top and tail sections:

1 Introduction

2 Position

3 Problem

4 Possibilities

5 Proposal

6 Summary

INTRODUCTION

Here's your chance to make an impression, grab attention and show how polished and well prepared you are. Your first impression will, of course, be your strongest – so if you make it good, the rest follows far more easily. There's no need to be clever; just be confident and friendly and cover the essentials.

1 Say hello and thanks for coming.

2 Introduce yourself.

3 Say what your objective is (yep, the one you've established already).

4 Explain how long the presentation will be, and roughly what form it will take. ('I'll spend about ten minutes going through why we need to address the problem of staffing levels in the despatch department, and what the options are. Then I'll outline what I believe is the best option, and why.')

5 Tell your audience what you want them to do about asking questions (for example, 'Please ask as we go along if you don't follow anything, but would you please save any other questions until the end.').

Making an entrance

There is a folklore belief that you should always start a presentation with a witty remark: like so many folklore beliefs it isn't true, but there is truth somewhere at the root of it. The fact is that every speaker needs some sort of acceptance from the audience. If they are to accept what you say, they need some grounds for believing that you are in most ways the same sort of person as them.

A good witty line or a funny anecdote that is not obtrusively dragged in, that is relevant and amusing and gets a big laugh, is an excellent way of giving the audience this sense of all belonging to the same group along with you. However, a funny story or line that fails has exactly the reverse effect and may be very hard to recover from. An opening joke is therefore particularly dangerous with very small audiences, with unfamiliar audiences, when you haven't the time to practise it on colleagues, or if you have any doubts about whether it will get the laugh you intend.

There are many alternatives to humour which will still help you to create an accepting kind of atmosphere. All of these approaches work because they show that you are just as ordinary as the rest of them, and not setting yourself up as a superior person:

- **any expression of personal feelings**
- **some honest self-revelation**
- **a self-deprecating remark.**

Some people believe that you should do something really headline-grabbing at the opening of a presentation. Don't get hung up on this one – you haven't time. If something brilliant springs to mind, great. But it really isn't essential – it's just a bonus.

If you think of something you can do or say that will get a big reaction (such as entering the room through the third-floor window, or appearing in drag) just follow these guidelines.

- **Make the opening directly relevant to the presentation – if it's going to be memorable, make sure that when the audience remember it, they simultaneously remember the point you were making.**
- **Don't make the audience feel nervous or uncomfortable.**
- **Don't use humour unless you are certain it will work, and never crack a joke at the expense of the audience.**

 thththin **thinkingsfast**

GET SOMEONE ELSE TO DO THE WORK

If you are a little shaky on the background, and don't have time to research it fully, you could ask one of the audience to state it for you. If it is at all controversial, ask someone with authority: 'Mr Fuller, as Managing Director you've overseen all aspects of this project right from the start. Perhaps it would be helpful for everyone if you could briefly explain the thinking behind it which has brought us to this point? (Then you just nod along sagely as if you knew it all already.) Obviously you shouldn't try this unless you're confident your audience will co-operate.

POSITION

The members of the audience at the start of a presentation are like the horses before the start of a race – scattered all over the place and facing in different directions. The starter at a race meeting has to bring them all up to the line together so that they start level and all go off in the right direction at the same time.

A presenter has to do much the same: if you gallop straight off, you may hurtle along splendidly without realising that you left everybody else behind at the starting gate. So you have to gather your audience together and connect yourself up to them.

The way to do this is to outline the present situation: describe the way overseas distribution is currently organised, or the way the pattern of home demand has been changing, or the way we order stationery at the moment – whatever the purpose of your presentation, it is essential that everyone should start with the same knowledge, and important that you should demonstrate to them all that you know the situation and background. It also enables everyone to focus on the specific part of the present situation which you are addressing. This not only helps comprehension: it also helps you to get accepted by the audience by showing that you understand their situation.

This part of the presentation may take no more than a couple of sentences, or it may need quite a long analysis of how things came to be the way they are. But some statement of the present situation has to be made and agreed upon.

PROBLEM

This is where you introduce the need for change by showing why the present situation cannot continue, or why it would be unwise to continue it. There must be some significant change or danger or worry or opportunity, or you wouldn't be making the presentation. You need to express this in terms your audience can relate to. Here are some typical catalysts for change:

- ▶ **Demand is shifting.**
- ▶ **Staff are leaving.**
- ▶ **Competitors are gaining.**
- ▶ **Profits are falling.**
- ▶ **Technology is changing.**
- ▶ **Delays are lengthening.**
- ▶ **Costs are rising.**
- ▶ **Buildings are leaking.**

This is the stage at which you dig the hole in which you intend to plant your idea.

A computer salesman once explained, rather convincingly, why his job was very like a missionary's or an evangelical minister's. Both he and they, he said, succeeded by unearthing or implanting some unease, guilt or fear in the person they were trying to convert. He himself did not deal in hellfire and torment, only in business rivals doing things cheaper, better or quicker and some people being left behind, but he felt that the principle was the same: nobody was interested in salvation until they had a fear of damnation.

thinking smart

THE POWER OF PERSUASION

If you have five or ten minutes to spare, read the appendix at the back of this book on techniques for persuading the audience round to your point of view.

I am not suggesting anything so extreme; nevertheless if your audience is rather cool it is a great help if you can make them aware, from the very start, of the ways in which what you are about to present is important to them. They arrive prepared to listen: by the end of the first few minutes they should be wanting to know.

This is one of those times when a little thought goes a long way. However pushed for time you are, taking a few minutes to think through what you will say here is always worth it.

POSSIBILITIES

The two previous sections may be brief: the remaining two form the bulk of the presentation. If you are outlining various options before making a recommendation, you will need to include this section; if you have only one possible course of action to propose you can skip this bit and go straight on to the 'proposal' section below.

Suppose you are asking the board for three new posts to cover what you see as an increased workload. There are other options, too, at least in the board's eyes, and you need to outline these. You could leave things as they are. You could take on just one or two more staff. Or you could even take on four. Your audience needs to understand all these options in order to choose between them.

In this part of the presentation you should aim to conceal from the audience what your preferred option is. Of course they may know perfectly well what it is, but by trying to keep it quiet you will necessarily have to observe the key rules for this part of the proceedings.

 Give facts and not opinions.

 Be fair to all the arguments.

 Be unbiased.

You need to explain what each option entails, and any statistics or data which back this up. So you need to outline the cost, the timescale, the benefits, and so on. But your audience have to make up their own minds (or at least that's what they should think they are doing), and they can't do that if you keep telling them what to think – they will simply resent you and, by association, your recommendation.

The point about outlining the other options, even if you don't want to propose them, is that your audience will consider them whether or not you do. At least if you include them in your presentation you take the business of analysing them under your control, on an equal footing with your personal recommendation.

In this section you may:

- give a product demonstration (or several)
- describe the products, services or packages
- meet objections (before they are voiced)
- compare prices
- give evidence and supporting data
- quote examples.

When expressing the possibilities, you need always to talk in terms of direct benefits to your audience, not merely features of the product or package. To give you a simple example of the difference, a *feature* of a car might be that it has ABS brakes, but the *benefit* is that it brakes more safely, without skidding. Your audience doesn't want to know what each option does, but what it can do *for them*. So three extra staff isn't about getting through the paperwork faster, it's about reducing complaints or improving cash flow.

PROPOSAL

Now, finally, it's time to come clean about your recommendation. Mind you, it doesn't do to denigrate any of the other options – some members of your audience may have favoured those, and won't want their judgement criticised. So imply that all the options are valid, but show why your favoured one is the best. Obviously if there are no other options this section makes up the bulk of your presentation.

If you omitted the previous section on possibilities, you will now want to do at least some of the following:

- give a product demonstration
- describe the product, service or package
- meet objections (before they are voiced)
- give prices and timescales
- give evidence and supporting data
- quote examples.

SUMMARY

The ending of a presentation, like the opening, is too important to be left to the mercy of chance or the whim of the moment. True, you may think of an improvement on your planned ending while you are speaking, but it is still vital to have a planned ending to improve on. This does not mean that it has to be long, complicated or clever, only that it has to be worked out in advance and rehearsed as well as you have time for.

It doesn't do to denigrate any of the other options – some members of your audience may have favoured those, and won't want their judgement criticised

TOP AND TAIL

If you don't have time to script your whole presentation, at least decide what you will say at the beginning and the end. These are the two most vital moments for making and cementing a good impression.

When working out your ending you must, again, go back to your original objective, since this will dictate it. The ending should normally include:

- ▸ **a summary of the salient facts and arguments**
- ▸ **a summary of the recommendation**
- ▸ **a proposal for the next step, if the recommendation is accepted, with target dates**
- ▸ **a description or explanation of any handouts you are about to distribute**
- ▸ **thanks for listening patiently.**

You will probably want to invite questions at this point as well. Incidentally, you may well want to repeat any key visuals along with the summary, and if you have a single summarising visual (perhaps your only one if you're really pushed for time) you might leave it on display after you have finished as a reminder.

QUESTIONS

You can't stop your audience asking you questions; nor should you want to. It is their opportunity to express doubts so that you can reassure them. Without that opportunity, any doubt will continue to fester in the minds of your audience. The fear, of course, is that they will ask you a question to which you don't know the answer.

Later on we'll look at how to handle particular types of difficult question. But at this stage, it's a good idea to think through what questions you are likely to be asked. Yes, this is another one of those moments when, even with the clock ticking, you still need to stop doing for a moment and just think. In their position, what would you ask?

Some likely questions you may think of should suggest to you that you go back and put the answer in the presentation proper ('What's the name of your product again?'). But you may well come up with questions which aren't likely, or which are too detailed or specialised to put into the presentation itself, but for which you should nevertheless be prepared. For example, there may be one audience member who wants a detailed breakdown of costs, or specific data on your safety record.

There are two particularly good key ways of spotting likely questions.

- ▸ **Run through the job titles or remits of the members of your audience – people tend to ask questions related to their own specific field. If the finance director, health and safety officer, or personnel manager is going to be there, this should give you a big clue about what to prepare for.**
- ▸ **Phone someone else – a colleague or your boss – who knows something about the subject of your presentation but has a different perspective or a fresh eye, and ask them to give you a quick rundown of anything they think you are likely to be asked.**

thinking smart

PART OF THE PACKAGE

If you can say everything you feel you need to in about five minutes, but feel you ought to go on longer, why not make the question and answer session seem like part of the allotted presentation time? Introduce it at the beginning as part of your presentation – 'I'm just going to talk for a few minutes first, and then allow your questions to help me make the most of the time we have' – and stay standing up with your last visual still on display; it will look like part of the presentation rather than something else which follows on.

The danger, especially if you are preparing your presentation in something of a hurry, is that you will miss the obvious. No one is going to mind if you can't answer detailed, specialised questions on the spot (although it looks great when you can). But it doesn't look so good if you don't know how you arrived at your costings, or how long it will take to deliver the product if the customer decides to place the order. This is what you are investing your time – however precious – to avoid.

thinking fast

FACT FINDING

No matter how pushed for time you are, you are inevitably going to have to come up with certain hard facts for each of the options. You should have collected these during your research stage, but there is always a possibility that you will find you don't have a vital piece of data which you need. To establish the minimum you can get away with, go back to your objective. You need the facts which directly help you achieve this. So, for example, if your objective states that you are demonstrating that your recommendation is the best value for money, you need comparative costs more than you need comparative performance data for all your options.

for next time

If you have time, as I mentioned earlier, it is a good idea to write each point you wish to make on a separate piece of paper. It can also help to write on the reverse of the paper what your source for the information is so that you can find it again easily.

When it comes to structuring your presentation, the first thing to do is to organise all these pieces of paper into just a few groups. You might have one group of points for each of the possible options, for example, or one for cost issues, one for time issues, and one for performance data – along with one for the problem section of the presentation and one for the summary, and so on.

Once you have reached this point, it is very easy to work through the structuring process, moving around whole groups at a time until you feel you have the order right. Individual points can easily be swapped or relocated, and a fresh point added if you think of something else you should have included. But at any given moment your presentation has physical shape which doesn't require you to rely on holding the information in your head where a chance interruption can push it beyond your grasp.

4 notes and scripts

Now you know what points you want to make, and in what order. You're doing well – you've laid the groundwork for your presentation now. The next step is to find the words to make your point.

When you're in enough of a hurry you may start with a handful of scribbled notes and launch straight into your presentation. From the point of view of the language you will use, that's terrific. But of course it carries the risk that you will miss out certain important – if not crucial – arguments. And that you will get stuck trying to find a good way to express a complex idea off the cuff.

So start with as much of a script as you have time for.

- ▶ **In an ideal world (which you don't inhabit just now) you would write out your full presentation and then reduce it to note form.**

- ▶ **Failing that, write only notes, but script any important areas you can find time to – the toughest examples, explanations or ideas to express – along with the opening and the close of the presentation.**

- ▶ **Whatever happens, at least try to script the opening and the close.**

Write your notes out by hand on index cards, or using a word processor. You want to include all the key points and any phrases, analogies or metaphors you have identified for explaining complex ideas (see the next chapter). Don't make your notes too detailed, however (as if you had the time), since this makes it harder to find your place in the heat of the moment. You might like to go through and underline the main section headings, or colour-code red for key arguments and green for phrases, for example. Too many colours and underlinings, however, are likely to give you an indecipherable jumble.

Giving a presentation from notes is an excellent way of showing your audience that you have prepared thoroughly, which flatters them apart from anything else. It actually looks more professional and polished than working without notes at all (which can look a bit fly), even if you are one of those lucky people who can do it. You clearly thought your audience were worth the effort. You may know that you were obliged to leave the preparation until the last minute, but they will imagine you have been working on this presentation for several days.

thinking smart

SCRIPTING SECTIONS

One of the plus points of scripting your presentation in full is that certain points may be difficult to express clearly, and there will be a best way of saying them. A proper script identifies these and finds a clear wording which gets your point across. So identify these sticking points and script at least these sections of your presentation.

thinking smart

STEADY HAND

If you type your notes, cut the paper down to a smaller size as this is less obtrusive. If you get shaky during presentations, index cards are better than paper for concealing the fact. Staple your cards or sheets of notes in the top left-hand corner so they can't get out of order.

Giving a presentation from notes is an excellent way of showing your audience that you have prepared thoroughly

485

5 language

On the printed page you may get away with all sorts of things you can't possibly say in everyday speech – so don't try and say them in your presentation. It is clarity that impresses people, not long words and convoluted sentences. If you use unnatural spoken language, the people in your audience are likely to feel 'Whoever this person is talking to, it isn't me.' Show you are one of them by speaking their language.

Writing good spoken English can mean writing ungrammatically. In fact, grammatically correct English can be bad spoken English; just count how many times anyone says the word 'whom' to you tomorrow. Very few people can say it and get away with it. Conversely, you can get away with language face to face which you would never allow on the printed page. Slang can be very effective face to face ('Compared with our expenditure on exhibitions, it's peanuts'; 'During peak order times, with our current system, there are frankly far too many cock-ups').

Write this type of language into your first draft – whether it is a full script or you have time only to make notes – and you can be sure that it will follow right through to the presentation itself.

USING SPOKEN ENGLISH

OK, this bit is important even if you're racing the clock. In a presentation you are offering a structured series of arguments, and it requires some effort from the audience to follow. The easier you make it for them, the more likely they are to listen attentively and take it all in. So here's a quick rundown of the key techniques for helping them along the way.

▸ **Use short words and short sentences.** Do not say: 'Circumstances occasionally arise involving a situation in which one or more of the contributing personnel wishes to exercise the option of continuing in employment beyond the normal retirement date as specified in their formal contractual agreement, in which eventuality suitable arrangements can be concluded for the further maintenance of contribution and consequent enhancement of eventual benefit.' Just say: 'Sometimes people want to stay on after they're 60. If so they can still stay in the pension scheme.'

▸ **Avoid abstract words.** Abstract words send people to sleep. They are, by definition, hard to get a concrete grasp on, so they tend to wash over the audience's heads. 'Transportation' is an abstract noun: better to say 'car' if that is what you mean. Don't

thinking smart

e-STYLE

Written and spoken English always used to differ widely. But in the last few years an overlap has emerged – e-mail English. Almost all of us use a more relaxed writing style in e-mails than we ever do in proposals, letters, reports or even memos. So use this as a guide – write your presentation in the style you would write an e-mail.

say 'When you take into consideration...' but 'When you consider...'. Words such as 'situation', 'operation' and 'facilities' should all be banned, and either removed or replaced with more specific, concrete terms.

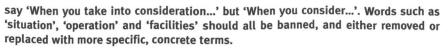

- *Use active verbs (in other words, 'doing' words).* It is better to say 'we need your help' than 'your help is needed by us'. Active verbs are more dynamic and interesting to listen to than passive ones. So say: 'The department will meet the budget' rather than 'The budget will be met by the department'.
- *Avoid jargon and technical terms.* Unless you are certain that *every* member of the audience is thoroughly familiar with them, avoid these ruthlessly.

It should be becoming clear why scripting – when you have time – is worthwhile. It is far easier to observe these rules in the methodical atmosphere of a scripting session on the word processor than in the heat of the moment at the presentation itself, working from what notes you had time to fling together.

AN AUDIENCE WITH NO SCRIPT

Whether or not *you* have a script, your audience doesn't. This makes a big difference to them. When we read, we use the written format – often unconsciously – to help us find our way around the document. We know how much there is left by the thickness of it, we skip the bits we can see we don't want to read, we go back and re-read parts we didn't get first time, we check back a reference we think applies to this section too. But when we listen to a presentation, we can do none of these things. As a presenter, you have to do all this for your audience.

Signposting paragraphs

Keep them posted. Tell your audience what's coming up. Don't just say 'Here's why we should do this…' and then list eight reasons. Say 'There are eight reasons for doing this…'. Give them signposts. Tell them where they have come from, and where they are going. Use plenty of phrases such as:

- 'So that's where we are now. Let's see why we need to change...'
- 'There are three key reasons for this. Firstly...'
- 'There are three options to consider. I'll outline each one briefly, and then we'll look at which is the best...'
- 'I'm going to explain what the machine does first, and then I'll turn it on and let you see for yourselves'.

thinking smart

PLANT YOUR FACTS

An invaluable device for signposting is the rhetorical question. For example: 'Our present warehouse capacity won't be anything like enough. So what do we do? Well…'. You must have noticed that it is much easier to assimilate information if you wanted to know it than if it's just presented to you. The rhetorical question is a good way of digging a hole to plant a fact in.

Signposting sentences

Signposting applies to individual sentences as well as to the structure of your presentation. For instance, if you say, 'Dickens, Socrates, Drake, Lincoln, Henry VIII – they all had beards', your audience doesn't know why all the names are being mentioned until the last word of the sentence. When it comes you are asking the audience to go back and mentally draw beards on all five of them – if they can remember who they were.

If you say, 'Dickens had a beard, and so did Socrates, Drake, Lincoln and Henry VIII' the audience is drawing the beards on all the time. I'm not saying you can't ask them to make this mental effort, only that you must be aware you are demanding it.

Similarly, if someone tells you 'In the last year Harry Smith has climbed the Matterhorn, swum the Hellespont, crossed the Sahara, run from London to Brighton and shot the Niagara Falls in a canoe, and all this blindfold and with one hand tied behind his back', they may provoke a certain shock effect, but they are asking you to go back and do all those things again in your head in the light of the later information.

EXAMPLES

Another way to help your audience along is to give them plenty of concrete examples of what you are talking about. Describe how other clients in their position have benefited from changing over to your system, how other companies or divisions have been successful working in the way you propose, or give examples to your board of what you could offer customers if you installed integrated online ordering: 'They could track their orders online, and check the items are in stock. And if they place an order online and then want to speak to us, our call centre can see their order on screen instantly.'

METAPHORS

Metaphors convert an abstract or difficult idea into a concrete image which the audience can grasp. For example, when we talk about persuading people by 'showing them you are on their side', and then 'leading them over to your side' during the course of the presentation, that is a metaphor which gives you a concrete image.

The one danger with metaphors is mixing them, and making a laughing-stock of yourself in the process. Mixed metaphors combine two or more pieces of visual imagery which don't go together – here are two genuine examples of mixed metaphors, both from journalists.

▶ **'After shooting himself in the foot last week, he has now scored an own goal.'**
▶ **'President Reagan has left a legacy that may yet turn sour in the mouths of those who rode to victory on it.'**

thihihihithihfhffts **thinking fast**

BUYING TIME WITH EXAMPLES

When preparation time is really short, you may have to cut the length of the presentation itself. I would never advocate cutting it so short that you cannot say everything that needs saying. However, sometimes you can genuinely get your point across in seven or eight minutes – all you have time to prepare – but feel obliged to talk for longer. When you need to fill time fast, examples are a great way of doing it. An audience is always grateful for three or four concrete examples or anecdotes to illustrate key points.

ANALOGIES

These tend to start 'It's a bit like…' or 'It's as if…'. They are great for explaining complicated or unfamiliar ideas or concepts. Suppose you're trying to explain how white blood cells work. You could say: 'They're a bit like a school of piranha, swimming gently along. As soon as anything alien appears in their river, they descend on it and attack it mercilessly until they've eaten it. Then they go back to drifting in the current again.'

for next time

Despite the slight risk of sounding as if you're reciting by rote, it is still worth scripting your presentation fully if you have time. You don't need to agonise over every word, since you won't actually work from the script anyway. But it gives you a baseline to work from, means that you have found a way of making each point which you can refer back to if no better phrasing comes to mind off the cuff, and means that all the points you want to make are included in the best order.

Many people find that a script gives them a sense that the job is complete, and boosts their confidence accordingly. If you never get beyond note form, there may be a niggling – if unfounded – worry that you have missed something out. The mere act of writing the script is an important mental stage in the process of preparing your presentation.

Once you have your script, *do not attempt to memorise it.* Turn it into notes as soon as possible (we'll look at notes in just a moment). But use the script to refer to regularly throughout your (leisurely) rehearsal time, as a reminder of the points you are making, and an *aide-mémoire* when you can't find a comfortable way of expressing a particular point.

6 visuals

Averbal message which is reinforced with a visual one is stronger than the verbal message alone. This is why visual aids are an important part of most presentations. They help you make your point more strongly and more clearly. At least they should do. Whatever medium you use to present your visuals – PowerPoint, flipchart, OHP or anything else – the guidelines are the same. The extraordinary thing is how few people seem to follow these guidelines in their presentations.

The problem is that while a good visual gives a huge boost to your presentation, a poor visual leaves it worse off than no visual at all. It distracts at best, and baffles at worst. So if you're going to use visuals, make sure you use them well. If you haven't time to do this, don't use them at all.

DESIGNING VISUALS

The first question when you plan your presentation shouldn't be 'What visuals do I need?' but 'Do I need any visuals at all?' The answer may well be no, in which case you have saved yourself a load of time (hey, have another coffee). Here are the reasons for avoiding all visuals.

- **They take time and thought to design.**
- **They can divert your attention away from what you want to say and on to how you want to say it.**
- **They diminish your flexibility during the presentation.**
- **They can cost money.**
- **If they go wrong the result can vary from mild confusion to the ultimate in catastrophe and humiliation.**

So why do we ever think of using them? Well…

- **A picture is worth a thousand words.**
- **They can portray vividly and instantly things that are impossible to convey verbally.**
- **They can save time (aha! tricky paradox here) – it can be quicker to come up with a visual to illustrate a complex point than to think of a clear analogy.**
- **They create interest.**
- **They lend variety.**

thinking fast

BUYING TIME

Good visuals can take time to prepare. Simply devising the idea can take a while. So if you're preparing your presentation against the clock, visuals are often the first thing to go. This is great if it stops you cobbling together ill thought-out visuals, but it can mean missing an opportunity to reinforce an important argument. So aim to produce just one visual, and then put all the time you have into making it a really memorable one which reinforces the central message of the presentation.

- ▶ **They add impact.**
- ▶ **They remain in the memory long after the words have left it.**

All in all, the balance generally comes down in favour of visuals (good ones, that is). But it is reassuring to know that there are disadvantages, and many excellent presentations include no visuals at all. If you do have time to include them – however few – think about them at the start and build them into the structure of your presentation. Decide where you need a visual to help reinforce an argument, not just where there's a point which makes you think of a really funny cartoon. A visual which does not back up the argument it accompanies will distract from it.

THE MISSING VISUAL

One troublespot you need to look out for – even when you're in a hurry – is the visual which isn't there and obviously should be. If you are trying to explain something complicated – from the inner workings of a machine to the comparison of financial statistics – it can beg for a visual to make it clear. In this case, I'm afraid you must provide one.

THE IMPACT VISUAL

A good discipline for any presentation is to ask yourself what single message you most want the audience to take away with them. This will identify the one visual you most need to include in your presentation. It should be the most visually memorable of all, and is the one you would choose to leave on display at the end of the presentation.

WORDS ARE NOT VISUALS

How often have you sat through presentations and seen endless visuals listing abstract nouns: PREPARATION, PLANNING, PRODUCTIVITY, PROGRESS and the like? Visuals are not there to provide words; that's your job. You do the words, the visuals do the pictures. Just occasionally they need to incorporate words as labels to help identify what is going on in the picture, but words alone do not constitute visuals. Luckily, you probably don't have time to make this mistake. One way to avoid this trap (for future reference) is always to ask yourself 'What will this visual *show*?' rather than 'What will this visual *say*?'

If you do have to use words – for example to label a pie-chart – write them horizontally. Never use them at any other angle, whatever the temptation.

KEEP IT SIMPLE

A popular error with visuals is to make them too complicated. It is just about impossible to put too little information on a visual, while including too much is very easy. This is one of the risks with copying existing material – it can need simplifying before it is suitable. If this is the case, and you haven't the time, you are probably

II ~~thinkingfast~~ thinkingfast

SECOND-HAND VISUALS
So long as a visual is neat and makes its point clearly, that's all that counts. You can scan or copy a graph from a management report, or a diagram from your production development team's files. You don't have to redraw it from scratch. Just make sure you don't breach any copyright by copying from books.

DOUBLE UP

You can save time by using fewer visuals and repeating them. If you reiterate an important point, repeat the visual which accompanied it too.

better off scrapping the visual than using it as it is. If it is absolutely essential then make the time to get it right.

Some visuals are such a mass of boxes and arrows and feedback control loops that you might as well show a maze from a children's comic ('How can teddy get back to his house without crossing any lines?'). This distracts the audience from whatever you have to say, unless you work through it laboriously. Don't try to include everything in the process on your visual; include only the bits which the audience really wants to know about.

If you have something complex to impart, such as a flow chart, diagram or detailed chart, use build-up visuals which add a section at a time to create a new visual. PowerPoint is obviously the ideal medium for doing this, but you can do it with flipcharts or OHPs too. If you are too rushed to prepare a decent visual in advance, you can draw it on a flipchart as you go along (but make sure you know when you start exactly what you are going to draw).

USING VISUALS

Once you have your visuals (or, for the hard-pressed, your single visual), you must be able to show them in a way which enhances your performance and your message. So here are the principal errors to avoid.

- ▶ **Unless a visual is blindingly simple, it should at least be referred to, and probably talked through. It is quite astounding how many presenters display and then remove a visual without referring to it or apparently noticing it.**

- ▶ **Make sure you don't block your audience's view of the visual.**

- ▶ **Once the visual has made its point it should be removed unless there is a positive reason for keeping it there; otherwise it becomes a distraction.**

- ▶ **Don't use any kind of pointer or cursor if you can possibly help it. If it really is essential as the only means of pointing out something important, move it straight to the spot, keep it still while you are discussing the point, and then remove it completely.**

DON'T GET CLEVER

When you're deciding what kind of visual to use, opt for the simplest equipment. You haven't time to learn new techniques. If you're not thoroughly *au fait* with PowerPoint, now is probably not the time to learn to use it. Use visuals which will work on a flipchart, and save the PowerPoint until you have more time. A flipchart prepared in advance, using different colour pens, can look very slick.

thinking smart

LOOK COOL

If you keep looking to check that the right visual has come up, you will look under-rehearsed and ill-prepared (surely not!). You must be – or at least appear – entirely confident that the next visual will be the correct one.

PROPS

Of course, you don't have to restrict yourself to two-dimensional images when you're looking for aids to add interest and value to your presentation. Grabbing a handful of objects to pass round as you leave the office can give your presentation that well thought-out and prepared look. It might be the widgets from inside your new machine, or a sheaf of colour swatches, or a sample of the house wine you would offer if you got the catering contract.

The point is, don't forget the 3-D option. Once people can touch and hold something it becomes more real to them. It's much harder to say no to ordering half a dozen of the really luxurious leather directors' armchairs after you've sat in one rather than merely looked at a photo of it.

PRODUCT DEMONSTRATIONS

Handing round a swatch is very different from demonstrating a product, but this is something else you may well have to do at a sales presentation. And in the end the product itself will be far more persuasive than all the rest of your presentation put together. But its ability to persuade the buyer to sign the order form relies heavily on you.

Just about the worst thing that can happen during a product demonstration is that the product fails to work. So whether you are demonstrating a blender or a computer, on your premises or on the customer's, make absolutely certain that the product is working and that you know how to use it, and have any accessories or materials you need to demonstrate it fully.

No matter what the time pressure, don't go into a product demonstration without testing it out yourself first. In a sales presentation this is the core of the whole thing, and you should give it top priority. If the demo is bad, you will probably lose the sale. So here are the key guidelines you'll need to follow.

- ▶ **Treat the product respectfully – don't slam the doors, or toss a small product nonchalantly from hand to hand.**
- ▶ **Don't talk and demonstrate at the same time. Talk before and after the demo, but shut up while the product is doing its bit.**
- ▶ **Let the customers have a go at using it.**

thinking fast

BUYING TIME

How about handing out something which you can go out and buy quickly? I've handed out toffee apples before now to reinforce a presentation for which they were relevant.

Choose material which is hard for the audience to throw away

493

STANDARD FARE

Remember that standard sales literature such as brochures and price lists make perfectly good presentation handout material with no preparation at all on your part. They are often better than any alternative you could have come up with even given more time.

- **Encourage questions – you want any doubts brought to the surface so that you can answer them.**
- **Provide backup literature.**

HANDOUTS

A handout makes it much harder for your audience to forget your presentation after they've left. They'll think of it when they see the handout – even if they're only thinking about what the hell to do with the damn thing. Providing a handout also gives the impression you've been doing your homework. And on top of all that, of course, it should also contain a message which reinforces what you were saying in the presentation.

- **What will your audience want you to hand out? They may want price lists, backup information, sheets of performance data and so on which you didn't elaborate in detail during the presentation itself. Make sure you have thought of anything they are likely to want.**
- **If you're in a hurry, you can hand out previously printed material, or scan, copy or take digital photographs (making sure you don't breach anyone's copyright).**
- **Choose material which is hard for the audience to throw away. A beautiful photo, a miniature sofa, or a sample of the ingenious new giggle-widget that makes your product's performance so incredibly smooth are all harder to throw away than a piece of paper.**

HANDOUTS

If time is short, providing just one handout will make a big difference. Print out your key points on a single sheet, in a large enough point size to fill the page without cramping it. Hand this round at the end of the presentation as an *aide-mémoire* for your audience.

for next time

If you have time, it's worth thinking through your handout material more fully. What do you really want the audience to take away from the presentation? Have you used any high-impact visuals which you could reproduce? Do you have product samples you can give out? Handouts do a valuable job, so give them the thought they deserve.

Find ways to make it harder to throw away or even file away the handout. Laminate a really good cartoon you used as a visual so people can pin it up on the wall. Or find something relevant and memorable, even if it isn't permanent – from food or fresh flowers to a packet of tissues.

7 the presentation

DELIVERY

When you're giving a presentation to a relatively small group the whole matter of delivery ought to be simple. You just talk as you would if you were chatting off the cuff, or making a point in a meeting. Curiously, though, most of us find this hard to do. As soon as we are in the more formalised setting of a presentation, we adopt a different tone.

The key to a good delivery, therefore, is not to do anything specific, but simply to avoid this formal, grown-up voice. Alongside this, there are half a dozen particular mannerisms to avoid, which often creep into presentations despite being absent the rest of the time.

- ▶ *Mumbling*. It's better to be too loud than too quiet.
- ▶ *Gabbling*. Watch the tendency to speak faster than usual if you are nervous, and especially if you are a fast talker anyway.
- ▶ *Hesitating*. Excessive pauses, usually filled with '...er...'. Apart from being tedious to listen to, these almost always suggest that you have not rehearsed sufficiently (heaven forbid).
- ▶ *Catch-phrases*. 'As I say...', 'Basically...', '...like...', '...you know', 'and that sort of thing...'. These phrases are fine in themselves, but if you use them so frequently that they become a verbal mannerism they can distract your audience. (I had a history teacher at school who used to say 'you know what I mean?' so frequently that it became a great game to count the repetitions each lesson and see if she could beat her last record. I can still remember to this day that her all-time record was 23 in a 40-minute lesson, but I remember nothing at all about the corn laws.)
- ▶ *Poor eye contact*. Do your best to look at people as you would in normal conversation. Make natural eye contact with everyone – not just the person in the middle at the front who you feel is on your side. People will naturally follow your gaze, and if you keep looking at the ceiling, so will they.

thinking smart

AND NOW THE GOOD NEWS...

While I would never advocate preparing a presentation at the last minute if you can avoid it – as I'm sure you wouldn't either – you might find it reassuring at this juncture to know that you have given yourself one advantage. It is easier to sound natural when you speak off the cuff than it is when you spend a long time preparing. Even if you work from notes and not a script – as you always should for a small presentation – repeated rehearsal over time leads to the danger that you will end up almost word perfect in your head. This can lead to a stilted, over-practised delivery.

REPEATING YOURSELF

A close friend or colleague will be able to tell you instantly if you have any noticeable and distracting verbal mannerisms such as catch-phrases. Just ask someone you know will give you an honest answer.

- *Mannerisms.* Like verbal mannerisms, frequent physical mannerisms such as scratching your ear, or trying to put your hand in a pocket you haven't got on this outfit, will distract the audience. Don't get hung up on removing every personal gesture: just be on the lookout for frequent distracting habits, especially those you only acquire under stress such as foot shuffling or manically adjusting your glasses.
- *Swallowing words.* This is a mannerism which you are unlikely to detect in yourself (assuming you have it) unless you make an audio recording of your presentation. It is generally the last word or two of each sentence that gets swallowed, and it gives the impression that the presentation is repeatedly grinding to a halt. Once you hear yourself do it, however, you should find it an easy habit to overcome.

REHEARSAL

Rehearsal is essential for several key reasons.

- It shows up whether there are chunks of your presentation which don't work, are too long, or don't make sense.
- It gives you a chance to practise your delivery.
- It means you can time your presentation (but bear in mind that you almost always go faster in the real thing).
- It helps reduce your nerves – once you know what you're doing your fears subside.
- It gives you a chance to make sure that any technical equipment such as PowerPoint will work smoothly and slot into the presentation easily.

However little time you have, make time to rehearse if you possibly possibly can. Don't just go through the presentation in your head (although this helps as an extra while you're travelling, for example). Hold your notes in your hand, and stand in front of a mirror. Tape record yourself (if you have a dictaphone you can do this really quickly). If you can manage it, rehearse in front of a colleague, friend or partner and ask them to be honest in their comments. But you must rehearse, or all the rest of your preparation could go to waste when you gabble through the presentation, or the visuals come up in the wrong order, or you burst into tears with panic, or your presentation lasts all of 90 seconds.

thinking smart

BUYING REHEARSAL TIME

Go to work by car if you can, even if you don't normally. Unless you are remarkably unselfconscious you won't want to rehearse out loud in the train, but you can practise your presentation aloud in the car all the way to work. Or you can tape the presentation if you have time and then play it back to yourself in the car.

QUESTIONS

The vast majority of questions are very simple to respond to. They will be straightforward requests for information, which you will be able to impart. But occasionally someone will ask a question which contains a hidden doubt, or a challenge. So here's a quick rundown of the most common types of difficult question, and how to respond to them.

The concealed objection

It may indeed be only thinly concealed: 'Won't this mean weekend working?', 'Why is the price so high?', but it can be dealt with according to the standard rules for handling objections.

- ▶ **Don't get defensive.**
- ▶ **Make the objection specific – ask what makes them feel the price is too high, for example.**
- ▶ **Put it in perspective – for example, 'It may mean some weekend work, yes, but only Saturdays, and only once every couple of months'.**
- ▶ **Give the compensating benefits – 'and the new system will mean that there's no more coming in at 7 o'clock every morning'.**

The test question

This is designed to probe your knowledge and experience: 'What are the stress characteristics of this new alloy?' The golden rule is not to try bluffing or excusing your ignorance. If you don't know, say so, and promise to find out for the questioner. Then make a note and keep your promise.

The display question

Quite often a questioner's real motive is to show their colleagues how well informed they are. Nothing will make them happier than to have their expertise publicly commended, so don't be afraid to agree and tell them how clever they are. 'Of course you're right. I didn't mention it because it's too technical for some people and, as you'll know, it doesn't affect performance.'

The challenge question

You make an assertion which trespasses on the territory of one of the audience. It is best to retreat immediately and with deference, concede them full territorial rights, and perhaps consult their wisdom. 'I'm sorry, of course I was only talking about the US market in general, not the US market for hot water bottles, which obviously you know much more about than I do. What in fact has been the sales trend over the past two years?'

The defensive question

Something you are proposing may mean a cut in staff, budget, status, authority, patronage or perks for one or more of the audience. 'What makes you think we can trust area managers to do their own purchasing of technical equipment?' may in fact mean 'Central purchasing is the part of my job I enjoy most, quite apart from all those bottles of Scotch around Christmas, and I'm damned if I'm going to let you take it away from me'. One way to deal with this is to question the questioner ('Could you explain your concern a little more fully?') and get them talking more, and then if you have difficulty dealing with the point at the factual level try to throw it back to the rest of the group by asking them to give their experience – do they feel area managers are up to the job? On what basis are they making their judgement?

With any kind of difficult question, your first reaction should be to quell any emotional response you may feel rising in you, and your second should be to explore the question and ask the questioner to elaborate or refine it. You then have the following options.

- **Answer the question.**
- **Admit ignorance and promise to find out the answer (and do so).**
- **Defer it to deal with privately at greater length afterwards (and make the time for it later).**
- **Refer it to an expert colleague if you have one with you.**
- **Throw it back to the person who asked it.**
- **Throw it back to another member of the audience.**
- **Put it up for general discussion.**

COPING WITH NERVES

However bad your nerves are before a presentation there is a cure, although I have to tell you that the more time you have the more effective the cure (sorry about that). The key lies in understanding what causes an attack of nerves. And the root cause is fear. Fear of what could go wrong – from you drying up to the PowerPoint slides playing up. The more remote these failures and catastrophes seem, the more remote will be your fears. This is why you often notice a couple of minutes into a presentation that you're not nearly as nervous as you were just before you began: things are going fine, you realise you're not making a prat of yourself and the visuals seem to be co-operating normally.

thinking smart

DIFFICULT QUESTIONS

If these are your particular bugbear, get someone to role- play a question and answer session with you and brief them to make their questions as difficult as possible. That way, the real thing will be a breeze by comparison. If time is tight, call up a colleague and get them to interrogate you down the phone.

If you can minimise the likelihood of things going wrong, you will minimise your fears. Of course there will still be a small irrational panic at the very back of your mind, at least until the presentation is under way, but it need cause no more than a touch of adrenalin which simply keeps you on your toes.

Your best bet is to rehearse as thoroughly as you can. But even when you have plenty of time, you will still want to take other precautions. And when you don't have as much rehearsal time as you would like, this becomes even more important. Your motto should be: be prepared. Expect disaster, consider every possible emergency or embarrassment you can, and plan for it. The checklists which follow should be a big help, but you will also want to consider one or two other classic stress-inducers.

▸ **Notes: staple these together so they can't get out of order, and have a spare copy as back up if you have time to prepare them.**

▸ **Signs of nerves: actually no one cares if you look nervous so long as you still do the job well. But we often fear appearing to be nervous. If you are inclined to shake at the start of the presentation, memorise the first few points so that you don't have to look at your notes.**

As far as coping with the physical symptoms of nerves is concerned, try to eat before the presentation. Don't binge, but a light breakfast or lunch will help (unless you really think you'll bring it straight back up). Nerves are always worse on an empty stomach. And on the subject of food and drink, don't mix alcohol and presentations. If you must have a drink, have it now.

You may also find relaxation exercises helpful. The way to reduce stress is to relax, and slow breathing is a quick fix for this. Here's an exercise which you can do moments before your presentation.

1 Sit down if possible, but you can do this standing up if necessary.

2 Relax your arms and hands. If you're sitting down, put your hands in your lap.

3 Close your eyes if you can, but again this isn't essential.

4 Breathe in through your nose, slowly, to a count of five. Breathe in as low down as you can, pushing out your diaphragm and stomach.

5 Breathe out through your mouth to a count of seven. If you are sitting down, don't slump as you breathe out.

6 Allow your breathing to return to normal and open your eyes.

You can repeat this at intervals as often as you need to, but always let your breathing return to normal in between. If you don't, you may hyperventilate. This doesn't matter at all, except that it can make you feel a little light-headed, which may make you more nervous rather than more relaxed.

thinking smart

BE REALISTIC

Almost all of us suffer from nerves to some degree. But if you are one of those who reacts very strongly, to the point of being sick or passing out, design a presentation where there is as little as possible to go wrong. Given plenty of preparation time, copious rehearsal will help you. But if this isn't possible, cut out anything nerve-wracking that you can. For example:

- ▶ Forget the flipchart: devise just one visual with plenty of impact.
- ▶ Keep the presentation as short as you can and fill out the time with a question and answer session.
- ▶ Bring in a colleague to do part of the presentation for you (the moral support alone is a big help).
- ▶ Don't distribute handouts – put them on the table in advance and invite the audience to help themselves later.

Analyse what it is that worries you most, and eliminate or minimise it. You should really notice the difference in your stress levels.

CHECKLISTS

We all know things can go wrong at presentations, and we've all seen it happen to other people. When you prepare in a hurry, one of the biggest worries is that this time it will be your turn to feel like a prat. And of course, the risk really is greater when you have little or no rehearsal. So here are a few checklists to cover the most likely problem areas. Run through these shortly before your presentation (in other words now) to make sure you have everything covered, and again at the very last minute.

There are five main areas to consider:

1 interruptions

2 staging

3 equipment

4 appearance

5 last-minute checks.

Interruptions

- ▶ **Arrange for phones to be diverted during the presentation.**
- ▶ **Make sure someone is briefed to prevent anyone barging into the room, and put a sign on the door.**
- ▶ **If anyone else regularly uses the room, check they know it will be out of bounds. Include in this not only colleagues but also cleaners, window cleaners, catering staff, postal staff, and so on.**
- ▶ **Check there are no regular interruptions such as fire alarm testing, or break time in the school playground just outside the window. If there are, try to reschedule the presentation.**
- ▶ **You cannot prevent every possible interruption. The golden rule if you are interrupted is to acknowledge the fact. Don't try to talk through the fire alarm test – wait for it to stop.**

Staging

- Make sure you have enough chairs, including a couple extra in case someone else decides to come along too. Arrange the chairs in an arc facing you.

- Check there will be a table for your papers, handouts, briefcase and anything else you have. You may also need another table for equipment, such as a working model or your computer.

- Don't put any barrier, such as a table or desk, between yourself and your audience, unless you are obliged to present around a large boardroom-style table.

- Don't stand with your back to a window or you will appear in silhouette to your audience.

- Sit in each of the chairs in turn to make sure that the view of you or any visuals is not obscured.

- Make sure you know how to dim or black out the room if you need to.

- Try to make sure that if there is a clock in the room, you can see it but the audience can't.

- Except for the most informal presentation, it is better for you to stand. It looks more professional and is a mark of respect to your audience. If you find this very nerve-wracking, and are aware of a tendency to shuffle your feet distractingly, make sure there is a table positioned where you can lean back on the edge of it. (Don't sit on it properly, however, as this will look too casual.)

Equipment

- Test all your equipment in advance.

- Test it all again *in situ* immediately before the presentation.

- Make sure you know exactly how to operate your equipment and are confident with it.

- Find out – if you don't already know – what is most likely to go wrong with the OHP, PowerPoint, demonstration model or whatever you are using. And make sure you know what to do when it does.

- Make sure you have spares of everything you could need – backup disks, spare bulbs, spare batteries, handouts, pens and so on.

Appearance

The most important rule is to dress appropriately. All organisations have their own dress codes; a large firm of management accountants will dress very differently from a small company of record producers. People like people who look like them, so adapt your outfit to tone in with your audience's style. Get it ready the evening before the presentation. You want people to remember you for your presentation, not your appearance, so avoid extremes in:

II thinkingfast

KEEP IT SIMPLE

The less equipment you have, the less can go wrong. If you're in a rush, minimise the equipment. If your presentation calls for a demonstration, you must give one. But do you really need to use PowerPoint? Would a couple of enlarged printouts neatly attached to a flipchart be just as good? And do you really need the OHP, or would a prepared flipchart make the point just as well? Go back to your original objective again and see if the equipment is helping you to meet it, or simply putting obstacles in your way.

- fashion
- smell (strong perfume or aftershave)
- jewellery and accessories
- large patterns and bright or even lurid colours.

For your own comfort you should also avoid:

- new shoes or clothes that haven't been worn in
- tight clothes which inhibit your movement or gestures.

You may feel that you want to give yourself an additional air of authority, especially if you've had to prepare in a rush and are less confident underneath than you'd like to be. You can do this by wearing or carrying certain items:

- a jacket
- the darkest neutral colours that suit you, such as charcoal or navy
- good-quality clothes and accessories
- a good pen
- smart earrings for women
- heels on women's shoes – not totally flat, but not too high.

Last-minute checks

The venue
- Check all the equipment is working.
- Make sure it is set up and ready to go.
- Check the position of the screen for maximum visibility.
- If you are using any kind of lectern or stand, check it is at the right height.
- If you are using any sound effects, check the sound levels.
- Have a list of props, equipment, handouts, your notes etc., and check off everything on the list.
- Get a glass of water if you want one.
- Check you can locate and operate: lights, air conditioning, heating and windows.
- Check the phone is diverted and any likely interruptions have been forestalled.
- If you are on unfamiliar territory, check you know your way to the reception, lavatories, coffee machine and phone – not only for you, but also because one of your audience members may ask you for directions.

Yourself
- women: earrings, make-up, skirt (not hitched up)
- men: tie, shirt (tucked in), flies
- both: hair, nose, teeth.

... AND FINALLY

Have a spare set of notes, for peace of mind, if you can possibly find the time to write them out or copy them. And armed with all the preparation and advice in this book, you should be more than ready to go out there and knock 'em dead.

for next time

- Run through your presentation a couple of times on your own, in front of a mirror and with a tape recorder. Make any changes you feel are necessary as a result of this, and practise improving your delivery or dropping any repetitive mannerisms.
- Ask someone else to watch your presentation for you and to make comments. Ask them to be honest but not overly picky. If you find speaking in front of people painful and nerve-wracking, you are aiming for a competent, professional delivery. You don't want a colleague who will keep criticising until you have the public speaking prowess of an experienced politician or actor.
- Finally, if you possibly can, rehearse in the physical location where you will be giving the presentation. This final rehearsal can often wait until the morning of the presentation. You are checking that all the equipment works, that the acoustics in the room don't cause your voice to disappear or overpower, that there are no unexpected distractions to prepare yourself for, and so on. Technical problems, in other words.

It's worth carrying a kit with you to fix most things that could go wrong. You may not have time to put much together this time, but here's what to put in your kit in future. Once assembled, you can take this to any presentation with you, so it includes some items which may be more useful for slightly larger presentations. But then again, you never know when you'll need them...

- basic tools – hammer and nails, adjustable spanner, Stanley knife, screwdrivers (flathead and crosshead)
- gaffer tape (to tape down trailing leads that could be tripped over)
- PVC tape
- masking tape (to write on for labelling things)
- fishing line (to tie things invisibly)
- tape measure
- Blu-tack™
- spare felt pens and highlighter pens
- drawing pins, wire, safety pins
- nail scissors
- needle and thread
- spare tie for men/spare tights for women
- comb, mirror
- headache pills.

There are, ideally, three stages of rehearsal.

PERSUASION

Even if your customer is internal and not external you're still selling your idea – your way of doing things – to the boss, the board of directors or whoever. And selling is all about persuading people to see things from a particular perspective which will convince them to buy, or adopt the scheme, or agree the purchase or whatever it is you want your presentation to achieve.

There are two key stages in persuading people round to your way of thinking.

1 Show you're on their side.

2 Lead them over to your side.

The psychology

The process of listening to a presentation is more emotional (albeit unconsciously) than you might think. The audience needs to feel that you understand their position. In a sense, it shows that you accept them; it puts you both on the same team. This feeling of acceptance is surprisingly important, even to the most hard-bitten business people. In other words, you have to start by convincing them that you're on their side.

Once you're standing alongside your audience – they've accepted you and they're confident that you've accepted them – you can gently start to lead them where you want them to go. You can explain things from their perspective and guide them towards the right decision. They're much more likely to listen to you when you're standing next to them. If you were miles away shouting 'Come over here – it's much nicer, honest!' they could reasonably ask 'How do you know? You don't know what it's like over here.'

So that's the key to the psychology. Don't stand in your entrenched position shouting 'Come here!' If you want them to agree to the idea you're presenting, you have to do the work. Go over to them, take their hand and lead them back to your position.

Show you're on their side

 Talk from their point of view. Always describe their position and their problem, and make it clear that you accept it as such. Never give the impression (even if it's the truth) that you don't see their problem as a problem at all. Suppose the board has asked you to give a presentation. They're not happy with the cost of the food in the canteen; they think it's unnecessary to provide such a wide range at such a generous subsidy. You, on the other hand, think it's the least they can do for their hard-working and loyal staff. You should still explain the problem as they see it. Once you do that, they'll feel you're on their side; so they're far more likely to believe you when you explain later on that, unfortunately, any change in the arrangements would lead to more problems than it would solve.

thinking smart

DON'T GET CAUGHT OUT

If you have no objective measure, don't use subjective statements as an alternative – if you're asked to justify them you'll be in trouble. In other words, don't say your system is faster than the competition unless you can answer the question 'How much faster?'

▸ **Be objective.** Your own credibility is vital. No one is going to allow you to lead them round to your way of thinking if they don't trust your judgement. If the data suggested a different route, you would take it; you're only recommending your own product because you genuinely consider that it matches the criteria more closely than the others: that's the feeling you want your audience to come away with. So avoid subjective words like 'best' – choose an objective alternative. Say it's the 'fastest' or the 'most accurate'; these are statements you can prove. Keep away from fancy adjectives – 'its incredible speed' or 'stunning performance'. It's far more persuasive to specify: 'speeds up to 120 mph' or 'performance which, in tests, was consistently 6 per cent above its nearest rival'.

Lead them over to your side

So, by the end of the *position* and *problem* sections, you're standing shoulder to shoulder with your audience. They know you understand their situation and their needs. You have shown them that your judgement is sound and your information accurate. Now it's time to examine the possibilities. This is where you start to lead them back over to your side. But do it as if you were treading on eggshells.

▸ **Be fair.** Treat all the options fairly. If one of the other *possibilities* works out cheaper than the one you're recommending, don't attempt to hide the fact. It's not worth the risk of getting found out – which you almost certainly will. A false statement or the suppression of a relevant fact is like the thirteenth chime of a clock: it isn't just obviously wrong in itself; it also casts doubt on the previous twelve. If, on the other hand, the audience sees you being scrupulously fair, they will have far more faith in your judgement, and be happy to follow you to whatever conclusion you decide to lead them to.

▸ **Don't dismiss the other possibilities.** Your audience considers all the possibilities to be viable options. That's why you're listing them. If someone wants to soft-boil an egg for their breakfast and is deciding how long to cook it for, you might suggest three minutes, four minutes, four and a half, or five. But you're not going to bother suggesting they get up at 5 o'clock in the morning, coat it in wax so it can't breathe and leave it in the sun for three hours while they go back to bed. You know that option isn't in the running. Never forget that your audience is giving serious consideration to all the other possibilities. So if you criticise any of the options, however subtly, you are in effect insulting their judgement.

▸ **Give the audience an excuse to change their minds.** Suppose you're giving a presentation to the whole board, half a dozen or more people. Some of them may already have expressed strong views on the subject which your presentation is about. You know what people are like (we're back to the psychology again) – they don't like backing down. So give them an excuse. Explain that they are absolutely right that, for example, this new project will mean a lot of overtime, but that it will also make their jobs more secure. Now they can say 'You see: I was right. Hard work. But, of course, if there are long-term benefits we didn't know about...'.

▸ **Put your preferred option last.** Your approach to the possibilities you've laid out may vary. For a sales presentation it may well be that the only option you'll be happy with is the one you're recommending. If you're giving an internal presentation you might have a first choice, but several other options you consider to be perfectly acceptable. So don't back yourself into a corner by making one clear recommendation if there are others which you would settle for. But whether you're pointing up your number one choice subtly or obviously, put it last. That way it's freshest in your audience's minds at the end of the presentation.

If you express all the relevant points objectively, fairly and honestly, show respect for all the options, and give your audience an excuse to change their minds, then you have maximised your chances of bringing them over to your side. If that hasn't persuaded them, nothing will.

presentation in an evening

An evening? A whole evening? You're doing fine. You should meet the poor presenter who's busy reading the next section: presentations in an hour. An evening is long enough to cover the essentials, so there's no panic.

The first thing to do is to read this whole book through once. It won't take too long, and everything you need is here. Next, if you need to make any phone calls – for research, or role playing practice with a colleague – do it before everyone goes to bed. I know this sounds obvious, but it's surprising how fast the time can go.

Apart from that, the real question you need answered is 'What should I leave out?' Well, here are a few pointers for trimming down the preparation time to fit your schedule.

- ▶ **Do as much research as you can on the phone – in other words, pick other people's brains shamelessly. It's much quicker than looking things up. (But avoid any garrulous colleagues who are always impossible to get off the phone.)**

- ▶ **Keep the presentation as short as it needs to be to put across your argument clearly and persuasively. If this is shorter than you feel it should last, fill the time by coming up with relevant examples and anecdotes. These are interesting, useful, and easy to slot in without any restructuring of the presentation. You can also make the question and answer session part of the presentation time.**

- ▶ **Script the opening, closing and any complicated arguments or ideas only – just start with notes for everything else.**

- ▶ **Save time on visuals. Some things really need a visual to illustrate them, and of course you may have to give a product demonstration. But exclude any visuals which aren't vital. If you have time later, you can always add visuals back in. But generally, aim to have just one really good visual with real impact.**

- ▶ **Don't trim down rehearsal time more than necessary, and if you have a whole evening aim for an absolute minimum of two full run-throughs (more if you're using visuals or props). Make changes after the first rehearsal and incorporate them into the second run-through.**

You should find that this leaves you comfortable time to put together a professional and persuasive presentation, while still leaving you hoping for more preparation time for the next one. The important thing is to relax and not panic. An evening may not be ideal, but it is a perfectly realistic timespan.

presentation in an hour

You're not sure how you found yourself here, but now you're in this pit you need to start clawing your way out fast. Even though it may well be sheer pressure of work which has prevented you starting on this presentation earlier, the odds are that this got moved to the bottom of the pile because you know you're pretty good at thinking on your feet. Excellent. You'll need to be.

If you only have an hour or so, what can you usefully do to look good and polished, and to win your audience round to your view? Here are the vital stages – read them all through once before you begin. Oh, all right, I know you won't really do that. But at least read point 7 before you start.

1 Spend the first three minutes thinking about your objective (see chapter 1). Yes, yes, I know you haven't got three minutes to waste. It's OK, it won't be wasted.

2 I suggest you now cut straight to the structure of the presentation, and skip the preparation. Do the research (page 473) as you need it going along.

3 Jot down the key points you want to make, check them against your objective, and sort them into the right order as outlined in Chapter 3. Mmm, yes, I'm afraid you're going to have to find time to read Chapter 3.

4 Obviously you're not going to script this presentation, but look through your notes and see which key points need examples, or would benefit from metaphors or analogies to help illustrate them. A few of these will give your presentation both clarity and colour, and are worth the time investment (see pages 488–9).

5 Read the bit about signposting (pages 487–8) – it makes a huge difference to how professionally your performance comes across.

6 Forget the visual aids – and anything involving equipment. But if you want to look more prepared than you are you can always do a handout. Just print out your three or four key points in big letters on a single sheet and hand it round after the presentation.

7 Leave enough time to rehearse the whole thing once right through. This will show up any major problems, identify ideas or concepts you find hard to phrase well, and give you a timing.

8 Read the checklists (pages in Chapter 7), or at least the last-minute checks (page 502).

9 If you have any time left, read the bit about handling difficult questions (pages 497–8: you'll probably be leaving plenty of scope for questions).

10 Relax ... and good luck!

proposal

MAKE YOUR CASE

WRITE WITH FLAIR

GET A RESULT

ros jay

contents

introduction

Y ou've got a proposal to write ... yesterday. Well, today just about scrapes through but that's as far as you can push it. Someone important – your boss, your MD, a key customer – is expecting it on their desk by tomorrow. Obviously you *should* have started on it sooner, but there's always so much other work piling up, and then there's that awful sinking feeling you get whenever you think about writing proposals. It does nothing to galvanize you into action.

Now, however, the clock is going to galvanize you. Panic has risen to the point where you can't ignore it any longer and you just *have* to get on with the damn thing. But how? Part of the problem, I suspect, is that you're not sure how best to go about it – certainly not in the time you've got left. This proposal is important. It could make or break a sale or a business loan from the bank, or influence top management's opinion of you. What if it's no good? What if it doesn't convince them?

It's a funny thing, but no one ever teaches us how to write proposals. It's not part of the training. We get sent on courses to teach us everything from time management to maternity legislation – but proposal writing always gets left out. And yet it is a central management skill. We all have to do it, apparently without any help.

Well, the panic's over. This book will take you only an hour to read, and it will tell you everything you need to know to write a truly impressive and convincing proposal. No waffle, no unnecessary background – you haven't got time for all that. Just the essentials (but all of them, mind).

Of course it's better to have more time, and this book also tells you what to do with it when you *do* have it (next time ...). But what you need right now is the fast thinker's version. You want:

 tips for looking as if you know more than you do

 shortcuts for doing as little preparation as possible

 checklists to run through at the last minute

... all put together clearly and simply. And short enough to read fast, of course.

This book will tell you how to write a proposal in a day. Yes, it can be done – no sweat. In fact, at the end of the book, you'll find guidelines for writing a proposal in an evening if you're cutting things really fine. And if you like to sail truly close to the wind, there's even a one-hour version. So if it can be done in an hour, doing it in a day should be a breeze.

So relax, put the answerphone on, and don't panic. Everything you need to know is in here, and it will get you through the preparation in as little as an hour if that's all you've got. But the longer, the better. Any additional time you have over an hour is a bonus, so if you have a whole evening to write your proposal ... you've got time to make yourself a cup of coffee before you even start.

This book will take you through the seven key stages of preparing and writing a proposal:

1 To begin with, you'll need to set your objective. This makes everything that comes after it more effective.

2 Next, you'll need to collect together all the information you want to include – at least everything you can collect in the time.

3 Now you need to work out what order you're going to say everything in – in other words you have to give your proposal a structure.

4 Many people find the most daunting aspect of proposals is the actual writing bit. So we'll look at how to write in a clear, readable style which will get your point across.

5 The mechanics of writing English can be as fraught as the style, so the next chapter will fill you in on everything from vocab to punctuation.

6 However clear the structure, and however slick the writing, your proposal will let you down if it doesn't look good. So this is the next stage – presentation.

7 Finally, you need to finish off the proposal with summaries, appendices and all that stuff – so we'll run through everything you need to know about topping and tailing.

fast thinking gambles

If you can write a proposal in a day, or even an hour, what is the point of trying to make more time to do the job? Why not learn to do it in, say, an evening every time? That is certainly an option, but it's not the best one. The thing is that fast thinking will achieve your objective – to produce a convincing and professionally presented proposal – but it still has its limitations. When you limit your time, you limit your options.

And while you certainly want to be fast, you also want to be the best. After all, many managers can date the start of their success to a particular proposal which was admired higher up the organization. So what are the drawbacks of proposal writing at breakneck speed?

- ▶ For arguments to be convincing, they must be backed up by hard facts. So you have to research all the facts you need to support your case. You cannot lay your hands on as much information in an hour as you can in a couple of days. And suppose you can only get the data you need from someone else, and they are out of the office until next week?

- ▶ If you find the writing part tough, you're not going to find it gets any easier with the sword of Damocles hanging over you. It's one thing to find a good way of expressing what you want to say; quite another to find the *best* way.

- ▶ Although a proposal should rarely be very long, there is often enough information in there that the typing alone takes a fair while. When you're really under pressure, you may have to leave out information that would have been better included.

- ▶ The presentation of your proposal is hugely influential – you know what they say about first impressions. With more time, you can put finishing touches to your proposal which you simply can't find time for this time around. For example, it can look far smarter to retype data for an appendix in the style of your proposal rather than attach photocopies of figures or pages from other documents.

- ▶ It's always a good idea to get someone else – or several someone elses – to read through an important proposal before you submit it. The tighter the time, the harder it is to fit in this important stage.

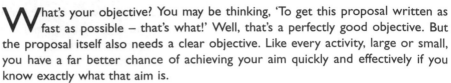

1 your objective

What's your objective? You may be thinking, 'To get this proposal written as fast as possible – that's what!' Well, that's a perfectly good objective. But the proposal itself also needs a clear objective. Like every activity, large or small, you have a far better chance of achieving your aim quickly and effectively if you know exactly what that aim is.

The more thinking you do at the start of the process of writing a proposal, the less work you will have to do later. Honest. And that's why you need to begin with a clear objective. Once you have a clear objective you can:

- **see easily what information to include in your proposal**
- **see easily what information to omit**
- **be consistent in content and style throughout the proposal.**

So your proposal will be focused and clear in its intent, and therefore far more likely to persuade the reader of your point of view. And you won't waste time researching or writing information which doesn't need to be there.

GETTING THE PITCH

To begin with, your objective should help you to pitch your proposal accurately at the people it is intended for. This makes a big difference. Think of it in a different context for a moment. Suppose you are trying to persuade two of your friends to go on a surfing holiday in Hawaii with you. One is adventurous, the other a lover of creature comforts. You would use very different arguments to propose the same holiday.

Selling adventure	Selling comfort
Great surfing beaches	Stay in a luxury hotel
Plenty of other water	Laze on the beach in the sunshine
sports on offer	Spend the evenings eating out
Exciting and unusual location	at open air restaurants

So you can see that you need to know the person – or people – you are writing your proposal for in order to pitch it as persuasively as possible. To do this, you should begin by asking yourself:

thinking smart

GET IT IN WRITING

Make yourself write down a clear objective before you start, following the guidelines here. It should take five minutes at the most. Then prop it up on the desk in front of you the whole time you're working on the proposal.

- Who is the proposal for?
- What is their level of knowledge on the subject?
- What will they use the proposal for (persuading someone else, justifying the cost, making a straight yes/no decision)?
- What aspects do they particularly want covered (costs, staffing, technical problems, logistics and so on)?
- What does the proposal *not* need to cover (technical details, justifications of cost when money isn't an issue etc.)?

This thought process should take you only a few moments, but will help hugely in setting a clear objective. Suppose you are proposing to your board that staffing levels in your department be increased. A statement of your aim might be simply that: To persuade the board to increase staffing levels in the department. But the more detail you add, the more helpful your objective will be. That means it will save you time and increase the chance of your proposal being accepted.

Compare it to a journey. Imagine you're in London and you want to go to New York. You could head off vaguely in a westerly direction and start asking the way somewhere around Cardiff. You might find a boat heading for the USA and when you arrived you could start hitching. I expect you'd get there eventually.

But that isn't what most of us do. We establish the best way to get there before we start. A way that doesn't only get us to New York, but does it comfortably, quickly, economically and according to any other requirements we have.

The same holds for writing your proposal. You need to decide not only where you are going, but also what the main requirements of your route are, and what aspects of the subject you want to visit on the way. So the objective needs to be fleshed out a little. Here's a fresh version: To persuade the board that increased staffing levels in the department would be more productive.

Now we're getting somewhere. But we need to be still more specific. What does 'more productive' mean? More cost-effective? Or will it generate more income? Or speed up the system? What benefit are you trying to sell to your board? What turns them on? Cutting costs? Increasing output? Improving customer service? Operating a faster system?

OK, let's try again: To persuade the board that increased staffing levels in the department would improve customer service and generate more income than it

thinking smart

THIRD TIME LUCKY

It often takes three stages to set a clear objective. Identify the broad objective first, then state a broad reason why your reader should accept it, and finally make the reason more specific. For example:

1 persuade the board to up staffing levels
2 to make the department more productive
3 in terms of customer service and income/cost balance.

thinkingfast

THE RIGHT PROPOSAL

Have you ever presented a proposal only to be told: 'No, no. That's not what I wanted.'? If you've been asked to write a proposal by someone else, it can easily happen. Your boss might say, 'I can't present this to the board. They've agreed the principle of extra staffing already. I want them to agree the logistics – which extra posts to create, who should fill them, who trains them … that sort of thing.'

But there's a simple way to avoid this colossal waste of time: write a clear objective and then show it to your boss (or whoever commissioned the proposal). If you've got it wrong, you've only wasted five minutes rather than hours or even days.

would cost. That's more like it. You've thought about who the proposal is for, what they want to hear, and you've given yourself an objective that tells you where you're going and the key elements to focus on en route.

So that's your one-sentence objective. It should have taken you only a few minutes to write, but you're going to be referring to it frequently over the next few hours.

for next time

You may not need any longer to set your objective next time. But sometimes it takes a little while to research, so it's worth allowing this time. You might need to find out more about your readers – are they technically minded or not? Are they broadly in agreement or are they likely to take a lot of persuading? What are likely to be the key sticking points in their minds?

You can usually find this out by asking. If you can't ask them directly, ask other people. Colleagues might tell you that the finance director is always a stickler for plenty of financial detail in proposals, or that this particular customer has had after-sales problems in the past and will need convincing that they won't recur if they sign this contract.

So allow yourself time to research your readers – all of them. Not just your bosses, but whoever they will pass your proposal on to. Not just your customer, but the people further up their organization they will show your proposal to. Not just your bank manager, but the regional manager too if you're proposing a sizeable business loan.

2 collecting the information

You can't write your report until you know what you want to say. So once you've set your objective, your next task is to collect together all the information you need. And already, your objective is going to come in handy.

The first thing to do is to create a list of areas you need to cover. Begin with the objective, since this covers the most vital aspects of the subject – current problems, staffing levels, customer service, income and costs, for example. You can expand the list with other areas you know you need to touch on as well: speed of service, line of accountability – whatever else applies.

These are broad subject areas of course, so the next step is to create a sub-list under each of these headings. Each of these is a list of specific topics to research. For example, under costs, you might list:

▸ **salaries**
▸ **recruitment costs**
▸ **induction costs**
▸ **overheads**

… and so on.

As we'll see in more detail later, you're going to have to come up with hard facts to back up every assertion you make in your proposal. So you're creating a list of all the hard facts you need to research before you begin to write it.

Now write down any other notes of your own of points you want to make, arguments you want to use or benefits you want to emphasize. These are all things you want to include in your proposal which don't necessarily have specific researched facts attached to them. Consider these points for inclusion in your notes:

▸ **Mention boost to departmental morale – happier staff are more productive.**
▸ **Accounts always complain paperwork doesn't filter through fast enough – this will help.**
▸ **Less pressure on staff creates more time to develop projects – customer surveys, improved systems etc.**

Write each of these down on a separate piece of paper (for reasons we'll get to in a moment).

thinking fast

WORKING TO TIME CONSTRAINTS

Ideally, every relevant fact should be in your proposal. But if you simply cannot make enough time to research them all, make sure you research the most important ones. How do you know which those ones are? They are the ones which support your objective.

YOU'RE NOT ALONE

If you think you may have missed out something important, you can always ask someone else to run through what they see as the key areas. Call up or e-mail your boss, your customer, a colleague or a member of your team and get them to tell you what they think should be included.

Now you have lists covering just about everything that's going to go into this proposal. Don't waste time you haven't got wracking your brain for anything you've missed out – you can always add other points while you're assembling your information. At the moment (just to summarize) you have:

- **a list of general areas you need to cover, compiled with reference to your objective**
- **a list under each of these headings of topics to research and data to collect**
- **your own notes – each on a separate piece of paper – of other points you want to make that don't require specific data to back them up.**

DOING YOUR RESEARCH

The next step is to assemble all the information you've just listed. You can get this information from a variety of sources:

- **talking to people – suppliers, customers, experts, colleagues**
- **books**
- **competitors' annual reports**
- **minutes of past meetings**
- **internal management reports and monthly figures**
- **other internal reports and survey results**
- **magazine and newspaper articles**
- **publicly available information and statistics – from trade associations, market research reports, government departments and so on.**

For each topic on your lists, you'll need to decide where you're going to get your information from. You may well have some of it collected already. After all, you may not have started on this proposal until a few minutes ago, but you've probably known it was looming for some time. So you should already have been collecting anything useful – from magazine articles to minutes of meetings – as you have encountered them.

The question of where to find the information is, generally speaking, easy – there is often only one place where it exists. But if you have a choice, consider which is the most convincing source. Would your readers be more persuaded by a quote from a newspaper article or a statistic from a trade association?

If you cannot track down the data you want, you should question the validity of the argument they were intended to support. Suppose you wanted to say that customers are more concerned about speed of response than about the nature of that response. If you can't back this up, are you sure it's true? And what are you going to say when the board call you in to discuss your interesting proposal and then ask you how you know this?

Some proposals need relatively few hard facts to be convincing, while others need a good deal. If you're under time pressure, you want this proposal to be in the first category. But if you do find yourself trying to research a lot of elusive data in a short time, you might be relieved to know there is a companion volume to this one entitled *fast thinking: finding facts*, which should be a big help.

ORGANIZING YOUR INFORMATION

No doubt you now have pieces of paper, reports, brochures, books, pamphlets, documents and the like all over your desk. This is the point where you start to sort it all out. The first thing to do is to transfer every piece of information onto its own slip of paper. This is why you wrote down your notes on individual pieces of paper earlier.

Stop panicking: this isn't going to take all day. You don't have to write all the data down – just a note of what is covered and where to find it. So you might have a slip of paper which says 'recruitment costs – *Management Today* article' and a corresponding post-it note in the magazine.

By the end of this process, you will have every single point you want to make in your proposal written down, and you can sort and resort them endlessly (not that you have time to), because each has its own slip of paper. And you should have a neat pile of reference material marked with post-it notes so you can find the data you want really quickly.

The final part of the process of collecting your information is to sort it into groups. Put all your slips of paper into logical groupings: costs, income, speed, current problems or whatever. This is where having each point written down separately is such an advantage – you can move them around until you feel comfortable with the groupings.

There's no point spending too much time on this, because these groups don't reflect the structure you're going to use for your proposal once you start writing it. But before you start to wonder why on earth, in that case, you have to do it at all, let me explain. There are three particular advantages in doing this.

1 As you work through the pieces of paper, you get the chance to check each one against your objective and make sure you are including only the information you need to. That is not to say that everything will get a specific mention in the objective, obviously, but it will be clear if you're including unnecessary data. You can also check you aren't repeating yourself or including information your readers will already know.

2 As a mental process, the exercise helps to give you a clear focus and to organize your mind.

3 Although these groups do not represent your final structure (which we'll look at in the next chapter), your information will largely stay in these groups as you go along, so you have saved yourself time later.

 thihfhikthikifsfast thinkingsfast

FAST FORWARD

If a document or magazine has several pages of useful data marked, number each one on its bookmark and cross-refer to the number on your slip of paper so you can find it fast.

Since you now have everything down on paper and organized into groups, this is a good point to congratulate yourself on having got this far, and to take a short break. You don't have to retain any information in your head any longer – it's all on your desk now and it's not going anywhere.

for next time

The more time you leave yourself, the more convincing the research you can come up with. Sometimes it may make no difference, but often it does.

Suppose one of your key arguments is that some of your competitors have increased the size of their customer service departments, and have seen a corresponding rise in their customer satisfaction ratings. Your readers will want some evidence of this, or at least clear figures on the number of new personnel and the percentage increase in the ratings. Your source for these data might be a colleague who used to work for one of your competitors, and who therefore knows all the relevant facts and figures … but is on holiday until next week. Whoops. And the proposal has to be finished tomorrow.

That's a big part of why it's always better to start work on a proposal early. This time you might get away with repeating the data from memory and catching up with your colleague as soon as they get back from their holiday. But for next time, it will help to set aside even just a couple of hours a week or two in advance to get the ball rolling on this sort of data which can take a while to track down.

3 structure

You're well on your way. You've collected all your information now, and you know exactly what you're going to say. The only question left is: what order will you say it in? This should be easy, but it doesn't always seem to be. You've probably read confused proposals yourself which left you barely more enlightened at the end than you were at the beginning. I remember wading through a pretty hefty proposal once only to find myself still asking at the end, 'Yes, but what are you actually selling?'

A lot of the trouble stems from the fact that it is so abundantly clear to *you* what you are trying to say that it can be difficult to see the issue from your readers' perspective. Maybe they know nothing about your product at all. Maybe what seems to you like a blindingly obvious idea somehow does nothing for them. So you have to keep reminding yourself of the differences between you and them. For example:

- **They don't know what your product, service or idea can do.**
- **They have different priorities from you.**
- **They don't know the background which brought you to this point.**
- **They don't know what the alternatives are.**
- **They don't see why things can't just carry on as they are.**

A proposal that doesn't address these differences – doesn't take the reader along the logical route through your argument – is never going to be a persuasive and influential document. Even if all the information they need *is* in there somewhere, it must be coherently presented and argued if it is to leave them clearer on the subject, let alone persuaded of your case.

The good news is that there is a way of presenting the information in your proposal that is clear, logical and persuasive, and that works every time. Whether you are proposing a major sale to a client, an idea for a product to a manufacturer, or a new system to your board of directors, this structure is always the best way to do it.

Just as a good story should always have a beginning, a middle and an end, so a good proposal should always follow the same structure. There are lots of different ways of expressing it: setting the scene, developing the story, resolving the story; or maybe situation, complication, resolution. Whatever terminology you use, they all mean the same thing. One of the easiest to remember is:

thinking smart

DEVIL'S ADVOCATE

It can help to put yourself in your readers' shoes for a minute. Suppose they are really resistant to your idea. Imagine what they would pick holes in: 'What's the point of that?' 'What's wrong with the way we do things already?' and so on. You can even get a colleague to play the role of Negative Reader In A Bad Mood for you. It should help you see that what is obvious to you isn't obvious to them.

521

- position
- problem
- proposal.

To begin with, you need to state the current position. Then you look at the problem – why the situation has to change. Then you make your proposal in the light of this background. Actually, there is often more than one possible solution, although you will have your own preferred one. If this is the case you will need to discuss the others too, so you can insert another section. Just for the sake of mnemonics (the four Ps), we'll call it possibilities. So now your structure looks like this:

- position
- problem
- possibilities
- proposal.

One reason this structure is so easy to follow is because we have all grown up listening to stories that follow this format – and reading books and watching movies that run along the same lines. To go back to basics, let's take Hansel and Gretel as an example:

1 **Position.** Hansel and Gretel were left in the woods by their parents who couldn't afford to look after them any longer.

2 **Problem.** They found a house made of gingerbread, but, unfortunately, it belonged to a wicked witch who imprisoned them.

3 **Possibilities.** They could try to escape or they could trick the witch. Otherwise they would be cooked and eaten by her.

4 **Proposal.** In the end the best option was to trick the witch by pushing her into her own oven so she burned to death, and then to run away. So Hansel and Gretel escaped and ran home.

See? All you're doing when you write a proposal is spinning a good yarn (and hopefully one which is a little more suitable for children). You don't have to follow an alien format – just the structure you've grown up understanding naturally. Boy meets girl, boy loses girl, boy finds girl. Manager wants something, boss says no, manager persuades boss.

And there's more good news. Yes, really. It is much quicker writing to a clear structure than floundering around trying to decide what to say next. The structure makes most of your decisions for you. So you can just get on with getting the proposal down on paper. Let's now look at each element of the structure in turn.

thinking smart

ARE YOU SITTING COMFORTABLY?

It can be easier to get a handle on the structure by telling yourself the contents of the proposal as a story. Begin with: 'Once upon a time there was a manager …' (or a business, or whatever). You should find it quite easy to slip into storytelling mode (especially if you have children), and you should find much of your proposal structure slots into place.

thihfthihthinkingsfast

> **PAPER CHASE**
>
> At this stage you can jot down what you want to say in draft form (we'll be looking at phrasing and language and all that later) as you go along. However, it can be quicker – and just as helpful – simply to organize your slips of paper as you go. Begin by creating a small pile of things to state in the 'position' part of your proposal and build the slips of paper up from there.

POSITION

Start your proposal by stating the current position. You might consider this to be stating the obvious, but do it anyway. For one thing, it may not be as obvious as you think. You may want extra staff in your department because you are struggling to maintain customer service standards, but some of your readers may not realize you're struggling. If you never explain this, they'll read the whole proposal on the assumption that you are asking for the luxury of extra staff rather than the necessity.

Or suppose you're proposing to a retail outlet that they stock your new range of citrus juicers. You might start by stating that juicers always sell well, especially in the summer. Tell them how many a typical outlet sells each week. Otherwise they might be working on the assumption that your juicers are terrific, but no one wants juicers these days.

So you need to make sure that all your readers are starting in the same position. But there are other reasons too for summarizing your position at the start of the proposal.

- **It helps people to focus on the right part of the issue.** If you've written a proposal for your board of directors, some of the non-executive members might know that your proposal is something to do with needing more company cars, say, but may not have realized that it was specifically about the need for the PR department to have cars.

- **It shows that you understand the background.** The readers are far more likely to accept your proposed solution if they can see that you understand the problem.

- **It gives you a chance to explain things to anyone who doesn't understand the problem without patronizing anyone who does.** The tone isn't 'I'm telling you this because you don't know it'; it's 'Let's just make sure we're all agreed exactly what we're talking about.'

- **Your intended reader might decide to pass your proposal on to someone else much less acquainted with the subject.** Your customer might be fully conversant in the state of the market for citrus juicers, but what if they pass your proposal on to their regional director who doesn't know a juicer from a squeezer?

- **It ensures that every reader has taken on board all the facts necessary to follow the rest of the proposal.** It's like checking that everyone embarking on a trekking holiday together has all the essential equipment in their rucksacks before setting off on the first leg of the journey.

You may find that you can state the position in a single sentence, or it may take a while to explain – you identified your readers' level of knowledge when you worked out your objective. Obviously if it's relatively low you may need to explain quite a lot. You may also have to run through a bit of history to explain how the present position was reached – that's fine, if it helps the reader.

Stating the position also gives you a chance to prove that you understand things from the reader's point of view. This is especially valuable if you're writing a sales proposal. Suppose your company sells photocopiers. Your proposal to a potential customer should not start by telling them *your* position – that your company 'started out selling printing blocks back in 1657 and now markets a range of photocopiers'. The idea is to state the *reader's* position. So you start by saying that they 'have a photocopier which they've leased for the last 12 years' and so on. Of course your position might be the same as the reader's; or it might not – it's not important. *Their* position is the one that matters.

From the start of your proposal onwards – in other words from here – you must deal in facts, not assumptions or unsupported assertions. It is facts that will persuade your readers, and facts alone. No matter how much of a rush you are in to get this proposal written, facts are not the place to economize.

So don't just say that the market in citrus juicers is very healthy – say precisely how healthy it is. State the rate of growth or the level of sales (and before you ask, no, it's not OK to make it up).

PROBLEM

The point of this section of the proposal is to establish why you need to do anything at all – why the present position can't continue. This could be something bad, but it doesn't have to be. It could be an opportunity that you mustn't miss. Look at these examples.

Bad
- **Demand is changing.**
- **Equipment is wearing out.**
- **Staff are leaving.**
- **Money is being wasted.**
- **There is new competition in the market.**
- **Offices are becoming overcrowded.**

Good
- **There is scope for a new product.**
- **A small investment in new equipment could increase profit margins.**
- **There's a new source of raw materials which is much cheaper than before.**
- **A perfect site has come up on the new trading estate.**

thinking smart

LYING WITH STATISTICS

You might think you can remember a particular statistic even though you can't quite track it down just at the moment, so you might as well include it. Or if you're a good bullshitter, you may even be tempted to embellish facts. *Don't do it.* What if someone asks you for evidence, or tries to check your sources? Sooner or later it will happen – if not this proposal, the next one or the one after. It would cast doubt on all the other facts you ever present, including the real ones. Just imagine what it could do to your reputation and your career ... and resist temptation.

- Trade barriers to Europe are coming down.
- New legislation means things are possible that weren't before.

This is the section of the proposal most likely to meet with resistance from the reader, so it's especially important to validate your statement of the problem with hard evidence. The idea is that by the time you've finished explaining the problem, the reader should be left in no doubt that Something Must Be Done. All that remains is to bring them round to your view of precisely *what* should be done.

POSSIBILITIES

You may or may not want to consider different options for resolving the problem that your reader is now convinced exists. Or rather, the reader may or may not want to consider them – that's the factor that should determine whether or not you include a 'possibilities' section in your proposal. Your reader is likely to be adopting one of two stances:

1 They will decide whether to do x, y or z.
2 They will either accept your proposal or leave things as they are.

In the first of these situations, they will consider other options whether you do or not. If you own a car wash, say, any potential customer will consider the options of using your car wash, washing their car themselves, getting the kid round the corner to do it for 50p, or leaving it dirty. You may only be offering one of the four options, but you'll need to discuss the other three with your customers in order to convince them that your option is better.

So if you're writing a proposal for a customer who is likely to be considering other options, you'll need to include a 'possibilities' section in order to discuss them. Or if the board is considering your proposal for restructuring, but also considering a more minor restructure, or the option of leaving things alone – you'll need to cover these in your report.

This section should cover the pros and cons of each possibility, such as:

- how each one works or what it does (just in case the readers do not already know)
- what it costs

thinking smart

KEEPING YOUR OPTIONS COVERED

It's always worth making sure you've considered all the options that may have occurred to your readers. If you discuss two other options but miss out their favourite one, you have missed an opportunity to compare yours favourably with it. So think it through for a moment. The most commonly missed option is … doing nothing at all. For example, you may have considered your two leading competitors, but forgotten that your customer might simply leave things as they are and stock no citrus juicers at all.

However, if your reader is simply going to say yes or no, there's no need to consider alternatives. If you're asking your bank manager for a loan for a new business you're starting, they won't be choosing between yours and someone else's – they'll give you both a loan if you both warrant one. It's a straight yes or no choice; you can't very well include a section on their other options when there aren't any.

- other relevant details such as how long it takes to implement, technical specifications etc.
- what its benefits are (it's the cheapest, it's very safe, customers seem to love it, it only takes two people to operate it)
- what its disadvantages are (delivery takes four months, the staff hate using it, there's no absolute guarantee it will work etc.).

You may want to look at these factors for each option in isolation, but you will probably want to compare them as well. Don't draw any overall conclusions at this stage – that comes later. You may have your own preferred possibility but it shouldn't be visible to the reader at this stage. You must describe all the possibilities fairly and impartially.

Preserve neutrality

I know it can go against the grain to give a fair hearing to a hated rival contender, but it has to be done. The thing is, one of your readers might have a secret – or indeed an overt – preference for another option. If you pooh-pooh it, they will resent you and won't be inclined to listen to your own preference. But if you demonstrate that their view is valid, they are more likely to give you a fair hearing in return.

Persuasion

The psychology of persuasion is worth considering. The process of reading a proposal is more emotional (albeit unconsciously) than you might think. The reader needs to feel that you understand their position. In a sense, it shows that you accept them, it puts you both on the same team. This feeling of acceptance is surprisingly important, even to the most hard-bitten business people. In other words, you have to start by convincing them that you're on their side.

Once you're standing alongside your readers – they've accepted you and they're confident that you've accepted them – you can gently start to lead them where you want them to go. You can explain things from their perspective and guide them towards the right decision. They're much more likely to listen to you when you're standing next to them. If you were miles away shouting, 'Come over here – it's much nicer, honest!' they could reasonably ask, 'How do you know? You don't know what it's like over here.'

So that's the key to the psychology. Don't stand in your entrenched position shouting, 'Come here!' If you want them to agree to the idea you're proposing, *you* have to do the work. Go over to them, take their hand and lead them back to your position. You can show you're on their side by being fair and objective, and not dismissing the other possibilities.

thinking smart

THE POSSIBILITIES ARE ENDLESS ...

You'll just confuse your readers if you include 25 possibilities at this stage. The ideal number is about three (including yours). But it could be two or it could be four. Maybe even five. Any more, and you're better off grouping them together – instead of listing all the options for restructuring in your proposal for extra staffing, simply include 'restructuring' as an alternative to extra staffing.

GIVE THEM AN EXCUSE

Some of your readers may already have expressed strong views on the subject your proposal is about. And people don't like backing down. So give them an excuse to change their minds. Enable them to say: 'You see, I was right. It will mean a lot of overtime. Mind you, if there are long-term benefits we didn't know about ...'

PROPOSAL

If you're not including a 'possibilities' section this will probably be the largest part of the document. It will include:

- **an explanation of what you are proposing (your business plan, for example, for your bank manager)**
- **answers to any objections which you anticipate from your readers (such as the bank manager saying, 'But why do you need as much as £25,000?')**
- **facts and figures to support your case (such as research showing there is a market gap for your proposed product).**

If you have listed the 'possibilities', you will already have covered these points. In this case, the 'proposal' section should read a bit like the television show *Call My Bluff*: 'I don't think it's the first one; it sounded rather implausible. A sort of medieval alarm clock? I think not ...' – that sort of thing. Except that you don't want to be rude about any of the options – if your readers support the other option, or if they did until they just read this stonking proposal persuading them otherwise, you are criticizing their judgement if you throw scorn on it.

You've already discussed the pros and cons of each option under 'possibilities', so now you simply make a choice and justify it: 'All in all the brick house looks like the best option. The straw one will blow over too easily and the wood one, while it is slightly more stable, is nevertheless also vulnerable to fire. The brick one, on the other hand, should withstand any amount of wind and it won't burn. It's true that it's the most expensive, but its durability means that in the long term, say ten years, it's actually the cheapest of the three options. What's more, it's the only one that's truly secure against wolves, as the survey figures show.'

for next time

The biggest danger when you prepare your proposal in something of a hurry is that you will miss out some key fact or argument, or even overlook one of the other options. If you have more time it is a good idea to draft out your proposal, however roughly, at this stage and ask someone else to cast their eye over it – your boss or a close colleague who knows the background is ideal. This should not only bring to light any important missing pieces, but will also reassure you that you have everything covered.

Apart from that, one of the great things about working to a clear and logical structure is that it is actually the quickest way of doing something. So even though you're fretting about the time, you have the satisfaction of knowing that more time wouldn't have helped you do the job any better – you've already done it perfectly.

You must describe all the possibilities fairly and impartially

527

4 good writing style

This is the scary bit for a lot of people – choosing the right words and phrases to sound articulate and intelligent, and to get the argument across strong and clear. Let's be honest, you're worried that the reader will stop thinking about the proposal itself, and start wondering where you were educated (if at all) and how on earth your career has made it this far.

If it's any help, this is most people's worry when they write a proposal, and yet they actually do fine. And so will you. However, we don't want to settle for 'fine'. So this chapter is partly about reassuring you of the right way to do things, and partly about making sure that your style really shines. The next chapter, by the way, is about using correct English – grammar and all that stuff – so we're not going to worry about that just now. For the moment, here's a crash course in becoming a skilled, articulate and persuasive writer.

CREATING AN IMPRESSION

Many people try too hard to impress when they write. They use long, convoluted sentences packed with long, convoluted words. But, in fact, this doesn't impress at all – it does quite the opposite. Your readers aren't marking an essay, they are trying to decide whether to buy into your idea or your product. They want the reading bit to be easy and straightforward, so they can concentrate on the content, not the style.

And that is the crux of it. Everything about using a good writing style is to do with making your proposal simple and easy to read. You're not James Joyce – the MD isn't going to take your proposal on holiday for a spot of thought-provoking and inspirational literature to read on the beach. Your readers want the message to come through clear and simple. They won't be impressed by 'clever' writing. If you keep all your words and sentences short and simple, they will be deeply grateful. Anyway, for all you know, they may not understand half those long words other people use, and making your readers feel uneducated and inadequate isn't going to endear you to them.

So the first rule of good writing is keep it simple:

- ▶ **short paragraphs**
- ▶ **short sentences**
- ▶ **short words.**

thinking smart

WRITE AS YOU SPEAK

As a rule of thumb, if you don't use a word in everyday speech, don't use it in your proposal. If you wouldn't say, 'Let me draw your attention to the aforementioned point …' don't write it. Just write, 'As I mentioned before …'

This is all pretty easy so far, isn't it? And that's how it stays. A good writing style is much quicker to write, because you don't have to agonize over constructing complex phrases or remembering little-used words.

Certain types of words are particular culprits when it comes to making proposals harder on the reader:

- ▷ **legal words (heretofore, notwithstanding and all that lot)**
- ▷ **pomposity (henceforth, thus and so on)**
- ▷ **jargon.**

Regarding this last point: *Never* try to impress with jargon. The only time you should use it is when there is absolutely no other word that will do. And then – unless your readers are all without doubt fully conversant in the jargon – add an explanation in brackets. If you have to use several jargon words you can add a glossary at the end.

STYLE THAT SELLS

All we're doing at the moment is knocking out all the complicated bits to keep your writing simple. But there are other types of word or phrase that are also best avoided. Look, if you're in a real hurry, I know it's tempting to skip this bit. But try to resist, because it's about how to make your proposal more convincing, and that's the most important thing here. You need to sell your idea to these readers, so don't waste any opportunity to do this through your style as well as your content. Here's a summary of the most important points.

Use concrete nouns. Ouch! Noun? That was definitely one of those words your English teacher used to use. In fact, it could even be defined as jargon, couldn't it? OK, I'll explain it in case you weren't concentrating hard enough at school (as if). Nouns are words for things: car, dog, holiday, phone, newspaper. And the ones I just listed are all concrete nouns – they give the reader a clear visual picture of something specific. They're fine.

The ones to avoid are the abstract ones, especially the ones that give no clear picture. For example: situation, activities, operation. Reading them just bores people. And it makes it harder for them to grasp what you are saying. You can't always avoid abstract nouns, but you often can. For example, instead of saying 'When you take into *consideration* …', say 'When you consider …'. Here's another example: Change 'the *operation* of this bulldozer isn't easy' to 'this bulldozer isn't easy to operate.'

Use active verbs. Done it again! More jargon! OK, a verb is a doing word: run, help, find, operate, over-exaggerate … and so on. Active verbs are ones where the

thinking smart

CHAT BUT NOT SLANG

Use idiomatic English when it comes to your vocabulary, although slang is pushing it a bit far. So you can talk about the lavatory (assuming it's relevant to your proposal), you don't have to call it the toilet or the washroom. Just don't call it the bog.

subject of the sentence is doing something – 'I *met* an important customer yesterday.' The baddies are the passive verbs, where things happen to the subject: 'I *was met* by an important customer yesterday.' Again, these are slow and plodding, while plenty of active verbs give your proposal a lively, dynamic feel, full of action.

Here are a couple more examples. Instead of saying 'I *was trampled* by the elephant,' say: 'The elephant *trampled* me.' Instead of writing 'The aeroplane *will be painted* by a team of people wearing magnetic boots,' say: 'A team of people wearing magnetic boots *will paint* the aeroplane.'

Avoid clichés. Overused phrases cease to mean anything because the reader's eye just skims over them. So you're wasting an opportunity if you use empty phrases such as *meeting customer needs* or *a wide range of products and services*. Almost invariably there's a better way of saying the same thing. Instead of 'a wide range of products and services', why not say what they are? Or at least give an idea: 'Over 30 different vehicles, from two-door sports cars to four-ton trucks'. It's much clearer, and gives the reader a concrete visual image (you're also changing abstract nouns – 'products' and 'services' – into concrete ones).

Avoid stock phrases. How often do you hear people say 'at this precise moment in time' when what they mean is 'now'? Business English seems to be full of this kind of cumbersome and slightly pompous phrase. The problem with using these phrases is that they give your reader time to lose the thread of the sentence, make you sound like everyone else, and give the whole document a slightly woolly feel. In other words, they do nothing for your image as an original thinker and a dynamic manager.

Here are a few more to avoid: there is a reasonable expectation that … (probably); owing to the situation that … (because); should a situation arise where … (if); taking into consideration such factors as … (considering); prior to the occasion when … (before). There. You should have the idea by now.

Avoid neutral words. Neutral words are inexpressive ones such as 'alter', 'affect', or 'express an opinion'. Your style will be much more colourful and interesting if you replace these with more expressive alternatives. So instead of writing 'the new flexitime system altered productivity' write that it 'improved' or 'boosted' it.

BROAD STYLE

So much for the individual words and phrases you use. But how about your broader style? We've already talked about using everyday language, which means addressing the reader as 'you' and yourself as 'I'. But there are a few other points worth making about your overall style.

GETTING IT THE RIGHT WAY ROUND

If you want to be sure you are using an active verb, just ask yourself what is doing the action in the sentence – and then put that first. If you were trampled by an elephant, the elephant is doing the trampling. So put the elephant first in the sentence, and it all follows naturally: The elephant trampled me.

YOU AND I

In the interests of a clear style, in which you write as you speak, address your reader as 'you' and refer to yourself as 'I'. It's fine to say, 'You'll be able to see the improvement within a few weeks' or 'I'd like to explain how it works…'.

Match the style to the reader

This is a general approach, not something to get hung up on. You don't have to write in the same style as your reader would. But be sensitive to them. If you are writing for most readers, the guidelines so far in this chapter will do you fine. Just skim through this section to make sure you don't need to read it. But some types of readers do need a slight tweak of style to keep them happy.

Adapting your style to suit your reader is one of the best subliminal techniques for showing you're on their side — it makes them feel that you're their sort of person. So if your readers are much older or younger than you, for example, adapt your style a little accordingly:

Old fashioned readers. If your readers were at school 40 years ago, they may be fussier than you about 'correct' grammar (that is to say, grammar that was correct forty years ago). So you're probably better off using words like 'whom'. And sticking to 'proper' sentences. If you've never met your readers but you suspect they're old fashioned — perhaps they're a group of elderly barristers, for instance — steer away from the most obvious modern colloquialisms. And don't start sentences with 'and'.

Young readers. Conversely, if you use words like 'whom' when you're writing for most young readers, you'll alienate them. Don't break the rules (outlined in the next chapter) completely, but feel free to stretch them. The readers will feel you're on their wavelength.

Readers with restricted reading skills. Perhaps some of your readers are foreign and their English is poor. Or maybe the report is for your boss who is mildly dyslexic. If, for any reason, your readers might have problems with standard English, or with certain words, adapt your style to avoid their problem areas. If your readers don't speak good English, the ideal solution is to have the proposal or report translated. Failing that, however, it would be better to replace the word 'livelihood' with 'job', for instance, or 'archive' with 'records'.

IT'S…

Unless your readers are very fusty and old fashioned, it's fine to elide words. In other words you can write 'it's' instead of 'it is', 'isn't' instead of 'is not', and 'can't' instead of 'cannot'.

Stock phrases do nothing for your image as an original thinker and a dynamic manager

531

SAY IT OUT LOUD

If you're not sure whether something goes in terms of your readers' own style, play safe. If you can't think of a safe option that says what you want to so succinctly, imagine standing in the room with your readers giving a presentation (which is, after all, only a spoken proposal rather than a written one). If you would use the word or phrase in a presentation, you can use it in a proposal. If not, not.

Be politically correct

This topic gets almost everybody incredibly heated – whatever their view. But it doesn't matter what *your* view is of course; it's the reader's view that counts. If you're in any doubt at all, don't take chances. The fact is that this particular subject is now so well discussed that anyone who doesn't follow the modern approach appears, at best, to be fuddy-duddy and out of touch. So make sure your reports and proposals are free of racism, ageism, sexism and any other -isms you can think of, regardless of your personal views.

Avoiding sexism is the area that can cause most problems. All the other subjects or words that are not 'pc' are pretty easy to avoid. But it can seem quite difficult to avoid any reference to gender except when talking about real people. So here are a few tips:

▸ **Rewrite the sentence in the plural: instead of 'England believes that every man will do his duty' write 'England believes that all citizens will do their duty.'**

▸ **It's now generally acceptable to use the pronoun 'they' in place of 'he' or 'she', so instead of 'Ask your boss if he or she wants a cup of tea' you can say 'Ask your boss if they want a cup of tea.' Occasionally, this construction can sound uncomfortable, however, in which case use one of the alternative techniques to avoid referring to gender altogether.**

▸ **You can use the phrase 'he or she' (or variations on it such as s/he). This can be intrusive, however, and tends to draw attention to itself. It's certainly correct, but it may not always be the smoothest approach.**

▸ **Say 'you' or 'your'. For example, instead of saying 'Every employee should leave his desk tidy' say 'Leave your desk tidy.' Apart from being more correct, this is also a much friendlier style to adopt.**

Explain new ideas clearly

You must know the old challenge: explain a spiral staircase without using your hands. Well, with reports and proposals you can never use your hands. Sometimes you can provide diagrams and drawings, but not if you're explaining an abstract concept. What's more, you won't be there when your readers see the document, so they can't stop you as they could at a presentation and ask you to run that one past them again.

One solution that frequently works is to use examples. A clear example or two can make all the difference between clarity and bafflement. For instance (you see, I'm giving you an example): I mentioned earlier that you should use concrete nouns. Now, if you didn't know what a noun was, you'd have been baffled. But as soon as I gave you some examples – car, dog, holiday, phone, newspaper – it should have become perfectly clear.

IF IN DOUBT ...

It's difficult to give too many examples. Something may be evident to you, but not necessarily so obvious to your readers. If you think there's any chance that the reader might benefit from an example, supply one or even several. No one's going to complain if you give them an example they didn't really need.

Use metaphors and analogies

These are also invaluable devices, especially for explaining abstract concepts and ideas. For instance (here we go again; I'm giving you another example!), I said earlier that the way to persuade someone round to your way of thinking was to 'show that you're on their side' and then 'lead them over to your side'. When you are trying to explain an abstract concept, the best way is often to find a concrete visual image to relate it to.

Analogies tend to start 'it's a bit like ...' or 'it's as if ...'. Suppose you're trying to explain how white blood cells work. You could say, 'They're a bit like a school of piranha, swimming gently along. As soon as anything alien appears in their river, they descend on it and attack it mercilessly until they've eaten it. Then they go back to drifting in the current again.'

The key thing with examples, metaphors and analogies is knowing when to use them. If you're writing about a new drug for treating heart disease, and your readership is a group of senior consultants who specialize in cardiac disorders, there's no point explaining where in the body the heart is located. But if you're writing for heart patients, they'll need things explained that the consultants would take for granted.

START WRITING

That's the end of the crash course in clear and persuasive writing. So now you can sit down and write your proposal, following these guidelines to make sure it is not only well structured but well written too. You can use the next chapter to help correct any technical points of grammar and so on after you've finished your draft. After that there's a little more to do, but you've done the bulk of the work.

NO NEED TO EXPLAIN?

If you're in any doubt about whether your proposal is as clear as it should be, ask a plain-speaking and honest colleague or friend to read your first draft and tell you if you need to explain anything more clearly. Obviously you need to ask someone whose knowledge of the subject is not substantially different from that of the readers.

Here's a checklist to help you keep your writing on course as you go.

CHECKLIST

Keep it simple
- ▶ **short paragraphs**
- ▶ **short sentences**
- ▶ **short words.**

Use a style that sells
- ▶ **use concrete nouns**
- ▶ **use active verbs**
- ▶ **avoid clichés**
- ▶ **avoid stock phrases**
- ▶ **avoid neutral words**
- ▶ **beware ambiguous words.**

Broad style
- ▶ **match the style to the reader**
- ▶ **be politically correct**
- ▶ **explain new ideas with examples, metaphors and analogies.**

◀◀ for next time

As with the structure of your proposal, this is both the best style to use and as quick as any other – certainly as quick as any other effective style. But you will find that when you have more time, you'll almost certainly feel more comfortable taking a couple of drafts to get to this stage. You might find it easier to write the proposal in a simple style first, then go through it looking for places where you could usefully add examples or analogies, and then go through it again checking for jargon, clichés and neutral words and all the other things on the checklist.

After this you can redraft the whole thing with all the changes, and then give it one final read through. And the last stage you should always incorporate if you can possibly find the time is to get someone else whose opinion you value to read it through for you.

5 using correct English

I don't suppose this is your favourite chapter heading. When you decided to read this book, I don't imagine this chapter was the clincher: 'Ooh, English grammar! That sounds fun. I must read that!' The only people who don't contemplate a chapter on correct English with a sinking feeling are the ones who don't need to read it in the first place.

So if no one's interested in this chapter, what is it doing in the book? Why don't we just gloss over this bit? Can't a spelling and grammar check do it all for you anyway?

We'll get to spell checks in a minute. But first, why are you supposed to read this stuff? If it didn't sink in at school, it's hardly likely to now, is it? Well, at school, nothing was riding on it. But now you have an incentive: your proposal – even your success – could depend on it. The trouble is simple: What if your readers can spell? And punctuate, and remember when to put the apostrophe in 'its' and all the rest of it? In other words, what if they notice when you get it wrong?

The answer is that they will be distinctly unimpressed. They may disregard a stray typing error, but their opinion of you will be diminished if they perceive you as someone who can't use English properly. Even if the proposal is otherwise excellent and they accept it, they will still be left with a feeling that you're not quite up to their standard. And if your bosses are reading the proposal, that might even affect your career.

You may yearn for the days of Olde Englande when there was no right and wrong in spelling and grammar. And you may argue convincingly that it's stupid to put a 'c' in practice some of the time and an 's' the rest of the time. But your protestations are wasted on the kind of directors and customers who know the difference between a compliment and a complement.

So this chapter stays in.

SPELL CHECKS AND GRAMMAR CHECKS

We'll begin by addressing this question. If you are in a tearing rush, you can use these. In fact, you can use them anyway if you like. *But they are not infallible.* Mistakes can still slip through. They are better than nothing, but they can give you a false sense of security.

The problem with spell checks is simple: If you mistype or misspell a word in a way which happens to be another word rather than gobbledegook, your spell check won't pick it up. If you miss the final 'o' off 'too' you are left with a legitimate word ('to'). Your spell check has no quarrel with this word, so it will leave it alone … even though it is grammatically wrong.

Grammar checks are quite often plain wrong. They have no common sense, and they often misinterpret what you have typed and try to change it when there's nothing wrong with it. If you are fairly confident on your grammar you might find them helpful for picking up errors so long as you know when to hit the 'ignore' button. But if you're very shaky they are likely to give you a bum steer as often as not. What's more, they can take ages, and you're in a hurry.

FINAL CHECK

The best way to use a spell check or a grammar check is as a final run through, *after* you have checked the proposal by eye. That prevents you relying on them too heavily.

So, while computer checks are useful as a safety net, they won't do everything for you. They'll correct you if you spell embarrass with only one 'r', but they won't tell you if you inadvertently spell principle with an '-al' at the end.

So the answer, I'm afraid, is to know for yourself when you are right and when you are wrong, just in case your readers can tell too. So let's have a really quick check through some of the main sticking points. If you're in a rush don't read this right through for the moment, just use the chapter as a reference for the bits you need.

If you do stick with it, you'll be rewarded at the end with a list of rules you are allowed to break. I bet your English teacher never gave you that.

VOCABULARY

If you're shaky, don't use words you're not sure of. That's the general rule. But sometimes you have to. So use a dictionary and look up anything you're not 100 per cent confident on. In addition to that, there are certain frequently misused words which it is worth making sure you know about. One of the most obvious examples is 'criteria'. This is a plural word, so if there is only one of them, you should say 'criterion'. Once you've learnt that, you're already in an elite group.

Here is a list of ten pairs of the most commonly confused words and their meanings – see how many of these pairs you already know.

affect verb meaning to influence: It affected me deeply	**effect** noun meaning result, or verb meaning to bring about: It had a deep effect on me / The new law will effect change in the country
adverse adjective meaning unfavourable: It had an adverse effect on me	**averse** adjective meaning opposed to or disinclined: I am averse to powdered eggs (formerly 'averse from')
principle noun meaning a standard or rule of conduct: It's against my principles to do that	**principal** adjective or noun meaning most important: the principal rule, the principal of the school
stationery noun meaning writing materials: I'm running out of stationery	**stationary** adjective meaning not moving: That is a stationary vehicle
complement noun meaning something that completes, or verb meaning to make complete: One more member of the committee would give us a full complement	**compliment** noun meaning praise or verb meaning to praise: She complimented me on paying her such a kind compliment

council noun meaning an assembly of people: The council meets every month	**counsel** verb meaning to recommend, or noun meaning recommendation: I counselled her to accept my counsel
dependent adjective meaning reliant: I'm dependent on my job for my income	**dependant** – noun meaning a person who depends: He has three elderly dependants
ensure verb meaning to make certain: I want to ensure that the water's not too hot before I get in the bath	**insure** verb meaning to protect against risk: I have insured my car against being damaged by circus animals
practice noun: I need more practice before I can do this	**practise** verb: I'm going to practise the double bass until I'm an expert
advice noun meaning recommendation: Let me give you some advice	**advise** verb meaning to counsel: I advise you to think twice before you do that

SPELLING

Use a dictionary, and a spell check for a final sweep of your proposal, but in the meantime here are some basic guidelines for spelling:

▸ **Why does targeted have one 't' in the middle and regretted have two? There's a rule you can follow here: If the stress falls on the final syllable of the word (regret), you double the final letter when you add -ed. If it falls on an earlier syllable (target) you retain the single letter at the end. Other examples of retaining the single letter include marketed, offered, focused, benefited. A final 'l', however is always doubled, as in travelled.**

▸ **If you are turning an adjective ending in a single or double 'l' (magical, full, special, dull) into an adverb, you always end up with a double 'll' in the middle: magically, fully, specially, dully.**

▸ **The rule 'i before e except after c' is worth remembering. The exceptions are, or can be:**
  - **words in which the 'ei' is _not_ pronounced 'ee' (such as heinous or inveigle)**
  - **the word seize**
  - **some names of places and people.**

ABBREVIATIONS

However fast you're trying to get this proposal written, there's no point saving time by using abbreviations such as approx for approximately (I hope you're not _that_ desperate). It implies the reader isn't important enough to bother writing it out fully for.

However, it is always worth shortening long titles to their initials, such as EC for European Community. It saves your reader having to wade through the whole thing

thinking smart

PATRIOTIC STYLE

The Americans tend to end words -ize which we end -ise (organise, rationalise, subsidise). If you think your readers would prefer the English form, use the -ise ending.

each time. The first time you mention the organization, use its full name. If you're going to refer to it later, add its abbreviation in brackets afterwards – for example, local education authority (LEA). After that, you can use the initials on their own.

APOSTROPHES

The apostrophe is probably the most frequently misused piece of punctuation in the English language. People most commonly misuse it when they want to pluralize a word, for example:

Wrong

▶ **Pick your own tomatoe's**

▶ **Back in the 1880's ...**

▶ **All the department's were represented.**

All these examples are wrong, for a very good reason – you don't need an apostrophe *anywhere* to pluralize a word. That isn't what apostrophes were invented for. They actually have two purposes:

1 to show possession
2 to show that a letter has been missed out.

The possessive

Add an 's' to the person, people or thing doing the possessing: the children's shoes, the tree's shade, the snake's eyes. The apostrophe goes after whoever is possessing, so in the last example, if you were talking about the eyes of lots of snakes the apostrophe would go after the final 's' of snakes: the snakes' eyes.

If the person or people (or snakes) doing the possessing already have an 's' on the end, you don't add another one; simply stick the apostrophe on the end – that's why you've never seen anyone write 'the snakes's eyes'. The only times when you would add an 's' after a singular word that ends in 's' are:

▶ **if it's a proper name (Mr Jones's, St James's)**

▶ **if the word ends in a double 'ss' (the boss's).**

Never use an apostrophe with a possessive pronoun. Oops! Jargon again. (It's a fair cop. A possessive pronoun is a word indicating possession which replaces someone or something's name.) These are words like yours, hers, its, theirs, ours.

thinkingfast

PLACING THE APOSTROPHE

A quick way to remember where the apostrophe goes is to say to yourself 'the ... belonging to the ... ':

▶ If they're the *eyes* belonging to the *snake* (singular) you would write: the snake's eyes.

▶ If they're the *eyes* belonging to the *snakes* (plural) you would write: the snakes' eyes.

Missing letters

You also use an apostrophe to show that one or more letters have been left out, as in: isn't, shouldn't (both missing the 'o' of 'not'), what's (meaning 'what is' or 'what has'), can't (for cannot) and so on.

Perhaps one of the most frequent confusions is between *its* and *it's*: they are two completely different words. *Its* is a possessive pronoun (you know what that is now) and therefore has no apostrophe, while *it's* is short for *it is* and does have one. The easiest way to tell each time you write the word is to say it in your head as 'it is'. If it makes sense, it's short for it is and has an apostrophe. Otherwise it doesn't. For example:

1 'I gave the dog its breakfast.'
2 Try the technique: 'I gave the dog it is breakfast.'
3 That was gobbledegook. It clearly isn't short for it is, so it doesn't have an apostrophe.

Here's another example:

1 'Its a great day to go potholing.'
2 Try the technique: 'It is a great day to go potholing.'
3 That makes sense – it's short for 'it is' so it *does* have an apostrophe, in place of the missing 'i'.

RULES YOU CAN BREAK

OK, I promised. So here it is. Three traditional rules of English grammar which haven't made it into the 21st century. If you're writing for well-educated octogenarians you might think twice about breaking them, but no one else cares two hoots any more.

Never start a sentence with 'and', 'but' or 'because

William Blake clearly wasn't too bothered by grammatic convention when he wrote

And did those feet, in ancient times.

And not only can you start a sentence with these words, you can start paragraphs with them too. They can be very useful for this purpose, as they tend to add emphasis to what you are about to say.

Never finish a sentence with a preposition

This was always quite hard to obey. Prepositions are all those little words that aren't anything else, like up, of, to, in and so on. There are times when the only way to avoid putting one of them at the end of a sentence involves twisting the sentence self-consciously around until it becomes harder to follow.

There is a story (no doubt apocryphal) about Winston Churchill's view of this rule. His secretary told him he should rephrase a sentence because he had finished it with a preposition, and he supposedly replied: 'There are some things up with which I will not put!'

Never split an infinitive

Apart from anything else, who on earth can recognize a split infinitive these days? People over 60 and creeps, that's all (unless *you* can, in which case there are also some very clever people who understand them). The most famous modern example of a split infinitive is in the title sequence of *Star Trek* where the voiceover says: 'To boldly go …' If it's good enough for the Starship *Enterprise*, it's good enough for us.

◀◀ for next time

Rather than check through your proposal several times for grammatical and spelling errors, how much nicer to get it right first time. If you write a lot of proposals or reports, it's worth teaching yourself to write more correct English.

Don't push it: just pick one or two stumbling blocks at a time and learn the right way to do it, starting with the guidelines in this chapter. Then practise (that's practise with an 's', of course). Once you've learnt it confidently, move on to the next weak point and strengthen that, too.

You might like a small reference library to help you with this. I can thoroughly recommend the following to keep on your shelf:

- ▶ a dictionary
- ▶ a thesaurus (which gives groups of words with very similar meanings – invaluable when you can't quite remember a particular word)
- ▶ *The Complete Plain Words*, Ernest Gowers, Oxford University Press
- ▶ *Fowler's Modern English Usage*, Oxford University Press
- ▶ *The Economist Style Guide*, The Economist Books Ltd
- ▶ *The Penguin Dictionary of Troublesome Words*, Penguin

It's difficult to overexaggerate the value of a small but good reference shelf like this. And if you're at all under-confident about your writing skills it will help you turn out high-quality writing. And don't worry if you think you're hopeless at writing clearly and following all the guidelines: English is a sod of a language and we all look things up from time to time.

6 presentation

Nearly there. You've written the whole proposal now, to the structure we outlined earlier, and you may be wondering what's left. The answer is: the look of the thing. It's the first thing your readers will notice, and the difference between a clear, attractive layout or a wodge of impenetrable text is going to have a big impact on their attitude to it. Poor presentation can even put them off reading it altogether.

Getting the layout right is a quick job (you'll be pleased to hear) in this age of word processors. You can add in the presentation features after you've completed the main text. You can also add any appendices you need at this stage. So this is a simple but crucial step in preparing your proposal.

LAYOUT

Not only does a well-laid-out proposal look more readable and inviting, it also gives the impression of being more organized than one which is badly presented. So what are the features you need to incorporate to give your proposal the right look? A key rule here is don't worry how many pages it covers – it's better to have an eight-page proposal with lots of space and white page showing through than to cram the same material into four pages. Here are the best ways to improve your layout; use it as a checklist:

- ▶ **Double space your proposal.**
- ▶ **Leave generous margins, and align the right-hand margin.**
- ▶ **Use plenty of headings and sub-headings: they give readers big clues at a glance, and help them to find any specific information they are looking for.**
- ▶ **Use plenty of paragraphs – a fresh one for each fresh thought, idea or concept.**
- ▶ **Use lists wherever you can – they are easier to follow than solid text when you are listing ideas, items or options. Give them bullet points, numbers, icons or whatever you choose to mark them.**
- ▶ **Summarise main sections briefly if it will help clarity: 'So those are our four key options ...' followed by a list, for example.**
- ▶ **You can give each paragraph or headed section a number if you wish, but don't get too complicated. It just confuses people if you number a paragraph 2.1.1.**
- ▶ **Put the odd point or piece of information in a box if you think this will help clarity – but don't overuse the feature.**

❚❚ thinking smart

PLAIN AND SIMPLE

Just because your word processor offers you 74 different fonts, this is not the time to play with them. Stick to one plain font, with perhaps one other for headings. You don't want to confuse your readers, or distract from the substance of your proposal.

LOOKING AHEAD

If you are including information in your proposal which is likely to be updated later, putting it in an appendix makes it easy to swap with the new data when the time comes.

APPENDICES

We've established, of course, that you need to back up all your arguments with hard facts. But if there are lots of them, you don't want to clutter your proposal with endless tables and charts. So put the key facts in the proposal and move the supporting data to the appendices. That way, those who want to can read it, and those who don't can avoid it altogether.

Technical information in particular is generally best moved to an appendix. Just make sure you direct readers to the appendix at the relevant point in the proposal. By the way, don't feel that if your proposal has no appendices that you have somehow failed. There's no point in including them for the sake of it, just because it looks more grown up to have an appendix.

LENGTH

It's worth mentioning length, because many people simply haven't a clue how long their proposal should be. You might feel that a long proposal will look more impressive, and as if you have worked harder, but in fact the reverse is often the case. How do you feel about the reports and proposals that land on your desk? With your busy schedule you probably like them to be as brief as possible.

Well, you're no different from your readers. They are equally busy, and they want quality, not quantity. Especially not quantity. That's why putting non-essential data in an appendix is such a good idea. So make sure you include everything necessary, but otherwise keep your proposal down to a few pages. Two or three pages is plenty if that covers everything.

The Duke of Wellington once sent a message to the War Office saying, 'I apologize for the length of these despatches but I did not have time to make them shorter.' You may be up against the clock right now, but you should still make sure your proposal is no longer than necessary.

◀◀ for next time

Arranging the presentation of your proposal isn't a long task, but you might find in future that you would like to experiment with types of bullet points, heading styles and so on. Please do so. But whatever you do, make sure the end result stays clear and simple.

Unless you're a designer touting for work, you should let the content of your proposal be the star of the show, not the cosmetics.

7 topping and tailing

This is the very last bit, I promise. Then you can sit back and breathe a sigh of relief before you print off your proposal and deliver it.

There are lots of little bits and pieces which you need to add to your proposal, many of them as a kind of garnish that makes the proposal look really impressive and helps the reader through it, too. They are the finishing touches. You won't need all of them every time — sometimes you will use very few of them — but you need to know what they are. And you need to add them last of all.

This book, like any book, has a title page, information about publishers and copyright, a contents page and so on. Some books also have a bibliography, or a useful addresses section. So what we're talking about is the proposal version of this packaging.

REGULAR FEATURES

We'll start with the features just about every proposal should include:

- **title page with title and author**
- **contents page (if the proposal is more than four pages including any appendices)**
- **the objective – here it is again. You may need to reword it slightly, but state it below the title, or at the start of the proposal somewhere**
- **summary (we'll look at this in a moment)**
- **page numbers.**

OCCASIONAL FEATURES

And now for the features that you will sometimes need to include. These can all go at the back, although you might prefer to put the acknowledgements at the front:

- **acknowledgements – of other people who have helped or contributed**
- **appendices**
- **glossary (if you have had to use jargon your readers might not understand)**
- **bibliography**
- **references – referring to the sources you've used boosts your credibility so list interviews, catalogues, books, reports, media sources, trade associations or anything else you think will convince or impress**
- **further addresses.**

SUMMARY

Unless your report is extremely brief, some of your readers may not have time to read it all. Even if they do, they may want to recap it later without having to read the whole thing again. What they need is a summary. Not a summary in the sense of a conclusion, but a précis or résumé that briefly summarizes the report or proposal.

UNDER COVER

Always put your proposal into some kind of report folder (through which the title shows) before presenting it. It looks smart, is easier to find among a pile of papers, and it will protect it from coffee rings and other damage.

Every report or proposal that runs to more than three or four pages should have a summary at the beginning, straight after the contents page. So what should you put in it? If you think about it, it's quite simple. If this is the only part of the report that some of your readers will see, you want to include everything. Only shorter.

The summary should be a miniature version of the report or proposal, complete in itself, so the key facts are clear to anyone who reads it, even if they read nothing else. This being the case, it should obviously follow the same structure as the full version:

- **position**
- **problem**
- **possibilities (if they apply)**
- **proposal.**

FIRST THINGS LAST

It is far more sensible and much quicker to write the summary *after* you've written the main body of the document. You've already covered the ground by then, and it's just a matter of pulling out the most central information.

for next time

If you are in a real rush, you may have to miss out a few of these. Make sure you retain the essential ones, but you might need more time to include a full list of references, further addresses, bibliography and so on. When you have more time, however, you should include these if you can since they give your proposal more weight, and can answer specific questions for your reader (such as, 'Where on earth has Jo dragged up these statistics from?').

proposal in an evening

If you feel panicky, read the last bit of the book: proposals in an hour. If that's possible, this should be a breeze. Begin by reading this book right through. It'll only take you an hour, so there's plenty of time.

One of your biggest drawbacks is going to be the difficulty of getting hold of the data you need to back up your proposal. If you already have them, great. If not, anything you can find out by phone needs doing first of all, before it gets too late. If you need to call colleagues and ask them to e-mail you facts and figures, do it now.

Other than that, writing a proposal at this kind of speed is all about knowing which stages in the process you can skip and still get away with it. So here are some suggestions for trimming down the time it takes to get this thing written.

▶ **Keep the proposal as short as you possibly can without sacrificing any essential points. It has to be quicker to write three pages than to write eight. It won't be much quicker at the planning stage, but when it comes to physically writing the thing it will save you time.**

▶ **If the proposal is short enough (three to four pages maximum) you can skip the contents page and the summary page.**

▶ **Drag in any help you possibly can. Come on! There must be plenty of people out there who owe you favours. Get suggestions from colleagues about arguments to use, advice about what issues your readers consider important, talk them into digging out facts for you and, if you know anyone who can write good English and is on e-mail, get them to go through your draft proposal for you and e-mail it back corrected. Offer bottles of Scotch, tickets to Wimbledon, a go on your playstation – whatever will persuade them to help you out.**

▶ **Don't economize on time spent on presentation. First impressions are vital – especially if you don't want the reader to spot any economies you may have made elsewhere.**

▶ **Don't economize on facts either. If you can't find the data, don't include the argument. If it's essential, and you have to include it, dig out the data tomorrow morning as soon as you have delivered the proposal. That way, if anyone queries it, you'll at least be able to come back with the goods.**

▶ **If it still looks neat, you may be able to copy or scan in data for appendices, rather than retype it. But be aware that this can contravene copyright law if you are using copyrighted material – even if it's only for internal circulation to a few people. Internal documents or copyright-free material, however, are fine.**

If you follow these tips, you'll have plenty of time to prepare your proposal in an evening, even if it doesn't leave you the time or the energy to follow it with a slap-up meal and a couple of videos. It may, however, persuade you to try even harder when you write your next proposal to find more time in which to do it. But, for now, relax and stay cool. People have written proposals in less time than this *and* come out looking smart and winning their case.

proposal in an hour

Even by fast thinking standards you're pushing it a bit, aren't you? Write a proposal in an hour? Are you serious? OK, then. If you're serious enough about it, it can be done. Especially if you're used to working under time pressure – which I guess you must be to have arrived at this point.

So what can you do in an hour? Write a very short proposal. And actually, as long as everything is in there, a short proposal can be every bit as effective and impressive as a longer one. You'll just need to employ great clarity of thought:

1 You need to start by working out your objective (Chapter 1). No, it's not a waste of time. It's the one thing you most need to give you clarity of purpose.
2 Forget research. I presume you've got a pile of facts and data fairly readily to hand or you wouldn't be cutting things this fine. If you haven't, it's too late anyway. Skip straight to the chapter about structure (Chapter 3), and fit what you need to say into this structure as succinctly as possible.
3 Now type it up on your word processor, if you haven't already done it as you went along.
4 Go through the proposal and look for any points which need explaining better (in which case see page 532). Change any words you're not certain you are using correctly. And make sure your words, sentences and paragraphs are nice and short. Don't try to be clever with language.
5 Bang through the thing and correct your English, check your spelling and all that stuff. Twice. (I know you won't really do it twice but I have to say it, because we both know you ought to. When you're in a rush you make more mistakes than usual.)
6 Now tart up the layout, according to Chapter 6. It's OK, it's a really short chapter. Just checklists really.
7 Same goes for Chapter 7, all about topping and tailing. You're going to need a title page, which should include your objective. And don't forget to add page numbers.
8 And finally … don't make a habit of this. My blood pressure can't take it even if yours can.

guide to time management

fast thinking

ros jay

guide to time management

When time seems to move faster than you, you need to use any trick you can to squeeze full value out of every minute. The fast thinking manager uses a host of clever techniques to force time to expand to fit the workload. Here are some of the top techniques for managing your time to the max.

LEARN TO SPEED READ

You can buy books or go on courses to learn speed reading – and some of them are excellent – but they take time. So here's the basic principle of doubling your reading speed. Practise it whenever you have papers, reports or journals to read, and before long you could be saving yourself hours every week:

1. Draw two vertical lines down the page to divide it into three equal columns (after the initial practice, you can imagine the lines).

2. Read the group of words in the first line of the left-hand column as a single unit, without moving your eyes from one word to the next.

3. Repeat this with the centre and right-hand columns. You are now reading each line in three passes, rather than one for every word.

4. When you've mastered this, simply draw a single line down the centre of the page. Read the group of words to the left of it on the first line without moving your eyes, and then the group on the right. Now you can read a line with only one move of the eyes.

5. Finally, focus on the single, central line (whether real or imaginary) and try to read the entire line, margin to margin, without moving your eyes.

DON'T LET OTHER PEOPLE WASTE YOUR TIME

Other people seem to have a knack of spending *your* time without your agreement. Here are the best methods of making sure you stay in control of your own time:

- **Always meet people on their territory rather than your own; it's much easier to leave than to turf them out.**

- **Keep your office door open when you can make time for people. That way, when you close it, they'll know you really mean it. Put a 'do not disturb' notice on it if you need to.**

- **Never let anyone put you on hold on the phone. Before they get the chance to do so, interrupt and ask them to call you back or pass on a message for you.**

- **When you launch into an informal chat with someone in an office or a meeting room, stay standing up. Once you've sat down, you'll never get through the conversation as fast.**

KNOW YOURSELF

We all work better at certain times of day, and some tasks suit us better in the morning than the afternoon. Learn to recognize your own mental patterns and allocate your work around them; you'll find you get through your workload much faster – and more effectively too. We're all different, but here's a typical mental rhythm many of us fit into. Use it as a basis for working out your own natural pattern:

- ▶ *Before 10 a.m.* **The peak time for energy and vitality, so the best time to tackle difficult tasks.**

- ▶ *10 a.m. to 1 p.m.* **A good phase for mentally demanding work, such as detailed analysis or working with figures.**

- ▶ *1 p.m. to 4 p.m.* **Your system is running a little slower, so it helps to revive it by interacting with other people – meetings, phone calls, dealing with customers or even negotiating.**

- ▶ *4 p.m. to 7 p.m.* **Not so sluggish, but past your most mentally energetic. This is a good time for routine work, writing and studying, or dealing with your emails and correspondence.**

- ▶ *7 p.m. to 10 p.m.* **You should have knocked off by now, but if you're still on the go, use this as thinking time for reviewing events or thinking through outline plans.**

introduction

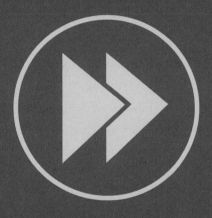

fast thinking you

So where do *you* fit into all this? This manual has looked at how to manage people, how to inspire them with your leadership qualities, and how to master the hard skills that enable you to bring success to your team and your organization. But what about you? What do you need to make your own working life a little easier, and to cope with the mad pace of modern life a little more comfortably? This final section has a couple of guides just for you.

One of the worst personal work nightmares – and a very common one – is an overload of work. A desk piled high with correspondence waiting to be dealt with, a list of phone calls to make that fills your whole notebook, and more unanswered emails than you can shake a stick at. Meetings to prepare for, reports to read, and events to attend. And in amongst all that, didn't you have objectives and targets you were supposed to meet in this job? *work overload* will tell you how to get on top of the work backlog fast, and bring it down to a level where you feel on top of it, instead of letting *it* get on top of you.

And suppose you decide to walk away from it all and get another job (well, it's one way to escape from a work overload). How are you going to kick off in your new job smoothly so that overloads don't happen and you stay focused on your objectives? How can you hit the ground running without tripping over any hurdles on the way? *flying start* will give you the cool manager's guide to stepping into a new job looking good and staying that way.

It's part of your job as a manager to stay on top of your own job and be seen to be in control. These are the skills that make your team members look at you with envy and dream about being as cool and as savvy as you … one day.

work overload

 CREATE MORE TIME

TACKLE THE BACKLOG

CLEAR YOUR DESK

ros jay

contents

introduction

Your in-tray is the height of a small tower block, you can't find your phone under the pile of to-do lists and post-it notes, your boss wants to see you in five minutes, you're due at a vital meeting in a quarter of an hour, and reception has just called to tell you there is a visitor to see you now.

Familiar? If you are one of the millions of people for whom work is always so frantic that there's no time to catch up with yourself, this is the book for you. There's plenty of advice around (much of it plain unrealistic) on how to make sure you never build up a backlog, but it's too late for all that. You've got the backlog *now*, and the only question you need answered is 'How do I get rid of it?'

This book will answer that question. Ideally, you need to be able to clear a day to get right back on top of things. In fantasy land you'd have several days to sort everything out and start again with a clear desk, but this is the real world, and you have to think fast and act smart. You want:

 tips for getting on top of things fast

 shortcuts for avoiding any unnecessary work

 checklists to make sure you have the essentials covered

… all put together clearly and simply. And short enough to read fast, of course. So here it is.

If time is really pressing (and when isn't it?), you'll find at the back of this book a checklist for getting through the whole process in half a day – maybe an evening when everyone else is off your back. And if you're up to your neck and you can't even find half a day, there's a one-hour version for creating time at the speed of life.

So take a deep breath, and don't panic. Everything you need to know is in this book. This will get your working life back to a manageable state in as little as an hour if that's all you have. You can regard any extra time beyond that as a bonus. So if you have a whole morning, you can already start to feel smug. And if you've had trouble finding the time to read this introduction, then the first section will give you a few tips for making time to read the rest of the book.

Throughout the book, we'll also identify ways of preventing the same situation bulding up again in future. So the contents of the book are both a cure for the present and a prevention against future pile-ups.

This book is going to guide you through the six key steps you need to take to clear the backlog of work fast:

1 You'll have to start by creating the time to deal with the pile-up, so we'll begin by doing just that.
2 The next stage is to identify your objective; this means you can tackle the work in the most effective and productive order.
3 After this, we'll establish how to sort all the hundreds (or even thousands) of individual tasks into just a few key groups.
4 The next step involves measuring these groups against your objective so that you can prioritise.
5 Now we come to dealing with the actual tasks themselves, and the options for doing this – do it, defer it, delegate it or dump it.
6 Finally, we'll look at how to handle the tasks you deal with yourself so that they take up as little time as possible.

fast thinking gambles

Obviously you're not supposed to get into this state in the first place – but then life was never meant to be this packed. And now you're here, you should ideally give yourself several days to concentrate exclusively on sorting out the piles of paperwork and the mounting voicemail messages. But let's get real. You're doing well to have found the time to read this book and start acting on it.

Just for the record, however, in case you ever find yourself in a parallel existence where work doesn't expand to exceed the time available, why should you allow more time to clear the backlog? Well, there are disadvantages to metaphorically putting a bomb under your desk and wiping out everything on it in a matter of moments.

- ▶ **Without the benefit of a time machine, there are still only 60 minutes to each hour, and 24 hours in a day. There is doubtless loads of junk on your desk, and plenty of things that are now too late to action, or that should be passed on. But there are still going to be tasks that you need to do, and the more of these there are the longer it will take to do them properly.**

- ▶ **Psychologically, the more time you have to deal with the pile-up, the more manageable and approachable the job seems. The only people who really relish tackling a backlog under time pressure are those irritating creeps who are so damn perfect they never have backlogs in the first place. Do you really want to be like them? (Well yes, actually ... but then, once this lot is cleared, you will be.)**

- ▶ **Of course, following the guidelines in this book you have plenty of time to clear your overload. But knowing that you are doing it under intense time pressure can still be stressful, and does nothing for your relaxation levels or your blood pressure.**

- ▶ **When you come to dealing with those tasks that really do need your attention, it is much less frustrating if you can get them all done easily. When people are out of the office when you call, or suppliers can't get back to you with the figures for at least 48 hours, or your laptop crashes – and all the other everyday irritations that life is peppered with – you are better off having a few days clear ahead of you than needing this all tied up by tomorrow afternoon.**

- ▶ **Some tasks will need to be delegated. However, if these are urgent, you'll hit problems when the person you want to delegate to isn't around. Even if they are around, it can be tough on someone to have an urgent task delegated at almost no notice – after all, their backlog may be even bigger than yours (there's a refreshing thought).**

So, although fast thinking will clear the work effectively, allowing more time for the job will make it even *more* effective and a whole lot less frustrating. Of course, the aim is to follow the tips in this book and avoid ever accumulating another backlog. But if life does catch up with you again, at least try to allow yourself more time to cope with it.

1 create the time

So you have six weeks, work to get through in the next two days, and now you've bought this book to help you and it's telling you to find *another* chunk of time to do what it says. Oh great. Just the kind of book you need.

It's a fair cop. It does seem to be missing the point to expect you to find even more time. But deep down, of course, you know that this work isn't going to evaporate by itself. There is simply no option but to take action – and taking action takes time. However, to show that I really am going to help I can start by giving you a few pointers for clearing the time you need.

THE MD WANTS TO SEE YOU *NOW*

You might think that you simply can't free up any more time, but I bet you could if a good enough reason came along. How many of the following could you find the time for despite the pile of work on your desk?

- ▶ **The MD is finalizing the decision on who to promote, and wants to see you for an hour first thing tomorrow morning.**
- ▶ **Your top client calls to say they are almost certain they want to double their last order – but they need you personally to come and meet their MD tomorrow afternoon.**
- ▶ **Ditto, and the customer is based on the other side of Europe.**

No doubt you could find the time for most (if not all) of these, however awkward the knock-on effect. OK, so clearing your desk isn't quite as urgent or as important as these, but the point is that it *is* possible to find time if you really need to. You just have to decide that you really need to. Having bought this book, I suspect that you don't need persuading. But in case you do, here's why it's so important to be on top of your work, rather than have your work getting on top of you:

- ▶ **If the work piles up, you are likely to miss important or urgent tasks until it is too late to do them properly.**
- ▶ **Being overloaded with work is extremely stressful.**
- ▶ **If you can't get the routine work out of the way, you can't make time for the important, proactive work.**
- ▶ **Successful people are those who get things done. People with piles of work on their desk are not getting things done.**

 thinking fast

CLEARING A WHOLE DAY

Tell yourself that an essential presentation to a key client or to the board of directors has just been scheduled for all day tomorrow. Can you make it? Great. Now here's some good news. It's just been cancelled. So you can use the whole day that you just freed up to clear your work backlog instead.

EARLY BIRD

If you absolutely cannot free up this much time at once, how about starting work an hour early each day for a week? This would buy you five hours before anyone else has arrived in the office to pester you. Be strict about forbidding yourself to do anything else in these five hours other than clear the pile-up of work.

▷ **When something important comes along, you cannot give it the attention it deserves without making something else suffer.**

FREEING UP TIME

You know it has got to be done; the only question is how can you make the time for it? Try to clear a whole day if you possibly can, and prevent interruptions:

▷ **Decide in advance which day you will spend on clearing your desk, and write it in your diary in indelible ink. Do not allow *anything* to displace it. Treat it as you would a diary entry for a vital meeting or the day you fly back from Australia.**

▷ **Enlist the help of assistants, secretaries or anyone else on your team to support you. Ask them to back up your assertion that you are not available to anyone who asks, to field all phone calls and visitors, not to bring you any new work, and not to disturb you all day – just this once.**

▷ **You may find that it helps to work some or all of the day from home if you can. Better still, work from somewhere else where no one has a number for you, but you can still make any calls necessary. Maybe you could work from a friend's house (making sure they will be out so they can't bother you, or tempt you with an invitation to the pub for lunch).**

▷ **Evenings and weekends are far from ideal, since it is often impossible to delegate at these times, or to action tasks that can be done only during working hours. But you can do the first part of the process – the preparation – out of hours, and arrive at work with a pile of tasks to delegate and another pile of tasks to do yourself (which you still have to allocate time for). This reduces the office time you have to dedicate to clearing the work overload, and can be a good option.**

You are clearly pretty committed by now to sorting out your workload, so you will find the time simply because you must. The longer you leave it, the worse it will get (which is what my mother used to say to me about tidying my bedroom, which is the same thing really; much as it galls me to say it, she was right). So the three key steps are:

 Pick your time.

 Stick to it.

 Eliminate distractions and interruptions.

Simple as that, really.

2 your objective

You may not have been expecting this one. In fact, you might wonder where setting objectives comes into the whole thing of offloading as much work as possible. But, in fact, it is central to the exercise. I'm not talking about the objective of this particular process – which we know is to turn the mountain of work on your desk, your computer, your voicemail and your mental list into something smaller than a molehill. I'm talking about the big stuff. Your personal objective. What are you here for?

You may have only a few hours to clear the backlog, but you still need to dedicate the first five minutes to this. It is easy to forget, among the weekly meetings, budgets, requests for information, invoices for approval and all the rest of it, that your core function is something else: to increase sales, raise customer satisfaction, boost PR, improve productivity, or whatever it is the company is really paying you to do. Of course all the other things are important, and I'm not suggesting they shouldn't be done. But if you are not achiving your core objective, all the rest is worthless. So identify a clear objective. Here are some possible examples:

- ▸ **sales: increase profits**
- ▸ **accounts: ensure accurate, helpful billing and payment systems**
- ▸ **production: improve productivity**
- ▸ **PR: increase positive public awareness**
- ▸ **distribution: ensure fast, high-quality distribution at minimum cost**
- ▸ **marketing: build customer loyalty and attract new customers.**

You may work in one of these areas and feel the main thrust of your job is slightly different – that's fine. These are only examples. For instance, as a marketing executive

thinking fast

TAKING TIME TO MAKE TIME
Identifying your objective doesn't have to take long – five minutes at the most and probably less. But the whole process of clearing the work overload will be much faster in the long run if you just give this the time it needs.

thinking smart

WHAT WILL YOU LEAVE BEHIND?
If you're not entirely clear what your objective should be, try asking yourself this question: when you move on from this job, what single aspect of your company's performance do you hope to have improved? Customer satisfaction? Sales figures? Productivity? Costs? Public awareness? The answer to this will tell you what your objective is.

you might be employed primarily to focus on attracting new customers, while your sales team is charged with building loyalty.

If you really haven't a clue what your objective is, there is something amiss in your organization and I suspect that you are not the only one with a work overload. Your job description ought to be clear on the subject, or failing that your boss should be able to give you a straight answer.

You need this objective to be clear, because you cannot prioritize your workload without it, as we'll see later. Clearly, work that directly helps you achieve your objective is more important than all the other mountains of work that don't. And you cannot identify which tasks belong in this category until you know your objective. So, however rushed you are, this is an essential step.

for next time

Once you have cleared the overload, your objective remains important for helping you prioritize in future. But that's not all. The smart way to work is to block in time in your diary every week which is dedicated directly to achieving your objective. Aim for a couple of half days a week, and during these times do only work that will further that objective. Include time for coming up with new ideas too.

It is the people who manage to do this who really make successes of their jobs. They don't simply keep things ticking over; they actively make things happen. They are the ones who are noticed by top management, and who rise up the ladder fastest. So, if you're not already one of them, now's the time to start.

3 organizing the tasks

I know, I know, you just want to get on and *do* the work, not mess about organizing it first. But trust me; this really will help in the long run. Not only will you get through the pile of work faster, you will also do the work better. Honest.

There are two reasons for this stage:

- Psychologically, a lot of the problem with tackling a work overload is that your mind sees a huge nebulous collection of tasks – some written down, some stored on computer or voicemail, some running loose in your head – and it all seems impossible to cope with. But once you organize it, you have taken control of it, and you have reduced it to a form that your mind can comprehend. This somehow makes the whole job seem manageable, and gives you a huge positive boost.

- Once you have sorted out the work logically, you will be able to do it more efficiently. If you approach it haphazardly, you will keep losing your thread, and you will miss opportunities to streamline tasks. You might find, for example, that one of the pieces of paperwork on your desk postdates another, and makes it redundant. But if you get to the redundant one first you'll act on it anyway, and then find later that you wasted your time. So organizing the work will speed things up later on.

So how are you going to organize it? Start by getting everything down on paper – yes, paper; forget about computer screens because you need to move things around physically. Write down any tasks that currently exist only in your head. Write each on a fresh piece of paper, because they may end up in different piles. Print out any notes, e-mails or anything else that needs action. You will also need to write down any key diary dates in the next few days, especially those that clash.

SORTING INTO GROUPS

Now you need to start sorting out piles of paper. Don't worry – it won't take long. This is the point where you should start to relax because you are getting on with something: creating order out of chaos. So what are these piles of paper? Well, that depends on your work. You need to create one pile for each key job you have in hand. You'll probably find that at least some of the paperwork is already sorted – you may already have half a pile of notes and papers to do with next week's presentation which you haven't started on yet, and a file bulging with data for your budget which you're supposed to have drawn up.

thinking smart

MAKE ROOM

Clear physical space for this part of the process, so that you have plenty of room. If the work looks visually organized, your mind will be more organized. If you are working among a mass of papers and files on your desk, you will continue to feel disorganized mentally. So find a clear table, or even the floor, to amass your piles of paper on.

These are the kinds of categories you are sorting everything into. You should create a pile for each major project or task:

- ▶ **a pile of applications, job description and so on for a post you are trying to fill**
- ▶ **a bundle of papers and post-it notes for next month's exhibition**
- ▶ **a pile of letters to sign**
- ▶ **a file of data to go into a report you are writing**
- ▶ **a collection of phone calls you should be returning**
- ▶ **all the stuff to be filed**
- ▶ **a pile of reading material**

… and so on. You'll have to decide what the exact groups are, but that's the general idea.

SORTING THE LEFTOVERS

It may have occurred to you that you will probably have some items that don't fit into groups – they are one-off tasks, or perhaps just a couple of related tasks that don't really constitute a group. Or, of course, they may be rubbish: out-of-date figures, e-mails that have been superseded, and notes to call colleagues who left the company over a year ago (I'm sure your backlog doesn't really go back that far). So you need another two piles:

1 *Miscellaneous*: This is where you put everything that doesn't go anywhere else. However, this becomes in effect a pile of everything that hasn't been sorted properly, which isn't a particularly good thing. So try to keep it as small as possible. If it starts to expand, you may find that you can create fresh groups from it. Suppose you had put in this pile a reminder to deal with a member of your team whose timekeeping is poor, and an email from a colleague asking you to allocate three people to help staff the exhibition stand next week, and a request from one of your team members to move to another desk further from the coffee machine where there are fewer distractions. These could form the basis of a group of tasks related to personnel matters.

2 *Rubbish*: Feel free to throw anything away that you can. Bear in mind, though, that there will be another opportunity to throw things away later, so don't spend ages dithering about it here. If you're sure you can chuck it – great. But don't waste time thinking about it. Better to get on and organize your groups fairly fast for now.

 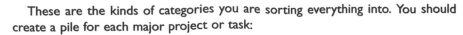 thinking fast

MORE RATHER THAN LESS

At this stage, you should go for more groups rather than fewer if you're in doubt. Maybe you are advertising two posts at the moment. Should all the stuff go in one pile or two? If you feel strongly about it, do what feels right. But if you're not sure, split it into two for now. Don't waste time agonizing over it. (You can always combine them later if you change your mind.)

thinking smart

POSITIVE PILE-UP

You can put your rubbish straight in the bin if you like. But if there's a lot of it, you may find it hugely encouraging to keep a pile for it so that you can see how much progress you're making. This is just the sort of positive boost that can make the whole operation more satisfying. And that, in turn, can help you to work through it faster.

thinking smart

Don't assume that everyone else maintains your high standard of organization. If someone says they'll call you back, make a note so that if they let you down you're still on the case. Otherwise it goes out of your head until, for example, two minutes before the meeting at which you need the information they were going to give you. The same goes for suppliers getting back to you with quotes and so on. Every week, when you clear your miscellaneous file, you'll catch up with these.

At the end of this process you should have, apart from your miscellaneous and rubbish piles, about half a dozen to a dozen key groups, and a few smaller ones. You've probably spent somewhere in the region of half an hour or so getting to this stage. And you should be starting to feel a whole lot better already.

KEEPING NOTES

If ever you find yourself with a serious overload again (as if!), it would be great to have a backlog that wasn't full of post-it notes and scraps of paper. The way around this is simple: carry a notebook with you and write down all your notes in it. These notes should include all those loose ideas and thoughts in your head – get them down on paper instead. If other people pass you post-its, you can stick them in the notebook.

As long as you don't leave the notebook on the train, you have everything in one place. And because it's portable, you have it with you all the time, so as a bonus you can take advantage of any spare five minutes when you're away from the office to catch up on some of the items in it.

for next time

It is more efficient to work on one project at a time, rather than to jump from one thing to another and back again. So, ideally, you need to keep a file for each project or logical group of tasks from the start. Each email or post-it note or piece of paper goes into the correct file from the offset. You can have a miscellaneous file too (commonly known as an in-tray), but allocate a certain amount of time each week to clearing it. How about doing it at 4.30 on a Friday afternoon, and you can go home as soon as the file is empty? It shouldn't take long.

4 prioritising

No, I'm sorry, it still isn't time to get on with your tasks. First, you have to know which ones to get on with. You're up against the clock, and you can't clear all the work instantly. Some will be scheduled for later. So you want to be sure that the work is tackled in the right order, the most important tasks are given the time they deserve, and nothing urgent is left till last. There are two aspects of prioritizing to address:

 importance

 urgency.

IMPORTANCE

This is where your objective is so useful. Simply take each group in turn and measure it against your original objective – increasing profits, raising customer satisfaction or whatever it is. Will this task help you directly to achieve your objective? Mark each group of tasks A, B or C, where A means that the task is central to your objective, and C means it is of little direct relevance.

Suppose you are an accounts manager: here are three groups of tasks to set against your objective – to ensure accurate, helpful billing and payment systems. You should be able to see which directly further it and which don't.

Remember: we are not concerned with urgency at the moment – that comes later. We are simply establishing importance at the moment. The presentation, for example, may not need preparing for a fortnight, but when the time comes it will be crucial.

A few people have more than one objective in their job. This is less common than you might think, because your objective is fairly broad and is generally very close to the objective of the department. Don't be tempted to think you have more than one objective when in fact both are part of the same overall objective. But perhaps your job spans two departments. Perhaps you work for both sales and marketing.

Group of tasks	Objective	Importance to objective
Prepare a presentation to persuade the board to invest in new invoicing software	Ensure accurate, helpful billing and payment systems	A
Plan move into larger office	Ensure accurate, helpful billing and payment systems	C
Plan selection of new accounts supervisor	Ensure accurate, helpful billing and payment systems	B

567

WHAT IF ...?

If you have trouble working out the importance of any group of tasks, try asking yourself what would happen if you simply didn't do it. What would be the effect on the organization? If it would mean a cut in profits, mounting costs or damaging PR for example, award it a grade A. If it would make little significant difference in the long term, give it a C.

In this case, any task that is vital to meeting *either* objective is an A-grade task. So you can prioritize in just the same way as you would with only one objective.

You should be starting to see how you were actually saving yourself time when you were sorting all those pieces of paperwork into groups. Instead of having to establish the importance of hundreds of tasks, you have only to deal with a dozen or so categories. All the tasks within each category fall into the same level of importance.

URGENCY

Urgent tasks are, obviously, those that must be done as soon as possible. When you prioritize you have to identify urgency separately from importance, otherwise you will become muddled. Some tasks merit only a C when measured against your objective, and yet you know you need to give them your attention, and soon.

So identify urgent groups of tasks as a separate issue. Arranging the move to a bigger office, for example, may be urgent even though it scored only a C. These urgent groups will be fed into the overall priority list, as we'll see in just a moment. However, they should not be allocated too much time (unless they are also important). These are the tasks to get out of the way first, that's all.

What if you have tasks on your list which you don't consider urgent but someone else does? For example, one of your colleagues can't finalize the details for the press launch until you decide the date of it. It's still a few weeks away and you're in no hurry, but your colleague is getting very edgy.

If the task is really quick, it's probably better just to list it as urgent and keep everyone happy. But it could be a long job. What then? In that case, be objective. Does your colleague have a valid point? How important is the press launch? How much does the precise date matter? Decide whether the task itself is urgent, not whether it is urgent to you or to somebody else.

YOUR PRIORITIES

You should now be able to put all your groups of tasks into order of priority. The first ones to tackle are the really urgent ones, even if they are not that important. (If they are both urgent and important, then they come right at the top of the list, of course.) Then come the remaining tasks in order of importance:

1 urgent and important
2 urgent
3 important (A)
4 important (B)
5 important (C).

thinking smart

WORD OF WARNING

It is very tempting to move the tasks you enjoy up your list, and put the tasks you don't want to do at the bottom of the list. Don't do it. Be brutally objective about ranking tasks, or you will end up back where you started before you know it – with unimportant jobs done and a pile of taks on your desk which are urgent and important and should have been done already. You've got to deal with it all sooner or later, so when it comes to your least favourite tasks, just bite the bullet.

Even the least important tasks will be dealt with in time, because they will eventually become urgent and thereby jump to the top of the list – that's if you haven't got round to doing them first (and if pigs have learnt to fly).

You presumably decided to read this book because you had a huge pile of things to do and you wanted to get rid of the backlog and make a fresh start with a clear desk. This book seemed to suggest, improbably, that you could do all these myriad tasks in as little as an hour if you only knew how.

But in fact – as may be becoming apparent – you don't have to *do* all of them now at all. You only have to do a few now, and either offload or defer the rest. The real exercise is in deciding which to tackle now, and how to handle the rest in a realistic timescale. There's a relief!

thinking fast

COLOUR CODING

Why not use three different colours of files for all your work, coded according to importance? This means you are constantly reminding yourself of where your priorities really lie, and it saves a lot of time whenever you come to prioritize your workload (even when it isn't piling up).

for next time

If you want to prevent overloads in future, one of the ways is to prioritise tasks as you go. Whenever a new project arises, or you start a new file, ascribe it a level of importance – A, B or C – by measuring it against your objective.

Each week, preferably on Monday morning, prioritise all your current files for the week. Not only will this remind you of which tasks are the key ones to focus on – perhaps that presentation is your main focus for this week – but it also means that the system will pick up any low-importance tasks that are becoming urgent.

When you schedule time for urgent tasks that are not important, don't allow more time than you have to. These are not tasks to hang around over – they need to be got out of the way as quickly as possible to make way for the important work.

5 the options

Now you know what order you need to work through your groups in, it is finally time to start doing it. Well, almost. First, you need to go through the tasks in each group and sort them into four categories. The point of this is to identify the tasks that you absolutely have to deal with now, and find an alternative way of coping with all the rest of them. This is where you really start to slim down your immediate workload so that it becomes manageable. This is time well spent, however little you have.

There are only four things you can do with each task:

- **dump it**
- **delegate it**
- **defer it**
- **do it.**

Which option to choose?

As you go through each of your groups, you can sort everything in it into one of these four categories. We'll look at delegating and deferring in more detail later in this chapter, and in the next chapter at doing the tasks you can't sensibly offload. But here is what you need to know to sort the groups:

Dump it. You've already had one quick dumping session, but now's the time to be brutal. Look, you've got a huge overload of work here, and you simply can't afford to be dealing with things that you don't need to, or even finding space for them on your desk. So, if in doubt, just dump it. Suppose you dump fifty things, ten of which you're not quite sure about. What are the odds on regretting it? Maybe one of the ten will rebound – so what? You can always ask for another copy of an invoice, or look up a phone number you thought you'd finished with. Better just to dump the lot now and take the minor consequences later. They probably won't happen at all.

Delegate it. Delegating is a skilled task (don't worry, you'll have learnt it by the end of this chapter). For the moment, you just need to know which tasks to delegate – we'll look at how to delegate them later. And the answer is very easy – does it have to be you who does this task? If not, pass it on to someone else, whether it is urgent or not. There's just one proviso: some tasks take longer to

 thinking smart

SAVE IT FOR LATER
Don't be tempted to address the most important tasks now simply because they are important. If they are not urgent, they can still be deferred. It will give you more time to do them justice.

explain than to do yourself. With proper delegation (as we'll see), this isn't generally an issue, but when you're racing to clear your desk as fast as possible, a few quick tasks might be better off in your 'do it' pile than in your 'delegate it' pile.

Defer it. Again, we'll look at how to handle these tasks later. But essentially, if a job needs to be done by you but it isn't urgent, you can do it later. Pretty obvious really. The only thing is that there's no point deferring ten days' work to be done by the end of next week, on to the top of next week's workload, or you'll find yourself going through exactly this process again next Friday.

Do it. Everything that can't be dumped, delegated or deferred will have to be done. However, by the time you've reached the end of this sort-out, your 'do it' pile should be looking refreshingly small compared to the mountain you started out with an hour or so ago.

SCHEDULE YOUR TIME

You'll need to do a quick sort-through of all your groups – or at least all but the very low-priority ones – before you go any further. In theory, you might think that you could do each group as you get to it. However, it is very hard to plan your time if you do this. Suppose you have four hours left to clear this backlog. How long can you spend on the first group? That rather depends on how much else you have to fit into the time, doesn't it? And that is determined by how many of the tasks in the other groups you are going to have to do today. So you'll have to do a basic sort-through of your key groups so that you can allocate your time appropriately.

Once you have been through your groups, and can see which contain the most time-consuming tasks that you are going to have to do now, plan out your time before you begin. Take into account both the estimated amount of work in the group and its importance. Work through the groups in order of the priority you have established. That way, if anything goes horribly wrong and your time is cut short, at least the most crucial tasks will have been done.

Here are a few guidelines to help you set a schedule after you've sorted everything into the four categories:

1 Do all your urgent delegating first (following the delegating principles we'll be looking at in a moment).
2 Separate out the tasks you can delegate later when your poor minions have got over the shock of the pile of work you've just given them.
3 Schedule your most urgent tasks next, but unless they are also important don't spend much time on them.
4 You may find you need to do one or two urgent tasks from a group first, before you get to the rest of the group. This is fine – tackle whole groups at a time otherwise, but obviously urgent tasks must be handled first. Maybe the pile relating to Friday's presentation can wait, but you may need to phone your supplier to talk about prices urgently to give them time to work out costs and get back to you later.
5 Look at the number of groups to deal with, and the amount of time, and schedule according to the average time per group. So, if you have four hours and eight groups, you should average half an hour per group.

Every task can be dumped, delegated, deferred or done

GIVE IT TIME

The earlier in the process you identify urgent tasks that you can delegate, the earlier you can set them in motion. It's no good giving someone a pile of tasks at 4.30 in the afternoon and asking them to have them done by 5.30. Better to have handed them over straight after lunch. And if you don't find the task until 8.30 in the evening, it will be almost impossible to delegate it for completion before tomorrow morning. You'll end up having to do it yourself. So identify early on those urgent tasks that you can delegate, and get the ball rolling.

6 Now you can do a few quick trade-offs. Suppose you want more time to work on next week's exhibition – up its allocation to an hour, and give two minor groups fifteen minutes each instead. Keep trading off like this until you are happy with the balance. This should be a quick process, but then I doubt you'll feel inclined to spend all afternoon on it.

7 Whatever schedule you draw up, *stick to it*. If you get ahead, that's fine. But don't let yourself slip behind. Keep checking the clock to make sure you are on course.

Scheduling your time may look like a huge job, but it isn't really. It should take you five minutes at the most, and you'll have a game plan to last you the rest of the day (or evening, or whatever it is you have).

thinking smart

INVESTING NOT WASTING

Drawing up schedules may not seem like a clever use of time. You are doubtless itching to get on with all those piles of tasks by now. But it is the only way to make sure you don't reach the end of your time before you reach the end of the workload. One of the first things we tend to do when we are rushing is to stop thinking. But by thinking *smart* – setting an objective, drawing up a schedule and so on – we are investing a few minutes now to save a load of time later. Trust me.

for next time

Learn to recognize the tasks, e-mails and post-it notes that will end up being dumped, and don't keep them in the first place. Delete e-mail messages after you've opened them whenever you can – without printing them out. Reassure yourself with the thought that you can always get them back if you have to. Just don't send them to the recycle bin. If you have a note with a phone number on, either bin it or enter it in your phone book, but don't keep it lying around.

Equally, delegate what you can even when you think you aren't overloaded. There are always more important things to free up time for – planning, developing ideas and so on. The earlier you delegate a task, the fairer you are being on the person you delegate it to, and the better chance they have of doing it well.

6 delegating

If you have staff you are authorized to delegate to, and you have a work overload, you are almost certainly not delegating as effectively as you could. In fact, delegation is a core management skill and the mark of a good team leader. Once you have learnt to delegate well, you are much less likely to build up a work overload in the first place (or at least it will happen a lot less often). The pace of the modern business world is so fast that unless you delegate whatever you can you are bound to be swamped quickly by your workload.

UNDERSTANDING DELEGATION

Delegation is often misunderstood. It is not just a case of offloading simple tasks which you haven't time for yourself (or don't enjoy). That is simply allocation of tasks and has no long-term value. Delegation, on the other hand, not only creates more time for you to get on with the important job of managing your team, but it also helps to develop your team members' skills, to make the team as a whole more effective – to your credit and theirs.

So, the whole business of delegating means delegating responsibility for tasks. Give your team member a target, with specified time, cost and quality constraints, and let them decide how to achieve it. That way they learn more, they get the boost of achieving a positive result, and they take some of your workload from you. You retain overall accountability, of course. If anything goes wrong, you carry the can – but then half the skill is in delegating well so that nothing does go wrong, as we'll see.

Many people fear that by delegating part of their workload they will lose control. But think about what you lose control of: the details and minutiae that occupy too much of your time; the phone calls and research and e-mails and paperwork. You are still in overall control of the tasks you delegate. And you have made time to stand back and look at the big picture. You can see opportunities to grasp, spot threats in time to stave them off, and develop ideas to boost your team's achievements and impress your boss.

thinking smart

PASS IT ON
Don't assume, simply because your boss has delegated a task to you, that you can't delegate it yourself. After all, you are still accountable for it and taking overall responsibility. So long as your boss gets the same result, what does it matter who performs the task?

thinking smart

WHEN YOU'RE NOT THERE...
Ask yourself this question: 'If I were away ill or on business for a month, which tasks simply couldn't be done?' There should be almost none. Everything else not on this list can be delegated.

DELEGATION SKILLS

When you're clearing the backlog and you're up against the clock, you may well end up delegating the odd boring but necessary task just to get it done fast. But not everything on your desk is urgent, and you should be able to apply the principles of delegation properly to most of them. So here are the key steps to delegating successfully:

1 Review the task and set the objective. Here we go, setting objectives again. Have you noticed how setting the objective is the first step in almost all management skills? That's because if you don't know where you're going, your chances of arriving there are seriously hampered. An objective is a destination: once you know it you can plan your route, estimate the time you will take, identify whether any alternatives or shortcuts will be helpful or not, and know when you have reached the end of the journey.

So start by identifying the task and setting an objective for it. Bundle together groups of tasks with the same objective. So if you need some research done for your proposal, get one person to do it all – costings, performance data, packaging options, competitor comparisons and all the rest. The objective is to find the data that will support your proposal and make it more convincing.

2 Decide who to delegate it to. Not every task suits every person. When time is not an issue, try to stretch people with the tasks you delegate to them. They will find it more rewarding. Even crucial tasks can go to someone skilled and capable but without experience of that particular task. That way you are continuously building the experience and capability of your whole team.

At the same time, there's no point giving someone a task that simply doesn't suit them and wastes their talents. If you want someone to do your research, find someone who is quite methodical and good with people if they need to coax information about competitors out of suppliers, or to persuade someone busy to spend time tracking down data. Don't delegate the tasks to a brash ideas person who is great at getting things started but then wants to move straight on to the next task without seeing the thing through.

3 Set parameters. You're giving the person you delegate this task to an objective. They need to know what they are supposed to achieve and why. But they will need more than just this. They will want to know how long they've got, what authority they have (to ask for input from other people, for example) and so on. So you need to provide:

WHEN YOU'RE PUSHED FOR TIME, GO FOR EXPERIENCE

If you're in a hurry, it's a good idea to delegate to someone who will already know how to do the task with relatively little support from you. When you have time, however, try finding someone who will be more stretched by it, and who will learn from it. Once you've trained them up, they will be encouraged and you will have one more skilled person to delegate to next time.

- objective
- deadline
- quality standards
- budget
- limits of authority
- details of any resources available.

You are not, however, telling them how to do the job. You are telling them everything they need to give you the results you want — including when you want them, at what cost and so on. But how they get there is up to them. To return to the analogy of the objective as a destination, they are free to plan their own route so long as they arrive on time, having consumed an acceptable amount of fuel and not crashed the car. By all means ask them to outline their route to you, but don't make them change it to suit you. If you can see a problem they haven't anticipated, point it out and let *them* find the solution.

4 Check they understand. Encourage them to talk to you about the task, so you can make sure they understand exactly what is required and why. You can suggest ideas, so long as you are not railroading them into adopting your approach.

5 Give them back-up. Help all you can. Clear the way with another department head for them to get support from their team; tell them where to find information that you know about and they don't; give them access to any useful documents; let them have a draft copy of the proposal that their research will go into (I take it you generally write a draft well in advance?)

6 Monitor their progress. Schedule feedback sessions for a major, long-term project. Even for a brief task, check how it's going — frequent, informal feedback often works better than a formal session. This gives them a chance to check with you that they are on course, that they aren't wasting their time on too much detail, or missing a key angle. It boosts their confidence in the job they are doing, and reassures you that everything is on track.

Monitoring, however, does not mean interfering. Look out for any sign that they have made an error and not noticed it, but don't fuss about trivial mistakes. These are almost inevitable, and you'd probably have made equivalent mistakes if you'd done the task yourself. You should intervene only if serious mistakes threaten, and then only for as long as it takes to get the job back on course. Taking a task away from someone is deeply demoralizing and should be done only in extreme circumstances. If you delegate well from the start it should never be necessary.

 thinking smart

DOUBLING UP

If the task is a major project, or even if it is relatively small but time is tight, you can always delegate it to more than one person. Generally, the best approach is to appoint a task leader, and brief everyone at the same time so they all know what's needed.

KEEPING TABS

Just because you're up against the clock, it doesn't mean you can't monitor progress. After all, you still need to be sure that the task gets done properly. If you've delegated an urgent task to be done by the end of the day, you can still call or pop your head round the door half way through the afternoon to check that it's going OK.

7 Evaluate their performance. After the task is completed, sit down with the team member involved and evaluate what they have done. Give praise and recognition where it is deserved, and even if the results were disappointing find aspects of their performance to praise. Make sure that they – and you – have learnt any lessons you need to from the exercise. And remember that the ultimate responsibility for failure, as well as for success, lies with you.

Those are the basic principles of delegation, so now do it, at least as far as you can under your current time constraints. Before you move on to deal with the rest of your workload, go and delegate anything that is really urgent and has to be done in the next 24 hours.

Now set aside all the rest of your work to delegate (still grouped in order of priority), so that you can delegate it later and give it the time to think it through properly according to the principles we've just looked at. There. That should be quite a large chunk of your backlog taken care of.

So don't view delegation as a way of offloading jobs you don't like or don't have time for. It is actually a key opportunity for you to exercise your skill as a manager in developing your team.

GET AHEAD

If you delegate work well in advance of when you need it completed, you can set a deadline that gives you plenty of leeway for building it into a subsequent project of your own. So, for example, you can get the research for your proposal completed and delivered to you ten days before you have to write the thing – giving you plenty of time to incorporate it into your own work.

for next time

Identify tasks for delegating as soon as they arrive on your desk, or as soon as you generate the work. This gives the maximum time to get ahead of yourself, and for the person to whom you delegate the work to get it done.

The aim is to build the skills of your whole team continuously, so always think hard about the best person to delegate each task to. Up against the clock, you just want to give the job to someone you know who can be left alone to get on with it. But, in the long term, this doesn't stretch or challenge anyone. The better you are at delegating, the better your team will become at performing delegated tasks, and the easier it will be for you to delegate future tasks. And your team members will feel motivated, confident and appreciated, which can only benefit their performance.

7 deferring tasks

Deferring might seem, at first glance, to be a bad idea. After all, it's just another word for putting things off, isn't it? And isn't that why you got into this mess in the first place? Too much work and too little time, so you've been putting things off until there's such a backlog that you can't find your desk under the heap of papers and notes.

Well, yes and no. Deferring is a sort of structured, organized putting things off, which makes a big difference. It means putting things off until there's time to do them – and making that time if necessary – rather than simply putting them off and then *not* doing them.

Let's just recap where we've got to, so you can see how much you've achieved already:

- You've found time to read this book, and at least a few more hours for actually doing the job – clearing your work overload.
- You've identified your core objective.
- You've got all your tasks down on paper, and organized them into groups.
- You've set the groups in order of priority according to both urgency and importance, by measuring them against your objective.
- You've sorted the contents of each group into four categories: tasks to dump, delegate, defer or do.
- You've scheduled your remaining time (check now to see how you're doing).
- You're dumping everything you can as you work through each group.
- You're also delegating whatever you don't need to do yourself – or setting it aside to delegate later if it isn't urgent.

You should by now be looking at a much smaller pile of work; and instead of being chaotic, it should now be neatly ordered. I hope you're starting to feel smug. All the remaining tasks as you sort through each group are ones that you need to do yourself – no more dumping or passing on. However, you still have two categories remaining: tasks to defer and tasks to do today. We'll start by finding out how to defer tasks effectively, and the next chapter will tackle tasks you have to do now.

Deferring tasks isn't about putting them in a pending pile: it's about allocating a specific time to do them. When life travels at the rate of an express train, almost any task that isn't scheduled will end up cluttering up your desk or your brain until an impending deadline impels you into last-minute action. So the answer is to schedule everything. Yes, everything.

In the long term, the key to keeping on top of the workload is to put everything in your diary, so we'll look at that in a moment. But right now, you're probably not interested in the long term. You just want to finish clearing this pile of work.

So look at the groups you have left. Look at your diary for the next couple of weeks. Now schedule in the tasks in order of priority, blocking out time in your diary. So you

SCHEDULE THE SCHEDULE

If you're really short of time now, just schedule in one block of time in the next couple of days to spend on planning your diary. That way, you can defer not only the tasks but the scheduling of them as well. You presumably don't need me to tell you that if you don't do your scheduling at the time you've allocated, you'll just end up back here again all too soon.

might block out half a day to plan your proposal, and another day the following week to write it. You might schedule a couple of hours to catch up on non-urgent phone calls. Perhaps you need to block in time to plan your budget or hold appraisals. And, of course, you'll need some time to delegate all the tasks in your non-urgent delegation pile.

I've already suggested allocating the last hour of a Friday afternoon to deal with miscellaneous tasks (if you had time to read that bit). So remember you can allow time for general tasks such as correspondence as well as for major projects. You will still need to keep your objective in mind here, and be sure you give each group of tasks the time it deserves. Schedule everything – even if it needs only five minutes – otherwise it's not going to get done.

You need to make sure of two things to make this deferring business work.

1 **Be realistic.** There's no point scheduling time that it isn't possible to find. You'll just be demoralized, the work won't get done, and instead of being overworked you'll be overworked *and* miserable. So, reckon to work as fast and as smart as you can, but don't expect yourself to work miracles, creating 30 hours in every day, or waving a wand so that your boss's interminable Monday morning meeting lasts only ten minutes. If you know it never finishes before 11 a.m., don't schedule anything else before then (unless you can get away with doing it during the meeting).

2 **Be firm.** If you don't adhere to the schedule you have set yourself, then the whole exercise will be a waste of time. Once you start to slip, you will become demotivated and slip further. So be really strict with yourself. If your working life is punctuated regularly with emergency calls that may have to interrupt your scheduled tasks, allow for this. Build catching-up time into your schedule.

And how do you know exactly what you have to do? Most of it should be in your diary already. Planning your diary means turning it from an occasional reference book into an indispensible interactive guide. Your diary should be a key tool for doing your job, and you should be making regular notes in it. Have a big desk diary if you can't write small enough for a pocket one. Every time someone says 'Call me next Tuesday,' down

DON'T GO HOME

Make a rule that you won't go home until you have completed that day's tasks. So if you don't stick to your schedule, you pay for it in the evening. You'll soon learn to schedule realistically, and in the meantime the work will still get done. The idea is not to keep staying late, but to make sure you never need to.

thinking smart

CANCEL WHAT YOU CAN

Regular meetings eat into your time in a big way. What's more, they can end up occupying a part of almost every day, so that you can never free up a whole day without several weeks' notice. So, see if you can reduce the number of regular meetings. For example:

- ▶ Could you make your weekly meetings fortnightly or even monthly?
- ▶ Could a conference call replace some meetings and occupy less time?
- ▶ Could fewer people attend? (This always speeds things up.)
- ▶ Can you excuse yourself from other people's regular meetings?

thinking smart

EARLY BIRD

It's a good idea to give yourself half an hour at the start of each day for planning the day's workload and dealing with any quick but urgent tasks – signing a couple of letters, returning a phone call from yesterday, checking a team member is coping with a task you delegated, answering urgent correspondence and so on. So if you start work at, say, 9 a.m., don't schedule any appointments before 9.30. This works better than leaving time at the end of the day, which often tends to be taken over by the afternoon's activities.

it should go in your diary entry for next Tuesday. Not on a post-it note that could get lost. And add a phone number if you have it to hand, to save looking it up again next week. So your to-do list should be half-written before you ever get there.

You should also note down in your diary when you are expecting call-backs, e-mails or answers from other people. Otherwise, if you leave the ball in their court and they let you down, the task is under no one's control. So, whenever someone says 'I'll get back to you by the end of the week,' make a note in the diary for Friday to check they have done so.

You can prioritize the tasks on your to-do list so that you do the most urgent ones first. Then, if a crisis happens, you've only got to delay the less urgent tasks. If they are of equal urgency, do the most important first (back to your objective again). You can prioritize in any way that suits you. For example:

- ▶ **mark the highest-priority tasks A, the next batch B, and the lowest-priority tasks C (three categories should be plenty);**
- ▶ **colour-code tasks according to priority using highlighter pens (again, three colours should do fine);**
- ▶ **list the tasks in order of priority so you simply work your way down the list.**

So, deferring tasks isn't the same thing as putting them off. It is the way to create time so that all your tasks get done efficiently and at the best time. And you never again have to deal with a work overload like this one.

WORKING JOURNEY

Why not plan your day on the way to work? If you travel by train or are driven, you can write out your to-do list and your phone calls as you go. If you drive yourself, you can think it through in your head – or talk it into a dictaphone – and simply jot it all down when you arrive.

◀◀ for next time

Diary planning is a crucial skill for staying on top of the work and – just as importantly – for making sure that you invest the bulk of your time in the really important tasks: those that further your core objective.

As soon as you get the chance (and you can schedule this in your diary now), you should take time to plan your diary for the rest of the year. No, that's not a printing error – I meant year. You should sit down once a year and plan key dates into your diary. Obviously you can't schedule everything that far in advance, so you'll also need to have a planning session at the start of each month. Then there's the weekly diary session too, and your daily planning, of course.

You may be thinking that you bought this book to pick up some fast tips on how to clear a hectic backlog of work. And suddenly you're being lectured to by some time-obsessed, crazed lunatic with a fascist desire to plan every last second of your day to the point where there's no time left to do any of the actual work.

But actually, this is a perfectly normal, sane approach to organizing your time (of course, I would say that). No, really. The point is that once you've got into the swing of planning it takes very little time. But it ensures that you are in control of your time and your actions. In particular, it ensures that you can spend time on the things that really matter; tasks that help you achieve your objective.

By the end of the planning process, every single task should have time scheduled for it. It may simply be part of 'miscellaneous' or 'correspondence', but there will be a window of time set aside for dealing with it. If there isn't, it won't get done. So let's go through the whole process.

YEARLY PLANNING

At the start of the year, spend half an hour or so entering in all the dates you already know about for the rest of the year:

- ▶ regular meetings
- ▶ special events (exhibitions or conferences, for example)
- ▶ regular events (such as a weekly pub lunch with the team, or an hour on a Friday afternoon to deal with miscellaneous tasks)
- ▶ holidays
- ▶ personal time (days you want to leave early for the kids' birthdays or your best friend's wedding).

You'll also need to set aside about fifteen minutes diary-planning time at the start of each month. Then also set aside whole days throughout the year for working on proactive tasks that will really produce results. This is when you will develop ideas and plan new projects geared to boosting your company's performance. This might be a strategic planning session with your team, preparing your annual budget, or working on a proposal for a new system to improve your department's productivity. This is what you are here for and this time is essential for the organization, and for you to shine in your own career. Start by setting aside at least a full day a month, but increase this if you feel you can.

Obviously, throughout the year, you will add in key meetings, customer appointments, presentations and so on, as dates are set for them.

MONTHLY PLANNING

This is your chance to schedule in all your key tasks for the month which you didn't know about when you did your yearly planning. In fact, we're talking about the type of tasks you are currently trying to schedule in. If you plan them at the start of the month, it's much easier to fit them all in with time to spare for routine tasks and things that crop up later. These might include:

- ▶ selection or appraisal interviews
- ▶ visits to customers or suppliers
- ▶ presentations, including preparation time
- ▶ time to prepare for reports and proposals
- ▶ time to delegate key tasks.

Your monthly planning sessions have another function too. They give you a chance to review your workload over the month. Not only does this give you an overview of your short-term priorities, but it also gives you a chance to check how much 'free' time you have left. You know how time gets filled with routine tasks, urgent problems, other people's demands on you, last-minute meetings and all the rest of it. So check you have plenty of time still available. If not:

- ▶ See if you can cancel or absent yourself from any meetings.
- ▶ Delegate any tasks you have scheduled for yourself.
- ▶ Reorganize your diary so it is more streamlined – reschedule those two meetings at the Hull office for the same day, or put two half-day planning sessions into the diary for the same day, freeing up a whole day elsewhere.

Whatever you do, though, do not be tempted to cancel or squeeze down any time allocated for key tasks, unless they can be delegated effectively. These are your raison d'être. The problem is, they are often the tasks it is logistically easiest to move or cancel. So never lose sight of your objective. The most successful managers are the ones who understand that these tasks are their absolute top priorities.

WEEKLY PLANNING

This is where you plan in all those other tasks that have to be done sometime. It should only take five minutes each Monday morning. You need to set aside time during the week for:

- ▶ delegating and monitoring delegated tasks
- ▶ dealing with correspondence and e-mails
- ▶ catching up with phone calls
- ▶ dealing with miscellaneous tasks
- ▶ being available on the phone (an assistant can put off callers during busy periods by saying that you will definitely be free to answer their calls on Wednesday afternoon, for example)
- ▶ being available face-to-face (a permanent open-door policy is a licence to interrupt you; better to schedule time when your staff and colleagues know you will be available so they don't need to bother you otherwise unless it's really urgent).

You might want to schedule some of these more than once in the week. Rather than being available on the phone or face-to-face for an hour once a week, it might be better to have two half-hour sessions so nobody has to wait more than a couple of days to pin you down. Or be available for the last fifteen minutes of every day.

DAILY PLANNING

At the start of each day, decide how you will allocate any spare time (yes, with this system you may actually have spare time – well, at the planning stage anyway). You should aim to have a walkabout every day (OK, you won't always succeed, but if you don't try you'll never succeed) among your staff so that you are in touch with them, and seen to be in touch (known as managing by walking about). You'll also have urgent tasks to deal with from writing up a brief report to making phone calls and dealing with problems. So decide when you'll do these.

Start the day by drawing up a 'to-do' list. This lists all the things you are going to fit in between your scheduled tasks, meetings and so on. You may find it helps to list phone calls separately; it is much more efficient to do them all at once if you can. So your list might read:

Phone
John Surrey, BTC (8812 6543)
Mike re report
Liz Kennedy
Robin South, Plimley Bros (01234 987654)

To do
Check up on Hedges account
Check Meg re proposal research
Prices from Onyx
Review schedule for exhibition
E-mail Paul re exhibition stand

---

8 do it

As you work through your groups in order of priority – according to your schedule – you are dumping, delegating or deferring everything you can. However, there will still be some tasks left over in most groups: those you have to do now, or almost now (in other words, too soon to defer). These might include phone calls and e-mails, documents to read, decisions to make, papers to approve, cheques to sign, and operational or personnel problems to solve. A mishmash of easy and difficult, quick and time-consuming tasks.

Essentially, you simply have to work through these as fast and effectively as you can, having cleared any potential interruptions out of the way. However, there are a couple of tips to help speed up the process:

▶ **Some kinds of brief tasks will keep cropping up throughout the groups. For example, there will probably be several e-mails to send, or several phone calls to make. It is usually much more efficient to do all these related tasks at the same time, so save them all up and have a blitz on e-mails when you get to the end of the groups, or sign off all the invoices at once. Of course, a few may need doing earlier – some other tasks may depend on the outcome of a particular phone call perhaps – but use your common sense and group together what you can.**

▶ **If any task in a group is dependent on any other, pick this up swiftly and make sure the primary task gets done first. If it takes time – maybe you need to get someone to call you back with a piece of information – get the ball rolling promptly.**

MAKING LISTS

You may well find that you need to make lists of things to do as you go through your workload. If you are working in your office, obviously you can't do, here and now, any tasks that require you to be on the shop floor – updating yourself on equipment problems, or talking to the production manager face-to-face – or at another branch, or down at the shops looking through your competitors' products.

Likewise, if you are working from home, you don't necessarily have access to everything you need, and may need a list of things to do as soon as you get back to the office. Or you might be working in the evening, and can't do anything that requires you to get hold of other people before tomorrow. You will also be saving up lists of phone calls, e-mails and so on to do together at the end of your clear-out session.

thinking smart

KEEP IN TOUCH
Making responses to people can sometimes be staved off if you're pushed for time by simply acknowledging their call, letter or e-mail. Send them a note or an e-mail that says 'Thanks for your letter/e-mail/call. I am giving it some thought and will get back to you in the next few days.' Make sure you do get back to them, of course, but you've bought yourself two or three days' grace.

DON'T GET CAUGHT

Sometimes you need to call someone who you know is likely to trap you on the phone. If you are one of those people who is under-assertive about extricating yourself, call when you're pretty sure they will be out and leave a voicemail message instead.

Anything you delay for more than a few hours should go into your diary, as we've seen. But there's no point writing every phone call in tomorrow morning's diary when you could simply write 'work through phone calls' and then make a separate list as you go along.

All the tasks to go on the list should already be written down somewhere in the relevant pile of papers, so your list might consist of a pile of notes and papers. But many people find their minds are clearer when their work is looking neater. If this is you, you may be happier composing a single list, and attaching to it any relevant papers to which you may need to refer.

Some people dread the look of a long list – it seems like such a lot to get through. If you need a psychological boost, put the following things at the top of your list:

- ▶ **something you will enjoy doing**
- ▶ **something that will be really quick**
- ▶ **a task you have already done.**

If you tick off each job as you do it, you'll find that almost instantly you'll have these first three items ticked. That will make you feel you're really cracking on.

MAKING DECISIONS

Most of the tasks you have to do will not necessarily be difficult; it's just a matter of getting around to them – as you now have. But the one category of tasks that most managers have piled up on their desks when time is getting the better of them is anything that requires a decision. The companion volume to this, *Fast Thinking: Decisions*, will help you to prevent this kind of pile-up. But in the meantime, here's a flash guide to making decisions fast.

Your current aim is to clear your work backlog. Now is not the time to make major decisions such as who to sack, or whether to switch to outsourcing your entire accounts function. If any decision of this magnitude needs to be made (and you're unlikely to be making it alone), schedule some time to do it later. At the moment we're concerned with more everyday – if important – decisions such as:

- ▶ **What level of raise should we give to a member of staff?**
- ▶ **Which model of van should we switch to as our fleet vehicle?**
- ▶ **Which of the applicants should we offer the telephone sales assistant job to?**
- ▶ **Should we go ahead with the plan to extend the car parking area?**
- ▶ **Should I accept a subordinate's proposal?**

These are the kind of decisions that can pile up on your desk ... until now. Of course, you don't only want to make these decisions fast, you also want to make them right. The ability to make good decisions fast is one of the cornerstones of success for managers. So what are the techniques for achieving it?

Many decisions are so easy that you barely notice you're making them: what time will you hold this meeting? Who will you delegate this task to? Others are straightforward because the answer is clear: there may have been only one really good applicant for the job, so there's no need to agonize over who to offer it to. But these, of course, are not the decisions you have been putting off.

Here are the key considerations to help you make any tricky decision you find lying in wait among your pile of papers:

- **Should you be making this decision?** Sometimes we put off decisions because we know deep down that someone else should be making them, or that the whole premise of the decision is wrong. For example, how can you choose which proposal to accept for designing the launch of a new product when you have serious doubts about whether the product should be launched at all? We may not want to take the decision because we know that we don't really have enough information to judge it. So remedy the problem – pass the decision on, instigate discussion about your reservations regarding the new product, ask for more information before you make the decision.

- **What is your objective?** Objective setting *again*? Yep, 'fraid so. Determine the core aim of taking this decision – what you intend to achieve by it. For example, your objective might be to pay your staff an affordable salary that reflects the value of the job they do and motivates them to do even better. Or it might be to ensure ample parking for staff and visitors within a certain budget. You cannot know what the right decision is if you don't know what you are aiming to achieve.

- **Collect all the data you can.** As I've already mentioned, you may need to collect more information. When the time comes to make the decision, make sure you are not missing relevant data. If you don't know what your staff member's performance has been like over the past few months, how can you meet your objective of ensuring that their salary reflects the value of the job they do?

- **Don't make a decision you can't implement.** Rule out all options that can't be achieved. There's no point deciding to extend the car park if there's nowhere for it to go without huge landscaping works, which will mean spending a fortune you haven't got in the budget.

- **Listen to your intuition.** Many people mock intuition, and others simply don't trust it. Generally it is not wise to make a decision on instinct alone, but if you have all the data and it doesn't point to a clear answer, intuition will often tell you which way to go. So listen to it as you would to an experienced advisor.

- **Don't force a decision unnecessarily.** Just because you have this load of work to clear off your desk, it isn't necessarily wise to make every decision now. If things aren't going to change, and no new data will turn up, you'll be no nearer to a decision in a month than you are now. But if the decision isn't urgent and you feel that more time will help in some way – if only so that you can sleep on it and clear your head – there's no point taking the decision just because it's there.

thinking smart

ASK ADVICE IF IT WILL HELP

Why not call someone else up? Others may have been through a similar decision-making process before, or may have more experience in this area than you. You don't have to take their advice, but you can feed it into the system.

thinking fast

TOSS A COIN

If there's really nothing to choose between two options, why not simply toss a coin? If you've looked at all the arguments and there's that little between them, it probably doesn't matter which decision you make – so just make one.

▶ **When you have to make a decision, do it.** If a decision needs to be taken now (if not last week), you *must* learn to do it. You may never have every last piece of information to guarantee a perfect decision, but speed is important too. A correct decision taken too slowly may be worse than a less perfect decision taken promptly. One of the biggest bars to successful decision-making is the temptation to weigh up all the pros and cons endlessly. But the dynamic manager must learn to say 'Enough!' Better to make an adequate decision than none at all. Sometimes every option has its drawbacks, but you still have to pick one of them.

▶ **Be committed to your decision.** Once you have made your decision, you must stick to it. And that includes being seen to stick to it. When your staff member rails against your decision not to give them the raise they wanted, don't waver. If that was the right decision you can be sympathetic, but don't allow yourself to be swayed.

▶ **Be prepared to sell your decision to other people.** The right decisions are not always the most popular ones. So be ready to persuade other people that even if it's not what they want, this is the right decision. They may have wanted better car parking or a different model of fleet vehicle, but be ready to explain why this is the best course.

Following these guidelines you should find it simple to make those decisions that are cluttering up your work pile. And in the process you'll be exercising a vital management skill.

READING

One of the real stomach-sinking ingredients of most piles of work is material that needs to be read. Those thick wodges of reports, proposals, research documents, publications, minutes of meetings you didn't attend, and all the rest of it. How on earth are you going to wade through all that in the few short hours you have? You're not – face it.

Do you imagine that every other manager, including your boss and your board of directors, doesn't have exactly the same problem? Of course they do. So what's their solution? There are two options. One of them – in the long term – is to learn speed reading. You haven't really got time to do that today, but I thoroughly recommend it if you regularly have a lot of material to read. (You'll find a fast thinker's guide to speed reading in the companion volume to this one, *Fast Thinking: Finding Facts*.)

The second option is to read only what you have to. You don't have to read every word of every document sitting in your in-tray, so don't feel you must. Here are a few tips for minimizing your reading:

thinking smart

BEDTIME READING

You obviously have to do some reading, even if you don't have to read everything that lands on your desk. So schedule some reading time into your diary each week for catching up.

thinking smart

THE ONE-PAGE RULE

Make it a rule among everyone who works for you that every report, proposal or other document must have a summary attached which is no longer than a single side of A4 paper. No memo or internal e-mail should exceed this length either.

- (▶) Just because someone gives you something to read, you don't automatically have to read it. *You* decide whether it warrants your attention. Measure it against your core objective – will reading this really help you to achieve it?

- (▶) Read the contents page and introduction to a book first and you may find it tells you all you need (or that you don't need to read it at all).

- (▶) Ask other people to read articles or documents for you, and give you a brief verbal or written report on them. They can highlight or clip any short passages they feel you should read.

- (▶) Many books, reports, proposals and so on have short summaries or chapter summaries. This is often all you need to read.

- (▶) If there is no summary, a well-written document often has a summarizing final paragraph to each section at least. Try reading only the first and last paragraphs of each section. This should give you enough information to see which sections you need to read more thoroughly and which you can skip with impunity.

- (▶) If you subscribe to trade publications or papers, just identify the top two or three most relevant articles. Read these, and throw the rest away.

You've done well to get this far, and the only challenge left is to avoid finding yourself in this situation again. Follow the 'For next time' guidelines in this book and you should find that when it comes to work overload, there isn't a next time.

for next time

In theory, you should never accumulate a pile of things to do in the first place (business theories are great, aren't they … when you want a laugh). But seriously, this one can work with a little practice and a lot of discipline. The idea is that we all push the same pieces of paper around our desks for days or even weeks before we finally deal with them (all right then, for months sometimes).

The solution is to have a firm rule that the moment a piece of paper reaches us, we deal with it and then get it off the desk. And there are only four options for dealing with it.

1 **Bin it.** You know all those papers you've just sorted out and dumped? How many of them could just as well have been dumped the minute they arrived on your desk all those weeks ago? Learning to identify rubbish at first glance is the smart thinker's approach.

2 **File it.** We've talked about having files for major projects from the outset. So if paperwork that needs keeping doesn't go into your archive file, it can at least go into your active 'presentation' file, or your 'budget' file, or your 'personnel' file.

3 **Pass it on.** If this can be passed on to a colleague or delegated to someone, do it now, instead of storing it on your desk for a fortnight and then doing it.

4 **Act on it.** Don't build up a pending file – act on everything you can immediately. If you don't, you simply build up a backlog (and we know all about that) so that you are continually acting on last week's or last month's paperwork. Now you've finally caught up, stay ahead of the game.

clearing a work overload in half a day

If you have only half a day to sort out your entire backlog of work, relax. You've got plenty of time. Even the heftiest overload can be straightened out in three or four hours. The first thing to do is to read this book right through. It'll only take you about an hour, and everything you need to know is in here.

You'll want to go through the stages in the book in terms of organizing the work, prioritizing and sorting through the groups, but you'll have to make sure the really urgent tasks get tackled today – schedule them first before you start to work through the groups. That way, however short the time is, the essentials will be covered.

After that, you simply need to go through the stages set out, but bear a few points in mind:

- ▶ **Setting your objective, organizing the work into groups and prioritizing your workload are essential stages: do not be tempted to skip them. In the long run they will save you far more time than they take up, and they will ensure the work is dealt with effectively.**

- ▶ **You may need to delegate a lot of work, so don't be hesitant about whether anyone else can do it. If you have a good team working with you – large or small – most tasks can be delegated. If you're not in the habit of delegating freely you may have to learn a new habit fast.**

- ▶ **Just because you can't delegate a whole task, it doesn't mean you can't delegate part of it. Maybe you have to remain actively involved in preparing for next week's exhibition, but someone else can liaise with the stand designers and the printers for you.**

- ▶ **You are also going to have to defer a fair amount of work. The important thing is to schedule it for as soon as possible, before it all gets out of hand again, but be realistic about how much you can fit in. There *will* be interruptions and emergencies, and if you haven't allowed for these you will quickly slip behind and become demoralized.**

- ▶ **If your half day is an evening, you have the advantage that you are less likely to be interrupted. On the other hand, it will be hard to get hold of other people. So make yourself a list of things to do as soon as the rest of the world is back in circulation. Start work early in the morning and get one of tomorrow's jobs out of the way before anyone else gets into the office. Use the time that this clears later in the day to make all your phone calls.**

You should find that half a day is ample time to get on top of a backlog of work. It won't all be done by the end of the session, but it will all be in hand and back under control. So don't panic; just relax and get started. Before you know it things will be looking a whole lot more manageable.

clearing a work overload in hour

You've managed to clear an hour – one single, solitary hour – to tackle several weeks' or even months' pile-up. You obviously do one of those jobs where the speed of life has overtaken you. Let's be realistic for a moment. Can you really get all this work done and out of the way in an hour? Of course you can't. So why have we put a page in this book headed 'Clearing a work overload in an hour'?

The answer is that although you can't do the work in an hour, you can prepare the ground for doing it. And that's all you need. So how do you go about it?

- ▶ **Don't even think about urgent tasks for the time being – they'll have to be subject to whatever system you operate all the rest of the time. Deal with them in the usual fashion *after* this one-hour blitz.**
- ▶ **Read Chapter 7 on deferring tasks – you're going to need it.**
- ▶ **Read Chapter 1 on creating time. Don't panic: they're the only chapters you have to read for now.**
- ▶ **On the basis of what these two chapters tell you, create an hour as soon as possible – bedtime would do nicely – to read this book right through.**
- ▶ **Now schedule at least half a day, but preferably a whole day, to put into action the contents of this book. Make sure you fit this time into the next seven days *no matter what*. You may well prefer to start work an hour early each day for the next week (I know you probably already have to get up half an hour before you go to bed), or to give up an evening to clear the workload.**

If you have any of your hour left at the end of this, feel free to sit and twiddle your thumbs. Or start reading the book now. You may not have your work overload cleared by the end of today, but you'll be making an essential start on it, and with a touch of fast thinking it will be clear by the end of next week. So relax!

Just because you can't delegate a whole task, it doesn't mean you can't delegate part of it

flying
start

HAVE FIRST DAY CONFIDENCE

KNOW THE RIGHT PEOPLE

SET OFF WITH STYLE

ros jay

contents

introduction

Congratulations on your new job! Feeling nervous? Starting a new job is exciting, but it can be nerve-wracking too. What if you make a fool of yourself? What if you can't do the job? What if you don't get on with anyone? What if you fail to make your mark on the organization? What if you make a bad impression?

These are typical fears that we all have when we start a new job, whether it's a move within the company or a move to a completely new organization. And you've got to get it right first time. It's no good getting off on the wrong foot and thinking you can have another go next week. This is crunch time. No wonder you're nervous.

But you needn't be. You've come to the right place. This book contains everything you need to know to get off to a flying start in the first two or three days (with the modern speed of work, that's all the time you'll have before you get stuck deep into the job). But that's all you need. This book will take you through all the different aspects of getting started in your new role – from getting to know the people to establishing your objective – regardless of whether your new employers also give you an induction course of their own.

You haven't got long. Maybe you start the job tomorrow morning. In any case, within a few days you'll be swamped with work. So you'll have to move fast to learn all you need to while you've still got the time. You need:

 tips for finding your feet fast

 shortcuts for learning what you need to know

 checklists to make sure you haven't missed anything

… all put together clearly and simply. And short enough to read fast, of course.

Well, you got it. Just follow the guidelines here and you'll make a stunning impression, and set yourself up to do a terrific job too. And if you're launching yourself into one of those jobs where you have hardly any time to settle in, you'll find a section at the back of the book on how to get off to a flying start in half a day. In fact, there's a section on how to make the best possible start in as little as an hour. So if you've got several days, you really are basking in luxury.

This book will take you through the six key areas you need to have covered when you start your new job:

1 To begin with, you need to get the practicalities – from loos to lunch breaks – sorted out, along with finding out everyone's names. And then there are the unspoken rules, philosophy and systems that you need to get to grips with.

2 You need some quick tips now on how to create a good first impression. This will make your job much easier when you get down to work.

3 Next, you need to find out exactly what your job is: your objective. That will inform everything else you do. And you need to establish the parameters of your job: what exactly your responsibilities are, what resources you have at your disposal, and so on. This means a meeting with your boss.

4 Now it's time to check out the history of your job and your department. You need to know precisely what you're taking over – the good bits and the bad bits.

5 You won't get far with your new job unless you know all about the people you're working with, from their talents to the internal politics. So that's your next task – getting to know your colleagues and team members.

6 Finally, once you've established what the job is all about, you need to assess your own ability to do it so that you can identify any weaknesses and remedy them before anyone else spots them. And, of course, you need to recognize where your strengths will come into play. You need to formulate an outline plan for your time in this job.

fast thinking gambles

This book is all about how to hit the ground running in your new job. You are likely to find yourself immersed in paperwork and meetings, budgets and special events within a few days, and you need to get through the essential background work of introducing yourself to the organization – and vice versa – as fast as possible.

In an ideal world (which you probably don't inhabit), you would spend about a fortnight settling into your new role before you started to schedule your time as though you were now fully integrated into the job. This is because when you induct yourself fast, there is always an element of gamble involved. Even if you have no choice in the matter, it's worth knowing the risks you take:

- ▶ **There's a lot to learn, and inevitably the faster you work through it, the more chance there is that at least something will get missed. If it does, you just have to hope it's something minor and not critical.**

- ▶ **You've got to get to know your team members, and they all have to get used to you too. The more time you and your team have to size each other up before you get stuck into the work together, the better chance you all have of getting on and not rubbing each other up the wrong way.**

- ▶ **The subtle, unspoken things – secrets, even – are the ones that are most likely to get missed in the rush, and they are often the most important. Maybe no one's telling you that the organization will be in huge trouble if the press find out about the damning safety report – and as PR manager, you really need to know. Or perhaps your department's dreadful figures for last year are about to be announced and you'll have to sort out the mess without any warning – unless you've found out about it ahead of time.**

With the help of this book, fast thinking should get you where you need to be in a couple of days rather than a couple of weeks, and no one but you will be able to tell the difference. But it's worth taking longer if you possibly can next time you start a new job – in a few months when you get promoted up the organization.

1 learning the ropes

It's nine o'clock in the morning, and you've just walked in on your first day in the new job. You've given your name to the receptionist, and your boss is on their way to meet you and take you to your desk. What are your immediate priorities?

Even without a formal induction process, your boss – or someone – is bound at least to show you where to hang your coat, where the loos are, and to give you any security codes you need in order to reach your office. Then they will, no doubt, whisk you round the part of the building you'll be spending most time in, and rush you through a whirl of introductions: 'This is Gabby; she's one of your sales assistants. And this is Mike, who handles several of the key accounts. Where's Doug? Doug seems to have popped out for a moment – well, you'll meet him later; anyway, he looks after the key accounts with Mike. And here's Ellen … '

With the best will in the world, people tend to dispense information faster than you can take it in. And you can find yourself being rushed – albeit kindly – to the point where you retain so little information you might as well have skipped this bit of the induction altogether.

SET YOUR OWN PACE

You can't afford to waste time being bombarded with information you can't absorb. It's far more time efficient in the long run to take a little longer but to end up remembering it all. So you need to set the pace yourself, politely but firmly, and find ways to help the information sink in. You can do this directly, simply by saying, 'I'm not sure I can take everything in at this speed. Can we slow down a little?' But there are also indirect ways of making the process more useful.

People

If you are swept through your department – and probably those other departments you'll be working closest with – with barely time to say more than 'Hi! Nice to meet you,' 'Hello,' and 'I'll catch up with you later,' you'll be lucky if you remember anyone's name or what they actually do. You may not even remember who is working under you and who is senior to you.

So resist the high-speed introductions firmly. As soon as you are told, 'This is Gabby; she's one of your sales assistants,' get in there fast with a question to Gabby before you can be hurried on to the next person. A question instantly sets

thinking smart

GET IT DOWN
Have a pen and a small notebook with you. Write down anything you can that you think you might forget, from the time the cafeteria opens to the security number to get through the doors. Once it's written down, it can't be forgotten and it's one less thing to have to retain in your head.

> **MEMORY BOOST**
>
> It is far easier to remember someone's name if you say it out loud. So as soon as you're introduced to anyone, repeat their name: 'Hi, Gabby. How are you?' Don't worry if it seems stilted: it won't sound it. And anyway, everyone knows you've got a lot of names to remember, and they'll appreciate the fact that you're bothering to try to learn them.

up a conversation, which Gabby will join in with, and your guide will be too polite to interrupt.

You can ask just about anything, so long as it is an open question. In other words, a question to which Gabby has to give more than a one-word answer. For example:

- **What exactly does your job entail?**
- **How do you manage to keep your desk so amazingly tidy?**
- **Was it you I saw getting out of that Frog-eyed Sprite in the car park?**

So long as the question is polite and friendly, its content doesn't matter much. You're not asking because you need the information. You're asking because a 15- to 30-second conversation with someone will do far more to imprint them on your memory than a rushed 'good to meet you' and on to the next person. Not only that, but having a brief conversation with each person slows the whole process down to a manageable speed, where you have a chance to take in the information you really need (that the name of the sales assistant who sits over by the window is Gabby).

Places

When it comes to finding your way around places, there's no substitute for navigating your own way around. So, if your guide is taking you there and back again, ask to be allowed to find your own way back with them at your shoulder to tell you if you go wrong. If you're on a round trip, ask if they'll accompany you on a repeat journey with you navigating to see if you can do it. If they can't, take someone else with you or simply go on your own and see what happens. You've got to do it some time, and the sooner you make mistakes, the sooner you'll learn.

Systems

At this stage, systems are going to be fairly practical and straightforward. No one is likely to launch into what your department does with each of its triplicate petty cash forms for another day or two. But it is important to remember the systems you're told, because even as a newcomer you can make a fool of yourself if you're found queueing in the shop-floor workers' queue instead of the managers' queue at the canteen.

Again, the best way to remember anything is by doing it. So, ask to punch the security code into the keypad yourself, or go and sit at the right canteen table for a moment. By taking a little longer, you'll imprint the memory of what to do far more strongly.

PLAYING SAFE

Don't write down anything uncomplimentary about the people you'll be working with, just in case your notebook falls into the wrong hands. If your team members find notes such as 'Gabby – talks too much' or 'Mike – fat one with b.o.' you may find your popularity falling off fast.

RECORDING TIME

As soon as you have time to sit down on your own for five minutes, write down everything you think you might forget. This might be a reminder of how to put names to faces, or a note of things to remember about people. If you meet 50 people today, and on Friday you still remember that Gabby is the one who drives the Frog-eyed Sprite, she'll be impressed and flattered. So jot down anything worth remembering about the people you've met.

You may also want to note down details of any systems you've been introduced to, such as how reception should be notified when visitors are expected, or how to find the fire escape where you're allowed to go for a smoke.

UNSPOKEN RULES

Every organization has unspoken rules to learn, as well as the ones you'll be told about. Perversely, these unspoken rules are almost always more important to the people around you. Here are a few examples, but remember that they will vary widely from one organization to the next:

▶ **Senior managers are addressed by title and surname, not forename.**

▶ **People always sit with their own teams in the cafeteria.**

▶ **Managers don't go into the rest room.**

▶ **Memos are always sent by email rather than hard copy.**

▶ **Managers always work through lunch.**

▶ **No one stays later than 6 o'clock in the evening.**

▶ **People work hard, with no gossiping round the coffee machine or over the photocopier.**

▶ **The manager treats the department to cream cakes every Friday morning.**

All organizations are full of unwritten rules of this kind. The reason you won't be told about these rules is that everyone is so used to them that they take them for granted – it's only when you break them that your team members will notice that you just called the marketing director Peter, or that you left the building for an hour at lunch time.

It's an alarming fact that much of what determines whether you fit into your new job is your ability to slot into the company culture. Sure, your performance will count, but if the rest of the crowd feel that you're not 'one of them', you're far less likely to succeed. Some research claims that as many as 90 per cent of sackings are due to failure to fit into the culture. So, listening and watching to pick up on the signs that tell you what's expected of you is a vital skill. You'll find that much of the advice in the rest of this book is also geared to helping you get in tune with the corporate culture.

The only way to learn these rules is by looking out for them, and asking questions whenever you suspect an unspoken rule applies. It is sometimes inappropriate to ask directly, since people have a strange aversion to discussing certain rules directly, but you can always find a way around the problem. For example, you may start to get the impression that all budget decisions seem to go through the administration director as well as the finance director. If you ask why, you may meet with an uncomfortable silence (perhaps the reason is that the admin director used to be the finance director's boss and, despite promotion to an equal position, the finance director is still in the admin director's pocket). Don't try to find out all the details straight away – just stick to the basics: 'Am I right in thinking that budget decisions should be referred to the admin director as well as the finance director?' Once you've established the facts, you're not going to put your foot in it. Sooner or later, you'll learn the real reason.

Some of the more simple unspoken rules, such as how to address senior colleagues, will start becoming apparent from your first day. So be on the lookout for them, and ask for clarification if you feel you need to.

First-day checklist

Before we finish this chapter, it's worth giving you a quick checklist of the practical things you can expect to cover, learn or be allocated in your first few hours (not all of them will apply to every job, of course). You can run through the list at the end of the day and make sure nothing important has been missed out.

- ▶ **Working hours (the real ones, which may not be exactly what it says on your contract).**
- ▶ **Lunchtimes and arrangements (eat in or out, or bring sandwiches?)**
- ▶ **Security codes and keys.**
- ▶ **Computer password and email address.**
- ▶ **Direct phone number.**
- ▶ **Business cards.**
- ▶ **Check you are conversant with the computer software (or make arrangements to learn it fast).**
- ▶ **Location of photocopier, fax machine, key personnel and meeting rooms, loos, canteen.**
- ▶ **Location of personnel files, departmental budget, minutes of meetings.**
- ▶ **Locker, or at least a place to hang your coat.**
- ▶ **Salary arrangements – do you need to pass on your bank account details?**

▶ for later....

One of the best ways to get a feel for the organization and immerse yourself into its philosophy – as well as picking up many of the unspoken rules – is by reading about it. So get hold of copies of company newsletters (including back copies), the annual report, press releases and press cuttings, sales literature and anything else you can lay your hands on.

If you're reading this ahead of starting your new job, don't wait until you get there. Phone up now and ask them to send you all the material they can to give you a feel for the place.

2 first impressions

We all know that stuff about never getting a second chance to make a first impression. And it's all true. As you're being rushed around the offices on your whirlwind tour, your new colleagues are getting their first chance to form an opinion of you. After you've left each room, the people in it will be saying to each other, 'What did you think?' I'm not trying to make you paranoid here – they really are all talking about you.

But you needn't worry. All you have to do is to make a *good* impression, and they will be saying just what you'd like them to. And once formed, a first impression is hard (though not impossible) to break. So you give yourself a flying start if those first few meetings with the people who matter – your team, your colleagues, your bosses – leave them feeling pleased you've joined the company.

So the 64 million dollar question is: how do you make a good impression from the start? Well, there are plenty of things you can do – none of them difficult – to make sure people decide from the off that you are likeable, trustworthy and talented.

THINK ABOUT YOUR APPEARANCE

This is really pretty straightforward. Keep your hair, teeth and nails clean and all that stuff. The most important thing is to fit in with everyone else. If you turn up in a smart suit when everyone else is wearing jeans and T-shirts, they will instinctively feel you're not one of them. Equally, if you turn up in a casual outfit and find all your colleagues dressed in tailored suits, you're not going to find it easy to slot into the company culture.

There's only one sure-fire answer to this dilemma: find out in advance what everyone wears at your new workplace. Think back to your interview. What was the interviewer wearing? Did you get a chance to see anyone else and, if so, what sort of clothes were they wearing?

If this line of thought doesn't help much, do you know anyone who works at the organization already whom you could call? If not, call the person who interviewed you, or their secretary. It's a perfectly reasonable question, so you've nothing to feel uncomfortable about. Just say, 'I want to make sure I fit in, so could you give me an idea of the dress code in the company?'

thinking smart

NEARLY NEW IS BETTER THAN BRAND NEW
Your first day in a new job is not the time to wear a new outfit, appropriate though it may seem. There are few worse times to find out that your new shoes are pinching and giving you blisters, or that your new top keeps riding up under your skirt, or that the collar on the shirt you bought yesterday is too tight. If you really want to wear new clothes – and for some people it is a psychological boost – at least wear them at home for an evening first to break them in.

BE ENERGETIC

One of the most vital and attractive characteristics – especially for a manager – is energy. You must have met people with limp handshakes who always sound wishy-washy and half asleep. Don't be one of them. You don't have to overpower people; simply come across from the start as someone with a positive attitude and the energy to carry your ideas through.

- ▶ **Don't speak too softly.**
- ▶ **Be ready with a firm handshake.**
- ▶ **Smile broadly when you meet people.**
- ▶ **Make eye contact.**
- ▶ **Say hello to people readily and with enthusiasm.**
- ▶ **Be ready to speak confidently without always waiting to be called on to speak – you can be the first to say hello.**
- ▶ **Sound interested in what you're saying, and in what other people say to you.**
- ▶ **Move and speak at an upbeat pace (without rushing).**

You don't have to turn yourself into something you're not – that never works – but we all have a range of behaviours we can call on, and the trick is to know which aspects of yourself to bring to the fore.

BE LIKEABLE

You hear all sorts of theories about what makes a good manager, some more convincing than others. But one quality that is essential in a top-class manager is likeability. When people like you, they want to work hard for you. The whole task of motivating your team is vastly easier and more effective if they like you.

So how do you get people to like you? It's pretty simple really. You know what qualities make people popular and which don't. But here's a run-down of the most important:

- ▶ **Be a good listener.**
- ▶ **Take a genuine interest in other people.**
- ▶ **Be fair (and be seen to be fair).**
- ▶ **Care about the people who work for you.**
- ▶ **Don't set yourself above the rest of the team (take your turn at making the coffee).**
- ▶ **Don't gossip about anyone in your team behind their backs.**
- ▶ **Make time for people when they need to talk to you.**

thinking smart

CALL ON YOUR EXPERIENCE

Think about people you know who always come across as energetic, and think about what it is they do that makes them seem so full of energy. Is it their tone of voice, their movements, their manner, their speed? And try the reverse, too. What makes low-energy people come across in this way?

- ▶ **If you have a strong sense of humour, that's great; but don't use sarcasm or direct humour against anyone you work with.**
- ▶ **Don't be arrogant or pompous.**

If you follow these guidelines – which anyone should be able to do regardless of their natural personality – your new colleagues will undoubtedly like you. You don't have to give in to them, sidestep necessary confrontations, or overlook poor performance. If you are liked, you will be respected even more for dealing fairly and squarely with uncomfortable situations when it is clearly necessary.

INSPIRE TRUST

There is a very simple formula for appearing trustworthy, and that is to be open and honest. If you are honest it will show, and people will recognize that you can be trusted to deal with them fairly and to be straight with them. You need to be open as well, so people can see that you're not the type to keep secrets, hold back important information, or be two-faced.

Your new team members will be looking for this quality in their new manager. They need to know that you will be a boss they can trust. You can demonstrate your honesty by being open about answering any questions they have, and by being open about your personal life too. That doesn't mean you have to bare your soul to them, but don't be secretive. Be comfortable mentioning where you went on holiday, or that you have a sister in Edinburgh, or how passionate you are about music.

CONVINCE THEM YOU'VE GOT TALENT

The key here is to show, not tell. If you go round bragging about how successful you were in your last job, or what an instinct you have for problem solving, you'll simply turn people off. They won't think, 'Wow, he must be good!' or 'She's just what we need round here.' They will actually think, 'What an arrogant little sh**.' You'll have blown all the hard work you put into being likeable.

And worse, it won't even work. If people don't like you, they won't want it to be true. So they won't believe it. 'I bet it wasn't really like that at all,' they'll whisper to each other.

So don't tell them. Show them. Remain modest and don't shout about past achievements, but act smart and they'll soon be saying to each other, 'That was a really neat idea – why has nobody thought of that before?' They will admire your achievements and your modesty. And they'll wonder what else you're capable of.

▋▋ thinking smart

READY ... AIM ... FIRE!

When you first arrive in a new job, do a lot more listening than talking. At those early meetings, don't say too much until you have something to say that you know is really smart. Then come out with it (without sounding as if you know you're being smart). This will be the first big impression you've made regarding your talent – so make it a good one. After that, it would take an awful lot of really pathetic ideas to shake everyone's view that you may not say much, but what you *do* say is worth listening to.

Don't get so hung up about making a good first impression that you end up too nervous. Remind yourself that you obviously got it right at the interview or you'd never have got the job. So feel confident without being cocky, and with a little bit of conscious effort along the lines we've just covered, it should all flow naturally.

for later...

Make sure that these initial impressions remain part of your everyday behaviour. No one will be fooled for long if the mask slips after the first couple of weeks. So make sure it's no mask. Work on being consistently energetic, likeable, trustworthy and talented … and you'll have the makings of a first-class manager.

3 meeting the boss

Once you've said hello to everyone and taken your coat off, it's time to crack on with the job. And the first thing you need to do is to have a meeting with your boss. With some luck, your boss will have set aside the first part of the morning for you anyway, so this is your best chance to have the meeting you want, as well as covering anything they want to discuss (which may well overlap).

But even if this meeting isn't already scheduled, you must have it. You may need to be assertive and explain to your boss that you don't feel you can really get your teeth into this job until you've covered certain topics together. Their input is sufficiently important (a bit of subtle flattery always helps, especially when it's true) that this meeting needs to come first. You shouldn't have too much trouble getting half an hour or so of their time on your first morning.

So, now you have your boss to yourself, what are you going to talk to them about? There are five key questions you must have the answers to before you can get on with the job:

1 What is your objective?
2 What is expected of you?
3 Why did you get the job?
4 What resources do you have?
5 What authority do you have?

WHAT IS YOUR OBJECTIVE?

Excuse me? Objective? What's this all about? What are we doing setting objectives before we've even found out what the job entails?

Well, we're not setting an objective for a particular project; we're setting the objective for your job. What are you here for? You can't do your job properly unless you know exactly what job you are there to do. But your objective isn't simply 'to run the department' – that isn't particularly helpful at all. And an objective should, above all, be helpful.

Your objective will also be the core objective of your department, and if none of you knows what it is, you're going to be floundering. So decide what you think it is and ask your boss to confirm it – or correct it – for you. Your objective clearly depends on your job, but here are a few examples:

Post	Possible objective
Sales manager	To increase profits
Accounts manager	To ensure accurate, helpful billing and payment systems
Production manager	To improve productivity
PR manager	To increase positive public awareness
Distribution manager	To ensure fast, high-quality distribution at minimum cost
Marketing manager	To build customer loyalty and attract new customers

thinking smart

GET IT IN WRITING

In a professional, up-together organization, your objective should appear on your job description. If you're lucky, it will be there already for you, in which case you may simply want to talk it through with your boss. If it isn't on your job description, ask for it to be added.

As you can see, the objective may not always be obvious. As a new marketing manager, you might think that your objective is to build customer loyalty while your boss might consider that it is to attract new customers. Maybe it's both – a joint objective. But if you don't discuss it with your boss, you could be in big trouble in six months' time when hardly any new customers have been acquired … while you were expecting to be congratulated on increasing customer retention.

Your objective needs to be clear so that you can keep an eye on it permanently. It is your way of making sure you and your team don't get bogged down in day-to-day work without ever really achieving anything worthwhile (you've seen it happen to other people often enough). Once you have a clear objective, you can ensure that the bulk of the work that gets done in your department is directed at meeting it.

WHAT IS EXPECTED OF YOU?

Your objective is your core aim – you can check any task against it to see that it meets your objective. This way you can ensure that you don't get sidetracked and waste time on unimportant activities (since you certainly don't have time to fritter). But your objective doesn't give you any detail. It tells you where you're headed, but it doesn't tell you how fast to get there, or what to bring with you. You need more specific guidance.

What you really need to know – and only your boss can tell you – is what you are expected to achieve in the job. Maybe you're the new production manager and your objective is to increase productivity. But by how much? If it goes up by 2 per cent in the next year, will you think you've done well? And will your boss think you've failed?

So ask your boss the two key questions:

▶ **What am I expected to achieve in the next three months/six months/year?**

▶ **How will I know if I've failed in my job after the next three months/six months/year?**

Ask for specific figures or targets, and don't settle for anything vague that you can't work to, such as 'Well, we'd like to see productivity go up, of course.' Insist – politely – on concrete targets. Without them, you can't be expected to do your job properly.

thinking smart

DO YOUR HOMEWORK

Before you meet your boss – even before you start the job – it's worth working out your own suggested answers to the questions of what your objective is, and what is expected of you. A really smart boss will have no trouble at all answering these questions (indeed they will be pleased to hear you ask them), but a less on-the-ball boss may need some prompting. It is easier for them to correct your proposal than to create their own out of thin air.

605

WHY DID YOU GET THE JOB?

When you applied for this job, you were probably not the only applicant. Some of the others may have been rubbish, but at least some of them will have been good – maybe all of them were. And yet you were the one they chose. Why?

You must have had some qualities, experience or skills that particularly attracted your new employers. Something that made them think you would be more valuable to them than any of those other promising candidates. Something they really needed bringing to this job.

Wouldn't it be helpful to know what it is? If they were particularly looking for someone who was a good diplomat after all the problems the last manager caused, or they were especially impressed with your experience of dealing with the press because improving press relations is high on their agenda, you want to know about it.

The answer to this question is going to give you a big clue as to where senior management's priorities lie when it comes to your new department, so make sure you ask it. Don't be shy: it's a perfectly reasonable – not to say intelligent – question. 'What was it that made you decide to offer the job to me? What in particular were you expecting I could bring to the job?'

WHAT RESOURCES DO YOU HAVE?

You wouldn't decide to bake a cake without knowing first what ingredients you had, and you can't start doing a job until you know what resources you have at your disposal. So ask your boss for:

- **a copy of the current budget for your department**
- **details of what staff you have and for what hours (if Gabby disappears every Friday for training, then you need to know about it)**
- **information about any other staff you can call on – can you bring in outsiders or call on staff from other departments for particular events? If you run big sales presentations, can you use in-house catering staff to provide coffees and lunches for your customers?**
- **information on access to other parts of the building, such as the conference hall or meeting rooms. Do you have to book? Do you take priority? What's the system?**

Depending on your job, there are all sorts of other resources you might need to find out about, such as:

- **time allocated to you on certain equipment**
- **use of company vehicles**
- **use of the in-house newsletter to post notices or information**

thinking smart

PERSONAL AUTHORITY

As with resources, many areas of authority will be specific to your job. For example, as PR manager, can you authorize any press release to be sent out yourself, or do certain releases have to be approved by someone else first? As distribution manager, do you handle crises such as postal strikes yourself, or do you have to refer such decisions to your boss?

... and so on. So make sure your boss tells you exactly what tools you are being given to do the job.

WHAT AUTHORITY DO YOU HAVE?

This question is very much the partner of the previous one. As well as knowing what tools you have, you need to know how freely you are allowed to use them. What decisions are you authorized to take yourself, and which do you have to refer up the line?

The kinds of areas that you'll need to know about are:

- **Staff – can you hire and fire them?**
- **Expenditure – what can you authorize yourself?**
- **Budget – how much room for manoeuvre do you have within your overall budget before having to check back with your boss or finance department?**
- **Other departments – for example, do you have authority to borrow catering staff for specific events (by arrangement, obviously), or can the catering manager refuse?**
- **Overtime – can you authorize it yourself so long as you stay within budget?**

Again, without this information you cannot either plan or execute your job. So pin your boss down to give you the answers to these questions so that you can meet your objective successfully.

for later....

Once you have been in the job for a week, it will be time to start planning for your first success (if you don't make your mark soon, you'll get so bogged down in everyday work it may never happen). This plan should be ready to put into action at the end of your first fortnight. You might plan to win a major contract, set and meet a new sales target, solve a long-standing problem left behind by your predecessor, organize a major event, or maybe streamline a system that will lead to cost savings or increased productivity. Only you can decide what your big success will be, but you will need the answers to the questions we've just covered to choose a suitable plan.

Whatever plan you choose, it should:

- meet the objective for your job
- fulfil what is expected of you – or work towards it
- utilize the strengths for which you were appointed
- use resources that you are in a position to allocate
- fall within your sphere of authority.

So you see, you need the answers to these questions to be able to make your mark early on.

There's one other criterion your first success should fulfil: it shouldn't take too long to come to fruition. You can also, by all means, embark on long-term plans that will show big profit increases, cost savings, PR advantage or productivity boosts in two or three years' time. But for your first success, you need to find a project or challenge that will demonstrate your talents within your first three months or so.

4 taking stock

So, what have you let yourself in for? Is this a thriving, successful department? Or is it already way over budget for this year, with plummeting profits and three unfair dismissal claims pending? Is team morale high, or are your staff already queueing up outside your door to hand in their letters of resignation?

Your next task is to find out what you can about the job and the department you've just taken on. Clearly this is a process that will take time, but since time is a commodity in very short supply at the moment, you can kick-start the process with an intensive research session that will get you a lot of information in the shortest possible time.

You will learn a lot of what you need to know when you talk to your team, but you need to have some level of forewarning before you sit down with them formally. Otherwise you will have no idea what to expect, or what topics they might try to duck or cover up.

THE FILES

A lot of the information you need to unearth will already be close to hand. You need to root out the most important files and have a good look through them. If there's a lot to go through, have a quick look now to pick up anything vital (you've got a lot of other things to get through today, too), and take the files home for a more thorough study later. But as you'll see, you need to have garnered at least some of this information in order to get the most from your team interviews, so this has to come first – even if only the fast thinking version.

The main paperwork you need to check out is the personnel files, key project files, customer/supplier relationship files and the budget.

Personnel files

As we'll see in the next chapter, one of your first tasks is to interview all the members of your team individually. But you need to have looked through their personnel files first, so you know what you're dealing with. This will tell you a great deal about their skills, experience, strengths and weaknesses.

thinking smart

CHECKING IN

Your top priority for the first few days in your new job (and indeed all your subsequent time in it) is your team. Learning the background to the job may be more urgent at the moment, but you should be seen to spend time with your team from the start. So, after you've finished your meeting with your boss, have a cup of coffee with your team and a few minutes of social chat before you start ploughing through files. And if this process takes a long time, take regular breaks to talk to your team – even start on the individual team interviews (covered in the next chapter) in between bouts of research.

If you find that there are clear problems with any of your key projects, make a note to discuss them with your team members

thinking smart

thhfhi thinking smart

DO IT YOURSELF

As you go through the files, you may want to mark certain pages or make notes. Often, your new desk isn't equipped with the basics when you first arrive, so take a supply of essentials into work with you on your first day:

- ▶ pens
- ▶ paper
- ▶ highlighter pens
- ▶ post-it notes

… and anything else you think you're likely to need. That way, you won't have to hang around waiting for stationery supplies.

Key project files

You haven't got time right now to memorize every detail of every project your department has been involved in, but you must know about the most important ones. So dig out the files on all the major current projects and initiatives, and go through them to give yourself a good working knowledge of what's going on. You may be asked to make an important and urgent decision on one of these projects in the next few days, so you'd better know the background. (You'll find a page at the back of the book to make your own notes about key projects.)

If you find that there are clear problems with any of your key projects, make a note to discuss them with your team members when you talk to them individually. You may learn all sorts of useful things that you'd never have uncovered if you hadn't known which questions to ask. So make notes of what you want to know, such as, 'Why did we handle the late delivery problems this way?' or 'Why are Jones & Co. so reluctant to sign up to this deal?'

Customer/supplier relationship files

You will have key customers and suppliers, whatever your department's role. If you don't deal with outside organizations, you must have internal customers and suppliers. So once again, go through the key files and find out which relationships are good and which are in trouble, and why. Note down questions to ask your team (or anyone else), such as, 'What's the history of the relationship between our department and accounts?' or 'Why are we dealing with AB&C when they don't seem to be giving us the kind of discounts I'd expect?'

Budget

It is essential that you find out what your existing budget is, and whether you are meeting it or not. It may be that you are arriving in a department that is already critically over budget. If so, you need to find out fast, and find out why. Again, you can question your team members or your boss: 'Why are we so over budget on overtime?'

Get acquainted with your budget as quickly as you can, and find out how soon you will be expected to put in your proposal for the next budget. (If you're not used to dealing with budgets, take a look at *fast thinking: budget*.)

RULE YOUR DEPARTMENT

When William the Conqueror won the English throne, he soon realized that it was impossible to rule a kingdom if you didn't know what was in it. So he commissioned a huge research exercise to find out exactly what he owned and what revenues he could expect. He called it the *Domesday Book*. Nothing's changed – if you want to run your department effectively, you must find out everything about it first.

YOUR PREDECESSOR

Assuming this isn't a new post you're filling, someone else was doing this job until recently. Even if it is a new post, most of the work may have been allocated to someone else. And that someone else could save you an awful lot of valuable time by telling you most of what you really need to know.

So, one of your most important tasks is to get hold of your predecessor and pick their brains. Your boss or your boss's secretary should be more than happy to tell you where to contact them. Of course, your predecessor might actually be your boss, or they might still be in the organization. But even if they're not, that's fine too. Your only problem is if they left under a cloud, or were moved reluctantly elsewhere in the organization. Assuming this isn't the case, most people will be more than happy to give help and advice to a grateful listener.

So what should you ask your predecessor, once you've made contact with them? If you've already looked through the files, that will give you a lot of clues. But whether or not you have, here are some key questions to ask:

- ▶ **What did you find were the strengths of your team?**
- ▶ **And what did you feel were their weaknesses?**
- ▶ **Did you run into any particular problems during your time in the department?**
- ▶ **How did you deal with them?**
- ▶ **Are there any difficult dynamics within the team?**
- ▶ **Did you encounter problems with other departments in the organization?**
- ▶ **Did you have any specific problems with the departmental budget?**
- ▶ **Are there any organizational secrets I ought to know about?**

CATCH THEM EARLY

Your introduction to this new job is hurried and busy enough. So if you can, talk to your predecessor *before* you start the job. Get their phone number and arrange to buy them a drink or at least talk on the phone, and get all the information you can out of them. If they're willing, get permission to call them if you have problems once you've started in the job. Don't – obviously – ask them how to do the job, but one or two calls over the first few weeks to ask what went wrong with the MPQ contract last year, or what the background is to the rivalry between your department and marketing, is perfectly in order.

Don't forget that your predecessor has an ego, and won't be half so helpful if there's any implication from you that they weren't doing a good job. So if they went way over budget, don't say, 'Blimey, you know how to blow a budget, don't you? Where did you go wrong there, then?' Far better to phrase it diplomatically: 'It looks as if you weren't given nearly enough overall budget to play with. What were your biggest problems with it?'

SKELETONS IN THE CLOSET

Not all organizations have worrying secrets, but many do. And it may turn out that you have just started working for one of them. They may be large or small skeletons; either way you need to be on the lookout for them. It is unlikely that you will be told about them officially – at least not in your first few days – so you need to find out about them in other ways.

So what sort of skeletons are we talking about here? Well, anything that could make your job particularly difficult or even unsafe.

Serious interpersonal or interdepartmental warfare

This can be a big problem for a manager. If the despatch department are traditionally at loggerheads with your sales department, you want to know about it sooner rather than later. Healthy competition is one thing, but unpleasantness, back-biting and having your authority or success deliberately undermined are a different matter. The chances are that your team will let you know about this, but it doesn't hurt to ask anyone – from your boss to the canteen staff – to tell you if this is a happy organization or a bitchy one.

Interpersonal problems in your team can also be very hard to deal with, especially when you barely know the people involved. At this stage, the most important thing is to identify the problem correctly. If you sense trouble, have a quiet word with your boss. Explain that you feel things aren't right, and ask what the problem is. Then you can do something about resolving it. (If you need help resolving such problems, try *fast thinking: difficult people.*)

⓫ thinking smart

YOU'RE THE PROBLEM

Sometimes, you yourself may unwittingly be the problem. Perhaps one of your team applied for the job you've just got, and resents you for displacing them. It never hurts to ask your boss about this as a matter of course: 'Did any of my team apply for this job?' That way, you're prepared. If ther's no problem, it's probably best not to mention to the team member that you know they were turned down in favour of you.

But if you do encounter this kind of trouble, talk to the person concerned frankly. Tell them you are aware that they too applied for the job, and you appreciate they are in a difficult position. Point out that you need them on your side, because they are clearly one of the most experienced and valuable people on your team.

Business or financial problems

Maybe your new employer is about to go bust. Or perhaps half the directors are about to be investigated for fraud. Maybe you're about to be taken over, or perhaps your department's biggest customer is going under. This is information you need to know about fast. It's likely that if you keep your ears and eyes open, you'll catch a whiff of something wrong pretty early on. People will drop hints: 'Our next big launch won't be until next year now (if we're still here).'

Make sure you pick people up on any comments like this, with an innocent 'What do you mean?' Sooner or later, someone will tell you what they mean. If you think there's trouble but no one's talking openly to you, socialize with your colleagues and do more listening than talking. Once they all but forget you're there, they'll start to talk more freely.

Dishonest business practice

From share dealing to operating a racist selection procedure, illegal dumping to cheating on overtime, there is never any excuse for getting involved in dishonest behaviour. Often, you may be personally liable even if you are only carrying out company policy set by someone else. If you suspect that there are dishonest dealings in your organization, don't jump to conclusions. But do ask questions to make sure nothing you are being asked to do is dishonest or illegal. An innocent question can often set your mind at rest: 'Where do we dump our toxic waste?' If you are still unsure, don't bury your head in the sand: make sure you find out what the score is.

If you discover that dishonest practices are going on around you, you will have to make your own decision on how that affects your position ethically. From a legal point of view, you may want to take professional advice.

▶ for later...

Your new organization is full of people who know more than you do about your department and even your job. So keep your ears open for clues, and take any opportunity to find out more about the history of your department. And bear in mind that it is the skeletons that will be hardest to drag out of the closet – it's not the good news that you'll have trouble eliciting from people.

Go for lunch or a drink after work with a couple of your colleagues who run other departments. They will often be the readiest to talk about past problems and successes – it's no skin off their nose to tell you that your predecessor was hugely popular with the team, for example, while your team members themselves might be too polite to ram it down your throat that you have a hard act to follow.

5 the people

This chapter may not have come first, but don't let that fool you. Getting to know your team is the most important part of your new job, followed by getting to know everyone else you will be working with closely. (You'll find a page at the back of the book for making notes on who you need to talk to.) As a manager, you are only as good as your team, and they are only as good as their manager. So you are mutually dependent.

If you could wave a magic wand, you would meet with your boss, study your paperwork and get to know your team simultaneously. Without a magic wand, you have to do them in sequence, and meeting the boss and researching the files have to come first because they inform your meetings with your team members. But be aware that if it didn't have to happen this way round, talking to the team would be your top priority.

Your team members are not going to be impressed with a new boss who turns up, says hello briefly, and then disappears into the secrecy of their office for a whole morning. So although you may have to cover some other ground before you talk to your team formally, find time to talk to them informally in between. Take a couple of coffee breaks and chat to them about work or anything else, just to get to know each other.

PREPARE THE GROUND

Your new team members may be understandably nervous if you summon them to your office, so warn them in advance what to expect. Call them together if you can – maybe over a cup of coffee – and explain that you will be talking to each of them individually. Tell them that this is largely for your own benefit: you're hoping that they will be able to tell you what you need to know to do the job. You're not going to be reviewing their performance, so there's nothing to worry about.

Take this opportunity to set the pattern by letting them know that from what you've gathered so far, you're lucky enough to have a good team behind you and you're looking forward to working with them. This will help them relax and recognize that they are in for a pleasant, friendly chat with you, rather than a formal, uncomfortable meeting.

thinking smart

RULE OF THUMB

Aim to start your individual sessions with your team members straight after lunch on your first day (or sooner if you can manage it). But during the morning, make sure you speak to everyone a couple of times at least – after the intial introductions – over coffee or just wandering around for a chat. So, by the time you see them individually they already feel they're getting to know you.

SHOW YOUR APPROVAL

You want to encourage your team members to spill the beans. Some information you're asking for is totally inocuous, but you might also want information that they might feel uncomfortable about giving you. Perhaps it makes them feel disloyal to your predecessor, or to one of their colleagues. Or maybe they are worried they will come across as inefficient or picky.

You can't make people break confidences or give you information they don't want to. So give them plenty of encouragement and approval, and absolutely no disapproval. If information is sensitive or difficult in any way, thank them for passing it on to you, and let them know it will help you do your job better.

To this end, you also need to make sure that you establish the right atmosphere in your office (or wherever you will be meeting them). Don't sit across a desk from them: this simply sets up a barrier between the two of you. Ideally, you should sit well away from a desk in easy chairs around a coffee table – and with a cup of coffee or tea each. Borrow a meeting room if you need to. If you really can't get away from the desk, sit at the side of it – at right angles to them – so that you are not in a dominant position. And make sure your chair is similar to theirs. No luxury swivel leather armchair while they sit on a hard plastic upright chair.

INDIVIDUAL SESSIONS

So now you've got your team members in front of you, one by one, what are you going to do with them? It's very simple, actually. You're going to ask them questions. Lots of them.

These people have most of the information you want to do your job well. So you need to get it out of them. This is no time to start telling them what you're going to do, or what you expect of them – you can't make those decisions until you have prised the information out of them. You're not asking them how to do your job – that's for you to decide. You're just asking them what you need to know.

And boy, is there a lot they can tell you. From why you're over budget to who gets on with whom, from what's gone wrong with a key account to why morale is low. Someone, perhaps everyone, on your team can fill in most of the blanks for you if you just ask the right questions. And they can all tell you about themselves too: whether their performance is as good as it could be, whether they are being stretched, whether they enjoy working in the team.

So what questions should you ask? You're best off relaxing them by asking them questions about themselves, before you move on to questions about the team and the organization (which might call on them to make criticisms they are uneasy making). You may well know what you want to ask, so take the following lists as a guide rather than gospel.

Questions about themselves

- ▶ **What is your job, and what is its purpose?**
- ▶ **What systems and people do you rely on to do your job well?**

thinking smart

- ▶ **How could you do your job better?**
- ▶ **Which parts of your job do you enjoy most?**
- ▶ **Do you feel you are stretched to the full?**

Your precise choice of questions will also be influenced, of course, by your study of each team member's personnel file, which will give you plenty of clues as to their strengths and weaknesses, problems and achievements.

Wider questions

- ▶ **What do you consider this team's greatest strengths to be?**
- ▶ **And its weak points?**
- ▶ **How would you describe the morale of the team?**
- ▶ **Do you feel the team is achieving the best performance it could?**
- ▶ **If you were in my position, what would you do to imporove the morale/performance of the team?**
- ▶ **How do you feel this team fits into the organization as a whole?**
- ▶ **What do you think are the greatest challenges facing this team at the moment?**

On top of this, you will also want to ask more specific questions, such as those we looked at in the last chapter arising from your study of the files and paperwork. This might include questions about the budget (particularly with senior team members), key projects and customer/supplier relationships.

You won't ask every team member exactly the same questions. And you will probably want to go into more depth with the most senior members of your team. If

thinking smart

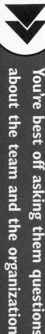

You're best off asking them questions about themselves, before you move on to questions about the team and the organization

615

there is a dominant concern – such as a failing relationship with a major customer – you may want to go into this thoroughly with the people who are involved most closely.

But you will need to ask each person something about themselves and something about wider issues. Not only are you informing yourself – you're also reassuring them that you're listening to their views. They may have been waiting months for a boss who might finally do something about the excessive workload in the department, or about the need to upgrade vital equipment. So let them see that you want to know what they consider priorities.

GROUP SESSIONS

Your first priority is to talk to your team members individually, for several reasons:

- **It gives you an in-depth view of them and of any problems they have.**
- **They may talk more freely when they are alone with you, especially about issues such as internal team difficulties.**
- **It helps you get to know them individually.**
- **It shows that you are interested in listening to each one of them.**

You will learn which issues concern all of them, and which are only raised by one or two of them. If you put them all together, one will raise an issue, the rest will join in the discussion, and you'll have no clear idea how much importance they each attach to it.

However, you will also gain a huge amount by listening to them talking together. You will get a quick feel for a subject, and learn fast what are the most important decisions or concerns around it. Once they get their teeth into a debate, they will begin to forget you are there, so they will talk much more freely than they might one to one with you.

And you'll learn something else, too. If you watch and listen, you'll find out a great deal about the personalities and relationships within your new team. A debate about problems will show you:

- **who is naturally respected by the rest of the team**
- **who are the natural leaders within the team**
- **who is less popular or less well respected**
- **any rivalries or factions within the team**
- **any person or group that tends to take a negative view**
- **your team's collective ability to analyze situations and solve problems**

… you get the picture. A group session to discuss an important issue will tell you far more than your team realize.

Arranging the sessions

So how about the practicalities? What sort of group sessions should you hold? When? And how? You want a situation formal enough for people to feel it is a proper meeting and they must stick to the subject, but relaxed enough for them to say freely what they think. The perfect situation is a working lunch, either in a company dining room or meeting room, or else at a nearby restaurant. Opt for whichever of these seems to fit the company culture best. Failing that, organize a

HOT TOPICS

You're under time pressure here, and you can't possibly hope to find time to discuss every important issue in a group session. So pick your top four to six topics, and aim to hold two or three sessions within the first week. The most burning issue may get a session all to itself, but otherwise try to fit in two topics per session – related ones, ideally (but when are things ever ideal?).

It should be perfectly obvious by day two – if you're following this book – what your key issues are. It may be the team's main project, or an obvious and major problem such as falling standards or a huge work backlog. If it isn't obvious, it shouldn't be on the list for discussion at this stage.

session in a meeting room, preferably where you can all sit round on comfortable chairs without a desk between you. Make sure everyone has a cup of coffee or a cold drink and can relax as much as possible.

You want to have completed your individual sessions before you launch into your group sessions. Failing that – if the individual sessions are going to take a long time to get through – hold your first group session before any of the individual sessions. The point is that everyone is then on an equal footing, both in their own minds and in your perception of them. From their point of view, people may feel at a disadvantage if others have met you one to one but they haven't. And from your perspective, you may prejudge some team members on the basis of their group performance, while others will have been fresh when you met them face to face.

You want to kick off these sessions as soon as you can, because you urgently need to hear what the team has to say about the most important issues and problems you're going to encounter in your new department. So, when should you start your group sessions?

▶ **The top time to hold your first group session is at lunchtime on day two, having completed all your individual meetings by then.**

▶ **If your individual meetings are going to go on beyond lunchtime on day two, hold it at lunchtime on day one before you start your individual meetings.**

▶ **If you can't complete the individual meetings by the middle of day two, and it's impossible to arrange a session on your first day, schedule your first group session for lunchtime on day three.**

Aim to have two or three sessions in all over the course of your first week or week and a half – it depends partly on how soon you need to collect all the information. If there are any really pressing issues, you won't be able to wait more than a couple

thinking smart

FULL HOUSE

You may have to be firm with your team about recognizing that they need to attend these group sessions. They are not optional, and you want everyone there. You won't get a proper feel for the dynamics of the team if some of its members are absent.

KEEP IT IN RESERVE

As time goes on, you are less likely to have any need for this kind of session. But if an old problem from before your time ever flares up, remember the option of calling a working lunch to get your team to fill you in on the background and come up with some useful ideas.

of days before filling yourself in on the background in this way. But don't wear your team out with three working lunches in a row – give them a lunchtime off between group sessions.

A working lunch will generally take an hour or so, so you should be able to discuss one or two topics in this time. If the lunch goes on longer, don't add more topics – have some social time at the end of the lunch instead. It's not fair on your team to wear them out too much over lunch, and it's not an example you want to set.

Running the sessions

Your role in running these sessions is a delicate one. You want to stay in the background as much as possible so that people will talk openly, but you also want to guide the discussion the way you want it to go. The way to achieve both of these aims is by asking questions. You will come across as someone who wants information, rather than someone about to start making snap decisions or issuing orders. And you can stay far more in the background as you direct the debate.

You'll need to start by introducing the topic briefly, saying why you want to know about it, and asking an initial question or two. You might say, for example, 'I've called this session because it's becoming clear from talking to you all individually that the biggest challenge facing this department at the moment is clearing the huge backlog of work. I'd really appreciate you filling me in on the background to this, and giving me some of your ideas on how to tackle it. How did the backlog build up in the first place?'

Now you can largely sit back, and simply prompt where necessary. If everyone clams up to start with, pick someone to kick off. Choose someone who isn't too shy, and who has a particular understanding of the issue (you see why you want to have held the individual sessions first if you can): 'Meg, you've been here longer than anyone, I believe. How did the backlog start to build up?'

You presumably know what questions you want to ask, but they will always include questions along the line of:

▶ **What's the history of this issue?**
▶ **Why is it causing such a problem?**
▶ **What can we do about it?**

You need to sit back and listen, without throwing in any comments. If you can see an option the rest of the team aren't raising, phrase it as a question: 'What would happen if we simply outsourced the backlog and started afresh?'

As well as asking the questions you want answers to, you also need to ask questions to steer the discussion if:

TAKE TIME OUT

You don't want an all-out row if an issue turns out to be more controversial than you realized. But if the discussion does become a little heated, it can help to slot in some social time for everyone to cool down at the end.

- ▶ **It is starting to go round in circles.**
- ▶ **The team are digressing.**
- ▶ **Things start to get personal (now is not the time to start allocating blame or making accusations).**

If any of these start to happen, stamp on them fast (and imperceptibly) by simply using a question to change the subject slightly.

At the end of the session, thank the team very much for filling you in on the issue. Tell them their ideas are appreciated and you will be taking them seriously, but don't announce any snap decisions about precisely how you will deal with the problem.

MEETING THE REST OF THE CROWD

Your team are the most important people of all, and you've already met your boss, of course. But there are still plenty of other people it will help to talk to as early in the proceedings as possible, especially the managers of other departments you're going to be working closely with.

An informal chat with these people is your best bet, and talk to them individually as they are more likely to be indiscreet that way – or at least not to bother so much with diplomacy – which will work in your favour. You want them to tell you, among other things, who is a pain to work with, where the system is failing, and what type of proposals the MD always blocks. This sort of information is far more likely to come out in private than in front of other colleagues.

WORKING LUNCH

Use your lunchtimes wisely for the first week or two. Unless the company culture is weighted very heavily towards working through every lunchtime, it's far better to be seen to take your lunch breaks. It makes you look more relaxed and in control, and sets a good example to your staff – you're not a slave-driver or a workaholic, and they don't have to feel guilty for taking their lunch breaks.

At the same time, the working lunch is one of those great institutions that create an atmosphere of relaxed, informal business that's hard to duplicate any other way. So don't waste your lunch breaks either.

The answer is to take time for a pleasant, relaxed lunch, but always in the company of someone you can talk to about work … and do a bit of socializing too. Hold group sessions or go for a drink with a colleague or even your boss; that way you can work and relax at the same time.

If there are one or two colleagues you expect to spend a lot of working time with, ask them out for a drink after work

Some colleagues will be discreet even in private, but they may still give you valuable hints. In any case, they can also give you plenty of other non-sensitive but highly useful information. If there are one or two colleagues you expect to spend a lot of working time with, ask them out for a drink after work. You haven't got time to do this with everyone, however, so ask the others for half an hour of their time over coffee or even a quick lunch. Half an hour isn't too much of their time, but it does give you a relaxed chance to go through a few questions and get to know them at the same time. You could get through the questions in ten or 15 minutes, but it would be more of a cross-examination than a getting-to-know-you session.

So what questions are you going to ask your colleagues? Obviously it depends partly on the working relationship you expect to have, but here is a guide:

- ▶ **In what areas do your team and mine work most closely?**
- ▶ **How has the relationship between the two departments been in the past?**
- ▶ **What do you see as the greatest challenges I'll encounter running my team?**
- ▶ **Are there any problems I'm going to meet that I ought to know about?**
- ▶ **If you were in my position, what would you consider your priorities for my department?**

In addition to this type of question, you might also have questions thrown up by your research into projects and your departmental history and so on.

Obviously, the job of getting to know people is an ongoing one, and you may well want to pick the brains of your boss, your colleagues or your team for some time to come. But this series of initial interviews and sessions should give you the fastest possible route to filling in as much background to your job as possible in a very short time. By the end of your first couple of days, you'll be feeling pretty well on top of things, and by the end of the first week you'll be raring to go.

▶ for later....

Once you've been in the job for about a week or two, it's time to set targets for each member of your team. You can't do this immediately, since you don't know enough about what needs doing or what they are capable of. But just as you needed to ask your boss what your objective was and what was expected of you, so each of your team members needs to know what you expect of them.

It may well be that your team members already have targets they are working to, set by their previous boss. If so, you will still need to review these (although you may decide to leave them as they are).

Call in each team member individually and discuss their targets with them. No one is going to meet a target that is unrealistic, and they are not likely to meet one they are unhappy about. So, the process is not a matter of you saying; 'Right, I want a 5 per cent increase in sales from you in the next quarter,' or 'I expect complaints from internal customers to halve by the end of the year.'

Discuss what they are achieving now, and how much more they could achieve. A target should be attainable, but should stretch the team member. Well motivated people like to be stretched, so you won't have any trouble getting them to agree to a realistic target if you've been doing your job well for the last week or two. They will want to give their best if you have inspired them.

6 the outline plan

By the time you've worked your way through the first five chapters of this book, you should be two or three days into your new job. But with fast thinking and smart action, you should already have established:

- ▶ **your objective**
- ▶ **what is expected of you**
- ▶ **what strengths you have been hired for (why you got the job)**
- ▶ **your resources and authority.**

You will by now have met and talked in depth with:

- ▶ **your boss**
- ▶ **your predecessor**
- ▶ **your team members**
- ▶ **your close colleagues.**

And you will have identified:

- ▶ **your key projects**
- ▶ **any major challenges or problems facing your department**
- ▶ **your budget position**

... and with any luck you'll have picked up at least a few hints about any skeletons that may be lurking in the company closet.

Good. That's enough information – packed into a very short time – to enable you to assess your ability to do the job. And that's the next step. Your career depends heavily on making your mark in this job, so it's time to assess how easy it's going to be.

THREATS AND OPPORTUNITIES

The starting point for this process is to identify the threats and the opportunites that face you in running this department successfully. So let's begin with the threats. List the most striking problems you can see are going to occupy your time for the next few weeks or months. (You'll find a page at the back of the book to do just that.) There's no point giving yourself an unmanageable list of 50 or 60 problems; just concentrate on the key ones – those that are going to get in the way of meeting your objective unless you resolve them.

Even when you encounter massive problems in a new job, that doesn't have to mean that there are a lot of them. You might have just one overriding problem. There's really no mileage in having a list of more than four or five threats: you haven't the resources to tackle more than that at one go. Once they're dealt with, you can move on to the next raft of problems.

Every job will obviously have a different list of key threats, but here's an idea of the kind of things that might appear on yours. You'll notice that the nature of the threats can vary widely:

- **work backlog**
- **failing contract with key customer**
- **major budget overspend**
- **bad relationship with production department**
- **plans for next month's big launch in disarray**
- **damaging rivalry between team members**
- **huge overtime bill**
- **serious software problems that are hampering work**
- **planned redundancies on the team.**

So that's the kind of threat you need to have on your list of key issues to tackle as soon as possible. Now it's time for more cheerful matters: the opportunities. You are in a position to score some successes for your department, but you need to decide what they are going to be. Again, you want to draw up a list of key opportunities that will help to further your objective. These are the projects that are central to your success.

Once again, you're looking for a list of up to four or five for the time being – once they're under way, you can move on to the next batch. Everyone's list is different, but this sample will give you an idea:

- **Increase market share by 3 per cent.**
- **Improve productivity by 5 per cent.**
- **Plan major showcase for new products for next year.**
- **Train more staff to operate new software to increase efficiency.**
- **Reduce complaints.**

thinking smart

SPOT THE DIFFERENCE

What's the difference between a threat and an opportunity? Suppose you list 'huge overtime bill' under threats. Why not list 'slash overtime bill' under opportunities instead? Can't you look at most threats as opportunities?

Yes, you can if you're into positive thinking; it's a great attitude to adopt. But there is a difference. If you're not sure which category to put any issue into, ask yourself this question: 'What happens if I do nothing?' If the result of inaction would be damaging to the department or the organization, then you are dealing with a threat. If the result would be no change at all – and the current situation isn't damaging – you have an opportunity on your hands.

Another way to look at it is that a threat demands a red light: it must be stopped. An opportunity needs a green light to make it go.

- ▶ **Cut overtime bill.**
- ▶ **Increase positive coverage in national and trade press.**

These are the successes you can start planning to notch up over the next few weeks and months in the job.

STRENGTHS AND WEAKNESSES

So, are you up to the job? Now you know what the key threats and opportunities are, do you have what it takes to meet them successfully? Each one is going to need a different set of skills, and the only way to be sure you can meet the challenge in each case is to list the skills you need. Here are a few examples:

Threat: Failing contract with key customer.
Skills: Negotiating, selling.

Threat: Overtime bill.

Skills: Financial, diplomatic, organizational, decision-making.

Opportunity: Train more staff to operate new software.
Skills: Training, IT skills, planning.

Opportunity: Increase positive press coverage.
Skills: PR, writing, event-planning.

As a professional manager, you should know what your strengths and weaknesses are. You need to go through your lists honestly, and identify the threats and opportunities that you are well equipped to tackle, and those that you may be weak in. Some managers are tempted to duck issues that they know they are going to be weak at handling, but smart managers address the weaknesses and develop the skills. If a threat is there, it must be met. And a good opportunity should never be missed just because you're not sure you're up to it.

Handling weaknesses

So what do you do if a threat or opportunity calls for a skill you don't have? There are three solutions you can apply (you may choose to apply more than one):

- ▶ **Go and train yourself. Enrol on an evening course, buy a good book on the subject, find an online training programme, ask a friend or colleague who is an expert to teach you.**
- ▶ **Ask for training. Talk to your boss. Explain that you feel you are weak in an area that is going to be important, and that you would like to be given training to help you do your job better.**
- ▶ **What's your team for? As a manager, you can't delagate discipline interviews or drawing up budgets. But if you have a top-notch negotiator on your team, or someone with a gift for organizing events, use them. It's what they're there for. What matters is that the team as a whole has the strengths to meet the threat or the opportunity – not necessarily that you personally have them.**

OUTLINE PLANS

You have your two lists of key issues to tackle: threats and opportunities. You've identified any weaknesses that may hamper your chances of success, and you're doing

COVER YOURSELF

Sometimes, you can see that something that is expected of you simply isn't possible. Maybe there is no way next month's launch can possibly succeed at such short notice without spending money that you don't have in your budget. Perhaps the backlog can't be cleared without cooperation from another department, which isn't forthcoming.

Talk to your boss and ask for the resources you need. If you get no joy, put your case in writing, stating that you cannot achieve what is expected of you without the additional resources. Then at least you're covered if there's any comeback later.

something about them. So now you need to draw up an outline plan for each issue on your list, so that you know how you're going to tackle it and in what kind of timeframe.

For example, let's take the threat that the plans for next month's launch are in disarray. You might decide that the only way to get them back on track is to:

- ▶ **Go through the plans with key team members in the next 48 hours and simplify them.**
- ▶ **Get all press and customer invitations out by the end of next week.**
- ▶ **Call in an outside event organizer to pull the rest of the plans together on time.**

Having drawn up your outline plan, you need to check what resources you need to carry them out. Do you have the resources and the authority? Can you bring in an outside event organizer off your own bat? And have you got the money to do it? Do you have the staff available to attend the launch, or will you have to find people from elsewhere?

For each of your key threats and opportunities, you need to draw up an outline plan and then list any resources you will need for it, or identify any areas where you need authorization from higher up the organization. This process shouldn't take too long, particularly since your lists shouldn't run to more than about eight threats or opportunities between them.

Once you have completed this outline planning, you're ready to sink your teeth into your new job. You've met the people, you've covered the background, and now you know where you're going. So off you go. Good luck!

for later....

Once you have your outline plans drawn up, you're ready to get cracking with the job. It is essential that you don't allow yourself to get so bogged down in everyday work that these key plans start to slip. You have already specified a timeframe for each one: mark key stages in your diary and make sure they happen.

Starting with the most urgent, work through each of these outline plans and flesh out the detail. You will probably want to bring in at least some of your team members to help you do this. Once the plans are worked out, you can start delegating tasks and getting things moving.

As soon as you begin to work through these threats and opportunities, add more on to the end of the list to replace those you have dealt with. This way you will always have about half a dozen or so core projects central to your objective under way at any time to keep your department moving towards its goals, and to keep you notching up fresh successes.

flying start in half a day

What if you're starting work on the day of some major event? You arrive at 9.30 in the morning, and by 2.00 in the afternoon you're expected to be shaking hands with customers or attending a conference. You've got half a day to get in, get settled, and get to know everyone. It's tough, but you can do it.

I hope you're reading this book before the morning you start work, so you should have time to read the whole thing comfortably. Here are a few guidelines for compressing its contents into half a day:

- ▶ If it's not too late, call your soon-to-be boss and ask for all the background material on the organization you can get hold of (corporate newsletters, annual reports, press releases etc.), including copies of your departmental budget and any key documents from project files.

- ▶ Get in touch with your predecessor – who may still be in post – and pick their brains for all the information you can get (see Chapter 4).

- ▶ It's tempting when time is tight to allow yourself to be rushed through the introductions. But since they may be your only chance this morning to talk to people, you should set a slower pace than you otherwise might so you can really imprint the key team members and colleagues on your memory.

- ▶ First impressions are vitally important whether you have half a day or half a year to settle in, so make sure that you appear relaxed and calm as far as possible, and follow the guidelines in Chapter 2.

- ▶ You'll still need to hold your meeting with your boss first thing; set this up before the day you start work if you can.

- ▶ Go through the files as outlined in Chapter 4, but give them just a cursory skim for the time being – you're simply looking for glaring problems or issues for now. Find a chance to go through the paperwork in more detail as soon as you can.

- ▶ You won't be able to hold individual meetings with each of your team members today – but schedule them in as soon as you can. However, try to fit in the first group session today, over lunch if possible, or else over coffee. It will give you and your team a feel for each other, and you'll start to get a valuable sense of the key issues and the company culture.

flying start in an hour

Wheeee! You're not hitting the ground running, you're hitting the ground from 30 000 feet without a parachute. They really have landed you in it, haven't they? Turn up at 9.00 and be stuck into the job by 10.00? Any organization that kicks off at that speed isn't going to slow down later; you can expect to do a lot of fast thinking between now and your next career move.

So what can you realistically achieve in an hour? A lot less than you can manage in two to three days, obviously. But all the work in this book is essential, so you're going to have to make sure it gets fitted in somehow, and within the next week or so at the most. But for now:

1 Call your boss a few days before you start (if it's not too late already) and ask for all the background information on the organization they can send you, and copies of any important files (see Chapter 4) that they are prepared to let you have.

2 Make an appointment for a 15- to 20-minute meeting with your boss to start half an hour after you arrive on your first day.

3 Get hold of your predecessor and pick their brains (see Chapter 4).

4 Turn up early. It may not be much, but it will help.

5 f you are early enough, and you can find them, spend this extra time looking through the files on major projects.

6 Spend your first (official) half hour meeting your team and talking to them (see Chapter 1). Decline any introductions outside your team for now, along with any guided tours, unless they seem essential. Remember the guidelines in Chapter 2 on making a good impression.

7 Spend the next quarter of an hour or so with your boss, getting answers to the questions outlined in Chapter 3.

8 Use your remaining time to have a quick look through the personnel files before you get thrown in at the deep end.

An hour isn't long, but this way you have time to cover a little of everything so at least you gain breadth of knowledge, if not depth. Although there are other essential areas to cover – such as meetings with your team – you can fit these in over the next few days. And bear in mind that you will arguably bond with people, and absorb the company culture, faster this way than if you had longer to find your feet.

key people

U se this page to list the key people you need to talk to in your first week. Tick them off as you meet each one so that you can make sure you miss no one out. Remember to include:

- ▶ **Your immediate boss**

- ▶ **Your predecessor**

- ▶ **All your team members**

- ▶ **Fellow managers of other departments**

- ▶ **Any other colleagues or ex-employees of the organisation who may be helpful.**

key issues and projects

Note down here the top issues and projects you need to get on top of in your first few days. You can also jot down any questions about them which you want to ask the people you talk to over the next few days.

threats

You need to keep a constant eye on the key threats facing your department, and give priority to addressing them. Note down here what they are so you can hold a quick mental review of them over the next few weeks.

opportunities

Missed opportunities are missed successes for your organisation, your department, and yourself personally. To make sure you can't miss any key opportunities, write them down here and then review them regularly to check you are making good progress on each.

contacts

fast thinking

ros jay

fast thinking contacts

When you're thinking fast, you need to be able to put your finger on the information you need in an instant. So here's your own space in which to record any contacts you might need when you're working at the speed of life, from emergency computer maintenance to website addresses to help you find facts under pressure. You'll also find the *fast thinking* website (**www.fast-thinking.com**) a valuable resource when you're looking for time-saving contacts.